AF412742

American Disguise

Cover image: Eric Renner, *Stripper Heart*, 10"x8" pinhole Polaroid 809, 2003
Back cover: Eric Renner, *Louis Armstrong in whiteface*, 10"x8" pinhole Polaroid 809, 2003
Back cover: Eric Renner, *Ku Klux Klansman*, 10"x8" pinhole Polaroid 809, 2003

FLYING MONKEY PRESS is an imprint of Pinhole Resource Inc.
Rt. 15 Box 1355
San Lorenzo, NM 88041
USA

email: pinhole@gilanet.com

Library of Congress Cataloging-in Publication Data
Application submitted

IBSN: 0-9791453-0-9

For information on FLYING MONKEY PRESS books visit our website at pinholeresource.com

First Edition printed in 1500 copies

Printed and bound by Decentmate Printing Co. Ltd., Shenzhen, China

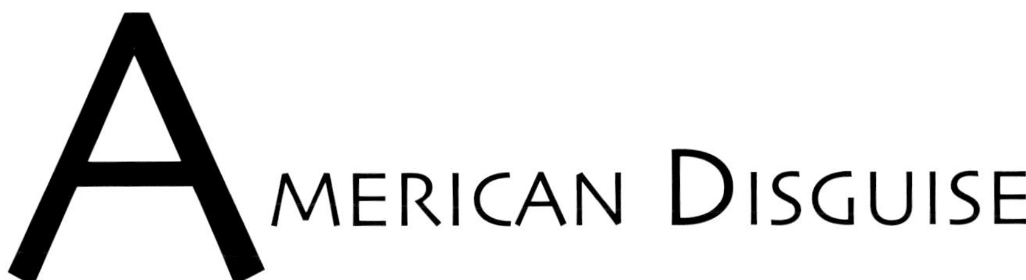American Disguise

Eric Renner

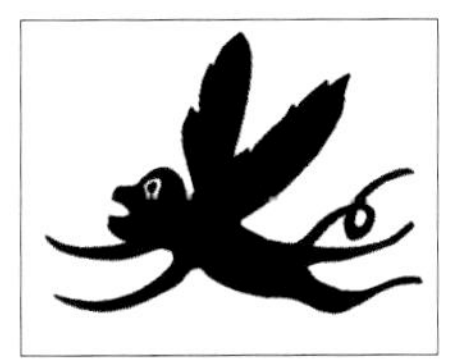

Flying Monkey Press

San Lorenzo, NM 88041

The past is never dead.
It's not even past.
—WILLIAM FAULKNER

To Nancy

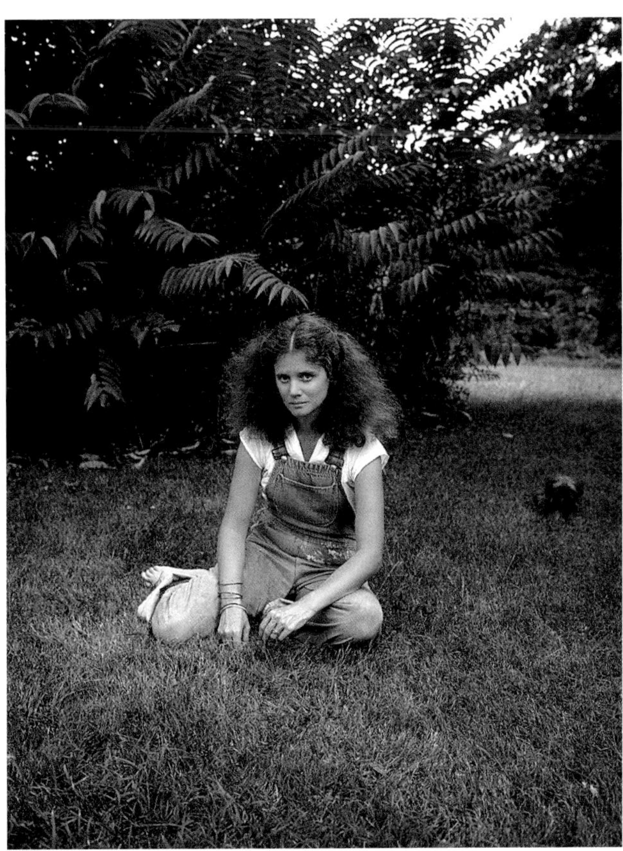

Self Portrait © Nancy Spencer

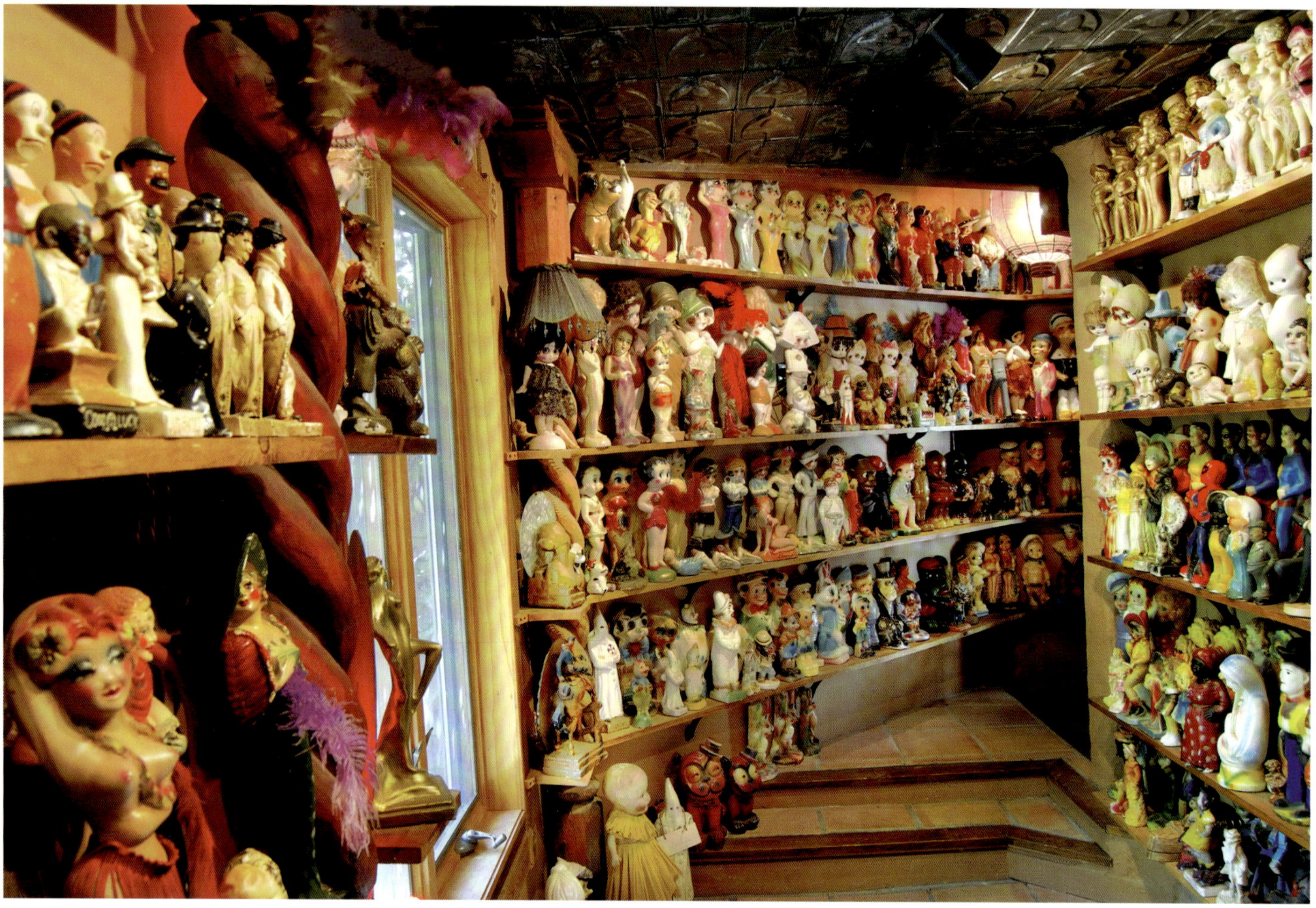

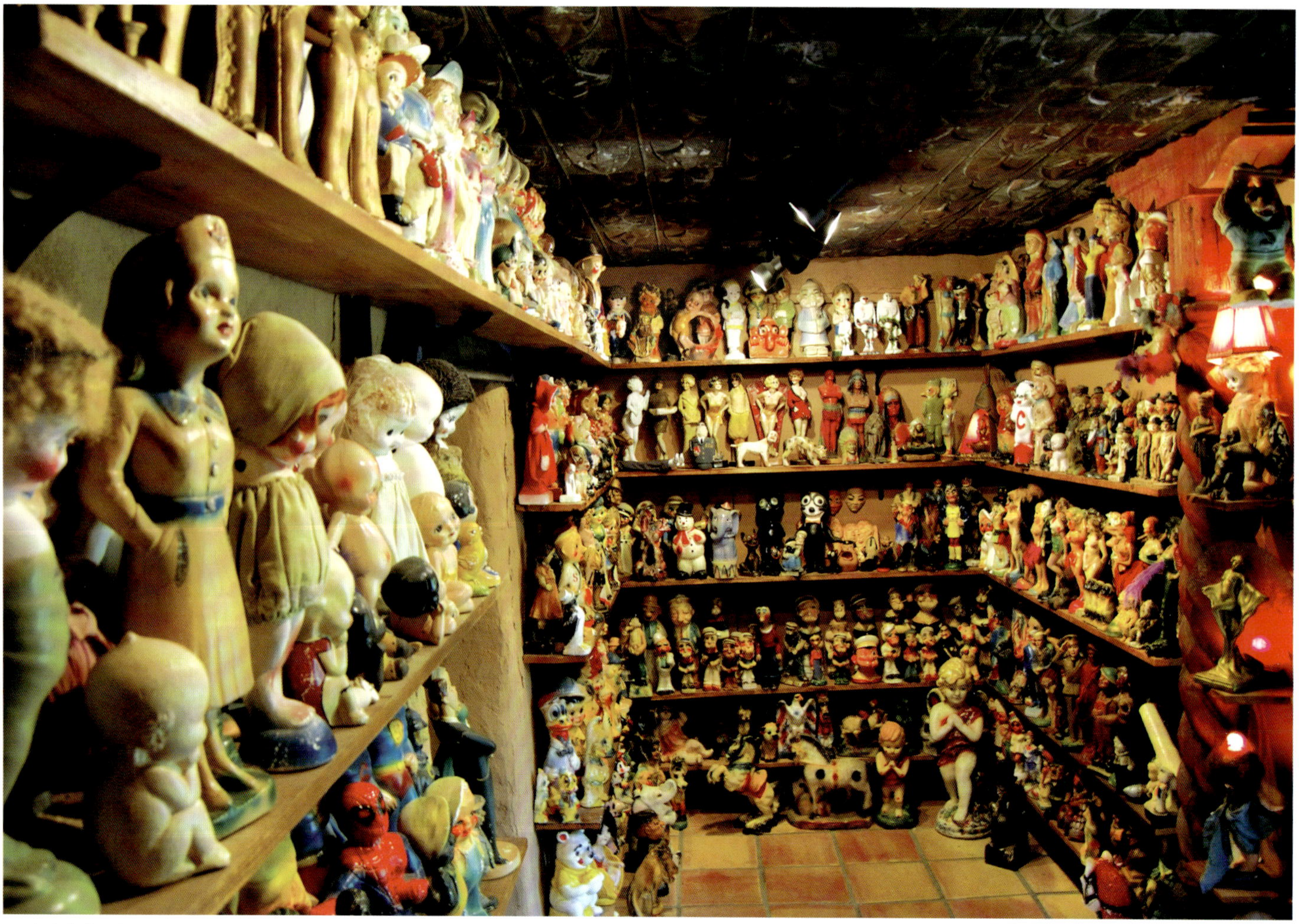

carnival chalk prizes

TABLE OF **C**ONTENTS

Acknowledgments

The least of things with a meaning is worth more in life than the greatest of things without it.
—CARL JUNG, *Modern Man in Search of a Soul*

This book could not have been done without the aid of five invaluable people: my wife, artist Nancy Spencer; collector and writer the late Tom Morris; religious scholar and writer Althea Aurandt; musician, artist, and writer Bolek Peplowski, and editor Karla Eoff.

Nancy lived with this project, day by day, month by month, and year by year. It was she, with her eye for an artifact with soul, who introduced me to antique and junk stores, the purgatory for carnival chalk prizes looking for a new home. After we met and married, we started collecting junk, including carnival chalk prizes, to use in assemblages we create together. Most of these assemblages were collaborative outcries against social unfairness and inequalities in the world. For meaning behind that group of object/image constructs, we gleaned useful passages from Barbara G. Walker's *The Woman's Encyclopedia of Myths and Secrets*,[1] describing discrimination, suppression, sexism, murder, and genocide. For instance, we learned from reading Walker that when someone says "rule of thumb," it actually referred back to Blackwell's Law in England where, up until the end of the nineteenth century, a husband was free to discipline his wife with a stick or whip no thicker than his thumb. What would have been considered assault under other circumstances was within the law if used to keep a wife in line.

I admit that I fell in love with carnival chalk prizes right away, due to their sometimes sloppily airbrushed caricaturesque quality, a less than elegant imitation of a well-known media star. (They were similar to winning a trophy.) Most of all they talked to me. I didn't really know why. But I couldn't resist purchasing a foot-high glittered Snow White painted red, orange, and blue, or a Lone Ranger painted lavender, green, pink, and yellow. These were the two most commonly found prizes in junk and antique stores. It took years to find a variety of prizes, and gradually I realized just how many of them were made from 1915 to 1955 (a few were made in the 60s) and are still available for collectors, usually on Internet auction sites like eBay. After eleven years of collecting about three hundred figures I began to see them not as the media stars they represented but as propagandized stereotypes and archetypes. That's the reason they are so seductive. Some of the prizes had stirred my subconscious instinctive feelings. Each figure had been frozen in time in its own media metaphor.

But I needed additional information about them. Fortunately I found Thomas Morris, whose generous guiding assistance has helped me in identifying prizes through his two valuable books, *The Carnival Chalk Prize I and II*,[2] and later through e-mails, for a number of the figures aren't in his books. The Lone Ranger is obvious and easy to identify, but for the Sophie Tucker prize, identification is much more difficult. Tom was the first to suggest Sophie Tucker. Then there are prizes in a more nebulous zone, for instance Johnny Appleseed. When a carnival side show owner was asked for that figure as the prize giveaway, maybe the customer saw it as Johnny Appleseed, or maybe the customer saw it as Gainsborough's *Blue Boy*. Who knows? The point is that each prize represented certain stereotypes with visual archetypes thrown in—that was its drawing power—and if the selected figure represented Jean Harlow plus Greta Garbo, then all the better. Some were more generic, like the hula girl.

There was also a "loser's prize" (if you lost at the side show games). It was a three-inch celluloid "Winky"—a remnant from the era of Jim Crow stereotypes—by the 1950s the NAACP had pressured carnivals to remove it.

Tom Morris had spent decades collecting and writing about carnival chalk prizes and helping many other people who collect them. Before we met him in Oregon, Nancy and I probably bumped into Tom in a junk shop and never knew it. Later, after I started this book, he went so far as to redefine the word "generosity" when he sent some of the rare, very fragile, delicate chalk figures to me to photograph (it was Tom's idea to loan them, I didn't dare ask). My ten-to-thirty-minute time exposures using a pinhole camera, Polaroid 809 color film, and two huge lights made it practically impossible to descend upon anyone's living space. In 2002, Nancy and I went to Medford, Oregon, to meet Tom and Yvonne Morris. It happened to be at a time when he was selling his collection. To my surprise, I ended up buying it. It filled in the gaps and made this book seem possible.

Each media personality is placed somewhat chronologically in this book, and each reflects manufacturing dates that are listed in Tom's *A Price Guide to Chalkware/Plaster Carnival Prizes*.[3] I say "somewhat chronologically" because there was often a long stretch of time in the media personality's career when they were famous, so the carnival chalk prize might have been made anywhere from one year to ten years after their fame began, depending upon the popularity of the person.

When Nancy and I exhibited our assemblages in a nearby gallery, we were interviewed by the local newspaper. In the interview we credited Barbara G. Walker's book for making us angry enough to inspire us to do the artwork. After the interview came out, Nancy got a phone call from someone who said, "I read about you in the paper. Why are you so angry about Barbara G. Walker? Are you for her or against her?" Nancy answered, "For her." A sigh of relief came over the phone—from then on I had the assistance of Althea Aurandt, whose scholarly knowledge of religion helped me through deep thickets of understanding that only her life of in-depth religious research could have brought to bear on this subject. Her book *Secrets the Church Never Told You*[4] showed me that she was the right person for the task. She shared her knowledge with me and corrected many blunders.

I owe a huge debt of gratitude to musician, painter, and writer Bolek Peplowski, whose music and ideas are a constant reminder that life is good. He deftly edited my lengthy writing without missing a beat. It is always a joy opening his e-mails and seeing how well he writes. One read:

It is, of course, literally true that every step we take, every motion we make and even the activity of our brains and other organs affects the universe, just as the universe affects us—it's a matter of physics. I guess what bothers me is humanity's endless attempts to control the universe and the events within it. It's a vain curse that spawns religions and all sorts of desperate notions of power in face of the bold fact that we are simply a part of, and not on top of, an incredibly complex system. The best we can hope to do, is to not hurt one another, or other entities in the system, and we fail miserably at that.

Lastly, I thank the final editor Karla Eoff, whose alchemy magically transformed the book.

Don't try to read the entire book holus-bolus (meaning all in one fell swoop), nor does the Introduction need to be read first! If a critic calls this book a *Mad* comic mind gone awry, I'd take that as a compliment. Once when I was young and sick in bed, my mother bought me *Mad* (at my request—we didn't usually have comics around the house, nor TV for that matter). I read it from cover to cover, quite a stupid thing to attempt (if you know how much retinal fatigue is involved in reading one *Mad* comic—brain fatigue too). Afterward I realized I was a whole lot sicker. That was my last *Mad* comic in situ. If this book makes you a whole lot sicker about what we weren't taught in school or the information that we don't receive through the conventional media, then I've done my work well, and my bleary eyes from lucubration (burning the midnight oil) will have been worth it.

I found quite a few unusual sounding words in the curious compendium by Norman Schur entitled *2000 Most Challenging and Obscure Words*,[5] so I included a number throughout.

Interpretations of symbolism are my own, an example being Little Red Riding Hood, where one more attempt seemed acceptable. Since she has been analyzed so many times in so many ways, what's one more?

My introduction into carnivalesque influences was my

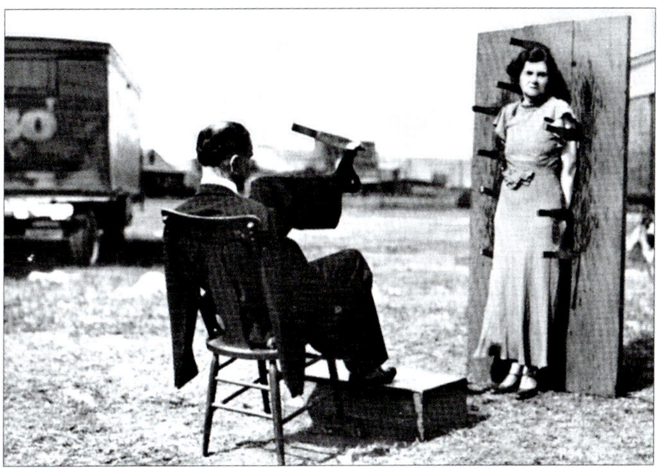

Knife thrower, Royal American Shows, 1934.

father's painting *The Barker* (1933), which hung in our dining room while I was growing up. I assume it had a lasting effect.

I would also like to give special thanks to my two book angels: Gabriel Berde and Peter Perrone.

Thanks to Jeff Robison of Hake's Americana, Division of Diamond International Galleries for use of their photographs on pages 11, 119, and 211; to Randy Johnson, Johnny Meah, Jim Secreto, and Teddy Verndell for the use of their image *Shooting Through a Woman* shown on page 10, originally published in their book *Freaks, Geeks, and Strange Girls*,[6] to Thomas Kempland who allowed me to reproduce the two J. R. Eike photographs on page 115, and to Larry Pogue who sent images of carnival chalkware string holders.

Thanks to Ann Lowe for help with the book jacket.

Thanks to Darien Putnam for proofreading.

Thanks to Nikita Chan for help with printing.

Lastly I thank my two sons Zephyr and Yarian whose sharp eyes helped find many carnival prizes on eBay and whose computer skills made this book possible.

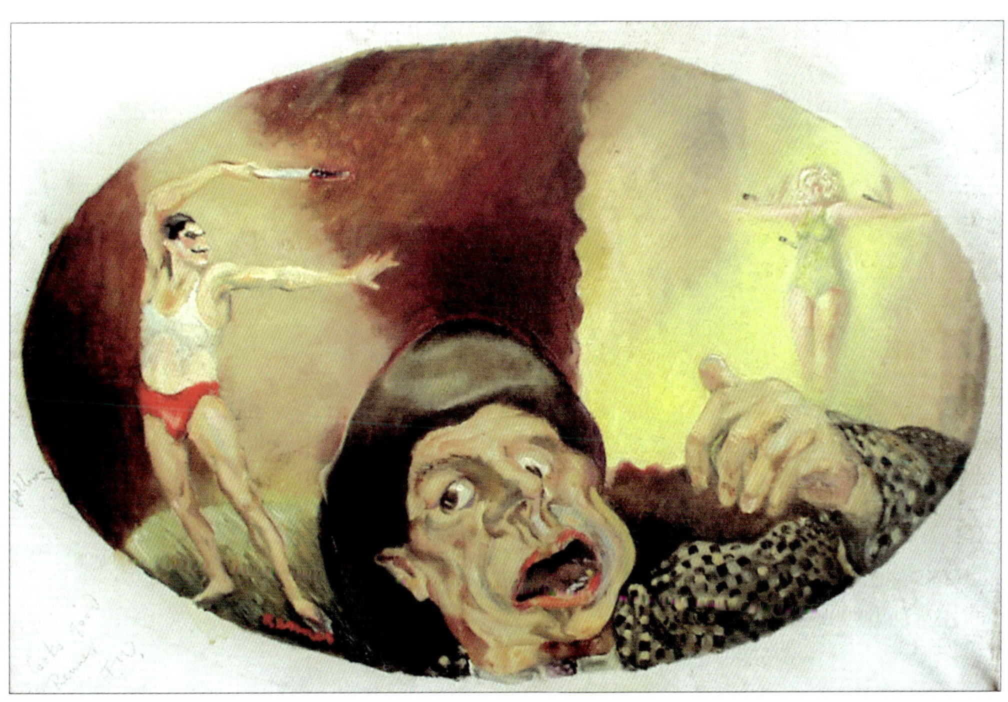

The Barker, Richard L. Renner, oil on canvas, 1933

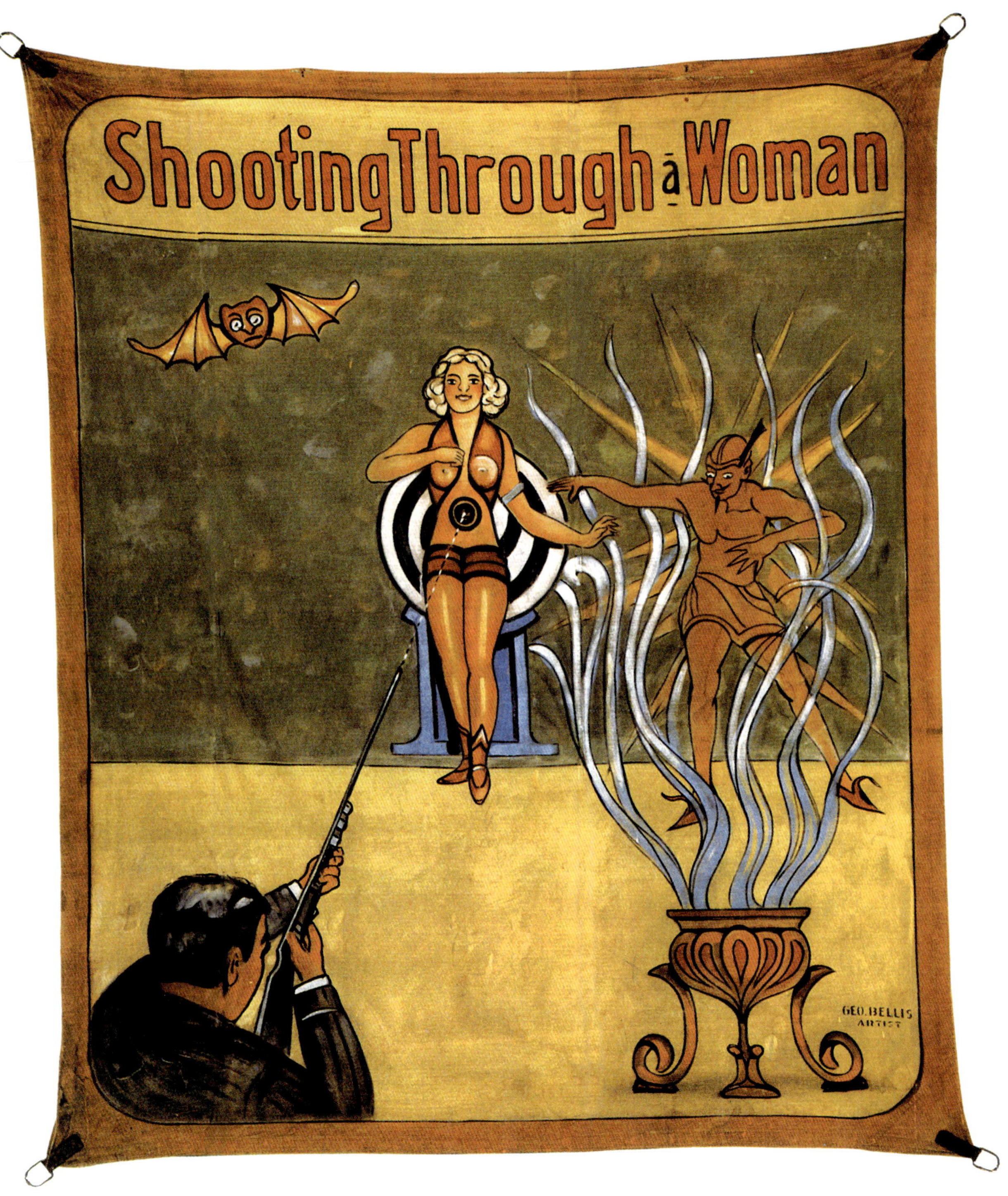

Shooting Through A Woman, carnival banner, oil on canvas George
Bellis, 1940. Courtesy: Randy Johnson, Johnny Meah, Jim Secreto,
Teddy Verndell, *Freaks, Geeks & Strange Girls: Sideshow Banners of
the American Midway*, Last Gasp Press, 2004, photograph Jim Secreto

Democracy passes into despotism.
—PLATO, *Republic*, Book VIII

*I*NTRODUCTION

I've put off reading Lolita for six years, till she's 18.
—GROUCHO MARX

I don't believe the war is simply the work of politicians and capitalists. Oh no, the common man is every bit as guilty; otherwise, people and nations would have rebelled long ago! There's a destructive urge in people, the urge to rage, murder and kill. And until all of humanity, without exception, undergoes a metamorphosis, wars will continue to be waged, and everything that has been carefully built up, cultivated and grown will be cut down and destroyed, only to start all over again!
—ANNE FRANK, *The Diary of Anne Frank*

T**HE** M**EDIA AND** U**S**

Instinct, as defined by *Webster's College Dictionary*:

> **Instinct**: Behavior that is mediated by reactions below the conscious level.

This book looks at more than one hundred of the most famous early media personalities. Some of these personalities were meant to be venerated, such as blond bombshell Jean Harlow; some were meant to be denigrated, like laughable Amos 'n' Andy, who epitomized black folks as inept citified adaptations with nineteenth-century Jim Crow attributes. These media figures aroused powerful instinctive feelings as they became assimilated throughout a diverse American populace. Instinctive feelings can be strong enough to make certain people want to fight and die for their country, as exemplified by the "Uncle Sam Wants You" poster. This book attempts to explain the lengthy evolvement of certain media stereotypes. For instance, the Marlboro Man didn't just ride out of the West one day—he is an invention with a long history, particularly within the Hollywood Western genre, representing feelings of freedom, toughness, and liberation.

Everyone is aware that famous media personalities become popular American icons. This transformation is as obvious today as it was in the nineteenth century, when early media personalities strutted across the stage in minstrel shows, vaudeville, theater, dance, and silent film, or as characters on the pages of prose, tabloids, pulp fiction, and comic strips. In the first half of the twentieth century, the availability of popular American icons had significantly increased, particularly because newer technologies— the mass media of film, radio, print, cartoons, and television—offered greater access to a consequentially greater amount of star power. This era should have been labeled the mass media age. Every American was under its influence, more rather than less. They still are.

One of the many ways that the original mass-media megastars—like the lovable Charlie Chaplin, the bawdy Mae West, or even the ominous Ku Klux Klansman—had their iconic significance assimilated into American culture was through the manufacturing of mass-produced carnival chalk statues that were won as prizes at traveling carnivals. People flocked to the carnival when it came to town, particularly

during its heyday of 1915 to 1955. The carnival was a vast sea of visually inviting archetypal motifs for arousing primal instincts. Flying through the air on the Ferris wheel, playing games of chance at the side shows, watching coochie dancers, snake handlers, knife throwers—these heart-pounding moments and glimpses of a more daring life were the carnival's draw. Winning at the ring toss in the side show meant you could have your very own chalk prize—it could be the risqué (sexist) fan dancer Sally Rand, a funny (racist) Sambo holding a watermelon, an all-powerful (macho) Superman, or an obnoxious (patriotic) Hitler portrayed as a skunk. Most of the prizes were about a foot high, very cheaply made of plaster, and painted in garish colors with glitter thrown on to make them look more inviting. Any prize (a souvenir) is an archetypal motif for feeling the excitement of winning. Although historically obscure, their significance completely unrecognized, carnival chalk prizes were some of the first caricatures of the most important of these early American media stars.

Carnival chalk figures evolved from figurative 19th century cast iron doorstops, an example being the caricatured figures of Ally Sloper and his wife. His creators over 40 years: Ross, Dalziel, Baxter, and then Thomas became the fathers of mass marketing by utilizing "product placement," coupons, and the Ally Sloper Fan Club (1904).

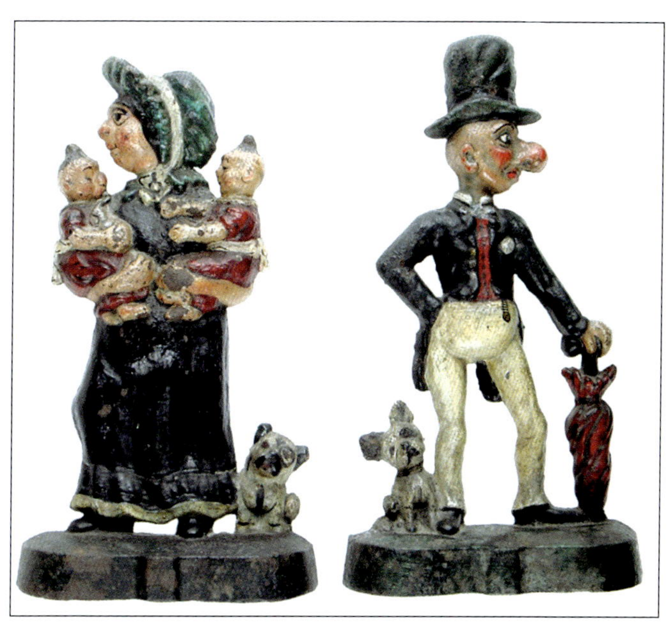

Ally Sloper and his wife doorstops, England, circa 1880s. Courtesy: Hake's Americana, Div. of Diamond International Galleries. Ally Sloper's antics, as well as his marketing, spread his popularity in cartoon format throughout the western world. Marketeer Charles Ross created the cartoon *Ally Sloper*. His personality was appropriated and evolved from Dickens' Wilkins Micawber in *David Copperfield*. Ally Sloper was a con man, a drunk, and a trickster, but not the alienated type—he believed in and spoke for royalty as well as empire building. He was against the gainfully unemployed. W. C. Fields appropriated much of Sloper's costume as well as persona.

Mostly unknown today, plaster carnival prizes were cherished back then; they operated as visual metaphors for each star's stereotype and various underlying archetypal motifs from the era. Since many of the most important media stars were caricatured in chalk, in sum total they give a reasonably full picture of an America in its mass-media infancy, its population influenced by invention, promotion, merchandising, and disguise.

There is deception at work here. First of all, mass-media stars are easily made famous as stereotypes. Secondly, it is their underlying archetypal motif, connected to certain instinctive feelings, which give them their real power, assuring them of mass appeal. Yet often little of the history surrounding the individual as a stereotype is really known. Much is generated as myth. The carnival chalk figure of Paul Revere stereotyped the American Revolutionary minuteman ready to fight for his country. His myth was generated by Longfellow's poem, written as a rallying cry for the Civil War, which piqued instinctive feelings of nationalism, bravery, honor, and patriotism—particularly during time of war. It is rarely mentioned that Revere did not complete his famous ride all the way to Concord. He was turned back by the British and was later court-martialed for another, rather unpatriotic matter during the Revolutionary War. I am not suggesting that Revere was not a hero—he was—but his full story needs to be part of history too. When "The Midnight Ride of Paul Revere" became widely read, he was looked upon almost as a Founding Father. But political stereotypes tend to be overtly propagandist—Jessica Lynch is a contemporary example.

If you had chosen the miniature Mount Rushmore as a carnival chalk prize, would it have surprised you to know that three of the four figures depicted there were not Christians? They were Deists—a now forgotten religion of morality and reason, usually practiced by the aristocrats during eighteenth-century to mid-nineteenth-century America. Founding Fathers Washington and Jefferson actually practiced Deism, and Lincoln was also a Deist. To Deists miracles were not possible unless they could be substantiated. Deists did believe in a God, but their Christian peers thought Deism was definitely not Christian. Freedom of religious thought throughout a young America was of the utmost importance to Thomas Jefferson who proclaimed:

> Millions of innocent men, women and children, since the introduction of Christianity, have been burnt, tortured, fined and imprisoned; yet we have not advanced one inch toward uniformity. What has been the effect of this coercion? To make one half the world fools and the other half hypocrites. To support roguery and error all over the earth.[1]

George Washington did share a church pew with Martha—though she was considered a Christian, he was usually not. Mary Todd Lincoln was a Presbyterian; her husband, although born poor, was a Deist. This humorous anecdote in Franklin Steiner's *Religious Beliefs of Our Presidents* describes Abraham Lincoln's beliefs:

> In 1846, when Lincoln was a candidate for Congress against a Methodist minister, the Rev. Peter Cartwright, his opponent openly accused him of being an unbeliever, and Lincoln never denied it. A story is told of Mr. Cartwright's holding a revival meeting while the campaign was in progress, during which Lincoln stepped into one of his meetings. When Cartwright asked the audience, "Will all who want to go to heaven stand up?" All arose except Lincoln.
>
> When he asked, "Now, will all who want to go to hell stand up?" Lincoln still remained in his seat. Mr. Cartwright

then said, "All have stood up for one place or the other except Mr. Lincoln, and we would like to know where he expects to go." Lincoln arose and quietly said, "I am going to Congress," and there he went.[2]

By the time of the Civil War, Deism had lost most of its followers. Much had changed, reflecting what John O'Sullivan, a newspaper reporter, had written in 1845, the year his phrase "Manifest Destiny" was coined[3]—one year before Lincoln ran for Congress. O'Sullivan explained why Americans deserved the beautifully unspoiled land that they had so clearly taken away from its natives. In the *United States Magazine and Democratic Review*, O'Sullivan proclaimed:

> The American claim is by the right of our manifest destiny to overspread and to possess the whole of the continent which Providence has given us for the development of the great experiment of liberty and federative self-government entrusted to us. It is a right such as that of the tree to the space of air and earth suitable for the full expansion of its principle and destiny of growth.

His beautifully worded argument is arrogant and false. It was specious propaganda tying God—that is, O'Sullivan's "Providence"—with three and a half centuries of horribly brutal colonization and the U.S. Constitution. Within his Providence-given experiment, labeled as "liberty and federative self-government," O'Sullivan completely left out or whitewashed the African American slaves, whose own liberty had been thwarted. Obviously he swept away the Native Americans, whose lives the colonists had exterminated and whose lands they had stolen. O'Sullivan's words were spoken with eloquence, as if his was a directive from God and he himself owned the voice of the prophet, which was just how he wanted his message to sound—by subtly adding "Providence has given," his God forgave all white colonists' sins. But O'Sullivan's God was not what the Deist Founding Fathers had in mind when they drew up the constitution—they clearly wanted a separation of church and state, and went so far as to make their desires known through that document. O'Sullivan discreetly added religious propaganda into his message. Over the years when Americans thought of their Founding Fathers, they began to be restereotyped as Christian Founding Fathers. Now, in the twenty-first century, when tourists visit Mount Rushmore in the Black Hills of South Dakota, they see it in terms of the patriotic feeling of American freedom and O'Sullivan's Providence-given right for those four presidents to be enshrined and carved in that mountainside.

Mount Rushmore's sculptor, Gutzon Borglum, knew he had placed his patriotic project in the heart of what was originally Native American land. He also knew that the Black Hills had been stolen through a fraudulent treaty that Sitting Bull had never signed and an arrogant war had been illegally started on Native American land by a gold-hungry freebooter named General George Armstrong Custer, who was backed by wealthy nineteenth-century capitalists in what was hoped to be another rich gold rush. In a speech in 1940, just before he died, Borglum decried: "We are standing on territory once belonging to the Sioux Indians . . . on their very land, for which we never paid a cent—just stole it from them and lied about it."[4]

By 1861, with the eventual disappearance of Deism, Christian guilt and sentiment increased due to the grisly horrors of the Civil War. It was then that the Reverend M. R. Watkinson, minister of the Gospel from Ridleyville, Pennsylvania, wrote to the Secretary of the Treasury requesting the words "God Liberty Law" be added to U.S. coins:

> You are probably a Christian. What if our Republic were not shattered beyond reconstruction? Would not the antiquaries of succeeding centuries rightly reason from our past that we were a heathen nation? What I propose is that instead of the goddess of liberty we shall have next inside the 13 stars a ring inscribed with the words PERPETUAL UNION; within the ring the all seeing eye, crowned with a halo; beneath this eye the American flag, bearing in its field stars equal to the number of the States united; in the folds of the bars the words GOD, LIBERTY, LAW.
>
> This would make a beautiful coin, to which no possible citizen could object. This would relieve us from the ignominy of heathenism. This would place us openly under the Divine protection we have personally claimed. From my hearth I have felt our national shame in disowning God as not the least of our present national disasters . . .[5]

It was ironic that "In God We Trust" was created due to war, but by 1864, these words were added to the two-cent coin. By 1888, *Laus Deo*, Latin for "Praise be to God," was placed on a plaque at the very top of the newly constructed Washington Monument. By 1938, all U.S. coins bore the inscription "In God We Trust." When the words "under God" were added to the Pledge of Allegiance in 1954, during the end of McCarthyism, the Christian Founding Father stereotype was further reconfirmed and again unconstitutionally recontextualized, far from the original ideals set out in the constitution.

Most Americans feel an instinctive need for a belief in God, as do most other people throughout the world. This need was explained by Sigmund Freud in his statement: "Religion is an illusion and it derives its strength from the fact that it falls in our instinctual desires." The God of which Freud speaks is symbolic of an ancient archetype.

Confronting DNA

Some popular U.S. icons have gradually become internationally recognized symbols—Mickey Mouse, Ronald McDonald, the World Trade Center, Marilyn Monroe, George Washington on the dollar bill, and the Statue of Liberty. These are probably as well known as the religious icons of Jesus and the Christian cross. What Americans see daily, if not hourly, whether they know it or not, is a constantly updated reaffirming of ancient archetypal symbols and stereotypes.

The American government wants us to believe in patriotism, corporations want us to buy their products, religions need membership, and the mass media is there to spread the news—good and bad. It is up to us to understand the depths of our instinctive feelings that often allow us to be exploited. Propaganda relies on instinctive association, not on learning. Strong feelings of nationalism and revenge are instinctively aroused by the sickening replaying of the 9/11 terrorist-piloted airplanes hitting the World Trade Center Twin Towers. Feelings of lust and liberation are aroused by the bikini-clad women on TV programs such as *Baywatch*, which is a compendium of *Playboy* stereotypes. Feelings of control, power, lust, and deadly humor are aroused by the portrayal of the Mafia on *The Sopranos*.

What is it that creates these feelings? At first glance, the carnival prize Conestoga wagon looks to be nothing more than a somewhat primitive, outmoded historical vehicle. In a larger sense, the horse- or ox-powered Conestoga wagon was an ATV transporting pioneers, who by their sheer numbers overran Native American cultures. The Conestoga was much more versatile than any present-day RV (no need to find gas stations along the way, only streams and grass). Grouping them in a circle created a fort that could be mobilized on the spot. They were also carriers of disease. In an even larger sense, the Conestogas were weapons of mass destruction (our newly coined WMD). They were, in every respect, America's nineteenth-century archetypal motif symbol for a weapon of power and change. Very few Native Americans who saw Conestogas heading their way thought of them as primitive vehicles, nor did many manage to live through the onslaught, as rising tides of Conestogas crossed from east to west. Those Native Americans who did live witnessed the destruction of most of their culture, as well as the arrival of that foreign thing called Christianity. And on the bleak horizon were the debilitating reservations.

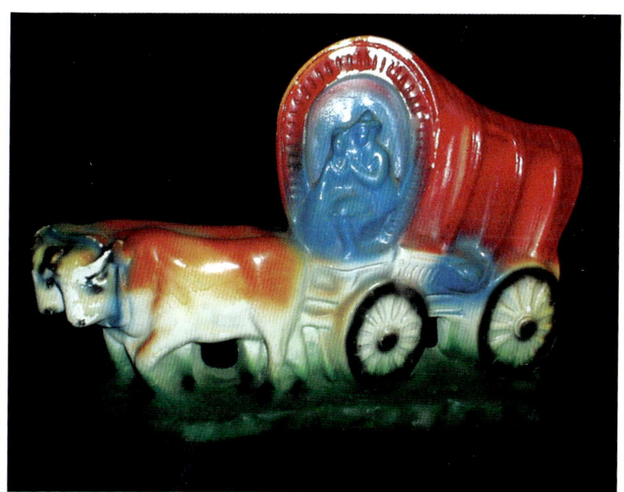

Conestoga Wagon six-inch carnival chalk prize

All of our instinctive feelings come directly from our inner file cabinet of DNA sensory identification tags that we are born with. Each and every tag can be triggered by an ancient or updated archetypal motif. Some motifs arrive unrequested—like the eternal highway patrolman who might stop us. If we are unlucky enough to be stopped, then instinctive feelings of fear, disgust, hate, and embarrassment are quickly aroused within us, because a policeman represents an archetypal symbol for an official with power. He is also a stereotype (a "cop"). For this reason highway police with radar are not too popular. Don't tell the next cop who stops you for speeding that you are an abecedarian (a rudimentary beginner) at trying to understand and reevaluate those instinctive feelings within yourself evoked by his symbolic attire, screaming siren, flashing lights, attitude, and ever-present deadly handgun. He'll think you just used a smear word. Driving a car offers feelings of freedom, and just about any car that runs is an updated archetypal motif for feeling that freedom. Those who drove the Conestogas felt a similar freedom. Driving literally means liberation (unless you're stuck in rush-hour traffic). If you break the law, even for something as seemingly commonplace as driving ten to fifteen miles an hour over the speed limit, then you have let your instinctive DNA feelings that are connected to liberation get slightly out of control. Or you might be feeling entitlement, which allows you to go faster than the next guy. Or maybe you're just in a hurry. Cops can drive faster than we are allowed to, which summon our feelings of disgust creating resentment towards them and their double standards.

Instinctive feelings are always much stronger than any logic we can summon against them. But if we can begin to understand that much of what we feel comes from seeing revised symbolic motifs and stereotypes, then we can make an attempt to place a somewhat enlightened perspective upon what we feel. Then, and only then, will we have the possible freedom of choice to confront ourselves. In that way, we will actually be confronting some of our own DNA.

This book may appear to be suggesting alienation or a quasi-rebellion against our political and religious institutions, corporations, and mass media, but it definitely is not. More than an outward rebellion against the omnipresent, it is suggesting an inner rebellion against our own DNA. This rebellion against our inner makeup is very hard work. At least in my attempts at confronting my own DNA, I have found it difficult. Separating the instinctive me from the thoughtful me is not easy. It takes time and thought.

Confronting DNA involves self-study of reactions to all our human senses. All that we do during every moment of our time here on Earth is part of our intrinsic being. Media is not only the outward popularized mass-media extensions like TV, film, music, the Internet, and so forth. It is everything we encounter from waking to sleeping to reawakening. For me, it is the entire life process I encounter.

This book is not meant to promote a repression of instinctive feelings. It is meant to help explain where these feelings come from and how many millions of them there seem to be. It's up to each of us to figure ourselves out. Possibly Anne Frank's statement at the beginning takes on a deeper meaning—war and a lot else functions as a group dynamic. We all have somewhat similar DNA identification tags.

STEREOTYPE

Stereotype, as defined by *Webster's College Dictionary*:

> **stereotype:** A standardized mental picture that is held in common by members of a group and that

represents an over simplified opinion, affective attitude or uncritical judgement.

A stereotype connects to something that has a specific time-honored look, as in handsome hero, beautiful heroine, sly villain, or cute baby.

A country can easily be stereotyped at any particular point in time. For instance, presently Americans equate France with wine and recent anti-Americanism, Cuba with Castro, and so on. People from other countries presently equate America with Disneyland, McDonald's, 9/11, and George W. Bush. Instantaneous media changes these generalized stereotypes at any given moment.

Decades ago, during the mid-1930s, countries were usually stereotyped as: France equals mistresses and the Eiffel Tower; Spain equals bullfighting, flamenco and Franco; Italy equals the Mafia and Mussolini; Germany equals Hitler and fascism; China equals communism and Confucius; America equals the Hollywood blonde, Shirley Temple, the Statue of Liberty, and FDR.

Some of the carnival chalk figures poked fun at a country's stereotype. There was the mad bullfighter that poked fun at Spain.

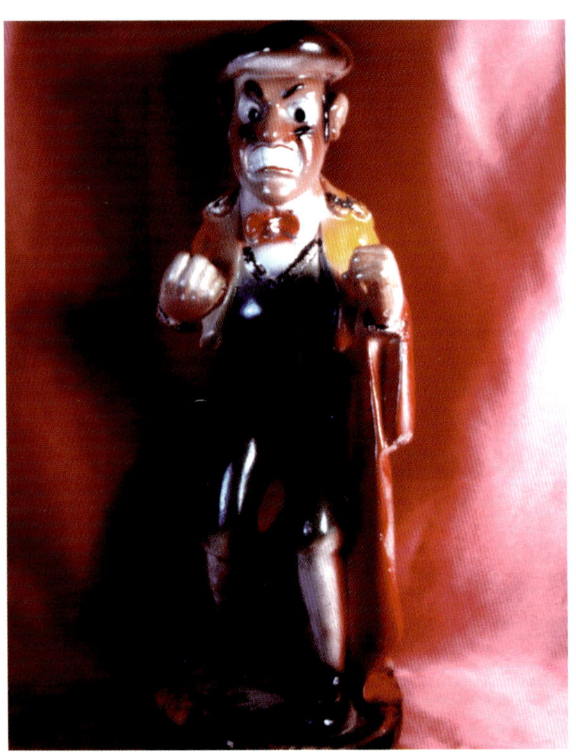

Mad bullfighter fourteen-inch carnival chalkware prize. The bullfighter plays into *The Story of Ferdinand*, by Munro Leaf (1936). Ferdinand is the rare peace-loving bull who doesn't want to fight, so the frustrated bullfighter gets angry.

Usually tourists go to a foreign country to participate in what they see and feel as culturally significant positive otherness. They might go to France to see Paris and the Eiffel Tower, to Italy to see Rome, Florence and the Vatican. What they expect is a positive learning experience about another culture's way of life.

A country's otherness can also be stereotyped as negative. William Scott Green states, "A society does not simply discover its others, it fabricates them, by selecting, isolating, and emphasizing an aspect of another people's life, and making it symbolize its difference."[6] If this concept of negative otherness is understood, the implications are very disturbing. As Elaine Pagels points out in *The Origin of Satan*:

> What may be new in Western Christian tradition is how the use of Satan to represent one's enemies lends to conflict, a specific kind of moral and religious interpretation, in which "we" are God's people and "they" are God's enemies, and ours as well . . . Such moral interpretation of conflict has proven extraordinarily effective throughout Western history in consolidating the identity of Christian groups; the same history also shows that it can justify hatred, even mass slaughter.[7]

Conflict feelings involving hatred toward a stereotyped enemy can begin with archetypal motif symbols, like the destruction of the World Trade Center (the Twin Towers represented world power). Conflict feelings are much stronger than the learned abilities of forgiveness, reconciliation, acceptance, and appreciation. This is the core of problem in finding and accepting nonviolent solutions, particularly if those conflict responses connect to images as grim as war, ethnic cleansing, or control of the earth's resources. These are areas that automatically involve politicians, propaganda, and what the mass media wants to promote or is pushed to promote.

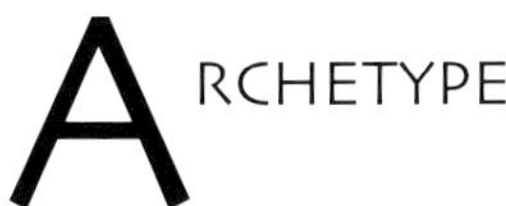

Archetype

Archetype, as defined by *Webster's College Dictionary*:

> **archetype:** (in Jungian psychology) an inherited unconscious idea, pattern of thought, image, etc., universally present in individual psyches.

An archetype is something that we see, hear, or even touch, smell, or taste that then connects these senses to instinctive feelings within us. Archetypes can be words or symbols that promote feelings of fear, lust, love, protection, power, greed, competition, survival, honor, bravery, heroism. Some of these instinctive feelings are knee-jerk responses, some are similar to feelings created by what we often refer to as our demons inside. The roots of archetype go deep within ourselves—so much so that the original source for the symbols cannot be identified, which explains why the feelings that an archetypal symbol arouse are always stronger than any logic surrounding it. For instance, love makes the world go around.

Explaining archetypes, the psychologist oneiroscopist (master dream interpreter) Carl Jung said:

> My views about the "archaic remnants," which I call "archetypes" or "primordial images," have been constantly criticized by people who lack a sufficient knowledge of the psychology of dreams and of mythology. The term "archetype" is often misunderstood as meaning certain definite mythological images or motifs. But these are nothing more than conscious representations; it would be absurd to assume that such variable representations could be inherited.

> The archetype is a tendency to form representations of a motif—representations that can vary a great deal in detail without losing their basic pattern. There are, for instance, many representations of the motif of the hostile brethren, but the motif itself remains the same. My critics have incorrectly assumed that I am dealing with "inherited representations," and on that ground they have dismissed the idea of the archetype as mere superstition. They have failed to take into account the fact that if archetypes were representations that originated in our consciousness (or were acquired by consciousness), we should surely understand them, and not be bewildered and astonished when they present themselves in our consciousness. They are, indeed, an instinctive trend, as marked as the impulse of birds to build nests, or ants to form organized colonies.

> Here I must clarify the relation between instincts and archetypes: What we properly call instincts are physiological urges, and are perceived by the senses. But at the same time, they also manifest themselves in fantasies and often reveal their presence by symbolic images. These manifestations are what I call the archetypes. They are without known origin; and they reproduce themselves in any time or in any part of the world—even where transmission by direct descent or "cross fertilization" through migration must be ruled out.[8]

By "fantasies" and "symbolic images," Jung was referring to dream imagery—night dreams, lucid dreams—all subconscious symbols woven into the zones of inner life. Equally, symbolic images are seen everywhere during the day. Any of these can be reinvented and even given a new name.

In 1955, Vladimir Nabokov created an enduring pornographic symbol when he described the entanglement between a middle-aged sexual pervert and an erotically charged twelve-year-old girl in *Lolita*: an imagined visual stereotype, descriptive of the nymphet—that is, nymphomaniac. From extended media exposure, the Lolita symbol has become so ingrained into social interaction that Lolita has become a cliché in everyday language used to convey that type of erotic behavior. Seeing an adolescent girl who has the body language, appropriate clothing, and a certain look evokes the Lolita stereotype. Her entire manner is operating within a combined set of visual archetypes that Nabokov gave name to. Her look arouses strong instincts which cannot be ignored by logic. In Jungian terms, Lolita could now be seen as a contemporary motif fitting within the set of archetypal symbols that promote and define instinctive feelings elicited by feminine pubescent lust.

A further example of intense social interaction with symbol exposure is Hitler's form of the swastika. So evocative are its heinous qualities that the swastika has been banned because of its connection to the Jungian hostile brethren motif for hate, the Holocaust, and Fascist superiority, although certain others cultures saw it as a symbol denoting good luck.

In *Man and His Symbols*, Jung explained that human archetypes cross international boundaries; people everywhere instinctively feel fear, lust, love, protection, power, greed, survival, honor, bravery, heroism. As each world culture evolves and becomes more diverse, it builds a slightly differing set of traditions and value systems around similar instinctive feelings and archetypes, even though the motifs may change.

By the 1970s, media popularizer Marshall McLuhan interpreted the term archetype into dense word twists saying: "The archetype is a retrieved awareness or consciousness. It is consequently a retrieved cliché. Since a cliché is a unit extension of man, an archetype is a quoted extension, medium, technology, or environment."[9] His writings often mused specifically on what he considered were the opiate effects of instant mass media: "Man has become essentially discarnate in the electric age. Much of his own sense of unreality may stem from this. Certainly it robs people of any sense of goals or direction."[10]

In the context of this last quote, McLuhan did not take into account the all-powerful role instinctive feelings and reactions play when aroused by the mass media's subtle use of archetypal motifs promoting various propagandist agendas. Where McLuhan thought the media fully narcotized its subjects, this book suggests that its use of stereotypes and archetypes stimulates them, whether they know it or not. McLuhan also stated: "There seems to be a deeply willed ignorance in man. 'Sin' might also be defined as lack of 'awareness,' 'resistance to learning,' and mankind being 'threatened by understanding.' "[11]

The Beginnings of Mass Media 1900–1950

In the first half of the twentieth century, the media of silent film, comic strip, radio, tabloid, sound film, comics, and television were popularly established. Sometimes the mass media unintentionally created new stereotypes for the American public. Jean Harlow partially created the enduring stereotype of the Hollywood blonde. She was Hollywood's number-one sex symbol for a few short years before her tragic death at twenty-six. Her unique look was appropriated by other lusty blond stars—Mae West, Marilyn Monroe, and Madonna to name a few. Harlow's Hollywood-blonde stereotype eventually became a very specific American identity symbol for many people from foreign lands. Hollywood and the Hollywood-blonde became aspects of America's otherness.

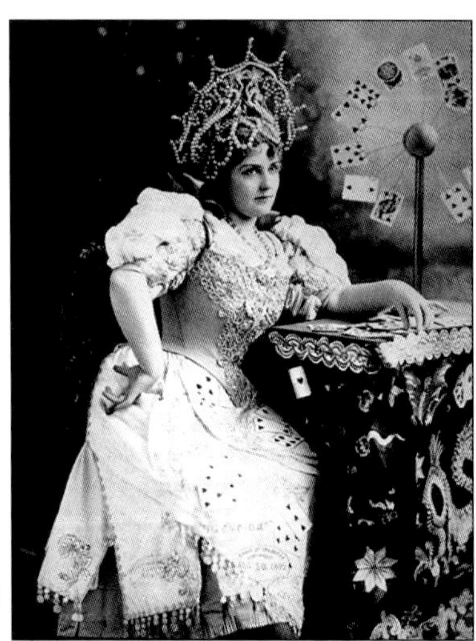

Lillian Russell, 1895

It should not come as a surprise that the qualities attached to a sex symbol are always shifting. A mere thirty years before Jean Harlow, the singer Lillian Russell was America's number-one sex symbol. As an opera soprano and actress, her romantic music reflected deeply into archetypes that could easily inspire lust for an extravagantly charismatic, booming-voiced, robust, 200-pound female star.

Probably the earliest sex symbol for lust, at least in Old Testament terms, was assigned to a modest Eve—with her fig-leaf-covered pubic area and exposed breasts—who was tricked into eating the apple. Eve can be remembered through a variety of ancient paintings and drawings, in most of which she looked pathetically skinny, almost gaunt to us today. Yet her modest skinniness must have stereotyped Eve for sex appeal when she was painted. Surely she was an object of lust, since the authors of the Old Testament desired her to be so, therefore she was—not only to the artists who painted her but also to those who viewed her in paintings during that era.

Most of the stereotypes in evolving twentieth-century media were traditional continuations in a long line of historical developments, as their personas were already formed in the existing media of fairy tales, newspapers, magazines, books, primers, theater, dance, music, fashion, oral history, circus and minstrel shows, as well as toys and other objects.

Stereotypes can be created adventitiously, simply because of the technical achievements within that specific medium—for example, take Mickey Mouse. He was an overnight sensation when he starred in the first sound cartoon, *Steamboat Willie* (1928). Much of the story line behind *Steamboat Willie* was taken from the 1924 Buster Keaton film *The Navigator*. Before sound was added, Mickey Mouse had basically flopped in his previous silent-film cartoon, *Plane Crazy* (1928), even though its story was appropriated from the sensationally successful flight and worldwide popularity of Charles Lindbergh, whose accomplishments fed right into archetypal motif symbols connected to feelings of bravery, courage, and nationalism. Mickey Mouse became a star because Walt Disney did such a perfect job of blending into his cartoons the new technique of sound with action. Slightly later, when Mickey Mouse's personality became fully realized, he combined a supernaturally determined heroism with an aw-shucks attitude. Historical antecedents for the determined hero archetype can also be found in the Old Testament figures of David who slew Goliath or Daniel in the lion's den.

Stereotypes are often created from various parts and pieces of the media. The flapper stereotype in the Jazz Age of the 1920s was a paradigm for the tough, open-minded, fully realized American woman who had gained equality. A lot of her flapper persona came from the apache dance. That incredibly violent dance, although little known today, presented women as super-tough. Other parts of the flapper persona came from publicized or polarized events, such as the suffragette's struggle, which presented woman as an open-minded and a fully realized being. By putting these media pieces together—super-tough, open-minded, fully realized—gender equality began to be achieved. If one identifying word were to describe the flapper, it would be liberated—she is an archetypal symbol and a stereotype for a liberated woman.

Stereotypes do not always evoke the same feelings

in everyone. In fact, many stereotypes are viewed one way by one group of people, while being viewed very differently by another group. The boxer Joe Louis, nicknamed the "Brown Bomber," was viewed very differently by white Americans than by African Americans when he beat the German Max Schmeling in 1938 to retain his title as Heavyweight Champion of the World. At that time, for white America the Brown Bomber represented racial harmony, since he had just won. But for the black Americans, Louis was a symbol of black triumph within a racist society. These are two very different cultural stereotypes. African Americans knew they had a long way to go before gaining racial harmony. But for both black and white Americans, Louis's opponent, Max Schmeling, represented and stereotyped a metaphor for Germany's otherness—an updated archetypal motif for Jung's hostile brethren—simply because he was a citizen of Germany and expressed feelings of macho superiority from the Fascist Hitler regime. Boxing itself is an archetypal motif symbol for life versus death, for survival feelings—at least for the boxer who could die. If he wins, he is the strongest fighter. For the gambler, boxing dredges up many feelings, such as vicarious fear of fighting or greed and power, and probably a whole lot more.

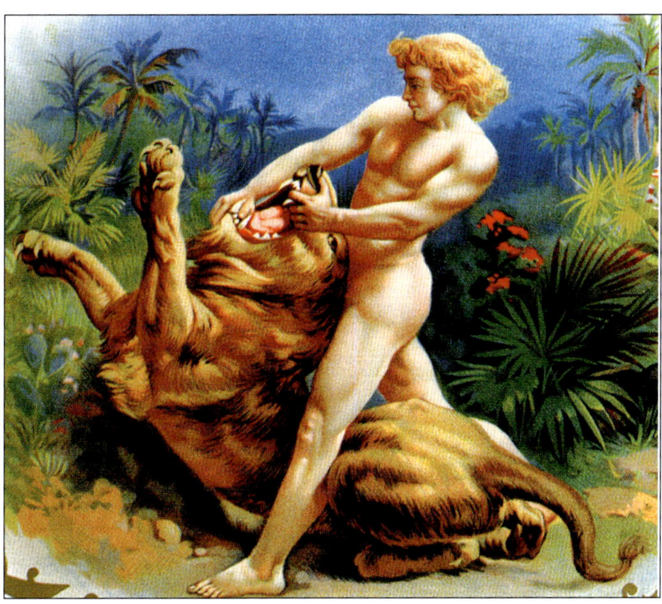

Daniel in the Lion's Den, cigar box label, circa 1900s

Stereotypes are tricky, to say the least. Most seem to be created from a natural evolution within different media at the same time. Most more or less retain their look, as in the Miss America Pageant, where a new stereotypical Miss America is crowned yearly. Only when the pageant was pushed to factor intelligence and equal rights into the winner's attributes did the stereotype change slightly, though not too much. Miss America was always equated with a bathing-suit mentality, continuously reinforcing the archetypal motifs toward youthful, lust eliciting perfection.

Stereotypes like the Ku Klux Klan, which had close to 9 million followers in the mid-1920s, have shown little change. They depended upon hooded fear symbols for vigilante power, wherein dreaded feelings of fear are honestly aroused. The KKK did more than just believe in its superiority.

D. W. Griffith's hugely successful film *The Birth of a Nation* (1915) jump-started the gratefully dead, (if only temporarily), KKK movement that was left over from the 1880s.

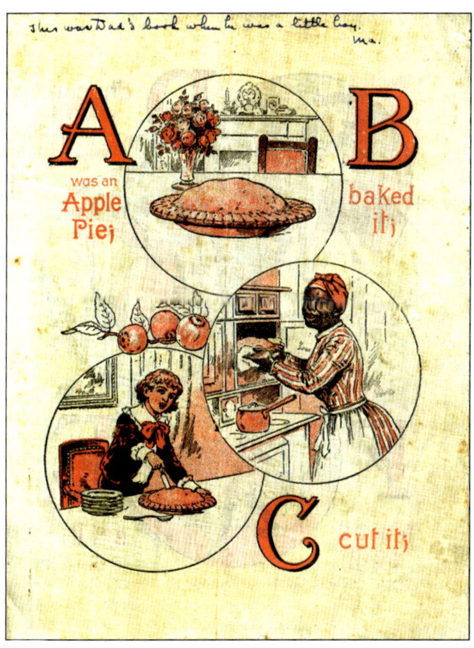

Primer cover, circa 1890s, publisher unknown

Another enduring stereotype is the Jim Crow symbol of Aunt Jemima. There was an early image of her in my grandfather's 1890s primer in which the alphabet letter "B = Baked It" showed Aunt Jemima baking. Primers, as an instrumental part of the media, were some of the first and deepest influences on young children. Aunt Jemima has quite a history: "Aunt Jemima" was a famous show tune in the racist minstrel shows of 1889. That same year, the Pearl Milling Company in St. Joseph, Missouri, placed her image on pancake mix. One year later Davis Mills bought Pearl Milling. Three years later, a real-live Aunt Jemima was found, as an advertising gimmick, in the person of fifty-nine-year-old Nancy Green, a former slave who became a gigantic sensation selling pancakes for the Davis Mills booth at the 1893 World's Columbian Exposition in Chicago. From then on Green was known as the "Pancake Queen." She signed a lifetime contract and traveled on promotional tours all over the United States. Her arrival in various cities was announced on giant billboards. In 1925, Quaker Oats bought Davis Mills. Two years earlier Green had been accidentally hit by a car and died on the South Side of Chicago. In the 1950s, the Aunt Jemima logo came under intense criticism because it portrayed a negative image of a black mammy in a kerchief. To appease criticism, Quaker Oats removed the kerchief—so like it or not, Aunt Jemima still lives on in just about every American supermarket. Corporate power and greed, rather than honest corporate acceptance of a mistaken, outdated racial slur, has kept her century-old stereotype on the shelves.

Over time, archetypal motifs are often generated into new forms. A perfect example is the exotic Middle Eastern woman known as Sheba. The name "Sheba" referred to the exotically dressed, international foreign women who worked as belly dancers in the Middle Eastern side shows of the 1893

World's Columbian Exposition and later in traveling carnivals within the United States. In the minds of most Americans, all Shebas referred to the ancient Middle Eastern Sheba from Solomon's Song of Songs in the Old Testament. The Sheba motif elicits extreme lust, reaffirmed by Salome dancers of the early decades of the twentieth century. Sheba was popularized through Hollywood films of that era. She was further altered by feathered Ziegfeld Follies dancers around 1919, during the early flapper years. When Follies dancer Gilda Gray startled America with her dance craze known as the shimmy, she was attired in an exotic Egyptian revival look. By 1923 she added a wiggling form of Hawaiian hula into her shimmy, as seen throughout America in her shimmy-hula film *Aloma of the South Seas* (1926), which earned a whopping $3 million in the first three months at movie theaters. By the 1930s the Egyptian revival craze was over. During the Great Depression, Betty Boop continued the South Seas escapist archetype in her shimmy-hula cartoon *Betty Boop's Bamboo Isle* (1932), as did Dorothy Lamour in her film version of *Aloma of the South Seas* (1941).

By 1941, the South Seas became the theater of operations for Americans fighting against the Japanese in World War II. A year after the war ended, the South Seas were dramatically transformed by the United States with Project Able, the first peacetime atomic test bomb exploded in the atmosphere near Bikini atoll. The bomb was nicknamed "Gilda," after Rita Hayworth, who starred as a liberating erotic dancer/femme fatalé in the popular postwar Hollywood film *Gilda* (1946). *Life* magazine's 1941 pinup picture of Hayworth had been lustfully viewed by millions of servicemen in World War II. That same pinup picture was painted onto Gilda's bomb casing. The name Gilda, of course, also subliminally referred to Gilda Gray and Sheba (belly dancing), Gilda Gray (shimmy dancing), and the South Seas woman (hula dancing). Each dance had been blended and slowly transformed starting two decades earlier. Four days after Gilda was exploded at Bikini atoll, French auto engineer Louis Reard brought out the erotic bikini bathing suit, named after Bikini atoll and the atom. When bikinis were seen on the beaches of France, the shock was felt worldwide. Those same beaches had been closed for the war years, so the suit added a sense of liberation—an instinctive archetypal feeling that has always surfaced after the devastating visual archetypes of a war.

It was not a coincidence that Gilda was Hayworth's movie title in 1946, because it was Gilda Gray who created the liberation archetype in her shimmy dance of twenty years earlier, as an instinctual visual response to the horror symbols of World War I. Hayworth's *Gilda* was a re-creation of that same need. By 1957, Bridget Bardot's bikini-clad sex symbol added an increased sense of the sweet life of liberation to Westernized audiences worldwide, most of whom were also moved by the new sounds of American rock and roll. By the 1960s bikinis were on America's beaches. Again it was Liberation (with a capital L) from the uptight, suppressed 1950s and the Korean War. Three decades later, bikini-clad women were the stars of the television show *Baywatch*, which has been shown in 148 countries and translated into 41 languages. By 1999 a billion viewers saw each episode. *Baywatch* sensibilities of the bikini motif pranced heavily

into Middle Eastern Islamic cultures, whose women and men saw it in entirely different ways than Westernized viewers saw it. Ironically, those symbols of erotica, which started out with exotically dressed Middle Eastern belly dancers at the 1893 World's Columbian Exposition, went full circle back to the Middle Eastern cultures as liberated women in the bikini motif. All this was done through the combined media forms of dance, theater, magazine pinups, fashion, film, posters, and TV.

THOSE WHO CHOOSE TO USE STEREOTYPES AND ARCHETYPES

Julia Roberts starred in the title role of Steven Soderbergh's film *Erin Brockovich* (2000), which was based on a true story; Roberts won the Oscar for Best Actress. The real Erin Brockovich was a genuine American heroine, courageously fighting against corporate greed and deadly environmental pollution. To make the film successful, Soderbergh cast Roberts as an antagonistic, brash, down-home heroine with courage and a conscience. With her vociferous obscenities, in-your-face body language, and direct honesty, she brilliantly copied the aw-shucks little guy; in her case she was the sexy, brash woman fighting the big-bully world. Her foil in the film was always the attorney, who told her many times that she shouldn't be doing what others could do better. In the years preceding *Erin Brockovich*, Roberts had developed her own Hollywood stereotype of the American aw-shucks beauty next door. She was cast perfectly for her role. Few other actresses have successfully incorporated that Mickey Mouse attitude into their charisma. Soderbergh might well have known that Erin Brockovich was a revived ancient motif of the little guy who owned the determined hero archetype. She was a new female, empowered David against Goliath.

Martin Luther King Day and Columbus Day are two important American holidays honoring extremely different archetypal symbols. As late as 1983, no African Americans had been honored with a holiday in their name. Until then, America had honored only three individuals with national holidays—George Washington, Abraham Lincoln, and Christopher Columbus. At that time, Martin Luther King Jr. was a symbol for the power of nonviolence from racism's struggle, as typified in his "I Have a Dream" speech. King championed the struggle for civil rights during a crucial time, then he was grievously assassinated. His contemporary, Malcolm X, who believed in self-preservation, had also championed the struggle for civil rights during that same crucial time, then he, too, was grievously assassinated. Some of us are old enough to remember that the legislation for Martin Luther King Day was highly controversial for Congress to pass, even though King preached nonviolence to white America and was a supremely important figure at that time. The mass media had cast Malcolm X out; he was thought by white America to be a symbol for the power of violence and was not being considered for a holiday. When King received the Nobel Peace Prize, Malcolm X said: "He got the peace prize, we got the problem . . . If I'm following a general, and he's leading me into a battle, and the enemy tends to give him rewards, or awards, I get suspicious of him. Especially if he gets a peace award before the war is over."[12]

King as a nonviolent symbol was greatly empowered by his untimely assassination; his death made him a justified martyr, somewhat similar to an African American Jesus who had died for America's sins. What of Malcolm X? He died too, but American officialdom never wanted Malcolm X to become a justifiable martyr. To most white Americans, Malcolm X remained rebellious. When Congress finally approved Martin Luther King Day, it was an archetypal motif for black and white Americans. White Americans could feel guilt release because Martin Luther King Day, now that it was official, represented guilt removal—a release from the white man's centuries-old burden for being the oppressor during slavery. For African Americans Martin Luther King Day was an archetypal motif for honoring their courageous heroic leader and a step in overcoming racism.

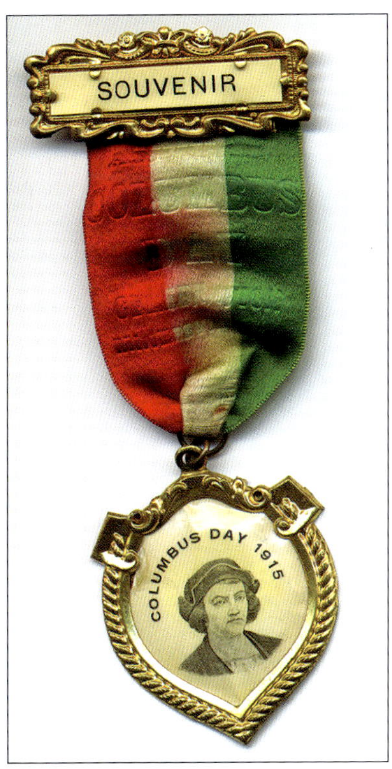

Columbus Day souvenir pin, 1915

On the other hand, on Columbus Day we are supposed to feel honor for Christopher Columbus as an archetypal symbol for the courageous discoverer of America. We are told that Columbus discovered America in 1492 using three ships that were paid for by Spain. Few people know that Columbus was a slave trader before he became an explorer, transporting and selling West Africans to Portugal. Few know that the *Santa Maria* ran aground at Hispaniola on his first voyage and had to be abandoned. The brutal sadism and intentional genocide Columbus performed on native peoples when he returned on his second voyage, during his thirst for power and wealth, is almost never mentioned. American schoolchildren are not told how he cut off the hand of every native who did not bring him gold, nor of the war dogs he used, which had been trained to rip out the natives' entrails. By 1536—due to Columbus's complete disregard for human

life, the diseases he inadvertently brought to the islands, and the natives who committed suicide rather than become slaves—at least 8 million natives had died and their island cultures were almost extinct. If anyone should be thought of as a monster or madman connected to Jung's hostile brethren motif, look no further than Columbus. Jung's motif should be bumped up a notch, identifying murderers like Columbus (or Hitler) as a archetypal symbol for genocidal warrior. There needs to be a Martin Luther King Day, but never again should there be a Columbus Day.

Similarly, no American citizen would want to have a town or college named after the pre–Revolutionary War British general Jeffrey Amherst (as in Amherst College; Amherst, Massachusetts; and at least seven other states that have a town named Amherst). It was Amherst who ordered smallpox scabs be inserted into blankets that were later given to Native American tribes, thereby condoning genocide through the use of biological warfare. He was probably America's first bioterrorist, who caused entire tribes to become extinct. He, too, fits the mold for an archetypal genocidal warrior. In his letter ordering smallpox, he even alludes to Columbus's killer dogs (the letter from Amherst is shown on page 89).

In building empires around the world, as Spain, Britain, and other European nations attempted, there were catastrophic effects on many cultures in their path of conquest. By the early 1800s Britain had gained control of its inroads into most continents. Had they wanted to, the British could have boasted of being the major slave traders to the United States while controlling much of Africa and the Orient. Britain outlawed slave trading using its own vessels in 1807, then outlawed slavery within its own territories in 1834. Ironically, just five years later Britain became involved in its first of two Opium Wars with China, which occurred because Her Majesty's English were also the major drug-trafficking criminal organization in the world at that time (very few drug cartels of the twentieth century begin to compare to England in the early nineteenth century in volume and criminality). Growing opium in India, a country then stereotyped as the Jewel of the Crown, was the way India repaid Britain for being a territory—paid through Britain's East India Company, which shipped thousands of tons of opium illegally through Canton, then Macao, illegally trading opium for manufactured Chinese goods and tea. A century of British smuggling had forced opium dependency upon the Chinese. Opium was and is connected to an ancient archetype for feeling escape through rare narcotized dream pleasure, rather than pain. The Chinese government was well aware that opium was Britain's major control mechanism over its slowly decaying population—any Chinese person caught selling or using opium was executed. During that same time period, opium was outlawed for use in Britain. China fought its two Opium Wars against Britain's illegal opium imports, yet to no avail. In losing both wars, China had to accept treaties that further weakened their government. In the first treaty they gave up Hong Kong. By 1844, the United States and France were granted access to China (at that time the Shakers were the major growers of opium in the United States). The most disgraceful parts of the second Opium War treaty of 1860 were the complete legalization of opium in China and the humiliating provision allowing unrestricted propagation of Christianity throughout all regions of China. By 1906, 27 percent of adult Chinese men had become addicted opium smokers—that was approximately 135 million people of the 500 million population. No wonder Napoleon Bonaparte called China "the sleeping giant."

As a result of these debilitating Opium Wars, a great human exportation began, shipping indentured and smuggled Chinese men and women into the western United States. Chinese men were used for mining during the 1850s Gold Rush and were 95 percent of the workforce in building railroads, while 85 percent of the women were used for intensive prostitution. Meanwhile, Christian missionaries spread throughout China.

Surprising to many is that Christianity's archetypal symbols have permeated American culture to the point of oversaturation, so much so that paradoxically almost no one is aware of them—simply because they are everywhere. Consider Christianity's devil. When the world watched Jack Nicholson playing the Joker dressed as a clown in *Batman* (1989), most people who had seen Nicholson act before knew he was some sort of joker/clown/devil stereotype that penetrated our psyche, as it crossed unhappy humor with happy horror, easily connected to a very sadistic archetypal motif. Certainly many clowns have been made up with devilish faces before. Subconsciously, Nicholson's Joker and the devil were one. As it was, Nicholson had always performed with his intentionally reinvented devilish persona, an important archetypal motif symbol for the hostile brethren, as well as a heavy-duty otherness stereotype. It is obvious when you see Nicholson cast as the alienated pianist turned redneck/lover in *Five Easy Pieces* (1970), or the bandaged-nose private detective/lover in *Chinatown* (1974), or the demented writer/lover in *The Shining* (1980). All three films showed us that his creative demonic depths made him a much stronger psychological madman force than the simple Hollywood stereotypical sly guy or sly villain. Nicholson's devil persona is just one of many variations on the devil motif. Some devil motifs are much less humorous and some so hideous—as in the Black Mass—that the media has yet to fully promote them (as far as I am aware). There are also Hollywood actresses who have created various forms of the femme fatalé, otherwise known as the dangerously empowered woman motif, into their archetypal persona.

In opposition to the hostile brethren/devil motif is Christopher Reeve cast in the title role in *Superman I* (1978) and *Superman II* (1980). The superhero archetype that penetrated viewers' psyches was one that connected him to the ultimate savior or great indestructible protector. For many people of the Christian faith, Superman might have been an archetypal motif for a low-flying Jesus. It was a coincidental reawakening in 1995, when an astonished America gasped upon hearing that Reeve had broken his neck in a fall from his horse. Everyone in America probably felt blessed that he miraculously lived. The idea of the miracle worker, a savior, was there already in Superman, vis-à-vis Reeve, in much more than a just a simple remembrance. Had Nicholson fallen from a horse and broken his neck, the world would not have thought of him as a godlike miracle worker. Later Reeve took on advocacy work; he was named chairman of the American Paralysis Association and vice chairman of the National Organization on Disability. He created the Christopher Reeve Foundation in 1996, which focuses on the quality of life for the disabled. Reeve remained a special kind of great indestructible protector until his death in 2004. His tragic fall added a deeper feeling to his Superman charisma. It would be hard to go back and watch a Superman movie without thinking that Reeve was some sort of true superman. Had he walked again, he could have probably won a bid for the American presidency. Ronald Reagan did just that, with a lot less Hollywood charisma going for him (Reagan was an undercover agent for the FBI in the 1940s for the House Un-American Activites Committee). That's how much people are fooled by disguised Hollywood stereotypes and archetypes; that's just part of how much Christian symbolism plays into American life.

Many people state that comic-strip characters like Superman should only be viewed as fantasy and enjoyed for their pleasant escapist entertainment value. They also say comic-strip characters are not there to present role models and that no one would, or should, seriously apply cartoon characters to any simulacrum of real life. After all, they say, cartoon characters are only ducks, mice, rabbits, or superheroes. But in real life, when was the last time you heard a duck, a mouse, or a rabbit talking, or saw a person flying over a building? Because animals and superheroes are made human in comics strips, cartoons, and films, they become real. They rely on human attributes and replay a variety of stereotypes that intrinsically involve archetypes, so they are real. They evoke instinctive feelings within the viewer—so they are very real.

Superman first appeared in the comics in 1939 and has been part of the American landscape for a long time. Unfortunately, Americans needed Superman when the World Trade Center Twin Towers were hit by jumbo jets. Seeing TV footage of people who were trapped desperately leaping from upper-story windows created a symbolic and tragic reality check that will never be forgotten by those who bore witness. It looked like the perfect moment for Superman to appear as our archetypal ultimate savior. Had he been able to stop the planes before they hit, he would have performed the ultimate deus ex machina in his role as the great indestructible protector.

In truth, what the world really knows about Nicholson and Reeve, as just people, is very little. And America itself, even with its diversity of cultures, its poor as well as its rich, and its overcrowded jails (a not-so-novel form of racism because a disproportionate number of African Americans are in prison), is still represented by the stereotype of the rich American, a label programmed into many people throughout the world. It is easy to see America's otherness in terms of wealth and greed, particularly since Americans use so much of the world's resources in comparison to other countries. Yet stereotypes are a shallow device in an inappropriate attempt to sum up an entire nation's personal diversity. As such, national stereotypes are easily manipulated for political means and, consequently, have immense power. A case in point might be Walt Disney's cast of characters, in particular Mickey Mouse.

Much of the world connects Mickey Mouse as an otherness stereotype associated with the United States as a bully, whereas most of America thinks it loved or still loves Walt Disney. Rarely has Disney been viewed as a propagandist and marketeer of Christian morality. Less is he understood as a political force, but that he was, and one of the most influential in the twentieth century. Disney controlled a special slice of the mediums of film, cartoon, comics, and television from 1930 until his death in 1966 (we are still part of the Disney whitewash/backlash). Although his animated cartoons look to be simple re-creations of old fairy tales (*Snow White*), they are also complex political and religious propaganda. Often the characters he chose to re-create (Davy Crockett) are inflated individuals who he used to promote America's Manifest Destiny, otherwise known by many nasty-sounding names: overt American imperialist expansionism, multinational capitalism, whitewashed world of fundamental Christian homogenization. When Mickey Mouse became an internationally recognized icon, he became a way to stereotype America's otherness. Mickey Mouse easily represented the bully because he was a paradigm for Disney, whose films had saturated the world and created an empire. Inherent in every Disney film, at least until 1966, was a disguised media blitz of patriarchal white Christian moralist myths. Unless you are willing to analyze the ancient fairy tales and American legends that Disney interpreted, his whitewash might not be readily apparent. His films helped to legitimize the McCarthy era, the House Un-American Activities Committee, the strength of the FBI, the Christian right, and, most important, the powerful neoconservative forces of the twenty-first century.

Up until now, the Christian morality that Disney attempted to strengthen has been counterbalanced by gains against racism through civil rights, by gains against blind patriotism through the Vietnam antiwar effort, by gains against sexism through the feminist movement, and by gains against homophobia through gay rights. All of these polarized forces are anti-Disney. At present all Americans are faced with a new Christian morality tool: the Patriot Act, disguised to look as if it protects American citizens. What forces can be assembled to balance it, only the future will show.

Stereotypes and archetypes can be used in many ways. If an actor or actress who performed in charismatic stereotype/archetype roles or a disguised politician who mimics a charismatic stereotype/archetype can be elected to high office, then the American form of democratic government is in serious trouble. And it is. Ronald Reagan proved that a Hollywood actor can become president. George W. Bush, the oil-baseball floccinaucinihilipilification (a trifle—that's a real word!), proved that the Prince Charming stereotype could become president. For he was the ideal Prince Charming, pulled right from Disney's *Snow White and the Seven Dwarfs*. His first "win" proved that Prince Charming was, and still is, a very viable stereotype (with symbolic archetypal edges, because a Prince Charming has family wealth, connections, and great power behind him)—even though America is supposedly not an oligarchy (or is it?). His running for any office, of course, was dependent upon his father having been president before him. All George W. Bush did was sprinkle in a touch of aw shucks to make himself a more appealing country-boy stereotype to a wider American populace. That he spoke in twisted words only proved to his

admirers that he was a bona-fide down-to-earth good old boy who could relate to the needs of the common man—he was one of them. He wasn't eloquent. He played dumb. All the better to not play up his Harvard and Yale education. George W. Bush's Prince Charming stereotype won the 2000 election by disguised deception (particularly when his cousin on Fox news made him the winner before the Florida vote was fully counted and the rest of mainstream TV media went along with this premature announcement). First of all, enough Americans that vote were fooled by the well-disguised George W. Bush to make his total vote tally only 500,000 less than Al Gore's. Secondly, the all-powerful and wise Supreme Court was composed of a slim majority of conservative Republicans, like his father, so that the American ideal of elective honesty was destroyed. We all know Bush's final vote tally was five votes cast by Supreme Court conservatives to four votes cast by Supreme Court liberals. Those five who voted for Bush let their archetypal instinctive feelings of greed and power go out of control against all logic of fairness. A Florida recount should have been taken. However, if fugacity (a fleeting moment) reigns, history may well fault Bush, stereotyping him as an illegitimate president who, as an evolutionary archetypal dirty-trickster motif, stole not one but two elections (although the winner writes the history). An earlier dirty-trickster president, Nixon, in pure hugger-mugger fashion (secrecy and disorder), was forced to resign, his own tapes delivering the coup de grace. He will always be known by his nickname—the "Crook." Nixon let his DNA feelings of greed and power get out of control.

Archetypes and stereotypes can be used as divisive weapons to elevate one group while pushing another group down by using prejudice. The archetype of an alluring woman was meant not only to elevate women to a high pedestal (which is a patriarchal phallic conquest symbol—like the steeple on a church or a tall monument) but also to demean her beauty into a trophy that sat on a shelf or lay in the bed of her male patriarch. If her figure and face were beautiful enough, then she qualified to offer her other talents. The various sex symbol stereotypes shown throughout this book worked, and still work, because they reflect directly into contemporary archetypal motif symbols for propagandized superficial projections of one's self worth, vis-à-vis beauty, meant to attract another person's lust, which when demeaned deeply denotes misogyny. A divisive prop-man-up analogue was John Gay's poem from *The Beggar's Opera* (1728):

> Man may escape from rope and gun,
>> Nay, some have outliv'd the doctor's pill:
> Who takes a woman must be undone.
>> That basilisk is sure to kill.
> The fly that sips treacle is lost in the sweets,
>> So he that tastes woman, woman, woman,
>> He that tastes woman, ruin meets.

To add even further damage to women, the word "basilisk" refers to an ancient dragon whose figurative evil eye can kill by breath, gaze, or gossip (the modern cliche archetype "Dragon Lady" came from the 1934 comic strip *Terry and the Pirates*). Poems as horrid as Gay's make their highest contribution to the literature of constantly evolving human relationships simply by giving insights into how deeply ingrained misogyny really was (and still is). The poem could have come from the Bible, which also seriously demeaned womankind. Violence against women has many subtle forms—witness the postcard, a conventional media format for slurred humor, of the World War II sailor getting a shot into his hula girl tattoo (right into her breast), saying: "Give 'er a good shot Doc, she can take it!"

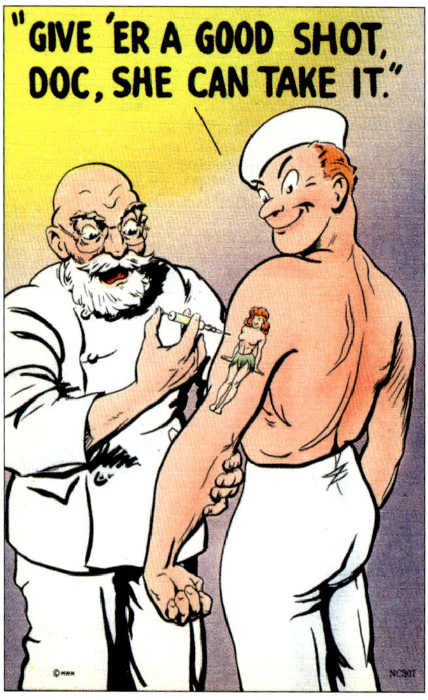

Postcard, M W M Color Litho, Aurora, Missouri., 1940s

Stereotypes can often be used to promote conformity in thought and action. A simplistic example would be the Lana Turner sweater-girl stereotype, worn and conformed to by most American adolescent girls and young women in the 1940s and 1950s. Anyone intent upon forcing conformity on others at any cost, or arbitrarily, or violently, is committing what is labeled procrustean behavior.

Francis Bellamy was a Christian minister and the powerful chairman of the Committee of State Superintendents of Education in the National Education Association when he wrote the Pledge of Allegiance for the Columbus centennial in 1892. Bellamy exemplified the use of procrustean behavior after he published his Pledge of Allegiance in *The Youth's Companion*, a magazine he owned, and then offered incentives for all schools who placed it into practice. His Pledge of Allegiance played into archetypes that promoted a superior country—including the U.S. flag, which is a strong archetypal symbol for patriotic feelings (as well as placing your hand over your heart). All this is regimented, indoctrinated devotion to God and country, beginning in first grade. Unfortunately officialdom needs patriotic youth to fight in their wars.

An incongruous example of eliciting conformity into children with the idea of creating peace was promoted by Dr. J. Stanley Brown, National Thrift Director, who in 1919 had 15 million surplus World War I hand grenades dismantled, turned into piggy banks, and distributed free to children. Knowing

of the allure created by the look and feel of weapons, this idea seems oxymoronic, thereby going against the instinctive feelings that archetypal war symbols always generate, which is a fascination with power and death. There is nothing nonviolent about a hand grenade turned into a piggy bank.

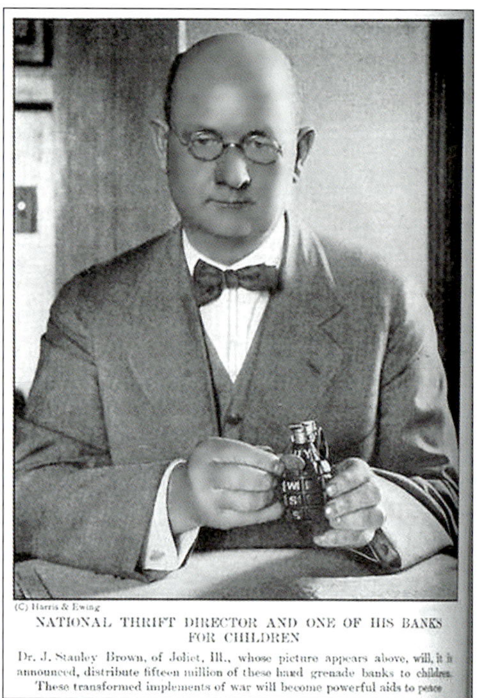

NATIONAL THRIFT DIRECTOR AND ONE OF HIS BANKS FOR CHILDREN

Dr. J. Stanley Brown, of Joliet, Ill., whose picture appears above, will, it is announced, distribute fifteen million of these hand grenade banks to children. These transformed implements of war will become powerful aids to peace.

The text reads: "National Thrift Director and one of his banks for children. Dr. J. Stanley Brown of Joliet, Ill., whose picture appears above, will, it is announced, distribute fifteen million of these hand grenade banks to children. These transformed implements of war will become powerful aids to peace." *Outlook*, June 18, 1919

An extreme example of draconian conformity would be what Harry Hamilton Laughlin, head of the Department of Eugenics in Washington, D.C., devised in his diabolic sterilization laws of 1910, and which states adopted and used by the 1920s (slightly later, Hitler reused Laughlin's model in Germany).

STEREOTYPES IN CONFLICT : ARCHETYPAL MOTIFS OUT OF CONTROL

Twentieth-century media, when it had profitable stereotypes, often excessively developed them. Because of Superman's popularity, there have been more than four hundred attempts at superheroes in the comics. Another case in point would be the redundant cowboy, which became a stereotype in the Hollywood Western: Broncho Billy, William Hart, Tom Mix, Buck Jones (the first smoking "cool" cowboy), Hopalong Cassidy, the Lone Ranger, Roy Rogers, Gene Autry, John Wayne, Clint Eastwood, and hundreds of others. The continued presence of cowboys in the media and the sheer volume of public exposure to them leaves us with an archetypal motif symbol promoting feelings of freedom and toughness, whether or not we even like cowboys. That feeling, sitting inside us, is free for anyone to manipulate and plunder. Enter advertising and twentieth-century international market globalization. Bring on the Marlboro Man. What was he exactly? A disguise of Hollywood's western cowboy stereotype. When Marlboro cigarettes came out in the 1920s, they were aimed at glamorous women, but the product sold poorly. By the 1930s, the ivory tip was changed to red as an advertising gimmick—to not show lipstick. This advertising ploy was unsuccessful too. The brand was then removed from the market.

Marlboros were reintroduced in the 1950s, when initial information about a possible link between lung cancer and cigarettes developed, and its filter suggested a safer choice than the big-three leading brands: Camel, Lucky Strike, and Chesterfield. At first the filters were seen as effeminate, then Philip Morris enlisted the Leo Burnett Agency who, in 1955, introduced the macho "Tattooed Man" ads. In each of these ads, the tattooed wrist of a virile cattle rancher, airman, or navy officer was shown, with his hand holding a lit Marlboro. (Having various macho men advertise cigarettes had been used successfully by Camel cigarettes in the 1940s.) A large part

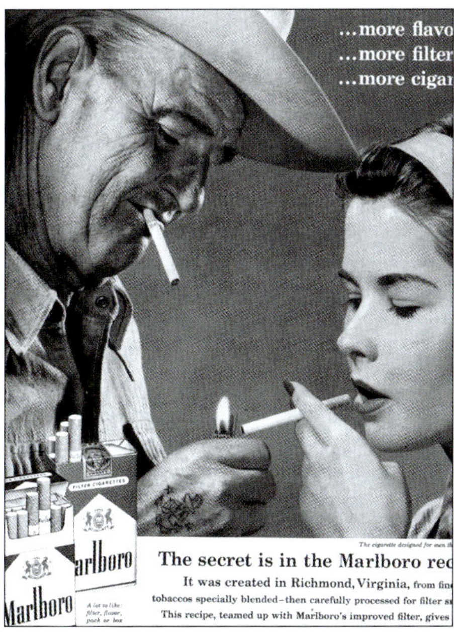

Marlboro ad, detail, 1956 © Philip Morris Inc.

of Marlboro's new appeal was the box's strikingly simplified colors, the immediacy of the flip-top box, and the instant recognition of membership into the group who displayed it. In a brief eight months, Marlboro was the top-selling cigarette, its sales increasing 5,000 percent. From marketing studies developed during the first three years, Philip Morris realized that the public most identified with the cowboy Marlboro Man. He became the prevalent advertising figure along with the box, which was a carrying card available to everyone, visible proof of participation in or appreciation for the cowboy's idealized way of life. It meant that its smoker felt a sense of freedom and toughness. Through instinctive association, the Marlboro Man was a hugely successful analogue to the cowboy stereotype. From 1960 to 1995 the Marlboro Man was ever present in advertising throughout the media. If we saw

an ad with a cowboy with a cigarette in his hand, we knew it was the Marlboro Man. His stereotype was one of the world's most identifiable, probably second only to Mickey Mouse. By the late 1990s, when tobacco companies were being sued for lying about nicotine addiction (they are still hiding that cigarettes are radioactive when lit) and the cancer-causing effects of cigarettes, Marlboro was able to have ads where the Marlboro Man didn't even have a cigarette in his hand. He had achieved his infinite possibilities.

Here's the irony and here's the point. By the 1970s most of America had lost interest in Westerns; few films and TV programs were made promoting that cowboy image. It had been tremendously overdone. The archetypal motif symbol promoting the need to feel freedom and toughness, however, had not disappeared in the least. So Philip Morris and the disguised Marlboro Man basked in the glorious Western sunset, while people rapidly got lung cancer (and died). Sadly, corporations, without a moral obligation or conscience, violate humanity. The Marlboro Man is probably the easiest case in point in understanding this concept of disguising one thing for another. To them money was more important than the smoker's life. Statistically, many more Americans have died from cancer and diseases caused by smoking than have died fighting for America in all its twentieth-century wars; and in fact, since cigarettes were given free to soldiers in the two world wars, cigarettes managed to kill many of the veterans too.

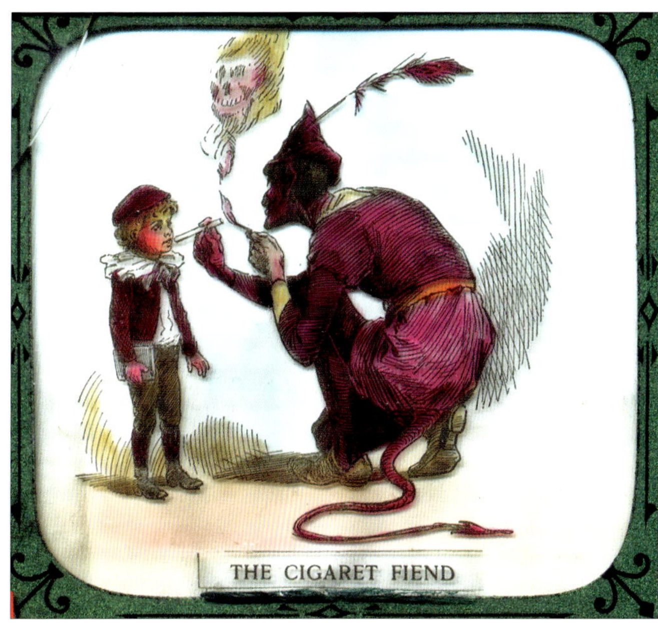

"The Cigaret Fiend," anti-smoking lantern slide, circa 1890s

Capitalism's growth, through media manipulation of American stereotypes that promote feelings of liberation like the Marlboro Man or a bikini-clad Pamela Anderson in *Baywatch*—have become America's disguised way to continue its expansionist role. Multinational corporations' need for more of the global market share has pushed American products beyond its shores into foreign lands. Many who work in poorer foreign countries are multinational corporations' slaves forced to live on a poverty wage. America's disguised stereotypes have taken on the power that was previously reserved for religious missionaries, the church, and the colonizers' gun and plow. Capitalism's limits are the outer edges of other cultures who have not accepted all of America's mass media stereotypes. These edges reflect the ever-changing boundaries of American Manifest Destiny.

When the archetypal sex-symbol pinup of Rita Hayworth as Gilda was painted onto the casing of the first peacetime atomic test bomb, little did the scientists and government realize what weapon they really were testing. Was the weapon the atomic bomb or the pinup painted on the bomb casing? This is truly the ultimate paradox and irony of these two important twentieth-century archetypal motifs. Although it occurred nearly sixty years ago, the Bikini atoll atomic explosion was symbolized worldwide by the tangential invention of the bombshell bikini bathing suit, which has defined the limits of mass media's acceptable stereotypes when forced into cultures like Islam, where women are usually seen fully clothed. The fundamental question is quite simple: What is present-day America's ultimate mass-media propaganda weapon toward the Islamic culture? Is it the nuclear bomb, which is a device of war whose archetype elicits fear of mass death, or the bikini, which is just one of many archetypal motifs that embodies feelings of lust? Most people would quickly answer that it was the nuclear bomb, thinking the question was semi-ridiculous. But unless it was used for genocide, the nuclear bomb is not specifically aimed toward changing a culture's traditions. Whereas disguised stereotypes like the pinup or the bikini—ones that embody cultural motifs that elicit lust and offer liberation—are really the basic inner issues at conflict. If Islamic women wore bikinis, there would be a profound loss of their cultural traditions.

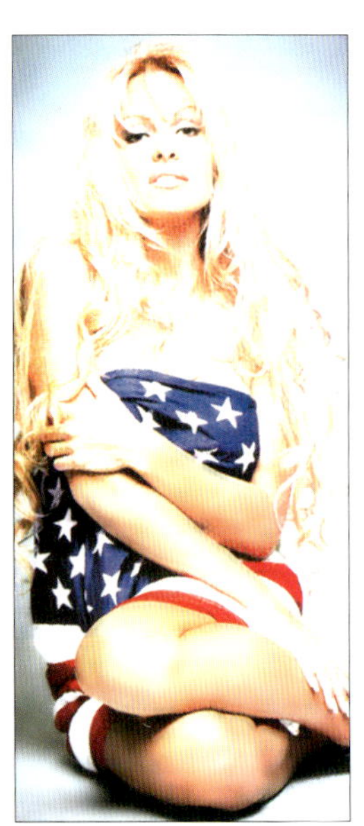

Pamela Anderson, poster, 2003

When the Taliban took control in Afghanistan, it outlawed media such as film and television. Only radio was acceptable within their law and the most joy radio offered the Afghan population was the soap opera *New Home—New Life*. Their Muslim fundamentalist political leaders knew *Baywatch* offered a lustful life and a sense of liberation that was unquestionably out of control. It defied and defiled their one God, Allah. This was an identity crisis. When America's war with Osama bin Laden and the scapegoat Taliban did occur, Pamela Anderson, the *Baywatch* superstar, became the flag-draped pinup for American soldiers; she was displayed on page 74 of *Newsweek* on November 12, 2001, then made into a popular poster. Whoever chose Anderson as the American pinup undoubtedly followed their unconscious and subliminal thought processes in making her the people's choice. Anderson was the perfect disguise for feeling liberation as well as the openly patriotic archetypal motif for a U.S. war against fundamentalist Islam.

Following that war the United States went to war against Saddam Hussein, knowing that there is competition for attaining oil for America and other industrialized nations. The world no longer lives on a gold standard. Oil, not gold, is what lubricates world economies. And oil happens to be under the earth of several Middle Eastern Islamic nations who believe in only one God—Allah—who presides over a religion that does not want pictorial representations. As such they are iconoclasts, whereas Christians are iconodules (those who believe in pictorial representations of their religious icons); two very different visual/spiritual concepts that have been in place for many hundreds of years.

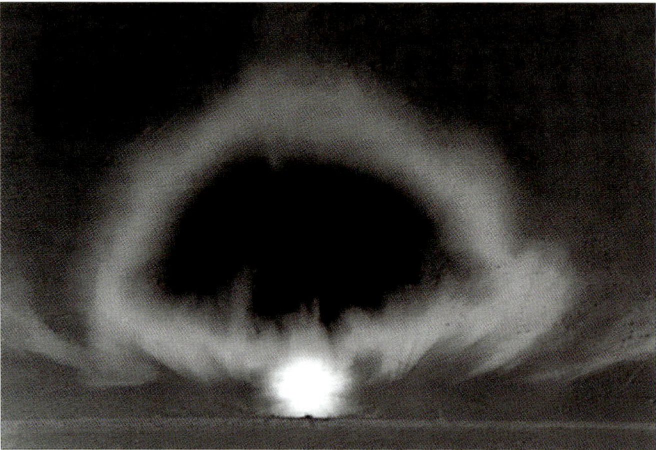

Trinity Site atomic bomb test, 1945, pinhole photograph, Julian Mack. Courtesy: Los Alamos National Laboratories

Besides, George W. Bush knew that a war against a propagandized (propped-up and false) enemy like Saddam Hussein was an instinctive archetype, helpful in Bush's own reelection campaign because war begets archetypal feelings of fear that are easily promoted—the American public instinctively wants to be safe. Bringing democracy to the world is simply a neoconservative disguise for keeping and maintaining America's oil needs by expanding Manifest Destiny just a little farther. World control through greed, not democracy, is what the neoconservatives are after. Oil is just one of many assets connected to superiority, power, and longevity.

Ironically, war is probably easier for Americans to understand than peace. If any country or group or person were to invent strong mass-media peace stereotypes using new archetypal motifs, ones that encroached upon Americans in profound ways, would that not be a monumental cause for many Americans to consciously go to war? Most Americans are not ready to understand nonviolent peace. Charlton Heston, when faced with the question of even minimal gun control, held his weapon over his head and emphatically retorted, "From my cold, dead hands!" There would be an even more cataclysmic outcry and rampage if anyone invented a strong media stereotype that encroached upon Christianity's many icons, particularly if it was available within the boundaries of the United States. Yet God-stealing, which involves cultural change, has always been acceptable to most Americans—so long as *we* do it to *them*.

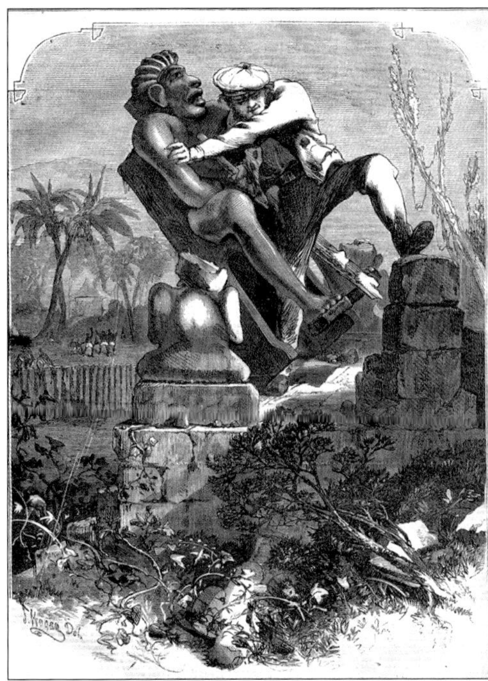

"Daley's raid among the idols . . . exerting his strength with a Yo-Ho! which was half-patriotic, half-national, down came the ponderous mass." *Frank Leslie's Boys' and Girls' Weekly*, etching, September 24, 1870

It was no coincidence that the World Trade Center's Twin Towers (proudly the world's tallest buildings until 1973) came down. Why were they so tall? So Americans could be proud that we are the best. For the terrorists the destruction of those buildings represented a monumental act against what they considered was America's God—the almighty dollar connected to world trade. The almighty dollar is an archetypal symbol for feeling superiority. When its value is decreased, there is fear.

America now increasingly clings to Christianity so desperately because ever since the mass media age began fear has been promoted and propagandized into so many political, social and commercial messages. Fear is the politician's and the evangelical's tool—a disguise used to hold a population in limbo. Why? Because fear is inherent in so many superiority archetypes, vigorously reinstilled into the American puritan work ethic. In his refashioned specious statement mawkishly copying John O'Sullivan's Manifest Destiny from 1845, Eric Johnston, then president of the United States Chamber of Commerce and later head of the Motion Picture Producer's Association exclaimed (ninety-nine years after O'Sullivan) in 1944:

> If ever humankind and geography have been brought
> together under the most propitious circumstances, it is here
> in the United States of America. One feels almost that the
> kindly Providence which contrived this miracle is watching
> . . . to see how the epic test of man's capacity for grandeur
> is working out. Can man, thus richly dowered with all
> the prerequisites of greatness, live up to his magnificent
> opportunity? Can we temper his spirit and lift his mind to
> new and unprecedented levels?[13]

In the near future the next real U.S. crisis might become a war about water, or air, or humanity itself (the lowering sperm count or cancer to reproductive systems). How these multiple crisis situations can be resolved without continual struggle is the major question. Certainly the United States cannot continue forever on the same path that was devised—and is still, remarkably, in place—by Foreign Policy Planning director George Kennan in 1948 who perceived:

> We have about 50% of the world's wealth but only 6.3%
> of its population. In this situation, we cannot fail to be the
> object of envy and resentment. Our real test in the coming
> period is to devise a pattern of relationships which will
> permit us to maintain this position of disparity. We need
> not deceive ourselves that we can afford today the luxury
> of altruism and world benefaction—unreal objectives
> such as human rights, the raising of living standards, and
> democratization.[14]

Answers will only be possible when stereotypes, archetypes, and their aroused instinctive feelings are understood. Until then, exploitative propagandism, greed, power, and war will be inescapable. This book suggests that all people, not only Americans, be concerned about the various disguised as well as undisguised stereotypes and archetypal motifs that the media (governmental, institutional, and corporate) reinvents, recontinues, redefines, and reinforces through regenerated archetypal motif symbols to arouse instinctive DNA feelings. Mass media is certainly aware of what instinctive feeling will be unconsciously probed and excited. Mass media does this easily with each changing era. A new life should not mean a new person to propagandize.

This book is not so much about the people in it as it is about the instinctive feelings generated by the media using them as stereotypes and archetypes for disguised agendas.

Humanity has discovered almost every square inch on the planet, little has been left undiscovered—except for a fuller understanding of the human or inhumane within oneself.

Is this what Albert Einstein meant when he pondered:

> The world that we have made as a result of the level of
> thinking that we have done so far, has created problems we
> cannot solve at the level of thinking at which we created
> them . . . We shall require a substantially new manner of
> thinking if humankind is to survive.[15]

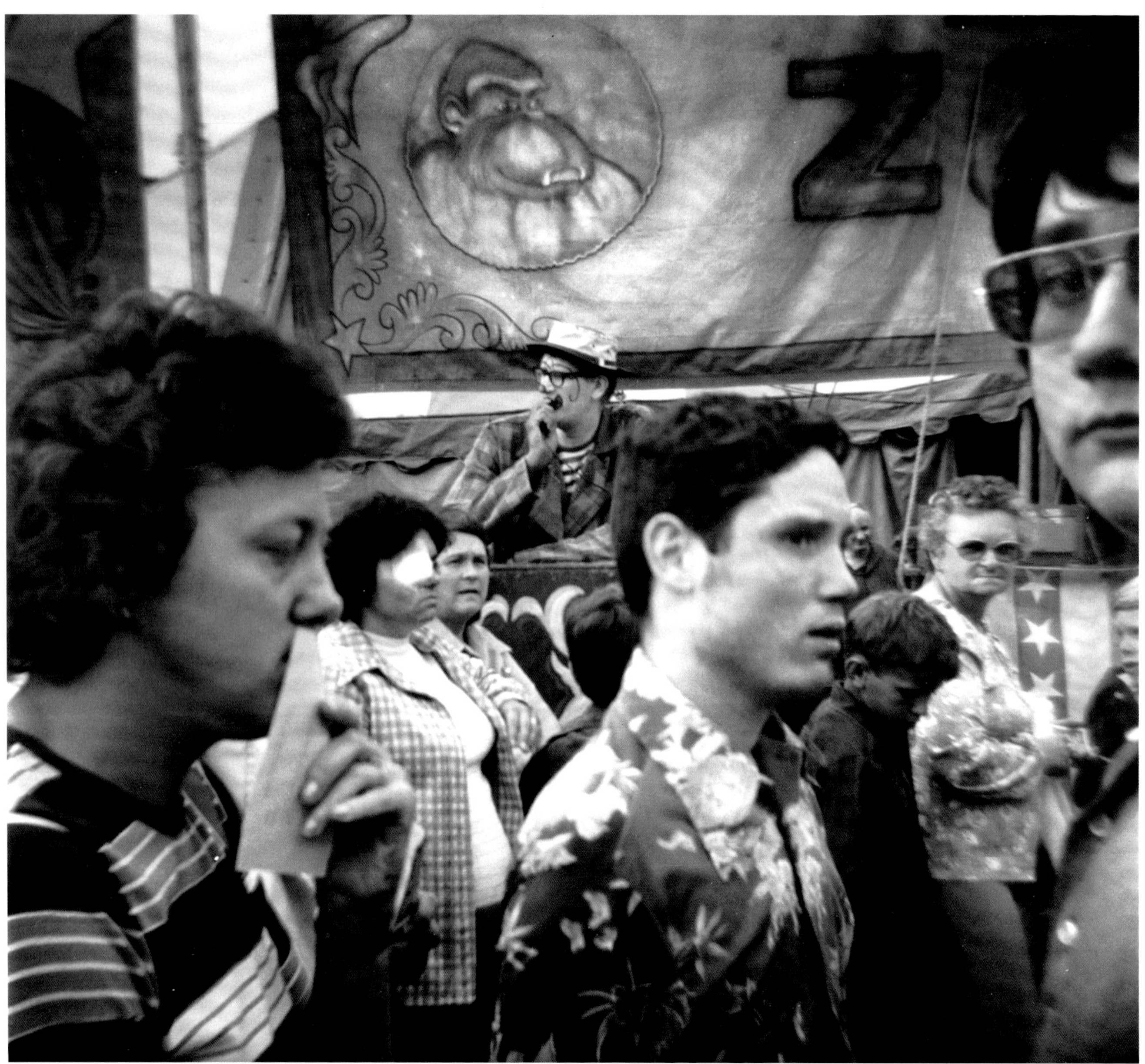

© Nancy Spencer *The Barker* 1980

AMERICAN DISGUISE

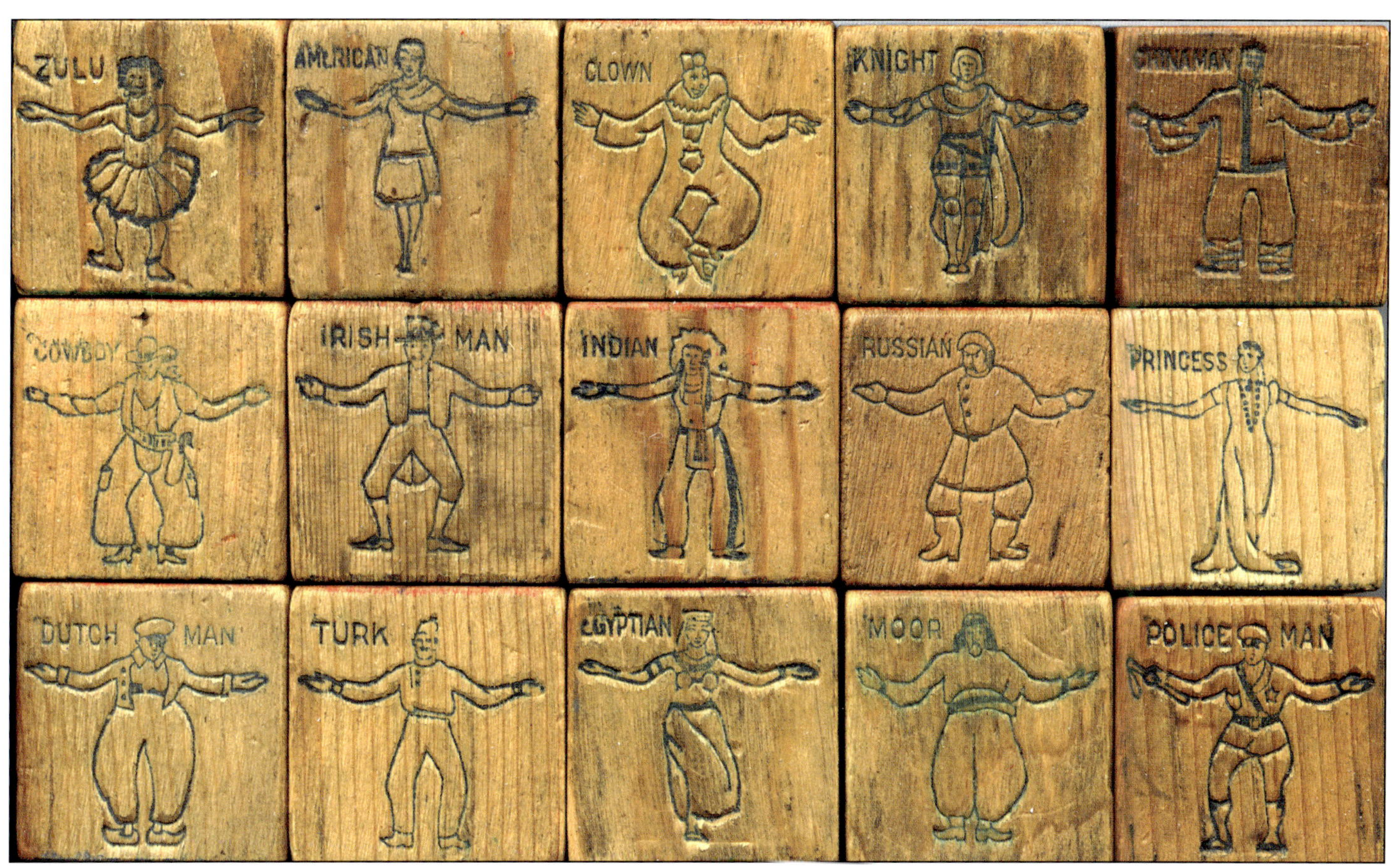

Alphabet blocks, USA, 1920s-1930s, displaying a variety of stereotypes

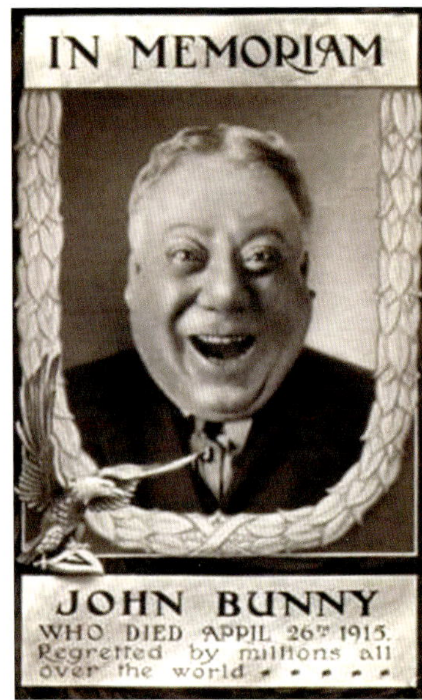

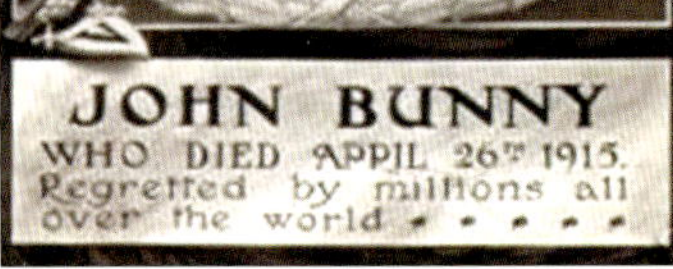

John Bunny, memorial postcard, 1915

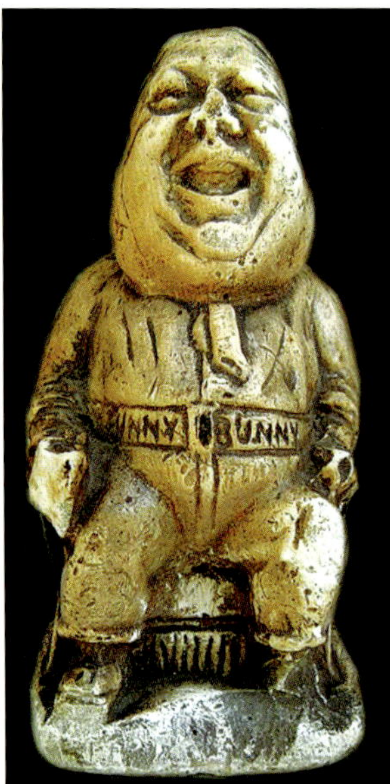

John Bunny (nicknamed Funny Bunny on his belt) five-inch carnival chalk prize, 1914. John Bunny made two hundred short films for Vitagraph from 1910 until his death in 1915. Although unknown today, Bunny is considered the first internationally famous silent film comedian (before Charlie Chaplin). Rotund at five-foot four-inch and weighing three hundred pounds, Bunny acted in the realm of jolly farce, flirting with his thin partner-comedienne Flora Finch. After his death the overweight-jolly stereotype was extended by Fatty Arbuckle, Oliver Hardy and others. By the 1930s, Coca Cola would promote the overweight-jolly stereotype through their increasingly rotund Santa Claus drinking Coke in Christmas ads.

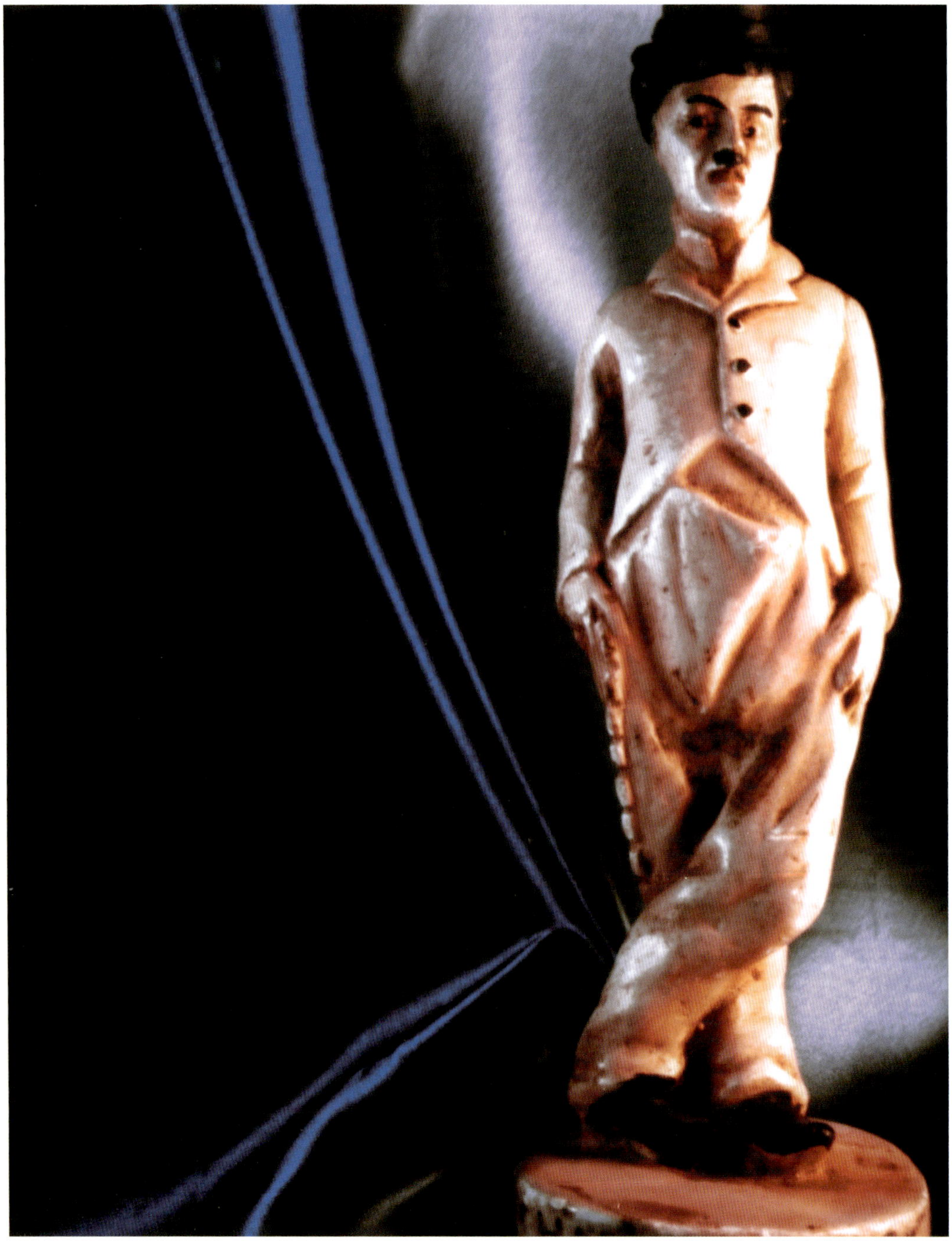

Charlie Chaplin seven-and-one-half-inch carnival chalk prize © Ambus Corp., 1915

Charlie Chaplin (1889-1977)
The Tramp (1914-1940)

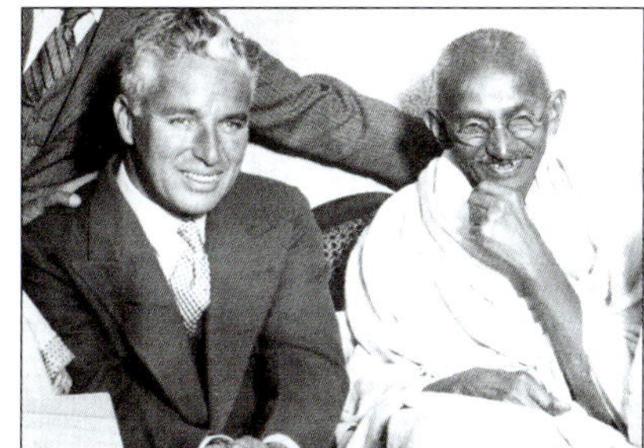

Charlie Chaplin and Mahatma Gandhi, 1932

Charles Spencer Chaplin was born in London and raised by his mother, Hannah Hill, a music-hall performer. His father deserted the family while Charles was still an infant. His mother's career was ruined, because of mental illness, when he was seven. He was placed in Lambeth Workhouse and later in Hanwell School for Orphans and Destitute Children. His half brother, Sid, encouraged Charles to develop his obvious dancing and singing talents and, through sheer determination, he transformed himself from an impoverished child of the London slums, into a star performer.

Chaplin toured the United States with the Karno Pantomime Troupe from 1907 to 1913. The Karno group moved on, but Chaplin remained in America and accepted an offer of $125 a week from Adam Kessel, who had part interest in Keystone Films. Chaplin first appeared on the screen in 1914 in the silent film *Making a Living*, directed by Max Sennett. Chaplin's signature character—the whimsical satirist, wearing baggy pants, enormous shoes, and a bowler hat while swinging a bamboo cane—first appeared in the 1914 film *Kid Auto*

Races at Venice. This was the film debut for his ingenious and autobiographical character the Tramp. Chaplin gradually developed his little tramp into a universally recognized archetypal motif—a symbol of indestructibility. The Tramp consistently triumphed over adversity and persecution. In many ways, he was a nonviolent motif for the David and Goliath legend and effectively symbolized America's immigrants and their struggle against poverty, low social status, and an aristocracy that subtly (and often openly) despised them in an era that espoused eugenics. The Tramp would prove to be very influential upon future media figures like Popeye and Mickey Mouse.

Chaplin had, through years of practice, perfected a very personal style of expressive gesture in his acting, one that combined circus clown, acrobat, and mime. By 1917, he was earning $10,000 a week and was the highest-paid actor in Hollywood. Chaplin, Mary Pickford, Douglas Fairbanks, and D. W. Griffith formed United Artists Corporation in 1919. In 1921, Chaplin completed his first feature-length film, *The Kid*, which starred child actor Jackie Coogan. The film was a year in the making, and Chaplin spiked it to perfection. *The Kid* created a legend out of Chaplin's tramp—an icon of human compassion that was loved by audiences the world over. The film also cemented Chaplin's stature as the most famous star of the silent era. His tramp became a stereotype.

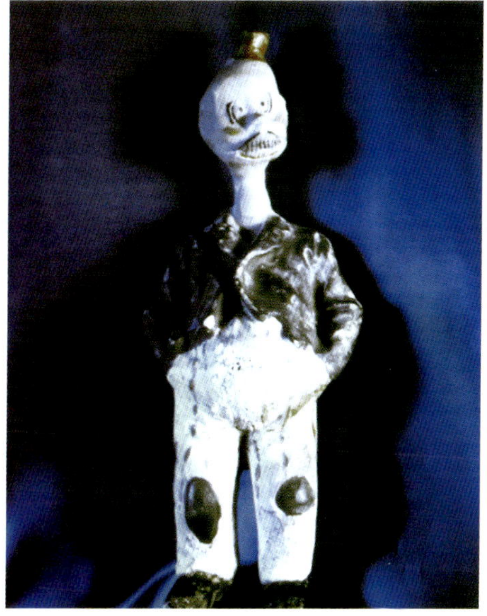

Happy Hooligan eleven-inch carnival chalk prize, circa 1910

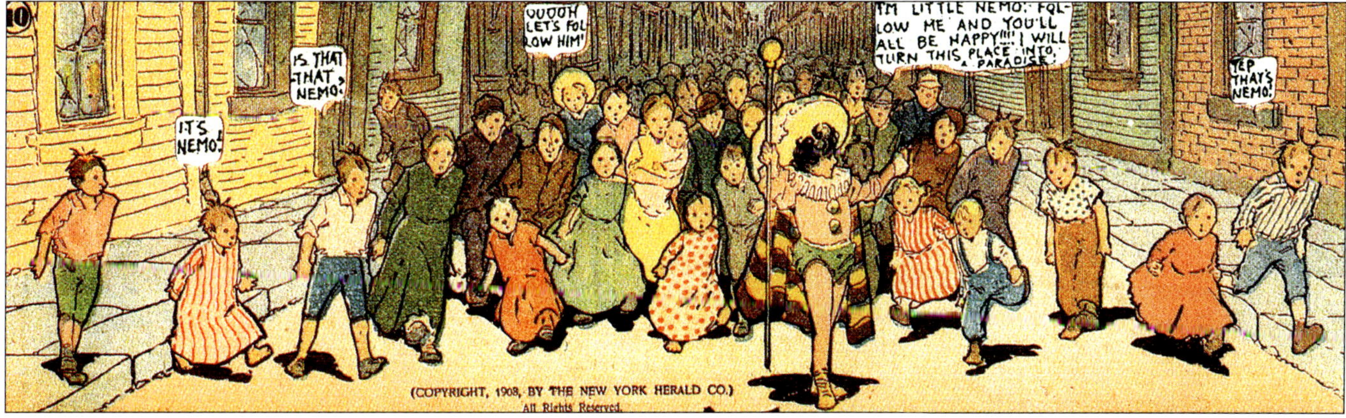

Little Nemo in Slumberland, comic strip detail, Winsor McCay, March 29, 1908 © *New York Herald*

Turn-of-the-century cartoon strips, such as Richard Felton Outcault's *Yellow Kid* (1897) and Frederick Opper's *Happy Hooligan* (1900), were extremely influential in creating public awareness of specific tramp stereotypes. Chaplin remarked that as a child he read *Ally Sloper* cartoons and credited some of Sloper's trickster persona went into his version of the tramp. Even Winsor McKay touched upon shantytown pathos with wealthy Nemo's visit to the poor side of town in the comic strip *Little Nemo in Slumberland*. Immigrants of the period regarded Chaplin's tramp as a symbolic masterpiece that exemplified the dreams, aspirations, loves, and hopes experienced in their own tragicomic existence. The once popular cartoon strip of two Frenchmen *Alphonse and Gaston* (1901) also by Frederick Opper, played upon silly aristocratic manners. Within a decade it lost its appeal to the more earthy immigrant-based strips.

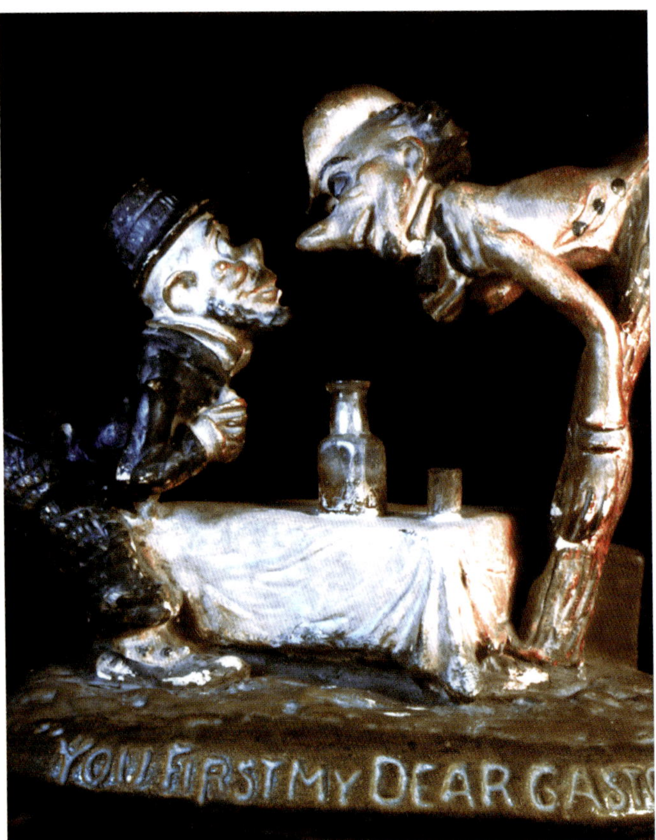

Alphonse and Gaston nine-inch carnival prize (?), circa 1905, uncopyrighted, with the cartoon strip's popular words "YOU FIRST MY DEAR GASTON" molded into the base

The Tramp didn't utter a word in his first two films of the sound era, *City Lights* (1931) and *Modern Times* (1936).

Hitler invaded Poland in September of 1939 (*Time* magazine had named Hitler "Man of the Year" in 1938), prompting Chaplin's first sound-dialogue parody, *The Great Dictator* (1940). Horrified by the nonaggression pact signed by Stalin and Hitler, Chaplin transformed the little tramp into "Charlie," a gentle Jewish barber whose fanatical look-alike was the dictator Adenoid Hynkel. Although greed, capitalism, and fascism were subtly referenced in the film, its bent was more toward themes that were popular and timely, and it attempted to suggest a far better world. The most creative

pantomime in it was enacted by the "Emperor of the World" caricature, where the world was a balloon revolving on Hynkel's fingertip. That scene reinforced America's stereotype of Hitler as Nazi madman. Kenneth Lynn, in *Charlie Chaplin and His Times*, described Hynkel's desperation:

As he holds the spinning world directly in front of the sick-wolf smile on his face, it becomes a metaphor of his tenuous psychological stability. An overly ecstatic embrace of the bubble finally bursts it. Hynkel breaks into tears and collapses across his desk. A dancer's physical grace; deliberate, almost slow-motion pacing; an ominously decorated office; Wagnerian music; and a madman's fantasy of global conquest: through this dreamlike combination of elements, Chaplin created an awed hush in movie theaters in the United States, Britain, and elsewhere in the year in which Hitler became the overlord of Europe from Norway to the Pyrenees.[1]

In the final moments of the film, the barber's girl-friend, Hannah (Chaplin's mother's name), hears Charlie:

Wherever you are, look up Hannah! The clouds are lifting—the sun is breaking through, we are coming out of the darkness into a new world—where men will rise above their hate, their greed, and their brutality. Look up, Hannah! The soul of man has been given wings and at last he is beginning to fly. He is flying into the rainbow—into the light of hope—into the future, into the glorious future that belongs to you—to me—and to all of us. Look up, Hannah, look up!

Chaplin's fame, riches, self-liberated actions, and rousing escapades did not go unnoticed, particularly by those who thought he had too much populist power (even though decades earlier Chaplin had raised funds for Liberty Bonds during World War I). As the tidal wave of anti-Communist conservatism and propagandist sentiment rose in America, Chaplin became the biggest fish to catch, and the tastiest to fry. On March 17, 1947, on the Senate floor, Senator William Langer slanderously asked:

Why is it that a man like Charlie Chaplin, with his communist leanings, with his unsavory record of lawbreaking, or rape, or the debauchery of American girls 16 and 17 years of age, remains?

Langer's goal was to make Chaplin a despicable scapegoat and an example of hedonism. Chaplin made a particularly attractive target because he was a Hollywood icon and he wasn't even an American. Furthermore, he had the audacity to rise to the top of the cinematic heap. Why should Chaplin be so free? Chaplin eventually supplied the bait for his own setup and was trapped by tricky questions and an antagonistic press. Expecting to be subpoenaed, he issued the chairman of the House Un-American Activities Committee a brief sarcastic note:

. . . view carefully my latest production, *Monsieur Verdoux*. It is against war and the futile slaughter of our youth. I trust you will find its humane message distasteful. While you are preparing your engraved subpoena I will give you a hint on where I stand. I am not a Communist. I am a peace-monger.[2]

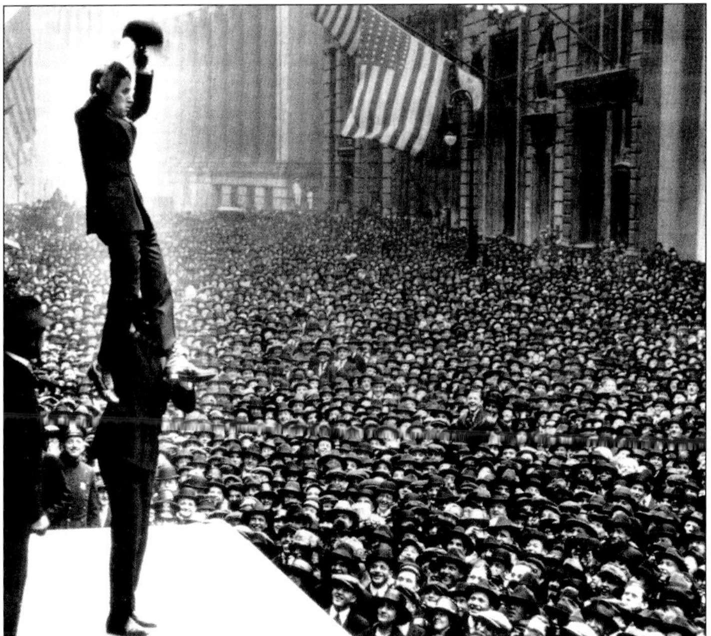

Charlie Chaplin being held aloft by Douglas Fairbanks to promote Liberty Bonds during a rally in Manhattan, April, 1918 © Museum of Modern Art, Still Photograph Section

On April 14, 1947, three days after *Monsieur Verdoux* opened to outright hostility, Chaplin agreed to meet the press. Their questions were aimed at destroying him.

C: Thank you ladies and gentlemen of the press. I am not going to waste your time. I should say—proceed with the butchery. If there's any question anybody wants to ask, I'm here, fire away at this old gray head.

Q: There have been several stories in the past accusing you more or less of being a fellow traveler, a Communist sympathizer. Could you define your present political beliefs, sir?

C: Well, I think that is very difficult to do these days to define anything politically. There are so many generalities, and life is becoming so technical that if you step off the curb with your left foot, they accuse you of being a Communist. But, I have no political persuasions whatsoever. I've never belonged to any political party in my life, and I have never voted in my life! Does that answer your question?

Q: Not precisely. Could you answer a direct question? Are you a Communis—

C: I am not a Communist!

Q: A Communist sympathizer was the question.

C: A Communist sympathizer? That has to qualified again. I don't know what you mean by a "Communist sympathizer." I'd say this—that during the war, I sympathized very much with Russia because I believe that she was holding the front, and for that I have a memory and I feel I owe her thanks. I think that she helped contribute a considerable amount of fighting and dying to bring victory to the Allies. In that sense I am sympathetic.

Q: Mr. Chaplin, did you intend to create sympathy for the character of Monsieur Verdoux?

C: No, I intended to create a pity for all humanity under certain drastic circumstances in times of stress, I think—in catastrophe—conditions bring out the worst in humanity and I've been intensifying that in this picture, and I wanted to show that any time we have a Depression or any time that we have a natural catastrophe, that it brings out these cancerous conditions like the figure of Verdoux, which to me is not—is a figure of pity and tragic from the point that you ask me now.

Q: Shouldn't there be somebody in a vehicle of entertainment for whom the public has sympathy?

C: As for sympathy, I think—unless I'm mistaken—I intended that the feeling should be that you have a sympathy for the whole human race. I think that's the doctrine of Christianity. My motive—if there is any sympathy for Verdoux, it is to understand crime and the nature of crime, I'd sooner understand it and the nature of it than condemn it.

By 1952, Chaplin had exiled himself. Chaplin alone stood up for the little guy, both in his private life and in his art. It was a cruel irony that he should become the victim of a mob of unsympathetic congressmen and like-minded headhunters hell-bent on pushing him out of the country simply because they were unable to reconcile his private life with the redeeming sociological messages of his professional life and his films. (It is an even greater irony that powerful people do not see that they actually lose power by treading on thoughtful messengers proffering solutions for social woes.)

Twenty years later Chaplin returned to the United States to extremely enthusiastic fans and with the quixotic reporters now by his side. Queen Elizabeth II knighted him in 1975. Sir Charles Chaplin died in 1977. Inept thieves mysteriously unearthed his coffin nine weeks after his burial and a ransom was demanded for his remains. The police eventually caught the body snatchers and found the coffin hidden in a wheat field near the village of Noville, Switzerland. The farmer who owned the wheat field placed a cross on the spot where the coffin had been found and decorated it simply with a symbolic cane. A bouquet of flowers was ritually placed before the cross for many years thereafter.[3]

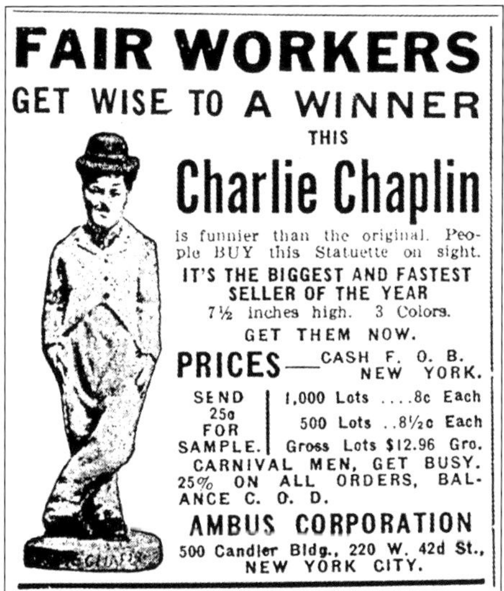

Ad for the Charlie Chaplin carnival chalk prize © Ambus Corporation, 1915. A similar Charlie Chaplin chalk figure without his legs crossed has © Mark Hampton & Co., 1328 Broadway, New York City, 1915 engraved on a metal plate inserted into the base.

Boy Scout (1910–

The people may be made to follow a course of action, but they may not be made to understand it.
—Confucius, *Analects*

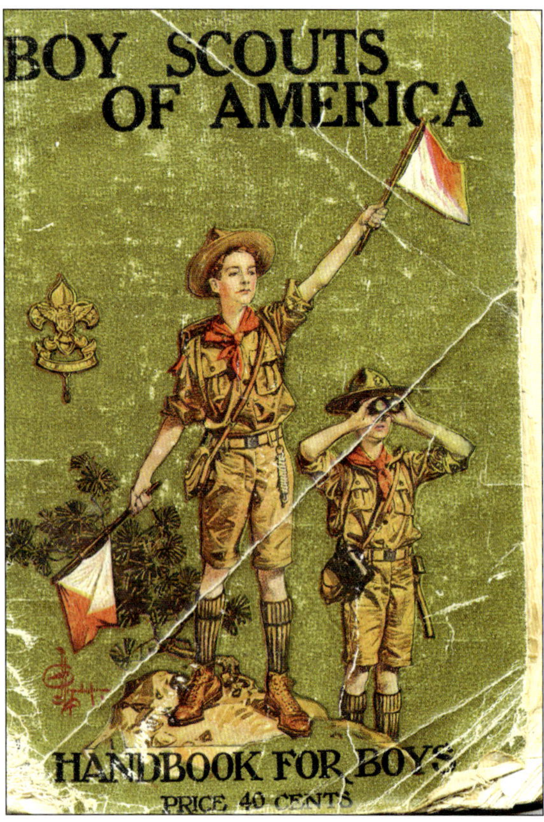

Boy Scouts of America: Handbook for Boys, cover, 1927 © Boy Scouts of America

William Boyce, a Chicago publisher, founded the Boy Scouts of America in 1910. The organization was modeled after an original concept conceived by British army officer Robert Baden-Powell, who first promoted "Boy Scouts" while stationed in South Africa. Baden-Powell's key endorsement for the new American organization was sought out and received, and the Boy Scouts of America was incorporated by an act of Congress on June 15, 1916, one year before the United States entered World War I. Page 4 of *The Handbook for Boys*, published by the Boy Scouts of America (1927), reads:

What Scouting Means
In all ages there have been scouts, the place of the scout being on the danger line of the army or at the outposts, protecting those of his company who confide in his care.
The army scout was the soldier who was chosen out of all the army to go out on the skirmish line.
The pioneer, who was out on the edge of the wilderness guarding the men, women, and children in the stockade, was also a scout. Should he fall asleep or lose control of his faculties, or fail on his watch, then the lives of the men, women, and children paid the forfeit, and the scout lost his honor.
But there have been other kinds of scouts besides war scouts and frontier scouts. They have been the men of all ages who have gone out on new and strange adventures, and

through their work have benefited the people of the earth. Thus, Columbus discovered America, the Pilgrim Fathers founded New England, and the early English settlers colonized Jamestown, and the Dutch built up New York. In the same way the hardy Scotch-Irish pushed west and made a new home for the American people beyond the Alleghenies and the Rockies.

Reading farther into the book, page 353 states:

A Boy Scout's Religion
The Boy Scouts of America maintain that no boy can grow into the best kind of citizenship without recognizing his obligation to God. The first part of the Boy Scout's oath or pledge is therefore "I must promise on my honor to do my best to do my duty to God and my country." The recognition of God as the ruling and leading power in the universe, and the grateful acknowledgment of His favors and blessings, is necessary to the best type of citizenship, and is a wholesome thing in the education of the growing boy.

The United States entered World War I on April 6, 1917. Could it be that Congress was looking toward an inevitable war when the Boy Scouts of America Act was passed? Could it be that the Boy Scouts Act provided moralists the opportunity to preen, prepare, and indoctrinate new military officers? Could it be that the Boy Scout, as an upstanding American citizen and an archetypal motif symbol, was answering the instinctive requirements for feeling patriotism toward one's country with a dedication to God? The Boy Scout Oath suggests that:

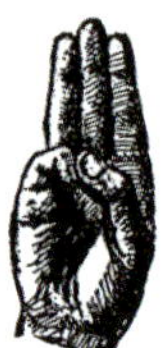

On my honor I will do my best—
To do my duty to God and my country, and to obey the scout law;
To help other people at all times;
To keep myself physically strong, mentally awake, and morally straight.

Could this have all been disguised, disingenuous, militaristic, moralist propaganda tying together the instinctive feelings created by archetypal symbols for patriotism (love of country) with God and religious morality (good versus evil), with macho superior strength (we're the strongest, therefore the best), so that young men would feel honor to die for God and country? During time of war, "Uncle Sam wants you" meaning Uncle Sam wants patriotic conformity and regimentation.

Additionally, did it make men think their primary function was to protect the weaker women and children? Did it reinforce instinctive feelings that women are secondary—because men, who are the strongest, do not give any of their power away to women? Men fight for God, country, and their honor to be sacrificed in war.

A personal anecdote: I grew up on the outskirts of Philadelphia. My father had been an Eagle Scout (the highest level and rank in Scouting). I didn't particularly like belonging to the Cub Scouts in the late 1940s when I was cajoled into joining, before I had much to say about decisions in my life. I weathered it and the natural progression into the Boy Scouts followed in the mid-1950s, but I was not a willing participant.

One of my Scout leaders lived in a large house with a high-fenced swimming pool, right next to the local police station. If lucky, we got to ride in his limousine, which boasted a spiffy, foldout booze bar in the backseat. This dandy didn't last long as a scoutmaster. It seems that he was a member of an organized group engaged in the profitable business of making porno pictures around his pool, which starred teenage girls from *Bandstand*. That was the *Bandstand* with Bob Horn, before it went national as *American Bandstand* with Dick Clark. Disc jockeys from a local radio station were also involved in the shenanigans. Unfortunately for us, this was the radio station that played the best black rock and roll. The entire station was removed from the air for a time. The exposé created a sensation that found its way into *Time* magazine. That was the end of Boy Scouting for me. (My fellow Scouts and I didn't have a clue as to what was going on nor did we see any of the pictures.) The scoutmaster was sentenced to six months in a mental institution; his wife (a retired stripper) got two years in a mental institution. And that was my moral tutelage under the honorable auspices of the Boy Scouts of America. Needless to say, I wasn't indoctrinated into thinking war was beneficial, nor was it worth dying for one's country, nor was the Boy Scouts of America sanctioned by God.

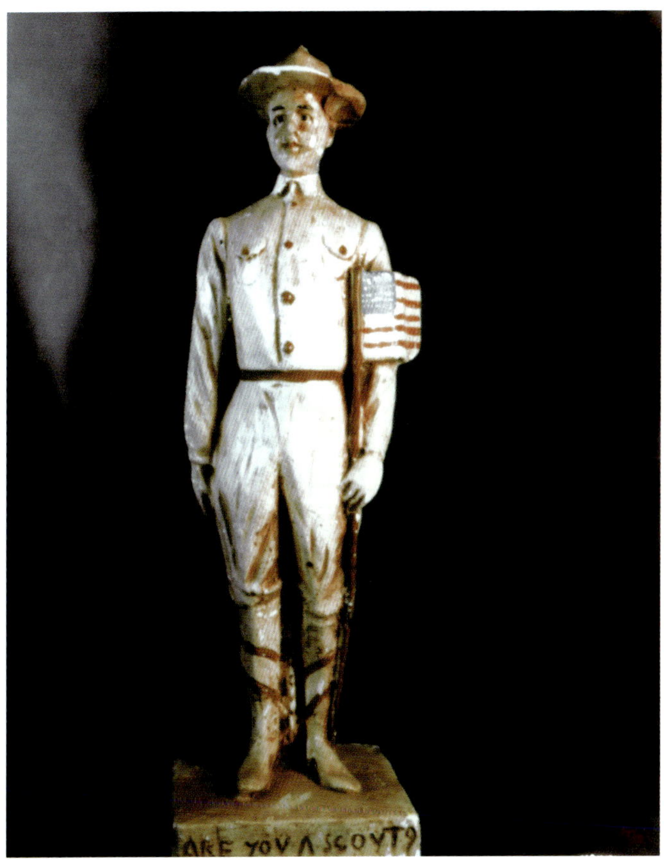

Boy Scout twelve-inch carnival chalk prize bearing the intimidating, guilt-provoking message, "Are You a Scout?" The U.S. flag by his side encourages the Boy Scout to feel patriotic. Every uniform creates an instant stereotype, cloaking the individual underneath.

Buster Brown (1902–1926)

So many gods, so many creeds,
So many paths that wind and wind,
While just the art of being kind
Is all the sad world needs.
—Ella Wheeler Wilcox, *The World's Need*, 1919

Buster Brown, in a comic strip of the same name, exemplified the rich American child born into aristocracy. He was created by Richard Fenton Outcault and appeared first in the *New York Herald* on May 4, 1902—one of the earliest cartoon strips published in a newspaper. Outcault had previously created *Yellow Kid* in 1895, which was about a poor immigrant child born into abject poverty.

Yellow Kid was possibly the first tatterdemalion (ragamuffin) to be characterized in a comic strip. The comic strip *Yellow Kid* (and all things alluding to the color yellow) abruptly vanished from the American scene with the onset of the Spanish-American War. Because it was the predominant color of the Spanish flag, yellow became the stereotypical symbol of otherness and the American abhorrence of all things Spanish. Yellow also referred back to the "Yellow Peril" used to label the Chinese who had been brought into America as indentured workers. Amazingly, schools across the United States even went so far as to banish yellow from crayon boxes. It is not uncommon for governments (once an enemy is identified or created) to stir the home pot with nasty symbols and connotations designed to elicit patriotic responses and provide improbable props of disdain representing the enemy. It's a blatant, if not transparent, homeland propaganda ploy. World War I produced a similar contempt for all things German, and America transformed sauerkraut, hamburgers, and German measles into "liberty cabbage," "liberty sandwiches," and (quite laughably) "liberty measles." This prejudice-producing tactic is not restricted only to enemies. It can be extended to those who do not support a government's policies or actions, as during the second Gulf War in 2003, when french fries were renamed "freedom fries" in a childish pout designed to demonstrate America's discontent with its nonsupportive ally, France.

Buster Brown wore fastidious Little Lord Fauntleroy outfits, unlike his predecessor, the decidedly inferior, poor immigrant, Yellow Kid, who was draped in the rags of a yellow feedbag. Buster Brown sparked bright, devilish eyes out of a face framed with long blond hair and Dutch-boy bangs. His spoiled-brat antics were acceptable simply because eccentric behavior was tolerated and acknowledged in aristocrats, being part and parcel of the prevalent stereotype for superiority. Buster Brown traveled through the world of comic-strip fantasy with his sister, Mary Jane, and his dog, Tige. Their doting mother fussed over Buster and Mary Jane constantly, and Buster was the quintessential archetypal symbol for a spoiled young aristocrat. The resplendent suits Buster wore were made of black velvet and trimmed with lace collars, imitating the costumes Oscar Wilde wore when he visited Washington, D.C., in 1882.[1] The suits were popularized by the British-born American author Frances Hodgson Burnett in her book *Little Lord Fauntleroy* (1886). She dressed her two real-life

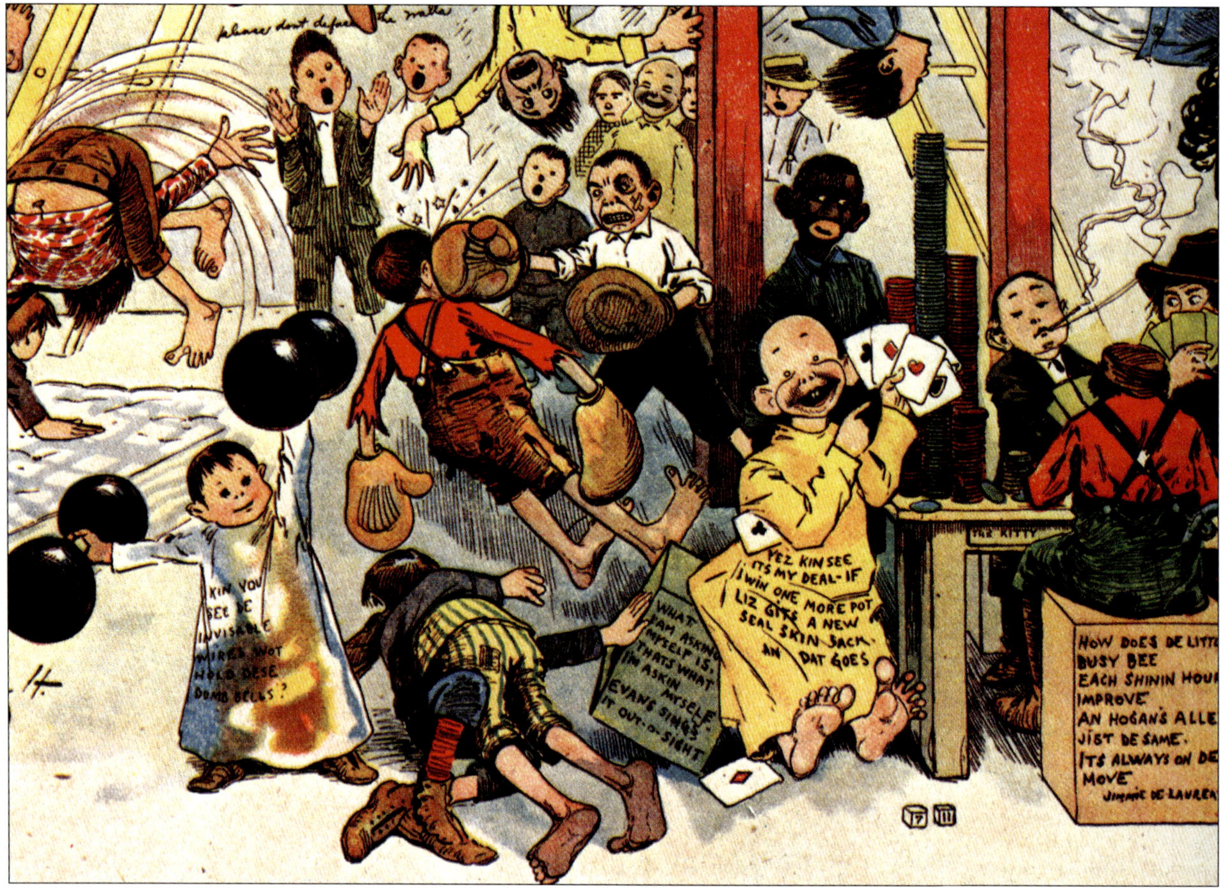

Yellow Kid, "Opening of Hogan's Alley," comic strip detail, Richard Felten Outcault, 1896 © *New York Herald*

sons in the same fanciful manner that Buster's mother dressed him. Burnett's book was immediately popular and sold more than a million copies, but the prissy suits (an analogue for wealth) never became fashionable. Evidently not all rich boys tolerated the frills and velvet masquerade and, rumor had it, one eight-year-old boy protested by burning down his parents' barn.

Buster's pranks were never purposely evil enough to sully his character, so Outcault was able to end his strips with preachy little homilies directed at young readers, or at young readers' parents. Buster continued appearing in the comic strips in one form or another through World War I, but he was too wealthy (worse—his family were snobs) and his popularity waned. The last *Buster Brown* comic strip was published in 1926.

In a large children's book entitled *Buster Brown in Foreign Lands*, published in 1910, Buster glues a dark-skinned Egyptian boy's hand to a donkey's tail to punish the boy for whipping the donkey. Outcault's pontificating sermon reads:

Resolved:
That Cruelty arises from ignorance. Small boys hurt animals because they don't realize the pain they inflict. If that donkey-boy had been licked when he was younger, he might have had more mercy for the donkey that he drives now. I've had my share of lickings, and they did me good, though I didn't appreciate them during the painful moments.[2]

Outcault's homilies were often simply inappropriate puritanical abuse. Equally disturbing in this book is that Outcault endowed his dark-skinned donkey-boy with a Jim Crow stereotype (while the sphinx laughs). When the donkey-boy says, "Stop minit, de tail stick to ma hand," the appropriated talk and sticking action comes directly from Joel Chandler Harris' tale *Brer Rabbit: The Wonderful Tar-Baby Story*.

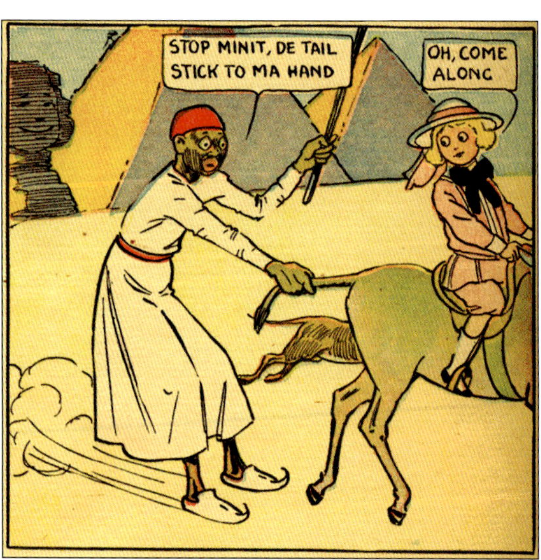

"Stop minit, de tail stick to ma hand!," *Buster Brown in Foreign Lands*, detail, Richard Felten Outcault, 1910 © *New York Herald*

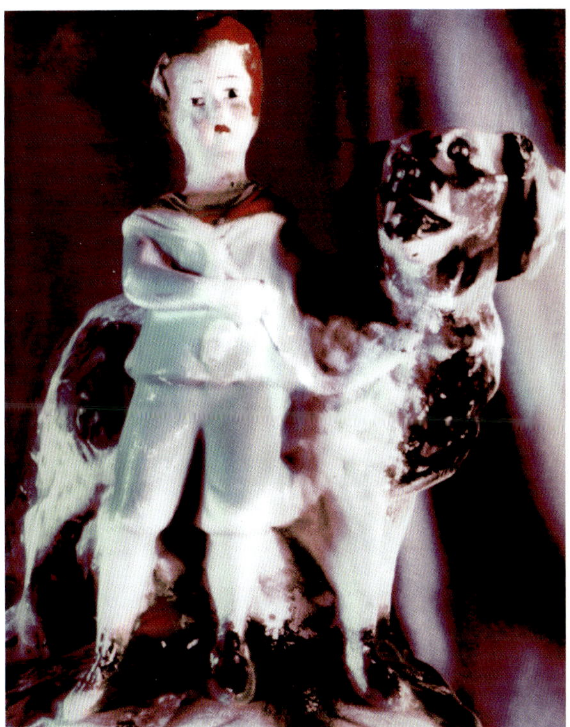

Buster Brown nine-inch carnival chalk prize (or is it Little Lord Fauntleroy?). Some can be found labeled "My Pal" on the base.

Homilies aimed toward strong discipline were often included in children's literature. However, Lewis Carroll in *Alice's Adventures in Wonderland* (1865) turned this idea around by stating "Speak Roughly to your little boy," which meant "speak the truth" rather than daily repetitions of insidious fairy-tale untruths.

Speak Roughly to your little boy,
And beat him when he sneezes:
He only does it to annoy,
Because he knows it teases.

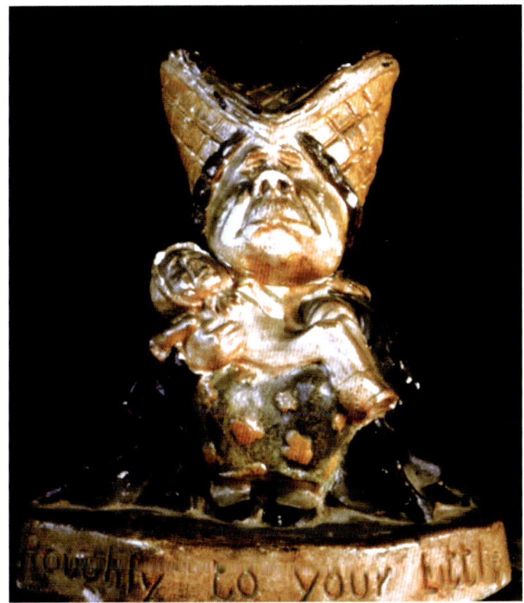

Duchess six-and-one-half-inch carnival chalk prize. The Duchess prize replicates John Tenniel's 1865 book illustration—an updated archetypal motif to Michelangelo's *Pieta*. The prize states "Speak Roughly to Your Little Boy" around the base. Where is the carnival chalk Alice?

THEDA BARA (1885-1955)

The first casualty when war comes is truth.
—SENATOR HIRAM JOHNSON, Speech U.S. Senate, 1917

Theodosia Goodman was born in Avondale, Ohio, on July 29, 1885, but very few Americans knew this when her first Hollywood film was released in 1916. Studio hype fabricated Theda Bara. As an easy anagram, the letters of her name spell Arab Death. Hollywood gave her an exotic lineage, entirely appropriated from the "Salomania" that was sweeping across Europe and America. Theda Bara was a homogenized titillated and titivated Salome stereotype, which was very much in vogue at that time. Hollywood re-created Bara as their vamp stereotype. Hollywood publicity said that she was born near the pyramids in 1892, the daughter of an Italian artist and French actress—maybe her mother was even an Arabian princess. Film historians, who thought they were wiser, incorrectly dated her birth as 1890. Her publicity was all disguise, yet it represented that blatantly primitive moment in early Hollywood, as in war, when truth is the first casualty. Her jaded director-producer, Frank J. Powell, claimed,

Those were the days we were importing stage stars by the carload, and studios were beginning to feel the financial strain. I thought, "I wonder if I could make a big star, all by myself." There was an extra girl around the Fort Lee studios that I spotted. She was angling for bigger parts, but halfheartedly, in fact everything she did was halfhearted. She had a sort of negative personality. But she had a body and she had big dark eyes that I though we could make even bigger with heavy kohl eye make-up we used then. I called her to see me, the big, stern, mysterious director, and said, "I've got work for you, and a future for you, but you've got to do exactly what I tell you. Here's some money. Go find yourself a little apartment in the Bronx and stay there and don't see anybody or talk to anybody you know until you hear from me." We started production with this little girl in the part of the Vampire, and she photographed just like I thought she would. There was hardly any advance publicity for pictures then, and we got away with the whole thing without anybody knowing what was going on. Then I got going. I announced that in *A Fool There Was* we had a new star, Theda Bara (the girl's real name was Theodosia Goodman) who the boob American public had never heard of but who was famous all over the civilized world. She was born in Egypt, half-French and half-Arab, she was not only an actress, she was also a sort of witch who could hypnotize people into doing things they oughtn't to do, and most important of all, she was going to knock the pants off all the men in the world, civilized and uncivilized. It worked, too. They not only swallowed it, they loved it.[1]

When Bara was interviewed by reporters she dressed the part in veils and furs, petted a python, and nibbled on raw beef and lettuce. Helena Rubenstein invented heavy mascara to create her Salome look. She was the exotic temptress, the vampire who overpowered her men and swallowed them alive. "Kiss me, my fool!" became her oft-repeated popular line. Bara was Hollywood's number-one sex symbol in a long line of number-one sex symbols, yet she and her fame

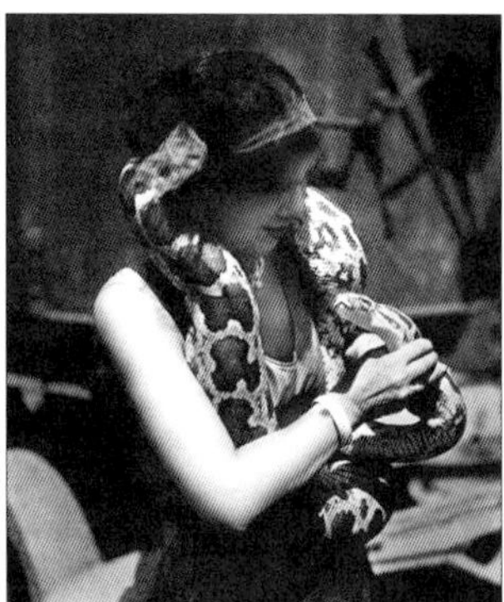

"A Python Makes a Shuddery Necklace,
Every Side Show Must Have its Woman
Snake Charmer," image caption from
"The Land of Sawdust and Spangles,"
© *The National Geographic Magazine*,
October, 1931, photograph Richard H.
Stewart. Connecting women with snakes
has taken many forms (other images are
shown on pages 157 and 225).

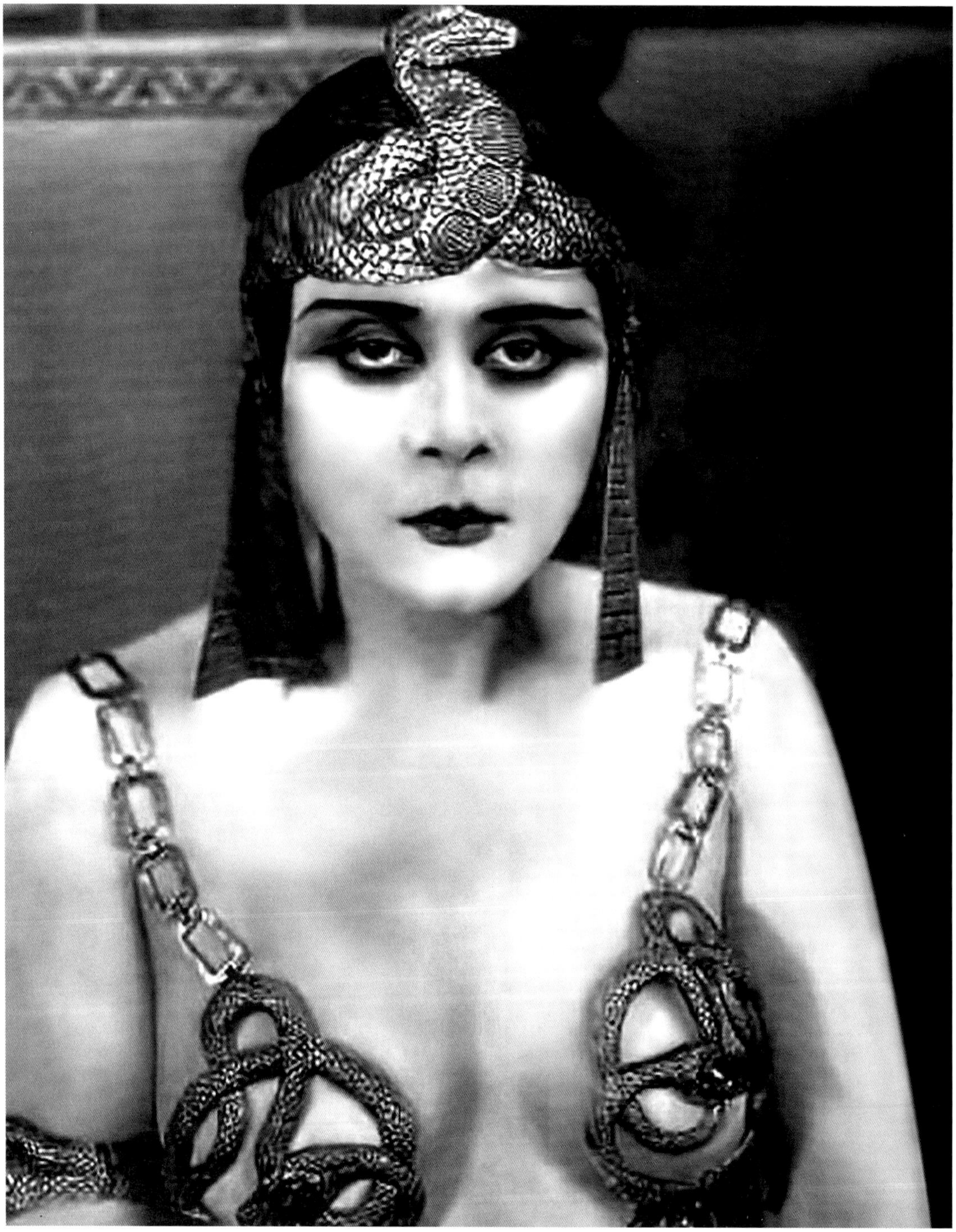

Theda Bara, *Cleopatra*, 1917 © Fox Film Corporation

have become obscure. Her portrayal of sex made Fox Film rich. She earned $4,000 a week at the height of her stardom in 1918. Her films constantly displayed her as an archetypal symbol of the extremely erotic woman for feeling dangerous lust—able to usurp any man's power. By the end of 1916, Bara had starred in six films, the last being *Carmen*. Her most exotic film was *Cleopatra* (1917). In it, she wore a gold snake on her head and gold snakes loosely wound around her breasts, each snake's mouth ended at a nipple. (The snake is an archetypal symbol, instinctive for feeling fear.) Displayed on her head and breasts, the snakes referenced sex and the garden of Eden, thereby doubling the misogyny.

Bara was not at all the vamp in private life. When America entered World War I, she joined the war effort, visiting camps, raising hundreds of thousands of dollars in war bonds, and contributing some of her salary to charity. She fought for better roles in film; one she attained was that of a poor Irish girl in *Kathleen Mavoureen* (1919). Unfortunately the film was surrounded by controversy, because Bara's Jewish heritage had been discovered. Irish and Catholic groups blasted the movie, protesting Hollywood's depiction of Ireland and the blasphemy that a Jewish actress could be playing an Irish role. Riots broke out and bomb threats closed the theaters, ending her career. After a total of forty films in four years, Fox dropped her contract. She spoke not a word on film; so no audience knows her voice. Bara died of abdominal cancer in 1955.

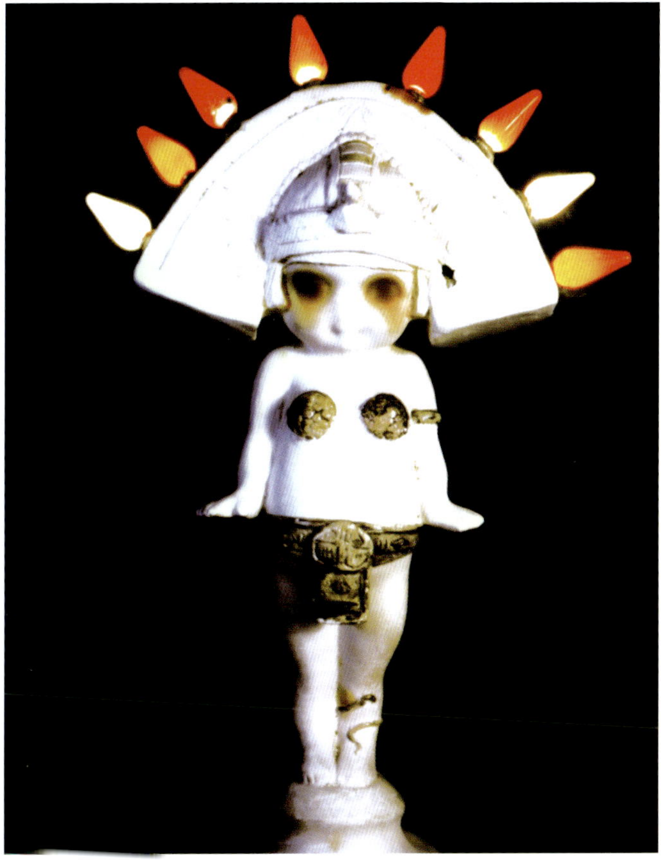

Cleopatria seventeen-inch carnival chalk prize designed by Julie Yates Jenkins as Theda Bara from her film *Cleopatra*. Jenkins copyrighted her "Cleopatria," circa early 1920s. She is pink chalk with subtle coloring. Many Kewpie-vamp carnival chalk prizes of the era had heavy make-up reminiscent of Theda Bara. Many had girl's faces with women's bodies, or the reverse—women's faces with girl's bodies. Most were clothed in alluring exotic faux Zeigfeld Follies attire.

Mutt & Jeff
(1907-1982)

A. Mutt was the initial comic-strip name for *Mutt & Jeff*, created by Bud Fisher in the sports pages of the *San Francisco Chronicle* on November 15, 1907. A. Mutt was a gambling enthusiast, following the almighty horse races—he perused the dailies—just like the readers who laughed at him. Since his strip was next to the racing schedules, his readers were, of course, laughing at themselves.

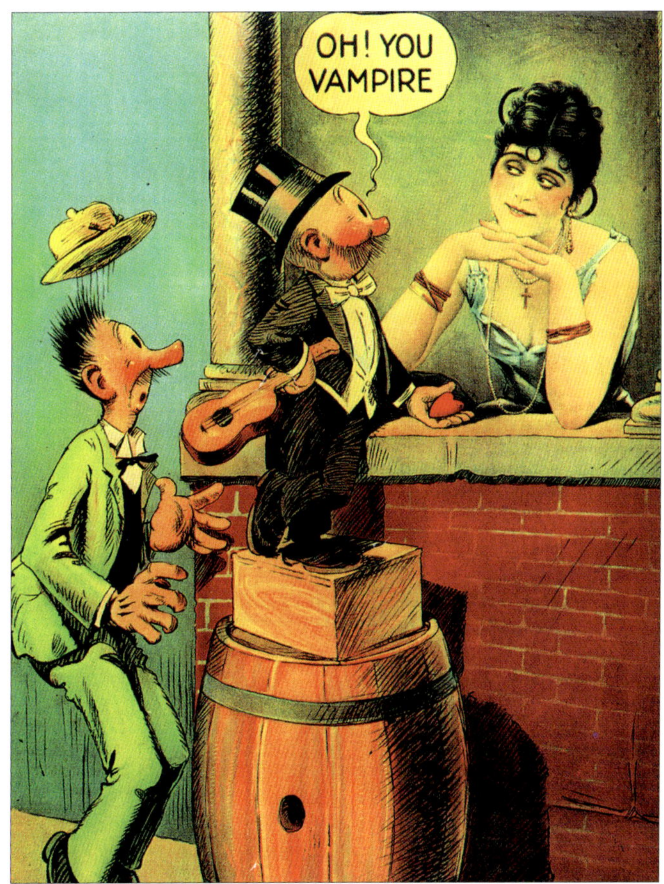

Mutt & Jeff in Meeting Theda Bara, lobby card detail, 1918 © Fox Film Corporation

A. Mutt was the first successful six-day-a-week strip appearing in panels placed horizontally across the page, a format that set the standard other newspaper cartoons would follow. A. Mutt was synonymous with the lowest member in the family hierarchy—the lovable but not very bright family dog. The "A" in his name stood for Augustus; he was tall and skinny. His daily gambling was a domestic issue and not held in high esteem by his suspicious wife. The diminutive Jeff appeared in the strip in 1908. Mutt had been shown as dim-witted; his new pal Jeff was certifiably insane; they met in a mental institution. Jeff added bizarre situations, making for increased popularity because it was a nuttier strip with archetypal symbols for feeling absurd humor and misogamy (a hatred of marriage). The strip's name was quickly changed to *Mutt & Jeff*, a term now embedded into American slang, used for anyone tall seen with anyone small. *Mutt & Jeff* portrayed immature emotional tendencies of "get away from the wife, so we boys can have fun." Wives were always shown as members of a specialist task force, whose main goal in life was to practice astute scrutiny; they were old-fashioned, and always, always, always nagging.

Mutt and Jeff's relationship depended on slapstick brutality at times. They rivaled each other. Who was actually the boss? Mutt was long suffering. Jeff might easily have suffered from a small-man complex, although he usually suffered from an in-your-face dementia. Their humor usually depended upon reader escape—wondering what illogical stunt they might perform that day.

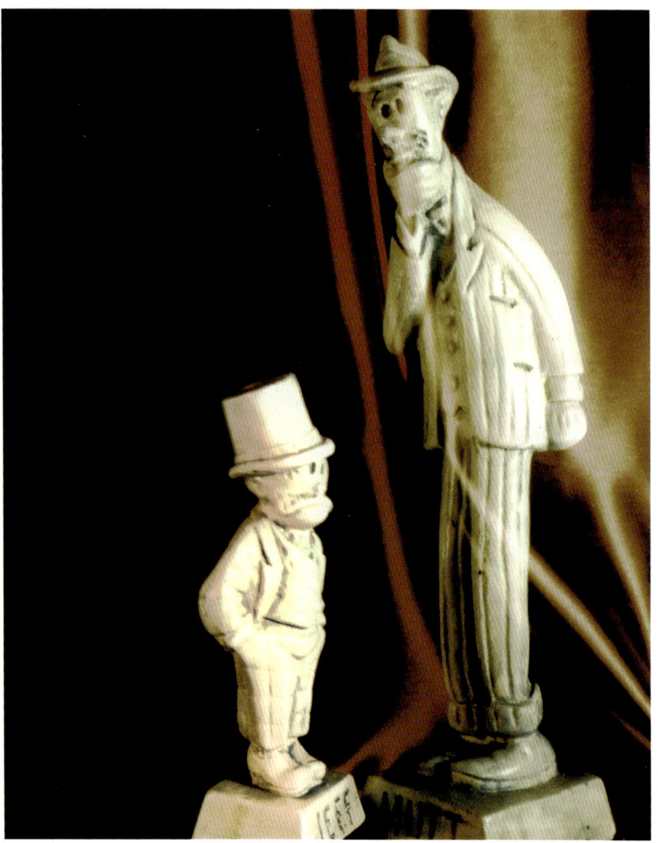

Ten-inch Mutt and six-inch Jeff carnival chalk prizes from about 1917

In 1911, the *Chicago American* issued a collection of *Mutt & Jeff* strips in a wide-view 18" x 6" book, available by sending in six newspaper coupons. Mutt and Jeff were featured on the cover of *Famous Funnies #1*, the first ten-cent comic, in 1934. They were popular in a series of animated films, although their greatest continued success was in the newspaper strip. They had their own DC All-American Comic from 1939 until 1958, when it was taken over by Dell Comics. A year later they went to Harvey Comics, where they remained until 1965. After seventy-five years, *Mutt & Jeff* finally disintegrated in 1982—one of the longest-running strips in cartoon history.

Broncho Billy

(1909-1915)

—JANE AND MICHAEL STERN, *Way Out West*

You ask me to plow the ground. Shall I take a knife and tear my mother's bosom? Then when I die she will not take me to her bosom to rest. You ask me to dig for stones! Shall I dig under her skin for bones? Then when I die I cannot enter her body to be born again.
—WAVOKA

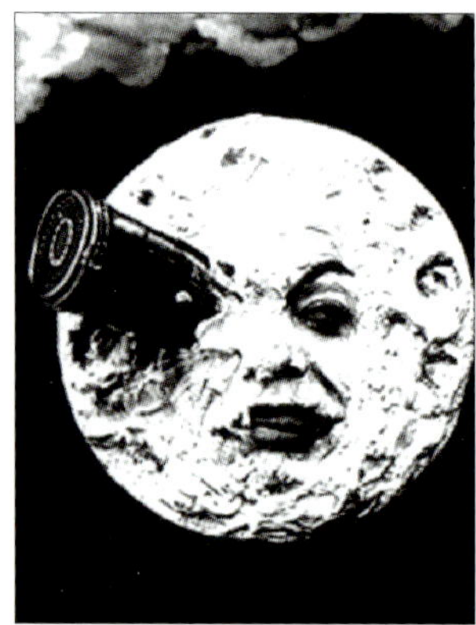

A Trip to the Moon, Georges Méliès, 1903

History will not look at it this way, but to be the first human to step foot on the moon is hardly a more extraordinary distinction than to be the first famous American movie star and, even more memorably, to be the first American cowboy hero and prototype of the classic Western cowboy phony. Who dares claim this breathtaking and venerable historical distinction? Why, none other than Broncho Billy Anderson. You knew it all along, right? Well, probably not. (Broncho Billy is even less famous than the early Georges Méliès film *A Trip to the Moon*, released in 1914.) Bronco Billy Anderson is not a name recognized today by anyone but avid cowboy-film buffs. Yet Broncho Billy's 300 short Western films, made between 1909 and 1915, cemented the cowboy stereotype: the true-grit-sin-and-redemption gallant man of action, the save-the-world dust-buster hero born of the wild, wild, and wilder West. Broncho Billy set the stage and provided the original mold, although he was eventually paled by Hollywood's seemingly endless sculpting and resculpting of phony cowboys. Broncho Billy dressed to the nines in his films (in the typical melodrama manner), but under the polished and sparkling veneer, there dwelled the heart of a simple, straightforward, hard-ridin', dust-lovin' cowboy.

Thirty-three-year-old Broncho Billy eventually relinquished his cowboy crown to a grittier, tobacco-spittin'

William S. Hart, and the moral dilemma /redemption themes persisted in the Westerns that followed, continuing to buttress the tough-guy-makes-a-fresh-start cowboy stereotype. Trends change, being the temporary façades they are, and the fresh-start formula was inevitably destined to play itself out—that image was deemed not useful for future cowboys, particularly in the series films that were to become so popular. Hollywood understood the need to instill respectful ideals and incredible prowess in their cowboy heroes. For daredevil Tom Mix, the persona embodied unbelievably polished (albeit outrageous) horsemanship; for clean-living Hopalong Cassidy, it was moral faultlessness In thought and deed, with the added accoutrement of amazingly intuitive criminal profiling; for the singing cowboys, Roy Rogers and Gene Autry, it was romance on the range; and for the most impeccable, white-bread-immaculate cowboy ever, the Lone Ranger, it was simply his God-given mask, undisputed authority, and, of course, the William Tell Overture. (All of these cowboys, plus the momentarily cool 1930s Buck Jones who smoked onscreen, set the stage for the devastatingly effective marketing success of the Philip Morris cigarette-sucking cowboy, the Marlboro Man.) It was not all that difficult for Clint Eastwood to re-create grit, sin and redemption in *Unforgiven* (1992) because he harked back to the original true-grit, William S. Hart, cowboy-redemption stereotype, first created by Broncho Billy (sans the gaudy duds, of course).

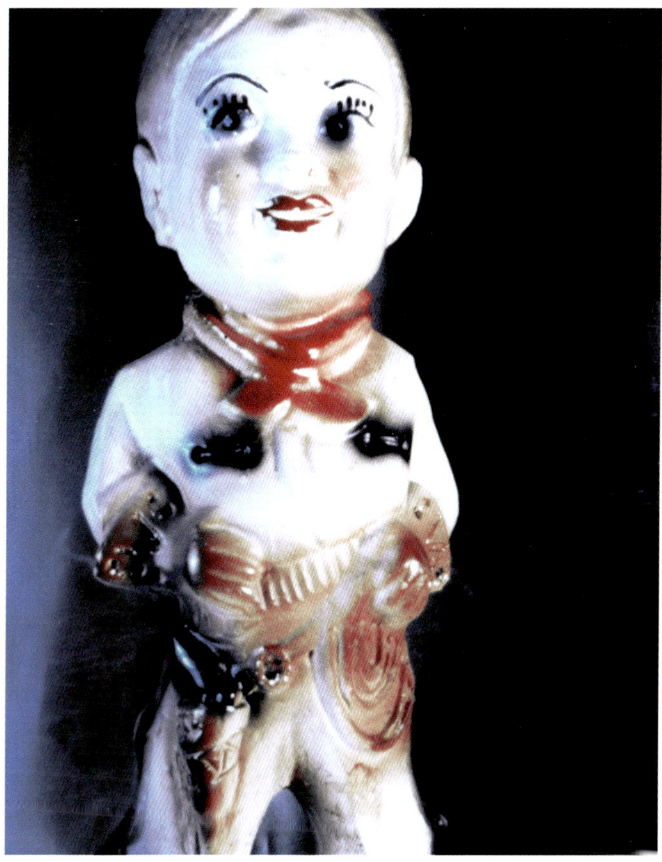

Broncho Buster fourteen-inch carnival chalk figure with "Broncho Buster" inscribed on its base. Had it been spelled "Bronco Buster," without the "h," it could have referred to any number of generic Western stars, but since it is spelled "Broncho," this prize is most certainly a memorial and homage to the great Broncho Billy.

The Hollywood Western provided the perfect vessel for injecting guns, gunplay, vicarious thrills, and violence into films, and the bleak atmosphere of an untamed Western landscape created the perfect austere, alien backdrop. Early mystery/crime/suspense films were also a natural medium in which to display flashing guns—albeit citified guns, like snub-nose .38s and machine guns, not the long-barreled Western varieties of pistols and rifles. Guns symbolize the most significant archetypal emblem in all of these films. They created violence and chaos and, more important, were emblematic of a control and power archetype. All guns were, and still are, a patriarchal surrogate—analogues for the authority of threatening penises—meant to promote feelings of fear. By the time Roy Rogers and Gene Autry crooned their way across the Western plains with their guitars (and backup vocal groups) in tow, everyone in the audience understood that their guns were loaded and the guns were the real deal. Their guitars and voices were sweet romance archetypes for instinctive feelings of admiration and love, but it was their guns that showed them as men with archetypal power. The inventive Lash Larue used an eighteen-foot-long bullwhip to ascertain his power, which demonstrated his sadomasochistic supremacy.

Broncho Billy was born Gilbert Max Aronson, in Little Rock, Arkansas, in 1882. His first theatrical experience was in vaudeville, under the stage name Max Anderson. In 1903 he played several parts in Edison's ten-minute film extravaganza *The Great Train Robbery*, directed by Edwin Porter. Anderson led the posse and George Barnes starred as the leading robber. *The Great Train Robbery* was filmed along the Lackawanna railroad in New Jersey. Films made before *The Great Train Robbery* were about one minute long—so, with the luxury of ten minutes at its disposal, this lengthy new feature marked a great departure and really told a story.

The Great Train Robbery was based on an actual holdup that occurred on August 29, 1900, when four members of Butch Cassidy's gang stopped the No. 3 train on Union Pacific rail tracks in Wyoming. They forced the conductor to uncouple the passenger cars from the rest of the train, blew open the safe in the mail car, and escaped with $5,000 in cash. In the film's final scene, the gang is captured and the courageous men in the posse kill every one of the scoundrels. For cinematic effect, the last robber killed fired his gun directly at the audience. People screamed in terror thinking they'd truly been shot. (Such was the illusionary nature of film to a public not yet hardened by the deceits a screen could perpetrate.) *The Great Train Robbery* was the most popular film of its era. Joe McKennon, in *The Pictorial History of the American Carnival*, explains how it was presented to a massive American audience:

> *The Great Train Robbery* motion picture was the featured carnival show that 1905 season . . . The carnival showman had special black tents made especially for motion pictures and electric spectacle shows. The townspeople came out early in the morning and lined up in front of the motion picture tents. Some of them would see *The Great Train Robbery* over and over again, paying admission each time. One carnival carried five moving picture shows that season, and all of them showed *The Great Train Robbery*. These outdoor showmen who had so recently created a form of mass entertainment for the common working people were

now introducing and tenderly nursing another new form of amusement that would almost put them out of business a few years later.[2]

New projection technology provided carnival showmen with an opportunity to downsize and they cut back their number of showgirls.[3] The film's popularity proved that a Western stereotype could easily be found in true stories and the gates to a cinematic dam had been opened. Much of the "wildwest" stereotype relied upon media saturation of archetypal evil icons like the gun-crazed outlaw Billy the Kid or the Butch Cassidy gang. By promoting murderous misdeeds law and order throughout the U.S. was creditable and Hollywood's cowboy heroes were born (good won out over evil).

By 1909, Anderson was no longer a supporting actor and was vaulted into stardom under the cowboy name Broncho Billy Anderson. His last silent film was *The Son of a Gun* (1919). In 1965, eighty-three years old and still going strong, Anderson played a cameo role in his first talking picture, *The Bounty Killer*, starring Rod Cameron. Anderson died in his sleep at the wizened age of eighty-nine. Much earlier, Anderson admitted to being the first Western phony: he hated to ride horses and chose to fake as many riding stunts as possible—causing the accidental invention of the stuntman and double. What he loved most about his roles was the opportunity they gave him to wear gaudy duds.

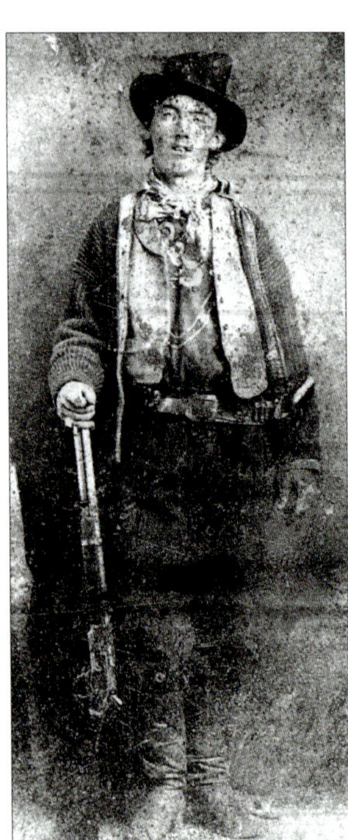

Billy the Kid

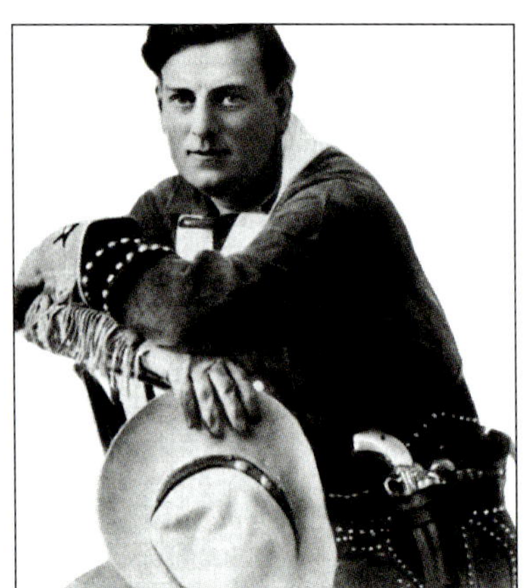

Broncho Billy, still © Essanay Film

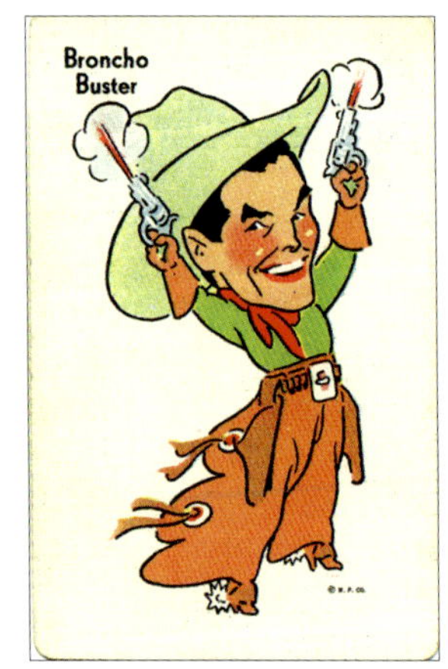

Old Maid Playing Card © Parker Brothers, Inc., 1950s

Kewpie Dolls (1908-

The famous American illustrator Rose O'Neill designed Kewpie dolls in 1912. She originally saw them in a dream, slightly after the turn of the century. She modeled them after her baby brother and, by 1908, after her second marriage failed, she began inserting them into her illustrations for *Ladies' Home Journal*. She called them Kewpies because they looked like cupids. She said, "Cupid gets you into trouble and Kewpies get you out." That must have meant: if love is difficult, that is, problematic and sad, then a Kewpie will make you feel good. Kewpies were a archetypal motif symbol for a lucky love angel that aroused instinctive uplifting feelings of happiness and joy. O'Neill played into the same instinctive feelings bank that country-and-western tunes play into: "Lovin's hard, I'm feelin' bad, this littl' tune'll pick you up." Until 1920 all her Kewpies were male, then she started making females. Kewpies were so influential that their looks were appropriated for use in all types of media and merchandising.

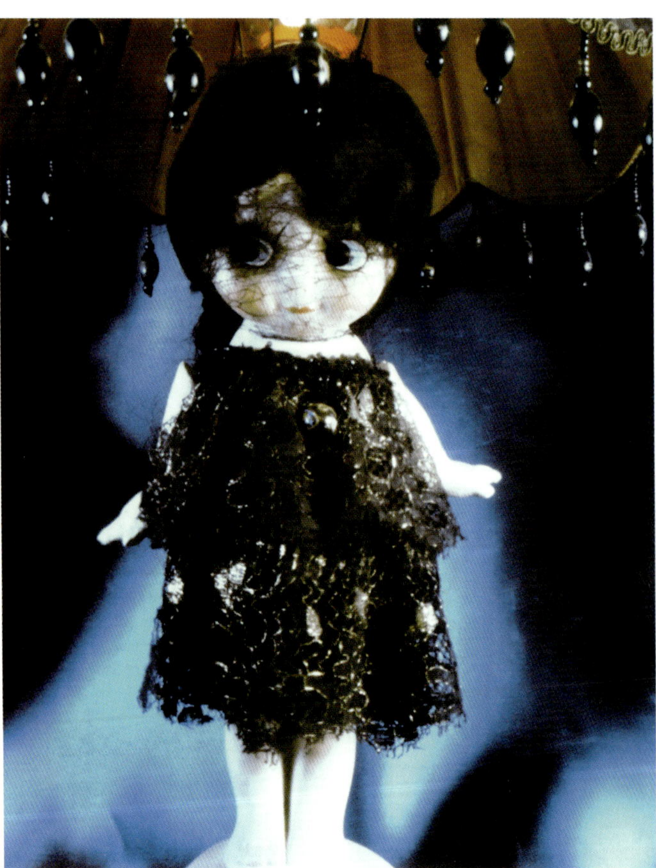

Kewpie thirteen-inch carnival chalk lamp prize, movable arms, circa early 1920s

When the popularity of Kewpies increased, O'Neill had three-dimensional bisque doll-like Kewpies made in Germany, some as small as buttonholes, others seventeen inches tall. Her original Kewpie looked like a chubby child with its legs molded together and arms outstretched, with a tuft of hair on the head, small sprouting wings on either side of the neck, and webbed hands. During the Kewpie craze, between 1912 and 1920, they were made to represent soldiers, bakers, gardeners, and musicians, or they came in pairs hugging each other, called Huggers. They could no longer be imported from our enemy, Germany, during World War I, so she had them produced in America, made from celluloid, plaster, or rubber. Approximately 5 million Kewpie dolls were sold with O'Neill's signature across the sole of one foot. To most Americans, the 1920s squeaky-voiced singer Helen Kane, of "Boop, boop, a doop" fame, represented a living Kewpie doll.

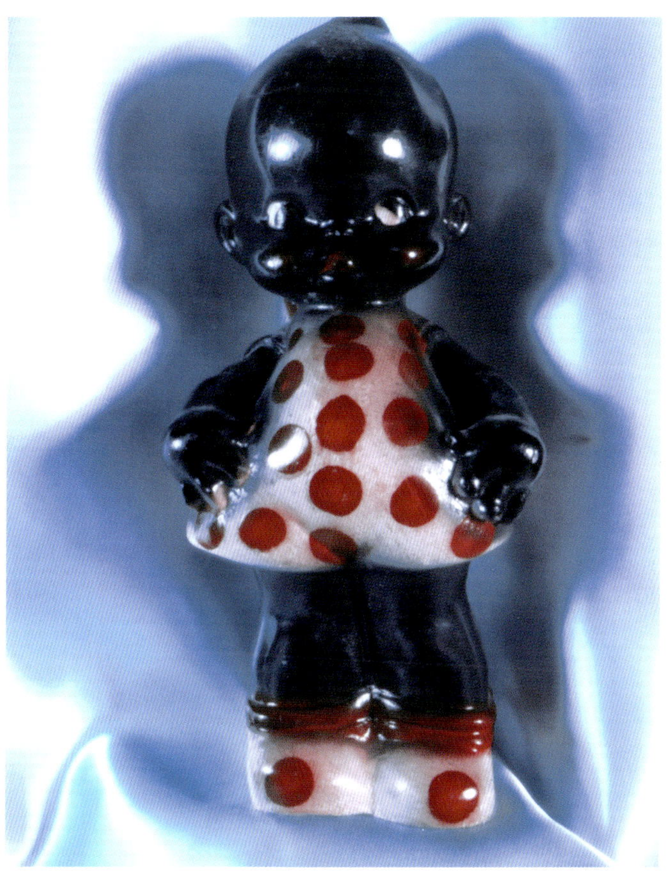
Kewpie bank twelve-inch carnival chalk prize, circa 1930s

So widespread was the Kewpie craze, that their features influenced many of the carnival chalk baby banks made after the Kewpie era. O'Neill must have been horrified that the carnival chalk black baby's shifty eyes reinforced stereotypical Jim Crow features, since she was known to be antiracist. Also, she would have been disappointed that so many of the chalkware fat baby banks were made with unhappy facial expressions. The Kewpie Riding a Bullet chalk figure that reads "Hatched in USA" on the bullet and "Columbia Egg" on the casing probably was not from the carnivals but some kind of patriotic World War II giveaway from a company named Columbia Egg. Its idea played upon O'Neill's stereotyped love Kewpie, but totally reversed it. This Kewpie was steering its

deadly bullet, rather than its love arrow, into an enemy destination. Subliminally, the Kewpie Riding a Bullet was suggestive of Japan's kamikaze pilots—a martyred warrior archetype—a symbol having powerful influence; one that touched upon strong instinctive feelings of honor, patriotism and nationalism.

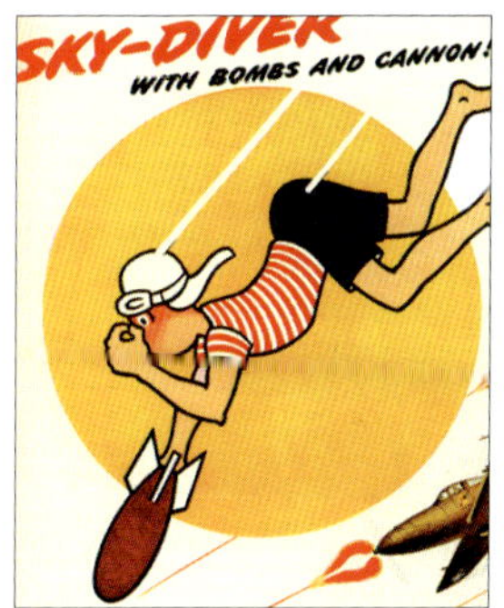

Insignia 500th Fighter-Bomber Squadron, World War II

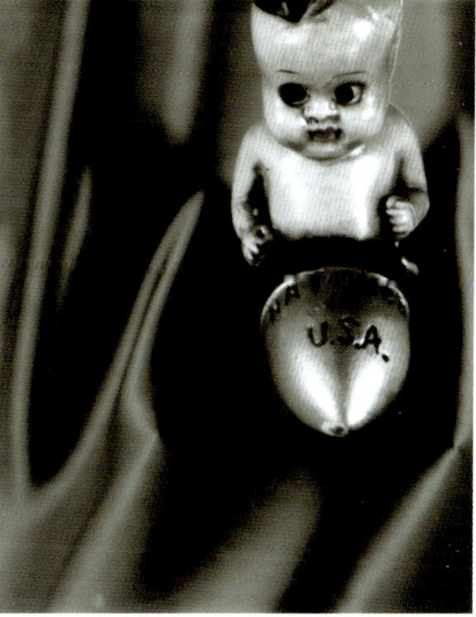

Kewpie Riding a Bullet © Columbia Egg, 1940s

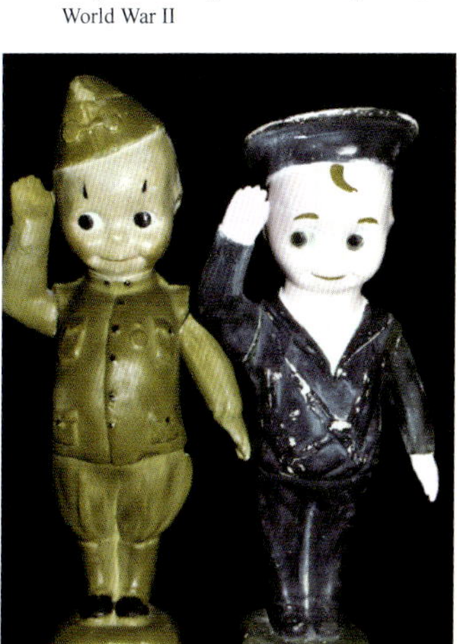
World War I kewpie soldier and kewpie sailor fifteen-and fourteen-inch carnival chalk prizes with movable saluting arms, circa 1918.
Collection: Kathie and Lanny Patrick

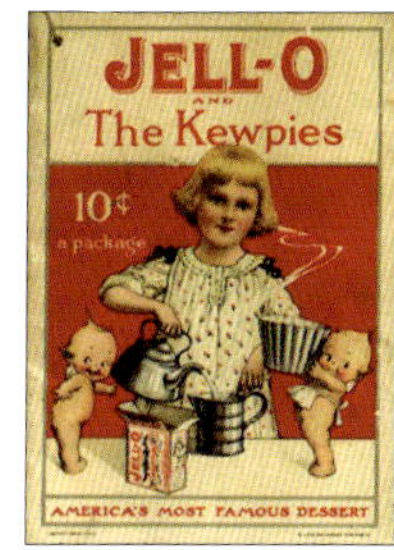

Jell-O Box, Rose O'Neill with her Kewpies, designed by O'Neill, circa 1920s

Rose O'Neill was born in 1874, in Wilkes-Barre, Pennsylvania. Her family soon moved to Nebraska. At age thirteen, she entered a drawing contest sponsored by the *Omaha World Herald* that was specifically for children under the age of fifteen. Her drawing easily won but, before she was proclaimed winner, the judges, who did not believe any child could have produced her drawing, asked her to submit to a drawing test. She quickly turned them into believers. She moved to New York in 1893 and her work appeared in *Harper's Monthly*, *Harper's Weekly*, *Harper's Bazaar*, and *Collier's*. *Puck* hired her in 1896 and she created more than seven hundred illustrations for them. Her illustrations centered on the shifting roles of women, ethnic groups, and children, and were atypical of the era's familiar derogatory, racist stereotypes that demeaned blacks and immigrants. She strongly supported the suffragist movement. She was the "Rose" in the popular song "Rose of Washington Square." She traveled widely and studied in Paris with the sculptor Rodin and the writer Kahil Gibran. The popular small carnival prize chalk Kewpie of the 1920s, whose chin rested in its hands and whose elbows were propped against its knees, was entitled "The Thinker" in homage to Rodin's famous sculpture of that name. O'Neill died in 1944.

Battlin' Bert

(1917-

There died a myriad,
And of the best, among them,
For an old bitch gone in the teeth,
For a botched civilization.
—Ezra Pound, *Hugh Selwyn Mauberley*, 1920

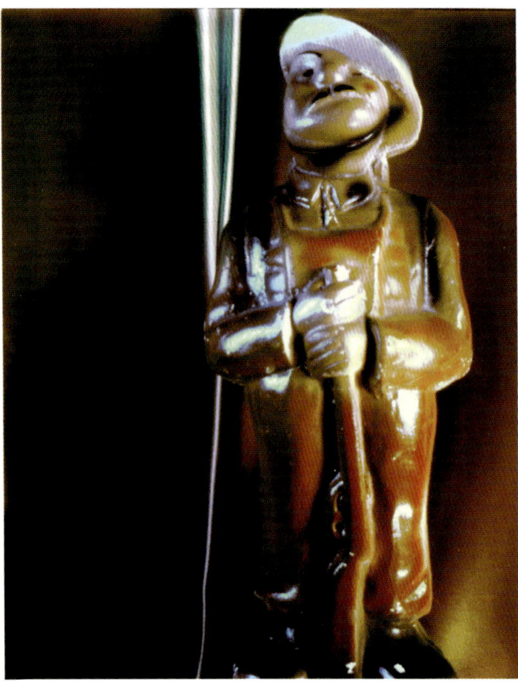

Battlin' Bert thirteen-inch carnival chalk prize

Reminiscent of British soldiers in World War I, Battlin' Bert is a famous war character depicted in Bruce Bairnsfather's cartoons, collected in book form in *Fragments from France*. His cartoons honestly presented the devastation, loneliness, and emotional horrors of World War I, through the only way possible—with stereotypical *M*A*S*H* humor. Bert is everyone's common man. His every breath is humorous, because in the next breath he may be blown away. The cartoons are meant as a transparent disguise, barely hiding the soldier's

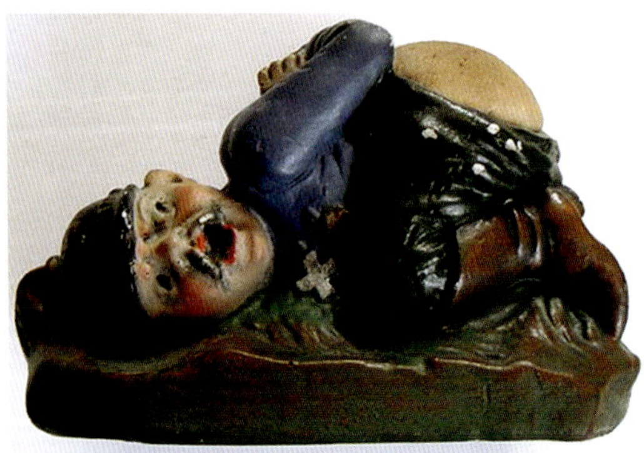

Kaiser Wilhelm pincushion WW I carnival chalk prize, hands tied behind his back, by A. Sylvestri. Pincushions have always been used to negate an enemy's power.

fear, endured, if possible, during wartime hell.

World War I was not fantasy—nor was death made easier—by repeating Peter Pan's most famous line, "To die will be an awfully big adventure," spoken by Pauline Chase to the many London audiences in J. M. Barrie's *Peter Pan* from 1906-1914.

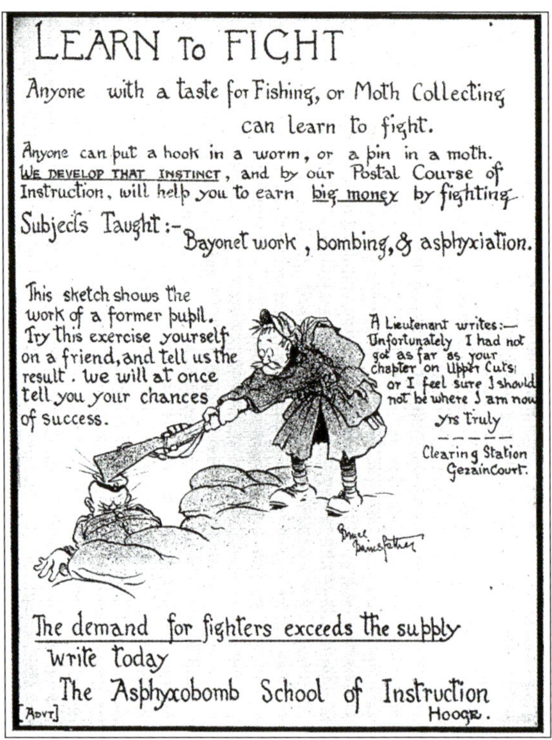

Bruce Bairnsfather, *Fragments from France*, cartoon 1917 © G. P. Putnams & Sons

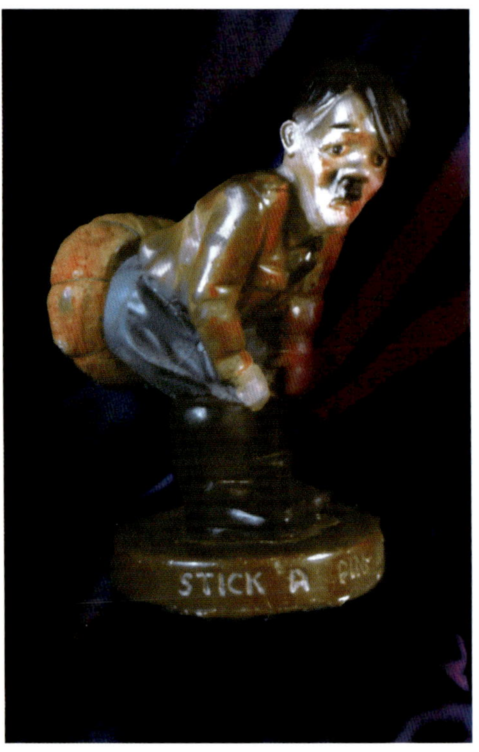

Hitler pincushion WW II six-inch carnival chalk prize, text on the base "Stick a Pin in the Axis." (Tojo Rat Pincushion page 212.)

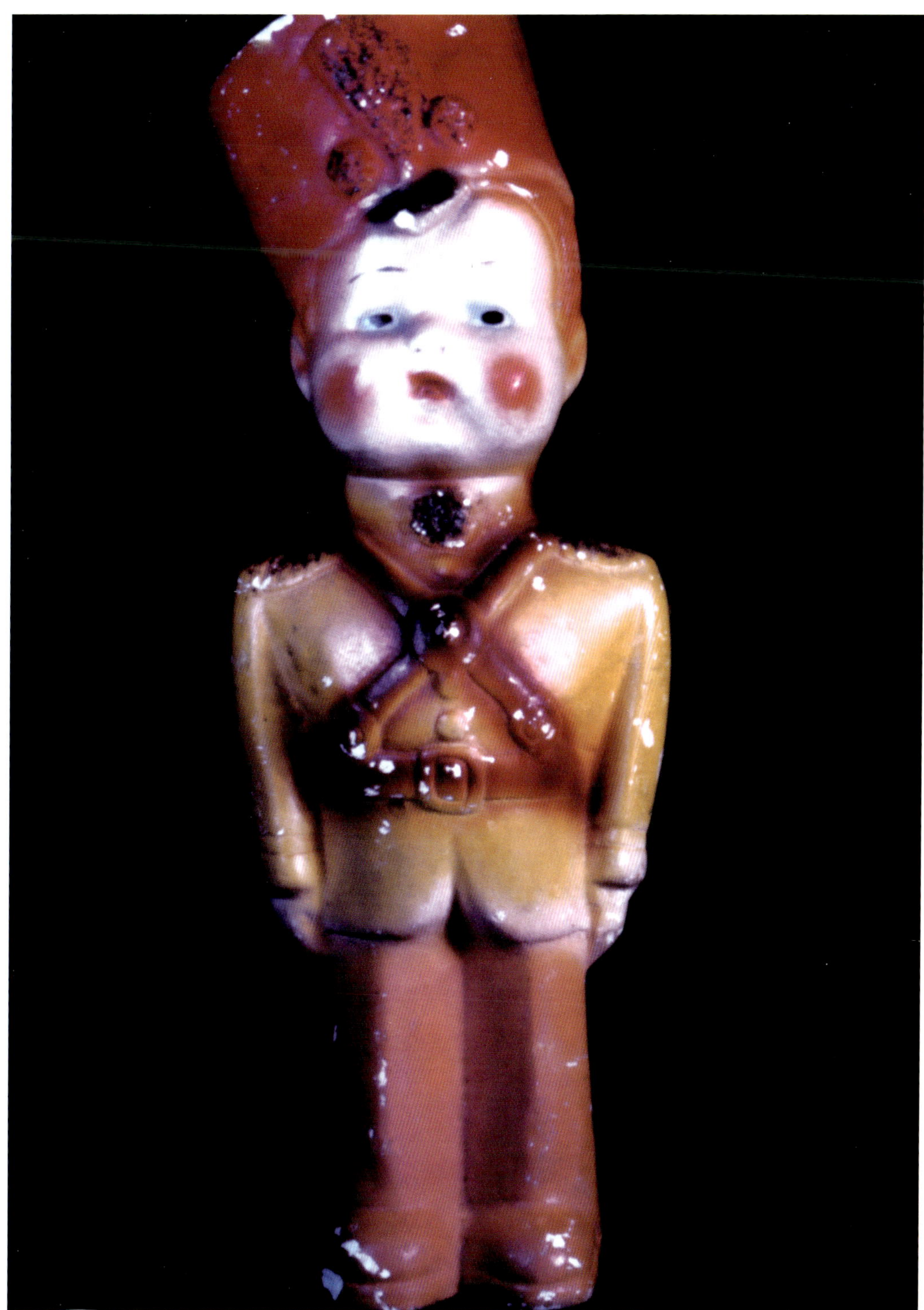

Tin Soldier sixteen-inch carnival chalk prize with remnants of silvered glitter, now tarnished, on his hat and epaulet. As playtoys they suggest war is a game of fantasy. From the 1930s onward many carnival chalk prizes were glittered to make them even more visually appealing. As early as the 15th century (and probably much earlier) ground-up mica was mixed into paint used to create a glowing aura to religious figures in Tibetan paintings.

. . . and these atomic bombs which science burst upon the world that night were strange even to the men who used them.
—H. G. WELLS, *The World Set Free*, 1914

LITTLE BLACK SAMBO
(1890-1950)

As you live, believe in life. Always human beings will live and progress to greater, broader and fuller life. The only possible death is to lose belief in this truth simply because the great end comes slowly, because the time is long.
—WILLIAM DuBois

Some people thought the Sambo character in Helen Bannerman's *The Story of Little Black Sambo* was the first black child hero to show up in white children's literature. Alleging that a black boy was a hero in a racist book is simply oxymoronic hypocrisy.

Bannerman was born Brodie Cowan Watson in Scotland, the daughter of a minister. She married a surgeon serving in the British army in India, where she spent thirty years. *The Story of Little Black Sambo* was originally written and drawn to amuse her two little girls during a long train ride in the 1890s. A friend saw beauty and simplicity in Bannerman's illustrated pages and offered to take them to the British publisher Grant Richards, who immediately made an offer to purchase the copyright for five British pounds. Lacking the time to write Bannerman for approval, and not wanting to jeopardize the publication of the book, her friend reluctantly sold the copyright. (One can imagine the pennies lost from the five pounds gained.) *The Story of Little Black Sambo* was first published in 1899. At that time, Bannerman's bright but unrefined illustrations, suspenseful narrative, and rhythmic repetitive sentences were considered unique, as was the small size of the book, which made it easy for children to hold.[1] Unfortunately, *The Story of Little Black Sambo* reinforced American Jim Crow stereotypes of black children's looks and names, features that were already placed maliciously into many cartoons beginning in the 1870s. The story's racist bent was weighted more heavily than were Sambo's heroic qualities, although Bannerman claimed she did not mean it to be. Misunderstood intentions were, and still are, a standard retort from those who do not understand their own, as well as others' instinctive responses from archetypes. Her claim that she did not mean her book to be racist is the perfect illustration of archetypal unexamined superiority verses an examined understanding of archetypes—therefore an appreciation of those who have been placed in an inferior position. Since Bannerman foolishly lost the copyright, a surfeit of racist editions of *Little Black Sambo* were released in the United States from the 1910s through the 1940s—all with increasingly degrading illustrations of Sambo, by then a stereotype.

Similarly, Thomas Edison probably did not want others to think of him as racist in 1904, when he released his film *Ten Picaninnies*, which showed unnamed black children playing and running. Nor did the cartoonist Winsor McKay want to be thought racist when he invented a Sambo motif to stereotype his "wild child" character Impie in the highly praised comic strip *Little Nemo in Slumberland*, which began as part of the Sunday comics section slightly after 1900. McCay's comic strip is probably the most creative from a standpoint of artful perspective; yet on July 14, 1907, the African child Impie was shown packed in a box, then stolen from his African parents by Flip, Nemo's malicious accomplice. Impie became an important part of McCay's traveling troupe of dissimilar characters for several years running. Impie was always shown as troublesome and sometimes very destructive. His speech balloons contained garbled letters. Impie basically stereotyped what white Americans thought an uncivilized black child might look and act like—one who came directly from Africa. Hal Roach probably didn't want to be thought of as a racist either when he released *Our Gang*, first produced in 1922. In it Farina,

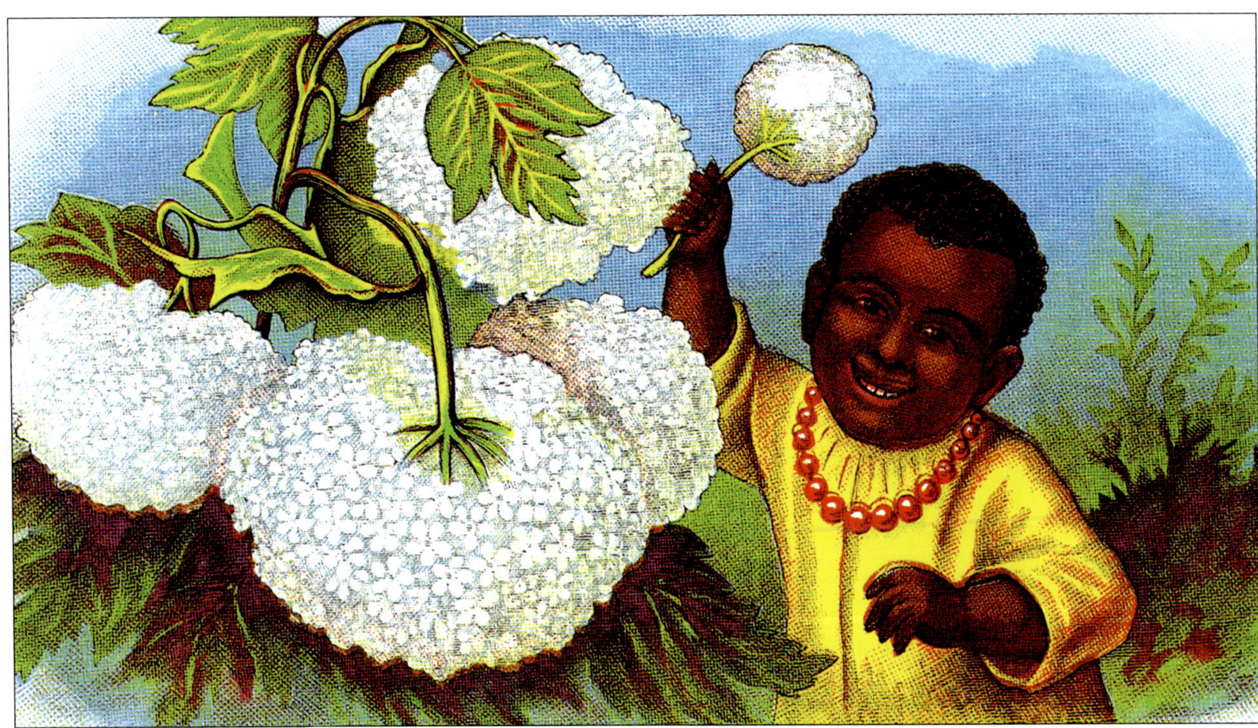
Little Black Sambo, cigar box label, circa 1900s

a little black boy, was often seen eating watermelon just like
Sambo. And so the black stereotypical slurs cascaded on and on.

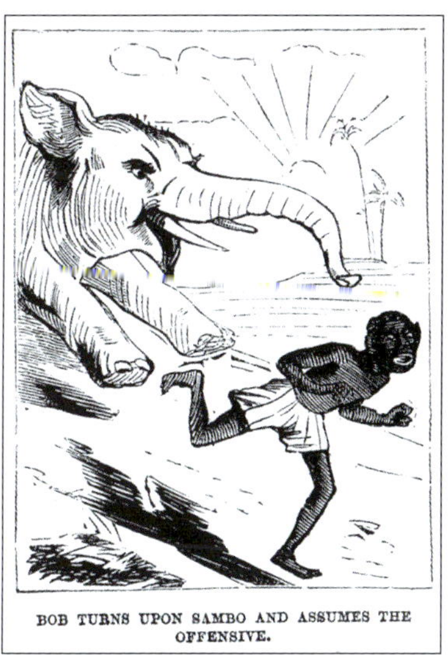

Sambo, *Frank Leslie's Boy's and Girl's Weekly*, comic strip
detail, April 30, 1870

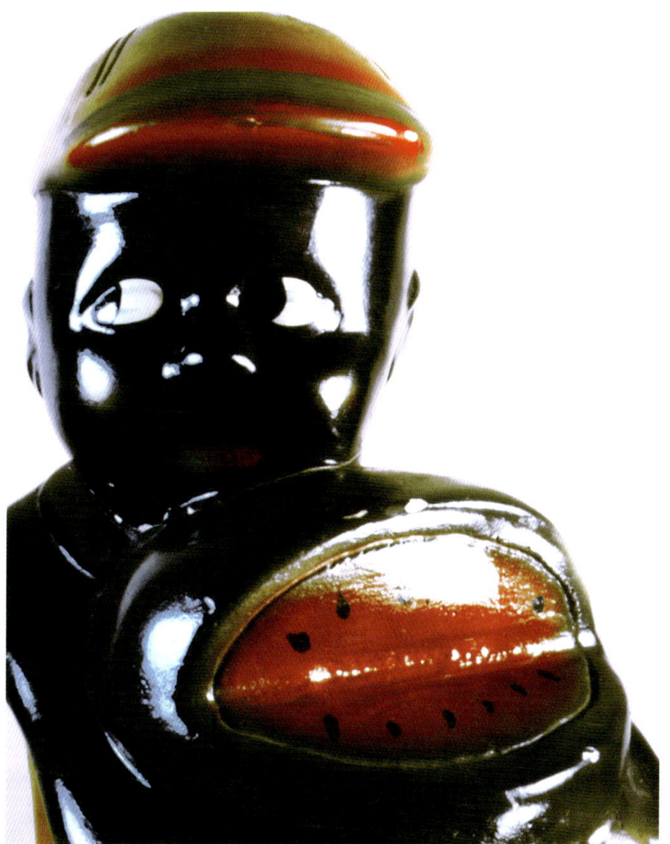

Little Black Sambo twelve-inch carnival chalk bank prize. There is no plug for removing
the money, so to get your money out, Sambo had to be broken (not unusual for the
carnival prizes). Go to the carnival, win another!

CAPTAIN KIDDO (1909-1936)

PIRATE WOMAN

*Actions receive their tincture from the times,
And as they change are virtues made of crimes.*
—DANIEL DEFOE, *A Hymn to the Pillory*

Grace Drayton, one of the first and most important
American women cartoonists, created the comic strip *Captain
Kiddo* in 1909. She also designed the Campbell Kids (1904)
and Dolly Dingle. Along with her sister, Margaret Hayes, she
co-authored *The Terrible Tales of Captain Kiddo*, replayed as
the silent film *Captain Kiddo* (1917).

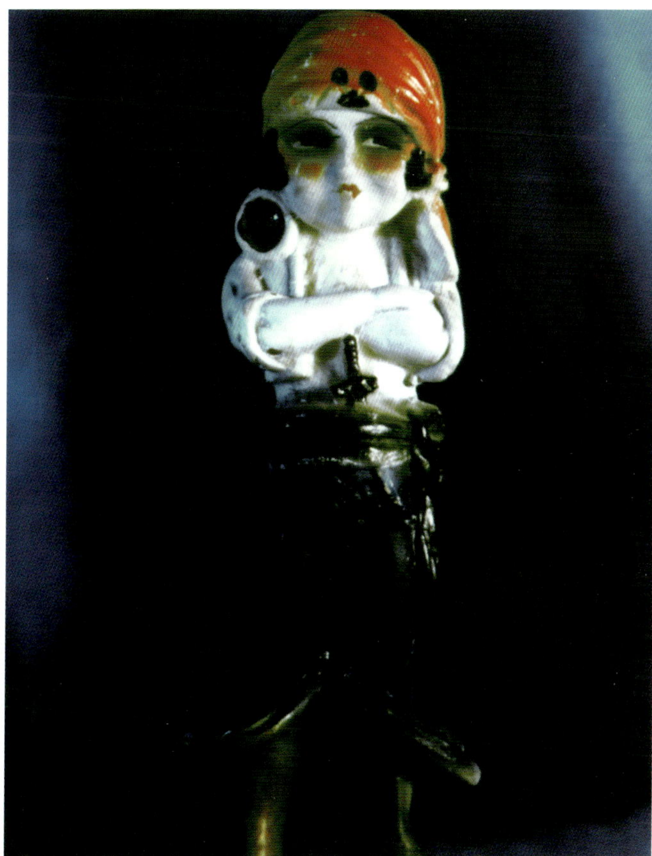

Captain Kiddo fourteen-inch carnival chalk prize, mid-1920s

Pirate Woman (page 46) is the continuum prize from
the Captain Kiddo pirate stereotype—a novel macho role
reversal for the sexes. No longer a child, as in the earlier
Captain Kiddo pirate girls, this fully developed Pirate Woman
displayed herself with cleavage, bared legs, and tight short-
shorts, rare for that time. With arms akimbo and legs defiantly
spread, this dagger-wielding Pirate Woman looked muscular,
aggressive, and well equipped for any battle of the sexes. Her
face resembled Mae West's. Pirate Woman, a newfound power
woman archetypal motif symbol, offered instinctive feelings
of liberation for women and dangerous lust for men. Of all the
carnival chalk figures of women, Pirate Woman says more
about the future role that feminists expected to play, and did
play, in American society.

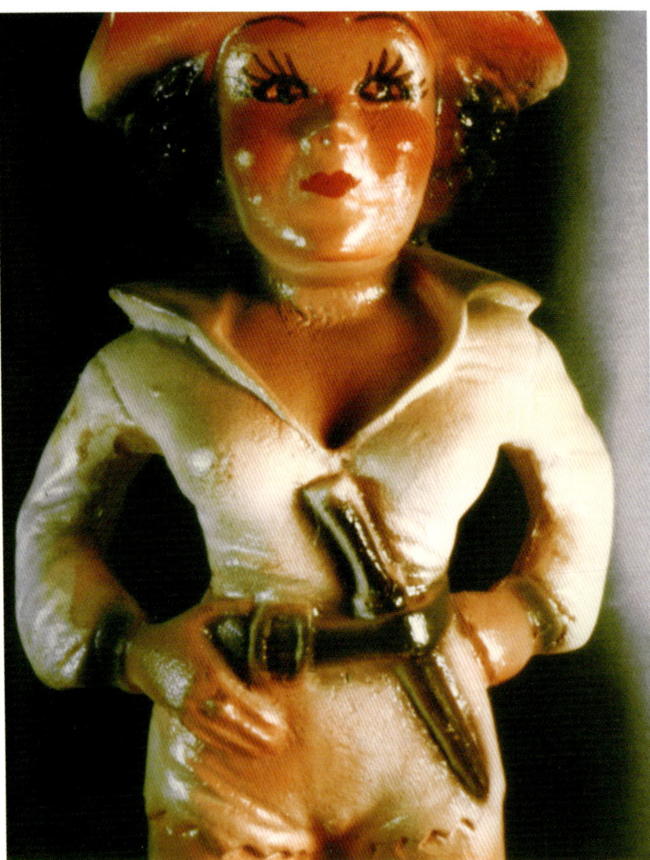

Pirate Woman fifteen-inch carnival chalk prize © William Rainwater (original figure carved in wood by Clarence DeWitt)

History tells of two early famous American women pirates: Anne Bonny (1698–?) and Mary Read (1684–1721). They were both cross-dressers and looked much like male pirates when engaged in battle, but while aboard ship, living their daily lives, they dressed as women. Much of their histories are mythopoeic writing and little of their activities are fully documented, therefore the tale's historical authenticity cannot be fully ascertained. What is known does indeed seem to prove that "truth is stranger than fiction."

Anne Bonny was the illegitimate child of William Cormac, a wealthy Irish lawyer, and his family maid, Mary Brennan, who lived in Cork, Ireland. Anne's birth proved scandalous and exposed Cormac as an adulterer. Cormac, Brennan, and their baby, escaping community wrath, immigrated to Charleston, South Carolina, where they were married and began a plantation. Anne was known as hoydenish (a high-spirited girl) and a tomboy. While still quite young, she eloped with James Bonny, a penniless sailor and fortune hunter.

Because she eloped, Anne was disinherited. Slightly later, Bonny became an informer for Governor Woodes Rogers. Bonny set out to rid the seas of sailors he disliked by accusing them of being pirates. Meanwhile, Anne fell in love with "Calico Jack" Rackham, a dashing pirate who bought her lavish presents and even offered to purchase her from her husband. Bonny asked Governor Rogers to step in and order Anne back to him. The governor agreed and told Anne she would be flogged if she did not reunite with Bonny. To avoid flogging and also to avoid being reunited with Bonny, Anne and Calico Jack escaped, beginning their years of pirating as husband and wife. Anne was an expert with pistol and cutlass and could better any of the male pirates, except perhaps, the other famous woman pirate, Mary Read. Records show that Anne gave birth to a child fathered by Calico Jack. The baby was left in Cuba to be raised by friends, but the rest of the child's history is lost.

The accepted pirate's rule of battle was that captured sailors from a defeated ship would become forced crew on the victorious vessel. It was under these circumstances that Anne met and fell in love with another pirate, Mark Read, who was in actuality the cross-dressing pirate, Mary Read.

Mary was an illegitimate child too, born in Devon, England. Her mother dressed her in boy's clothing so that "he" might illegally receive a family inheritance that was customarily left only to sons. She named "him" Mark Read. The funding from the inheritance ran dry when Mark was twelve years old and he entered the king's service in 1696, working on the docks as a cabin boy. Two years later he served as foot soldier and dragoon in the War of the Spanish Succession. He fought bravely and fell in love with his tent mate. Their romance was discovered and for this unconventional act (Mark was supposed to be a boy, after all!), they were both cast out of the service. Mark Read became Mary Read at last, and the couple went to Holland, married, and ran an inn named the Three Horseshoes. Mary's husband soon died of fever, forcing her to return to the sea. At sea, she was once again Mark Read, since women were not accepted as ship's crew. The British pirate Charles Vane captured the ship Mark was crewing on around 1717. Vane recognized Mark's fighting skills, kept him on his ship, and marooned the rest of the captured crew. Later, when Calico Jack and Anne defeated and took control of Vane's ship, Calico Jack made Mark his lieutenant. Anne fell in love with Mark, and they made each other privy to their hidden gender (a true Hollywood moment). They became lovers, a situation that seemed to be acceptable to Calico Jack. Together the women became even more notorious as pirates and were generally thought to be men, except by their own crew.

Their ship was attacked by a British sloop off the coast of Jamaica in October 1720. The sloop had been specifically designed to destroy pirate ships and operated in known pirate waters. Giddy after a raid on another ship, most of the pirate crew was drunk, including Calico Jack. Anne and Mary put up a valiant fight against the British, while those who were drunk hid below. When all seemed lost, Mary turned on her fellow pirates, killing two and wounding Calico Jack, screaming ,"Come up and fight like men." Captured by the British, all were put on trial in St. Catherine, Jamaica. Mary and Anne were sentenced to be executed. Both women were pregnant at the time and, when asked if they had anything to say to the court, they pleaded, "Milord, we plead our bellies." This served to stay their execution, since it was against British rule to hang a pregnant woman. Calico Jack was executed November 17, 1720. Mary died of fever in prison on April 28, 1721 (before giving birth), at the age of thirty-seven. Parish records for the District of St. Catherine indicate she was buried in a cemetery there. No records of Anne's execution or death exist, and it seems that she bore a son, as his birth date in 1721 was recorded in the parish records of St. Catherine. It was rumored that her wealthy father, John Cormac, bought Anne's release just after the birth of this son. It is also conjectured that the son inherited an estate in Princess Anne County, Virginia. Some historians suggest there are records showing that Anne remarried into a Charleston family in 1721 and lived on a plantation in York County, Virginia. Bible records apparently show Anne gave birth to eight children during this marriage. Her death was not recorded.

The first to write of these incredible exploits was Captain Charles Johnson, thought to be a pen name for Daniel Defoe, whose *A General History of the Pyrates* was published in 1724. His tale of Anne ends with her imprisonment. In Johnson's book, just before Calico Jack's death, Anne said to him: ". . . if you had fought like a Man, you need not have been hang'd like a Dog."

In 1961, the Italian film *Le Aventura di Mary Read* was made by Umberto Lenzi and starred Lisa Gastoni. Now obscure, the film does not follow any of the historical stories, although Mary is shown as a cross-dresser; her romance with Anne is not included in the film. On July 25, 1978, *The Women-Pirates*, a play by Steve Gooch about Anne and Mary, premiered at the Aldwych Theatre in London, performed by the Royal Shakespeare Company.

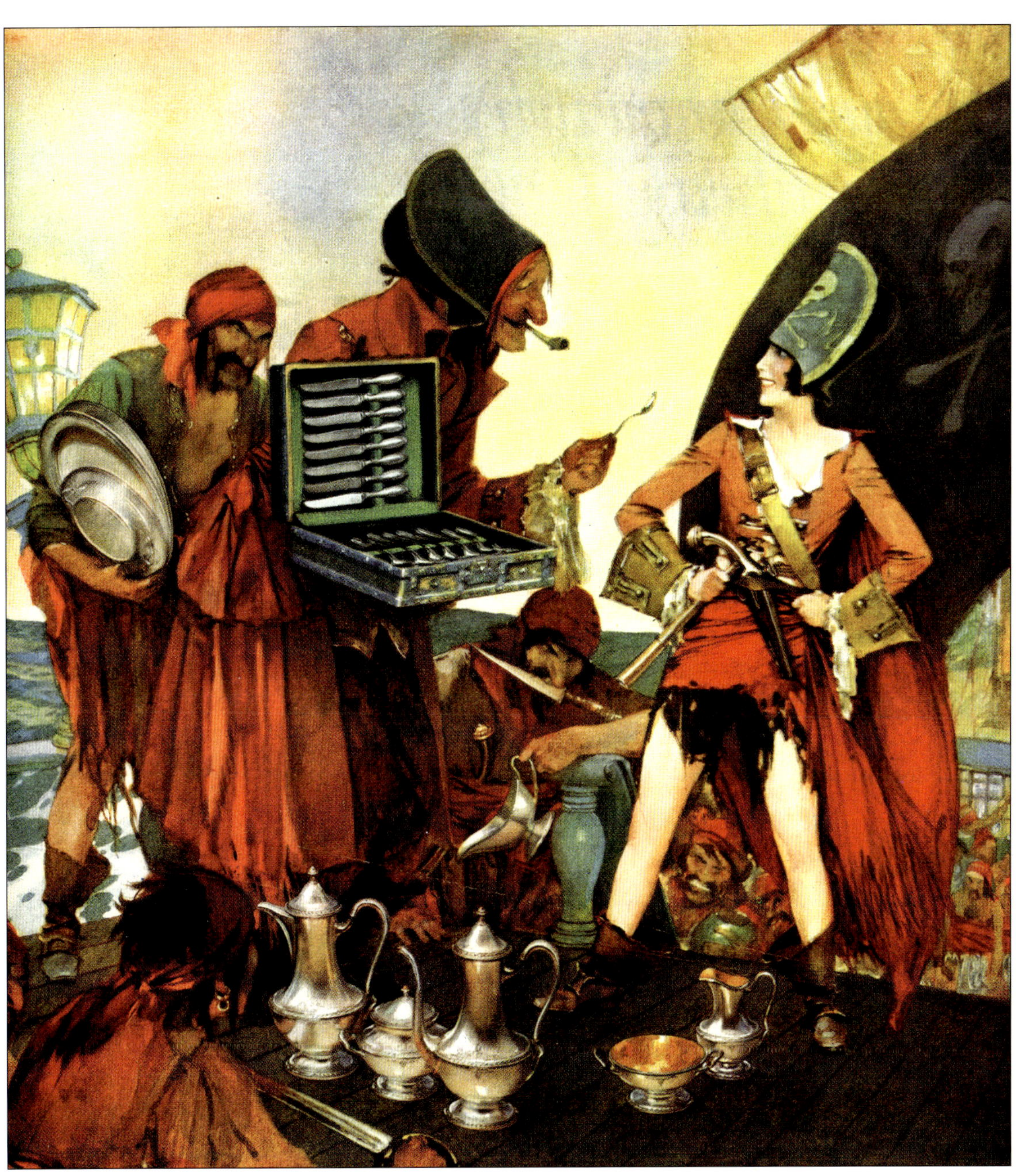

Rogers Brothers silver-plate ad, *Ladies' Home Journal*, April, 1927, illustration Gustaf Tenggren. In 1936, Tenggren worked for Walt Disney creating backgrounds for *Snow White* and *Pinocchio*.

Topsy (1852–

*Ignorance and depravity, and the inability to rise from degradation to
civilization and respectability, are the most usual allegations against
the oppressed. The evils most fostered by slavery and oppression are
precisely those which slave holders and oppressors would transfer
from their system to the inherent character of their victims. Thus the
very crimes of slavery become slavery's best defense. By making the
enslaved a character fit only for slavery, they excuse themselves for
refusing to make the slave a freeman.*
—Frederick Douglass

*Twenty centuries before the Christ a great cloud swept over sea and
settled on Africa, darkening and well-nigh blotting out the culture
of the land of Egypt. For half a thousand years it rested there until
a black woman, Queen Nefertiti, 'the most venerated figure in
Egyptian history,' rose to the throne of the pharaohs and redeemed
the world and her people. Twenty centuries after Christ, black Africa,
prostrated, raped, and shamed, lies at the feet of the conquering Phi-
listines of Europe. Beyond the awful sea a black woman is weeping
and waiting, with her sons on her breast. What shall the end be? The
world—old and fearful things, War and Wealth, Murder and Luxury?
Or shall it be a new thing—a new peace and new democracy of all
races: a great humanity of equal men?*
—William Du Bois, *African Roots of War*

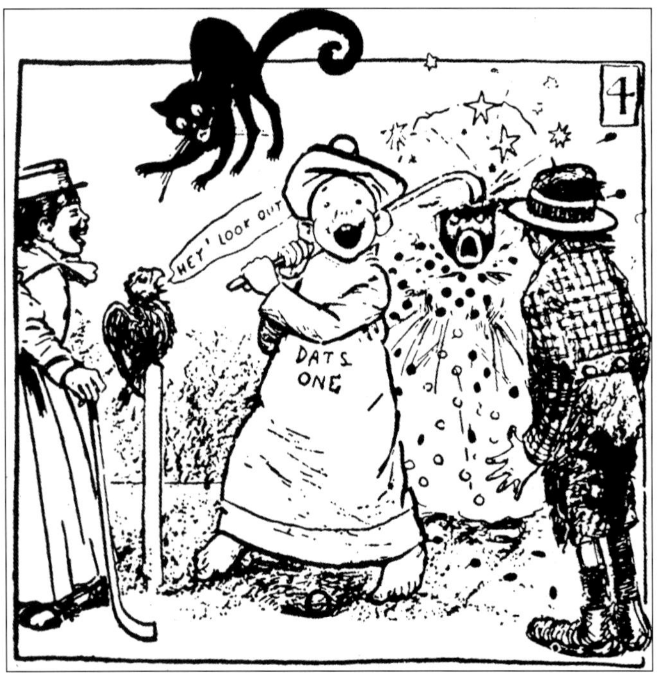

Topsy, "The Yellow Kid Takes a Hand at Golf," comic strip detail, William Felten Outcault, 1896

In his widely read two-volume book *Democracy in
America*, this is how Alexis de Tocqueville described the slave:

This man born in degradation, this stranger brought by slavery
into our midst, is hardly recognized as sharing the common
features of humanity. His face appears to be hideous, his
intelligence limited, and his tastes low; we almost take
him for some being intermediate between beast and man .
. . To induce the whites to abandon the opinion they have
conceived of the intellectual and moral inferiority of their
former slaves, the Negroes must change, but they cannot
change so long as this opinion persists.[1]

Africans were first brought to the Caribbean as slaves
in 1502 and to British-ruled North America in 1619. In 1662,
the Royal African Slave Company received a monopoly from
Britain's King Charles II.[2] The last slave ship, the *Clothilde*,
arrived in Mobile Bay, Alabama, in 1859. During that 357-
year period, it is estimated that 30 to 60 million Africans died
or were killed, either while being captured, chained, and
forced to ports for shipment, or en route when they were
again chained inside the ship's hulls. The stereotype of a
slave being an uncivilized, uneducated African native was a
derogatory myth; many who were forced into slavery were
educated, practicing Muslims, later thought by the Spanish to be
rebellious, but not so by the French and British who brought
Muslim slaves to this country.[3] The first recorded slave revolt
by Africans in the Americas was in 1552 by the Woloffs, black
slaves who had been raised by the Moors and were Muslim;
they revolted against Christopher Columbus's son, Admiral
Don Diego Colon, on his sugar plantation in what is now the
Dominican Republic.[4]

Woloff, one of the least-complicated African languages,
was easily tailored to meet the need for hidden communication
between slaves, who spoke a variety of African languages.
The Woloff language made its way to America and later,
in New Orleans, through the auspices of black jazz music,
infiltrated common English usage and has been adapted into
current slang expressions. The familiar slang word "dig," as
in "I dig it, man," is theorized to be a derivative of the Woloff
word "digga," which means "to understand." "Wow" in Woloff
means "yes" and is commonly repeated as an expression of
exclamatory affirmatives: "Wow-wow!" Another word, now
used in cultures worldwide, is "okay." Opinions vary, but
some theories suggest that "okay" is derivative of the Woloff
compound word "wow-kei," meaning the equivalent of "yes
indeed." Okay? Can you dig it?[5]

Once in America, Africans were given scores of derivative stereotypical name slurs; not even the children were
spared. The word "picaninny" (from the Portuguese word
pequenino—wee, small) was the smear word or racial slur
that whites used to caricature a useless black child. A pica-
inny could be depicted in many derogatory ways, but usually
he or she had most of the following characteristics: bulging
side-glancing eyes, kinky hair, and a wide mouth with oversize
red lips, portrayed slurping a large slice of watermelon. Eating
watermelon suggested two things: that it had been stolen from
a farmer's field, and that it was all there was to eat.

Black children were often portrayed completely naked
or sitting on a chamber pot, which added the insult of primordial incivility. Smear words like picaninny increased in use
after the Civil War, and as a result of the late 1870s Jim Crow
laws, were created to keep the freed slaves down—stereotypes
were resplendent for this. By that time, picaninnies symbolized
and stereotyped black children as being so stupid that they

were uneducable, and because of genetically inherited naïveté, they could never become smart enough to vote. Innumerable copies of the picaninny stereotype instinctively promoted discrimination and kept a stranglehold on the Jim Crow condition. All were archetypal symbols of white superiority for feeling pride or denoting black inferiority for being despised.

Topsy, the first widely known black stereotype, appeared in Harriet Beecher Stowe's famous antislavery novel *Uncle Tom's Cabin* (1852). Topsy was a poorly dressed, wretched slave girl, horribly denigrated by slavery. When the reader is first introduced to Topsy, she is asked to perform her dance routine, which consisted of spins, claps, and odd singing, concluded with a somersault. All her antics, including stealing, gave her the amoral and immoral "wild child" appearance as compared to her white counterpart, the civilized, educated, and sophisticated young Eva. Stowe hoped that readers would feel pity for Topsy's entrapment in slavery, and hardly dreamed that racists would turn Topsy into a negative stereotype. Stowe wrote of Topsy:

> She was one of the blackest of her race; and her round, shining eyes, glittering as glass beads, moved with quick and restless glances over everything in the room. Her mouth half open with astonishment at the wonders of the new Mas'r's parlor, displayed a white and brilliant set of teeth. Her woolly hair was braided in sundry little tails, which stuck out in every direction. The expression of her face was an odd mixture of shrewdness and cunning, over which was oddly drawn, like a veil, an expression of the most doleful gravity and solemnity. She was dressed in a single filthy, ragged garment, made of bagging; and stood with her hands demurely folded in front of her. Altogether, there was something odd and goblin-like about her appearance—something as Miss Ophelia afterwards said, "so heathenish."[6]

Topsy did manage to push some readers to question the brutality, inhumanity, and barbaric nature of slavery. When Stowe visited President Lincoln in 1862, legend claims that he greeted her as "the little lady who made this big war." Topsy and Eva inspired the black/white Topsy-Turvy doll, which came with one dress that was turned topsy to show black Topsy or turvy to show white Eva. Unfortunately, others took the image of Topsy's misery and exploited her further into degraded prejudice. She became a widespread comic dancing prop for minstrel shows. In these first minstrel adaptations her name remained Topsy, and she became an ever-too-happy, spirited, blackface girl (a white girl in blackface) who enjoyed life just by doing her playful, dazzling little acrobatics. Her dances, spins, and somersaults proved hilarious, so much so that later shows had two Topsy performers onstage simultaneously. By the 1900s, their dances evolved into two cooch dancing/stripping black Little Egypt look-alikes. The first film adaptation of *Uncle Tom's Cabin* was *Slavery Days* (1903), then *Uncle Tom's Cabin* (1913). Topsy's film dance became a much enhanced production, altered by years of minstrel adaptations. Blackface Topsy and white Eva were played by Rosetta and Vivian, the white Duncan sisters, in the popular Broadway musical *Topsy and Eva* in 1926.

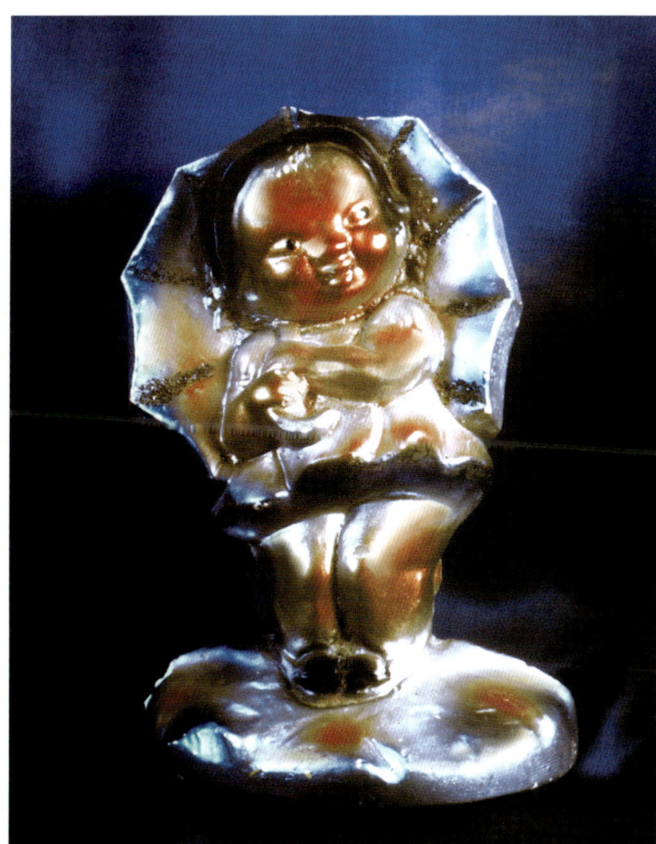

Topsy eight-inch carnival chalk prize

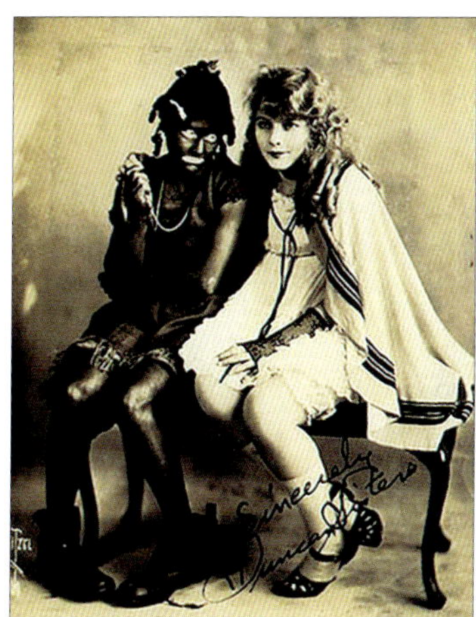

Rosetta and Vivian Duncan, *Topsy and Eva*, 1926

A change came when Shirley Temple parodied both characters in *Dimples* (1936). This began Topsy's transracial crossover from a black girl to a white girl. To perform this rarity, Temple played a Topsy-Turvy white girl who danced for pennies (like black Topsy). She then imitated the gallant white Eva, particularly when she was shown dying—a Hollywood swipe from *Uncle Tom's Cabin*. In 1939, the always incapable servant girl Prissy was cast as a stereotypical older Topsy in *Gone With the Wind*. Prissy was reminiscent of earlier picaninny stereotyping. In the film, Prissy deceitfully tells Scarlett O'Hara she has midwife experience, but when the birthing time arrives, Prissy, in her squeaky, excitable voice, squeezes out her famous line, "Lordy, we got to have a doctor! I don't know nuthin' 'bout birthin' babies!"

A real change came to Topsy's character when, for the first time, Topsy's song-and-dance routine was spoofed in Tex Avery's cartoon film *Uncle Tom's Cabana* (1947). This time Topsy had fully completed her transracial crossover. Avery had her play the part of a high-spirited white nightclub singer/dancer named Red, who sang "Little Eva got the penthouse suite, and that ain't all she got, yow-zuh!" It's unlikely that viewers realized that Red was really a disguised Topsy turned Eva. In this film, young black boys and girls watch the main storyteller showing Uncle Tom turning his sharecropper's shack into a nightclub where Red sings to pay the mortgage to that nasty white man Simon Legree. Legree cuts long-suffering Uncle Tom in half in a sawmill, runs him over with a steamroller, and shoots him from the back of an elephant. Mild-mannered Tom finally loses his temper and hurls the Empire State Building into space with Legree scrambling toward the top. Obviously, Legree is a switched, recognizably disguised analogue for King Kong. Maybe the viewers understood *that* reference.

Topsy has generally disappeared from Hollywood films, although civilized remnants are sometimes visible, particularly if the African American girl in the film is shown as difficult. The film *Paper Moon* (1973), set in the 1930s, sports a lovable, although sullen, Topsy character named Imogene, played by P. J. Johnson, maid to the white carney dancer Trixie Delight, played by Madeline Kahn. When Imogene describes her dislike of Trixie, she utters her best line: "She like that littl' bitty white thing on top a chicken doodle dey call chicken shiiiiiiiit!"

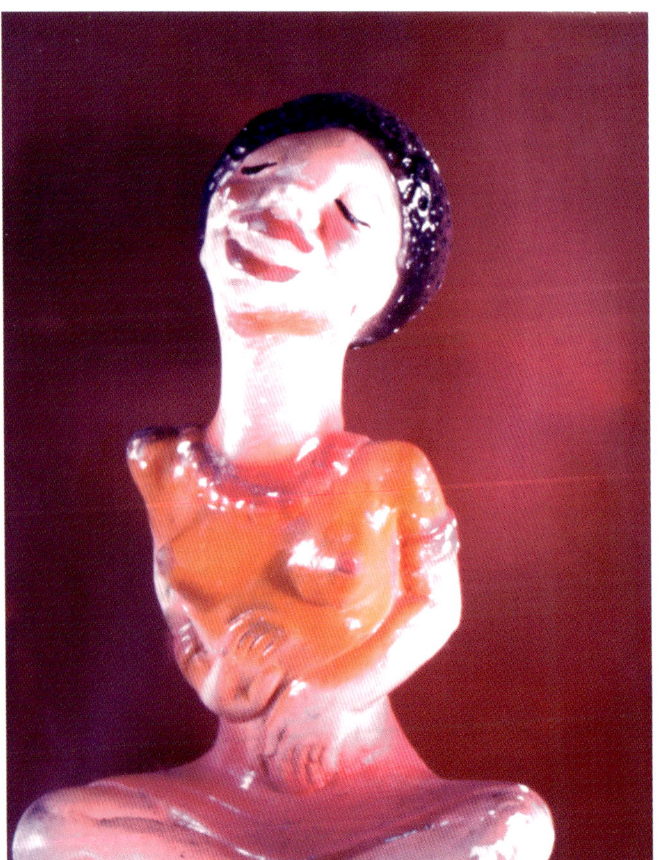

Topsy (caricatured as an uncivilized adolescent) ten-inch carnival chalk prize

JACKIE COOGAN *THE KID* (1921)

Jackie Coogan's star performance in Charlie Chaplin's first feature-length film, *The Kid* (1921), is acclaimed by many critics to be the greatest child performance of all time. Coogan, as the Kid, stereotyped the heart and courage it takes for an orphan to get past the unfair toss of the dice life had thrown him. The film opens as a scorned, unwed mother is being discharged from a charity hospital with her newborn baby in her arms. She spots a luxury car and puts the baby in it, hoping that a rich couple will find it and give it a good life. Bandits steal the car and then abandon the baby in a poor neighborhood. The kindhearted Tramp, Charlie Chaplin, takes the baby in.

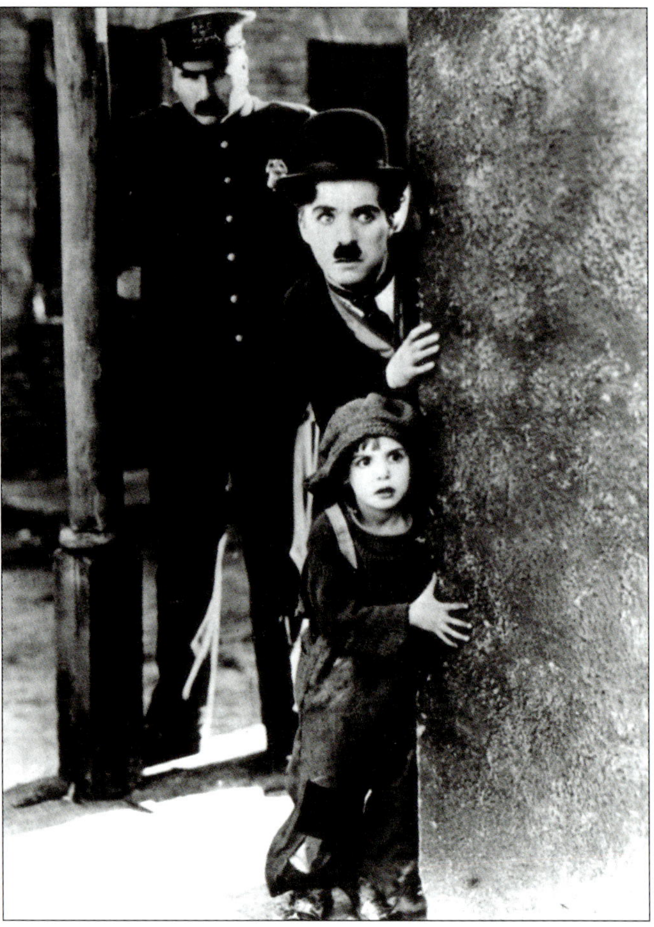

Jackie Coogan and Charlie Chaplin, *The Kid*, still, 1921 © United Artists Corp.

The film segues to five years later with the Tramp and his adopted son, the Kid, working together as window-glass installers. They use a clever scam to drum up work. The Kid acts the part of a brat who breaks windows with stones. The Tramp coincidentally strolls past the vandalized scene and gets hired to fix the windows, but authorities eventually catch on to their scam and they are nabbed. In one of the most poignant of all Hollywood scenes ever created, the orphanage police come to take the Kid away, the Kid gasping and crying uncontrollably as he's whisked away from the only daddy he ever knew. The scene created intense feelings of unfair loss, heart-wrenching when it happens to an orphan who is an archetypal symbol for feelings of unfair loss and who already is stereotyped as at the bottom of the heap.

By the film's end, it was obvious to most viewers that Coogan had stolen the show from the greatest comedian and top Hollywood star of the era. The young Coogan did this with natural screen presence, instinctive acting ability, and his pure depth of expression in depicting human emotions, and he was catapulted into instant stardom. He had been well trained by his vaudeville-actor father and his child-star mother, and also by Chaplin, who groomed him for the part.

Diana Sera Cary, in her book *Hollywood's Children*, describes how the Kid was made to cry for the famous scene with the orphanage police:

> Jackie had come to work that day in exceptionally high spirits . . . Nothing Chaplin described could douse his cheerfulness . . . If Jackie was too good-humored to sense it, his father was not . . . Not wanting to know what means brought on the indispensable tears, Chaplin disappeared into his dressing room . . . Moments later he heard the brokenhearted wail of a child. Without delay the cameras turned, the officials came to drag the boy away . . . The scene ended and a beaming cameraman signaled the perfect take . . . Walking out of the set, a shaken Chaplin asked Jack Coogan, "How did you get the boy to cry?" . . . "I just told him if he didn't, we'd take him away from the studio and really send him to the workhouse." . . . Chaplin ventured a tentative consolation. "They're not going to take you away," he smiled. "I know it," Jackie replied tremulously, and then, turning his great melancholy eyes on his father, he added, as though explaining away a parental embarrassment, "Daddy was only fooling."[1]

Jackie Coogan was born in 1914 and was performing onstage by the age of four. He acted in seventeen silent films between 1917 and 1928, but never again with Charlie Chaplin, who knew only too well who the most popular actor onscreen would be. Chaplin did help him behind the scenes, particularly in Coogan's film company, Jackie Coogan Productions. Coogan's huge popularity faded after he starred in *Tom Sawyer* (1930) and *Huckleberry Finn* (1931). He was overcome with emotional problems that began in 1935, when at age twenty-one his life seemed to imitate his role in *The Kid*. He was in a car accident with his father at the wheel. Another child star, Junior Durkin, aged seventeen (paired with Coogan in *Tom Sawyer* and *Huckleberry Finn*), along with two other passengers were in the car. Only Jackie survived the crash, miraculously walking away from the wreckage. Hollywood was plunged into deep mourning and Jackie was shattered. His father had meant everything to him. His only consolationswere the trust fund that his father had set

up and his engagement to the gorgeous starlet Betty Grable, whom he married in 1937. The marriage lasted only three brief years.

When he attempted to get the money he had earned in his early career, his mother refused his request. Coogan filed a lawsuit to regain the approximately $4 million that he had earned. In 1939, he had no rights under California law to the money he made as a world-famous Hollywood child star. Worse still, he discovered that his father had never set up a trust fund and had gone through most of the money. Coogan was awarded $126,000, which was half of what was left. The public outcry at the unfair decision forced the California legislature to pass the Child Actors Bill, also known as the Coogan Act, which set up a trust fund for any child actor or actress to protect their earnings. Coogan worked in bit parts and regained a small amount of his earlier fame, but it was much later, as the grotesque but good-natured Uncle Fester in the television show *The Addams Family*. He married four times and died of heart disease in 1984.

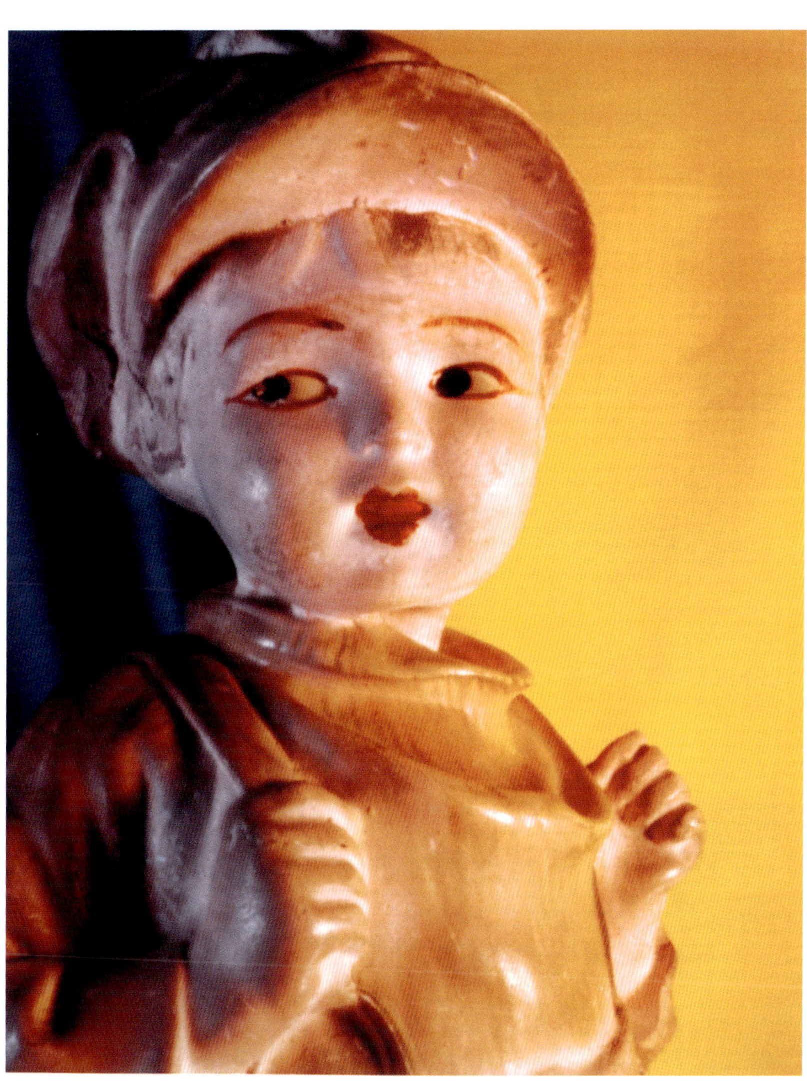

Jackie Coogan seventeen-inch carnival chalk prize, possibly designed by June Yates Jenkins

Little Egypt Cooch Dancer (1893-

The only unnatural sex act is that which you cannot perform.
—Alfred C. Kinsey

Congress approved Chicago as the site for the 400th anniversary of Columbus's discovery of America, a celebration known as the World's Colombian Exposition. The site, which covered one thousand acres, opened May 1, 1893, slightly late for the anniversary. Superb imitations of world-renowned architecture were erected along the Midway Plaisance, a graceful walkway that stretched for more than a mile. Initial attendance was very low, since many of the buildings were not quite completed on opening day. But by June, two magnetic bits of information spiked attendance: the Ferris wheel was finally working, and word had spread that there were exotic dancers in the international bazaars. The belly dancers drew immense crowds. The wildest dancer at the fair was Fatima in the Turkish village. She was actually a female impersonator (last heard from in 1933, the father of five children and grandfather of seven[1]). The most famous belly dancer was Fahreda Mahzar, who originated the "muscle dance." Mahzar made her last appearance at the 1933–34 Chicago's Century of Progress as Queen of the Midway. She always referred to herself as Little Egypt—she was not a cooch dancer, nor a stripper, she was simply a muscular belly dancer.

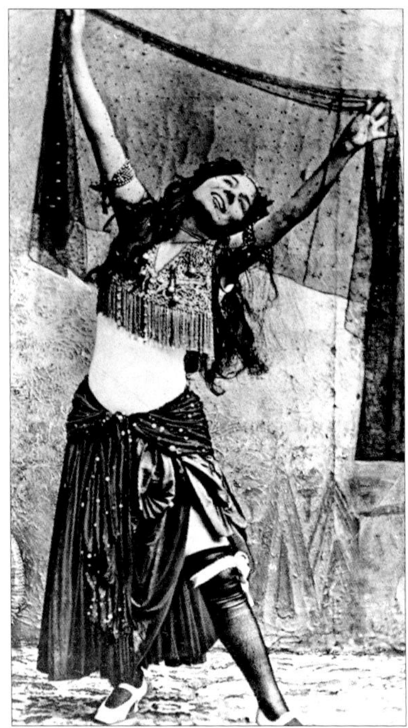

Fahreda Mahzar, World's Columbian Exposition, 1893

Many who came to see the exotic belly dancers quickly heard there were even more risqué dancers just out-side the fairgrounds. These were the cooch dancers, a stereo-type gleaned from the term "hootchy-kootchy." To see the cooch performed, people went past Buffalo Bill's Wild West Show to the small midway booths where strippers gyrated. Joe McKennon, in his encyclopedic book *The Pictorial History of the American Carnival*, subtly explained:

Another amusement area had been set up just outside the gates of the Midway Plaisance itself. In his story of Ferris' Wheel in the August 1893 issue of *Illustrated World's Fair*, editor John McGovern uses these words to describe this midway, "A little Ferris wheel, and still a littler one, work their unlovely motions in that vast and unlovely region that has been fastened to the Fair on Cottage Grove Avenue— a huge barnacle of entertainment, avarice and sin."[2]

It was here that the cooch dancer Little Egypt (not Fahreda Mahzar) got her name, and her stereotype. In later years, many dancers claimed they performed the cooch dance under the name Little Egypt, which was not true.[3] This myth was further developed by enthusiastic promoters who promised they would "bring the stripper, Little Egypt, direct from the 'Streets of Cairo,' from the 1893 World's Fair." These barnacles of entertainment were mentioned in lines of the popular song "Streets of Cairo." In 1895, James Thornton copyrighted his misogynist version of "Streets of Cairo":

I will sing you a song,
And it won't be very long,
'Bout a maiden sweet,
And she never would do wrong,
Ev'ryone said she was pretty,
She was not long in the city,
All alone, oh, what a pity,
Poor little maid.

She never saw the streets of Cairo,
On the Midway she had never strayed,
She never saw the kutchy, kutchy,
Poor little country maid.

She went out one night,
Did this innocent divine,
With a nice young man,
Who invited her to dine,
Now he's sorry that he met her,
And he never will forget her,
In the future he'll know better,
Poor little maid.

She never saw the streets of Cairo,
On the Midway she had never strayed,
She never saw the kutchy, kutchy,
Poor little country maid.

She was engaged,
As a picture for to pose,
To appear each night,
In abbreviated clothes,
All the dudes were in a flurry,
For to catch her they did hurry,
One who caught her now is sorry,
Poor little maid.

She was much fairer far than Trilby,
Lots of more men sorry will be,
If they don't try to keep way from this
Poor little country maid.[2]

This poor little country maid was advertised naked as a prostitute and, as the strident ditty intimated, one who carried some type of venereal disease.

Cooch dancers, fan dancers, burlesque strippers, and nudes accompanied most carnivals with their specific erotic side shows. They delivered body heat and burning desire—seductions that embody erotic female symbols for feeling instinctive lust. In the simplest of the nude acts, viewers paid an entry fee to get into the show and, after a slight dance performance, the women disposed of their tops. If the viewers wanted to stay, they paid a second fee, for which the show-girls removed their clothing below the waist. Only transient and easily transportable carnivals could get away with extremely outrageous sexual acts, like strippers picking up dollar bills with their vaginas—an archetypal gesture of the defamed woman, with strong undertones of misogyny. Sometimes these acts included bestiality, such as the "donkey show," which was performed in carnivals at least into the 1960s. Lewd acts depended upon where the carnival played and whether local officials had been paid to look the other way—or were treated to a private viewing.

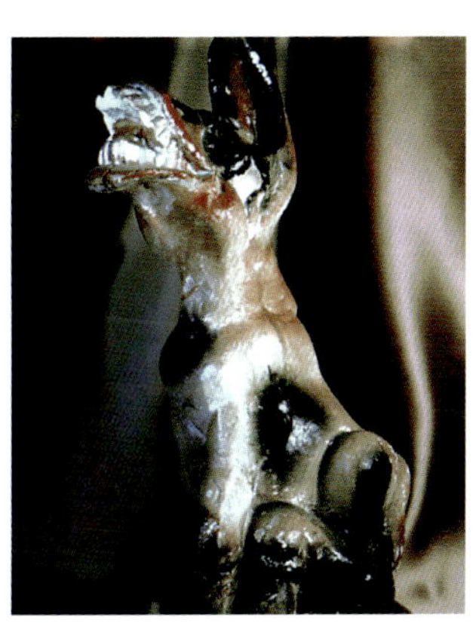

Grinning Donkey twelve-inch carnival chalk prize

BABY SNOOKUMS (1904-1933)

In 1904, "Da" was spoken by Baby Snookums in *The Newlyweds—Their Baby*, created by comic-strip artist, twenty-year-old George McManus for the *New York World*. After 1912, when McManus changed syndicates to *The New American*, Snookums appeared in *Their Only Child*. In the 1930s, Snookums was co-featured with McManus's successful comic strip *Jiggs*.

Snookums pin, circa late 1920s

During its run, Snookums was the best-known comic baby in the United States. At times Snookums was the adorable/terrible infant, a pleasurable problem found creeping around in many households. A baby is an arche-typal symbol for feeling unconditional love.

The hugely popular child-actor Sunny McKeen (born Lawrence David McKeen Jr.) played Baby Snookums, by then a stereotype, in the Stern Brothers Comedies short film series *The Newlyweds* (1926-29). Snookums candy bars were named after him. Tragically, McKeen died of a blood infection at the age of eight in 1933.

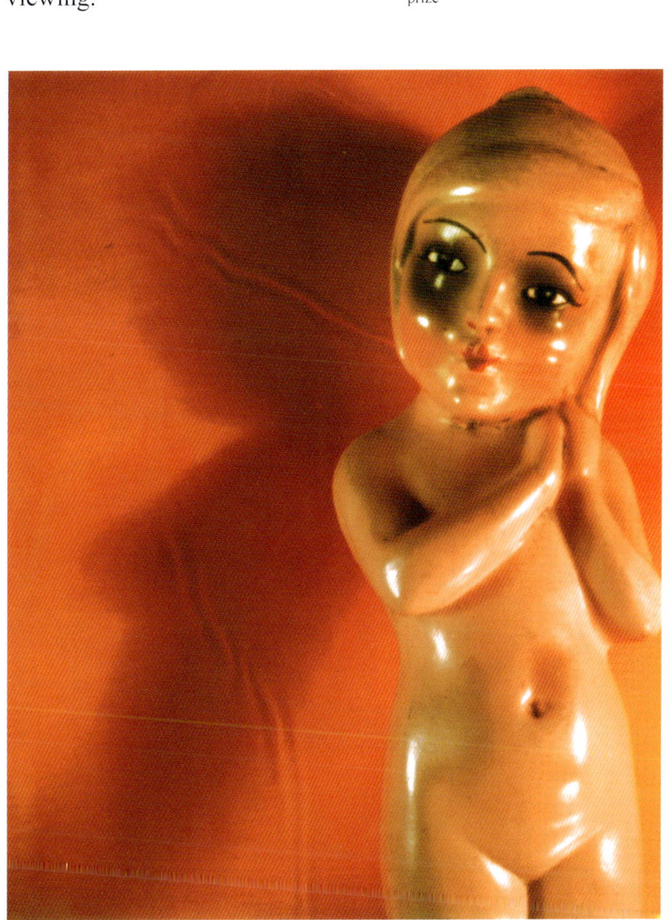

Little Egypt fourteen-inch carnival chalk prize. Many carnival chalk prizes represented the strippers and nudes who kept the carnivals financially afloat. Probably only one or two symbolized Little Egypt, the nude Lolitaesque figure shown above. She originally came with clothes or was sometimes delineated with the barest of glitter and wearing a feathered headdress.

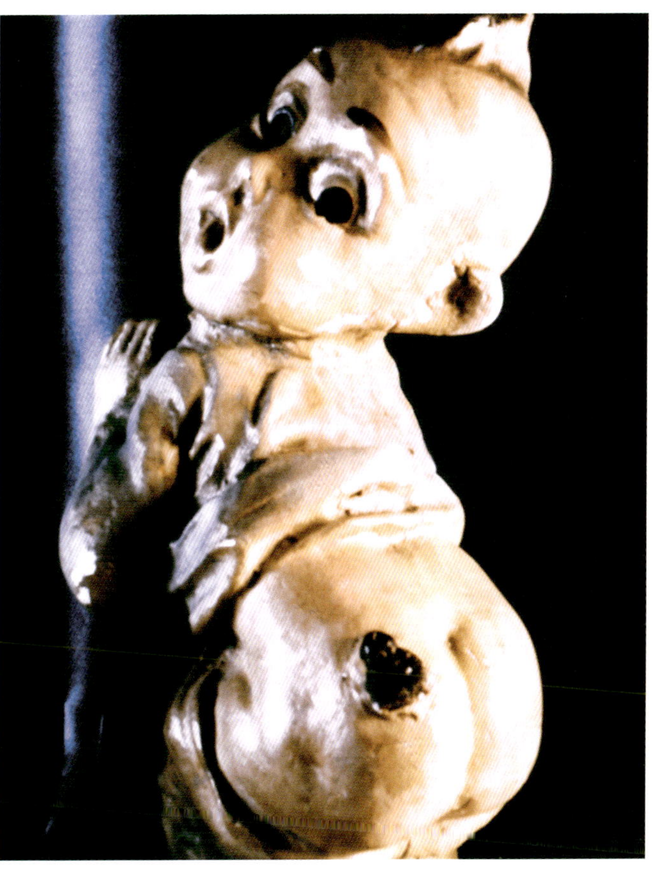

Baby Snookums eight-inch carnival chalk prize in a compromised position, pants down with a fly perched on his bottom. Coppertone used the same "cute baby bottom" look to advertise their suntan lotion for decades.

Maggie & Jiggs
(1913-2000)

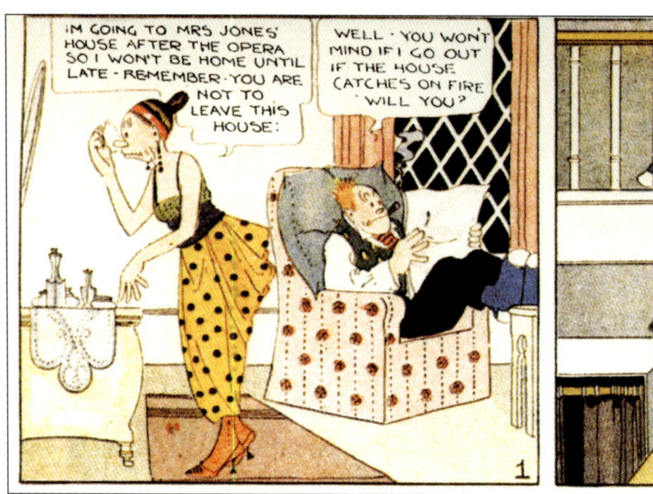

Maggie and Jiggs, comic strip detail, George McManus, 1918 © *Star Company*

Maggie and Jiggs, in George McManus's comic strip *Bringing up Father*, were a testimony to statistical ignorance. They bet on the lottery—supposedly the Irish Sweepstakes (but the Irish Sweepstakes wasn't started until 1930). Whatever lottery it was, they won. Someone does win lotteries; the money-making scheme has evolved since ancient times, and the group who runs the lottery usually makes a lot of money too, but that is not the point. The point is that anyone with an instinctive dream of winning it all can, in a lucky moment, win and feel the thrill of escaping from the ordinary, thus going from having everyday money troubles to being comfortably rich—and no longer ordinary. A lottery is an archetypal symbol for the lucky person. The media comes into play by announcing the lucky winner, which continually reinforces the fantasy of winning. During the 1930s, Irish Sweepstakes winning tickets were based on the results of four horse races. Tickets were sold on the black market (a slur) to mostly Americans and Canadians. Part of the money raised was used for Irish hospitals—a lottery became a good-cause stereotype.

Bringing up Father was a burlesque on catapulting poor people like Maggie, who was a washerwoman, and Jiggs, a bricklayer, into rich people. The great American dream becomes complete . . . almost. At least they can live in a mansion. Maggie gained socially ambitious snobbery, and Jiggs stayed the drinker and poker player that he always was, though now he could wear fancy clothes. Maggie, with the devastating use of her rolling pin (the female weapon archetype), kept watch over the mischievous Jiggs. The strip used standard stereotypes: woman as vigilant battle-ax (misogamy) and man as the corruptible little boy who was always getting into trouble by trying to find a means to escape—poster children for co-dependency and escape. Isn't that what sports and poker are for—as well as the opera (Maggie needed an escape too)?

George McManus was a child prodigy at drawing. By the age of sixteen he worked as a newspaper artist for the *St. Louis Republic*, where his first assignments were to draw hangings, murders, and suicides. Sickened by these violent atrocities, he went to New York in 1904 where he won $3,000 on a long shot named Hamburg Belle in the Futurity Stakes at Belmont Park. In 1913 McManus created *Maggie and Jiggs*. He admitted to being inspired by a touring production of William Gill's *The Rising Generation* performed at the Grand Opera House in St. Louis, where his father was employed as manager. It told the story of an Irish American bricklayer who becomes wealthy as a successful contractor. His socially ambitious wife and daughter remained ashamed of him because what he loved most of all was playing poker with the boys. Sound familiar?

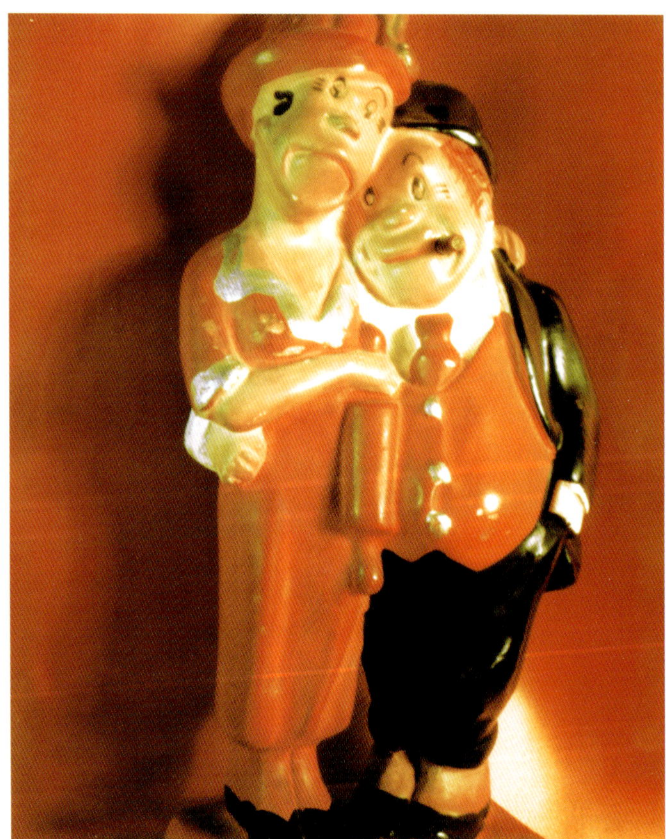

Maggie and Jiggs nine-and-a-half-inch carnival chalk prize. Other prizes included their daughter Nora (who eloped with Duke Nevere Worthnotten), as well as a figure of Jiggs's crusty friend Dinty.

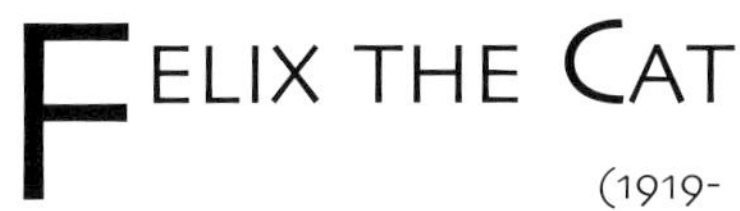

FELIX THE CAT

(1919-

There are two means of refuge from the miseries of life: music and cats.
—ALBERT SCHWEITZER

Felix the Cat was the world's most famous film cartoon star for almost a decade—long before Mickey Mouse (animated films should have been called catoons rather than cartoons).

Felix the Cat always was an archetypal symbol for the "good luck" cat (as in a cat has nine lives). His resonance with good luck was so embedded that in 1927 Charles Lindbergh carried a small Felix doll with him in *The Spirit of St. Louis* when he crossed the Atlantic on his world-famous flight. Felix had already been enlisted as the lucky mascot for the 1922 Yankees, who (as luck would have it) lost the World Series to the Giants that year. Being lucky, as a stereotype, was later copied by Walt Disney for his cartoon *Oswald the Lucky Rabbit* (1927), and also by Elzie Segar in his lucky baby, Swee' Pea, the adopted son of Popeye and Olive Oyl, born in the comics in 1933.

What was it that precipitated the embracing of Felix as the "good luck" cat? It had taken good luck and nine lives to live through World War I. Felix was not an accidental creation—he was a hopeful answer and a desperate archetypal symbol for feeling hope and luck in the face of difficult times, just as the devil-may-care flapper era was an instinctual response born from the horrific war archetypes that preceded it. Puffed up with its privileged, intellectual arrogance, humanity realizes the distasteful, core truth: that chance and happenstance controls one's lot to a great degree and that clinging to the weak straws of superstitions provides a modicum of comfort.

Superstitions surrounding a lucky person are deeply embedded cliché archetypes. There are hundreds, perhaps thousands, of ancient good luck superstitions, some still in use. A few of the most common ones are a rabbit's foot, a four-leaf clover, a horseshoe, clothes worn inside out, wearing your birthstone, beginner's luck, a cricket in the house, a lock of hair from a baby's first haircut, Lucky Strike cigarettes (lucky if you don't die from them), finding a penny heads up. Then there's the Mother Goose rhyme meant to teach frugality and vigilance:

> See a pin and pick it up,
> All the day you'll have good luck.
> See a pin and let it lay,
> Bad luck you'll have all the day.

Believing in superstitions for having good luck or avoiding bad luck is an ideal example of the powerful instinctual archetypes that playfully inhabit human DNA. Why does it seem so difficult to apply logical thinking against them? Because superstitions are primarily connected to such archetypal absolutes as life and death, health and illness, wealth or poverty, winning or losing—all of which create strong instinctive feelings.

Felix the Cat was originally named Master Tom in his 1919 silent-screen debut, *Feline Follies*, created by Otto Messmer. He cleverly crafted Felix as a response to Charlie Chaplin's popularly successful tramp stereotype, a character Messmer had studied meticulously. As a cartoon cat, Felix could be more pranklike than the human Chaplin—mischievousness was part of his stereotype and a readily recognizable feline trait. Messmer's clever cartoons, made during the twenties, included such classics as *Felix in Hollywood* (1923), in which Felix played the pet of an out-of-work actor and spoofed the silent-film stars. Once in Hollywood, Felix ditches his owner to pursue his own career at Static Studio, where he meets Gloria Swanson and Ben Turpin, who teach him to cross his eyes. Hearing a cry of help from Douglas Fairbanks, who is being attacked by giant mosquitoes, Felix takes a gun from William S. Hart and wipes out the insects, delighting Cecil B. DeMille, who then signs him to a contract. At one point, Felix detaches his tail and uses it as a cane to perform a Chaplin-style pantomime routine.

Felix was the first highly merchandised, internationally famous cartoon character from the United States, taking the crown from England's Ally Sloper. He even stole the heart of England's Queen Mary, who named her cat Felix (not Ally). The very first TV image ever transmitted was a blurry Felix the Cat, sent to receiving TV sets in 1929—a historic moment during the Depression. RCA laboratories conducted the experiment; for it they used a thirteen-inch-tall composition statue of Felix the Cat that was a carnival prize. (Just that historic tidbit shows the power of media archetypes—RCA wanted good luck.)

The beloved Felix held the premier spot as the world's most popular cartoon character until about 1929, when Mickey Mouse swiped his Hollywood crown. Walt Disney's successful Mickey Mouse cartoons utilized sound technology. Felix took a catnap and did not.

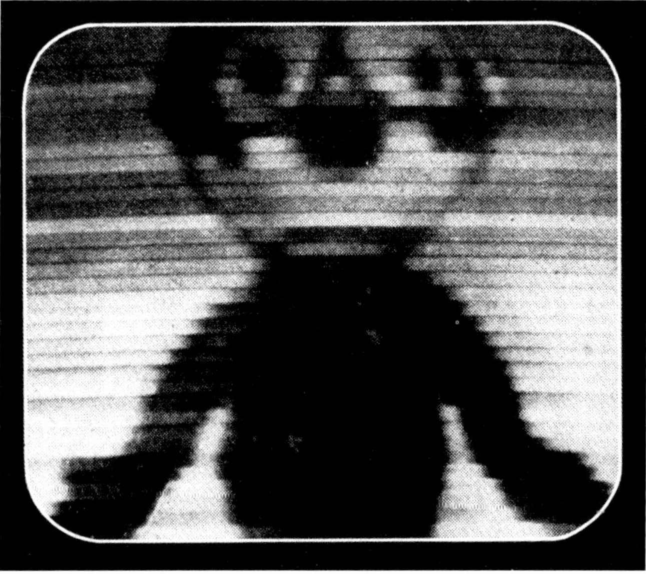

Felix the Cat, first transmitted TV image, 1929. Courtesy: RCA Laboratories

Otto Messmer was born in West Hoboken, New Jersey, in 1892. As a child, he attended Holy Family School, where his talent was recognized and he was encouraged to draw. He was greatly impressed when his brother took him to see Winsor McCay's vaudeville act in New York, featuring

McKay's animated films, beginning with *Little Nemo*. Felix was not the first cat to find its way into comic-strip form. George Herriman introduced Krazy Kat into his comic strip *The Family Upstairs* in 1910. By 1916, Krazy Kat was starring in his own color Sunday strip. Felix's fame came later through the medium of silent-film cartoons. Messmer began contributing his own comic-strip drawings to the Sunday papers, including *Fun* in the *New York World*, although he was more interested in film animation. Messmer's first released film was *The Travels of Teddy*, based on Teddy Roosevelt. He then joined the Pat Sullivan Studio in New York, but World War I intervened and Messmer served until May 1919. During the war, Pat Sullivan was sent to jail for rape. After serving nine months, Sullivan was released and later asked by Paramount Pictures to do a cartoon of a cat; Sullivan passed the idea over to Messmer and Felix was born.

Felix the Cat was the first animated animal in a silent-film cartoon that was intentionally created to be intelligent.

He contemplated problems and found solutions unique to the world of animation, where complete fantasy usually reigned (although Krazy Kat had preceded Felix as a profound thinker in comic strips). The unscrupulous Sullivan took credit as Felix's creator throughout Felix's early career, spreading a story of how his wife brought home an alley cat that became the model for Felix. The theft of origin was similar to Walt Disney later taking false credit for Mickey Mouse.

Felix's first comic strip in the United States began on August 19, 1923, in the *Boston American* and ran until 1943. When his screen career faded in the 1930s, Felix spent a few decades in a memorable series of comic books. By then, Messmer's assistant Joe Oriolo was sketching the drawings for Felix. Felix the Cat was resurrected from 1958 to 1960 as a television character, produced by Oriolo, who rightfully credited Messmer as Felix's original creator. Felix the Cat continues to be marketed and enjoyed. Messmer died in 1983.

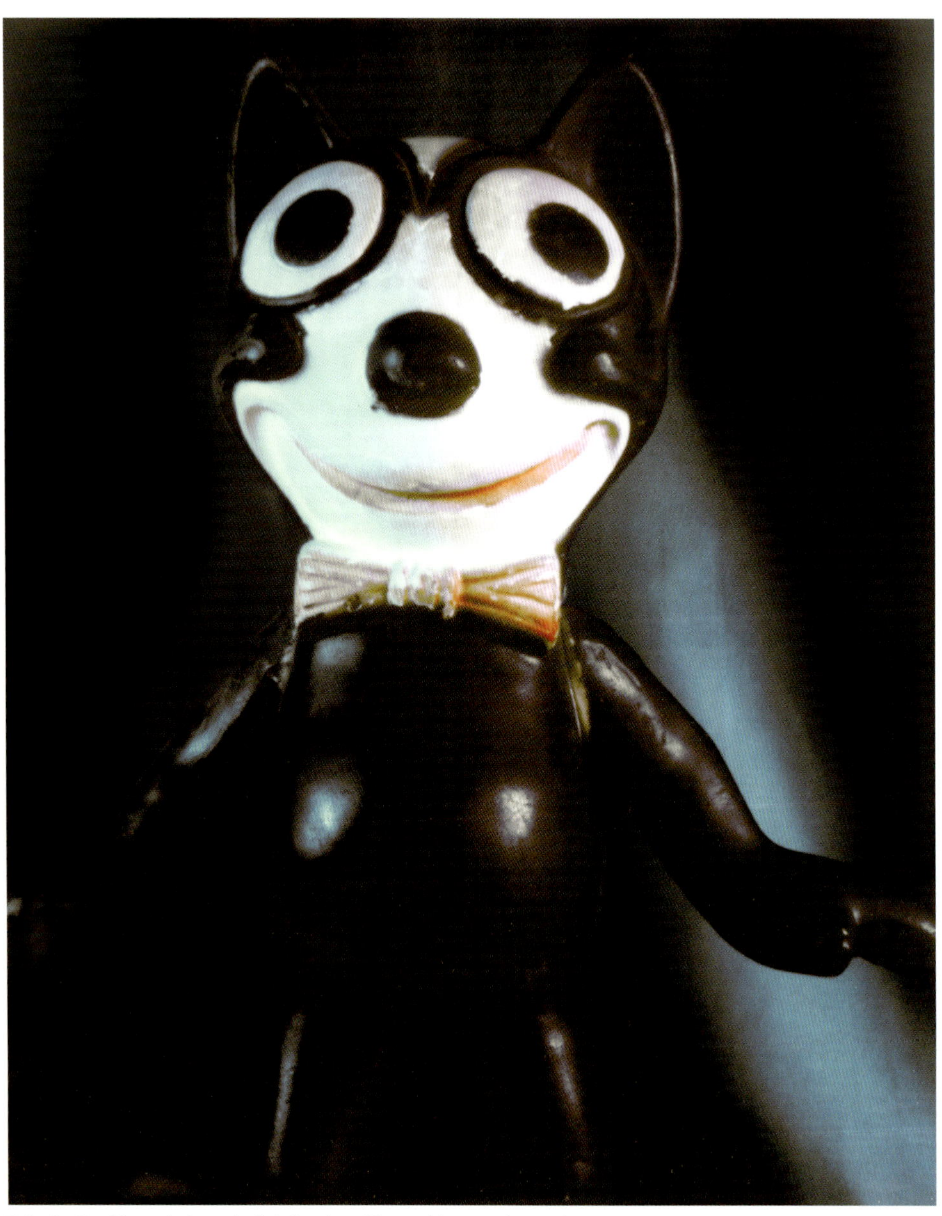

Felix the Cat thirteen-inch carnival chalk prize with movable arms, circa early 1920s

CROSS-DRESSER

The dress is a small, nay the least thing.
—JOAN OF ARC, spoken at her trial, Marina Warner, *Joan of Arc*

She was soon dead and her clothes all burned. Then the fire was raked back, and her naked body shown to all the people and all the secrets that could or should belong to a woman, to take away any doubts from people's minds. When they had stared long enough at her dead body bound to the stake, the executioner got a big fire going again round her poor carcass, which was soon burned, both flesh and bones reduced to ashes.[1]
—BOURGEOIS DE PARIS, anonymous peer of Joan of Arc, one who witnessed her death and wrote *Le Journal d'un Bourgeois de Paris, 1405-99,* Marina Warner, *Joan of Arc*

And the day came when the risk to remain tight in a bud was more painful than the risk it took to blossom.
—ANAIS NIN

The execution of Joan of Arc possibly elicited the most sympathy and notoriety ever accorded a woman. The various charges levied against her were grouped into twelve categorized, accusatory articles—two of which dealt with cross-dressing. Under pressure from her accusers, she recanted and agreed to never cross-dress again, but she later broke her word and reverted back to cross-dressing. The church sentenced her to be executed.[2] Just prior to her execution, when an explanation for her broken promise was requested by the church, she stated that she never meant to recant in the first place and that it was simply more convenient for her to wear men's clothing. This was the damning statement that provided the church with the dogmatic political excuse they needed to execute her: she had broken an oath to the church and, therefore, to God. It was, however, only a transparent ploy (a disguise), and the true reason she was killed was because she was highly visible, famous, and respected by her peers. It was a serious threat to patriarchy for a woman to have these qualities. Dressed as a man, Joan of Arc symbolized an archetype of the nonconventional person, which created fear. The church authorities stereotyped her as a devil witch, suggesting extreme fear. She overtly and unabashedly challenged female and male roles in a domineering, patriarchal society (even though it's unlikely that she perceived her image in that way). That image continues as the representative archetype of the present-day cross-dresser. Joan of Arc, a mere nineteen-year-old woman, was a threat to church control. Only twenty-five years later, in 1456, the next pope declared her innocent. Innocent of what crime, one might ask? Joan of Arc was canonized in 1920. Her tragic story presents tangible proof that clothing is paramount in the equation of stereotype and archetype.

The most famous cross-dressing American woman was Dr. Mary Walker, who insisted on wearing long trousers while serving as an assistant surgeon during the Civil War. She received a Congressional Medal of Honor for her selfless contributions. She wore a short dress over her trousers during the Civil War era, but by the 1870s, she appeared in male

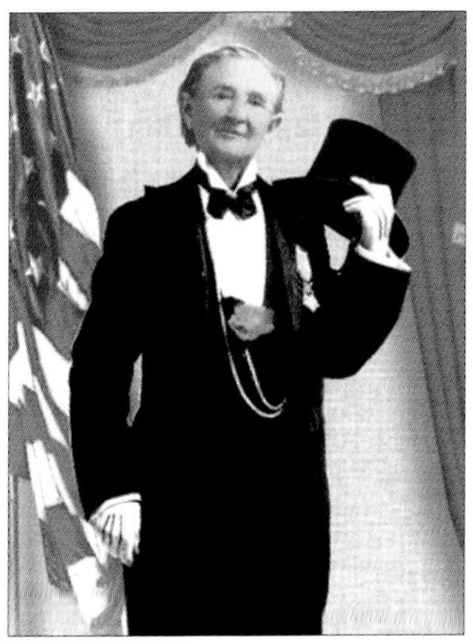

Dr. Mary Walker. She was purged from the Medal of Honor rolls in 1917, but she refused to return the medal, wearing it until she died.

attire only, in outfits that included a high silk hat. She became a notorious and controversial figure through the 1900s, and was so politicized because of her dress and her ideas that in 1917 her name was purged from the Medal of Honor rolls. Through style alone, in a fashion similar to that of Joan of Arc, Walker had challenged society's gender roles. She was also a very early antismoking advocate (so was Henry Ford) and the inventor of the return receipt for registered mail. She died in 1919.[3] President Jimmy Carter reinstated her medal in 1977.

Cross-dressing among men increased in popularity within flashier circles during the Jazz Age of the 1920s, when male admirers of the goddess Venus Castina began wearing wristwatches. Wristwatches were at the time universally regarded as braceletlike and effeminate—a pocket watch was a man's watch. Venus Castina was the goddess of sympathy and understanding to the yearnings of feminine souls locked in men's bodies. Rudolph Valentino blatantly wore a wristwatch, although he was not a cross-dresser. Lipstick, powder puff, and silk underwear were also available for men in suave men's stores during that era. One manufacturer of men's silk underwear labeled its products S-I-S, a feminine acronym for "step in suits." In a women's beauty contest in Lowell, Massachusetts, one cross-dressing male contestant appeared in décolleté. She almost won the contest, but lost when Rudolph Valentino, who was one of the judges, discovered the deception.[4]

Straight men scratched their heads over the rise in popularity of cross-dressing. One homophobic reason was that when prostitutes were removed from military bases, due to the May Act of 1910, men had to look elsewhere for enjoyment. A second reason was more plausible. During the suffragette era of the 1910s and 1920s, some men felt they were now free to express their gentler more feminine side, while some women felt they could express more aggressive masculine tendencies and be who they wanted to be. A third reason was that much of the freedom displayed by the liberated young women and men of the flapper era was a reaction to the horrors of war that they had witnessed and endured during World War I. For them, this was a valid way to feel freedom and liberation—an instinctive response to the brutality of war.

Wearing a red necktie hinted at homosexuality.[5] It is a popular misconception that cross-dressers are homosexuals. Historically some have been, but usually only a very small percentage. Homophobic nitpicks have always looked to the Bible for guidance and for a rationale for their extremist views on homosexuality. Of the many lines in the Old and New Testaments that supposedly speak against homosexuality, these are often quoted:

Leviticus 20:13: If a man also lie with mankind, as he lieth with a woman, both of them have committed an abomination:

they shall surely be put to death; their blood shall be upon them.

1 Corinthians 6:9–11: Know ye not that the unrighteous shall not inherit the kingdom of God? Be not deceived: neither fornicators, nor idolaters, nor adulterers, nor effeminate, nor abusers of themselves with mankind, nor thieves, nor covetous, nor drunkards, nor revilers, nor extortioners, shall inherit the kingdom of God. And such were some of you: but ye are washed, but ye are sanctified, but ye are justified in the name of the Lord Jesus, and by the Spirit of our God.

Most Christians have had difficulty with any form of cross-dressing or homosexuality, so much so that cryptic passages in the Bible pertaining to homosexuality have discreetly been dropped. In the King James version of the Bible, Acts 9:3–8, the story of Saint Paul's vision of Jesus is told: Paul, who was a Jew originally named Saul, had been persecuting Christians after Jesus' death. On the road to Damascus, Saul is blinded by a brilliant light and hears a voice saying, "Saul, Saul, why persecutest thou me?" Saul asks the voice to identify himself. The voice answers: "I am Jesus whom thou persecutest: it is hard for thee to kick against the pricks." Although the church has interpreted the word "pricks" to mean "ox goads" and claimed that the saying was a metaphor referring to Saul's rebellious nature, which was similar to that of a stubborn ox that needed to be prodded with divine nudges of the goad (which the ox might kick against), Saul /Paul, being an educated man, would have known that "it is hard for thee to kick against the pricks" was an ancient Greek phrase that was used only in homosexual contexts. This phrase for anal sex had been well known for more than four hundred years. Aristophanes used the phrase in his comedy *The Clouds*. In the play, Strepsiades pricks Amynias. Embarrassed by the homosexual phrase (and no longer able to pretend that "prick" did not mean "penis"), the church simply erased the phrase and, without any explanation to the public, omitted it from the more recent translations of the Bible.[6]

Every American state had laws against sodomy until the 1960s, when gay rights activists began challenging them. Thirteen states retained their laws. Four states—Kentucky, Arkansas, Oklahoma, and Texas—rewrote their laws so that sodomy laws applied only to homosexuals. In 1986, the Supreme Court ruled in the case of *Bowers v. Hardwick* that the right to privacy did not apply to homosexual and lesbian bedrooms. Chief Justice Burger vigorously noted that homosexuality was punishable by the death penalty under centuries of Roman law and that it had been condemned by British legal scholars as an "infamous crime against nature." To strike down state sodomy statutes on constitutional grounds would have been, in Burger's mind, "to cast aside millennia of moral teaching." The Supreme Court erased the Texas law against sodomy in 2003.

This is how the U.S. Health and Public Welfare Code identifies transsexual, homosexual, and transvestite behavior as it relates to equal opportunity for those individuals with disabilities:

UNITED STATES CODE ANNOTATED TITLE 42. THE PUBLIC HEALTH AND WELFARE CHAPTER 126—EQUAL OPPORTUNITY FOR INDIVIDUALS WITH DISABILITIES SUBCHAPTER IV—MISCELLANEOUS PROVISIONS
§ 12208. Transvestites
For the purposes of this chapter, the term "disabled" or "disability" shall not apply to an individual solely because that individual is a transvestite. A transsexual should be distinguished from homosexuals, who are sexually attracted to persons of the same sex, and from transvestites, who are most likely male heterosexuals who cross-dress for sexual arousal rather than comfort with gender identity. Both homosexuals and transvestites are "content with the sex into which they were born." Meriwether v. Faulkner, 821 F. 2d 408, 412 n. 6 (7th Cir. 1987); Ulane v. Eastern Airlines, Inc., 742 F. 2d 1081, 1083 n. 3 (7th Cir. 1984); American Psychiatric Association, DSM-III-R § 302.50, at 74 (1987); Wise & Meyer, *Transvestitism: Previous Findings and New Areas for Inquiry*, 6 J. Sex & Marital Therapy 116-120 (1980). A transsexual is also to be distinguished from a hermaphrodite, where an individual has both genital and sexual characteristics of both sexes. *Proof of Facts 3d: Tabor's Cyclopedic Medical Dictionary*, at 758 (15th ed. 1988). In addition, the Court observes that: A transsexual believes that he is the victim of a biologic accident, cruelly imprisoned within a body incompatible with his real sexual identity. Most are men who consider themselves to have feminine gender identity and regard their genitalia and masculine features with repugnance. Their primary objective in seeking psychiatric help is not to obtain psychological treatment but to secure surgery that will give them as close an approximation as possible to a female body. *Merck Manual of Diagnosis and Therapy* 1437 (14th ed. 1982). See generally *Comment, The Law and Transsexualism: A Faltering Response to a Conceptual Dilemma*, 7 Conn. L. Rev. 288, 288 n. 1 (1975); *Comment, Transsexualism, Sex Reassignment Surgery, and the Law*, 56 Cornell L. Rev. 963, 963 n. 1 (1971).

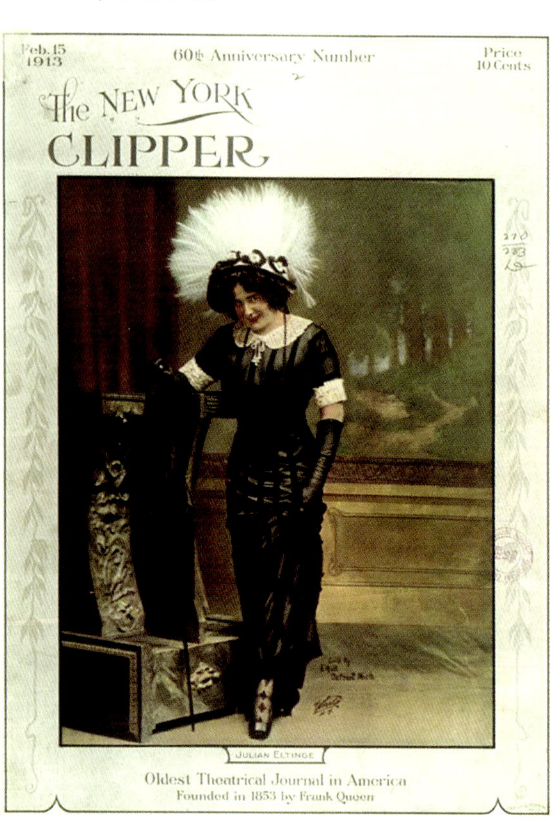

Julian Eltinge, *The New York Clipper*, cover, February 15, 1913

Satan was often identified as the ultimate cross-dresser in medieval times, depending upon whether he wished to seduce a man or a woman. He could change his pelvic apparatus, so he was actually a transgender. (Transgender surgery was not performed successfully until the twentieth century, so it took humans a while to catch up with Satan's procedures.) Whatever he was, Satan was always there to test the pious, and anyone who cross-dressed was thought to have Satan permanently implanted in his or her soul. It was the core reasoning underpinning the notion that cross-dressing constituted a threat to the church. There was a single exception, however: cross-dressing was acceptable in theatrical plays, and men were allowed to play women's roles. The only other exception was in certain holy men, like Saint Hildigund from the twelfth century, whose father disguised her to look like a boy when she was a twelve, so that his "son" could accompany him on the Crusades. He named her Joseph, and later in life she continued her disguise as Monk Joseph. Her ruse was discovered only after she died.

The saint who has the unenviable distinction of having the most preposterous pseudo-romance story was the bearded Saint Uncumber (known as Saint Librada in Spain and Saint Livrade in France). She was the child of a non-Christian Portuguese king and a Christian mother. When Uncumber was young, she decided to remain a virgin and a Christian. Her father decided she would marry the King of Sicily. She prayed to God for help. Her prayers were answered and she grew a long, drooping mustache and a beard. At her wedding, she lifted her veil just enough for her bridegroom to see her hirsute countenance. Aghast at the sight, he refused to proceed with the marriage. In anger, her father had her crucified. (Perhaps a fate better than marrying the bloke?)

The most controversial of all cross-dressers was Pope Joan. She, most certainly, caused the greatest anguish for the Catholic Church, more so than any other pope, which is not saying a little. She ruled under the name John VIII Anglicus around AD 850 for two years, five months, and four days. Thirteenth-century chroniclers recorded her life in great detail and her papacy was considered fact until John Hus, the Bohemian heretic, reproached the delegates at the Council of Constance in 1415 for admitting there had been a female pope. The church purged its records and had her erased from its history by the sixteenth century.

Joan was born in England; hence the title Anglicus. Her father took her to Mainz for schooling, where she fell in love with a monk named Ufilias. In order to stay with Ufilias, she dressed as a man and entered his monastery, but remained chaste. Later they traveled to the Holy Land and then to Athens where, for ten years, they were esteemed scholars. Ufilias died, and Joan, heartbroken, returned to Mainz via Rome. While in Rome, ex-students recognized her scholarship and ability (but not her gender) and persuaded her to remain. Her brilliance led to her immediate rise as notary, then cardinal, then pope after the death of Pope Leo. While pope, she fell in love with a Benedictine monk from Spain, who resembled Ufilias. She became pregnant and gave birth to a son. One version of the story claims that her son died soon after birth; another version claims he became Pope Adrian III. Because she had not remained chaste as pope, her sin was too great.[7] Most accounts end with her being stoned, while still pregnant, on a street between Lateran and St. Clement's church during a procession. There was a Christian sect in Milan whose followers believed in Joan's second coming, but the Inquisition exterminated the sect in 1300. The papess (priestess) of the tarot cards is thought by some to refer to Pope Joan.

A curious Vatican custom arose in the wake of Pope Joan's legend and provides a further proof of her reign and of the church's safeguard against it happening again. Subsequent candidates for the papacy were required to seat themselves naked on a stool with a hole in it. Cardinals, in a room below, looked up through a hole in the ceiling to verify the candidate's gender. Once satisfied with what they saw, the committee made its official announcement: "*Testiculos habet et bene pendentes*" ("He has testicles and they hang all right").[8]

A number of well-known male personalities cross-dressed in minstrel shows, vaudeville, and on Broadway during the 1900s through the 1930s. Not many women cross-dressed impersonating men, although the few who did were Vesta Tilly (circa 1906); German-born Salome dancer Gertrude Hoffman, who performed with Julian Eltinge (circa 1910); Kitty Doner, who starred in the silent short *A Famous Male Impersonator* (1928); and Betty Bronson as Hollywood's first *Peter Pan* (1925). Some of the men who cross-dressed as women were:

• Julian Eltinge was born William Dalton in 1883. Famous for her beauty and glamorous gowns, she was so popular that a Broadway theater was named after her (renamed the Empire, it still stands on 42nd Street). Female impersonators were among the most popular vaudeville headliners and she was the reason why. Eltinge was dubbed the "Mr. Lillian Russell" of her day. It took her two hours to transform herself into a woman. She made three Hollywood films for Jesse Lasky and became Charlie Chaplin's close friend.

• Bert Savoy was born Everett MacKenzie in 1888. Outrageously effeminate, both onstage and off, she referred to

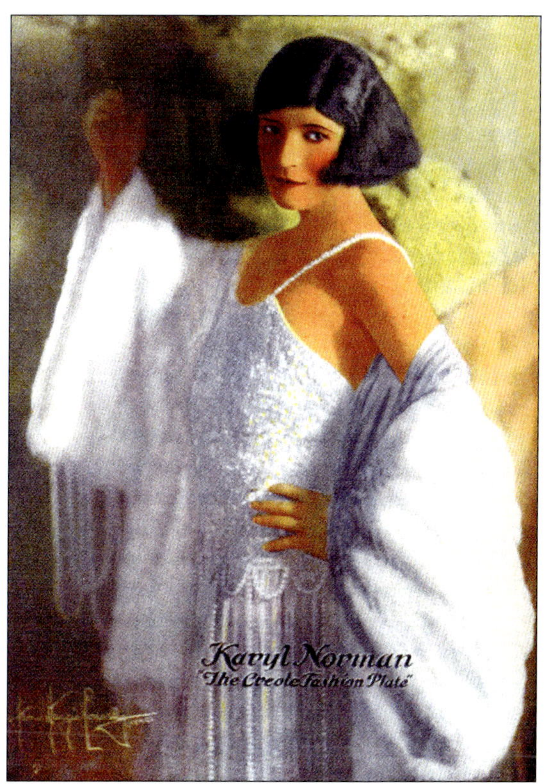

Karl Norman, Creole Fashion Plate, postcard, 1920s

men as "she" and camped it up at every opportunity. Her drag persona was as a hip-swaying quidnunc who dished out gossip about herself and the sordid exploits of her friend "Margie," while the dapper Jay Brennan (a former female impersonator) listened. Savoy appeared in several editions of the Shubert Theater's *Greenwich Village Follies*. She perfected her own erotic version of the cooch dance. Mae West "borrowed" her famous hip-swaying walk from Savoy, and several impersonators copied her act so accurately that Savoy went to court to protect her routines. One of Savoy's insinuating, hallmark lines was, "You must come over," also "borrowed" and altered by Mae West (who made it famous beyond all expectations). Struck by lightning while walking on the beach with friends in 1923, her last words were, "Mercy, ain't Miss God cutting up something awful?"

• Karyl Norman was born George Paduzzi in 1897. Billed as the "Creole Fashion Plate," she could switch voices from baritone to soprano while alternating sexes in her/his act.

• Barbette was born Vander Clyde Broodway in 1904. She performed brilliantly on the trapeze as a girl and went from circus performer to vaudeville. To soften the look of her bulging muscles, she wore silk tights over woolen tights. Part of her famous routine was a striptease performed before her flights on the trapeze. Barbette took off "his" wig at the end of "her" performance.

Hollywood films also presented cross-dressers. A few from the 1915 to 1950 era are:

• William S. Hart, who went from grimy, gritty cowboy to pretty lady in *John Petticoats* (1916).

• Charlie Chaplin appeared as a woman in *A Woman* (1915). The film was banned in Sweden in 1917.

• Jackie Coogan in *A Boy of Flanders* (1924) was the prettiest girl at her landlord's daughter's birthday party.

• Danny Kaye became a female star portraying a wildly effusive, ridiculous fashion photographer in *Lady in the Dark* (1941).

• William Powell shaved his trademark mustache and donned a dress in *Love Crazy* (1942).

• Bugs Bunny wore a blue ballerina skirt and matching blue bra in *A Corny Concerto* (1943).

• Cary Grant played "her" part in *I Was a Male War Bride* (1949).

Other famous stars from that era who appeared in drag were Groucho Marx, Stan Laurel, Jack Benny, Bob Hope, and Jerry Lewis.

The word "queen" is believed to have a double derivation, coming from both the standard English word meaning the wife of a king, and the obsolete word "quean," meaning prostitute.[9]

J. Edgar Hoover was the most infamous recent public figure in the United States who was a closeted cross-dresser. Hoover's cross-dressing was documented and it has been widely suggested that he shared a relationship with his constant companion, assistant director of the FBI Clyde "Junior" Tolson. Hoover, as head of the FBI from 1924 to 1972, became more than a self-imagined potentate. He wielded much power, perceived as well as hidden. His fifty-year legacy included the targeting of blacks and of being notoriously homophobic. Only 1 percent of FBI agents were black when he died in 1972. His years as director built a myth of invincibility and incorruptibility for the FBI. His own stereotype was that of the monster similar to the interrogators of the Inquisition. He must have adored the feelings of power that he symbolized as an archetype of the draconian official to everyone, whether his or her actions were being watched or not. Hoover and Walt Disney were two of the most influential people of the twentieth century, in terms of faithfully promoting what they believed to be Christian morality.

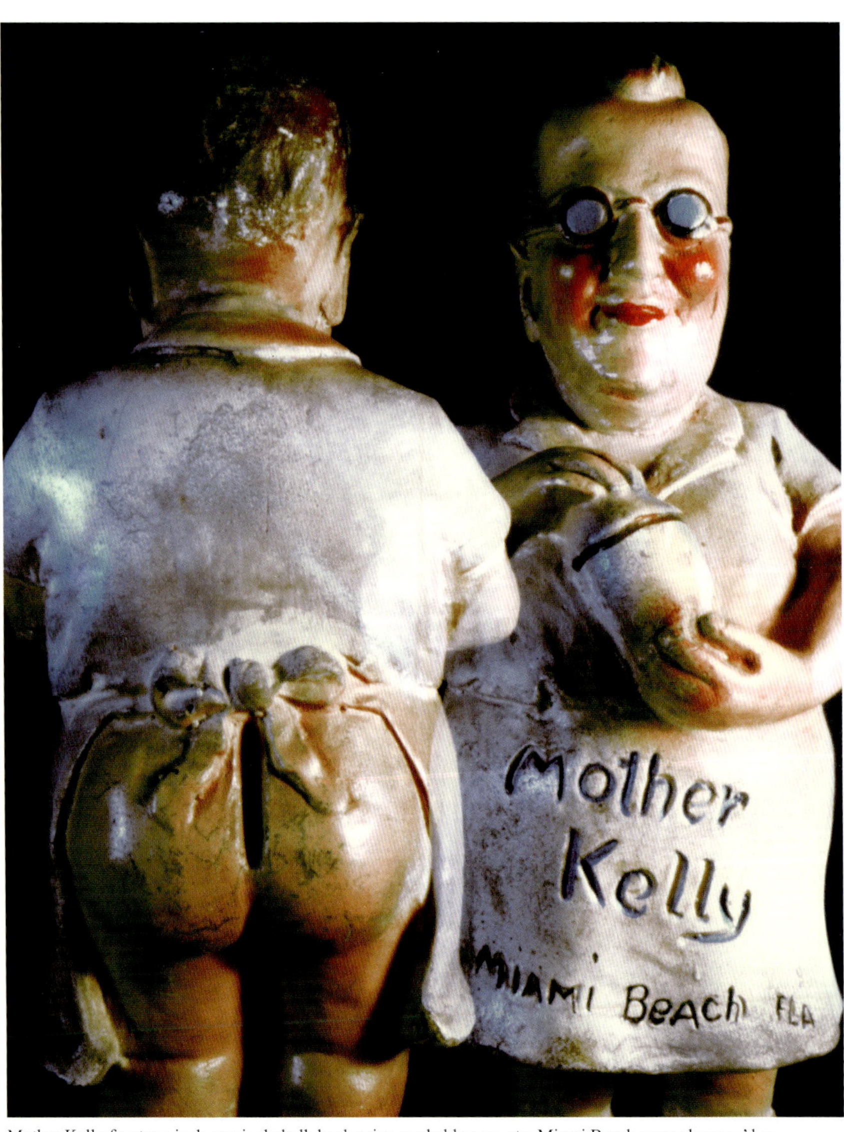

Mother Kelly fourteen-inch carnival chalk bank prize, probably won at a Miami Beach cross-dressers' bar (the origin of the Mother Kelly name is lost). A smaller version was also available. Double exposure

LITTLE RED RIDING HOOD

—JOHN GAY, Act 1 *The Beggar's Opera*, (1728)

In the puritanical ending of the Charles Perrault version of Little Red Riding Hood from his *Histoires ou Contes du temps passe* (1697), Red gets eaten by the wolf and joins her grandmother in the wolf's stomach. No one saved them: they are dead. And Perrault added a moral to the story:

> Now there are real wolves, with hairy pelts and enormous teeth; but also wolves who seem perfectly charming, sweet natured and obliging, who pursue young girls in the street and pay them the most flattering attentions.
>
> Unfortunately, these smooth-tongued, smooth-pelted wolves are the most dangerous beasts of all.[1]

The American version of the story, popular from 1900 to 1950, has Little Red Riding Hood and her grandmother saved (in patriarchal Disney fashion) by a heroic huntsman, who kills the wolf, allowing Granny and Little Red Riding Hood to climb out of the wolf unharmed. It is likely that most Americans saw this as a stereotypical tale: the naïve young girl being fooled by the evil wolf and then saved by the heroic passing huntsman. Just a simply crafted story with a happy ending, right? Hardly. This misanthropic American version was an assemblage of eerie stereotypes and Calvinist puritanical lessons particularly meant to scare young girls about their own sexual rites of passage. Little Red Riding Hood's symbolic name embodies these meanings: "red," blood and puberty's menstrual flow, signifying a girl on the threshold of her reproductive years, and "hood," a symbolic shield protecting her now that Little Red Riding Hood was vulnerable to desire—that is, sexual urges, the hymen, and virginity.

The options Little Red Riding Hood chose make a great difference.

Lesson One: Choose wisely—your destiny is in your own hands and your mother can no longer help. Her mother lets her walk through the woods without an escort, symbolizing the moment when a child is no longer a child, the lonely gateway through which she must pass and enter the difficult world alone. The gift she takes symbolizes her virginity: a gift that was at risk. The forest that Little Red Riding Hood was to travel through represented the larger world—the world of the unknown that a child experiences when she "goes out into the world."

Lesson Two: Beware the outside world—danger lurks there. Her grandmother's house represented a safe haven in the outside world, but a path (walk the straight and narrow) was followed to arrive there. Once in the forest, Little Red Riding Hood met the wolf. He was an archetype for the master of deception—the devil—creating feelings of extreme fear because he is always disguised. Not only did the wolf trick her into thinking he was a friend; he tricked her into telling him where she was going.

Lesson Three: Don't tell anyone anything, even if they appear friendly, because no one is to be trusted; and more specifically, don't tell them where you are going—the devil is out there to trick you. So the wolf rushed to Grandmother's house and she let him in because she too was deceived by the devil—and he eats her up. Meanwhile, Little Red Riding Hood smelled the flowers, watched the butterflies, enjoyed the beauty of nature, and took her time strolling through the forest in a circuitous and roundabout route to Granny's.

Lesson Four: Don't stop and smell the flowers (don't enjoy life). Life is a constant struggle; don't dally along the way. Go straight to your goal (again: walk the straight and narrow). Rigorous righteousness was the puritan's goal. Righteousness required serious work if you expected to bask in joys of heaven later. Little Red Riding Hood finally arrives at her grandmother's house and the wolf, disguised as Granny, lets her in. He invites her into Grandmother's bed (making the story's connection to seduction and sexuality rather obvious).

Lesson Five: If you are a girl don't climb into bed with anyone, even if you think they are as sweet as your wonderful grandmother. The bed symbolized sex, and to puritans, sex was evil.

Lesson Six: Don't succumb to the devil. Never, ever have sex with anyone prior to marriage. Not even in the bonds of matrimony was a puritan allowed to enjoy sex. Sex was "endured" only for procreation. Once in bed, Little Red Riding Hood had some troubling issues: "What big arms you have." Answer: "Better to hug you with." Question: "What big legs you have." Answer: "Better to run with."

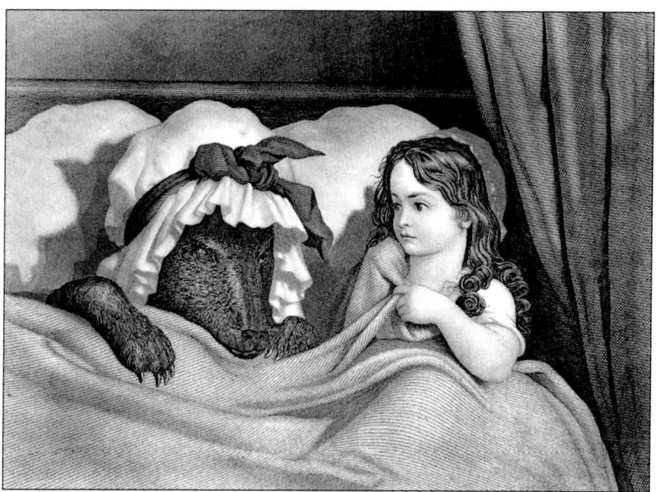

"What Big Eyes You Have, Grandma," *Peterson's Magazine*, engraving Samuel Sartain after G. Dore, circa 1890s

Lesson Seven: If you are a girl, beware of body parts, particularly men's body parts. Obviously Little Red Riding Hood's next statement might have been (subliminal to some adult readers): "What a big penis you have." Answer:

"Better to make love with." But of course the fairy tale could not be that explicit, although the bed and her series of questions certainly had cucumiform implications. Little Red Riding Hood's questioning continued to the point where she might be eaten up, to join her grandmother in the wolf's stomach.

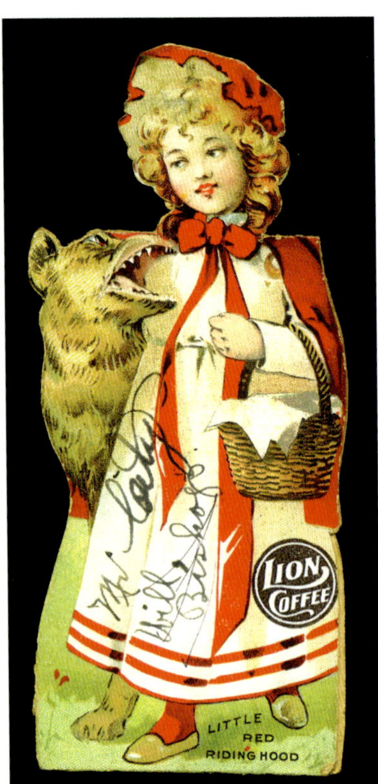

Little Red Riding Hood, Lion Coffee giveaway, *20 Stories for Children*, circa 1920s

Lesson Eight: If you have sex with someone, you will probably get eaten alive and die. Even as late as the 1940s in the United States, some daughters of Christian fundamentalist parents were told if they had sex before they married, they would be paralyzed for life. But the woodsman saved Little Red Riding Hood.

Lesson Nine: Men will save the day, they are strong and more than willing. The story was nothing less than a grouping of terror symbols that promoted a variety of dangerous fear archetypes—fear of men, fear of sex, fear of doing anything that was out of the ordinary.

Perrault's tricky original moral left young girls who had heard the fairy tale in a horrible quandary. It subliminally taught them that they would never meet anyone who could be trusted, and those men who were "perfectly charming, sweet natured and obliging" were the most evil. Perrault promoted a disturbing mind twist for all young girls, leaving them no way to gain an understanding with whom it was safe to fall in love. At the same time, he suggested disturbing ideas to young boys about being adult men, specifically saying that the best of men were really evil and "smooth-tongued." To Perrault all men were the devil because all men desired sex.

If Little Red Riding Hood seems like a strange and slightly grotesque story, try this earlier version, mentioned by Marina Warner in her book *From the Beast to the Blonde*:

For the famous fairy tale, "Le Petit chaperon rouge" (Little Red Riding Hood), Charles Perrault adapted a traditional story, in which a little girl takes food and drink to her grandmother and meets a wolf. It is likely that he set aside aspects which struck him as crude but which have survived in later retellings: in these, the wolf tricks the heroine into eating a piece of her granny's flesh and drinking some of her blood, but the little girl eventually manages to get away by refusing to get into bed, saying she has to pee. The wolf urges her to do it in the bed (!), but she refuses, so he ties her by a long cord to the bed post and lets her leave the cottage. Once in the woods, she manages to slip the knot and get away.[2]

However grotesque this story was, it was better than the Perrault version. At least Little Red Riding Hood became a heroine and escaped from the wolf to be the mistress of her own destiny. And it was better than the American version where the huntsman is the hero who saves her—she's not allowed to save herself.

The endings of fairy tales, as in the American version of Little Red Riding Hood, were very useful for the media to appropriate, for often the hero or heroine returned to the living, even after getting eaten, like Little Red Riding Hood and her granny. Death and resurrection became an easy formula for many film cartoons—when the hero, heroine, or adversary died, they could miraculously and believably be returned to life. How often do cartoon characters fall off a cliff, get blown up, or destroyed, only to return livelier than ever and ready

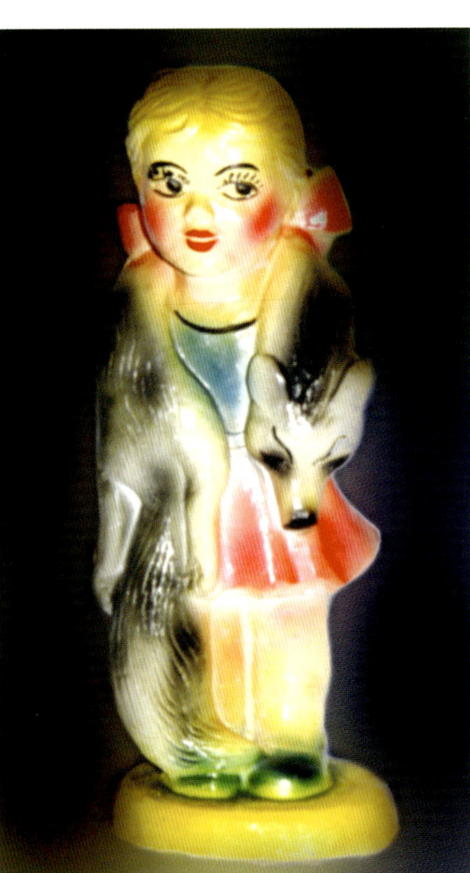

Little Red Riding Hood carnival chalk prize, the 1940s version shows her as a feminist champion—the wolf is around her neck as an adornment. Collection: Jo Wetmore

to do in the antagonist? This over-indulged genre made all violence seem acceptable and the results of violence humorously inconsequential.

Tex Avery's 1943 version of Little Red Riding Hood, entitled *Red Hot Riding Hood*, was an extremely rare departure in the cartoon genre. It was his third cartoon for M-G-M, and it parodied Walt Disney's version made in 1922 by starting with a kind and pleasant voice saying: "Good evening kiddies. Once upon a time Little Red Riding Hood was skipping through the wood. She was going to her grandmother's house to take Grandma a nice bunch of goodies."

We first see Avery's Little Red Riding Hood as a somewhat plump angel-faced girl, much like Disney's version. The Wolf is about to pounce on her, when he turns to the camera and unexpectedly proclaims how bored he is with repeating fairy tales. Grandma agrees. Little Red Riding Hood agrees too, saying, "Every Hollywood cartoon company has done it this way." So the cartoon begins all over again, but now with a deep voiced, "Once upon a time there was a wolf!"

Enter the mustached, zoot-suited, slick wolf on his way to a Hollywood nightclub where Red is performing as a chanteuse. When Red takes off her cloak, she reveals a more than child-like figure; the wolf's body springs up into the shape of a fantasized erection. He gets incredibly excited and attempts to seduce Red, who is not interested. But Grandma is. (She ain't seen one like that in a long time.) She chases the wolf around attempting to eat him—a complete reversal of the original Little Red Riding Hood. Avery did other cartoon versions of Red—*Little Red Walking Hood* (1937), *Little Rural Riding Hood* (1949), and *Uncle Tom's Cabana* (1947), where Red is still the sexy white chanteuse, but now a reversed stereotype of black Topsy.

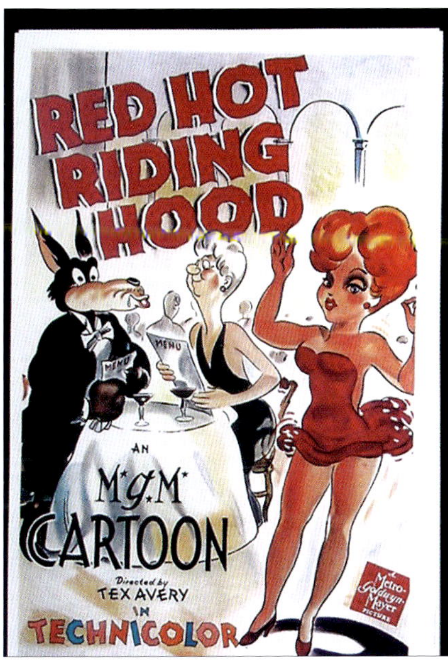

Red Hot Riding Hood, poster, Tex Avery, 1943 © M-G-M

KU KLUX KLANSMAN (1866-

I have just requested a book which I heard about. Believe it or not, somebody found out the Klan is still around. I could have told them that. The Klan never died. They just stopped wearing the sheets, because the sheets cost too much. When I say they, I think we all know who they would include. We have them in every phase of American life.
—THURGOOD MARSHALL

The Ku Klux Klansman archetype represents the super-vigilante. The Klansman believes he or she has a God-given right to crusade as a Christian knight or knightess. The group dynamic behind the white-robed figure with the cucullate (hooded) head was so powerful that a Klansman thought he was morally licensed to maim, burn, torture, and kill. Life in the South was not ideal after the Civil War, neither for whites nor for freed slaves. Many Southern whites viewed the freeing of slaves as their most bitter defeat—a defeat not only of their Rebel armies in the field but also of their economic and social customs. An age-old nightmare had become a reality for Southern whites: freed slaves were a potential threat and were now authorized to own property. As a result, and since slaves were no longer valued as plantation property, the freed slaves' lives were in constant danger.

A group of six Confederate veterans first organized the Ku Klux Klan in 1866 as a social club in Pulaski, Tennessee. The founders put white pillowcases with holes cut out for their eyes over their heads and then covered themselves with white bedsheets, even covering their horse's heads in similar

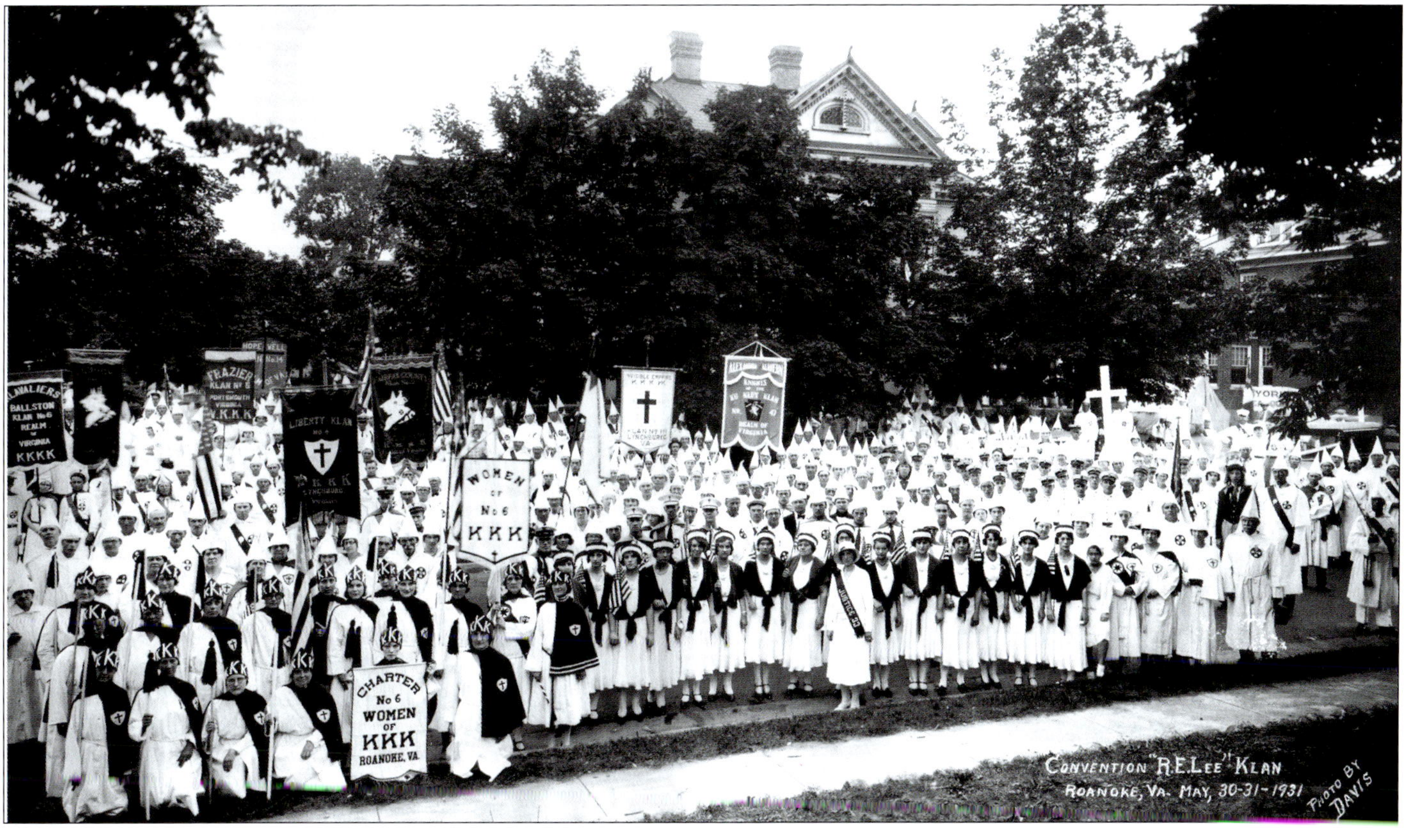

KKK Convention, "R. E. Lee" Klan, Roanoke, Virginia, May 30–31, 1931, photograph Davis, (a show of strength and vanity—they did not need or want to cover their faces)

fashion. They then rode together through their sleepy town, creating enough of a stir in surrounding communities to instill the notion of terror. That same year, new members were initiated into their secret organization in a ceremony very similar to the hazing and bullyragging used in college fraternities. Oaths and physical abuse were administered in front of a royal altar, which basically consisted of a large mirror. The initiate was then invested with a royal crown made from two large donkey ears.

The KKK was restructured along racial hate lines the following year, and Confederate general Nathan Bedford Forrest was selected as Grand Wizard. Sometimes called the Invisible Empire of the South or the Klan, the KKK was presided over by Forrest and his descending hierarchy of Grand Dragons, Grand Titans, and Grand Cyclopes. The KKK came from the Greek word *kyklos*, meaning "circle," and the English word "clan." After a time, mystical red symbols were placed on the white robes and hoods. The robes served the dual purpose of eliciting terror and providing concealment (a necessary disguise), since many of the members were ministers and other upstanding members in the white community.

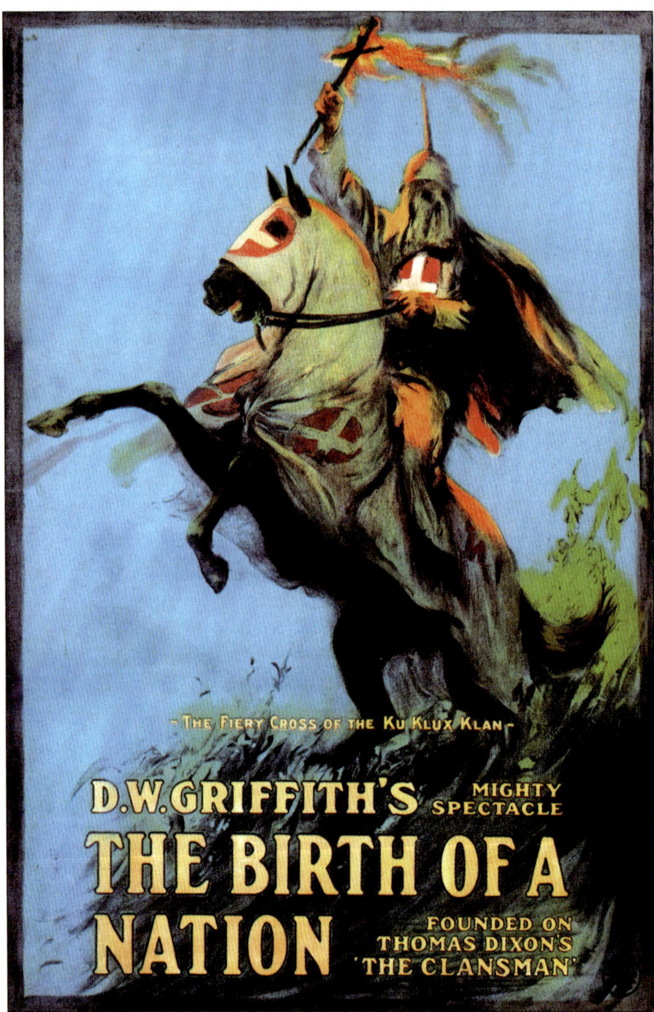

The Birth of a Nation, D. W. Griffith, lobby poster, 1915 © Epoch Studios. It was the first film to be shown in the White House.

When individuals were targeted as KKK enemies, white crosses were placed in their yard and set ablaze. These were archetypal warning symbols eliciting extreme fear. An unmitigated reign of terror would follow. Burning white crosses also symbolized the KKK's God-given power to be judge, jury, and executioner. Through intimidation, threats, and lynchings, Klansmen drove blacks and black sympathizers out of their communities, destroyed their crops, burned their houses and barns, and brutalized innocent people, simply because they could. At "spectacle lynchings," to make certain the person lynched went directly to hell and that no traces of the body remained, the person's body was cut up into small pieces and given away as souvenirs.[1]

By 1869, due to increased negative newspaper reports on the Klan's greater numbers of lynchings, the Grand Wizard ordered the national organization disbanded, but it was simply a foil. Local groups secretly remained active and the terror did not abate. The north reacted strongly to the increased violence and Congress passed the Force Act in 1870, then the Ku Klux Klan Act in 1871, authorizing the president to suppress disturbances by force and imposing heavy penalties on terrorist organizations. The KKK's white robes became more useful than ever, preventing federal troops from identifying individuals. The acts instituted to put an end to the Klan boomeranged, and prosecution of Klan members created widespread Southern sympathy on the Klan's behalf. Most white Southerners were members of the Democratic Party. As the Democrats' political power gradually increased during the 1870s, the need for secret organizations like the KKK lessened. The first KKK was anti-Republican, as well as anti-black. By the late 1870s, Southerners enacted Jim Crow laws to keep African Americans powerless in the South, resulting in a major migration by African Americans to cities in the north. (Jim Crow laws were named after the popular 1830s blackface minstrel Thomas Rice, who sang the Jim Crow song in his act. Its chorus went, "Weel about and turn about and do jis so, Eb'ry time I weel about I jump Jim Crow." When Rice performed the song, he took a wild jumping, turning-around leap off the stage just as he sang the words "jump Jim Crow.")

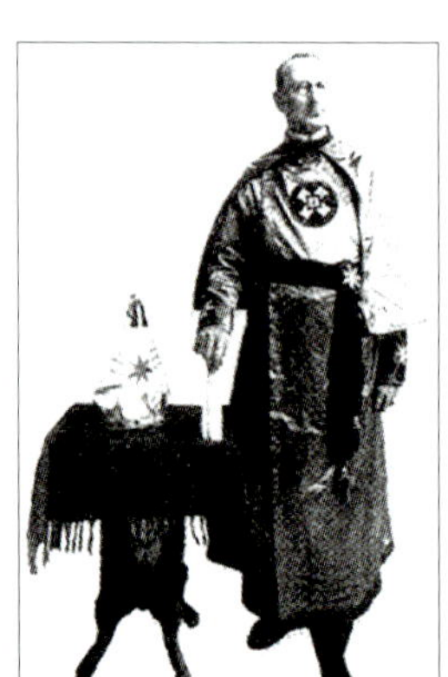

William J. Simmons

William J. Simmons, a Spanish-American War veteran turned preacher then salesman, reignited the KKK in 1915. This was easily accomplished because all of the earlier organizational structures were still in place, as well as the disturbing archetypal symbols—the white-robed figures and burning crosses, not to mention the reinforcement racist symbols of Jim Crow. Furthermore, D. W. Griffith's extremely popular 1915 film, *The Birth of a Nation*, had elevated racism and discrimination. It was seen by millions of Americans as a rousing archetypal adventure story in which the KKK were the saviors of all that was good, holy, and pure in America. Griffith showed blacks as endearing inferiors duped into rising above their accustomed station by misinformed abolitionists and vindictive reconstruction congressmen, who had betrayed Lincoln's benign plans for the defeated South. The film was so popular that it grossed an unheard of $18 million in fifteen years. People who thought they had the moral right and superior obligation to execrably intimidate those they considered inferior fell prey to all the stereotypical Jim Crow symbols that aroused these unmitigated instincts. *The Birth of a Nation* gave those who believed in it a reason to join forces. The film ends with a diaphanous Jesus rising above and approving of the Klan's power. It was not the first discrimination film, nor would it be the last, in which deceptive intentions propagated negative attitudes or where racist bias prevailed. It was the most popular film of the era.

By the 1920s the beginning of Prohibition and the flapper era had already polarized whites. Grand Wizard Simmons met Edward Clarke and Elizabeth Tyler, two KKK promoters from Atlanta, Georgia. With the Klan's membership at only a few thousand, Simmons signed a contract with Clarke and Tyler giving them 80 percent of the profits from the dues ($10 dollars) of new members if they could increase KKK membership. That they did! The promoters took an aggressive new stance—now the Klan was rabidly pro-America, which meant intensely anti-black, anti-Jewish, and anti-Catholic. As the Klan grew, its list of enemies increased to Asians, Prohibition bootleggers, owners of nightclubs and road-houses, violators of the Sabbath, and even downtrodden white women who were known sexual deviates (women having engaged in premarital sex or extramarital affairs).

The rejuvenated white supremacist Klan, with its mission of Christian social vigilance, adopted a more right-wing Protestant, Inquisition-like agenda. By the late summer of 1921, nearly 100,000 people had enrolled in the KKK and lynchings were once more on the rise. Congress publicly announced an inquiry into Klan activities, making it even more attractive to many. Texas voters sent Klansman Earl Mayfield, to the U.S. Senate in 1922 and membership rolls increased to 2 million. In the mid 1920s, Klan membership was comprised of people from both political parties—Democrats in the south and Republicans in the north and west. In 1924, 40,000 Klansman marched down Pennsylvania Avenue in Washington, D.C. Their numbers grew to as many as 4 million (some estimates put it as high as 9 million).

KKK marches and rhetoric increased, but the rest of the American public seemed to tire of their fanaticism by the late 1920s. Membership dwindled during the Great Depression, but the KKK still remained in the mid-1930s, particularly with the government's new Will Hays Production Code, which seemed to suggest that finger-pointing was good, not evil. In the early 1940s the KKK took a pronounced pro-Nazi stance. That, as well as major fractures within the Klan, caused immense drops in membership. With America's entrance into World War II, the KKK was finally reduced to only staunch but still dangerous fanatics.

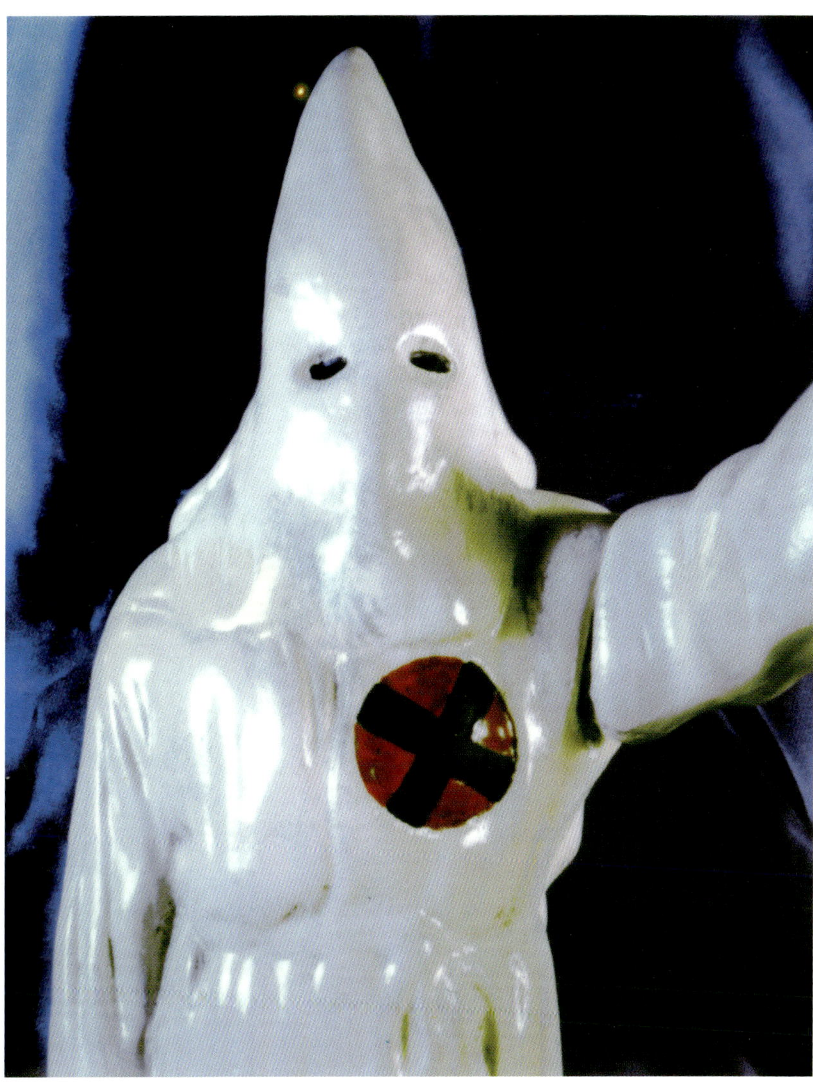

KKK fifteen-inch carnival chalk prize, circa mid-1920s, with a detachable left arm, meant for use in Klan ceremonies. If the candidate for membership was approved into the Klavern, the arm was then attached, if rejected, the arm was left unattached. KIGY on the base panel meant "Klansman I Greet You."

BUDDY LEE

(1921–1960s)

Buddy Lee dolls entered the commercial world first as promotional props created by the Lee Company in the 1920s. The cute babylike critters, costumed in miniature Lee overalls, were displayed in the window of Day's Department Store in Minneapolis. The dolls attracted so much attention and admiration from the public that, in 1922, the company decided to put them into production and merchandize them. Buddy came with little Lee overalls that could be put on and taken off—a sure sell because of people's endless fascination with ornamenting adorable dolls and cutouts. Buddy was an archetypal baby symbol combining feelings of love toward a baby with the puritan ethic stereotype of a hardworking everyday man. By 1923, there were three varieties of Buddy Lee dolls available: Buddy the cowboy, dressed in denim cowboy pants, plaid shirt, belt, bandanna, cowboy hat, and lariat; Buddy the railroad engineer (page 108), dressed in blue denim bib overalls, blue-and-white striped jacket, shop cap, and bandanna; and Buddy the blue-collar worker, dressed in a variety of shirts, pants, and belts. Buddy was not a replay of Charlie Chaplin's tramp, nor was he the executive type.

Hundreds of thousands of Buddy Lee dolls were sold in the following decades. Buddy became such a celebrity that carnival prize suppliers copied the doll in the 1920s and 1930s and simply painted his overalls onto the plaster, eliminating the need for manufactured Lee clothing, although the carnival Buddy did come with a hat. The name Buddy, a warm term usually reserved for close friends, was a carefully considered label for Lee's dolls and was designed to target the working class. It is likely that "Buddy" had its origins in the British colloquial "butty" meaning "workmate" from the earlys 1800s—a localized word in England and Wales associated with coal miners. The trendy Lee dolls infused the American language with the word "buddy." These days we are just as likely to yell "Hey, Buddy!" at the jerk driving the car that cut us off in heavy traffic, as to use it in an endearing way, as in "Bubba," which must be an adaptation from buddy.

The Lee Company was making Buddy out of plastic by 1949 and he was discontinued in the 1960s, just as Lee Riders and Levis jeans became fashionable.

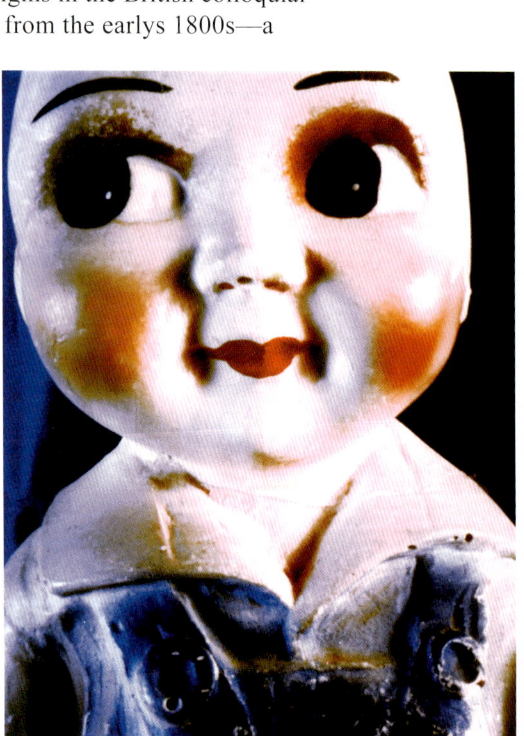

Buddy Lee twelve-and-a-half-inch carnival chalk prize, pink chalk, circa 1920s

The Strauss family opened a dry goods business in New York City after emigrating from Germany. Levi Strauss moved from New York to the boom atmosphere of San Francisco in 1853 and invented blue jeans, which were first called waist overalls. The "jeans" moniker was first used by the baby boomers in the sixties. Strauss established a dry goods business in San Francisco under his own name and began supplying cotton material and heavy, durable clothing to the rugged workers in the West. One of Levi's customers was a tailor named Jacob Davis, who solved the problem of garments tearing at heavy stress points by stamping metal rivets into strategic locations. His solution worked so well that he and Strauss applied for a patent and the riveted work clothes eventually led to the fashionable fame Levi's jeans enjoys today.

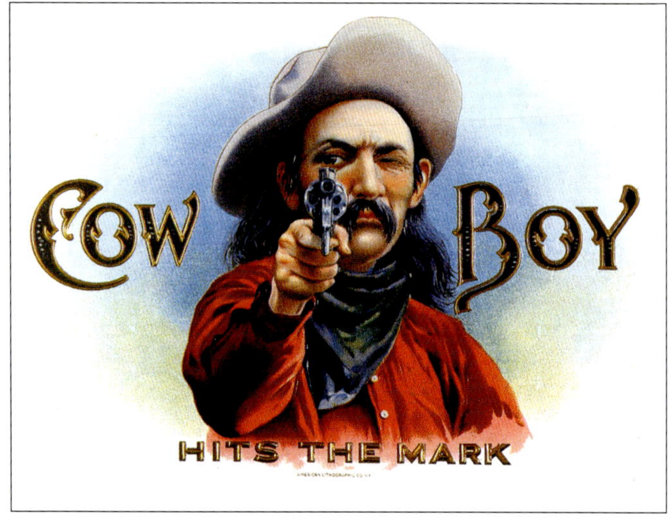

Cow Boy Hits the Mark cigar box label, circa 1920

Blue jeans remain an analogue for the West and characterize the cowboy as a stereotype for feeling freedom and toughness. The Buddy Lee "cowboy in blue jeans" idea was conjured thirty years before the Marlboro Man, who operates by the ingenious use of illusory projection. The Marlboro Man exploits the cowboy/blue jean paradigm and promises the instinctive sensations of freedom and toughness that are derived from the cowboy stereotype. He is the paragon of twentieth-century marketing design disguise.

Recent statistics show that 60 percent of those who begin smoking before the age of eighteen choose Marlboro cigarettes. That includes men and women. (No doubt, there are statistics from some study that tells us how many of that 60 percent wear blue jeans.) Wayne McLaren, one of the Marlboro Men from 1976 still photos and TV commercials, was later diagnosed with lung cancer. He then transformed his Marlboro Man advertising image and embarked on an antismoking campaign. It included a TV commercial sporting earlier images of him as handsome and youthful in blue jeans and Stetson hat, juxtaposed over shots of his withered body in a hospital bed just prior to his death in 1992. His brother, Charles, who provided the voice-over asked, "Lying there with all those tubes in you, how independent can you really be?"

David McLean, another Marlboro Man, appeared in many Marlboro TV commercials and print advertisements as their rugged, tough-smoking star (wearing jeans) in the early 1960s. He died of lung cancer in 1995 at the age of seventy-three. A year later, McLean's widow and son filed a wrongful death lawsuit against Philip Morris, claiming that McLean was unable to stop smoking because of his heavy addiction to nicotine—he was asked to smoke up to five packs per photo shoot.

Levi Strauss never dreamed that jeans would become a vehicle through which cigarettes could be hawked. Although it is quite clear to the public at large (and smokers in particular) that smoking is life threatening, it was not always perceived in that way, even though there was a vague understanding that the habit was not good for you. So what set the hook and created the costly craving for this devastating addiction? The explanation is embodied in one word: image. Probably no industry is more adept at connecting stereotypes/archetypes to their products than tobacco companies, and their techniques are pertinaciously subtle. Andrew Goliszek states *In the Name of Science*:

> What tobacco companies have desperately wanted to keep
> from the public was that more and more studies were show-
> ing that phosphate fertilizers contain natural radioactive
> particles that are transformed into radon, which then decays
> to radioactive polonium. During the growing season, the
> radon is taken up by the root system and accumulates in the
> leaves . . . Lighting a cigarette triggers a volatile reaction of
> radioactive particles . . . smoking a pack and a half a day was
> becoming equivalent to having almost one thousand chest
> x-rays a year[1]

The Knights of Columbus gave 57 million free cigarettes to men in World War I. Approximately twenty-three years later, during World War II, five cigarettes were included with each soldier's meal. Were hooks being set? Did cigarette companies understand that the stress of combat would tempt even nonsmoking soldiers to light up and continue to do so for the rest of their lives? Sports stars like Babe Ruth and Joe Louis were featured in cigarette ads. Until recently, baseball players were associated with chewing tobacco. By 1961, 68 percent of American men over eighteen smoked. Each year that percentage has declined; by 1999, only 24 percent of men over eighteen smoked. (Apparently the other 76 percent didn't believe they needed cigarettes to feel they were free or tough, or maybe they thought jeans alone could do the job.) There has been a surge in cigar smoking in recent years—another coup for the image-making tobacco industry. They sold the notion that cigars are less life threatening than cigarettes and reinstate the ingredient of the macho man archetype, generating feelings of superiority and power that were lost when society began winning its war against cigarettes. One cigar contains as much nicotine as three packs of cigarettes and the deceits of the image-builders rage on. The fashionability and staying power of jeans has been proven beyond a doubt, and the world is currently a community of look-alike "buddies."

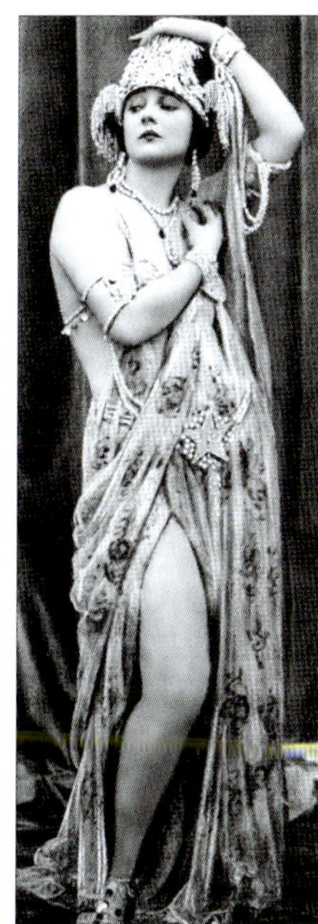

S HEBA (1890s-1925)

Z IEGFELD FOLLIES DANCERS
(1907-1931)

GILDA GRAY
(1901-1959)

THE SONG OF SONGS

Betty Blythe, *The Queen of Sheba*, 1921

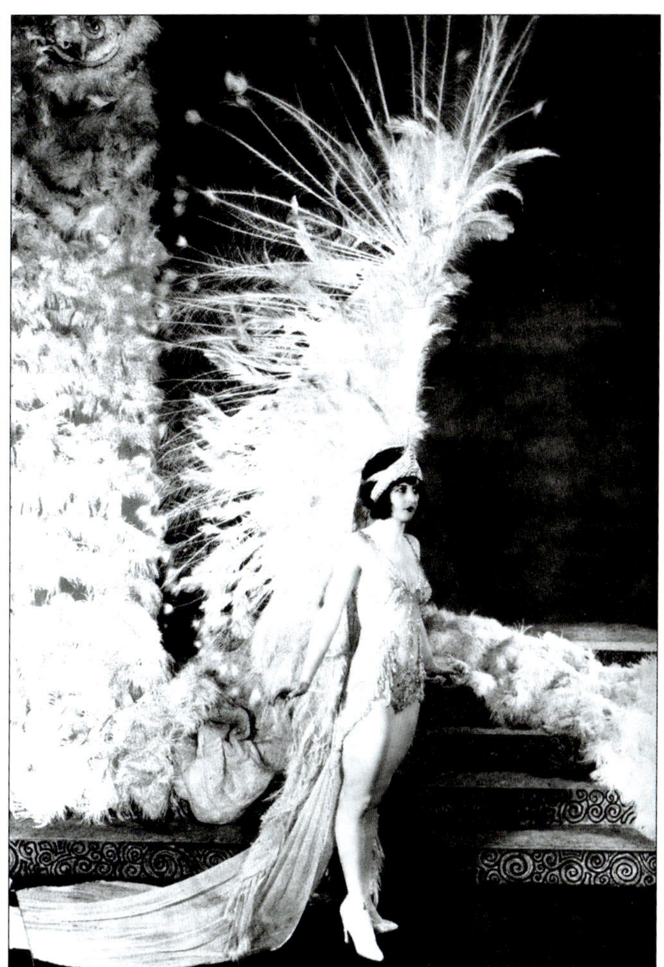

Ziegfeld Follies dancer, 1920s

Sheba is an exotic woman composite of 1920s fashion design. Seductive clothing created a strong archetypal symbol, giving Sheba a come-hither look that elicited lust. Her clothing was Egyptian revival, popular in the early 1920s, combined with Ziegfeld Follies dancers who wore extravagant costumes and feathered headdresses. Gilda Gray, known as the "Shimmy Queen" in the early 1920s, is at the edge of the visually astounding mix. Many actresses were bedizened in Middle Eastern attire: Theda Bara as *Carmen* (1916), *Cleopatra* (1917), and *Salome* (1918); and Betty Blythe as *The Queen of Sheba* (1921)—to name only two. This plethora of exotica was preceded by the Salomania of the early twentieth century—Mata Hari, Maud Allan, Gertrude Hoffman, and Alla Nazimova. Not to be ignored would be the many burlesque and belly dancers who acquired the name Little Egypt (page 52) and whose scanty attire was decidedly Middle Eastern. Put them all together and one comes up with a definitely generic Sheba by the 1920s.

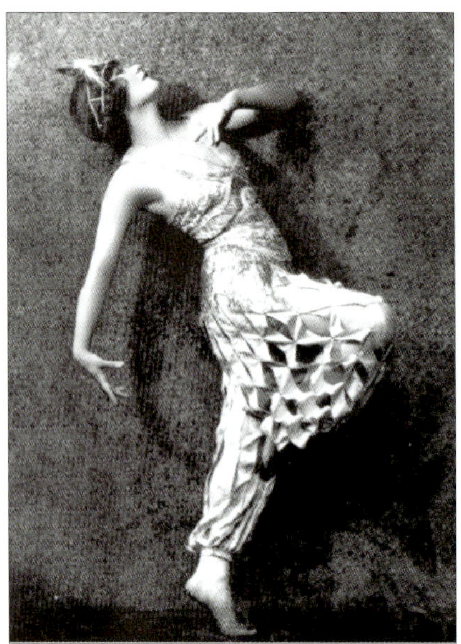

Gilda Gray, Egyptian revival costume, 1920s

The dancer Gilda Gray, although hardly known today, was infamous as a popular 1920s media figure. She is one of the most important liberated woman symbols of the early flapper era, and as such she could represent an aspect of the generic Sheba look. Gray's stage fright and nervousness in her first singing performances caused her to have the shakes. Audiences found her shaking to be evocatively sexual and it became her accidentally acquired identity. The word "shimmy" came from her chemise dress straps, which would slide (shimmy) down her shoulders as she sang and shook. The shimmy also had its roots in African ceremonial dance, and Spencer Williams's popular 1917 song "Shim-Me-Sha-Wabble"—literally translated: "chemise she wobbles"—is thought to have originated in an African American café in Chicago. The sixteen-year-old Gray left her young son and took her shimmy first to Chicago and then to New York, where she performed on Broadway in 1918. Her shimmy to the "St. Louis Blues" sparked a huge shimmy dance craze that spread and shook across America. She next starred in New York's Ziegfeld Follies, whose chorines wore exotic feathered head-dresses. During the beginnings of the flapper era, at the end of World War I in 1919, the now famous eighteen-year-old Gray took her shimmy to Hollywood, where she performed bit-part sexy-teaser dances in *The Virtuous Vamp* (1919), *Girl with the Jazz Heart* (1921), and *Lawful Larceny* (1923),—note that two of the three film titles are oxymorons. Gray's shimmy was a liberating instinctual response to the horrific visual archetypes of World War I and a welcomed respite from its angst. No wonder it became a craze. The shimmy was a new visual archetype. Any person who danced it experienced the energized thrill of freedom.

Gilda Gray had gained international fame by 1923 and starred again in the Ziegfeld Follies, where she set attendance records. Florenz Ziegfeld Jr. called her his golden girl because she drew large crowds and made so much money. Exotic Ziegfeld Follies dance lines were considered one of New York's most scenic attractions from 1907 to 1931.

Marianna Winchalska (Gilda Gray) was born in Kraków, Poland, in 1901. The family fled to the United States to escape the Russians when she was eight. They lived first in Bayonne, New Jersey, before eventually settling in Cudahy, a suburb of Milwaukee. Her father worked in a packing plant. Marianna married when she was fourteen, had a son, and began dancing in her father-in-law's saloon. She danced under the name Mary Gray in Chicago, but when she arrived in New York, Sophie Tucker told her to change her name to something more exotic, namely Gilda. She divorced her husband and by 1929, in tandem with the stock-market crash, her fame as the Shimmy Queen faded. She married twice again and died from a heart attack in 1959.

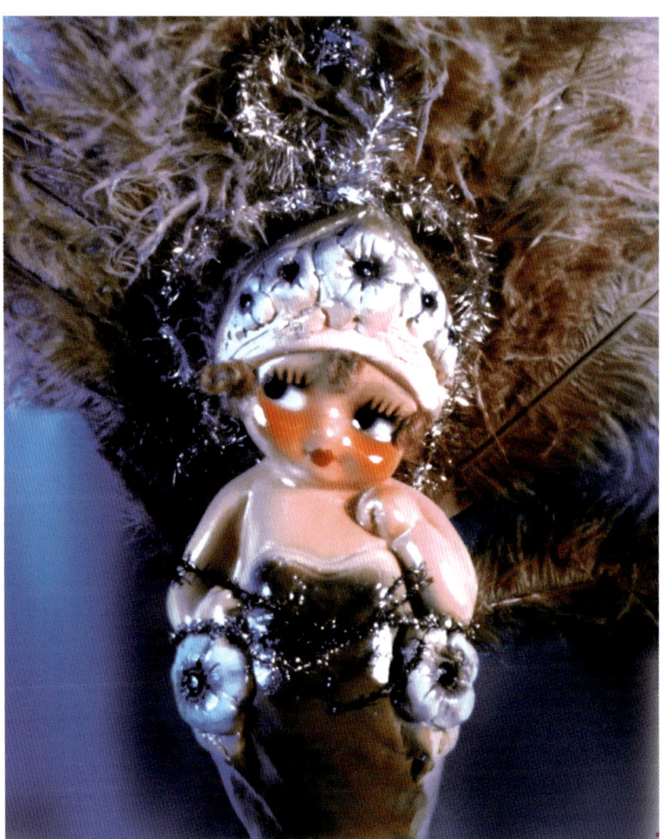

Sheba thirteen-inch carnival chalk prize © June Yates Jenkins

June Yates Jenkins entered "Marie" (now known as Sheba) as his first registry for a copyright patent on January 8, 1923. Marie[1] was not wildly different from Marianna (Gray's original name). Later, Jenkins's Marie figure was referred to as a Sheba doll, and still later as Little Sheba. All Marie and Sheba dolls came with exotic feathered headdresses.

In a generalized historical sense, the name Sheba referenced the Queen of Sheba in the Old Testament's Solomon and Sheba, from Solomon's Song of Songs. Liberal Christian scholars of the 1920s, as co-inheritors of the Jazz Age's desire for free thought, theorized that the Old Testament's Song of Songs was based on pagan Canaanite love poetry—with the explicit word images somewhat sanitized and placed into metaphoric form by the monotheistic Hebrews. Prior to the flapper era, and extending far back into Christian history, the Song of Songs endured with an orthodox explanation applied to it. The early church, from many dark centuries before, staunchly maintained that although Solomon wrote the Song of Songs, its meaning was strictly allegorical— the love of God for the church.[2]

Since the 1960s, scholars have revised the theory about the Song of Songs, now believing that it was influenced by Egyptian love poetry and that the poetry was almost certainly marriage or betrothal poetry.[3] It is thought that the poetry convincingly references human love in the literal, historical sense, rather than being written as an allegory about Christ's love for the church. Few scholars now believe that Solomon wrote the poetry.[4]

From the King James Bible (1873) Old Testament, Song of Songs 5:

1. I am come into my garden, my sister, my spouse: I have gathered my myrrh with my spice; I have eaten my honeycomb with my honey; I have drunk my wine with my milk: eat O friends; drink, yea, drink abundantly, O beloved.
2. I sleep, but my heart waketh: it is the voice of my beloved that knocketh, saying, Open to me my sister my love, my dove, my undefiled: for my head is filled with dew, and my locks with the drops of the night.
3. I have put off my coat; how shall I put it on? I have washed my feet. How shall I defile them?
4. My beloved put his hand by the hole of the door, and my bowels were moved for him.
5. I rose to open my beloved; and my hands dropped with myrrh, and my fingers with sweet smelling myrrh, upon the handles of the lock.
6. I opened to my beloved, but my beloved had withdrawn himself, and was gone.

Only a very few stanzas of the lengthy Song of Songs are reproduced above. Of the many sexual metaphors within it, a few examples are deciphered as follows: the "garden" is the vagina; Solomon proposes to unseal her, "unlock her door"; and "my head is filled with dew," "head" referring to the then popular symbol for the penis.

The Queen of Sheba can be found hidden under "Saba, Sabaeans," in *Harper's Bible Dictionary*. It reads:

The Sabaeans were ruled by priest-kings (Psalms 72:10) and Eponymous magistrates after whom the years were named. The ruins of their capital, Mariaba (Mareb), reveal the grandeur of their realm. Queen of Sheba, whose famous visit to King Solomon is narrated In I Kings 10:1,4, 10, 13 and II Chronicles 9: 1,3,9,12. She made the 1,200 mile journey to Jerusalem with a very great camel caravan,

laden with gold, precious stones, and spices . . . After she had enjoyed Solomon's royal bounty she returned to her Arabian home. Tradition, however, states that she became a wife of Solomon and bore him a son, Menelek, who later migrated to Abyssinia . . . The real significance of the visit of the Queen of Sheba to Jerusalem was probably the trade zone demarcation and alliance she worked out with Solomon, who with King Hiram of Tyre was then sending a joint merchant marine, "a navy of Tarshish" . . . and depositing their wares in Red Sea ports in competition with the Sabaeans . . . [5]

Althea Aurandt, author of *Secrets Your Church Never Told You*,[6] states:

. . . that the Church's emphasis was never on the Queen of Sheba, except to make King Solomon look even wiser and, as the great patriarch, more important. Here is the logic as presented in Sunday school lessons or Sunday morning sermons:

Premise I—King Solomon was the wisest and most important man alive to the Hebrews.

Premise II—Even non-Hebrews, such as the Queen of the Sabaeans (who had an impressive culture at the time), were impressed by the wisdom and importance of King Solomon.

Conclusion: Therefore, King Solomon and the Hebrews were more important than all other cultures. (That is, God loved the Hebrews best.) The Queen of Sheba was so impressed by the Hebrews and by their king that she valued Solomon personally. She may have become one of his many wives. She may have been the human female who inspired Solomon to write the "Song of Songs" about the love of God for His Church.

It is important to add that the Queen of Sheba was not a vamp. Solomon, who was promoted through the medium of the Old Testament was stereotyped into a status of powerful King, too important for any woman to be able to seduce.[7]

One line in the Song of Songs 1:5 adds another dimension to the story. It reads: "I am black, but comely, O ye daughters of Jerusalem, as the tents of Kedar, as the curtains of Solomon."

In the Old Testament's Song of Songs paragraph entry next to 1:5, it says, "She confesseth to her deformity." In other words, being black meant she was deformed, a racial slur cast by the 1873 version of the King James Bible (newer versions changed the poetry and paragraph entries).

Contemporaneously, most Bible scholars agree that the Queen of Sheba was black, a realization African Americans have been protesting for years. In ancient Israel there did not seem to be any prejudice over skin color and today, as always, there are black Jews. The prejudice was toward the descendants of Ham, son of Noah. Noah cursed Ham and swore that his descendants would always be slaves to his brothers' descendants. And so, the prejudice is against slaves, whatever color Ham's progeny might be.[8]

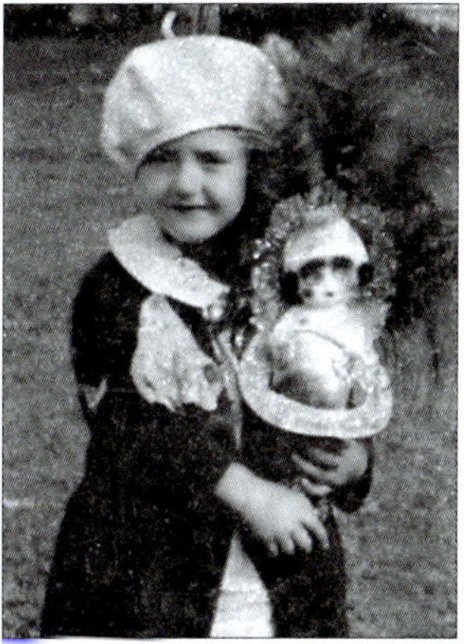

Child with Sheba doll, circa 1920s

Rebecca at the Well

Rebekah at the Well is an Old Testament replay of the
selected perfect woman archetype. She is there for the taking,
as a symbol eliciting chosen lust. Rebekah at the Well is what
happened (and still occurs) within a patriarchal society when
women (and girls) are not given a choice for position in life.

In Genesis 24:16, the servant goes out into the country to find a wife for Isaac, Abraham's son. The servant waits
by the well and prays for her appearance. When she appears,
it states explicitly: "And the damsel was very fair to look
upon, a virgin; neither had any man known her: and she went
down to the well, and filled her pitcher, and came up."

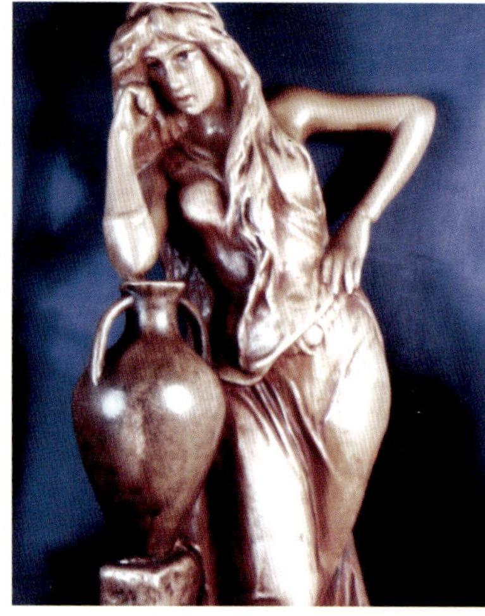

Rebecca at the Well eighteen-
inch carnival chalk prize, probably designed by June Yates
Jenkins. At first glance, this
figure looks too Romanesque
to be from the carnival. Looking closer, she has red lips and
is not just a cold ancient statue.
There was also a Rebecca
lamp carnival chalk prize made
by Pacini Novelty Statuary
Company in 1936.

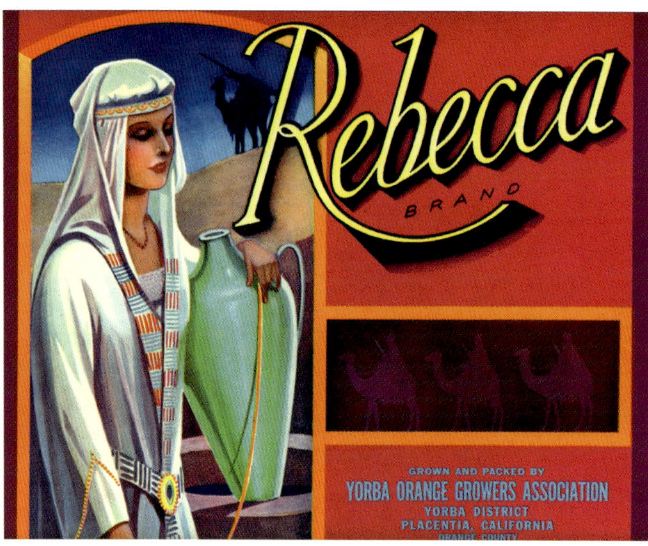

Rebecca at the Well, Orange Growers Association label, circa 1930s

As could be expected from Genesis 24:22, the servant
gave Rebekah "a golden earring of half a shekel weight,
and two bracelets for her hands of ten shekels weight in
gold," expressing an archetypal slur that any woman can
be purchased for a price, even the "very fair to look upon."
In this myth, beauty is glorified as a means to gain position and
wealth (a survival archetype—not a love archetype).

Finding a wife through direct purchase, as in the
Rebekah story, or through an arranged marriage was
an ancient custom in many parts of the world, generally
performed somewhat locally between families. The system
still operates, and in the U.S. it has a new twist: mail order
brides can be obtained—type in "mail order bride" on your
search engine, then type in "mail order husband" and note the
difference in gender availability. There's a second more subtle
21st century difference too—the marriage dating service now
gets the man's fee for a "mail order bride"—while the foreign
young woman just gets the man (sounds a little like the slick
corporate pimp takes the money while the young woman gets a
chance to be someone's slave or otherwise disadvantaged).

Hollywood was not averse to the idea of an arranged
marriage by creating a beautiful mate for their less than
handsome monster in *The Bride of Frankenstein* (1935),
considered a brilliant sequel to *Frankenstein*. His bride-to-be
is ressurected from a dead girl in the vain hope her machine-
made beauty will diffuse the killer/monster instincts in him
(keeping him busy—a lust archetype—not a love archetype).

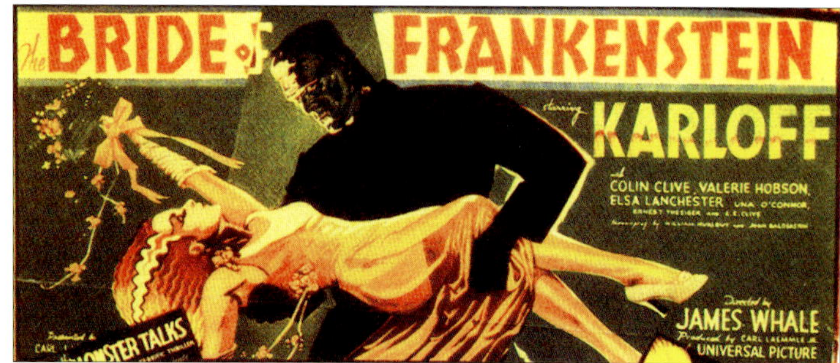

Poster, *The Bride of Frankenstein*, 1935 © Universal Studio

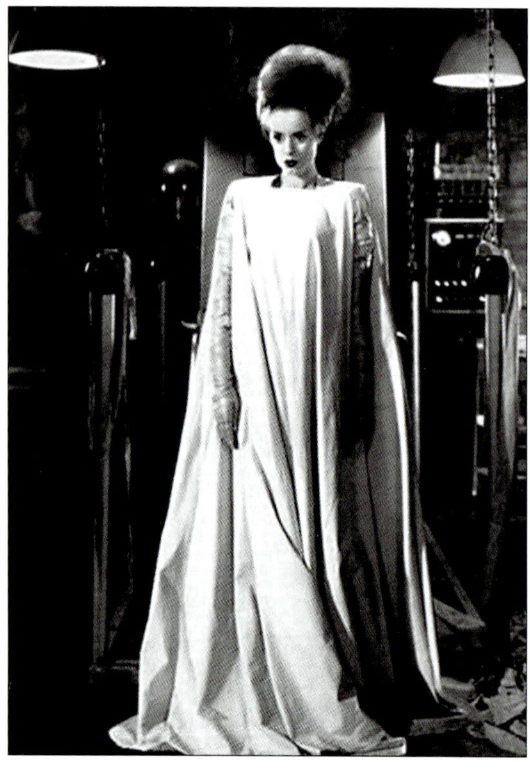

Elsa Lanchester, *The Bride of Frankenstein*, still, 1935 © Universal Studio

Lotus (1924-

Two bittee lookee, fo bittee feelee, six bittee doee!
—Enticement by Chinese Crib Girl Prostitutes, in search of a white male customer, spoken in San Francisco in the five to six decades following 1850

Killin' Chinamen ain't really the same as killin' people.
—Line from the TV Program *Gunsmoke*

The earliest Chinese to arrive in what would later be called the United States were conscripted sailors aboard Spanish ships traveling between Manila and Mexico from 1565 to 1815. A number of the sailors jumped ship and established a settlement on the coast of Louisiana; today their descendants live in New Orleans. A thriving Chinatown bustled in Mexico City in the early 1600s, but was pushed to the outskirts of the city in 1635.[1] The first known Asian American New Yorker was born in 1825, the son of a Chinese sailor and an Irish woman.

A large Asian migration to the New World began in 1806, one year before Britain outlawed the use of their vessels to carry slaves. Coolie (a slang slur stereotype) labor started arriving from China and India to island plantations on Trinidad and Cuba to work alongside black slaves. The same British slave ships were used to transport Chinese, who did not think of themselves as slaves since they were indentured for eight years to pay off their debt of passage, food, and clothing.[2] Cuba finally outlawed slavery at the end of the nineteenth century.

Chinese men were imported or smuggled into the United States to work for low wages and long hours in Western hardscrabble mining operations or in the construction of railroads during the California Gold Rush days, beginning in the 1850s. They were not considered coolies but simply semifree laborers who needed to pay back their debt of travel. By 1865, twelve thousand Chinese were hired by the Central Pacific to build the western half of the railroad—they accounted for 90 percent of the company's workforce. Most of the Chinese who did not work in the mines or on the rails lived in crowded housing conditions in San Francisco's Chinatown. Chinese were not eligible for U.S. citizenship until 1943.

Census figures taken in the last four decades of the nineteenth century showed that there were approximately twenty times more Chinese men than Chinese women living in the United States. Of the Chinese women, approximately 85 to 90 percent were prostitutes, the other 10 to 15 percent worked in areas of servitude. The importation of Chinese girls for prostitution, age fourteen and younger, began in 1850. Those only a few years old were used for servitude until they came of age. The number of young Chinese prostitutes rose to two thousand fairly quickly. Most lived and worked in San Francisco in what were called "cribs"—twelve-by-fourteen-foot structures divided into two rooms, where upward of eight girls lived and worked as prostitutes. Herbert Asbury, in *The Barbary Coast*, wrote:

> The backbone of Chinese prostitution in San Francisco
> was a system of slavery under which girls were owned
> and bartered as if they had been so many cattle; as, indeed,
> they were in the eyes of their masters. Practically every
> inmate of the Chinese parlor houses and cribs was a slave,
> and many had been in bondage since infancy. Usually they
> were owned by syndicates of Chinamen, or by women like
> Madame Ah Toy, who had themselves been prostitutes and
> had purchased their freedom. The slave holdings of some
> of these groups were extremely large. Four Chinamen in
> the middle of the eighteen-seventies owned eight hundred
> girls ranging in age from two to sixteen years . . . Six years
> was a long time for a girl to live after being placed in a crib,
> and since she almost invariably began her life of misery and
> degradation in her early teens, a Chinese prostitute of more
> than twenty years [old] was a great rarity. Moreover, she
> was, by that time, nothing more than a frightfully diseased
> old hag.[3]

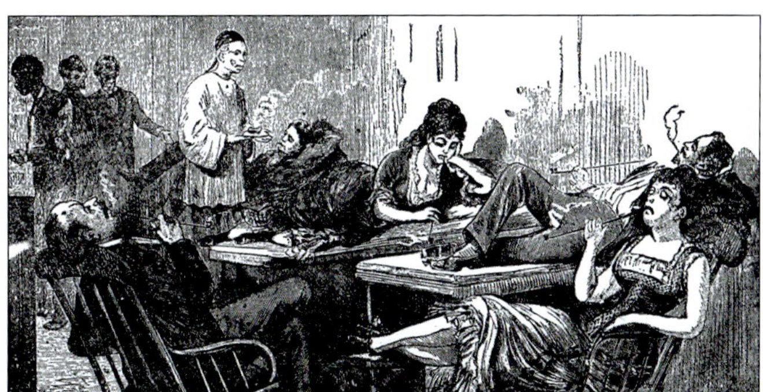

"Opium Den in San Francisco, 1880s," *The Barbary Coast* © Garden City Publishing Company, 1933

By 1870, San Francisco was notorious for opium, prostitution, and gambling. In order to protect the interests of Chinese brothel owners from police, an association of Chinese villains, known as "highbinders," was formed. They lived off the prostitutes by levying upon each girl a weekly fee and left behind them a trail of mayhem, blackmail, and murder. If the prostitutes did not work, they were beaten severely with sticks or burned with hot irons. As Albert Evans wrote in *A la California: Sketch of Life in the Golden State*:

> The girls cost $40 each in Canton, but are valued here at
> about $400, if passably good-looking, young and healthy,
> and they readily sell at that figure in cash, or approved
> paper. Each colony of half a dozen girls is under the
> immediate control of an "old mother," herself a retired
> prostitute, who jealously watches over each, and receives
> from them the wages of their shame as fast as earned. From
> each wicket all the way down the alley a female head may
> be seen protruding, and there is a constant fire of jokes and
> repartee going on between the occupants of the dens on
> each side of the alley, while every passer comes in for his
> share of personal notice. A girl, with hair carefully braided
> and decked with artificial flowers, and cheeks and lips
> cunningly painted so as to resemble those of her frail
> Caucasian sisters, notices us looking toward her wicket,
> and instantly raising her hand, taps at the window, but at the
> moment catches a glimpse of the policeman behind us, and
> shuts the wicket, and turns away as if she had not seen us
> at all. The alarm runs down the whole alley in an instant;
> there is a rattling of wickets, as if a hurricane was sweep-
> ing through the place, and in half a minute all is as silent
> as the grave, and not a head to be seen. It is a special

misdemeanor under our city ordinances for a China woman
to tap on a window to attract the attention of anybody on
the street; and the girls well know what is in store for them
if they are caught at it by the police.[4]

Those who partook of the prostitutes saw them as
archetypal symbols of the foreign exotic woman who elicited
impulsive lust. Their foreignness supplied a fantasy allure,
but they were also stereotyped as inferior cheap foreign goods,
since they were inexpensive and provided instant gratification.
During the 1860s and 1870s, any Chinese prostitutes who became diseased or too worn were carried to small dismal rooms
in the back alleys called "hospitals" and left to die. Locked in
the room, the lone occupant was given a cup of water, a cup
of boiled rice, and a little oil lamp. After several days passed,
the "doctors" who had locked the girl in the room returned.
Generally the prostitute had died or committed suicide; if a
spark of life remained, the visiting "doctors" killed her.

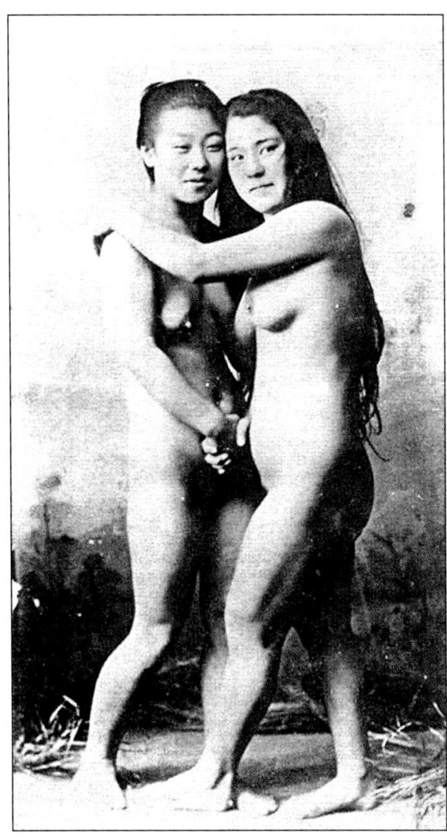

Chinese prostitutes, circa early 1900s. Courtesy: Jay Moynahan

When the yield from the gold mines waned and the
railroads neared completion, increased availability of cheap
Chinese labor in such industries as cigar rolling and textiles
became a source of tension for white laborers, who thought
that the Chinese were moving in to take their jobs and threaten
their livelihoods. An anti-Chinese movement began, known
as the Yellow Peril, and mass prejudice gripped the West.
Mob violence, murders, and rampant discrimination drove the
Chinese east to Chicago and New York, where more job opportunities were available and assimilation into an already diverse
population was easier to accomplish. In Tacoma, Washington,
hundreds of Chinese were herded onto ships with no captain or
crew and sent out to sea to their deaths. White mobs burned the
Chinese out of Denver.[5]

The Yellow Peril led Congress to pass the Page Law
in 1875, which stopped "women of ill-repute" from entering
the United States. Smugglers easily skirted around the law.
Congress passed the Chinese Exclusion Law in 1882, prohib-
iting Chinese from gaining American citizenship. In 1892,
Congress passed the Geary Act, which extended the Chinese
Exclusion Law for another ten years and also added the
requirement that all Chinese living in the United States obtain
certificates of residence.

Prompted by the Spanish-American War of 1898,
the yellow in Spain's flag represented the enemy and white
Americans' anxieties increased—there were too many people
with yellow skin spread throughout the United States. China-
towns were well established in major U.S. eastern cities, with
upward of ten thousand Chinese living in Manhattan. In
1902, Congress extended the Chinese Exclusion Law for yet
another ten years.

China inadvertently became an ally of the United
States during World War II— since China was also at war with
Japan and had lost millions of its citizens to the Japanese,
even before America became involved. (Chinese-Japanese
tensions exist to this day.) Embarrassed by the racist nature of the
National Origins Act of 1924, Congress finally eliminated it in
1943 and granted Chinese people living in the United States
the right to citizenship. China was finally given an immigration
quota of 105 immigrants per year.

In opposition to Oriental immigration, ultra-isola-
tionist Charles Lindbergh believed that a Germany at war in
1941 was the guardian of the eastern border of European
civilization against the perils of the "yellow men." Of Germany,
Lindbergh said:

> She alone can either dam the Asiatic hordes or form the
> spearhead of their penetration into Europe . . . It is time
> for us to build our White ramparts again . . . It is our turn
> to guard our heritage from Mongol and Persian and Moor.
> Aviation is a tool specifically shaped for Western hands . .
> . another barrier between the teeming millions of Asia and
> the Grecian inheritance of Europe.[6]

Until recently Hollywood painted yellowface onto
famous white actors and actresses because Asians were always
relegated to minor roles. The rare exception would be Anna
May Wong, born Luong Liu Tsong, a Los Angeles Chinatown launderer's daughter, who had many bit parts in silent
and sound films. She finally starred with Marlene Dietrich
in *Shanghai Express* (1932). Wong's career credits included
eighty films, yet it was practically impossible for her to get
starring roles competing against white actresses in yellowface. She was most often cast as the stereotypical Oriental
temptress—a slur. A brief list of white actors in yellowface
reads like a star-studded who's who: Loretta Young, Edward
G. Robinson, Lana Turner, Fred Astaire, Lillian Gish, Helen
Hayes, Bela Lugosi, Angie Dickenson, Shirley MacLaine,
Mary Pickford in *Madame Butterfly*, Katherine Hepburn in
Dragon Seed, Marlon Brando in *Teahouse of the August Moon*,
Anthony Quinn in *China Sky*, John Wayne in *The Conqueror*,

Mickey Rooney sporting buckteeth in *Breakfast at Tiffany's*, Boris Karloff in *The Mask of Fu Manchu* (horribly demonizing Asian features), and Warner Oland as Charlie Chan.[7]

Early Hollywood stereotyped Asian men as sexual predators luring white women into their depraved worlds. Mae West's film *Klondike Annie* (1936) is the perfect example— Chan Lo (played by white actor Harold Huber in yellowface)

To most white Americans in the 1920s, a beautiful Chinese woman stereotyped and symbolized the China doll—an exquisite Oriental prostitute or most likely a forbidden Oriental temptress. By 1934, with the advent of the catchall name Dragon Lady in *Terry and the Pirates* comic strips, a cliché stereotype was created—so the slang expression "dragon lady" (a slur) entered into the English language.

All three of Jenkins's carnival prizes represented Chinese women who were not wearing "Golden Lotus" slippers. Golden Lotus slippers on bound feet were usually prevalent among aristocratic Chinese women. To accomplish bound feet, at the age of three girls had their arches broken and their toes turned under, except for the big toe, then bound in a tight clawlike configuration. The manipulations were very painful, sometimes causing infections that resulted in death. Over a period of 1,700 years, that particular kind of beauty and control mechanism was distinctly perfected into a high-heeled archetypal motif for adornment worn by the "selected" bride, making a woman look sexy—and at the same time—incapacitated. Women were never seen without their Golden Lotus shoes, which were even worn to bed. Each foot had to be no more than three inches in length –if longer, the person had less worth.

High-heeled shoes have been worn by men and women in many cultures at various times and over many centuries— being "well-heeled" is a cliché intimately connected to their wearer. Dorothy's ruby red slippers from *The Wizard of Oz* were an archetypal motif—later a slightly higher heeled version adorned Marilyn Monroe and Jane Russell in *Gentlemen Prefer Blondes*.

Lotus thirteen-inch carnival chalk prize with metal earrings © June Yates Jenkins. In 1924, the same year as the National Origins Act, the thirteen-inch Ming Toy carnival chalk figure was patented by June Yates Jenkins on August 24.[8] There are at least three varieties of Jenkins's Chinese women carnival chalk prizes; the other two are named Tin Toy and Lotus. There was also a nine-and-a-half-inch carnival chalk caricature of a Chinese boy pejoratively named "Chinky."

controls singer/prostitute Frisco Doll (played by Mae West) until she finally kills him. When Hollywood showed Asian men as menial servants they were usually buck-toothed and baboonlike.

Recent Hollywood characterizations often make Oriental women and men into fantasy super-action figures analogous to violent real-life video games. One of the few recent films that honestly deals with white racism toward Chinese, as witnessed through an alluring young woman archetype who elicits escapist forbidden lust and then love, is Jean-Jacques Annaud's *The Lover* (1992).

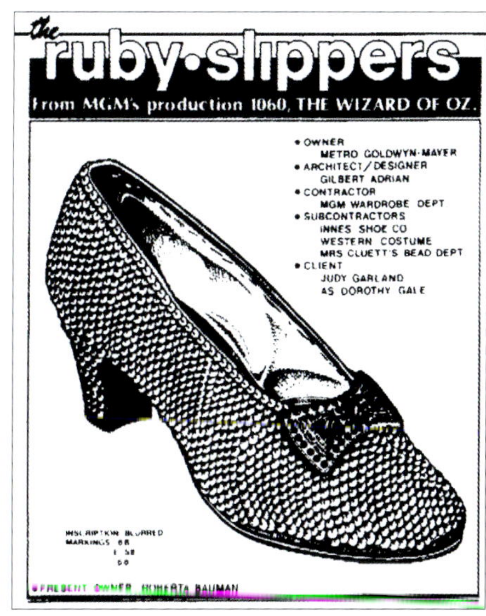

Ruby slippers design for *The Wizard of Oz* © M-G-M

SALOME

MATA HARI (1876-1917)
MAUD A$LLAN$ (1873-1956)

You shall die as everything must die. Live for the beautiful and glorious moments. It is better to live on Earth for a few short and intense instants and to pass away, than to drag about through old age without beauty or joy.
—MATA HARI

Salome's Dance of the Seven Veils is an archetypal symbol for the extremely erotic woman, eliciting feelings of dangerous lust so heightened that a transfixed viewer might be induced to commit murder at the dancer's request—the paragon of a femme fatalé. Salome referenced the beheading of John the Baptist in Mark 6:17 in the New Testament. This is one of the most memorable examples for the femme fatalé archetype; it was the Bible's way of demeaning irresistible, erotic women who supposedly possessed, through their beauty and charms, powers capable of usurping patriarchal control.

Salome's lasciviousness was reinvented by Oscar Wilde in *Salome* (1893). The play crystallized a 1900s Salomania that took hold throughout the Western world, when dancers known as Salomes were trained in both Europe and America. Canadian-born dancer Maud Allan debuted *The Vision of Salome* in Vienna on December 29, 1906, although some suggested she originally performed it in 1903. Allan became known internationally as the "Salome Dancer." Richard Strauss adapted Wilde's play into the erotic opera *Salome*, performed in New York at the Metropolitan Opera House in 1907, shocking the American public. Performances were canceled four days later. The Salome dance was popularized into vaudeville and American culture by the German-born Gertrude Hoffman, who danced *Salome and Her Seven Veils* at Willie Hammerstein's Victoria Music Hall in New York shortly after it opened in 1907. Police, using the charge of indecent exposure, shut down many Salome performances, but the added attention the raids produced only increased its popularity.

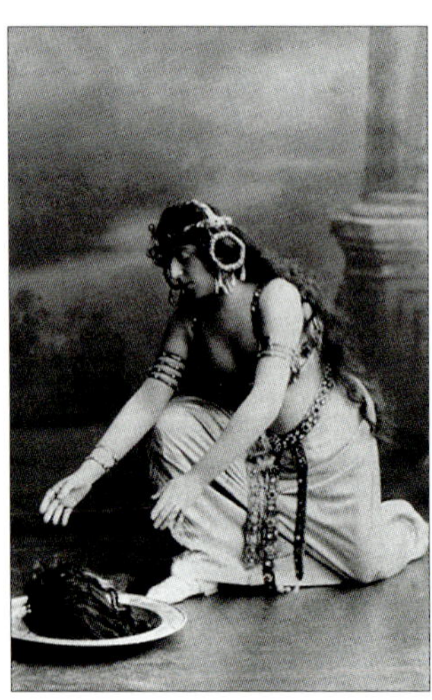

Oscar Wilde costumed as Salome in his play
Salome, circa 1894

By World War I, the name Mata Hari became synonymous with Salome, tragically making her the ultimate femme fatalé after the French arrested her and charged that she was a Salome dancer turned German spy. She was tried and executed. Films and stories dedicated to telling her story have kept the stereotype alive for decades. Her early dancing fame spread throughout Europe from 1905 to 1912—she danced as a Siva and then as a Salome dancer, with whirling shawls that she removed slowly, one by one, to the point of total nudity. Sometimes she wore a full-body stocking, including a covering for her pubic area. Mata Hari was tall, five foot ten, and dark, with an expressive face and dark eyes. She is considered a founding mother of the intellectual striptease. The name Mata Hari was Malayan for the sun—it meant "Eye of Dawn"—a name she attached to herself while living in Java. She invented a personal history of exotic birth in India (much like Theda Bara's history was invented). She proclaimed:

> My mother was a glorious temple dancer who died on the day I was born. When I reached the threshold of womanhood, my foster mother saw me a predestined soul and resolved to dedicate me to Shiva . . . It was on the purple granite altar of Kanda Swany, at the age of thirteen, I danced for the first time, completely nude.[1]

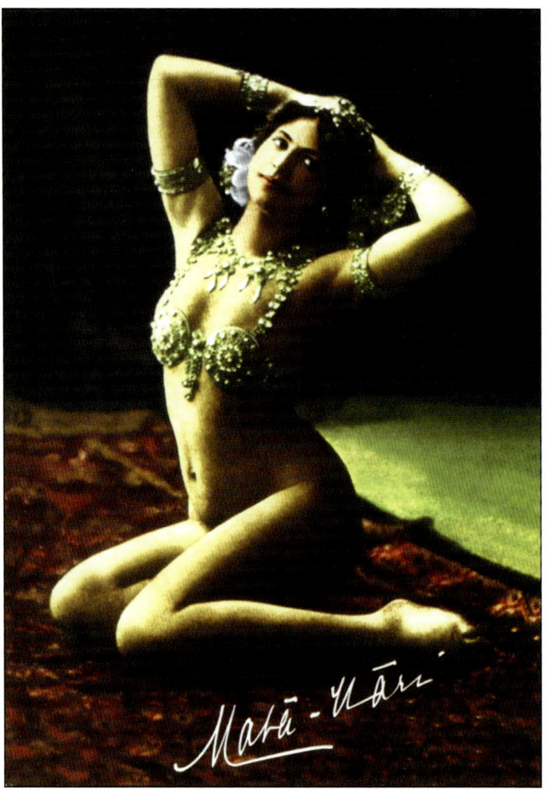

Mata Hari, hand-colored photograph, circa 1910. Courtesy: Fries Museum

In truth, Mata Hari was born Margaret Gertrude Zelle in Holland, the second child of Adam Zelle and Antje van der Meulen. She answered a mail order bride ad from an ancient monster of a military man who was placed in service in Java, where she learned Siva dancing. While there, she gave birth to two children; one died at an early age of poisoning. Returning to Europe, she separated from her husband, who then divorced her and took custody of their second child. During World War I, Mata Hari became a double spy, apparently working for France but actually working for Germany under the code name H21—at least that was what her French interrogators alleged. Toward the end of the war, she became one of the most infamous women spies in history. Word of her imprisonment, fate, and tragic story was reported worldwide; her execution increased her fame. Apparently the French became suspicious when she attempted to cross the French border to visit a German lover. They arrested her, she was interrogated, and at her trial was found guilty. During her three months of imprisonment, Mata Hari earned international respect for her courage in the face of imminent death. On October 15, 1917, she calmly faced execution, refusing a blindfold. Most who shot at her apparently missed on purpose. Only one bullet hit her. As her martyred fame grew, she was immortalized in films by Marlene Dietrich in *Dishonored* (1931), Greta Garbo in *Mata Hari* (1932), and Yvonne De Carlo in *Salome, Where She Danced* (1945). Years later it was shown that Mata Hari was a scapegoat for French war madness—an archetypal motif for feeling jubilant revenge against a war-spy. It was proven she had only gone to Germany for love. Spying is said to be the second oldest profession. This stereotype is derogatory to all women; it subliminally references the first oldest profession. It also intimates there is no woman you can trust. Mata Hari died because she fit the femme fatalé archetype, which could be easily adapted to a spy. To this day, the expression "Mata Hari" is still used as an a description denouncing an untrustworthy woman. And so the Bible's defamatory Salome tentacles persist.

self-taught and insisted that her dancing style was entirely her own creation. By 1908, Allan infatuated the dance circles of London, and then toured in America, Africa, Asia, and Australia. While in America in 1915, she played the title role in the silent film *The Rugmaker's Daughter*, which featured three of her dances, including "The Vision of Salome." No copies survive.

Allan is also remembered for the "Cult of the Clitoris" libel suit that she brought against Noel Pemberton Billing, a British newspaper publisher and member of Parliament, because he alleged that she was a lesbian, a slurred otherness stereotype. On February 16, 1918, his newspaper, *Vigilante*, had viscously headlined her as a member of a lesbian clitoris cult. As a lesbian, she represented a symbolic nonconventional woman archetype, eliciting fear within a patriarchal society. During the trial, Billing stated that he learned the word "clitoris" from a village doctor, who told him it was an "organ that, when unduly excited, possessed the most dreadful influence on any woman"—alluding to a she-devil stereotype. Allan's acknowledgment of knowing the word was presented as evidence of sexual perversion. Billing won the suit.

Hollywood has always loved the Salome archetype. A few who played it were Marguerite Snow in *Joseph in the Land of Egypt* (1914), Theda Bara in *Salome* (1918), Alla Nazimova in *Salome* (1922), and Rita Hayworth in *Salome* (1953).

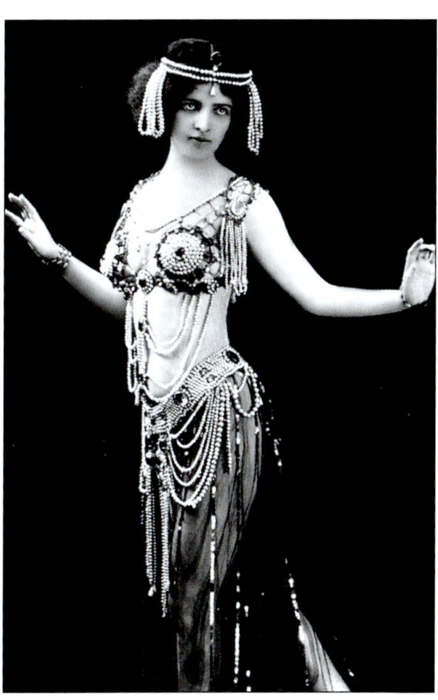

Maud Allan, *Salome*, postcard, 1920 © Beagles & Company

Maud Allan was born Beulah Maud Durrant in Toronto, the daughter of William Allan Durrant and Isa Matilda Hutchinson Durrant. The family moved to San Francisco in 1879, where Allan later studied to be a concert pianist. Her teacher, Eugene Bonelli of the San Francisco Grand Academy of Music, advised her to go to Germany for further study. It was there that she met Belgian musician and critic Marcel Rémy, who encouraged her to dance to his "The Vision of Salome" in 1903. This became her signature piece, gaining her international fame. She was actually

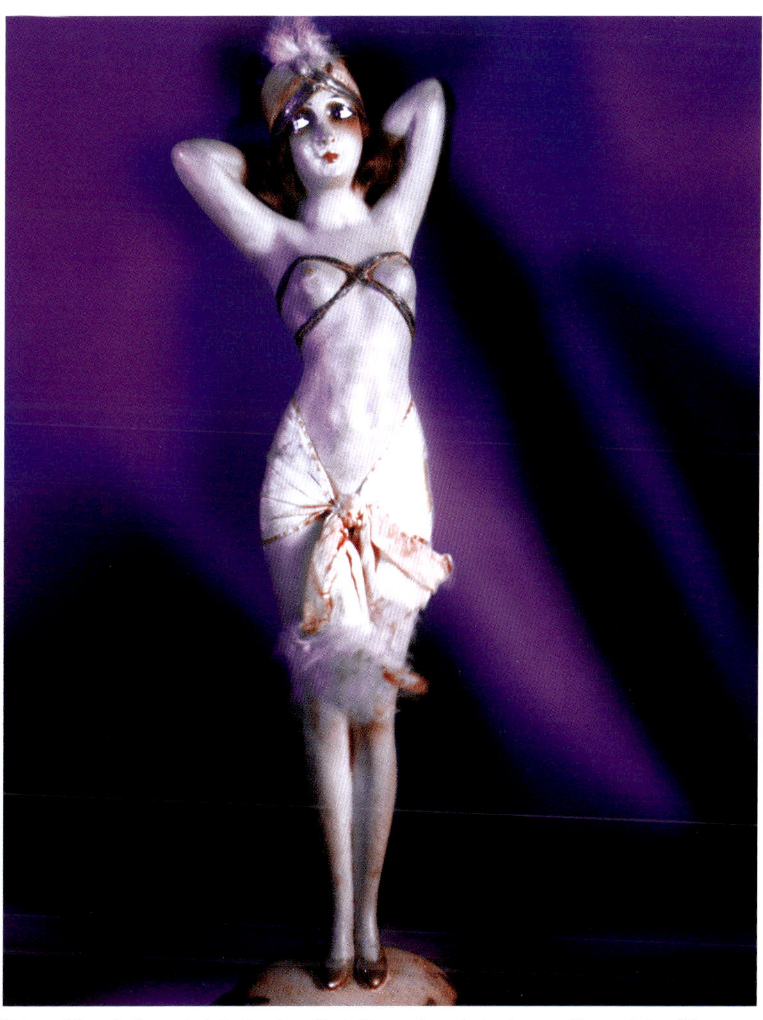

Salome fifteen-inch carnival chalk prize, silk clothing and a mohair wig, as well as mohair pubic hair—rare for any carnival chalk prize

Rudolph Valentino

(1895-1926)

Women are not in love with me but the picture of me on the screen.
I am merely the canvas on which they paint their dreams.
—RUDOLPH VALENTINO

*Suddenly it dawned upon me—I was too dull or it was too hot for me
to see it sooner that what we were talking about was really not what
we were talking about at all. I began to observe Valentino more closely: a curiously naive and boyish young fellow, certainly not much
beyond thirty, and with a disarming air of inexperience. To my eye,
at least, not handsome, but nevertheless immensely attractive. There
was an obvious fineness in him; even his clothes were not precisely
those of his trade. He began talking of his home, his people, his
early youth. His words were simple and yet somehow very eloquent.
I could still see the mime before me, but now and then, briefly and
darkly, there was a flash of something else. That something else, I
concluded, was what is commonly called, for want of a better name,
a gentleman. Valentino's agony, in brief, was the agony of a man
of civilized feelings thrown into a situation of intolerable vulgarity,
destructive alike to his peace and his dignity—nay, into a whole
series of such situations. It was not that trifling Chicago episode that
was riding him; it was the whole grotesque futility of his life. Had he
achieved, out of nothing, a vast and dizzy success? Then that success
was hollow as well as vast—a colossal and preposterous nothing. Was
he acclaimed by yelling multitudes? Then every time the multitudes
yelled he felt himself blushing inside.*
—H. L. MENCKEN, shortly before Valentino died, 1926

Rudolph Valentino created the fantasy Latin lover stereotype. He became Hollywood's number-one male sex symbol in his first starring role in the silent film *The Four Horsemen of the Apocalypse* (1921). Newly empowered American
women adored his foreign looks, graceful movements, and
seductive nature. He was hardly the rough-and-tumble Tom
Mix type.

In his next film, *The Sheik* (1921), Valentino played
the part of a gorgeous, hot-blooded Arab, conquering the love
of an Englishwoman. The intensity of his screen gaze caused
women to shiver and faint, which solidly cemented another
stereotype for him as the great lover. From then on, he and
his many stereotypes would endure. He became an icon for
a fantasized, forbidden, seductive lover. Valentino played the
part of a spirited bullfighter/lover in *Blood and Sand* (1922).
He displayed his muscular, lithe body naked (as much as was
allowable in films of the time) and his natural exhibition-
ism created the Hollywood beefcake stereotype. The word
"beefcake" did not exist in slang at the time, and the word
"priapic" (someone preoccupied with male sexuality) was
way too formal. The word "cheesecake" seems to have been
created around 1915 by combining "cheese," as said when
posing for a photograph (particularly obvious in sexy pinup
photos of smiling women), with "cake," something delicious.
Beefcake was the male equivalent stereotype and derived from
cheesecake, probably coined after 1938, when men's bathing
suits allowed their hairy, bare chests to show.

American women still travel to the Mediterranean in
search of their very own Valentino, and many Mediterranean
men (aware of the still-attractive Valentino stereotype) are

waiting and eager to provide this fantasy fulfillment. Valentino's
films quickly created a simplistic otherness stereotype—a way in
which Americans saw Italian and other Mediterranean men. It is
an unfortunately shallow and needy stereotype; sexism plays
an important part for those who hope to find a relationship in
this way.

American men were not as quick to take to Valentino's
magnetism. Many Tom Mix types found Valentino effeminate.
By 1926, after numerous starring roles in films, and slightly
prior to his tragic early death, the *Chicago Tribune* called him
a "pink powder puff." He reacted vehemently, challenging the
writer to a boxing match. Since Jack Dempsey had taught
Valentino to box, it might have erased the effeminacy label,
but the match never took place. H. L. Mencken, who had not
seen any of his films, interviewed Valentino and found him
a perfect analogue for the world of Hollywood hype—a sad
world wherein his fans could not or would not differentiate
between reality and fantasy. Valentino's public wanted and
expected him to be in real life the same person they saw in
films. His appeal had been molded and crafted, first by screen-
writer June Mathis, next by costumer/makeup artist/script-
writer/wife Natacha Rambova, and somewhere in there was his
own craftsmanship—the handsome Italian who had immigrated
to the States at eighteen years of age, a ready apache dancer,
gigolo, athlete, car mechanic, and agriculturalist turned mega
film star.

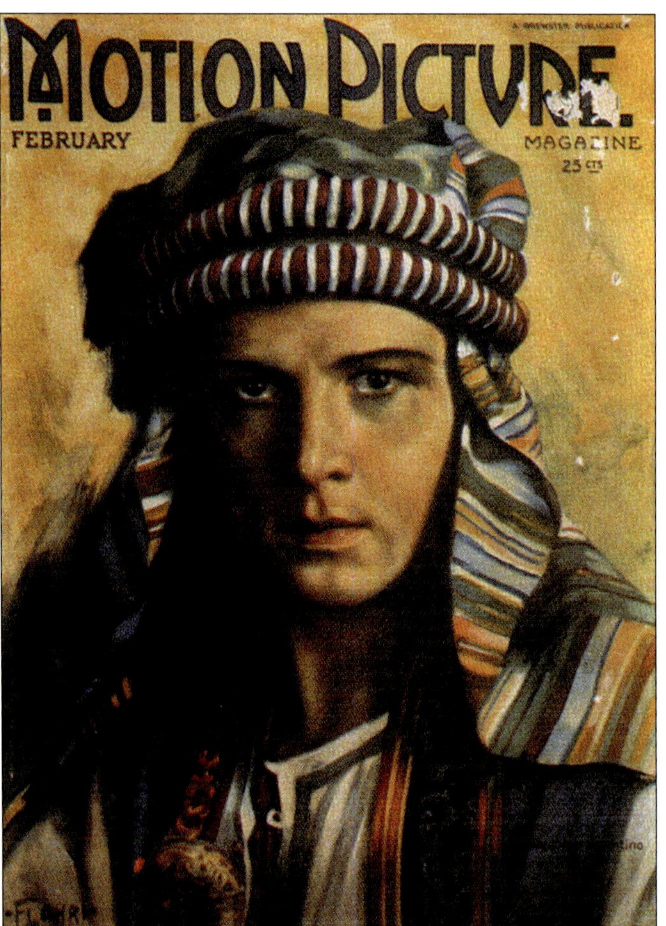

Rudolph Valentino, cover, February, 1922 © *Motion Picture* magazine

Valentino was the first superstar to cause mass feminine hysteria. No other star in the United States, except possibly Elvis, has ever matched that level of public hysteria. When Valentino died at the age of thirty-one on August 24, 1926, *The New York Times* wrote:

> The death of the silent-screen idol Rudolph Valentino sent his fans into a hysterical state of mass mourning. More than 100,000 of the faithful paid tribute at his open coffin in New York and a Mass was said in Hollywood.
>
> Mr. Rudolph Valentino, one of the foremost cinema actors in the United States, died yesterday from pleurisy following an operation for appendicitis, upon which peritonitis had supervened.
>
> The coffin is almost hidden by banks of flowers, among them being a wreath from Signor Mussolini. Four Fascists in black shirts keep guard, and an army of ushers and private detectives endeavor to keep in order the immense crowd of men, women and children that all day pass through the room at a rate of eighty a minute.

In his final film, *Son of the Sheik* (1926), he successfully parodied himself. He never lived to see it. He was probably the first major film star to die young, which set in motion an archetypal symbol for the remembered one, whose early death instinctively created feelings for death remembrance. The hysteria surrounding his death caused women to commit suicide. Frozen in time, his youthful looks and physique will never grow old, nor did he have to adapt to sound film—which provides an additional clue as to why his Latin lover stereotype remains so intact.

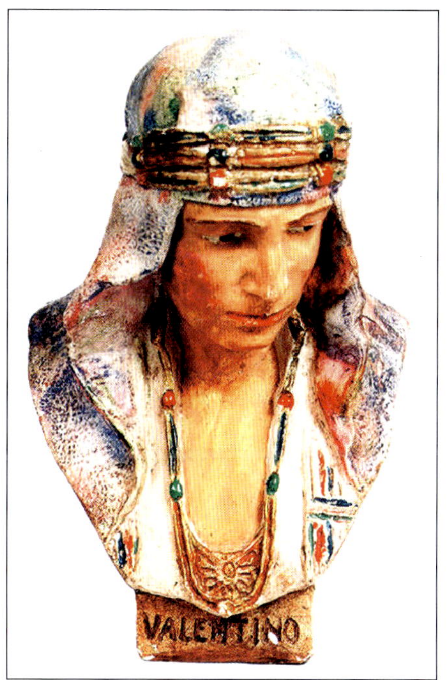

Rudolph Valentino carnival chalk prize © Leach Studios

Born Rodolpho Alfonso Raffaelo Pierre Filibert di Valentina d'Antonguolla Guglielmi on May 6, 1895, in Castellaneta, a small village in southern Italy, his numerous biographics allow readers to choose whatever vision of him they desire—reflecting their own image of Valentino, superimposed behind themselves onto the surface of the mirror of time.

Valentino was also a poet:

My tiny soul
Laughed daintily in its glee,
My heart sang a sweet little tune—
Chanting Time's first measure,
Frightened so—
Perplexed.
My new, new being tiptoed into life with hesitating step—
Wondered at the kaleidoscope of life—
Turning, turning, changing, shifting
Into mystic prophecies
Of the future.
Fate
Stood waiting.
Hovering over my cradle and pointing ahead
To the future.
Time Stood grinning—
Grinning merrily in the hour-glass of eternity;
And my small, small heart beat a sweet and dainty song
To the tender rhythm of the cradle,
Cradle rocking softly, patiently,
And someone humming
Such a lovely lullaby—
Someone lulling me
To sleep,
Sleep.
—"Babyhood"

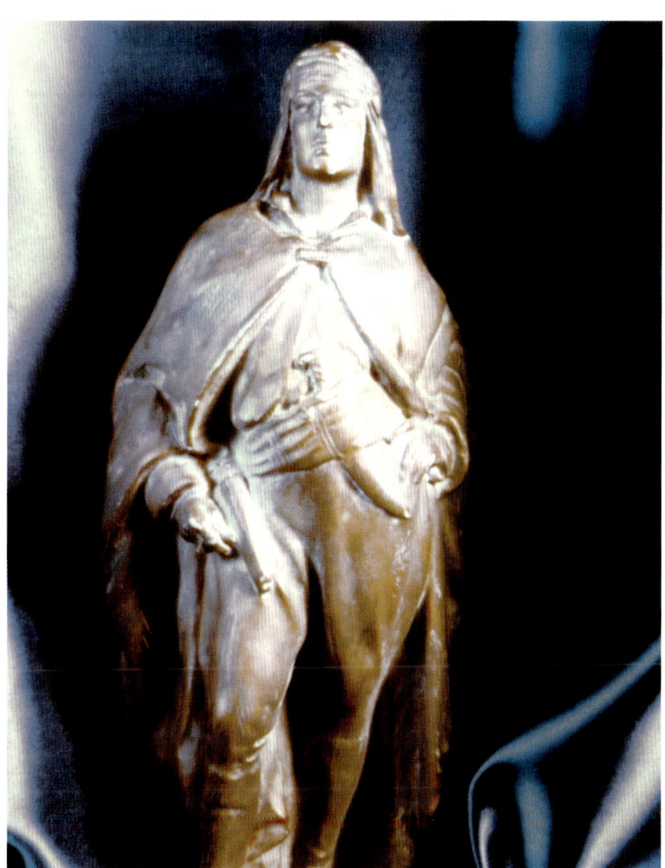

Rudolph Valentino carnival chalk prize © Davidson Novelty Company. Surprisingly, the nine-inch carnival chalkware prize is extremely rare, as is the eight-inch bust shown above.

A FRICAN EVE (1810-2002)

Doctor William Dunlop transported a twenty-one-year-old Quena woman from the East Cape of Africa to England in 1810. She was destined to be put on display at Bartholomew Fair and Haymarket Circus in London. She was evidently a bright woman, who was conversant in three languages. The "kind" doctor had persuaded her to travel with him by promising that she would make her fortune exhibiting her body to Europeans. Once in England, she was given the stage name "Hottentot Venus." ("Hottentot" subsequently became a racial slur, a stereotype synonymous with black female promiscuity, which persists to this day.) The Quena woman possessed physical characteristics typical of women from her region —protruding buttocks, huge breasts, and large genital lips that were lewdly billed by the show's promoters as "resembling the skin that hangs from a turkey's throat." She was paraded naked across a two-foot-high stage, led by her keeper and exhibited like a wild beast, obliged to walk, stand, and sit on command. She could be viewed for two shillings, but for an extra charge, viewers could also poke and prod her buttocks, which, of course, were the show's main attraction. Dunlop gave her a new Dutch name, Saartjie Baartman. The entire production made her an archetypal symbol for the inferior African woman, eliciting feelings of white superiority while reinforcing African inferiority.

Dunlop's racially exploitative exhibition took place at a time when the antislavery debate was raging in England, and Baartman's plight attracted the attention of a young Jamaican, Robert Wedderburn, founder of the African Association, an assembly that campaigned against racism in England. Under pressure from this group, the attorney general asked the government to put an end to the circus, saying Baartman was not a free participant. In 1814, it was decided that the show would move to Paris, but before it left, Baartman was baptized and given the English name Sarah Bartman.

She was then exhibited in an animal show on rue Neuve des Petits Champs in Paris. She died nine months later and her body was given to Doctor George Cuvier, surgeon-general to Napoleon Bonaparte. Pre-Darwinist social anthropology was the prevailing scientific notion of the day and Cuvier believed Bartman was the missing link, an example of the highest form of animal life and the lowest form of human life. He promoted the white supremacy dogma through what he called "advanced theories." For him, she was an archetypal symbol of the "least human one." He could then proclaim, through his intellectual disguise, his own unexamined racist feelings of white superiority. Curvier removed her brains and genitals, then made a plaster cast of her corpse. Her genitalia, preserved in a formalin bell jar, along with her skeleton and a cast of her body were on display in case 33 in the Musee de l'Homme in Paris until 1985. A stereoscopic, photographic view of Bartman's body cast was available at the museum store for purchase until as late as 1949. Her skin was sent back to England, stuffed by a taxidermist, and put on display. In recent years protests were launched to have her remains sent back to South Africa—finally in 2002 the French government agreed and she was returned to her homeland for a proper burial.

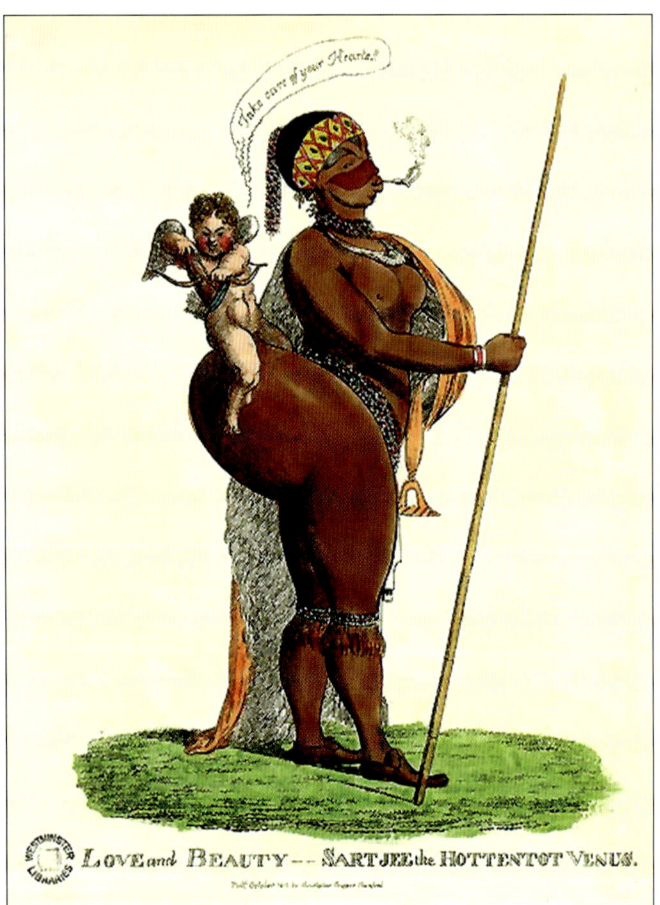

"Love and Beauty—Sartjie the Hottentot Venus." Courtesy: Westminster Library, U.K. Cupid is saying: "Take care of your hearts."

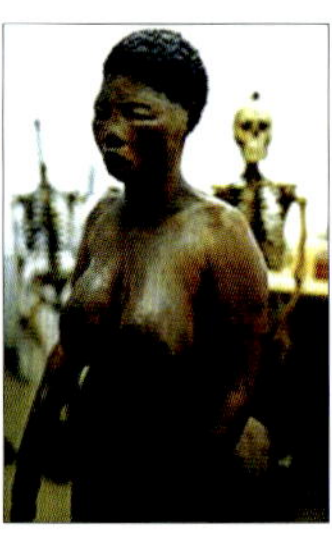

Sarah Bartman

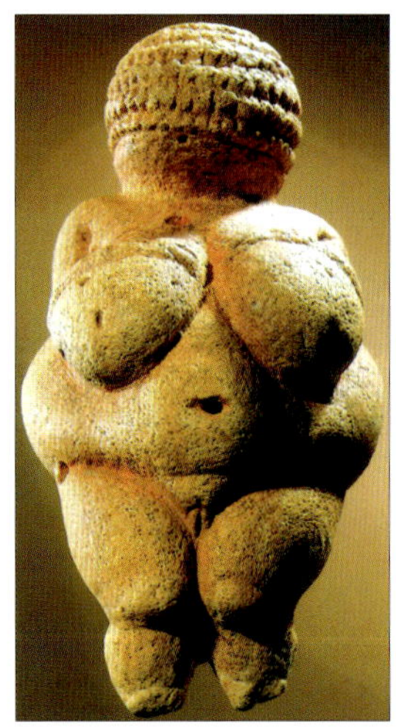

Venus of Willendorf

Archaeologist Josef Szombathy uncovered a goddess figurine in Willendorf, Austria, in 1908 that greatly resembles the Quena woman. It is made of limestone and is eleven centimeters tall. It is a carving of a corpulent woman with stout hips, a voluminous belly, and heavy breasts. It was given the name Venus of Willendorf.

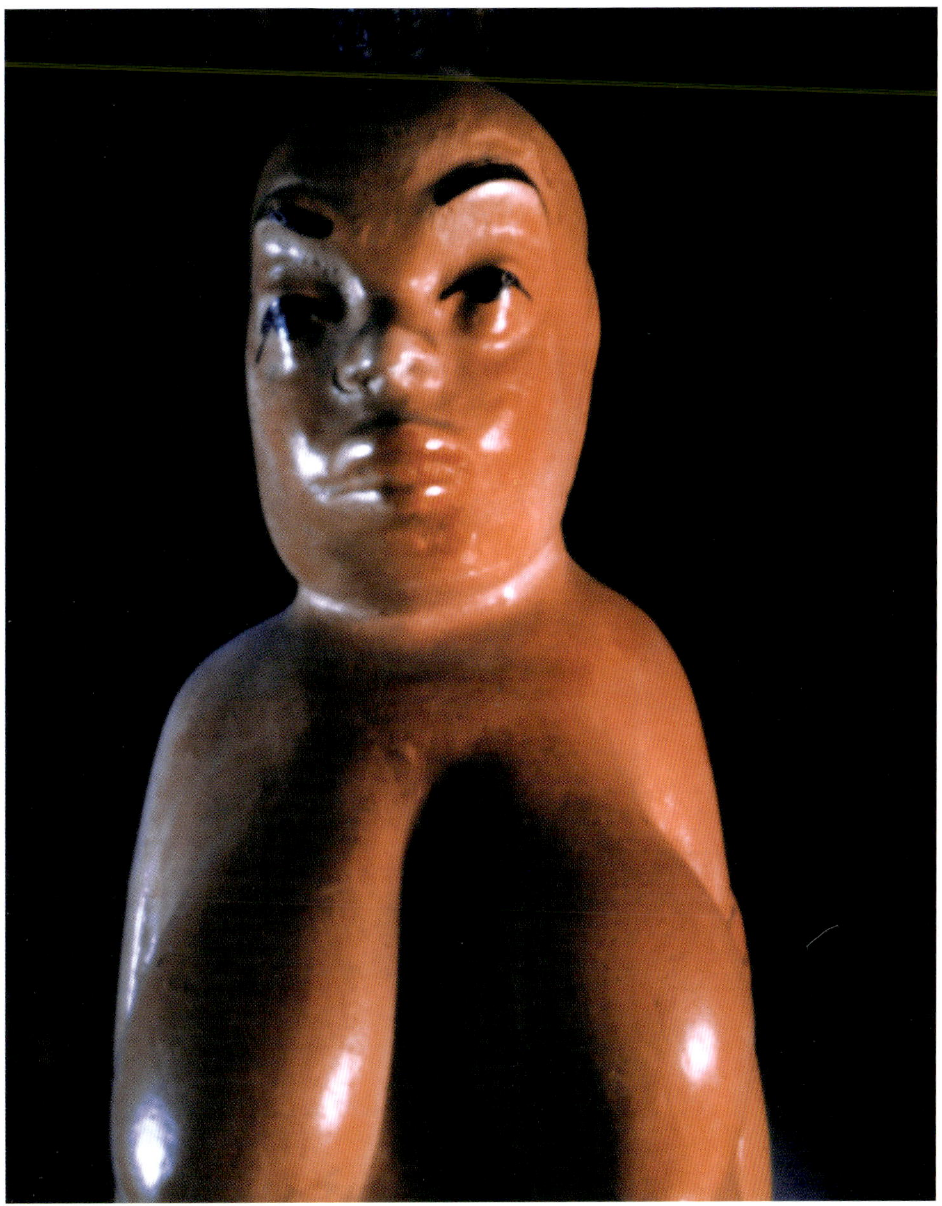

African Eve twelve-inch carnival chalk prize, a close copy of
the Quena body type and of the Venus of Willendorf figurine
(as well as Saartjie Baartman). African Eve has a twelve-and-a-
half-inch carnival chalk mate known as African Adam, wearing
barely more than a top hat and smoking a cigar.

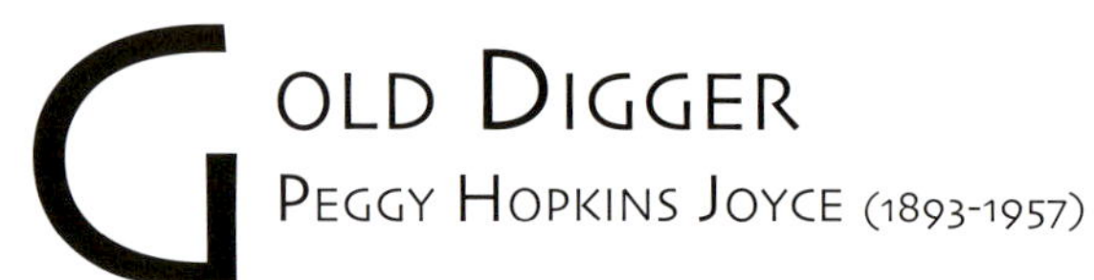Gold Digger
Peggy Hopkins Joyce (1893-1957)

Any girl who was a lady would not even think of having such a good time that she did not remember to hang onto her jewelry.
—Anita Loos, *Gentlemen Prefer Blondes*

I may be expensive, but I deliver the goods.
—Peggy Hopkins Joyce

Yet despite the obscurity into which she slipped so inexorably, Peggy Hopkins Joyce should be remembered. She was important not in what she accomplished but for what she represented. Quite simply, she stood as a harbinger of a new age. Her life illustrates what has emerged as one of the most significant phenomena of twentieth-century America—the rise and triumph of the modern celebrity in an image-driven culture and the transcendent role of the media in creating, anointing, and ultimately destroying these creatures. Peggy was, albeit inadvertently, a precursor of a breed that would become commonplace in the years and decades after her death.
—Constance Rosenblum, *Gold Digger*

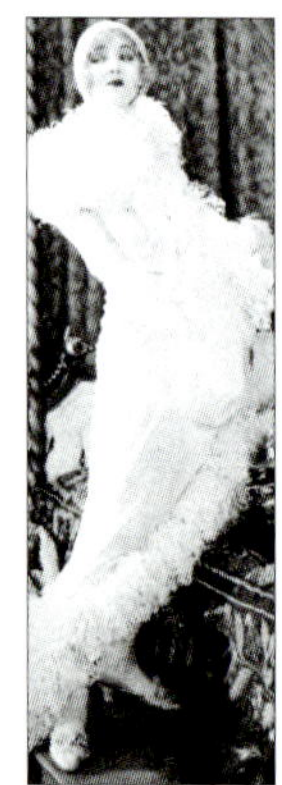

Peggy Hopkins Joyce, 1926

Tall, slim, and blond, Peggy Hopkins Joyce was one of America's most talked-about and gossiped-over personalities of the Jazz Age. She was the quintessential gold digger stereotype. She was not a kept woman. (The slang word for a kept woman was "sugar" and her wealthy keeper was called a "sugar daddy.") Peggy married six millionaires, one of them a titled count. Her greatest talent was self-promotion, trading principally on her good looks. Her sales pitch included boasts about her high-priced goods and she managed to snare more than a few high rollers.

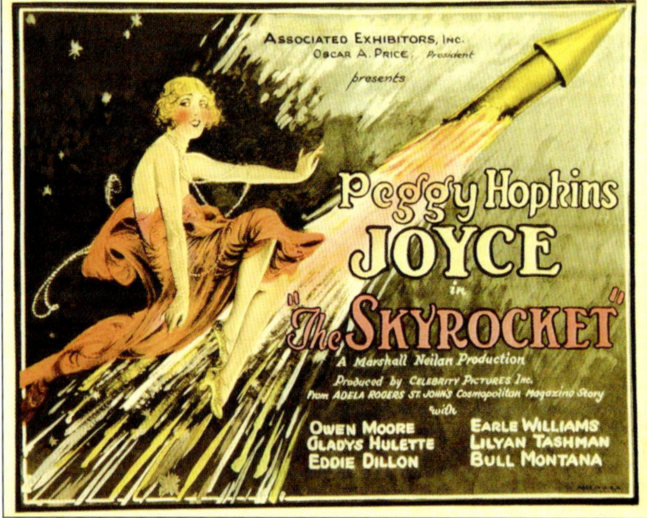

Peggy Hopkins Joyce, *The Skyrocket*, lobby card, 1926 © Associated Exhibitors Films

Peggy Hopkins Joyce was a barber's daughter from Norfolk, Virginia, born Marguerite Upton in 1893. At seventeen, she married her first millionaire husband, the wealthy

Everett Archibald Jr. of Denver. Three years later, she married New York millionaire attorney Sherburne Philbrick Hopkins. Her beauty also impressed Florenz Ziegfeld, who put her in the 1917 Ziegfeld Follies, where she became one of his stars.

Her beauty dazzled the eye of multimillionaire lumberman J. Stanley Joyce in 1920, and he won the dubious privilege of becoming her third husband—thus completing her stage name, Peggy Hopkins Joyce. Prior to her divorce from J. Stanley Joyce, Peggy had a flaming affair with Henry Letellier, considered the second-wealthiest man in Paris and a man whose riches and looks attracted many female admirers. One of Letellier's jilted mistresses sent Peggy an exquisitely wrapped gift just before she returned to America. Peggy opened it to find a dead cat (Meow~~~). She went back to America, and Joyce divorced her. The booty realized from the divorce included a $2 million home in Miami and $2 million worth of jewels (4,000 newspaper articles were written about their divorce).[1] She was then twenty-eight years old.

The era's brand-new medium of tabloid newspapers spawned scandal-hungry journalists who found Peggy's trashy, sugary charms irresistible—as did their escapist, love-starved audience. Her tabloid fame and notoriety created a surefire niche for her in Hollywood. She became a movie star in 1922 and acted in films for a decade. *The Skyrocket* (1926), one of her most popular films, was possibly the first to compare a woman to futuristic military hardware.

Her lascivious escapades made her the best-known woman of the 1920s. Peggy's charm connected to the blonde gold digger stereotype—she thought that her beauty could supply her life with more happiness from riches than happiness from simply being in love. She thrived on wealth and was recklessly lavish, known to spend $1 million in a week. She owned a dog collar that cost $3,000 and had love affairs with film stars and famous personalities, including Walter Chrysler and Charlie Chaplin. Her gold-digging personality was the inspiration for Chaplin's film *A Woman in Paris* (1923). By 1927, her fame was so great, because she was an archetypal symbol of an extravagant personality, that she was asked to sit in on the Ruth Snyder murder trial and report her thoughts on the proceedings. The front-page story involved a husband who had been bludgeoned and strangled by his wife and her lover. Snyder was found guilty and sentenced to death. The photograph of her execution was the most famous image of the decade, proving once again that the technologically advanced electric chair was a new archetypal motif symbol for a powerful death object—perfect for eliciting feelings of death fascination, which sells newspapers, particularly if it involves the death of a woman. (Snyder was not the first woman to occupy it.) Several decades earlier an elephant was used to prove that electricity could kill.

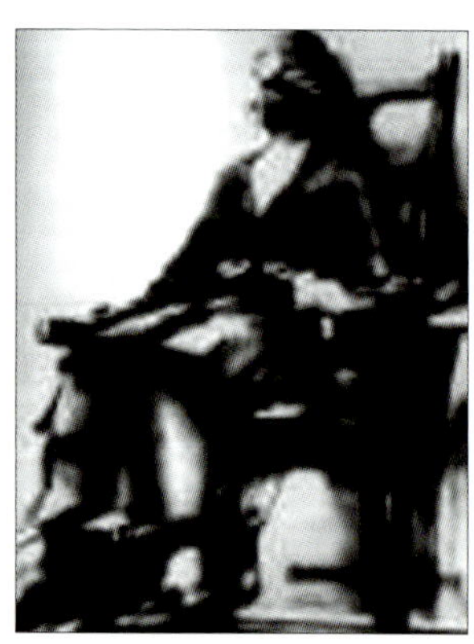

Ruth Snyder, execution photograph

It is not as obtuse a suggestion as it may seem at first to view a female gold digger (there are also a multitude of male gold diggers) as a brave heroine. While it's true that selfish striving for riches and what they can bring is their underlying propulsion and disguise, another less obvious factor comes into play. In a world where wealth is accumulated and controlled by men, it is not surprising to find women of extraordinary beauty and acumen willing to cross the gender line, brave macho posturing, engage in battle, and infiltrate patriarchal wealth using the best means at their disposal. In a sense, the gold digger represents an archetypal conquest victory symbol thrown at a male-dominated world.

Peggy unwittingly became a true American icon when fiction writer Anita Loos adapted Peggy's blonde persona for her gold digger character named Lorelei Lee in her famous book *Gentlemen Prefer Blondes*. *Harper's Bazaar* first published it in serialized form in 1925, making *Harper's* a top-selling magazine. When it was published in book form, Edith Wharton referred to it as the "great American novel" and it was preferred reading for the almost blind James Joyce during the brief time he was allotted to read each day. It also won praise from readers as varied as Winston Churchill, William Faulkner, George Santayana, and Benito Mussolini. Loos saw firsthand how her men friends preferred to move baggage for a blonde starlet, and she ironically complained:

Obviously there was some radical difference between that girl and me. But what was it? We were both in the pristine years of early youth; we were about the same degree of comeliness; as to our mental acumen, there was nothing to discuss: I was the smarter. Then why did that girl so far outdistance me in feminine allure? She was a natural blonde and I was a brunette.[2]

Busby Berkeley, the master of black-and-white film musicals, continued the blonde gold digger tradition during the Depression. He cornered the market for the popular stereotype with a surfeit of Gold Digger films: *Gold Diggers of 1933*, *Gold Diggers of 1935*, *Gold Diggers of 1937*, and the final *Gold Diggers in Paris* (1938). *In Gold Diggers of 1935* Berkeley's extravagant choreography, oversize stage sets, and synchronized dancing panoramas enlisted 150 dancers. Joan Blondell starred in the 1933 and 1937 versions of Berkeley's Gold Digger films. Like Peggy Hopkins Joyce, the flamboyant Busby Berkeley married six times.

On it goes. Carol Channing starred in the hit musical revue *Lend an Ear*, first in Hollywood in 1947, then in New York in 1948. In it, Channing spoofed Peggy Hopkins Joyce. This led to Channing's 1949 Broadway starring role in *Gentlemen Prefer Blondes*, where she dazzled audiences with her rendition of "Diamonds Are a Girl's Best Friend." Glitz lifted the United States out of post–World War II suffering. *Gentlemen Prefer Blondes* enjoyed a Broadway run of 740 performances in the Ziegfeld Theater, turning Channing into a colossal star. Marilyn Monroe studied Channing's performance and viewed the show many times, enabling her to imitate Channing's presentation in her own 1953 film version of Lorelei Lee in *Gentlemen Prefer Blondes* (with a Hollywood version of the red dress below).

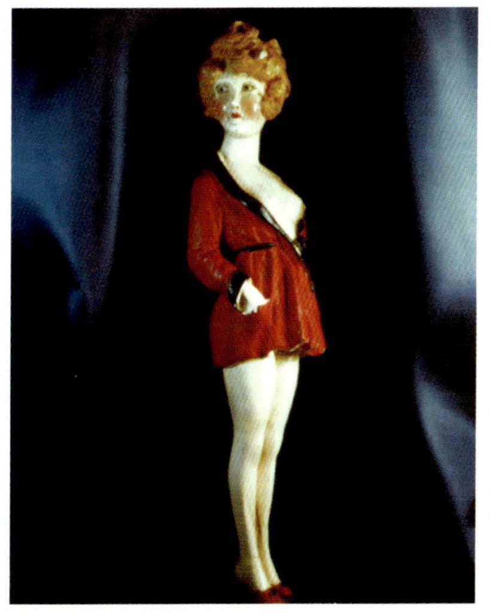

Peggy Hopkins Joyce sixteen-inch carnival chalkware prize. Her face is similar to other June Yates Jenkins' figures of that era.

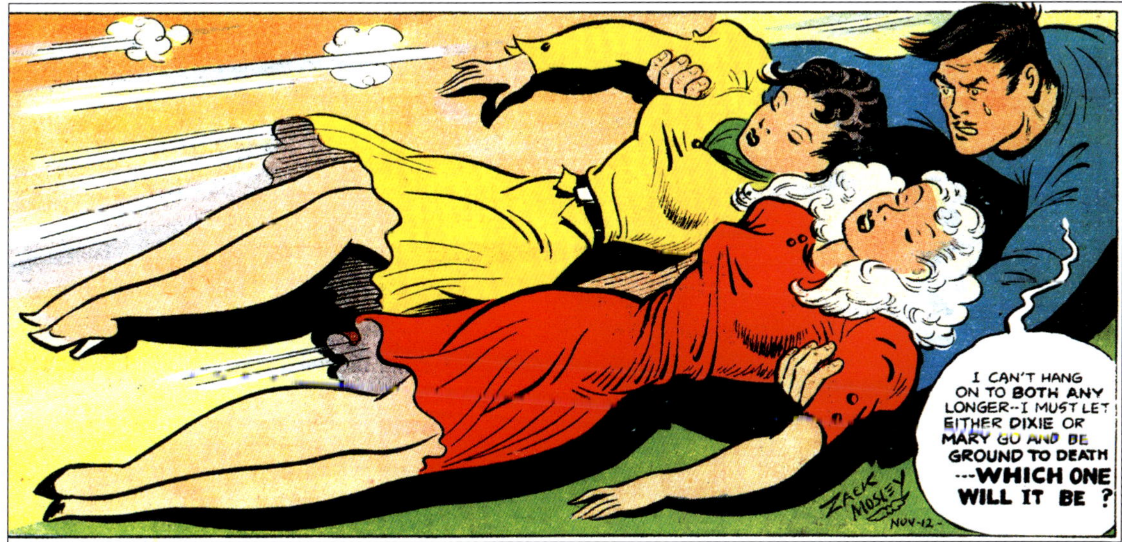

Cartoon detail, *Smilin' Jack* © Zack Mosley, Nov. 12, 1939

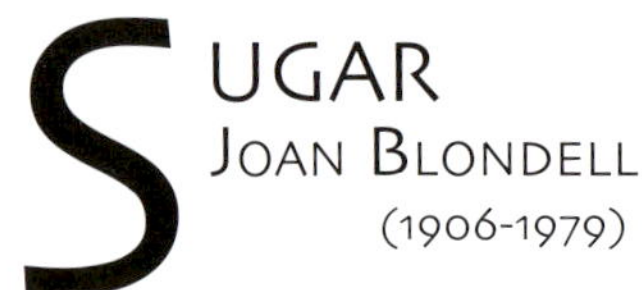

SUGAR
JOAN BLONDELL
(1906-1979)

. . . she was a mainstay at that studio for men, able to sing and dance as swap sour dialogue with gangsters, cops, or hustling stage managers. A pretty girl, she was given a cutting edge by so much dull work. . . . look back over the Warner's product and see how her slightly blowsy blonde, as round and shiny as cultured pearls, has lasted. Time and again, she brings life, fun, and worldliness to her scenes.
—DAVID THOMSON, *A Biographical Dictionary of Film*

You want my husband? Well, you can have him.
—JOAN BLONDELL to June Allyson, after she found out Dick Powell and June Allyson were having an affair.

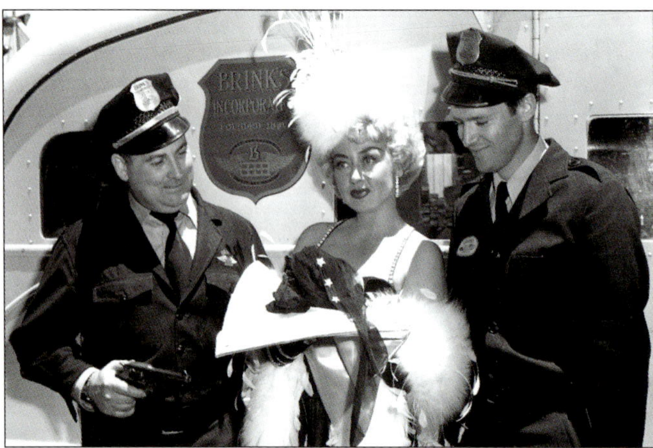

Joan Blondell © RKO Radio Pictures. When Blondell wore diamond-studded stockings designed by Willys of Hollywood in *The Blue Veil*, the producers hired guards (right out of central casting) from Brink's to safeguard her.

Rose Joan Blondell was born into a vaudevillian comic's family in New York City in 1906. At age three, she was put onstage by her ambitious mother. At seventeen she joined a theater company traveling across America, won a beauty pageant as Miss Dallas, and returned to New York for a debut in the Ziegfeld Follies. She tried Hollywood at age twenty-two, starring with Humphrey Bogart in *Broadway's Like That* (1928), but the unpopular film did little for either of their careers and both of them returned to Broadway. Her break came in 1929 when she starred with James Cagney on Broadway in *Penny Arcade*. Warner Brothers decided to film *Penny Arcade* and changed its name to *Sinner's Holiday*. Blondell and Cagney were coaxed to California to play their parts. The film was a success, turning Cagney into a major star. Blondell's supporting actress stereotype was formed, where the man in the film was consistently the major star. She parodied spunky, sexy, and faux-sleazy—on her way to the gold digger stereotype. Then she blessed her viewers with an erotic scene showing her dressing to go to work in *The Office Wife* (1930). She was paired with Dick Powell in ten films, including *Gold Diggers of 1933* (Blondell and Powell were married for nine years). She was consistently the archetypal symbol for an alluring woman, eliciting feelings of lust. When Blondell left Warner Brothers in 1939, her glittery,

jeweled career seemed to dim, but her wonderful, mesmerizing smile did not. She received an Academy Award nomination for *The Blue Veil* (1951). She persevered, continuing to act in film and TV, and completed her film finale, *The Woman Inside* (released in 1981 after her death). She married three times and died of leukemia in 1979.

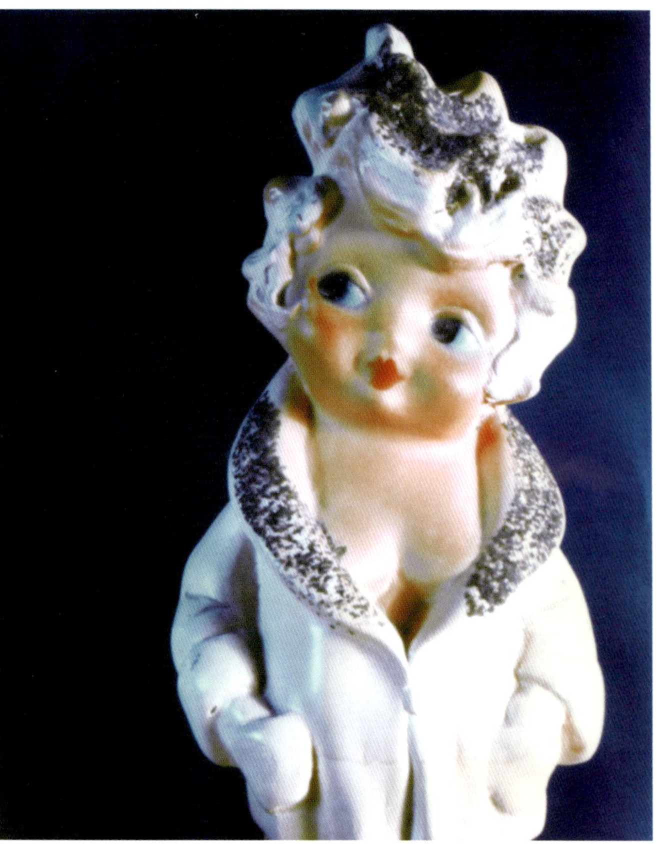

Sugar thirteen-and-a-half-inch carnival chalk prize © June Yates Jenkins May 19, 1948. Sugar was one of his last figures probably meant to partly caricature Joan Blondell as the composite blonde gold digger stereotype. It could have been drawn from many Hollywood films, Broadway productions, Anita Loos's book *Gentlemen Prefer Blondes*, and the one and only—the real-life Peggy Hopkins Joyce.

Hollywood had always found it beneficial to continued box-office successes to promote various sexual stereotypes, like the gold digger, the number-one sex symbol, the hula girl, or the femme fatale. In a patriarchal America, before true equality was achieved (which still remains to be seen), women's acting roles were and still are less varied than men's. Actresses are discovered who can portray these roles for a number of years, while they're still young, desirable, and hungry. Over time, another actress takes her place. Blondell easily fit into a pigeonhole. Rarely does Hollywood take risky leaps in advance of social change. One of the reasons Frances MacDormand received Best Actress for her role in *Fargo* (1996) was that Americans had never seen a pregnant woman as a chief of police. It was a new role and a stereotype reversal.

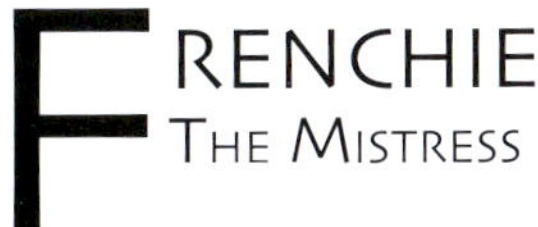

FRENCHIE
THE MISTRESS

If all the young ladies who attended the Yale promenade were laid end to end, no one would be the least surprised.
—DOROTHY PARKER, *While Rome Burns*

Frenchie's face was heavily made up, mimicking Theda Bara's thick applications of cosmetics in her Hollywood films of 1916 to 1919, when kohl makeup first appeared. The notion of keeping a mistress was easily popularized in the post–World War I flapper era and imparted a lascivious fantasy stereotype for France and, in particular, wealthy French men who could afford a mistress. Frenchie (the stereotype name given to sexy french women), closely resembles Sugar, which in some ways is a similar stereotype—both are kept women, famous in the 1920s and 1930s. The notable difference between them and a gold digger is that a gold digger gets her money through the wrangles of divorce while a mistress enjoys the luxuries of life paid for by her usually married consort.

One of the worst abuses of power connected to a mistress was associated with Marquise de Montespan, mistress of King Louis XIV, and her devotion to the unholy Black Mass, a heinous parody of the Catholic Mass. The Black Mass ritual was conducted for rich nobility as an affront to the Catholic Church. It was typically executed in reverse, either in its entirety or in part. The mass included inverting the cross, spitting and stepping on the cross, stabbing the host, and offering other obscenities. Urine was substituted for holy water or for the wine. Sliced pieces of rotted turnips or black leather were substituted for communion bread. Black candles were used instead of white. A defrocked monk generally performed the mass wearing vestments of black or the color of dried blood, and embroidered with inverted crosses, a goat's head, or magical symbols. All of these Antichrist actions were archetypal symbols of sadomasochistic supremacy, allowing participants to feel corrupted lust.

Catherine Deshayes, known as La Voisin— supposedly a witch who read fortunes and sold love potions—organized a Black Mass ritual for Marquise de Montespan, who wanted the mass performed because she thought King Louis XIV was interested in another mistress. While using the Marquise as a naked altar, Abbé Guiborg, a defrocked monk, said three Black Masses over her, invoking Satan and his demons of lust and deceit—Beelzebub, Asmodeus, and Astaroth—to grant the marquise whatever she desired. While incense burned, the throats of three babies were cut and their blood drained into chalices and mixed with flour to make the host. Whenever the mass called for kissing the altar, Abbé Guiborg kissed the nude Marquise de Montespan. He consecrated the host over her genitals, sticking pieces of it into her vagina. Later the bodies of the babies were burned in the furnace of La Voisin's home. Police records show that La Voisin obtained babies from orphanages, beggars, or prostitutes, and that she had killed 2,500 infants in previous Black Masses.[1] When the scandal of this horror broke, 246 people were arrested by order of King Louis XIV. Among them were some of France's highest-ranking nobility. They were brought to trial and confessions were achieved by means of torture. Most nobility received jail sentences or exile to the countryside. Thirty-six commoners were executed, including La Voisin, who was burned alive in 1680. She was an archetypal symbol for a corrupted woman who elicited dreaded fear—the devil's accomplice—a witch.

Frenchie thirteen-and-one-half-inch carnival chalk prize

Tom Mix
(1880-1940)

Tom Mix was the quintessential cowboy. His film image featured do-it-yourself daredevil horse-and-rider showmanship, and to his credit, he performed all the riding stunts. Pioneer silent-film producer William Selig elevated the thirty-year-old Mix from stock handler to a supporting role as broncobuster in *Ranch Life in the Great Southwest* (1910). Mix performed in one hundred of Selig's films by 1917, enough to establish his unique image of daredevil good-guy cowboy. Mix was always on the side of law and order, and rarely killed the villains, instead just roping them off their horses then giving them a good old-fashioned pounding with his bare fists. A Tom Mix film was always action packed, but at the same time it was proper family entertainment. Few of his films dealt with him as a romance figure. He gave the leading lady a kiss, but that was all. Women were added to his films only as pretty showgirls, and the dominant good guy (who else but Tom Mix) always got the showgirl. His lack of intimacy (except with his horse) was easily perceived as manliness by most men and boys in his audience.

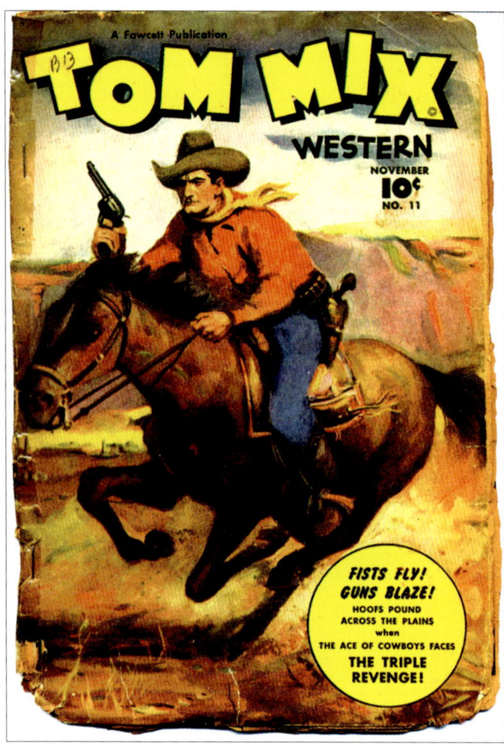

Tom Mix, comic book cover, 1948 © Fawcett Publications

Mix's main competition as Hollywood's top-billed cowboy star was William S. Hart, who in 1917 was the acclaimed King of the Cowboys largely due to his acting abilities and his desire to make authentic, earthy, slower-moving, "first you sin, then you get redemption" Westerns. Hart had been well trained on the smooth floors of the Broadway stage, whereas Mix had been trained through years of hardscrabble, dirt-in-your-face, daredevil horsemanship. He tended bar (and probably was the bouncer too); later he was a marksman in the army.

By 1920, Mix's fast-riding stunts and glorious costumes eroded Hart's crown and Mix became King of the Cowboys (at the youthful age of forty). He reigned (through clever reining) for ten years, playing in fairly simple formula films, many of which he directed. He should have been named "Testosterone Kid from Fashion City." No matter what trick he performed, his impeccably stylish Western clothes remained immaculate and dashing.

Mix's films were truly escapist sporting events. His first horse, Old Blue, held up until 1914, then came the even more amazing Tony, who soared through unbelievable high jumps, untied knotted ropes from around Mix's hands, and had a daredevil's heart to match that of his master. Mix could, in a wink of an eye, jump from Tony's back onto a moving train and back onto Tony again. He could stand astride two horses galloping at the same time, ride underneath Tony, ride Tony through a fire or a bar room window, leap with Tony from a collapsing bridge into swirling water, and on and on and on. The most difficult stunt looked easy. Mix boldly stereotyped the fashionable Western buckaroo—what most children in his audience, and most adults too, fantasized being. He was an archetypal symbol for the daredevil macho man, and his audience instinctively felt admirably breathless. Mix always played into the gallant hero stereotype, with numerous legendary antecedents in literature and oral history. Had he died, evil would have won. Using the backdrop of the Wild West, Mix clearly fantasized the life and morality of a bygone era.

Hollywood publicity agents glorified his earlier real life into super-legendary proportions with hyped-up, highly inaccurate stories. He did not dispute the glorification. They said he had seen action with Teddy Roosevelt's Rough Riders, and had been in the Boer War, the Boxer Rebellion, and the Philippine Insurrection. They claimed he had been a lawman in Oklahoma and a Texas Ranger.

Tom Mix was his real name. He was born in a little frame house near Driftwood, Pennsylvania, in 1880. When he was ten, he was inspired by Buffalo Bill's Wild West Show and received only two years of elementary schooling and a bunch of hard knocks learning to ride horses as a kid. He joined the army in 1898, the day after the Spanish-American War was declared, eventually reaching the rank of First Sergeant, though he never saw any action. He left the army as a deserter in 1902, but was never charged with desertion (ah—those were the days). Next he worked as a ranch hand and rider. When Hollywood beckoned, he was ready.

By the mid-1920s his Hollywood fame in silent films was so great that he and Tony made personal appearances in five countries on a European tour. But the 1929 stock market crash took away his savings of $1 million, his beautiful Beverly Hills mansion, and his golden-sunset Arizona ranch. He was left with his fancy duds. Even worse, his 1929 silent films were considered flops (he should have added the clopping of horse hooves, thereby using the new technology of sound).

Next he worked in various circuses and managed to achieve a minor film comeback with Universal Pictures from 1932 to 1935. Tony was retired in 1932 at the ripe old age of twenty-three when Mix was the ripe old age of fifty-three. Tony had at least five stand-ins at the height of Mix's fame—it was important to Mix not lose his favorite horse through an unfortunate accident whereas Mix himself suffered many injuries during his twenty-five-year film career, though he always lived to do another film and see another sunrise.

From 1935 to 1937, he traveled with his own Tom Mix Circus, which included side show acts and played in approximately two hundred venues each year. The *Tom Mix Ralston Straight Shooters* radio show ran from 1933 to 1951 (even after his tragic death in a car crash in 1940). His reincarnated, resurrected-Lazarus radio persona fought against every evil that the miracle-oriented radio producers could think up—giants, ghosts, saboteurs, invisible men, and, during World War II, many Japanese trick death plots.

Mix holds the rare distinction of being the first Hollywood cowboy to be put into comic books. *Tom Mix Comics* appeared from 1940 to 1942; later the name was changed to *Tom Mix Commando Comics*. Ironically, after his well-mourned death Mix reached the level of heaven-on-earth superhero. After World War II *Tom Mix Western Comics* survived from 1948 to 1953.

Mix was married five times. Of marriage anniversaries the daredevil cowboy turned love expert advised: "When a man's been married half a dozen times, any sentiment about anniversaries is as cold as the ashes of last year's campfire. Payin' all them alimonies sorta drowns out the romance."[1]

Vera McGinnis (1895-1990)

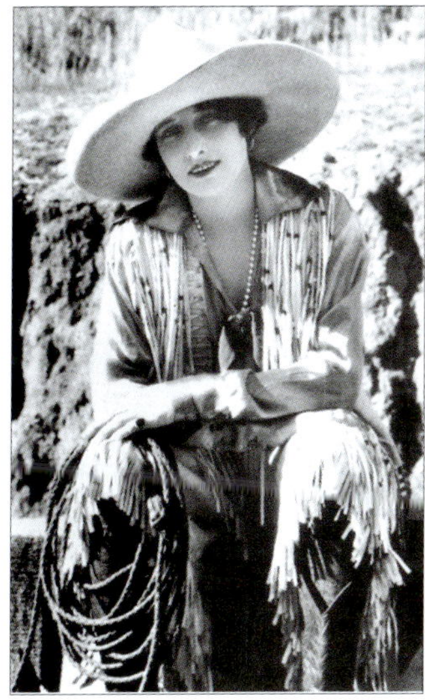

Vera McGinnis was America's premier woman rodeo champion and trick rider. Her abilities were so great that by 1924 she had won two championships at the First International Rodeo in London. As a true Western flapper stereotype, McGinnis introduced a new style of dress—long pants. She symbolized an archetypal daredevil macho woman and elicited feelings of macho thrills. By 1926, she was the U.S. National Woman Rodeo Champion. In trick riding she was famous for her ability to leap from one horse to another during a relay race and for riding under her horse's belly at full gallop. She was rodeo champion at bronco riding, bull riding, and Roman racing. Her rodeo career ended in 1934, when a somersaulting racehorse named China Rose crushed her. McGinnis survived but could never perform again. She was married three times, once for seven months when she was only seventeen. She was inducted into the Cowgirl Hall of Fame in 1979.

Vera McGinnis, circa 1925

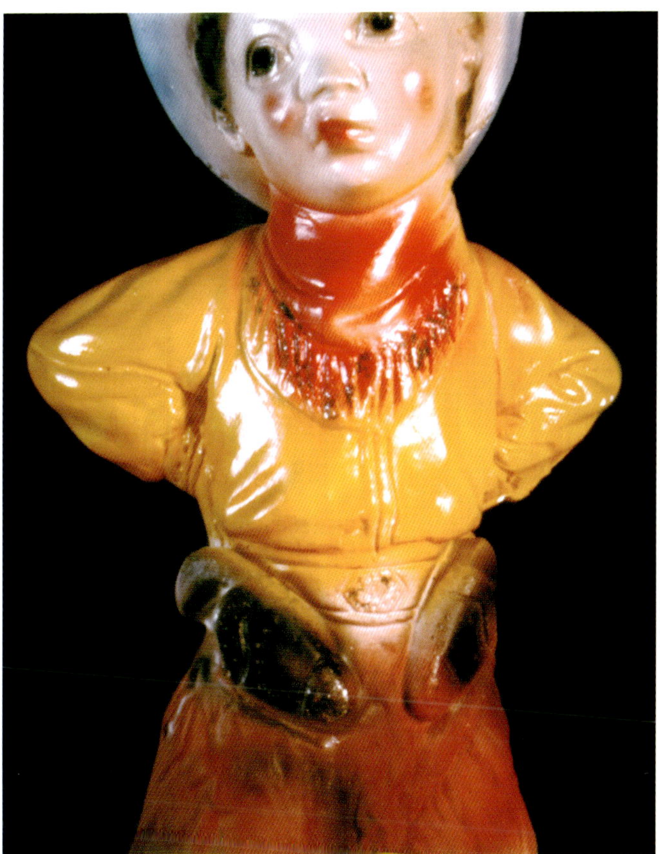

Tom Mix fifteen-inch carnival chalk prize. It portrayed a two-gun-totin' Tom Mix, probably made in the early 1930s and somewhat resembling his attire from the comics. His guns, ready to be drawn, symbolized a power and control motif.

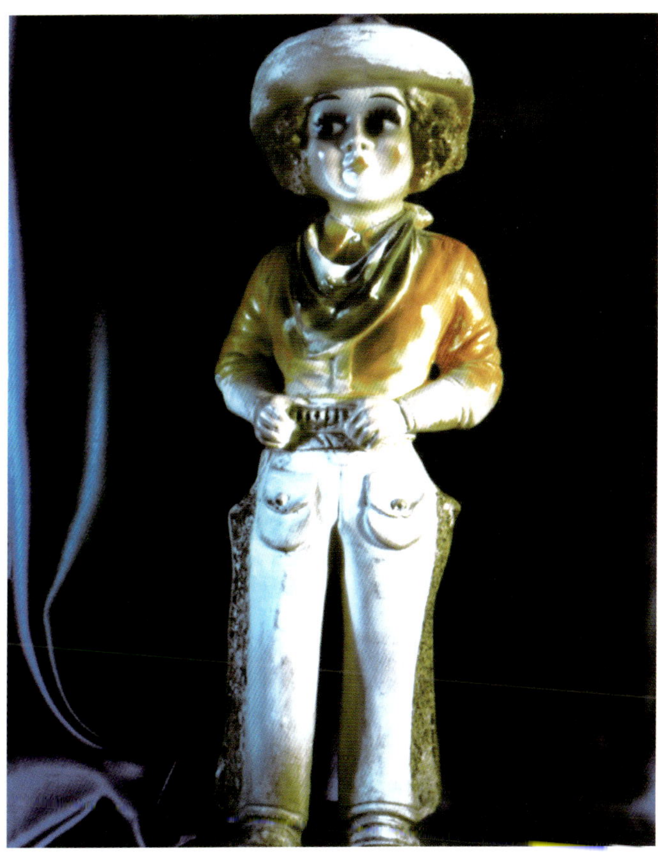

Vera McGinnis (?) fifteen-inch carnival chalk prize © William Rainwater (original figure carved in wood by Clarence DeWitt)

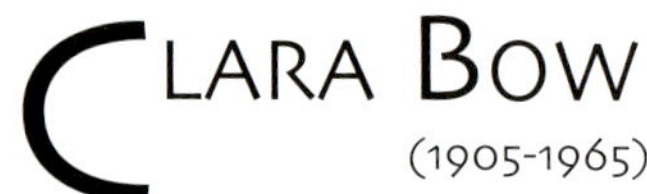

CLARA BOW
(1905-1965)

The true republic: men, their rights and nothing more;
women, their rights and nothing less.
—SUSAN B. ANTHONY, *The Revolution,* Motto

John-Paul Sartre labeled silent film "the frenzy on the wall," and Clara Bow was a key part of that early frenzy. Clara Gordon Bow was born in 1905 into severe poverty and exceedingly difficult family circumstances. She lived with her parents, Robert and Sarah Bow, in a Brooklyn tenement. Clara was the Bows' third daughter and the only one to survive. One daughter lived for two hours after her birth and another for only two days. As a result of the death of her children and poverty, Clara's mother was distressed and prone to destructive, unpredictable behavior. When Clara was only fourteen, her father, whose income barely supported the family, encouraged her to submit her photograph to a "Fame and Fortune" contest, sponsored by three motion-picture fan magazines. The national winner was to receive a silver trophy, an evening gown, and a contract for a part in one motion picture. The notion of Clara entering the contest greatly upset her disturbed mother and one night Clara woke up to the specter of her mother standing over her with a raised kitchen knife. Fortunately, her mother fainted. She was subsequently sent to a state mental hospital, where she died shortly thereafter.

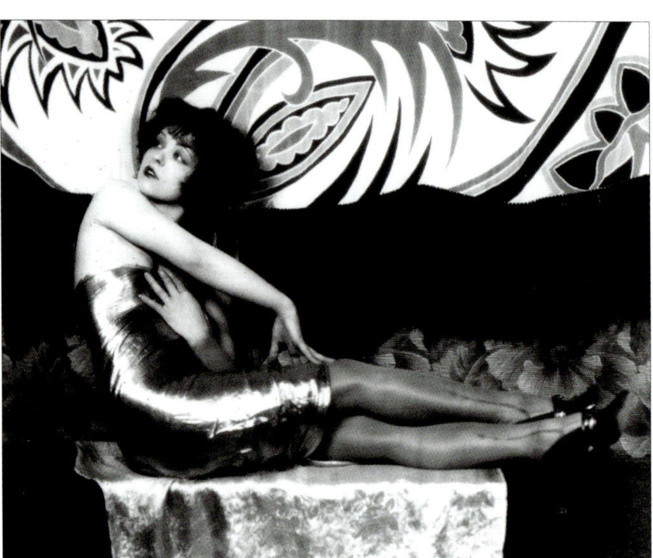

Clara Bow, 1920s

Clara Bow's auburn hair, brown eyes, and rare beauty won the contest. A screen test followed in which she impressed the judges with her remarkable range of emotional expression. She had already taught herself acting techniques in front of a mirror by mimicking parts from films she saw and studied in the cheaper theaters near her home. Many of her initial abilities were linked to imitating the sweet, young, slapstick comedienne Mabel Normand. As part of her contest prize, Bow got to act in *Beyond the Rainbow,* but her part was ultimately cut from the film. Still determined to be a silent-film star, she

eventually went to Hollywood, where she had another screen test with B. P. Schulberg, who was dazzled by her raw ability to laugh and cry almost simultaneously. Her natural brilliance as an actress was inspired by a combination of her horrendous childhood experiences and the intoxicating sense of liberation she felt while acting.

Bow was perfectly cast as the stereotypical easygoing flapper. She could be warm, flirtatious, and vivacious, but her conservative audiences consistently envisioned her as a young woman who was truly good on the inside. Her roles in her first films characterized the youthful, energetic fizgig (a flirtatious gadabout)—a working woman living in the moment in the wild Jazz Age, where she was cast as a manicurist, shopgirl, waitress, usherette, and dance-hall hostess. In *Parisian Love* (1925), she played a ragged and tough apache dancer. She made twenty-two flamboyant flapper films during 1925 and 1926.

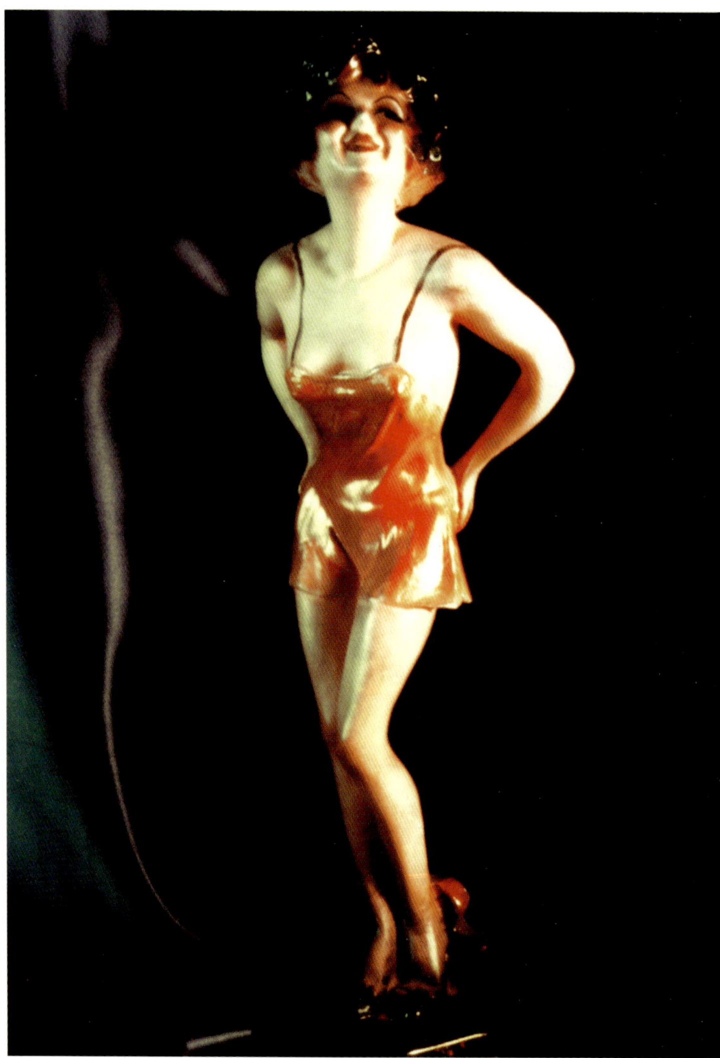

In 1924, June Yates Jenkins was commissioned by the Hollywood Chamber of Commerce to create a figure that promoted the movie industry. This fourteen-and-a-half-inch Clara Bow was his response. The conservative Hollywood Chamber of Commerce found it too risqué, but paid him for his time. He changed her name to "Frenchie" and marketed it to the carnival side shows.[1]

Portraying a woman only as an object of sexual desire was a far different role for her in the 1927 film *It*—"It" being a reference to sex. The film launched Bow as the "It Girl," a name she would never lose. She became Hollywood's number-one sex symbol stereotype for several years and thereby the most sexual woman archetype, eliciting extreme lust in her admirers. *It* opened with a corny title card that read:

> "It" is that quality possessed by some which draws all others with its magnetic force. With "It" you can draw all men, if you are a woman, and all women, if you are a man. "It" can be a quality of the mind, as well as a physical attraction.

That same year, Clara Bow made a nude appearance, lying in a gently flowing stream in the film *Hula*. The beginnings of the Great Depression ended the flapper era, although her role as Hollywood's sex goddess carried over slightly into sound films. Her voice was attractive, but the freedom she enjoyed in silent films, as the mistress of improvised wild gesture, was stymied by having to memorize dialogue.

The romantic comedies of the 1930s that followed looked backward at her outrageous, excessive Jazz Age as partly to blame for the financial crash. Bow, the flapper stereotype and important media icon, suffered unjustly as a scapegoat stereotype for the market crash. She had always been a loner in Hollywood and by then it was easy for the next generation of hungry stars to take advantage of her. Scandals surrounded her, but most were generated by unfair marketing exploitation invented by the tabloids. Clara Bow's exit marked Jean Harlow's entrance as Hollywood's next number-one sex symbol.

Film historians credit Bow with inventing her own mature, silent-screen image, as she had almost no help from her producers or scriptwriters. Using her uncanny instincts, she gave fully to her always improvised depiction of complete openness and to her genuinely offered healthy sexuality. Both assets combined to project a new and vibrant personality into silent films. Bow will always be remembered as the flapper and sex goddess of the mid-1920s silent era.

Mae West aptly caricatured Bow's techniques in the 1930s and used them to her own advantage. Bow's final film was *Hoopla* (1933), in which she portrayed a carnival dancer. Bow married once and died in 1965.

Many of the feminine carnival chalk figures dating from the mid-1920s combine three stereotypical looks into one figure: Clara Bow's flapper image; a Kewpie cuteness derived from Rose O'Neill's Kewpies; and a vamplike coyness, probably from Theda Bara. Many could possibly pass for Clara Bow.

NATIVE AMERICAN

Whoever kills you will think he is offering a service to God.
—JESUS, John: 16:2

Ralph Lemkin, a Holocaust survivor, coined the term "genocide" in his book *Axis Rule in Occupied Europe*, published in 1944. Prior to that, the only English words vaguely close to its definition were "extinction" or "massacre." Genocide is the coordinated and planned annihilation of a national, religious, or racial group by a variety of actions aimed at undermining the foundations essential to the survival of that group. In 1946, the United Nations General Assembly defined genocide as the denial of the right of existence to entire human groups.

While his ship the *Niña* (a long-range military transport vehicle) passed the Azores on March 4, 1493, Christopher Columbus, the ex-trader in African slaves turned explorer, finished his written description of the sights he had seen during his first voyage to the New World. Of the island he called La Spañola (Haiti and the Dominican Republic), he wrote:

> La Spañola is marvelous, the sierras and the mountains and the plains and the meadows and the lands are so beautiful and rich for planting and sowing, and for livestock of every sort, and for building towns and villages. The harbors of the sea are such as you could not believe it without seeing them; and so the rivers, many and great, and good streams, the most of which bear gold.[1]

Of the native people he had come upon he wrote:

> The people of this island and of all the other islands which I have found and seen, or have not seen, all go naked, men and women, as their mothers bore them, except that some women cover one place only with the leaf of a plant or a net of cotton which they make for that purpose. They have no iron or steel or weapons, nor are they capable of using them, although they are well built people of handsome stature, because they are wondrous timid . . . Of anything they have, if you ask them for it they never say no; rather they invite the person to share it, and show as much love as if they were giving their hearts; and whether the things be of value or of small price, at once they are content with whatever little thing of whatever kind may be given them.[2]

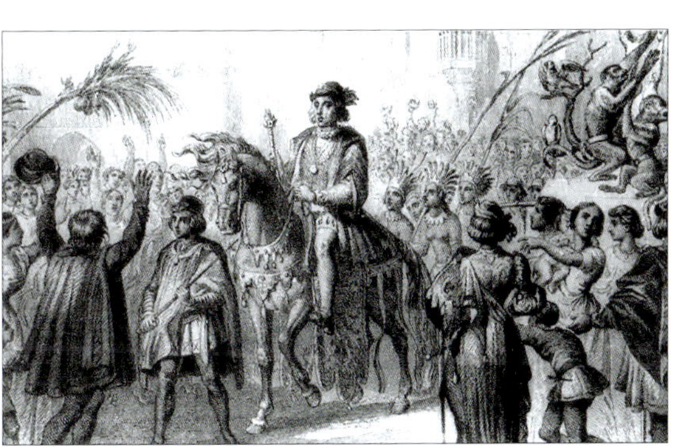

Columbus' return to Spain with natives and monkeys, etching, artist unknown

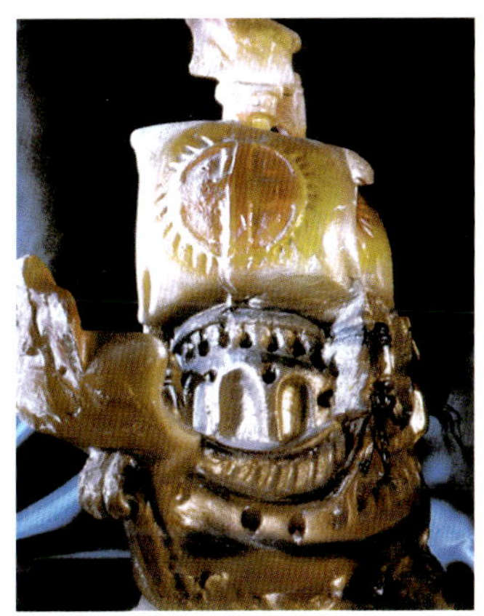

Santa Maria carnival chalk prize

Columbus left and returned in 1494 with an entourage of seventeen ships and 1,200 armed soldiers, sailors, and colonists (a military force). More passengers, including sheep, cattle, and pigs, were added when they stopped at the Canary Islands. His ships arrived on the island coasts of what was to be named Hispaniola. It has been estimated that approximately 8 million natives populated the islands. Whenever the Spanish arrived at a new location in the New World, a cross was driven into the earth and the dark document, the *requerimiento*, was read. It stated:

> I certify to you that, with the help of God, we shall power-
> fully enter into your country and shall make war against
> you in all ways and manners that we can, and shall subject
> you to the yoke and obedience of the Church and shall
> make slaves of them, and as such shall sell and dispose of
> them as Their Highnesses may command. And we shall take
> your goods, and shall do you all the mischief and damage
> that we can, as to vassals who do not obey and refuse to
> receive their lord and resist and contradict him.[3]

Wherever the *requerimiento* was read, whether the island natives understood it or not, the destruction commenced. In just two years, approximately 4 million of Hispaniola's natives died from influenza, probably brought in as swine flu. Those who did not die of disease perished by the sword, or the deadly crossbow, or by trained packs of dreaded attack dogs that were fed on human entrails. Columbus set up a tribute system whereby every adult native was ordered to deliver a certain amount of gold to Columbus's authorities every three months. Each native was presented a token to wear around his neck as proof that the gold had been properly delivered. Anyone found without the appropriate numbers of tokens had his or her hands cut off. Suffice it to say that the cutting off of hands became an everyday practice. Forty years later, almost all of the island's natives were dead. Many of the natives who did not want to be slaves to Columbus's cruelty committed suicide. Anyone wishing to read about the sickening Spanish, Portuguese, British, French, and post–Revolutionary War American brutality should see David Stannard's *American Holocaust* (and it's still happening).

The Spanish continued their search for gold and in 1525, led by Cortez, pushed inland into Mexico. The next to die or become enslaved were the estimated 25 million Native Americans in Mexico. The Spanish moved south in the latter half of the sixteenth century, invading South America, and then trampled far northward into lands that would later be named Virginia, New Mexico, and California. When the Native Americans at Acoma Pueblo defied Oñate, the penalty was either death or having one foot cut off; those who remained alive were sentenced to twenty years of slavery. (In the 1990s, a foot was symbolically cut off a towering bronze statue of Oñate on horseback, in a small town north of Santa Fe. The perpetrators were not found, and it was more than a kid's prank.) To build the Catholic Church at Acoma, the enslaved Native Americans were forced to carry, from a site twenty miles away, huge logs that were to act as beams spanning the church's ceiling. If a log accidentally touched the ground, it was cast aside, as it was now considered defiled and unholy; a new one was cut and the carrying process was started over again.

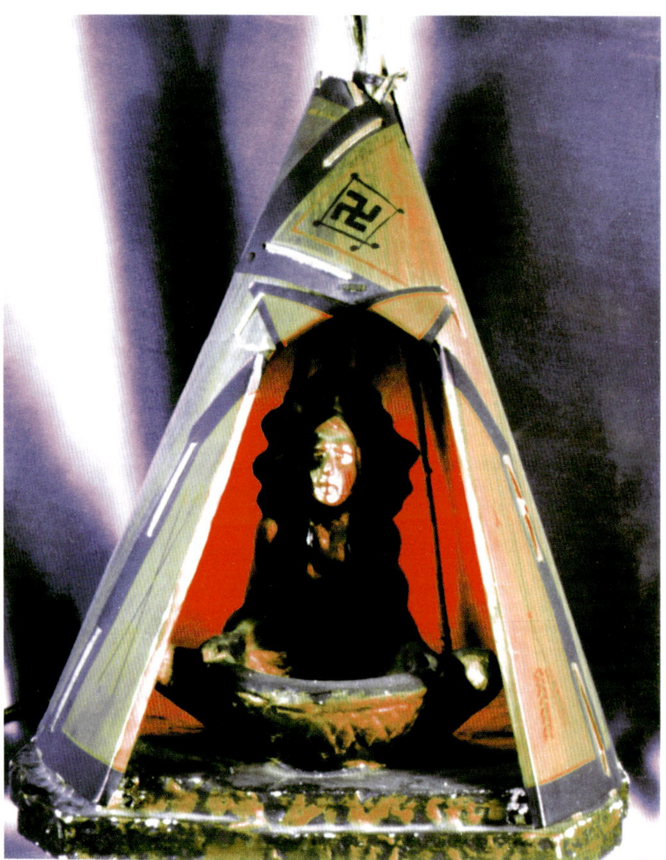

Tepee and Native American sixteen-inch carnival chalk lamp prize

The British (who considered themselves to be the most civilized people on earth) landed at Jamestown in 1607 and, in 1620 the Puritans landed at Plymouth Rock. Little by little, through disease (spread both naturally and through biological warfare—the Europeans were mostly immune to smallpox) or the sword, the gun, and dishonest treaties, almost all of North America's native peoples living on the eastern seaboard were ultimately destroyed. Stannard explains how this happened:

> The European habit of indiscriminately killing women and
> children when engaged in hostilities with the natives of
> the Americas was more than an atrocity. It was flatly and
> intentionally genocidal. For no population can survive
> if its women and children are destroyed . . . America's
> revered founding fathers were themselves activists in the
> anti–Native American genocide. George Washington, in
> 1779, instructed Major General John Sullivan to attack the
> Iroquois and "lay waste all the settlements around . . . that
> the country may not be merely overrun but destroyed," urg-
> ing General Sullivan not to "listen to any overture of peace
> before the total ruin of their settlements is effected."
>
> . . . Or Thomas Jefferson, for example, who in 1807
> instructed his Secretary of War . . . "if ever we are
> constrained to lift the hatchet against any tribe, we will
> never lay it down till that tribe is exterminated, or is driven
> beyond the Mississippi, in war they will kill some of us, we
> shall destroy all of them."[4]

Andrew Jackson taught his soldiers to slice off and save the noses of their Native American victims. He also commanded that they kill women and children and bragged, "I have on occasion preserved the scalps of my killed . . . the whole Cherokee Nation ought to be scourged." [5]

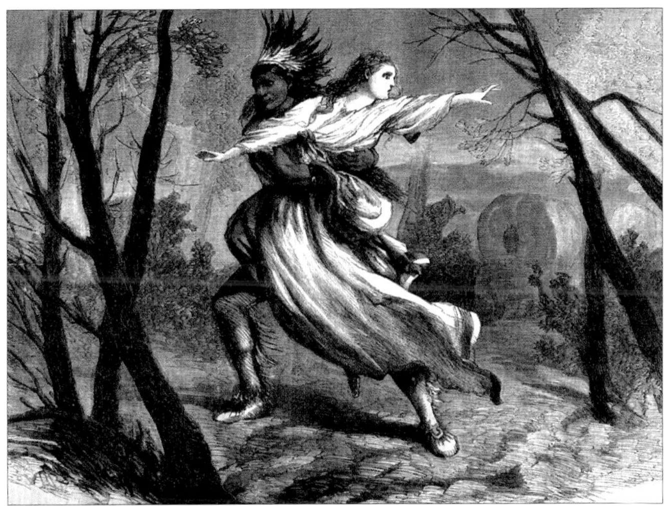

"The Scream," *Frank Leslie's Boys' and Girls' Weekly*, March 25, 1871

Stannard continues:

Consider the impact of some of the worst instances of modern warfare. General Douglas Haig sent his British troops into combat with the Germans at the Battle of the Somme . . . By the time that battle had finally ended, Haig lost 420,000 men . . . Yet between 1911 and 1921, Britain's population increased by about two million people . . . Or take Japan. Between 1940 and 1950, despite the frenzy of war in the Pacific, capped by the nuclear destruction of Hiroshima and Nagasaki, the population of Japan increased by almost 14 percent. The reason these populations were able to increase, despite massive military damage, was that a greatly disproportionate ratio of men to women and children was being killed. [6]

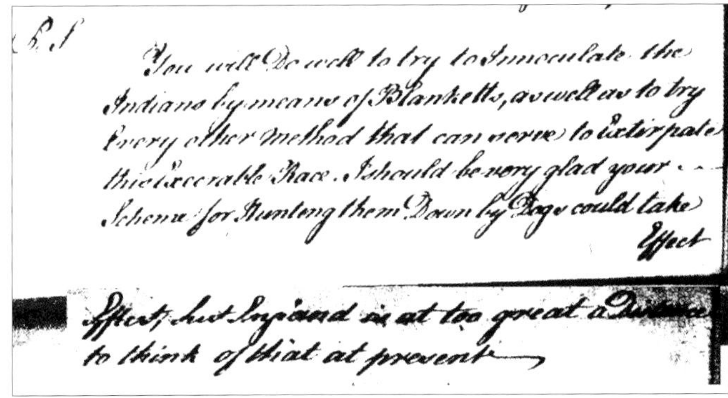

Sir Jeffrey Amherst, letter to Colonel Henry Bouquet, July 16, 1763: "P.S. You will Do well to try to Innoculate the Indians by means of Blankets, as well as to try Every other method that can serve to Extirpate this Execrable Race. I should be very glad your Scheme for Hunting them Down by Dogs could take Effect, but England is at too great a Distance to think of that at present."

The British, before the Revolutionary War, were not above using biological warfare. In a letter dated July 13, 1763, written to Sir Jeffrey Amherst, commander in chief of the British forces in America, Colonel Henry Bouquet suggested, in a postscript, the distribution of blankets to "innoculate [*sic*] the Indians." [7] On July 16, 1763, Amherst's return letter to

Bouquet suggested grinding the scabs of smallpox pustules into blankets that were to be distributed among disaffected tribes of Native Americans, and in a postscript he also suggested trying "Every other method that can serve to Extirpate this Execrable Race." [8]

At the end of the Revolutionary War, George Washington suggested that the tribes that helped fight against the British should be given an inviolate place in the West, where colonizers would never be allowed to cross (a momentary guilt removal archetype).

The horrific European invasion created a five-century genocide throughout both North and South America. It is estimated that 100 million natives were killed, which was 95 to 98 percent of the native population. Many tribes became extinct. The almost complete annihilation of the Native Americans from the Americas was the most massive act of genocide in the history of the world. Yet few Americans knew of these numbers and American history, as taught in schools, never described this immense loss of native life as genocide. Nor does it now. Even as late as 1890, a week and a half before the Massacre at Wounded Knee, the editor of the *Aberdeen Saturday Pioneer* in South Dakota, whose was none other than L. Frank Baum, the "gentle" author of *The Wizard of Oz*, urged:

The nobility of the redskin is extinguished, and what few are left are a pack of whining curs who lick the hand that smites them. The Whites, by law of conquest, by justice of civilization, are masters of the American continent, and the best safety of the frontier will be secured by the total annihilation of the few remaining Indians. Why not annihilation? Their glory has fled, their spirit broken, their manhood effaced; better that they should die than live the miserable wretches that they are. [9]

Four days after the Massacre at Wounded Knee, Baum editorialized: "we had better, in order to protect our civilization, follow it up . . . and wipe these untamed and untamable creatures from the face of the earth." [10]

Rebecca Blevins Faery in her book *Cartographies of Desire* [11] shows that when first described, Native Americans were depicted as white skinned; as the centuries of racist propagandism and annihilation wore on, their stereotypical skin coloring grew darker and darker, so that by the 1900s, Native Americans were shown to be dark reddish brown. With this disturbing historical backdrop, it is not surprising that Native Americans during the centuries of direct confrontation were stereotyped as "redskins." They were powerful archetypes of the hostile brethren, eliciting fear of the unknown. Only a rare few people during that time logically saw Native Americans for their resourcefulness, creativity, bravery, and beauty, eliciting admiration. After their civilizations were destroyed, Native Americans became fantasized and were archetypal symbols for feeling guilt release. Then, and only then, did their headdresses, clothing, and tepees become idealized and romanticized American icons.

From the 1930s to the 1940s, there were about ten carnival chalk prizes of Native Americans and ten varieties of Columbus's ship; some were fashioned as carnival chalkware prize lamps. Only a few of these carnival prizes are pictured. One was a tepee light with a Native American squatting inside.

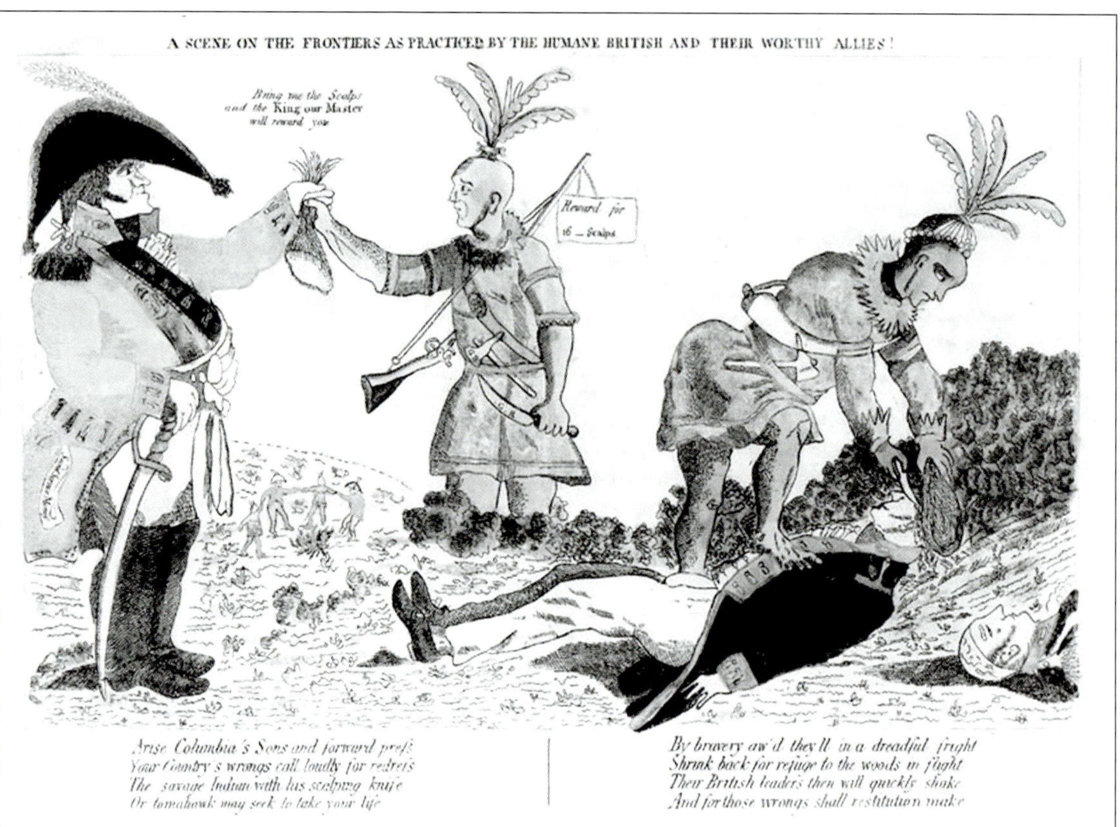

"A Scene on the Frontiers as Practiced by the Humane British and Their Worthy Allies," etching and watercolor William Charles, Philadelphia, 1812. Pictures like this promoted the archetypal feeling of fear: two enemy forces rampaging the young United States. A fat, rich British soldier is paying heathen Native Americans for scalps of Americans. The image was meant to stir up anti-British sentiment for starting the War of 1812 (anti-Native-American sentiment was always high—insinuating that heathen could be paid money or traded weapons for killing— 16 scalps equalled 1 gun). Scalps were an archetypal motif prize (a souvenir) for the hero in battle for feeling pride and excitement in victory. Collection: Library of Congress

A Native American version of the swastika (used centuries before Hitler's time by Native Americans) is printed on the tepee's paper shade, although it's not Hitler's form.

Little Beaver (certainly a questionable name) was the helpful Native American sidekick of the 1940s cowboy Red Ryder. So popular was Red Ryder in films, comics, and on the radio, that Little Beaver eventually had his own comic published by Dell from January 1949 until January 1958. Little Beaver was fantasized and became the white man's perfect little brave. A more accurate name may have been Little Ghost, reminiscent of the phantoms alluded to in four lines of James Fenimore Cooper's poem *The Last of the Mohicans* (1826):

Gone from the prairie, the forest, the stream.
Like the bodiless phantoms that people a dream;
Like the sparkes that round the cataract play,
Like the mists of the mountain, they've passed away.

As early as 1827, the Capitol in Washington, D.C., showcased art that represented the Native American as defeated in works such as Enrico Causici's *The Conflict of Daniel Boone* and, later, in Thomas Crawford's *Progress of Civilization* (1850), which depicted a seated Native American with his head heavily in hand, defeated and despondent.

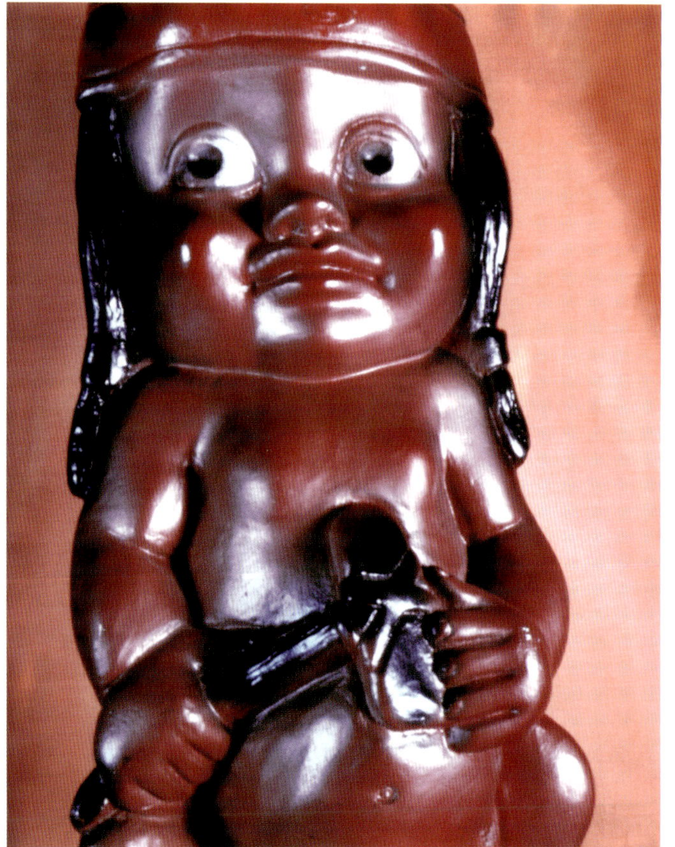
Little Beaver thirteen-inch carnival chalk prize

Devil

If I said that God did not send me, I should condemn myself; truly God did send me.
—JOAN OF ARC, statement at her trial, Marina Warner, *Joan of Arc*

I'm glad you like my Catherine. I like her too. She ruled thirty million people and had three thousand lovers. I do the best I can in two hours.
—MAE WEST, After her performance in *Catherine the Great*, speech from the stage

It is no good casting out devils. They belong to us, we must accept them and be at peace with them.
—D. H. LAWRENCE, *The Reality of Peace*

Throughout the centuries, Christianity has stereotyped as an Antichrist not only the devil but also social activists such as Mae West. The church points its accusing finger at those who plead for intelligence, reason, kindliness, and personal optimism for creative living and shun its self-flagellating sinner pessimism.

Few people are aware that the devil has not always been the Antichrist. Prior to the hierarchy of the church, very early Christians believed that devils possessed beneficent magic, and avowed that devils were known to restore health to the sick, teach the mysteries of the stars, and make people witty. (Leading us to wonder at whose altars the likes of Louise Brooks, Will Rogers, and Mark Twain might have knelt.) In Judeo-Christian tradition, diabolic acts were attributed to God, as great destruction by storms, earthquakes, tsunamis, etc., which are still commonly referred to as "acts of God."[1]

Later, when the church became a well-organized institution, it established the devil as a paradigm for evil. The Bible's scribes developed a hierarchal structure in which the devil functioned as the administrator, planner, head of job placement, chief warden, keeper of the darkness, and stoker of the fires in Hell. God functioned as administrator and keeper of the light in Heaven. In *The Woman's Encyclopedia of Myths and Secrets* Barbara G. Walker states:

> No Christian was permitted to disbelieve in the devil. His credibility rested on the same foundation as that of God. Indeed, the very concept of salvation depended on the devil. If there had been no Tempter, there was no original sin, no fall, no hell, no need of a redeemer or a church.[2]

Once a person believed in the devil, it was second nature to project that devil or Satan onto others. In *The Origin of Satan* Elaine Pagels explains Satan as a stereotype for "others":

I invite you to consider Satan as a reflection of how we perceive ourselves and those we call "others." Satan has, after all, made a kind of profession out of being the "other"; and so Satan defines negatively what we think of as human. The social and cultural practice of defining certain people as "others" in relation to one's group may be, of course, as old as humanity itself.[3]

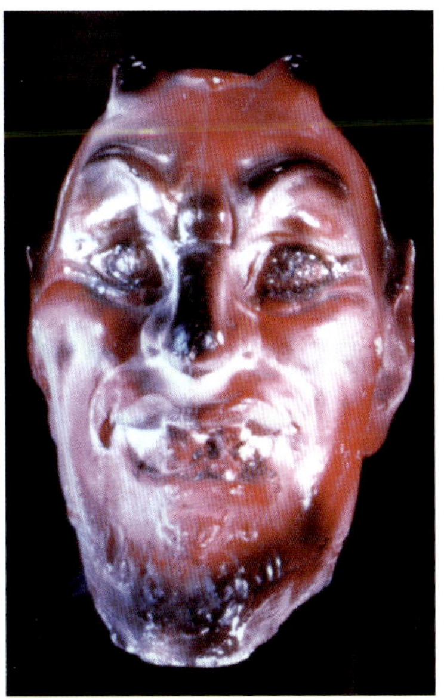

Devil seven-inch carnival chalk prize

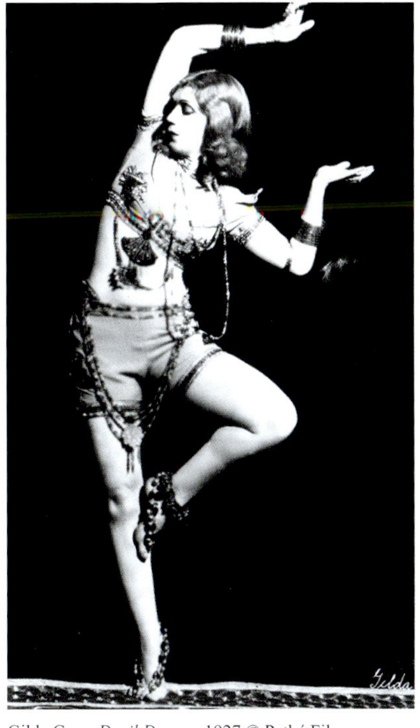

Gilda Gray, *Devil Dancer*, 1927 © Pathé Films

For a generalized feeling of hell, most Christians from the 1400s onward sought the popular *Divina Commedia* by Dante Alighieri. The *Catholic Encyclopedia* defines the poem *Divina Commedia* as:

> an allegory of human life, in the form of a vision of the world beyond the grave, written avowedly with the object of converting a corrupt society to righteousness: "to remove those living in this life from the state of misery, and lead them to the state of felicity." It is composed of a hundred cantos, written in the measure known as terza rima, with its normally hendecasyllabic lines and closely linked rhymes, which Dante so modified from the popular poetry of his day that it may be regarded as his own invention. He is relating, nearly twenty years after the event, a vision which was granted to him (for his own salvation when leading a sinful life) during the year of jubilee, 1300, in which for seven days (beginning on the morning of Good Friday) he passed through hell, purgatory, and paradise, spoke with the souls in each realm, and heard what the Providence of God had in store for himself and the world. The framework of the poem presents the dual scheme of the "De Monarchiâ" transfigured. Virgil, representing human philosophy acting in accordance with the moral and intellectual virtues, guides Dante by the light of natural reason from the dark wood of alienation from God (where the beasts of lust, pride, and avarice drive man back from ascending the Mountain of the Lord), through hell and purgatory to the earthly paradise, the state of temporal felicity, when spiritual liberty has been regained by the purgatorial pains. Beatrice, representing Divine philosophy illuminated by revelation, leads him

thence, up through the nine moving heavens of intellectual preparation, into the true paradise, the spaceless and timeless empyrean, in which the blessedness of eternal life is found in the fruition of the sight of God. There her place is taken by St. Bernard, type of the loving contemplation in which the eternal life of the soul consists, who commends him to the Blessed Virgin, at whose intercession he obtains a foretaste of the Beatific Vision, the poem closing with all powers of knowing and loving fulfilled and consumed in the union of the understanding with the Divine Essence, the will made one with the Divine Will, "the Love that moves the sun and the other stars."[4]

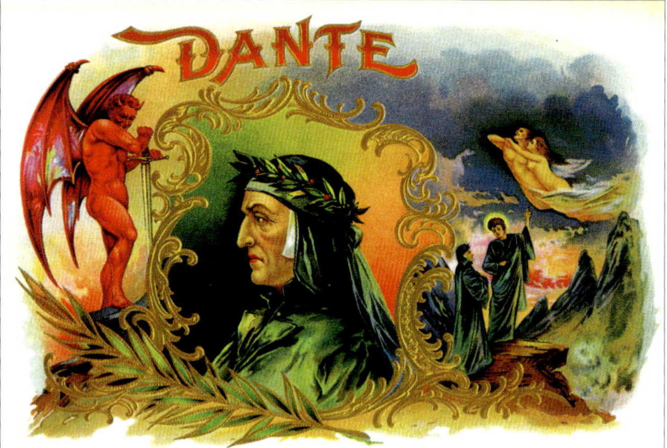

Dante, cigar box label, circa early 1900s

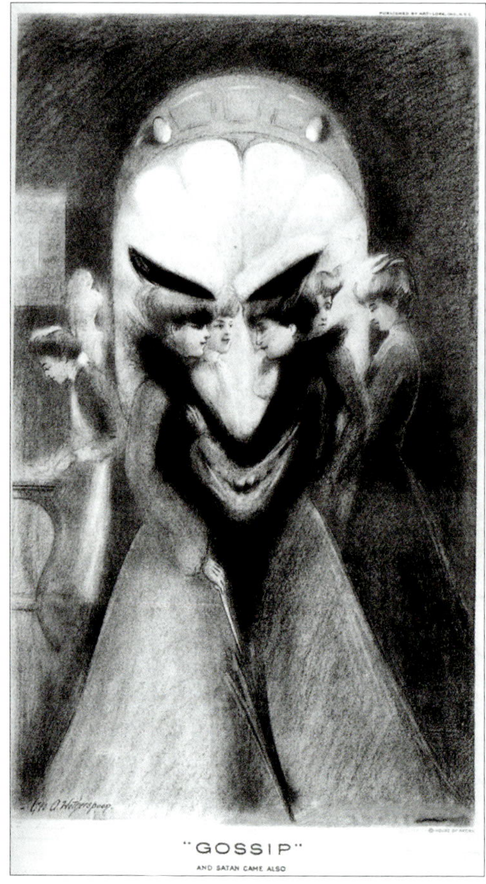

Gossip and Satan Came Also, illustration G. A. Wotherspoon, House of Art, 1900

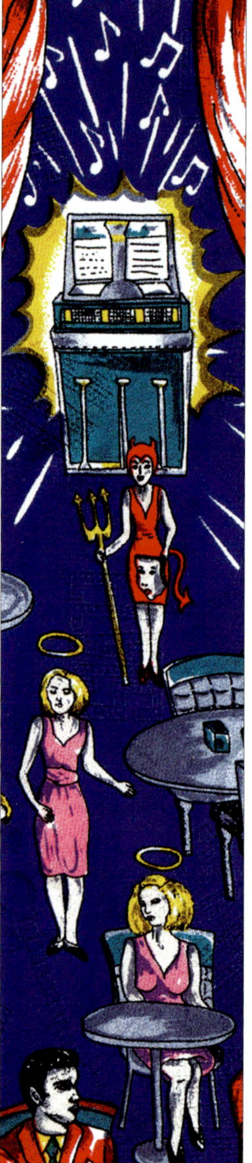

"Devil in Disguise," necktie, detail, 1950s

A more inventive image of hell can be found in the phantasmic paintings by Hieronymus Bosch. Few realized that heaven and hell could be states of mind, as propounded by the practitioner of deep-trance meditation Emanuel Swedenborg.

Early American Puritan ministers said the devil was a metaphor for the demons within all people which, when followed, created sin. The devil's master plan was to draw victims either into despair, so they would lose hope in their own salvation, or into carnal security, a state wherein sinners would follow the worldly path to hell but, at the same time, imagine that they were good people on the pathway to heaven. The latter state, carnal security, was thought to describe the condition of the vast majority of human beings. The devil would appear as an angel of light, presenting sins as good things or at least as innocuous trifles and gradually luring people deeper into sin, until the sins finally became habitual. To combat such a formidable foe, Puritan ministers insisted that Christians must have a clear understanding of the devil's mode of operation and of the precariousness of their situation. They must, above all, recognize that they are sinners and that they are wholly corrupt and unable to resist the devil without God's grace and spirit. They must also expect to be spiritually assaulted by the devil anywhere and everywhere. The ministers depicted the life of a Christian as warfare, a relentless battle against the devil, the world, and sins of the flesh. Although such a life of struggle brought anguish of mind, it also brought comfort and assurance of salvation. The experience of spiritual turmoil was a sign of special selection; only those with God's grace could fathom the depth of their own sin or discern the temptations of the devil. Simplistic puritanical lessons were promoted, as in this poem from *Mother Goose Rhymes,* still in print in a readily available 1898 edition:

> When I was a little boy, I had but little wit,
> It is some time ago, and I've no more yet;
> Nor ever, ever shall, until that I die,
> For the longer I live, the more fool am I.

It's rather simplistic to say that there is no such thing as a protagonist without an antagonist. Still, a world free of antagonists is the utopian scheme many people hope for and express through lamentations for peace. A powerful enemy is the best friend a politician, or an evangelist, can have. For them enemies are here to stay. The notion of an enemy provides power control over large groups of people. Nations constantly seek enemies for just this reason, but are often forced to change enemies as one or the other is overcome and peace befalls them. Christianity sidesteps the problem of constantly finding new enemies through the rather simple device of owning only one extremely powerful enemy that can never be seen and shows its face only to those who accept its existence. After all, the word devil is not far from the word evil.

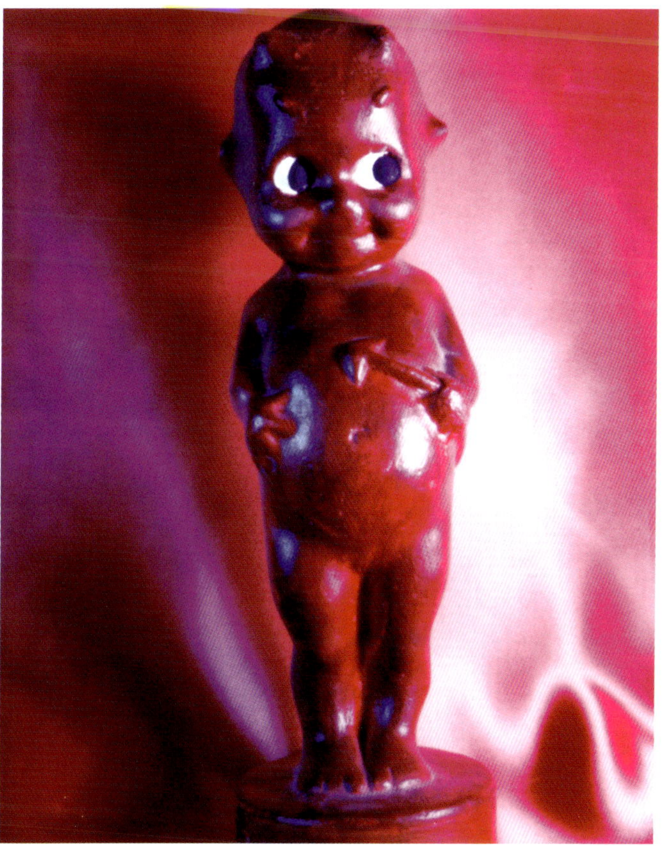

Kewpie Red Devil ten-inch carnival chalk prize. Combining a Kewpie with a devil would have made Rose O'Neill aghast; her Kewpie image was one that symbolized feelings of joy and love, whereas this red devil symbolized feelings of trickery and deceit.

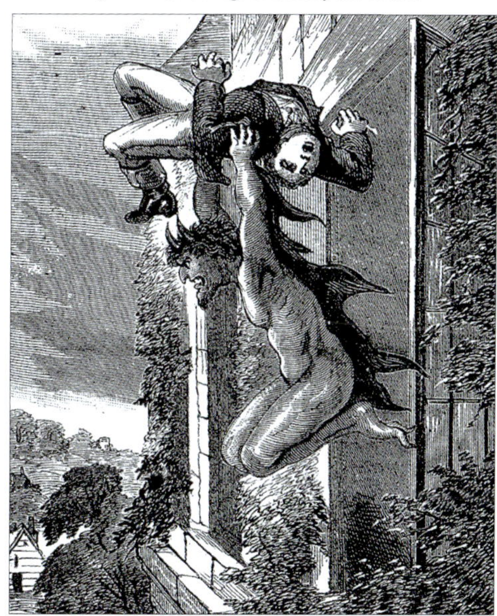

"The Window Shivered as Spring-Heeled Jack Leaped Bodily Through it." *Spring-Heeled Jack, the Terror of London,* detail of anonymous cartoon, circa 1860s when Spring-Heeled Jack was thought to have rampaged innocents throughout London.

Hula Girl

With bare breasts, painted nipples, and swaying grass skirt, the hula girl's charms suggested an exotic come-hither to carnivalgoers, and the carnival chalk prize of her was extremely popular in the 1930s and 1940s. She represented an archetypal symbol for feelings of exotic escapism for those prizewinners who selected her from the shelves of glittering trophies. Escapism was a much-needed instinctive response to the horrors of economic loss caused by the Great Depression. The hula girl was sex in the natural, in the same way that *National Geographic* magazines used in-the-buff, dark-skinned natives to stir up sexual desire within a country boy's naïveté—a boy gratified that there was at least one place on Earth where the sight of a partially nude woman was free for the viewing, even if it was racist (sex helped sell the magazine in those days). This hula girl was for male hedonists whose archetypal desires were aimed toward pleasure, not pain: escape, not involvement. Paul Gauguin fulfilled this same escapist ideal when he left Paris and moved to Tahiti to paint in its primitive, unspoiled, erotically charged setting, with natural young vahinés. (Adolescent girls became infected with syphilis from him—he did not tell them of his prior infection.)

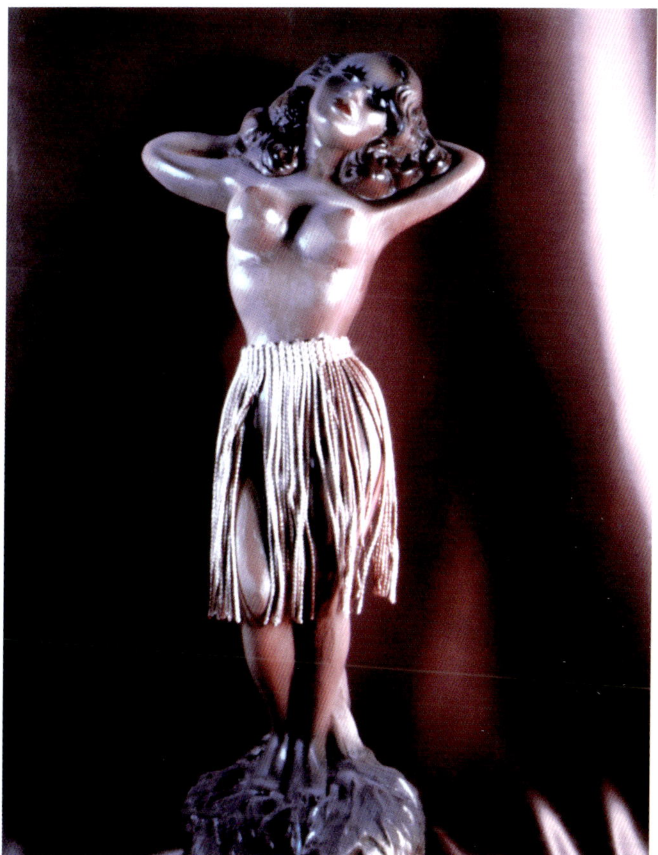

Hula Girl thirteen-inch carnival chalk prize, many varieties were available between 1930 and 1950

The American escapists who chose the hula girl prize were also happily removing themselves from the cultural remnants of puritanism in America, whether they knew it or not. The puritan ethic of living simply, working hard, and being thrifty also included hostility toward many forms of pleasure, particularly sexual delights. The Puritans literal belief in the Bible told them that Jesus promised salvation only to those who were filled with gloom, as in Luke 6:21: "Blessed are ye that weep now: for ye shall laugh." (In Luke 6:25, Jesus said it again, "Woe unto you that laugh now! For ye shall mourn and weep.") Laughing in this life caused eternal damnation of one's soul, promoting the ascetic philosophy "wait until the afterlife, then there will be fun" (causing one to wonder what the Puritan's notion of heavenly fun might be). Suffering was the required path. Those who devoutly followed it knew right from wrong, good from evil, and relentlessly flogged the rest of the world for not understanding the difference.

John Calvin was the founder of Puritanism and the creator of the puritan ethic. His theocracy, established in sixteenth-century Geneva, Switzerland, prohibited dancing, drinking, card playing, ribaldry, fashionable clothes, and many other amusements. Calvinism required religious instruction, public fasting, austere living, and an evening curfew. Its doctrine was severe beyond imagining. Calvinists beheaded adulterers, burned Puritan dissenters at the stake, and even beheaded children who struck their fathers. The Puritans gained temporary control in England and imposed their ruthless beliefs on English society. They banned all manner of entertainments, closed theaters, and prescribed the death penalty for sex outside marriage. Oliver Cromwell's Bible-carrying, hymn-singing Puritan army was notorious for slaughtering Anglicans in England and Catholics in Ireland. This harsh and extremely dogmatic society was soon to be injected into the soil of another continent and become the seed that would thrive and blossom into the United States of America.

The Puritans who landed at Plymouth Rock in 1620 emphasized that the human body was inherently impure and depraved. They shared a deep-seated suspicion of any type of pleasure, particularly those pleasures associated with sex. Sex was to be suffered through in marriage once or twice a year, and then only as absolutely needed for procreation. Puritans in Massachusetts set up a religious state and deviation from basic tenets resulted in flogging, pillorying, hanging, banishment, having one's ears cut off, or having one's tongue bored through with a hot iron. They had a law, based on Leviticus 20:9 from the Old Testament, which stated that a child who cursed his or her parent was to be put to death. Puritans were responsible for the Salem witch trials, which led to twenty people being executed and 150 imprisoned after confessing under torture to such acts as flying through the air to attend witch gatherings, partaking of witch sacraments, signing a book presented by the devil, and receiving Satanic baptism. The hardships of life in the American wilderness, combined with the austere aspects of Puritanism, made life especially difficult for Pilgrim mothers—they had to endure not only everything that the Pilgrim fathers suffered but also the righteous Pilgrim fathers as well. What difficulties, what traumas, lay in store for a child born to a Puritan household?

By contrast, the ancient Polynesians celebrated not only the mysteries of their heritage and existence but also the tastes and joys of life. Hawaiian religious dances were sacred rituals known as *ha'a*, performed only by men inside specific temples. The public form of dance known as hula was enjoyed by all members of Polynesian society. It provided a vehicle for looking back at the accomplishments of their ancient ancestors through its movements, motions, and chants. The hula rhythm was precipitated by lovely natural sounds and danced to thrumming drums, rattling gourds, and sounds of the surf. Traditionally the hand was extended at shoulder height, the head was bowed, and one bare foot was placed at a right angle to the instep of the other. *Lehua* flowers adorned the hair, while leis, consisting of flowers decorously strung together, were draped around the shoulders. *Ti* leaves swung from the waist to partly reveal the hips and legs. Legend held that Laka, goddess of the hula, gave birth to the dance on Molokai at a very sacred place in Ka'ana. The motions danced and expressed in the hula embody symbolically potent representations: a circular motion with the hands depicts spiritual continuity; the triangle depicts a Hawaiian value called *Lokahi*, a balance between humanity, nature, and God; diamond shapes are the eyes of the gods; and fingers wafting in front of the eyes are a depiction of the past, indicating ancestors who still looked upon them and guided them in their present life.

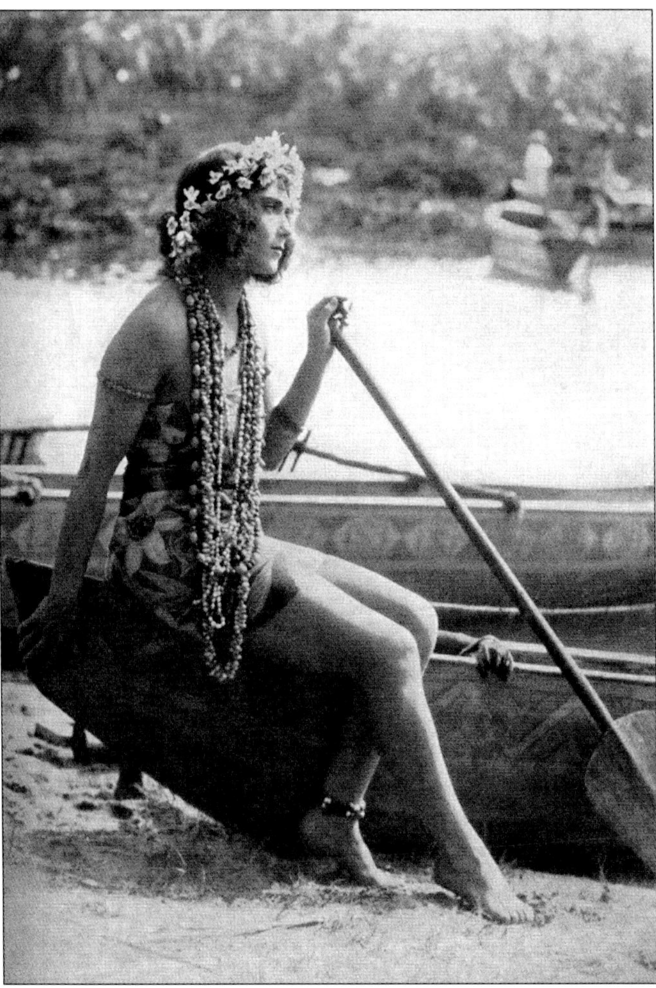

Gilda Gray, *Aloma of the South Seas*, book, photographic illustration from the film, 1926
© Grosset & Dunlap

British explorer Captain James Cook discovered the Hawaiian Islands in 1778 and named them Sandwich Islands, after Britain's Earl of Sandwich. A year later, Cook was killed in a dispute at Kealakekua Bay near Kona. That same year, a number of Chinese sailors jumped ship and were the first Chinese to land on the islands. Protestant missionaries arrived from New England in 1820 aboard the *Thaddeus*. The first sight of the hula dances shocked the staid Protestant missionaries. They remonstrated and complained that the dancers were blasphemous, lascivious, and depraved. Hawaii's puppet queen Ka'ahumanu was forced, by the same missionaries, to suppress the hula dance in the 1830s, but the *ha'a* continued to be performed secretly in remote village temples.

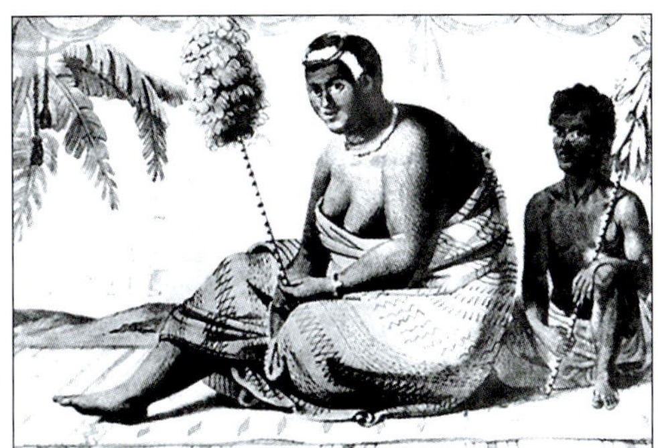

Queen Ka'ahumanu

King Kalakaua, known as the "Merrie Monarch," defied prohibitions and gave his royal sanction to the hula in the 1870s in an effort to revive his culture. He readily perceived that Hawaiian culture was dying, as were native Hawaiians: 90 percent of the natives had died from disease and cultural change which accompanied the evangelical imperialists. Colonial powers from America forced Queen Liliuokalani to surrender the kingdom to the United States in 1893. By 1898 Hawaii was annexed to the United States and only 45,000 of its original natives were still alive.

The first nonstop air flights from the U.S. mainland to Honolulu began in 1927, increasing tourism. American tourists mistakenly thought, and still think, that the hula is a welcoming dance performed in their honor.

Hollywood has always loved to use the hula as its pseudo-native/sexy-cheesy performance to create the South Seas stereotype. Some of the early mainstream Hollywood hula attractions were Gilda Gray in the silent film *Aloma of the South Seas* (1926) and Clara Bow in the silent romantic comedy *Hula* (1927). Then came the natural bare-breasted Reri, Hollywood's most authentic French-Polynesian hula dancer, in her only film, *Tabu* (1931). Florenz Ziegfeld put her in his Follies, but she quickly returned to Tahiti to escape and remain undiscovered. Betty Boop, the animated cartoon sex symbol, danced the hula-shimmy in *Betty Boop's Bamboo Isle* (1932) wearing only a lei and a grass skirt. The lei strategically covered her nipples but showed her breasts and cleavage. In 1941, Dorothy Lamour starred in a remake of *Aloma of the South Seas*, using the stereotypical sarong-clad image. Betty Grable Broadwayized it in *Sing Me a Song of the Islands* (1942).

The Flapper (1918-1930)

Resolved, that the women of this nation in 1876, have greater cause for discontent, rebellion and revolution than the men of 1776.
—Susan B. Anthony

I had no idea of originating an American flapper when I first began to write. I simply took girls whom I knew very well and, because they interested me as unique human beings, I used them for my heroines.
—F. Scott Fitzgerald

Propelled by the liberating Armistice Day of World War I, a newfound media image, the Jazz Age, and most of all women's right to vote, the young and restless American woman was for the first time free to do whatever she wished. The Gibson girl was a has-been, meant for the older generation. Resounding winds of a new femininity swept throughout America. Upon its wings, the flapper era was born. The word "flapper" was originally a British expression for pre-debutantes. Finally, the flapper had removed the centuries-old archetypal shackles, mentioned only too clearly in Genesis 3:16: "Unto the woman he said, I will greatly multiply thy sorrow and thy conception; in sorrow thou shall bring forth children: and thy desire shall be to thy husband, and he shall rule over thee."

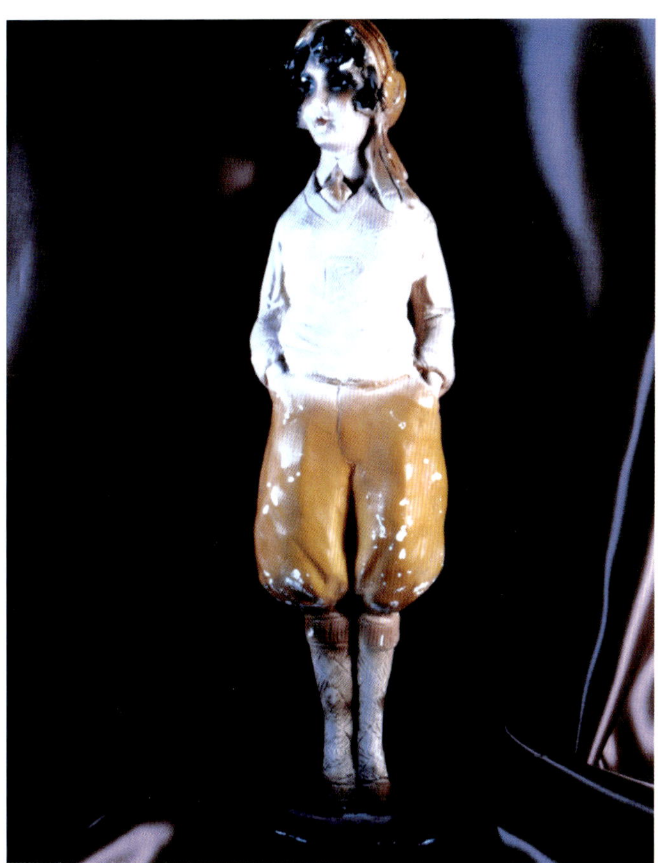

Ruth fifteen-and-one-half-inch flapper carnival chalk prize © June Yates Jenkins

As a stereotype, the flapper represented a liberated woman. An end to war. An end to traditions. Possibly even an end to the patriarchal idea that cars were made for men only. (Some early cars had warnings placed on the steering wheel that read "For men and boys only" because cars were hard to crank, there was no power steering, and the roads had many ruts—thus the stereotype of women as bad drivers was born.) Fashions encouraged a wilder look. Arms and legs could actually be exposed. Clothes were baggy. Hair could be short. Young women could be sexually brazen. They wore makeup. A few years earlier Theda Bara had unlocked Pandora's cosmetic box, which was never to be closed again. Bruce Bliven wrote in *The New Republic* in December 1925:

> . . . let us take a look at the young person as she strolls across the lawn of her parents' suburban home, having just put the car away after driving sixty miles in two hours. She is, for one thing, a very pretty girl. Beauty is the fashion in 1925. She is frankly, heavily made up, not to imitate nature, but for an altogether artificial effect—pallor mortis, poisonously scarlet lips, richly ringed eyes—the latter looking not so much debauched (which is the intention) as diabetic. Her walk duplicates the swagger supposed by innocent America to go with the female half of a Paris Apache dance. And there are, finally, her clothes . . . underwear—one piece, light, exceedingly brief but roomy. Her dress, as you can't possibly help knowing if you have even one good eye, and get around at all outside the Old People's Home, is also brief. It is cut low where it might be high, and vice versa. The skirt comes just an inch below her knees, overlapping by a faint fraction her rolled and twisted stockings. The idea is that when she walks in a bit of a breeze, you shall now and then observe the knee (which is not rouged—that's just newspaper talk) but always in an accidental, Venus-surprised-at-the-bath sort of way . . .
>
> The corset is as dead as the dodo's grandfather; no feeble publicity pipings by the manufacturers, or calling it a "clasp around" will enable it, as Jane says, to "do a Lazarus." The petticoat is even more defunct. Not even a snicker can be raised by telling Jane that once the nation was shattered to its foundations by the shadow-skirt. The brassiere has been abandoned, since 1924. While stockings are usually worn, they are not a sine-qua-nothing-doing. In hot weather Jane reserves the right to discard them, just as all the chorus girls did in 1923.

nude chorus girl. When Earl Carroll's play *Vanities* premiered in New York in 1923, rows of chorus girls could be seen clearly naked from the waist up amid bedizened costumes and lavish sets. His play was a measure of titillating sexuality. Erich von Stroheim's 1925 silent-film operetta, *The Merry Widow*, featured seminude musicians, and that same year on Broadway, only fig leaves were worn onstage. On February 9, 1926, police arrested the entire cast in Edouard Bourdet's *The Captive*, a story of lesbian love that was running at New York's Empire Theater, starring Basil Rathbone and Helen Menken. That was it—enough was definitely enough for the conservative politicians and their sheepish followers.

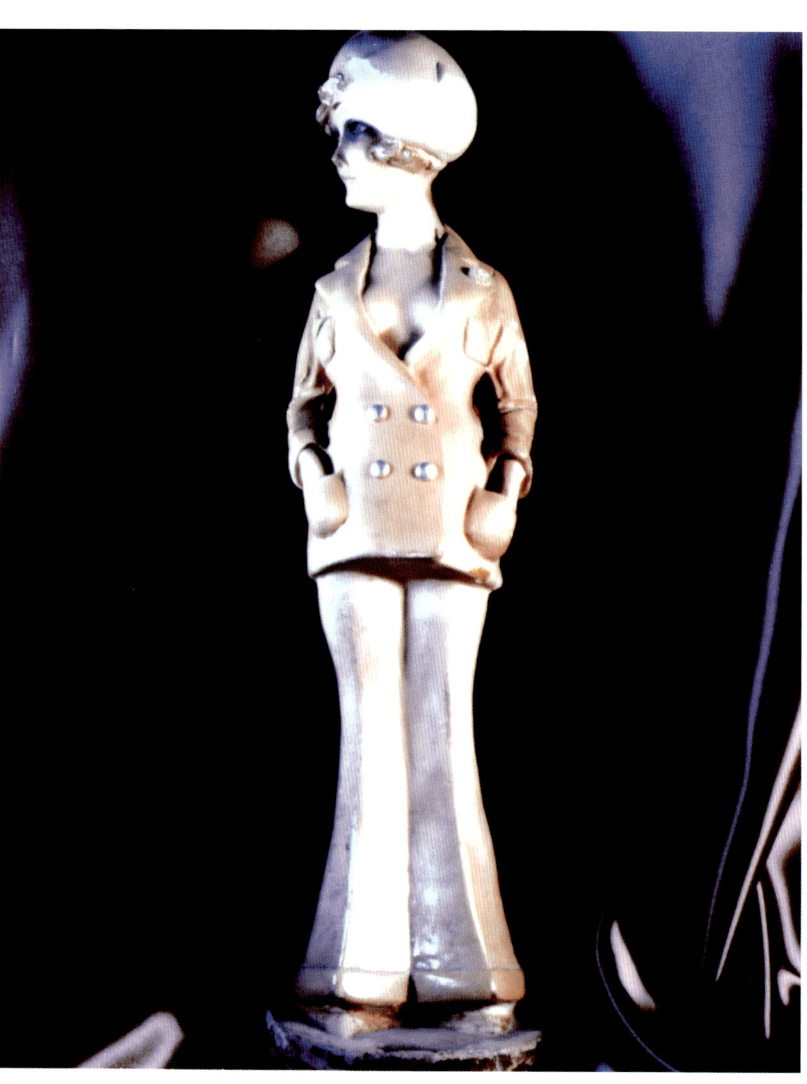

Flapper fifteen-and-one-half-inch carnival chalk prize © June Yates Jenkins

Like it or not, it was clear that the tides of sexuality and tolerance had risen. If you had lived through World War I, then LIVE! Music and theater were the media mainly responsible for these changes. Jazz was on a roll. Broadway pushed the limits of liberated sex. As early as 1904, the sexual content in George Bernard Shaw's *Mrs. Warren's Profession* caused the play to be halted by police. The air changed and fifteen years later, Shaw's explicitness was considered acceptable. In 1919, the character Madame Lucy in James Montgomery's *Irene* was a flamboyant male dressmaker who made no apologies for his apparent homosexuality, and on Broadway, *Aphrodite* caused a sensation with its minute-long, dimly lit view of a

In 1926, New York mayor Jimmy Walker signed the Padlock Law, which stated that a theater's doors would be padlocked and its cast imprisoned for presenting material that was found offensive to the public. For the mayor (who represented the public), offensive material included sex outside of marriage, homosexuality, prostitution, and any other outward portrayal of sexuality. In 1927, the padlock law sent Mae West to jail, where she spent eight days of a ten-day sentence in prison for writing and starring in her Broadway play *Sex*. The tide of newfound sexual freedom was ebbing, and intolerance, once again, was rising.

LOUISE BROOKS (1906-1985)

She made a flurry of comedies in which she was a capricious femme fatalé playing with a reserve that unfailingly monopolized attention amid so much mugging . . . Quite simply, she appreciated that the power of the screen actress lay not in impersonation or performance, in the carefully worked-out personal narrative of stage acting, but in the movements of thought and soul transmitted in a kind of intense isolation.

—DAVID THOMSON on Louise Brooks, *A Biographical Dictionary of Film*

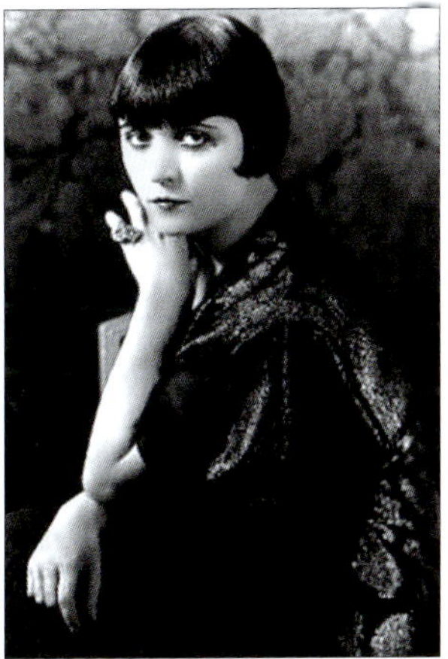

Pola Negri, 1920s

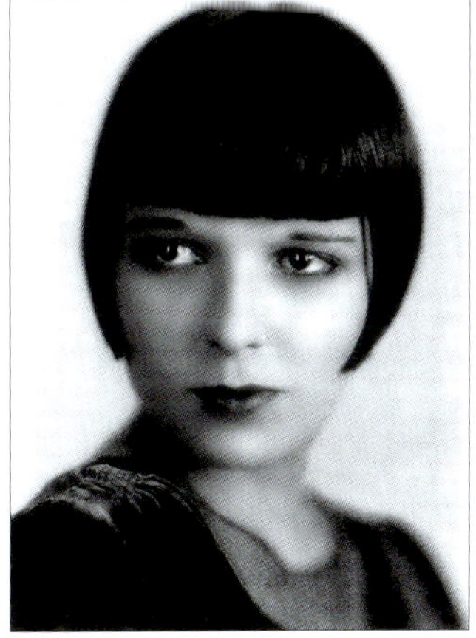

Louise Brooks, 1920s

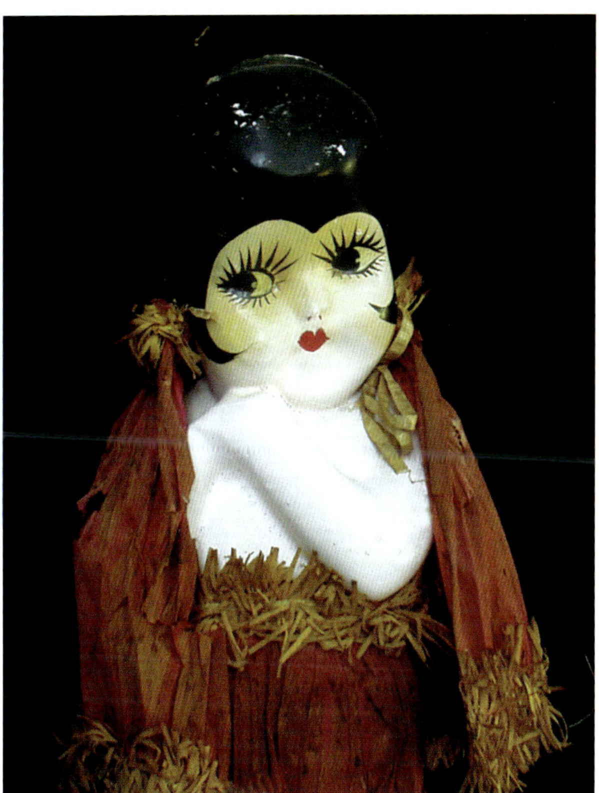

Vamp eighteen-and-a-half-inch carnival chalk prize, pink chalk. Because of the hairstyle, this "I Love Me Girl," resembled Pola Negri and Louise Brooks. Negri wore the style briefly, for Brooks it was her signature.

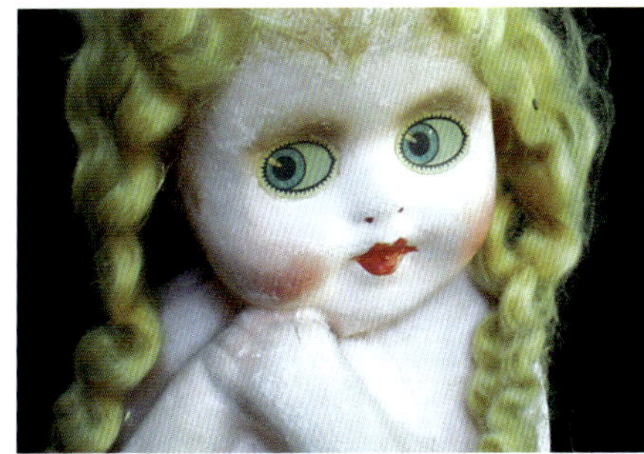

Several other "I Love Me Girl" carnival chalk prizes had long flowing marcelled hair similar to Mary Pickford's during her "Little Mary" roles playing a twelve year old (she was actually 24-34 years old at the time).

Louise Brooks's stark beauty was ever-present in many silent films from 1926 through 1928; her first starring roles were in *The American Venus* (1926) and *A Social Celebrity* (1926). Her meteoric rise as a film star and her exuberant social life were consistent with her image as a vivacious, intelligent flapper. Her social circle included such notable figures as George Gershwin, F. Scott Fitzgerald, Robert Benchley, H. L. Mencken, Anita Loos, and Charlie Chaplin, with whom she had a torrid love affair.

In a move that was widely frowned upon, she left Hollywood to play Frank Wedekind's intense sex-driven Lulu for the German filmmaker G. W. Pabst in his remake of his 1904 stage production *Pandora's Box* (1928), which was thought of as one of the most erotic films made during that era. The supposed eroticism was more symbolic of sadomasochistic fantasy, an archetypal replay based on feelings of fear and paranoia. In this early film noir, she seductively bumps into the tabloid monster/killer Jack the Ripper—that's enough to make the audience jump! *Pandora's Box* is considered one of the most important of all silent foreign films. An interesting evolvement is Ken Russell's *Crimes of Passion* (1984).

Much like the dancer Josephine Baker, who found American productions too puritanical or repressive, Brooks found freedom in Nero-Film of Berlin in 1928. By 1938 she had abandoned her film career altogether. Brooks's stature remains today, with a wide cult following, most likely due to the clarity of her vivid facial beauty and her liberated ideals. Brooks died of a heart attack in 1985.

By the mid-1920s children acted in short films that parodied their elder stars playing in the main feature. In many of these, young girls acted as Hollywood's vamps (Hollywood turned a blind eye to pedophilia). As these films became popular they were known as "Baby Burlesques." The most famous girl child star, Baby Peggy (1918-) even had her own film company.

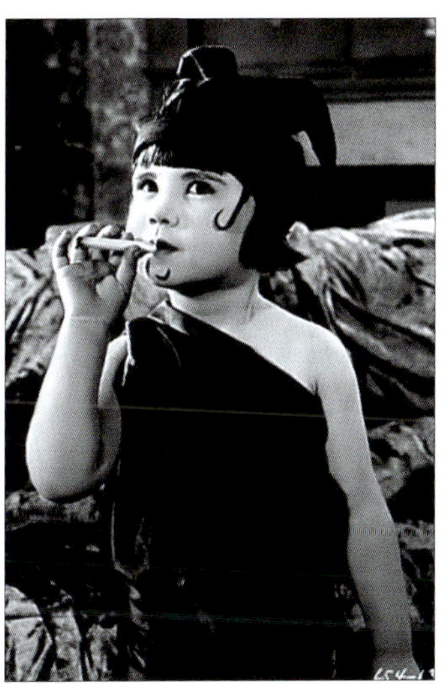

Baby Peggy with her hair styled to resemble Pola Negri, smoking in *Peg O' the Movies* (1923)

Barney Google & Spark Plug
(1919-1950)
Snuffy Smith

The expression "Where did you get those gu-gu-googly eyes?" was invented by Billy De Beck and then popularized in 1923 with the song "Barney Google" by Billy Rose. De Beck's comic strip *Barney Google* (initially named *Take Barney Google, F'rinstance*) premiered in 1919 in the *San Francisco Herald-Examiner*. Barney Google was characterized as the hen-pecked, diminutive, city-slicker husband, lover of prize fights and horse races. His wife was three times his size (sounds like a setup for misogamy *and* misogyny). Barney was the hard-living, hand-to-mouth, noisy, common city guy of the bustling 1920s. Spark Plug joined the comic strip's cast on July 17, 1922, when Barney happened to be standing in front of the Pastime Jockey Club. A loud argument erupted inside the club and ended abruptly when a man sailed out through a window and right onto Barney—flattening him. The soft landing saved the man's life and, in gratitude, he gave Barney the generous gift of a horse named Spark Plug. Spark Plug added a certain comic zest to the strip and the strip's popularity increased so much that it was renamed *Barney Google & Spark Plug*. Spark Plug's first horse race became a hyped and eagerly awaited national media event. Parents, enamored with the comic strip, named their children Sparky. De Beck, by virtue of his wit, injected many new words and phrases into the American vernacular, including "bodacious," "time's a-wastin'," "sweet mama," "balls o' fire," "horsefeathers," "heebie-jeebies," and "hotsy-totsy."

Spark Plug could have claimed that his racing blood originated in horses ridden by the prehistoric nomadic tribesmen of Central Asia who first domesticated the horse around 4500 BC. The archetypal motif of horse racing has flourished as the sport of kings and nobility for thousands of years. It is hardly any different today than it was in the past: only the rich can afford to own racehorses. Modern racing exists for the same reasons it existed in ancient times—as a major venue for gambling and an archetypal symbol for feelings of thrills and power.

The risk-taker/thrill-seeker gambling archetype depends upon a number of factors: alienation from the puritan work ethic, exuberant excitement, and the projected fantasy of winning through either skill or luck—or both.

The first American racetrack was laid out on Long Island in 1665, but organized racing did not begin in America until after the Civil War. By 1890, there were 314 tracks established in the United States. Antigambling sentiment in the early 1900s almost led to its demise and by 1908 the number of tracks had dwindled to only twenty-five. That same year, with the introduction of pari-mutuel betting in the Kentucky Derby, tracks suddenly began to reopen. Many state legislatures recognized the fountain of gambling money that promised showers of revenue into the public coffer, and they agreed to legalize pari-mutuel betting in exchange for a share of the money wagered. By the end of World War I, prosperity and horses like Man o' War made horse racing even more popular.

All track betting is now done under the pari-mutuel wagering system, developed by Frenchman Pierre Oller, where a fixed percentage, usually 14 to 25 percent, of the total amount wagered is taken out for track operating expenses, racing purses, and state and local taxes. The remaining sum is divided by the number of individual wagers to determine the payoff on each bet. The odds are continuously calculated and posted during the betting period before each race. Odds of 2 to 1, for example, mean that the bettor will receive $2 for every $1 wagered, if his or her horse wins.

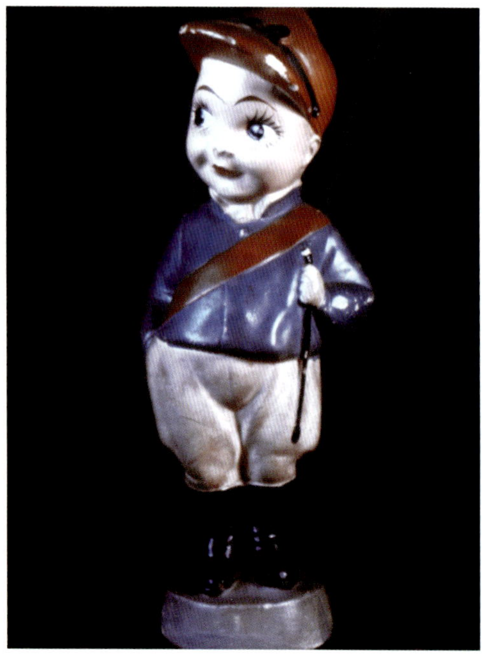

Jockey nine-inch carnival chalk prize © 1921 on the back. This figure is probably meant to resemble one of the two jockeys who rode "Man o' War" by 1921: Johnny Loftus or Clarence Kummer.

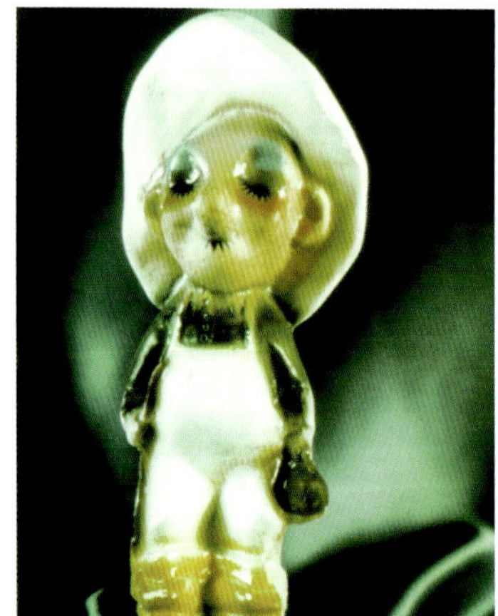

Snuffy Smith ten-inch carnival chalk prize

Billy De Beck's comic strip changed again in 1934. Hillbilly strips like *Li'l Abner* and *Joe Palooka* were popular, so Barney Google conveniently inherited his relative's rural estate (probably just over the hill from Dogpatch). Barney and Spark Plug meandered to Hootin' Holler, where they met Barney's ornery, sawed-off cousin Snuffy Smith and Snuffy's wife, the gossipy Loweezy. Eight years later, in 1942, De Beck up 'n' died. Fred Lasswell took up the strip and it continued as *Barney Google & Snuffy Smith*. Twenty-two years later it would become simply *Snuffy Smith*. Lasswell established a loving backwoods relationship between Snuffy,

Loweezy, and their family. Warmth and tenderness was not
what Barney, his wife, and Spark Plug always shared in the
original De Beck strip. Times changed, Lasswell kept up
with them, and he made Snuffy very popular. There was an
animated version of *Barney Google* in the 1930s, produced
by the Charles Mintz Screen Gems. *Barney Google & Snuffy
Smith* had an off-and-on career in comic books, starting with
Ace Comics in 1937. They also appeared in their own comics—
three issues from Dell in the 1940s and four from Toby Press
in the 1950s.

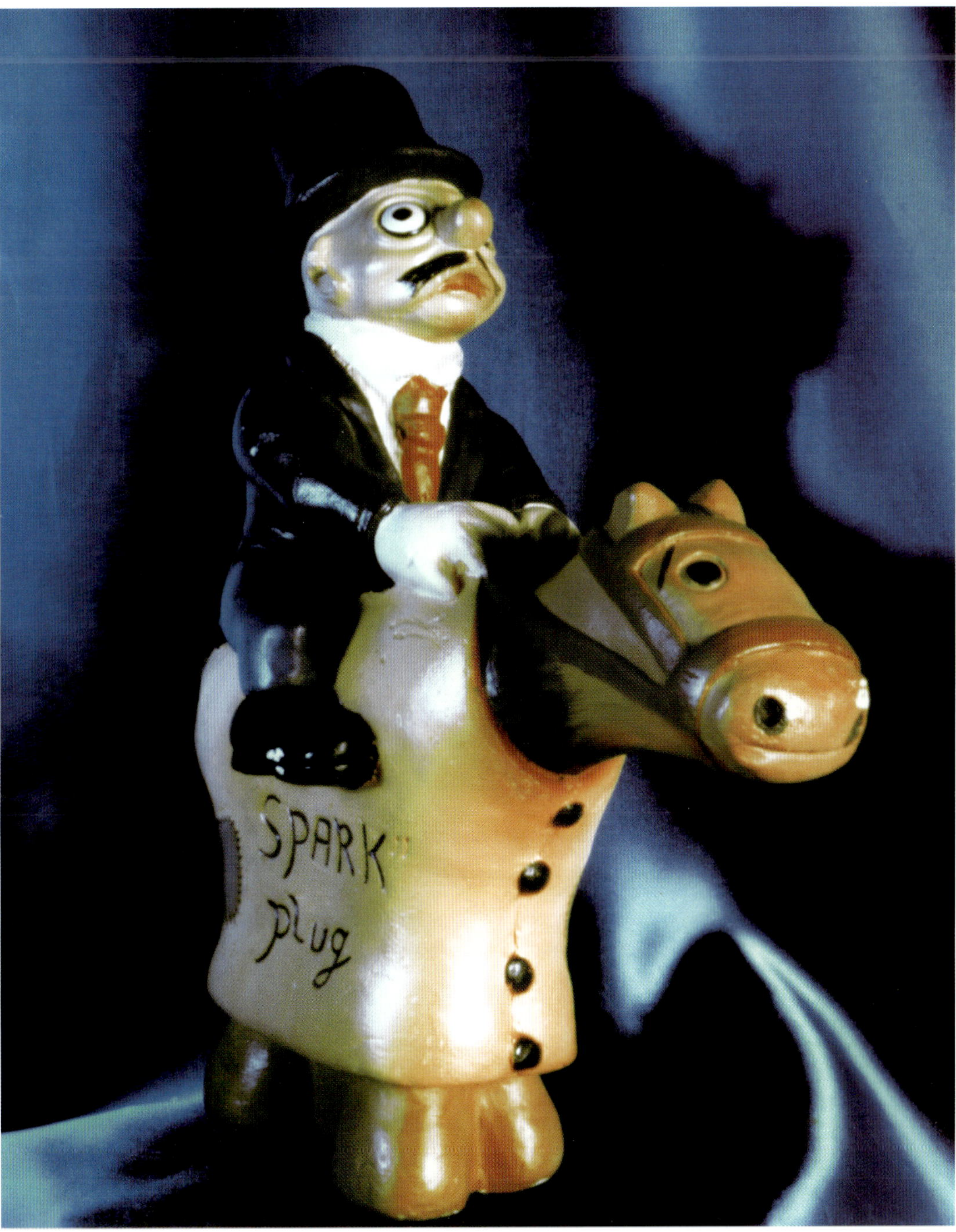

Barney Google and Spark Plug eleven-inch carnival chalk prize

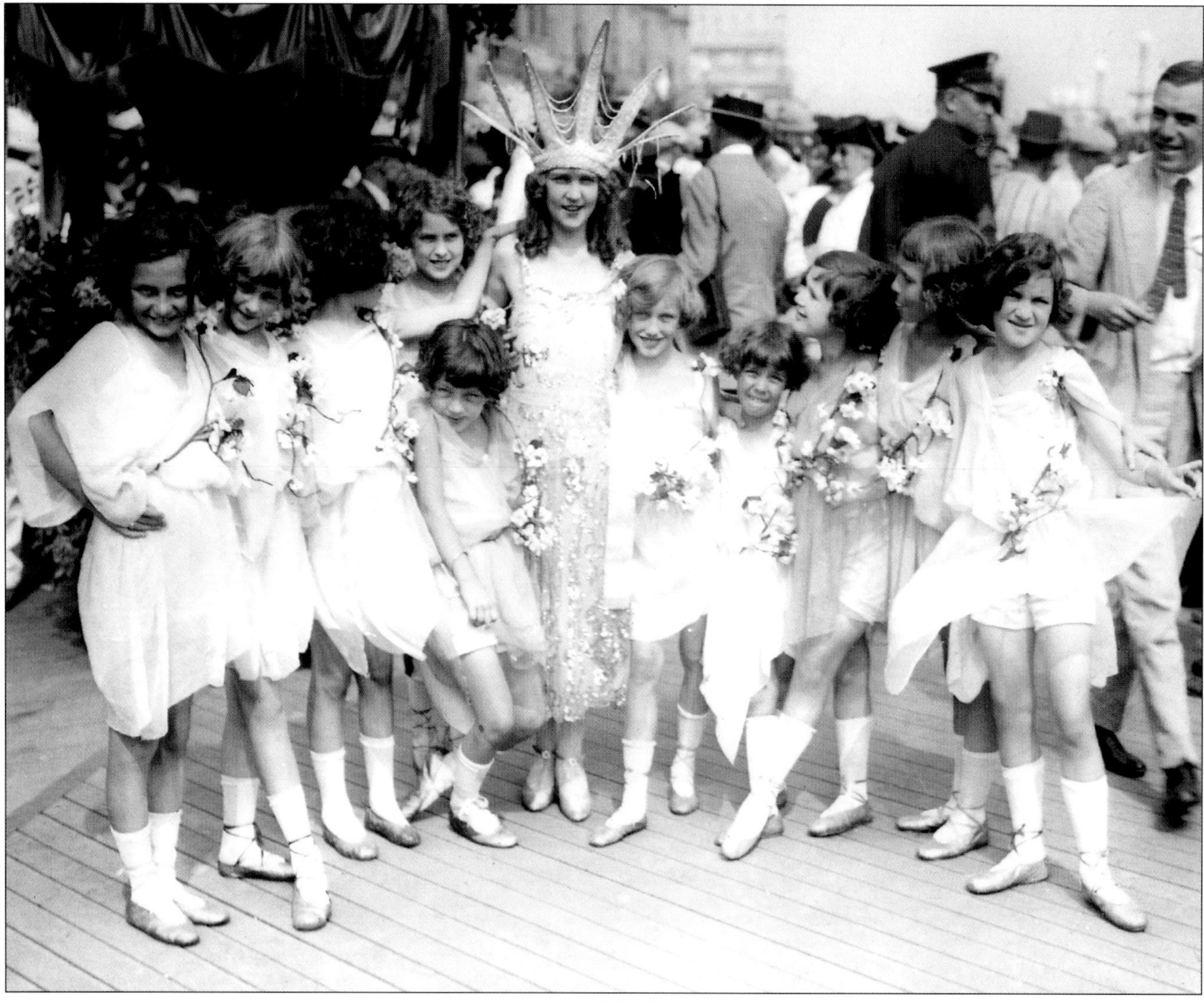

The first Miss America: Margaret Gorman, center, as "America's Most Beautiful Bathing Girl," 1921

Can there be a stereotype/archetype more obvious than Miss America?

A yearly competition for the perfect young woman's face and body began in Atlantic City, New Jersey, in 1921—the women were dressed in one-piece bathing suits (which were popular around 1915 to 1920). In the first years of the competition orchestra players donned bathing suits during the bathing revue.[1] In 1922, illustrator Norman Rockwell, the "Mr. America of Apple Pie," was a judge. Why Atlantic City? Because Atlantic City hotel owners came up with the idea of a bathing-suit competition to entice summer tourists to stay until Labor Day.

All early Miss America winners were crowned in their bathing suits. The first sixty-three winners of the pageant were white.

Some of the more unusual facts about the yearly competitions and its winners are:

• 1921: The first very young woman to win the Grand Prize—the Golden Mermaid Trophy for "America's Most Beautiful Bathing Girl"—was Margaret Gorman, who at the time of her crowning had just completed the tenth grade.

• 1922: The Grand Prize winner was renamed "Miss America." It went to fifteen-year-old Mary Katherine Campbell, who won again in 1923.

• 1924: The pageant passed the rule that previous winners could not compete.

• 1927: Winner Lois Delander accidentally held the crown longest, because the pageant was discontinued for six years; bad press had revealed that the competitions were rigged.

• 1932: Wildwood, New Jersey, sponsored a knockoff Miss America Pageant, infuriating the Atlantic City hotel owners, who in 1933, resurrected their Miss America Pageant. Apparently this time it was not rigged.

• 1936: Winner Henrietta Leaver eloped during her winning year.

• 1937: Winner Bette Cooper, immediately after being crowned, snuck away from the pageant with her male chaperone in a motorboat. The promoters panicked. A huge police search was organized. A day later they found her just where she wanted to be—back in high school.

• 1938: Pageant rules were changed so that one-third of the judges' vote went for talent. The new rule could have been stated differently—they could have said just two-thirds of the judges' vote went for breast size, body shape, and overall beauty. It also was ruled that a competitor had to be at least eighteen years old.

• 1943: Winner Jean Bartel chose to never "officially" pose in a swimsuit again.

• 1945: Due to increased negative publicity, complaints were heard that the Miss America prize was too anti-intellectual, so a college scholarship was added to the winner's prize. The winner was Bess Myerson, the first Jewish winner.

• 1951: Winner Yolanda Betbeze chose to never, ever pose in a swimsuit again—officially or unofficially. In doing so, she declared, "I'm an opera singer, not a pinup!" Her rebellious words did little to change the pageant. The reverse happened—Catalina Swimwear withdrew its support as a major sponsor, and founded two rival beauty pageants, Miss USA and Miss Universe.

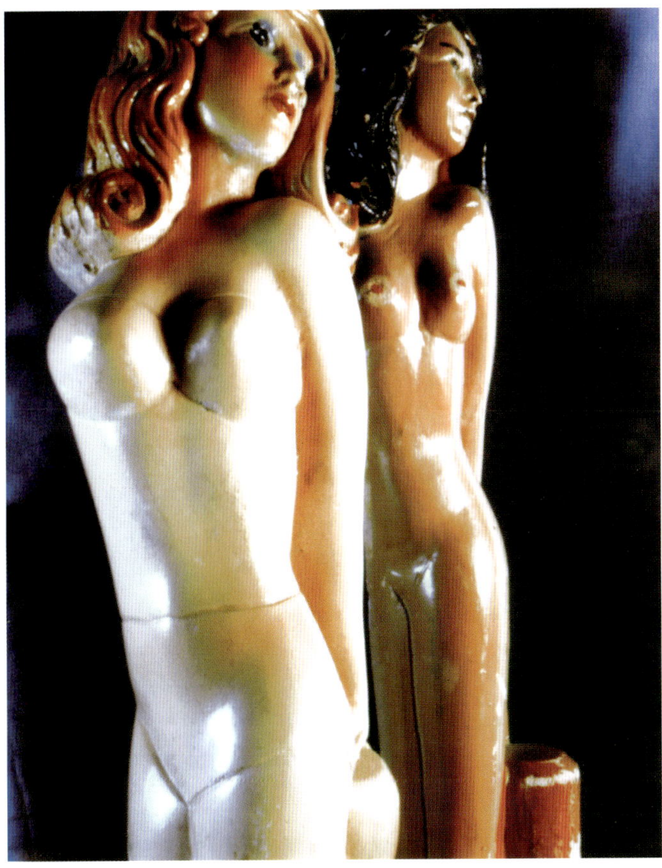

Miss America sixteen-inch carnival chalk prize, with "Miss America" inscribed on the base. To add a little playfulness, an inch taller Nude Miss America was available.

The Miss America Pageant became more glitzy when live television coverage began in 1955. Songwriter Bernie Wayne wrote the theme song, "Here She Comes, Miss America," in one hour. With live television coverage, Miss America became just about every white family's yearly event, much like Oscar night in Hollywood, and many American girls who watched dreamed of someday being crowned Miss America.

Miss America is an archetypal symbol that embodies the fantasized young woman of perfection. She maintains the perfect body for feelings of eternal lust—forever a fountain of youth.

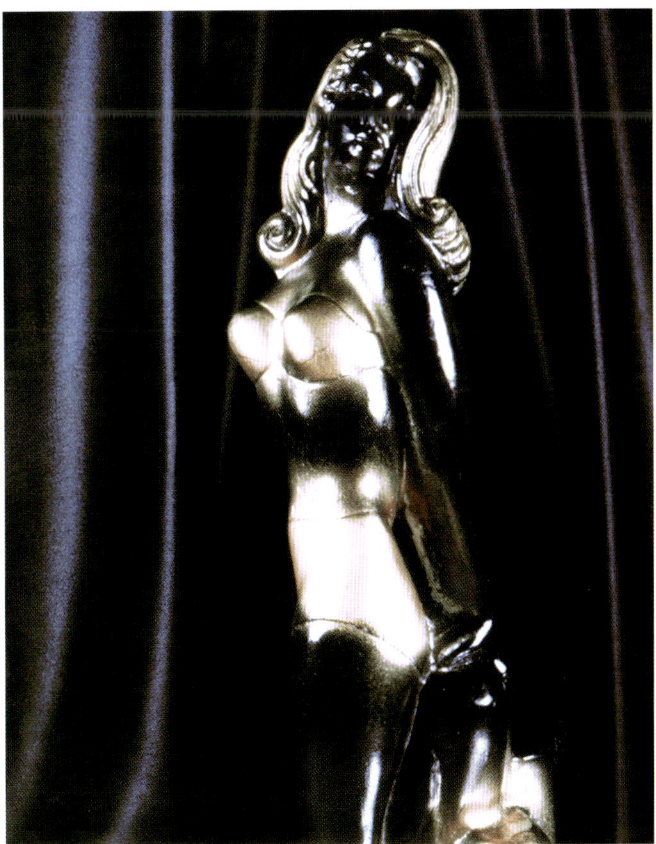

Black Miss America sixteen-inch carnival chalk prize, 1940s. African Americans were not allowed to compete in the pageant when these prizes were available.

In 1968, the first Miss Black America Pageant was held in Atlantic City, as a protest against the absence of black women in the all-white Miss America Pageant. By 1970, Cheryl Browne, Miss Iowa, was the first African American in the Miss America Pageant. Vanessa Williams was the first African American to win in 1984—although she lost her title after nude photos of her, from years earlier, were found and published in *Penthouse*. Humiliated, she was forced to announce her resignation on national television. The chairman of the pageant, in a fit of indignant self-righteousness proclaimed, "I have never before seen anything like these photographs. Ugh . . . I can't even show them to my wife." Williams has always been listed as the 1984A winner. Many people have tried to satire her injustice stating the "A" should have been written in scarlet. Later it was proven that no winner's past was investigated as much as Williams's had been, because she was black.

W illiam Jennings Bryan

(1860–1925)

The final moment in the limelight for the fundamentalist William Jennings Bryan was when he appeared for the prosecution in the famous 1925 Scopes evolution trial, aptly nicknamed the "Monkey Trial." Earlier that year, the state of Tennessee made it unlawful for anyone "to teach any theory that denies the story of the divine creation of man as taught in the Old Testament, and to teach instead that man descended from a lower order of animals." In other words, any theory that ran counter to belief in the divine creation of man according to Genesis was outlawed. John T. Scopes, a biology teacher, was tried for teaching Darwinian evolution in a Tennessee school. Apparently his statements in class had been preplanted as a publicity stunt to bring fame to the little town of Dayton, Tennessee. If convicted, the fine was to be $100.

Clarence Darrow, an agnostic and renowned iconoclast—and the most famous lawyer of the time—arrived in Dayton fresh from his success in the Chicago Loeb-Leopold murder trial to defend Scopes. Darrow had been contacted by the American Civil Liberties Union. Press coverage of the Scopes trial exceeded that of any prior event, as ten thousand people descended upon Dayton. H. L. Mencken, who came from Baltimore to cover the trial for *The Sun*, labeled Bryan the "fundamentalist Pope." As a promotion for the new technology of radio, the trial was broadcast live, making it America's first media circus.

performed in a side show on Main Street. Anti-Evolution League members sold copies of Bryan's book *Hell and the High School*. Religious fundamentalists camped in the surrounding hills and on the riverbanks.

At what proved to be the major point of the trial, Darrow began his agonistic (competitive) interrogation of Bryan with a quiet question: "You have given considerable study to the Bible, haven't you, Mr. Bryan?" Bryan replied, "Yes, I have. I have studied the Bible for about fifty years." Thus began a series of questions designed to undermine a literalist interpretation of the Bible. Bryan was asked about a whale swallowing Jonah, Joshua making the sun stand still, Noah and the great flood, the temptation of Eve in the Garden of Eden, and the creation according to Genesis. After initially contending that "everything in the Bible should be accepted as it is given there," Bryan finally conceded that the words of the Bible should not always be taken literally. In response to Darrow's relentless questions as to whether the six days of creation described in Genesis were twenty-four-hour days, Bryan said, "My impression is that they were periods." The highest moment came when Bryan, who began his testimony calmly, stumbled badly under Darrow's persistent prodding. Exasperated by Darrow's questions, Bryan said, "I do not think about things I don't think about." Darrow then asked, "Do you think about the things you do think about?" Bryan responded, "Well, sometimes." Derisive laughter from the spectators followed. After twelve days of hoopla, the judge had heard enough. Darrow was charged with contempt; Scopes lost, but the verdict was later remanded on a technicality.[1]

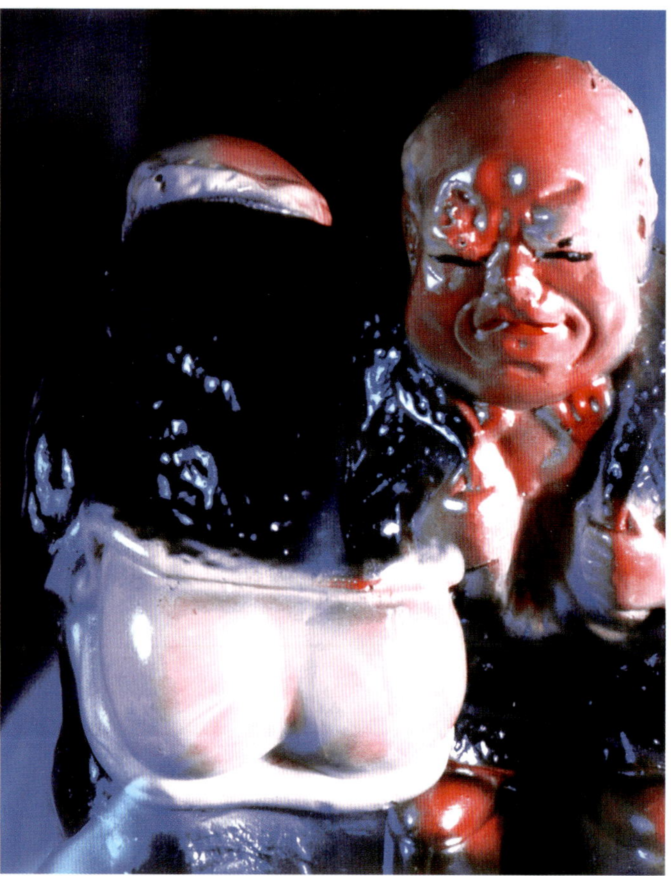

William Jennings Bryan nine-inch carnival chalk prize, showing Bryan caught with his pants down ("I do not think about things I don't think about"). Double exposure.

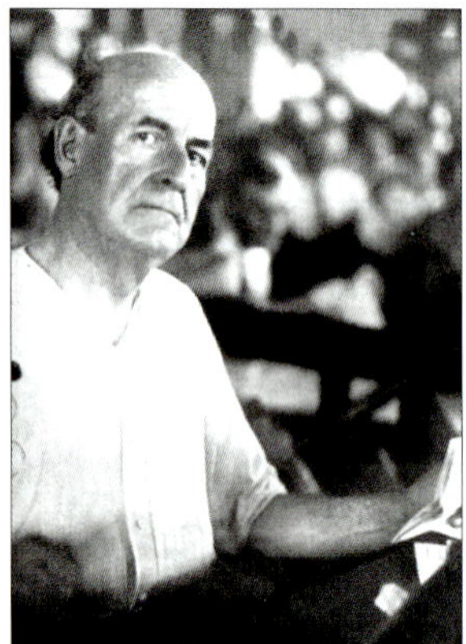

William Jennings Bryan, 1925, Scopes trial

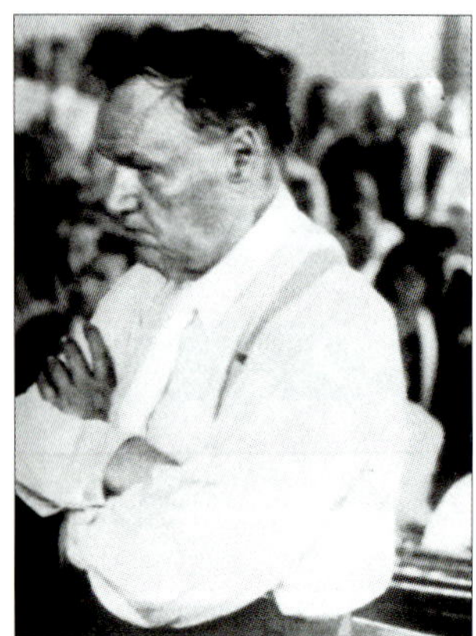

Clarence Darrow, 1925, Scopes trial

A carnival atmosphere pervaded Dayton as the trial began and banners decorated the streets. Chimpanzees, said to have been brought to town to testify for the prosecution,

Darrow's examination of Bryan, as well as the entire issue, went far to discredit the fundamentalist interpretation of the Bible. The result was that only two states, of thirteen other states that had laws pending, dared pass a similar law. The two that did were Arkansas and Mississippi. Five days after the trial ended, the edacious (gluttonous) Bryan died in his sleep, apparently after consuming a huge dinner.

Of the scatological William Jennings Bryan carnival chalk prize, Tom Morris, author of *The Carnival Chalk Prize* wrote:

> The first time I saw this figure, I passed on it, then several years later, our son picked one up at a garage sale and gave it to me—both were marked, on the bottom, paper hand written sticker, "William Jennings Bryan, caught with his pants down." It is also marked "very old chalkware"! I've seen them since, with the same writings on the bottom—all have a very old look to them. I couldn't prove they were ever carnival prizes. In recent years, a newer looking figure has come out, and this is when they began saying they were Winston Churchill.[2]

Ironically, this early prize of the famous American politician would have been a real slap in the face for Bryan, the iconodule (one who venerates icons), a leader in the Fundamentalist Movement of the 1890s and a three-time Democratic presidential candidate. Bryan's most famous "Cross of Gold" speech on July 9, 1896, against the gold standard ended with this famous line:

> Having behind us the producing masses of this nation and the world, supported by the commercial interests, the laboring interests, and the toilers everywhere, we will answer their demand for a gold standard by saying to them: You shall not press down upon the brow of labor this crown of thorns, you shall not crucify mankind upon a cross of gold.[3]

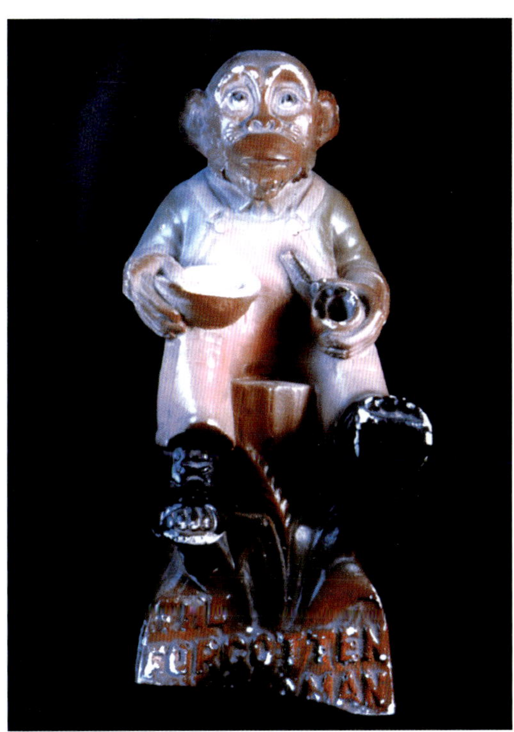

Forgotten Man eleven-inch carnival chalk prize

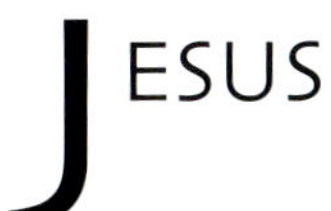

Jesus

Everything good that I have done, I have done at the command of my voices.
—Joan of Arc, statement at her trial, Marina Warner, *Joan of Arc*

Religion is what keeps the poor from murdering the rich.
—Napoleon

I have been into many of the ancient cathedrals—grand, wonderful, mysterious. But I always leave them with a feeling of indignation because of the generations of human beings who have struggled in poverty to build these alters to the unknown god.
—Elizabeth Cady Stanton, *Diary*

Then Christ says, 'The Son of Man shall send forth His angels, and they shall gather out of His kingdom all things that offend, and them which do iniquity, and shall cast them into a furnace of fire; there shall be wailing and gnashing of teeth;' and He goes on about the wailing and gnashing of teeth. It comes in one verse after another, and it is quite manifest to the reader that there is a certain pleasure in contemplating wailing and gnashing of teeth, or else it would not occur so often. Then you all, of course, remember about the sheep and the goats; how at the second coming He is going to divide the sheep from the goats, and He is going to say to the goats, 'Depart from me, ye cursed, into everlasting fire.' He continues, 'And these shall go away into everlasting fire.' Then He says again, 'If thy hand offend thee, cut it off; it is better for thee to enter into life maimed, than having two hands to go into Hell, into the fire that never shall be quenched; where the worm dieth not and the fire is not quenched.' He repeats that again and again also. I must say that I think all this doctrine, that hellfire is a punishment for sin, is a doctrine of cruelty. It is a doctrine that put cruelty into the world and gave the world generations of cruel torture; and the Christ of the Gospels, if you could take Him as His chroniclers represent Him, would certainly have to be considered partly responsible for that.
—Bertrand Russell, March 6, 1927, speech delivered to the National Secular Society, South London Branch, at Battersea Town Hall

Christianity's gathering places and ceremonies—churches and graveyards, marriages and funerals—have always been an important contextual aspect of mass media. Christianity's major symbol, Jesus, is an archetypal savior, as are all other saviors. Devout Christians look upon Jesus as the most important spiritual being in their lives, but rarely do they look upon him as an archetypal motif, reflective of all archetypal saviors. For Christians, Jesus on the cross represents humility, martyrdom, and resurrection. His cross, worn on a necklace, usually stereotypes its wearer as Christian, whereas the double-arc fish symbol seen on American car trunks, bumper stickers, and business cards stereotypes its owner as a member of the Christian faith. The *Catholic Encyclopedia* notes that the bleeding heart symbol on the chest of both Jesus and Mary was initiated in nunneries and monasteries during the 1700s; "Indeed one of the essential phases of the devotion is that it considers the love of Jesus as a despised, ignored love. He Himself revealed this when He complained so bitterly to Saint Margaret Mary in a vision in 1675."[1]

Devotion to the sacred bleeding heart was made

official in the 1700s and 1800s. It was said that people despised and ignored Jesus' love through various transgressions, such as questioning the truth of the doctrines, becoming Protestants, or either leaving the Catholic Church or not supporting it with money, dedicated time, and obedience. These transgressions, heresies, and indifferences broke and wounded Jesus' and Mary's hearts. Jesus required reciprocity for his love, but the majority of people refused such reciprocity. This emphasis, the preying upon emotions and guilt, was instilled shortly after the Middle Ages. Before and during the Middle Ages, the Roman Catholic Church focused upon the formal and legal aspects of the crucifixion: God demanded harsh punishment of sinners; Jesus became the legal substitute. He died in the place of human sinners.[2]

When one compares the savior Jesus to the savior Mithra—an early Persian God of Light worshipped many hundred years before the birth of Christ—there are shocking similarities. The Mithraic religion reached Egypt around 200 BC and Rome around the turn of the millennium. Some of the mind-boggling similarities are:

• Mithra's birth on December 25 was witnessed by shepherds.[3]

• It was believed Mithra sprang from the union of the Sun-God and Mithra's mother; she remained a virgin. Others believed Mithra was born from a female rock fertilized by God's lightning.[4]

• While on earth, Mithra performed many miracles: raising the dead, curing the sick, and casting out devils.[5]

• Mithra's ascension to heaven was celebrated at the spring equinox. In memory of this, his worshippers took a sacramental meal of bread marked with a cross—one of their seven sacraments.[6]

• Mithra had a "Last Supper" with twelve disciples, each of whom represented one sign of the zodiac.[7]

• Mithra's priesthood consisted of ascetic, unmarried men.[8]

• Women were forbidden in Mithra's temples. Mithraic women attended services in their own temples, dedicated to Isis, Diana, or Juno.[9]

• Mithra's image was buried in a rock tomb, which represented his mother's womb.

• Mithra was resurrected from the tomb to live again.

• Those who followed the teachings of Mithra would be saved to join the spirits of light.

• Those who sinned by not following Mithra would be cast into a hell, very similar to the later Christian hell.

• Followers of Mithra were baptized.

More on Mithra (and also Osiris, an Egyptian Savior-God whose texts formed many of the Christian tenets) can be found in Barbara G. Walker's *The Woman's Encyclopedia of Myths and Secrets*.

There were some differences—one was that Mithra was a castrate and Jesus was not, although many early Christian fanatics did have themselves castrated.[10] That Mithra was a castrate was not ill considered, as many early pre-Mithra saviors were castrates. In AD 190, under Roman Emperor Commodorus, Mithra was proclaimed the supreme patron of Roman armies. Christians began to be persecuted under Emperor Decius, around the year 250. The Roman co-emperor

Maxenthias declared Mithra the "Protector of the Empire" in 307.

But everything changed in 312. Co-emperor Constantine converted to Christianity after having a Christian-like vision during a battle against Maxenthias, and became the first fully Christianized Roman Emperor in 324. That year he also defeated his co-emperor, Licinia, in the west (his vision did not teach him nonviolence). Constantine began a systematic integration of all pagan traditions (his concept for earlier religions, like Mithraism) into Christian dogma. He supremely presided over his Council of Nicaea. There was no division of church and state. The council, composed of three hundred bishops, issued an official statement of creed affirming Jesus' absolute divinity. Constantine, ending any future dispute over the presentation of Jesus Christ, enforced their declaration politically. They drafted the defiant, religiously intolerant Creed of Nicaea, which read:

> We believe in one God, the Father, Almighty, Maker of all things visible and invisible; and in the one Lord Jesus Christ, the Son of God, begotten of the Father, only-begotten, that is, from the substance of the Father; God from God, Light from Light, Very God from Very God, begotten not made, of one substance with the Father, through whom all things were made, both in heaven and in earth; who for us men and for our salvation came down and was incarnate, was made man, suffered, and rose again on the third day, ascended into heaven, and is coming to judge the living and the dead; And in the Holy Spirit. And those who say: "There was a time when he was not," and: "Before he was begotten he was not," and: "He came into being from nothing," or those who pretend that the Son of God is "of another substance" or "created" or "alterable" or "mutable," the Catholic and apostolic church places under a curse.[11]

Simply stated, any person was damned and cursed if he or she did not believe that Jesus was the first and only son of the only God. In 354, the Church of Rome proclaimed that Jesus Christ's birthday was to be celebrated on December 25 of every year. Christians seized Mithra's cave temple on the Vatican hill in 376. Most other pagan holy places were destroyed or Christianized. Many ancient miracles, myths, phrases, and rituals were adopted and infused into Christian mythology. Much was taken from the 4,000-year-old worship of Osiris, a practice still very much alive during Roman times:

• The Lord's Prayer was derived from an earlier Egyptian hymn to Osiris.

• The 23rd Psalm was taken from an Egyptian text, also to Osiris.

• Rosary beads were Egyptian.[12]

• Buddhism was well known to Rome. Poverty and humility were copied from Buddha, as well as walking on water—a Buddhist sign of the true ascetic.[13]

• Turning water into wine was a Dionysian ritual.[14]

• Healing the sick and raising the dead was performed by magical healers of Egypt.[15]

• Curing the blind was performed by priestesses at Nineveh.[16]

• The double-arced fish symbol was pagan, as was

the Latin cross, which was not accepted by Christians until the seventh century.

    • The scarecrow, a man's figure hanging on a cross, was from distant antiquity. It represented a sacred king whose blood fertilized the earth and protected the crops.[17]

The largest problem facing the purveyors of Christianity was Jesus' credibility. Not one person wrote about Jesus while he was (supposedly) alive, and a suspect four hundred years passed before written accounts of his existence emerged. Books about him came only after the establishment of the church and no manuscript can be accurately dated earlier than the fourth century; most are from much later. If he did exist, he would most likely have been one of the many slain proclaimed saviors, well within established Middle Eastern traditions. Constantine's Council of Nicaea imparted the Jesus deity with the credibility he needed to justify his being humanity's sole savior, while Constantine's armies gave the Christian Church the political power and enforcement it needed to conquer and flourish. Had Christians not said that there was only one God and that all other religions beforehand, even ones that seemed incredibly similar, were mere devilish prior imitations (how does that work), then the history of Christianity might have been less brutal and bloody.

Catholic policies in the first People's Crusade, initiated in 1095 by Pope Urban II (Pope Schadenfreude), rallied against all non-Catholics. Those who participated in the pope's crusade were promised forgiveness for all their sins and offered eternal bliss in heaven. (Power-hungry religious despots throughout history, and even today, consistently dangle gossamer promises of everlasting happiness to the wretched souls they need to carry out their self-serving machinations.) Up to three hundred thousand Christian zealots set out across southern Europe to rid the world of heretics and insure their own places in heaven. Ten thousand Jews were killed in what would later become Germany. When they finally reached Constantinople, the number of Crusaders had decreased tremendously. The stronger Crusaders sold off the weaker ones as slaves to raise money for return passage. Of the seven thousand Crusaders who tried to return, all were killed in Turkey. Over the next four hundred years, other Crusaders were better prepared, possessing stronger weapons, greater numbers, and better organization. As always, those who joined the Crusades were granted heaven's eternal bliss and forgiveness for their sins. In 1209, Jews, many pagans, and half of the people living in what is now France were killed (for the Children's Crusade, page 260). It is estimated that the Crusaders took at least 10 million lives during their centuries of enlightened murder.

Added to the Crusades were the various Inquisitions, the first being the Medieval Inquisition, established in 1184. The four major Inquisitions were some of the most elaborate extortionist, torture, and murder schemes ever devised and carried out. Throughout Europe, anyone who was arrested for questioning for heresy immediately lost his or her property to the church. Once arrested, church authorities tortured the person until they confessed. The cliche phrase "make a clean breast of it" was derived from a pretorture rite, whereby religious authorities shaved all the hair from a man's or woman's body before he or she was interrogated—church

authorities thought the devil lived in a witch's hair. Once a person confessed of heresy, he or she was handed over to local secular authorities and then summarily executed—the church did not perform the executions. If a suspected heretic could not be tortured into a confession, the secular authorities usually killed him or her anyway. Few suspects escaped. The Spanish Inquisition, on the other hand, supposedly was not ecclesiastical. King Ferdinand and Queen Isabella initiated the Inquisition in 1481 to investigate and punish the Jews and Moors who publicly converted to Christianity but privately continued to practice their prior religions, making them, by definition, heretics. Prior to their expulsion from the country in 1492, Jews or Muslims who did not become Christians were not subjected to the powers of the Inquisition. Added to these Inquisitions were the Portuguese Inquisition, beginning in 1532 and used throughout its colonies, and the Roman Inquisition, beginning in 1542.

In light of this purging, it is no wonder that so little is known today of the pagan religions that were in existence only a thousand years ago. A Christian church was usually erected on or near practically every important pagan site. Another 8 million lives were lost over a five hundred year period during the Inquisitions. Amazingly, no subsequent pope has repealed the original edicts that established the Inquisition. Pope Gregory XV founded the Congregation of the Propaganda in 1622, a committee of cardinals charged with overseeing the propagation of Christianity by missionaries sent to non-Christian countries.

The Church insured that its iconography would be exemplary by commissioning the greatest painters of the time (what choice did the painters have?) By 1425, the church was given an even greater gift for visualization. That was the year Filippo Brunelleschi (the architect who ably designed the huge dome for the Cathedral in Florence) invented what would become the instrument of choice for creating perfect one point perspective. His pinhole viewing device gave painters the ability to place exact perspective into two dimensional paintings, similar to the way the human eye sees. The church promoted consistency in perspective, knowing it would make their miracles look all that more miraculous, thrilling to most viewers. Brunelleschi's device was furthered by Leon Battista Alberti who named it the intersector and later Leonardo da Vinci who used it as a window (a similar perspective is used in cameras). The most well known example of this "divine" perspective is in Leonardo's *The Last Supper*, where the vanishing point goes to Jesus' right eye.

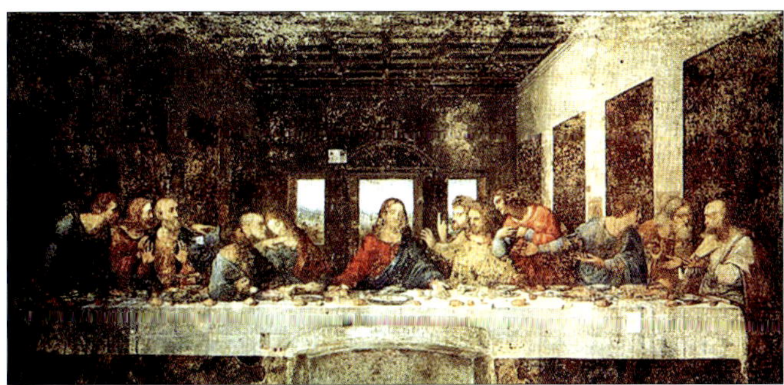

The Last Supper, Leonardo da Vinci, Church of Santa Maria delle Grazie, Milan, 1490s

Yet what of papal morality? To give an idea, one need only consider Pope Alexander VI, who reigned during the high point of the Italian Renaissance. That was the auspicious moment when Leonardo da Vinci began painting the *Mona Lisa* (a superb example of archetypal divine presence). Pope Alexander VI's biography reveals his incest with his daughter Lucretia, many murders, orgasm competitions, multiple mistresses, illegitimate children, and even the purchase of his papacy. Pope Alexander VI died as the result of poisoning. The church has always refused responsibility for its errant cast of characters, including unsavory popes saying, "The dignity of Peter suffers no diminution even in an unworthy successor."[18]

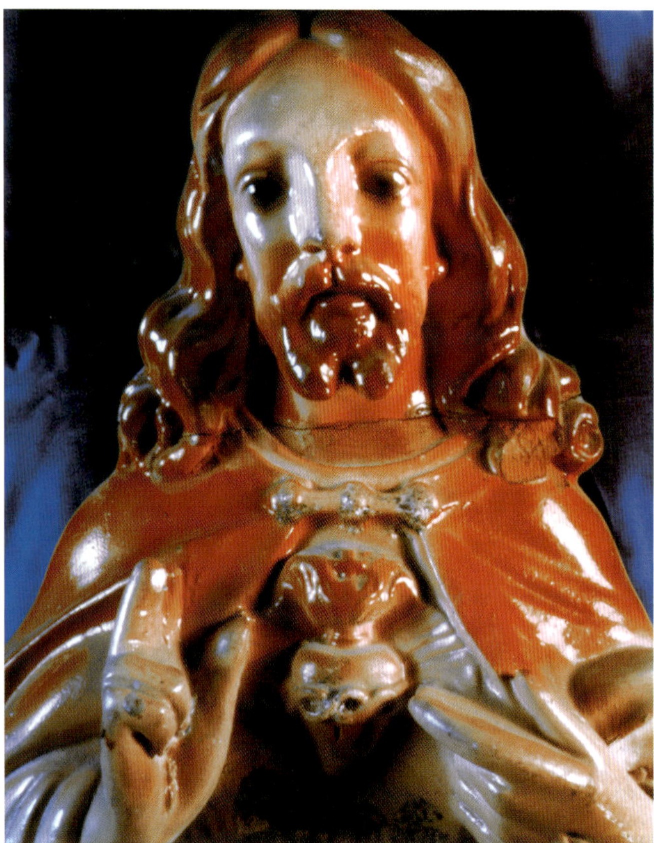

Jesus Christ nine-and-one-half inch carnival chalk prize, the Catholic version with the bleeding heart of Jesus

Between 1900 and 2000, more than 100 million people of various Christian denominations died fighting in wars—a number tremendously higher than any other religion (George W. Bush seems to be working to change that in the 21st century). Most of the twentieth century's Fascists, including Mussolini, Franco, and Hitler, had a Roman Catholic education and upbringing. Stalin was a seminary student, studying to be a Georgian Orthodox priest. So the question must be asked: Why have so many political extremists raised in the Christian faith felt the need to exterminate those they consider to be execrable or unnecessary?

Only sixty-some years ago, in 1939, the SS *St. Louis*, carrying 900 Jewish refugees seeking political asylum, was turned away from the United States and forced to return to Nazi Germany; most of its occupants eventually died in concentration camps. Protestants and Catholics alike never made an outcry. Jews living in America fought in World War II but were generally ostracized by the military's non-Jews. The pope never criticized Hitler's Third Reich during World War II for its Fascist, anti-Jewish propaganda or its deadly concentration camps.

The institution of Christianity, using Jesus as its archetypal savior, offers its followers answers to the great mystery surrounding death. Thoughts of dying instinctively create fear of the unknown. Security is needed. To abate that fear and gain security, guidelines are in place concerning morality. Those who follow the guidelines go to heaven. Those who don't go to hell. Those who sin along the way can get redemption (it generally costs a little more). Knowing you are on the right path (to heaven) offers feelings of superiority. (You'd have to feel superior, everyone else who dies is going to hell. If you don't want to look superior, there are ways to disguise yourself as humble.) To help those stereotyped as others (heathens), missionaries are there to gather the sheep. Fear, security, and superiority have always been Christianity's most effective tools, though fear might be number one. All of these instinctive feelings connect to the savior archetype.

And it all costs money.

The church gratefully "rakes in the money." But because it is dirty money, the priests who were connected to the building of St. Peter's at the Vatican used rakes to gather the money sent by their missionaries from around the world. They were not allowed to touch it.

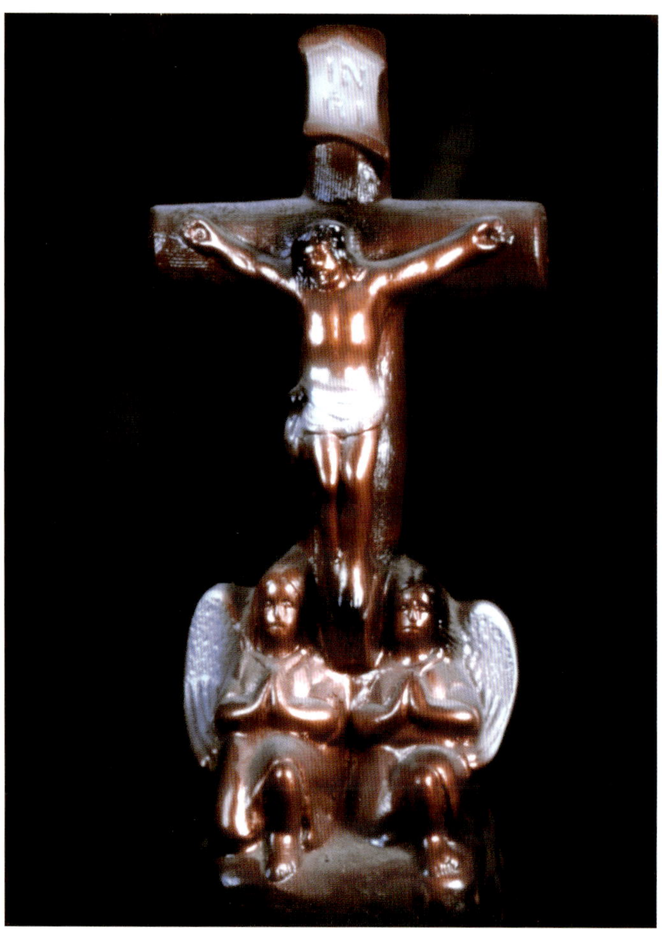

Crucifixion of Jesus thirteen-inch carnival chalk prize, symbolizing his miracles, humility, martyrdom, and resurrection

CASEY JONES (1863–1900)

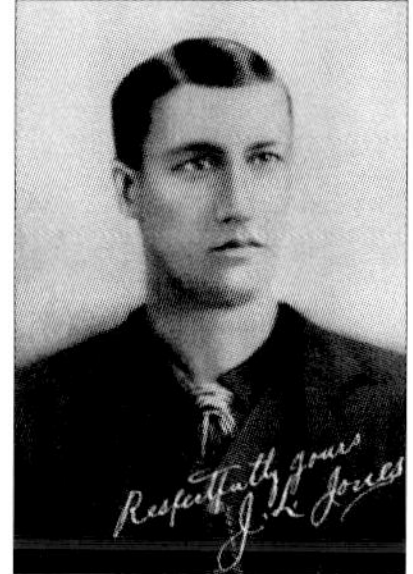

Casey Jones, circa 1895

Come all you rounders, for I want you to hear
The story told of a brave engineer;
Casey Jones was the rounder's name
On a six-eight wheeler, boys, he won his fame

Caller called Jones about half-past four,
Jones kissed his wife at the station door
Climbed into the cab with his orders in his hand.
Says, This is my trip to the Promised Land.

Through South Memphis yards on the fly,
He heard the fireman say, You've got a white-eye.
All the switchmen knew by the engine's moans
That the man at the throttle was Casey Jones.

It had been raining for more than a week
The railroad track was like the bed of a creek.
They rated him down to a thirty mile gait,
Threw the south bound mail about eight hours late.

Fireman says, Casey, you're running too fast,
You run the block signal last station you passed.
Jones says, Yes, I think we can make it through,
For she steams much better than I ever knew.

Jones says, Fireman, don't you fret,
Keep knockin' at the firedoor, don't give up yet;
I'm goin' to run her till she leaves the rail
Or make it on time with the south bound mail.

Around the curve and a-down the dump
Two locomotives were a-bound to bump
Fireman hollered, Jones, it's just ahead
We might jump and make it but we'll all be dead.

Twas around the curve he saw a passenger train;
Something happened in Casey's brain;
Fireman jumped off, but Casey stayed on.
He's a good engineer but he's dead and gone

Poor Casey was always all right
He stuck to his post both day and night
They loved to hear the whistle of old Number Three
As he came into Memphis on the old I.C.

Headaches and heartaches and all kinds of pain
Are not apart from a railroad train;
Tales that are earnest, noble and grand
Belong to the life of a railroad man.
—WALLACE SAUNDERS, engine wiper and friend of Casey Jones, 1902.

Music has the power to create legends and legends have the power to create music. Casey Jones became a folk hero shortly after dying in a train accident in 1900. He was an excellent engineer and twelve years of first-rate service whisked him to a top position with the railroad (although some people considered him a daredevil). African American Sim Webb, the train's fireman who lived through the accident, wrote the first song lamenting Jones's fatal run. Wallace Saunders, another friend of Casey's, wrote the first version to become popular. The accident report placed the entire blame for the accident on Jones, but the song's lyrics defied that finding and held him in good stead. It is reported that an estimated 2,500 railroad employees died in accidents that year.

Casey Jones was born John Luther Jones in Jordan, Kentucky. He moved to Cayce, Kentucky, when he was seventeen, which accounted for the nickname "Casey." He worked for the Illinois Central Railroad in 1888 as a locomotive fireman, and was promoted to engineer in 1890. At his death, he left a wife and three children.

Railroad engineers were important figures in the community, with statures similar to today's airline pilots. (A huge railroad engine is in itself an archetypal motif for unstoppable strength and power, particularly since it cannot brake quickly and destroys smaller objects in its path.) General Superintendent A. S. Sullivan's letter reporting the Casey Jones accident read, in part:

> Reports received to date indicate that Engineer Jones of the passenger train, who lost his life in the accident, was alone responsible for the accident as train No. 83 which was obstructing the main track at Vaughan sawing by train No. 26 was properly protected by flagman, who had gone back a distance of 3,000 feet, where he had placed torpedoes on the rail; then continued north a further distance of 500 to 800 feet, where he stood and gave signals to train No. 1; which signals, however, were apparently not observed by Engineer Jones: nor is it believed he heard the explosion of the torpedoes as his train continued toward the station at a high rate of speed, notwithstanding the fact it was moving up a grade; collision occurring at a point 210 feet north of the north passing track switch. It is also stated that Engineer Jones of train No. 1 failed to sound the whistle for the station when passing the whistle board.[1]

Becoming a legendary person is an archetype. The legend shifts over time, for reasons known only to the storytellers, as do the feelings that it generates. That is the inherent beauty of legends, and the song "Casey Jones" has been rewritten many times over to reshape the legend. The Grateful Dead sang it this way:

> This old engine
> makes it on time
> Leaves Central Station
> at a quarter to nine
> Hits River Junction
> at seventeen to
> at a quarter to ten
> you know it's trav'lin again
>
> Drivin' that train

High on cocaine
Casey Jones you better
watch your speed
Trouble ahead
Trouble behind
and you know that notion
just crossed my mind

Trouble ahead
The Lady in Red
Take my advice
you be better off dead
Switchman sleepin
Train hundred and two
is on the wrong track and
headed for you

Drivin' that train
High on cocaine
Casey Jones you better
watch your speed
Trouble ahead
Trouble behind
and you know that notion
just crossed my mind

Trouble with you is
The trouble with me
Got two good eyes
but we still don't see
Come round the bend
You know it's the end
The fireman screams and
The engine just gleams

Drivin' that train
High on cocaine
Casey Jones you better
watch your speed
Trouble ahead
Trouble behind
and you know that notion
just crossed my mind.[2]

A negative song version, slurring Jones legend, is "The Union Scab," written by Joe Hill, first published in 1912, when 35,000 shop men were on strike on the Harriman and Illinois Central Railroad, which included Southern Pacific. In it Jones becomes the scapegoat stereotype.

The Workers on the S. P. line to strike sent out a call;
But Casey Jones, the engineer, he wouldn't strike at all;
His boiler it was leaking, and its drivers on the bum,
And his engine and its bearings, they were all out of plumb.
Casey Jones kept his junk pile running;
Casey Jones was working double time;
Casey Jones got a wooden medal,
For being good and faithful on the S. P. line.
The workers said to Casey: "Won't you help us win this strike"
But Casey said: "Let me alone, you'd better take a hike."
Then some one put a bunch of railroad ties across the track,
And Casey hit the river bottom with an awful crack.

Casey Jones hit the river bottom;

Casey Jones broke his blessed spine;
Casey Jones was an Angelino,
He took a trip to heaven on the S. P. line.
When Casey Jones got up to heaven, to the Pearly Gate,

He said: "I'm Casey Jones, the guy that pulled the S. P. freight."
"You're just the man," said Peter, "our musicians went on strike;
You can get a job a'scabbing any time you like."

Casey Jones got up to heaven;
Casey Jones was doing mighty fine;
Casey Jones went scabbing on the angels,
Just like he did to workers of the S. P. line.
They got together, and they said it wasn't fair,
For Casey Jones to go around a'scabbing everywhere.
The Angels' Union No. 23, they sure were there,
And they promptly fired Casey down the Golden Stairs.

Casey Jones went to Hell a'flying;
"Casey Jones," the Devil said, "Oh fine":
Casey Jones, get busy shovelling sulphur;
That's what you get for scabbing on the S. P. Line. [3]

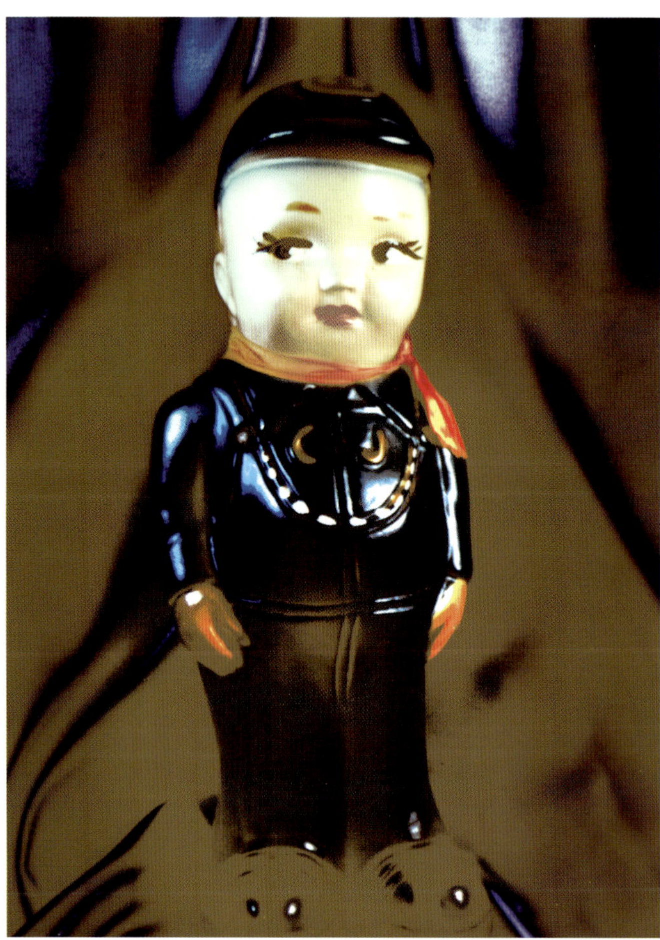

Buddy Lee eleven-inch railroad engineer bank souvenir from the Chicago Junction Railroad Convention (although it looks exactly like a carnival chalk prize). The initials C J on his chest and hat referred to Chicago Junction and were possibly a play on Casey Jones.

WILL ROGERS (1879-1935)

Here is a queer streak in me, I am no hunting man or fishing either. I just don't want to be shooting at any animal and even a fish I haven't got the heart to pull the hook out of him.
—WILL ROGERS

I don't care how little your country is, you got a right to run it like you want to. When the big nations quit meddling, then the world will have peace.
—WILL ROGERS

Herbert Hoover was elected President of the United States in 1928, but the Editors of Life *concluded that Will Rogers was the unanimous, if unofficial, choice of what they called the Great Silent Vote. The newspapers, they wired Will on election night, might say that the other candidates had piled up millions of votes, but that had little to do with the true sentiments of the country 'You're in.' the message read, and, in a sense, they were right. By now he was one of the most popular and best loved of all Americans.*
—RICHARD M. KETCHUM, *Will Rogers: His Life and Times*

Will Rogers's father was one-eighth Cherokee and his mother one-quarter Cherokee. He was born on a 600-acre ranch in Oklahoma and taught how to rope by a freed slave named Uncle Dan Walker. Rogers keened his roping skills to unsurpassed excellence and was put in the *Guinness Book of World Records* for the amazing feat of throwing three lassos at once—one looped the horse's neck, another the rider, and the last the horse's body. He worked with gauchos in Argentina in 1902 and a year later called himself "The Cherokee Kid" when he joined Texas Jack's Wild West Show in South Africa. Returning to the United States, Rogers worked in the Zack Muhall Show at the 1904 St. Louis World's Fair. He gradually learned to pepper dialogue into his roping act, finding that the audience warmed appreciably to cowboy witticisms.

Eventually he married Betty Blake, his longtime sweetheart, saying, "The day I roped Betty I did the star performance of my life." He worked in vaudeville with the Ziegfeld Follies in 1915, and it was there that he met star performer Elsie Janis, known as the "Queen of Vaudeville." She became fascinated with his roping act, practiced it on her own, and was able to impressively impersonate it (not a small accomplishment).

Rogers was cast in his first film, *Laughing Bill Hyde*, in 1918, resulting in Goldwyn Studios hiring him to star in Westerns made on Hollywood sets rather than in the east. By 1919, he had published his ideas and opinions in *The Cowboy Philosopher on the Peace Conference* and *The Cowboy Philosopher on Prohibition*. On his first radio broadcast in 1922, referring to radio's invisible airwaves he remarked: "It's the bunk. I don't think you can hear. If it isn't the bunk, let me know whether you can hear me." His first syndicated newspaper stories also appeared that year.

Fox Film Corporation hired him for their first sound film, *They Had to See Paris*, in 1929. He was back on the radio by 1930, a medium he never enjoyed until KHJ radio in

Los Angeles gave him a live audience. On his April 6, 1930, show he spoke about the World Disarmament Conference:

> Tonight all I know is this—just what I read in the papers during the day. Since Europe is so warlike, why not have the countries of the world trade places? Let Germany trade places with Mexico, France move to where Canada is, England switch with Cuba, and Japan with Hawaii. Now just surround us with those four gorillas and see how much disarmament we start hollering about. See if we want any disarmament.[1]

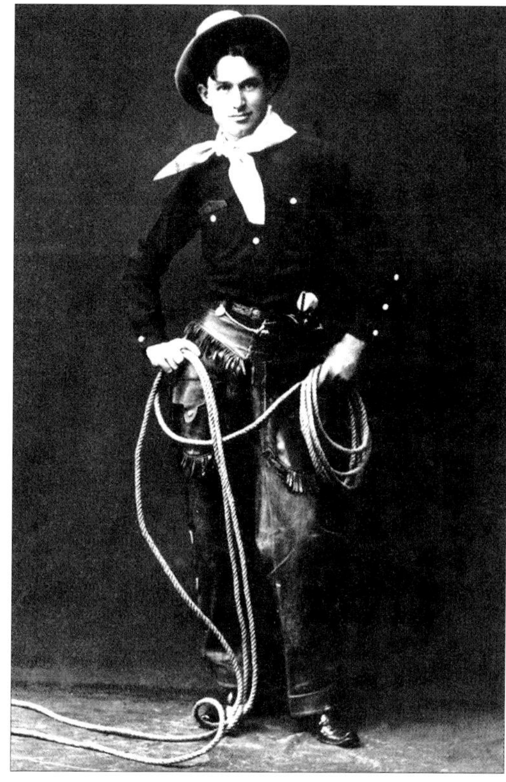

Will Rogers. Courtesy: Will Rogers Memorial, Claremont, Oklahoma

Always generous, Rogers gave his radio fees to charity. He went to Managua, Nicaragua, for a benefit for earthquakes and fire victims. As he traveled throughout the world, Rogers was a friend to everyone—presidents, kings, the poor. His was the voice of sharing rather than greed.

A shocked and saddened world listened in disbelief upon hearing that Rogers died in a small plane crash in Alaska in 1935. He had starred in seventy-one movies, published six books, toured the globe three times, and written four thousand newspaper columns. His small portable typewriter, found in the crash, displayed the last word he was to write: "death."

Rogers is considered the "father of radio commentary." His credo was "I never met a man I didn't like," and his love and respect for humanity were sincere. He symbolically represented the genuine man archetype —someone without a disguise, a rare person indeed. He epitomized one of the century's first superstars—a cowboy genius turned philosopher humorist, who spoke for and lived egalitarianism.

Will Rogers on the radio with a live audience

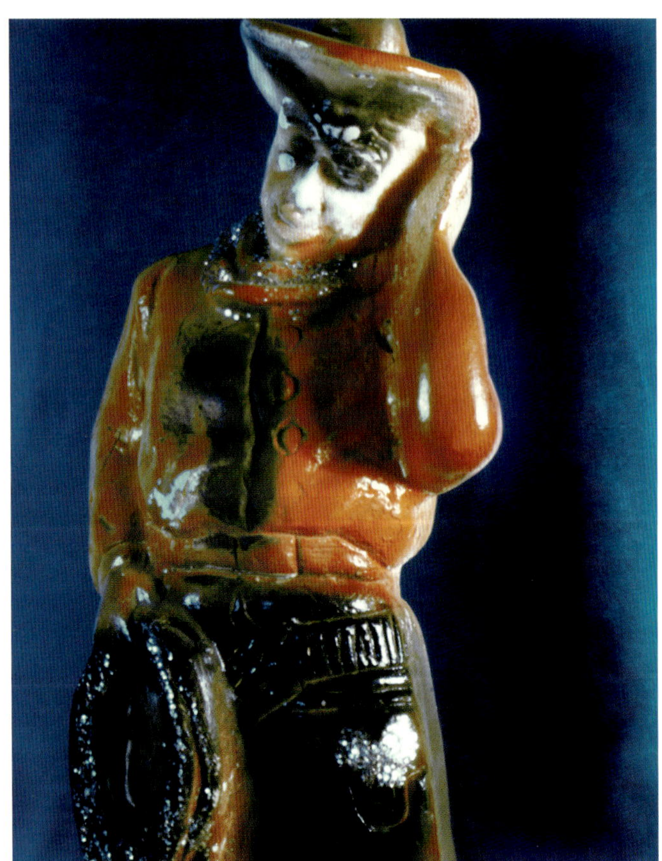
Will Rogers thirteen-inch carnival chalk prize, extremely rare

ELSIE JANIS (1889-1956)

Don't expect to do the Will Rogers act the first week. It took me two months and I'm fairly quick at grabbing other people's stuff.
—ELSIE JANIS, *Cowboy Roping and Rope Tricks*

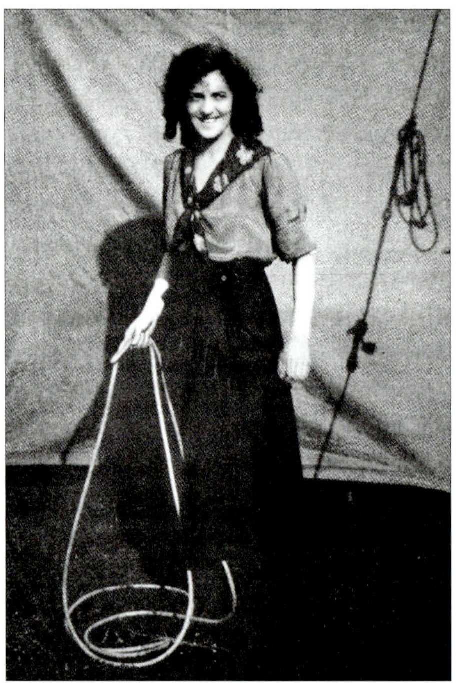
Elsie Janis, circa 1918

Born in Columbus, Ohio, Elsie Janis Bierbower was coached by her ambitious mother almost from the time she could walk. She was one of the most famous of all child stars. At age ten, she performed for President McKinley at the White House. At fourteen she began her long association with New York vaudeville, singing, dancing, and doing impersonations. First known as "Little Elsie," she later became the "Queen of Vaudeville." At the start of World War I, she was the most famous American actress on the London stage.

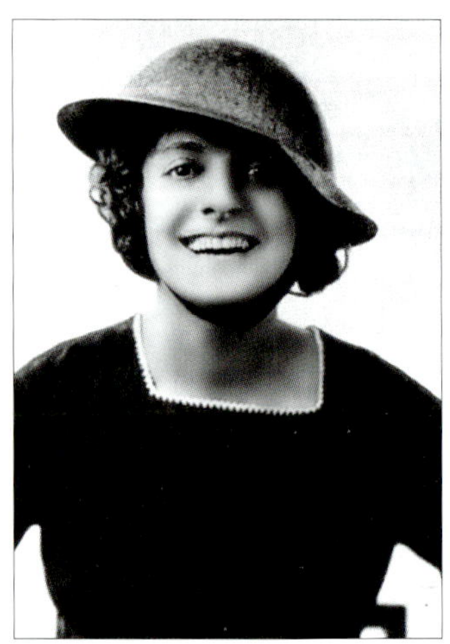
Elsie Janis as she appeared at WW I Army bases

On May 15, 1915, with the sinking of the *Lusitania*, Elsie's innocence abruptly ended. During the war she was the "Sweetheart of the Doughboys"—the first actress to perform at advanced U.S. army bases. Earlier in the war her British lover Basil Hallam was torn from her when he enlisted in the British army. As he was departing, she wrote this poem that he read onstage:

Where are you God,
In whom I have believed?
Are you in heaven?
Have I been deceived?
With poison gas and crucifixion
Battles have been won,
And yet upon this earth of yours
There still exists The Hun.
Where are you God?[1]

In her 1932 memoir, *So Far, So Good*, she wrote of the last time she saw Hallam: "I left him standing on the platform of Euston Station, chin up, clear eyes blue and fearless. In my hand I held a photograph he had posed for at the last moment in uniform and on it he wrote: 'If we still love those we lose, can we ever quite lose those we love.' "[2]

He died at the front in France, and she never got over him. Elsie Janis died in 1956.

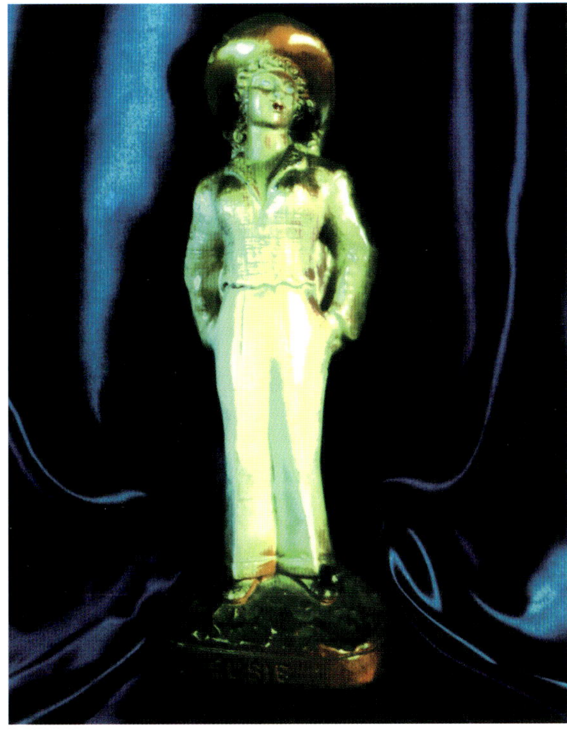

Elsie Janis twelve-inch carnival chalk prize

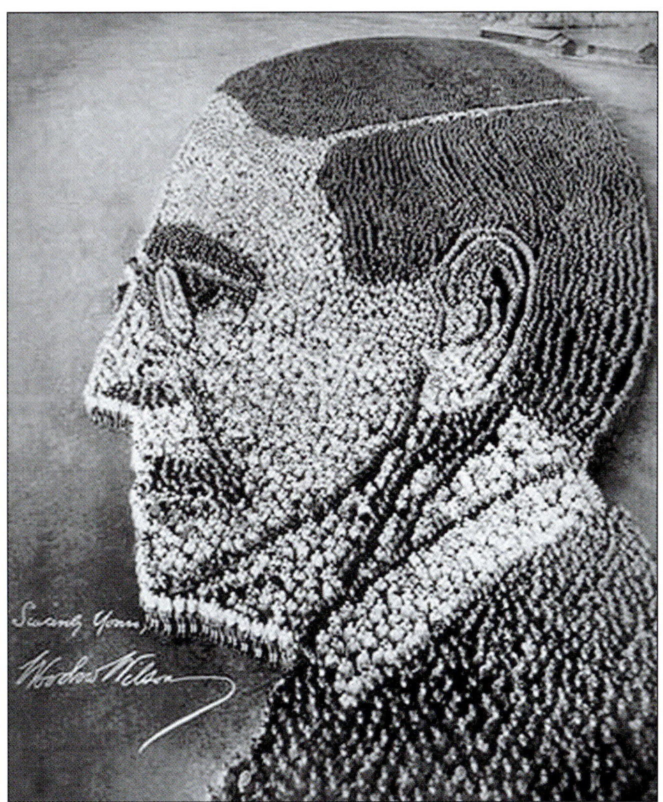

World War I postcard of twenty-one thousand soldiers at Camp Sherman, Ohio, staged and photographed by Arthur Mole, 1918

There are, it may be, many months of fiery trial and sacrifice ahead of us. It is a fearful thing to lead this great peaceful people into war, into the most terrible and disastrous of all wars, civilization itself seeming to be in the balance. But the right is more precious than peace, and we shall fight for the things which we have always carried nearest our hearts—for democracy, for the right of those who submit to authority to have a voice in their own governments, for the rights and liberties of small nations, for a universal dominion of right by such a concert of free peoples as shall bring peace and safety to all nations and make the world itself at last free. To such a task we can dedicate our lives and our fortunes, everything that we are and everything that we have, with the pride of those who know that the day has come when America is privileged to spend her blood and her might for the principles that gave her birth and happiness and the peace which she has treasured. God helping her, she can do no other.
—WOODROW WILSON, *War Message*, 65th Congress, 1st Session, April 2, 1917, Senate Document #5 Serial #7264, Washington, D. C., page 8. Four days later the U.S. entered World War I.

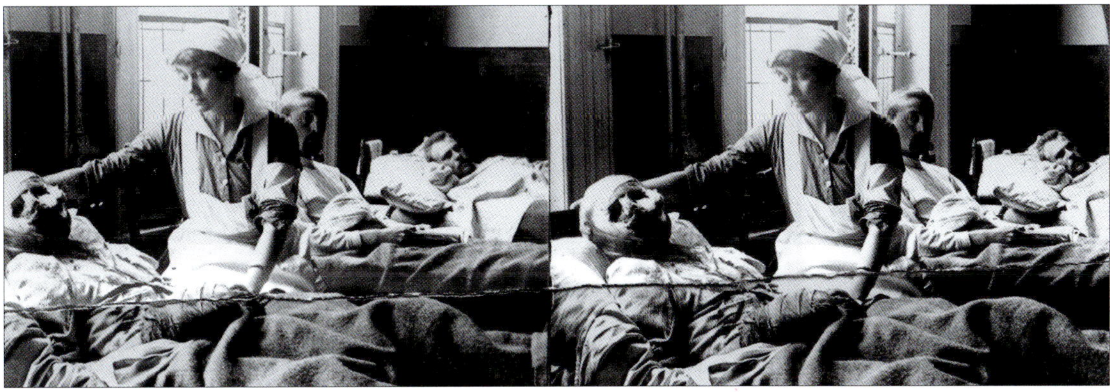

Detail, Stereo Card, World War I: "The Horror of War—Ghastly Glimpse of Wounded," Keystone View Company, Underwood & Underwood, U.S.A.

Virgin Mary

One cannot resist the thought that the level of normal morality is different for women. Their superego never becomes so unshakable, so impersonal, so independent of its affective origins, as we demand it of a man. Critics since time immemorial have reproached women of certain character traits: that they exhibit less of a sense of justice than men do; that they are less prepared to submit to the great necessities of life.
—Sigmund Freud

The prolonged slavery of women is the darkest page of human history.
—Elizabeth Cady Stanton, *History of Woman Suffrage*

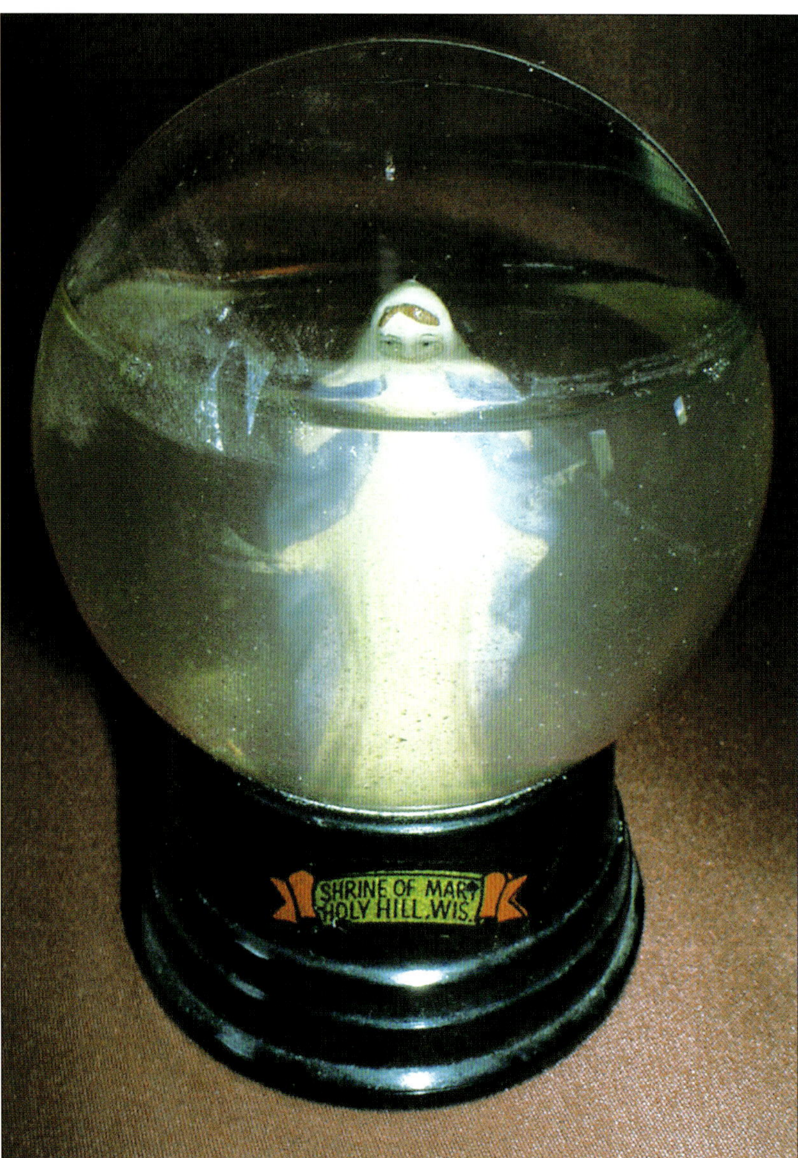

Snow globe, Shrine of Mary, Holy Hill, Wisconsin, circa 1940s

Early Christian scribes had a difficult time adding a woman into the story of God and Jesus—he obviously had to be born in some way. Since goddess worship was strong during the first few centuries of Christianity, the early Mary was a composite of previous goddess figures. The architects of the church, however, did not want Mary to represent motherhood, for that would have left her open to emulation as a goddess figure. Mariolatry has plagued Christian patriarchy throughout its history, as the need to worship the symbolic mother archetype has always arisen.[1] Up until the fifth century, Christians persecuted their own Marianite sect, who wanted Mary to be divine. In an effort to make Mary as sexless as possible, Christian scribes made her a virgin, knowing that many earlier saviors or pagan gods—such as Zoroaster, Perseus, Zeus, Heracles, Mithra, to name only a few—had been virgin born. The Christian scribes summarily dismissed all saviors and pagan gods celebrated before Christianity simply by declaring they were the work of the devil.

Christian ascetics invented curious ways for God to have impregnated Mary—the most unusual of these methods described God's seed as going into Mary's ear after having been transferred from Gabriel's mouth through a sacred lily.[2] But the Bible had problems with women in general, not just Mary. In 1 Corinthians 11:3, St. Paul said: "The head of every man is Christ; and the head of every woman is the man."

Saint Thomas Aquinas insisted that every woman was birth-defective, an imperfect male begotten because her father happened to be ill, weakened, or in a state of sin at the time of her conception.[3]

Martin Luther said:

> Men have broad and large chests and narrow hips and more understanding than women who have but small and narrow chests and broad hips, to the end they should remain at home, sit still, keep house and bear and bring up children. If women get tired and die of bearing, there is no harm in that; let them die as long as they bear; they were made for that.[4]

Over the twenty centuries of Christianity, Mary's place in the hierarchy has slowly ascended to her original heights prior to AD 400. It was only after 400 that she was omitted from the Trinity. Gothic cathedrals were often dedicated not to God or Jesus but to Mary, as evidenced by the many cathedrals that bear the words "Our Ladies of . . ." Many Christian cathedrals were built over pagan shrines to the goddess: the cathedral of Santa Maria Maggiore in Rome was erected over the sacred cave of the Magna Mater.[5] Some of the earliest churches dedicated to Mary were actually staffed by priestesses rather than priests.[6] But that practice soon ceased and was decidedly forgotten. In February 1977, Pope Paul VI again refused to ordain women as priests, although on June 30, 1968, he had reconfirmed the dogma of the Assumption of the Blessed Virgin Mary, saying that Mary, like Jesus, had risen bodily from the earth and ascended into glory, renewing her with a special equality through an eminence usually bestowed only on Jesus.[7]

Althea Aurandt, author of *Secrets Your Church Never Told You*, states:

Many present-day Catholic feminists say that the Virgin Mary historically had always been given the titles addressed to the Holy Spirit. They point to two Old Testament books of the Bible which are in the Catholic Bible but not in the Protestant Bible: Ecclesiasticus (NOT Ecclesiastes), and Wisdom. In these two books, which were Jewish not Christian writings, the Holy Spirit is equated with Wisdom and metaphorically described as a wife or daughter of God; as the breath of as God; as a cloud or mist; as tall; as a tree, a vine, a blossom; as sweet; as a mirror of God; as an educator; and as a friend of righteous men. All of these terms which describe the Holy Spirit or Wisdom were applied to the Virgin Mary, the Catholic feminists say. What is most bizarre was what the Church Fathers said about Mary. Because they hated non-virgin women, they insisted that Mary and Joseph, her husband, never had sexual relations even after Jesus was born. Even though the Gospels clearly said that Jesus had brothers, the Catholic Church claimed that these siblings were only half brothers, children of Joseph by an earlier marriage. In addition, they insisted that after Jesus was born, God miraculously healed Mary's stretched vagina and uterus and replaced her hymen![8]

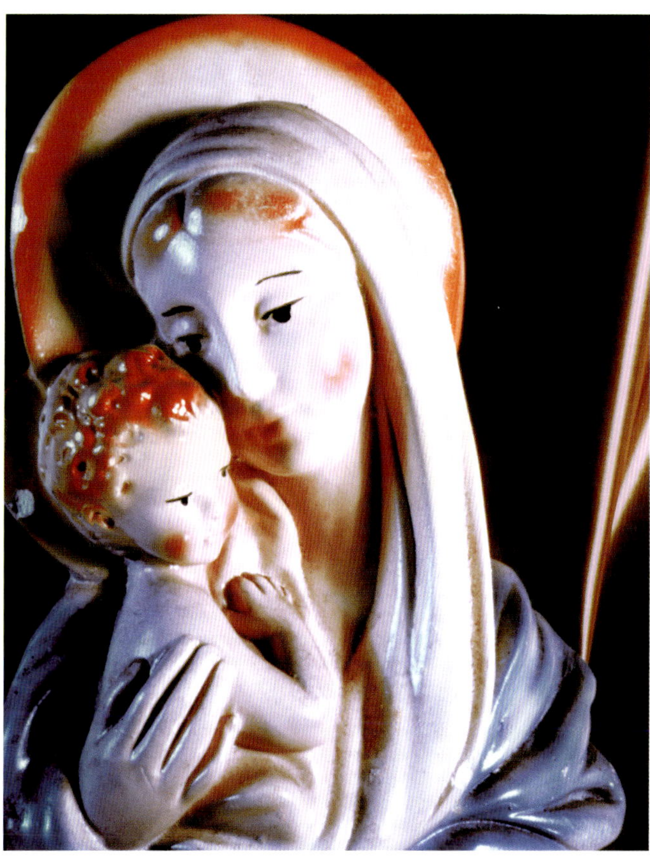

Virgin Mary ten-inch carnival chalkware prize. To those with an orthodox Christian view the Virgin Mary symbolized the merciful and compassionate virgin; to those more liberal, she was the mother archetype.

AL JOLSON (1886-1950)
SONNY BOY (1928)

When there are gray skies I don't mind the gray skies.
You make them blue, Sonny Boy.
Friends may forsake me, let them all forsake me.
You pull me thru, Sonny Boy. You're sent from heaven and I know your worth.
You made a heaven for me right here on the earth.
When I'm old and gray, dear, promise you won't stray, dear,
for I love you, Sonny Boy.
—AL JOLSON, *Sonny Boy*

Al Jolson called himself the "World's Greatest Entertainer." His popularity reached an all-time high in 1927 when he starred in Hollywood's first sound film, *The Jazz Singer*. His prophetic lines "Wait a minute! Wait a minute! You ain't heard nothin' yet!" were the first words spoken in any widely distributed Hollywood sound film. The story line in *The Jazz Singer* paralleled events in Jolson's personal life and followed a Jewish blackface minstrel who was trying to become a Broadway star despite his cantor father's disapproval. The film was hugely successful and an ecstatic Hollywood rushed him into another blackface film, *The Singing Fool* (1928). It was an even bigger box-office hit—thanks to his million-selling recording of the sugary, sentimental song "Sonny Boy," which was actually written as a joke by Jolson's collaborators, Brown and Henderson. *The Singing Fool* grossed more than $5 million.

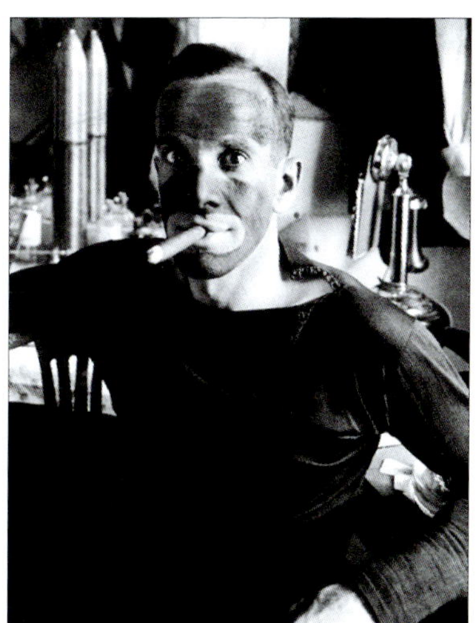

Al Jolson, circa 1915

Al Jolson was born Asa Yoelson in 1886 in Seredzius, Lithuania. In 1894, at age eight, his family immigrated to the United States. A year later his mother died—a very traumatic event for young Asa.

Jolson began singing in 1904 and toured in musical comedies and vaudeville revues. He received top billing at the prestigious Winter Garden Theater in New York City in 1911. He ad-libbed his comic material, improvised his music, and jumped into the aisles, engaging his audiences in a deeply personal way and leaving them spellbound. Jolson was the most popular singer from 1911 through the 1920s, just before the era of radio and sound film. His songs were indelibly sappy, and because he had to project to a large audience without the aid of microphones, he developed a "booming-moaning, crawling-groaning" vocal style, which became his signature. He worked almost entirely in the blackface minstrel genre, using burned cork makeup. Some entertainment critics have suggested that he used blackface more as a theatrical mask than as an expression of racial prejudice. Apparently he was never really comfortable performing without it. After his debut in *The Jazz Singer*, he starred on the radio and in other Hollywood films until 1939, when his popularity faded. He experienced a mild comeback performing for U.S. troops during World War II, which led to his dubbed voice-overs for *The Jolson Story* (1946) and *Jolson Sings Again* (1949), films that were about him.

Jolson's unique singing style inspired many imitators and, strangely enough, continues to do so. He died in 1950.

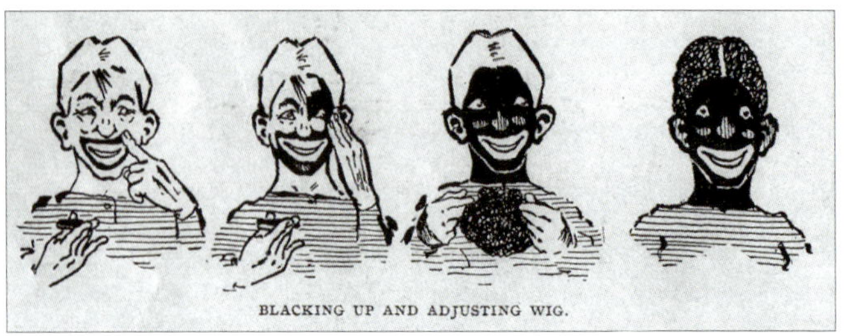

"Blacking up and adjusting wig," Frank Dumont, *The Witmark Minstrel Guide,* M. Witmark & Sons, Chicago, 1899

the minstrel repertoire, including such immortal tunes as "Oh! Susanna," "Camptown Races," "My Old Kentucky Home," "Old Black Joe," and "Massa's in de Cold, Cold Ground." As the Civil War drew closer, issues became more heated and the characterizations more exaggerated. The stereotype of the cowardly, sniveling, uneducated black man, later to be known as an Uncle Tom, came mostly from minstrel shows and preceded Harriet Beecher Stowe's *Uncle Tom's Cabin*. Blacks also performed as black minstrels. One group, the Real Nigs, took to the stage and advertised themselves as "the real thing." Blackface was a testimonial to archetypal denigration through emulation.

By the flapper era, black jazz stars and singers became a more accepted form of true entertainment. It was generally agreed that blacks were more capable singers and more facile dancers than their white counterparts (a racist compliment). Blackface minstrels imitated the uninhibited hip black jazz singers and dancers. During this time, minstrel shows allowed for a somewhat appreciative view of the black performers. That was Jolson's era. There is no doubt that the entire history of the minstrel medium was racist; it altered only slightly with the passage of time. With the advent of the civil rights era the minstrel show became unacceptable, but blacks continued to be portrayed with negative racial stereotypes in other venues. A lingering problem was that African-American actors and actresses were not accepted as stars in any of the media forms until well past the 1950s, and then just barely.

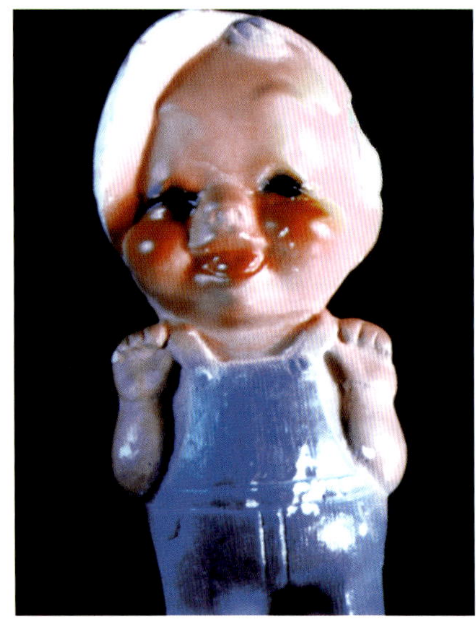

Al Jolson (Sonny Boy) carnival chalk prize © June Yates Jenkins. There were two eight-and-a-half-inch Al Jolson (Sonny Boy) carnival chalk prizes—in one he is in blackface; in both, he is marked "Sonny Boy" on the base.

Blackface was a political and entertainment tool from its inception in 1820. In the 125 years following its birth, blackface dramatically changed, keeping in tandem with the fluctuating political climate. In early productions that used blackface, the black person was stereotyped as lazy and shiftless. Later groups like the Virginia Minstrels invented caricatures, such as Mr. Bones and Mr. Tambo, who fidgeted and spoke totally inane lines in a negative, racist way. Stephen Foster, considered one of America's great songwriters during the 1840s and 1850s, contributed many racist songs for

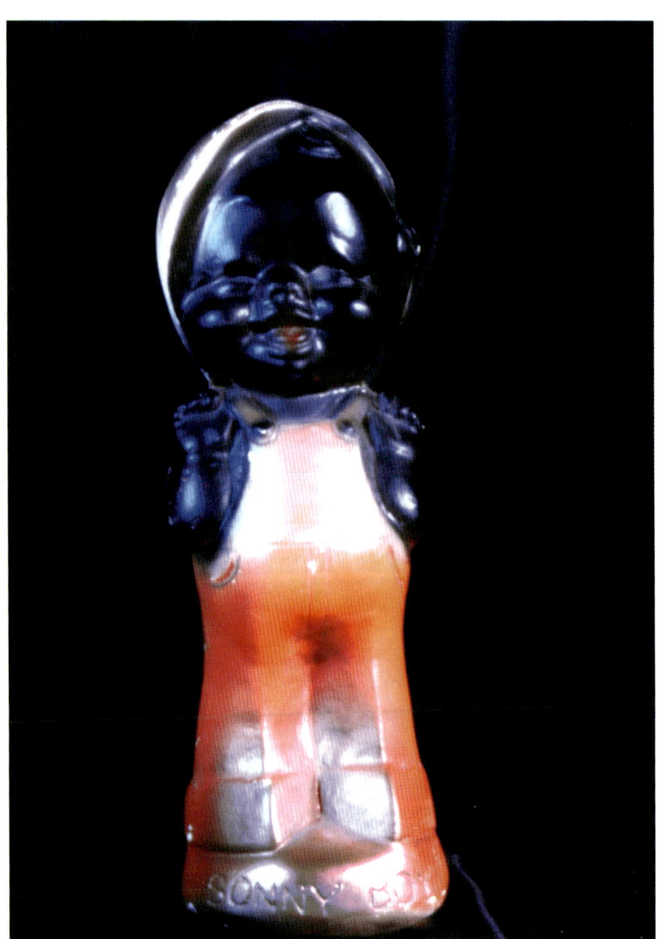

Sonny Boy in blackface carnival chalk prize

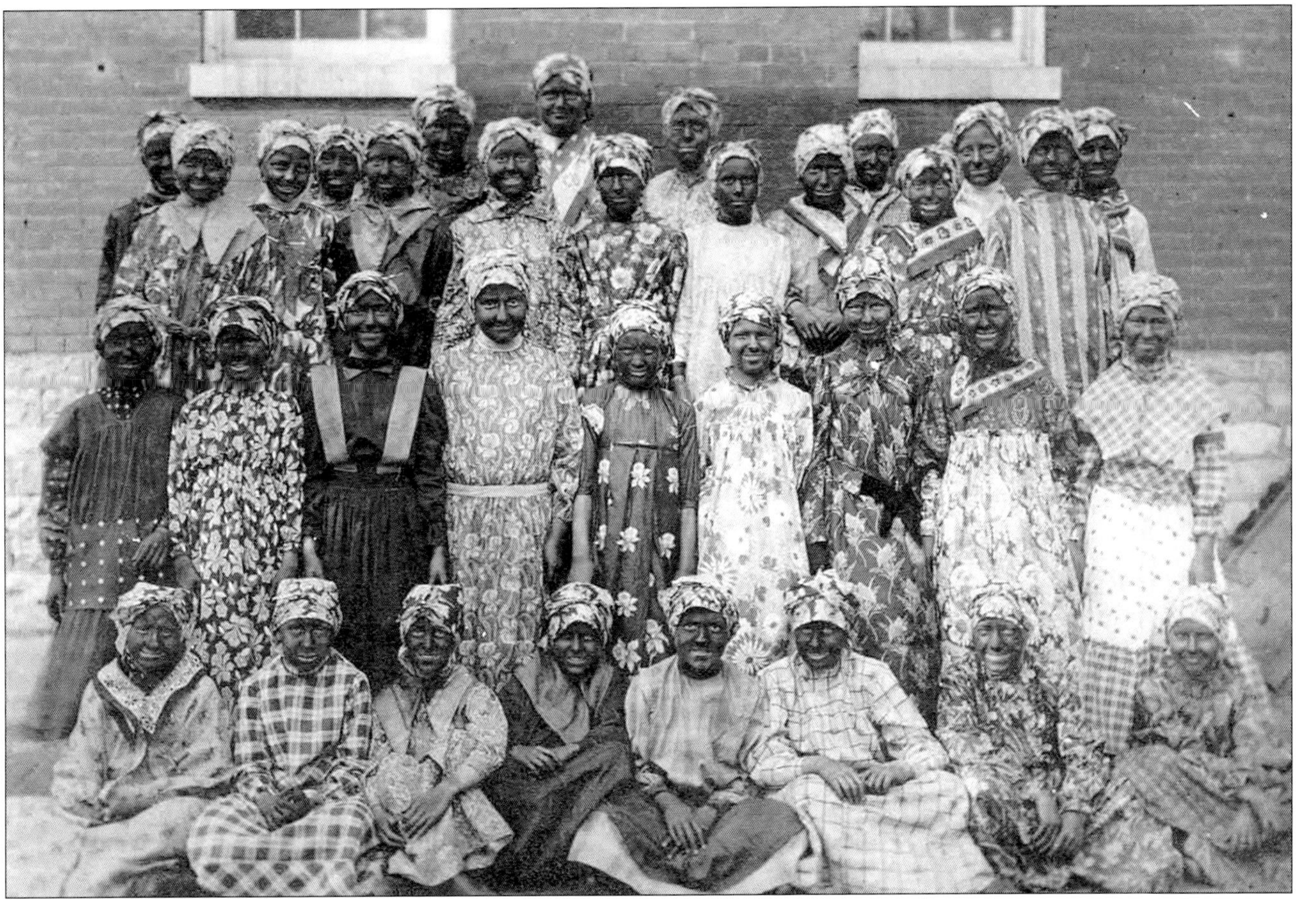

Girls in blackface at St. Anthony's School, Dutchtown, (St Louis), circa 1917, photograph J. R. Eike. Courtesy: © Thomas Kempland Collection

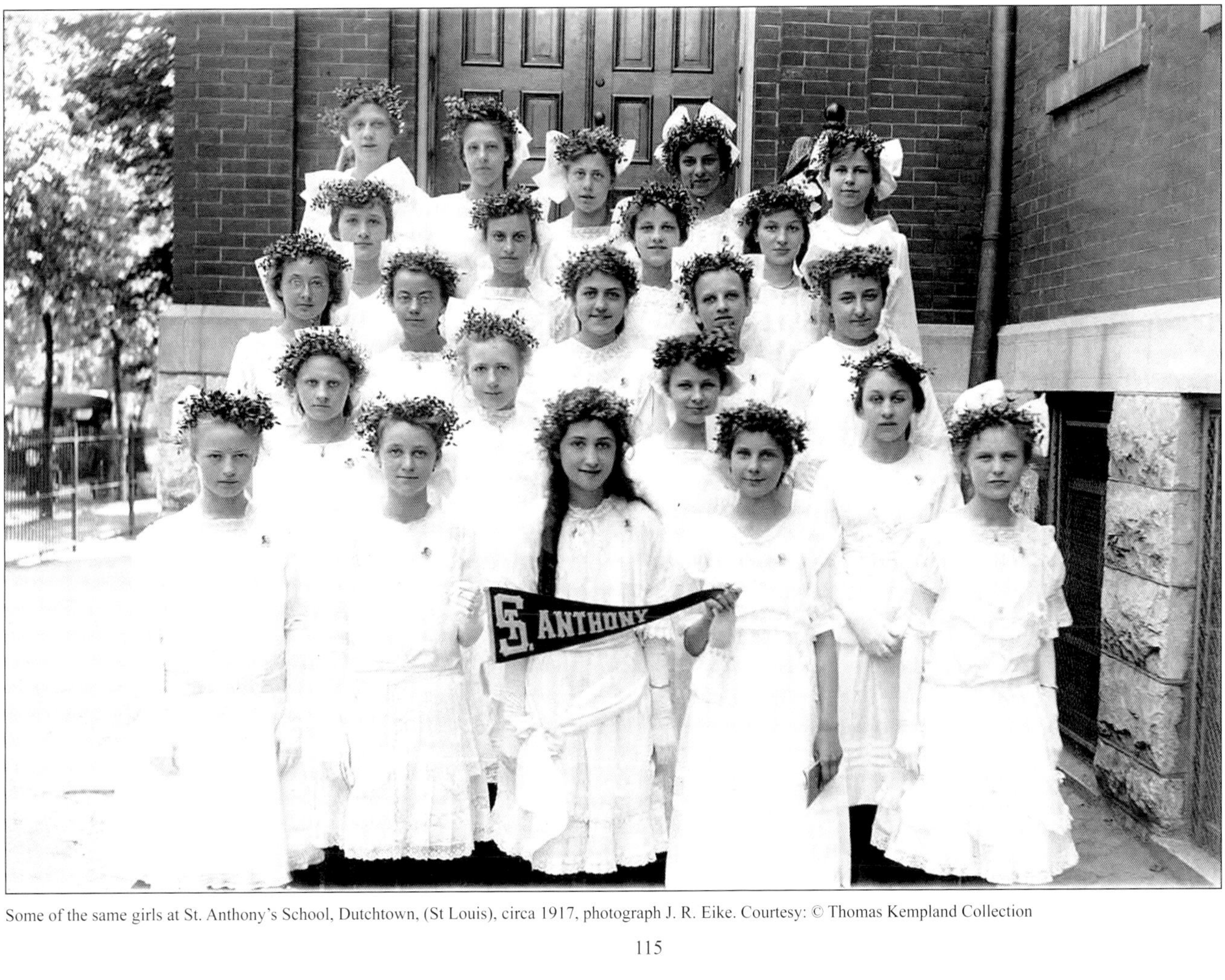

Some of the same girls at St. Anthony's School, Dutchtown, (St Louis), circa 1917, photograph J. R. Eike. Courtesy: © Thomas Kempland Collection

Humpty Dumpty

Humpty Dumpty sat on a wall,
Humpty Dumpty had a great fall;
All the King's horses and all the King's men
Couldn't put Humpty Dumpty together again.

It was not the working classes that brought on the economic crisis,
it was the big boys that thought the financial drunk was going to last
forever, and over bought, over merged and over capitalized.
—WILL ROGERS

As one of the ancient, lingering Mother Goose rhymes, the fairy-tale man-egg Humpty Dumpty's comic-tragic message has shifted slightly over the centuries. Now we see him as too satisfied—we all know that his insipid smile won't last long. Sooner or later he falls. No more Humpty Dumpty. His popularity as a fairy-tale icon was revived during the Great Depression—his smile aptly represented the happy fool, the overindulgent and inflated excesses of the flapper era. His fall was analogous to the stock market crash. Humpty Dumpty was symbolic of a broken America. Who could put it back together again?

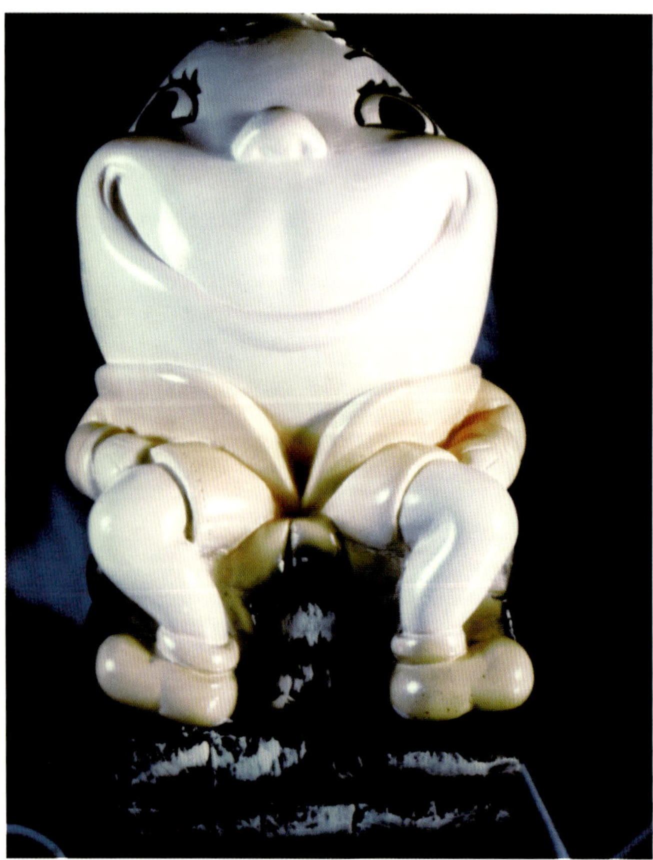

Humpty Dumpty twelve-inch carnival chalk bank prize

In American collections of Mother Goose rhymes in print, Humpty Dumpty can be traced back to 1719 to *Songs of the Nursery; or, Mother Goose's Melodies for Children* by

Thomas Fleet of Boston. During that harsh puritanical era, Humpty Dumpty's satisfied smile presented a horrid reminder of the Bible's account of the fall of man. Moreover, Humpty Dumpty referred to Adam and Eve's original sin. What could be more difficult to balance than an upright egg? Sooner or later the egg had to fall. Most likely sooner. What could be more easily broken and impossible to repair than an egg? Comparing an upright egg to humanity's inability to remain free of sin was an ominous paradigm. Humpty Dumpty is a puritanical archetypal scale model for a negative view of a world inhabited by an imperfect man and an imperfect woman.

Humpty Dumpty analyzed line by line:

• **Humpty Dumpty sat on a wall:** An analogue representing Eve's precarious quandary of whether or not to eat the apple from the tree of knowledge.

• **Humpty Dumpty had a great fall:** A reminder to Christians that when tempted by the snake, Eve ate the apple and had sex with Adam. Therefore, humanity angered God and "had a great fall" into Hell. Eve was held responsible for the miseries of lust and the horrors of death.

• **All the King's horses and all the King's men:** Who represent God's heavenly host.

• **Couldn't put Humpty Dumpty together again:** This final destruction represented Saint Paul's message in the New Testament that only Christians could be saved and put back "together again," and only if they believed in their savior Jesus, and only through the grace of God. The poem inferred that non-Christians would remain fallen forever, never to be put back together again. Humpty Dumpty represented feelings of fear of the unknown, easily promoted by many institutions.

Many Mother Goose rhymes were meant as harsh lessons and reflect cliché archetypes. For instance, to teach the Puritan work ethic to little boys:

> See saw, Jack-a-daw,
> Johnny shall have a new master;
> Johnny shall have but a penny a day,
> Because he can work no faster.

Or what does the message in this one teach? Snooping? Irreverence? Adultery? Brutality?

> Goosey, goosey, gander, whither shall I wander?
> Up stairs and down stairs, and in my lady's chamber.
> There I met an old man, who would not say his prayers;
> I took him by the left leg, and threw him down the stairs.

On cleanliness and discipline:

> Little Polly Flinders sat among the cinders,
> Warming her pretty little toes!
> Her mother came and caught her,
> and whipped her little daughter,
> for spoiling her nice new clothes.
> When a man marries, his trouble begins.

On an early accidental death:

> Little Tee Wee,

He went to sea,
In an open boat;
And while afloat
The little boat bended—
My story's ended.

The use of rhyme to project morals to youngsters will most likely always be part and parcel of the social conditioning tools used in all cultures. Singsong dialogues provide easy access to the short attention spans of children and are the perfect vehicle for injecting subliminal morality training. Of course the same method can, and is, used to teach communication skills, such as rhyming alphabet letters and numbers. The much-touted Dr. Seuss books use the same device to make children aware of social and environmental issues. The early messages and seemingly benign entertainments we drill into our children are later subtly telegraphed into their adult lives—hardly the innocuous ditties we perceive them to be. The power of suggested moralities to young people can never be underestimated, for who can predict when a silly rhyme sung to a four-year-old might eventually direct the thinking of the leader of a country?

Nor is a baby a dunce, as this harsh, judgmental, carnival chalk prize claimed. In the 1940s a dunce cap was an otherness stereotype for problematic stupidity. A pointed cap is an archetypal motif. Joan of Arc was made to wear a tall pointed mitre cap (the dunce cap comes from that shape) as she was taken to be burned at the stake. The pointed Ku Klux Klan cap is related to it, as is the witch's hat.

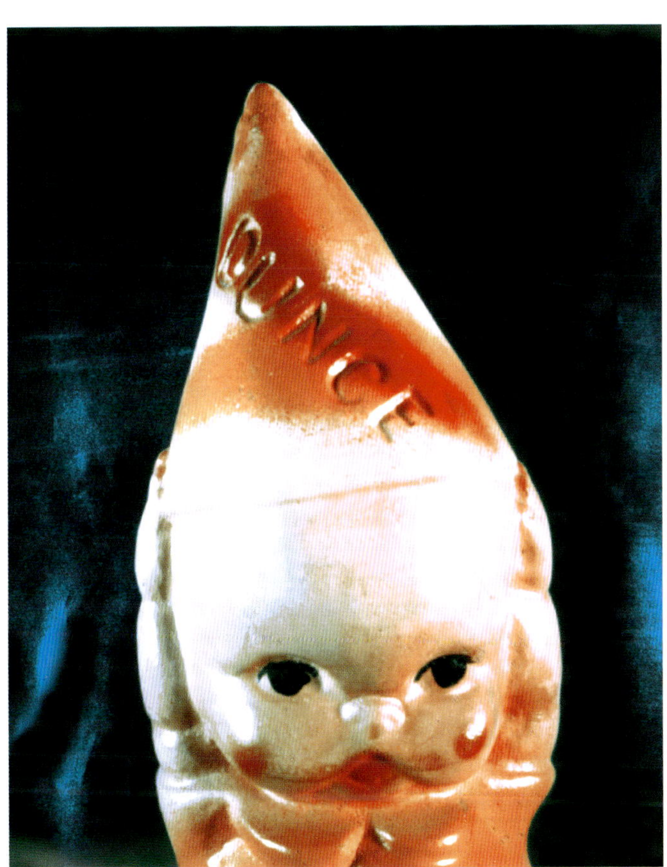

Dunce ten-inch carnival chalk prize

Jean Harlow (1911-1937)

Underwear makes me uncomfortable and besides my parts have to breathe.
—JEAN HARLOW

I used to look at movie magazines and cut out the pictures of Jean Harlow. That's what I wanted to be someday—a Jean Harlow.
—MARILYN MONROE

There is a vitality, a life force, a quickening that is translated through you into action, and there is only one of you in all time, this expression is unique, and if you block it, it will never exist through any other medium; and be lost. The world will not have it. It is not your business to determine how good it is, not how it compares with other expression. It is your business to keep it yours clearly and directly, to keep the channel open. You do not even have to believe in yourself or your work. You have to keep open and aware directly to the urges that motivate you. Keep the channel open. No artist is pleased. There is no satisfaction whatever at any time. There is only a queer, divine dissatisfaction, a blessed unrest that keeps us marching and makes us more alive than the others.
—MARTHA GRAHAM

Marilyn Monroe confessed to being fixated with Jean Harlow from her early childhood. In *Bombshell*, David Stenn describes Monroe's attempt to make *The Jean Harlow Story*:

> Given their similarities, it was inevitable that Monroe portray Harlow in a "biopic" of her life. "She should be done humanly," Monroe stipulated as Ben Hecht, Adela Rogers St. Johns, and Sidney Skolsky drafted separate treatments of *The Jean Harlow Story*. In a special *Life* feature, Monroe posed as Harlow for photographer Richard Avedon.
> *The Jean Harlow Story* stalled when Monroe read its script. "I hope they don't do that to me after I'm gone," she told her agent and refused the role. Still interested in playing Harlow, she agreed to see Skolsky on August 5, 1962. Early that day her death was announced.[1]

Jean Harlow bulldozed Hollywood's ridiculous taboo regarding blonde actresses; few blonde-haired women were cast in leading roles before her glistening hair sparkled onto the silver screen. It was about time. Harlow cast a golden spell over America that still holds sway—the Hollywood-blonde stereotype. Mae West, Carol Channing, Marilyn Monroe, Madonna, and many more attest to it.

Harlow's hair was actually platinum blonde, not blonde. Naturally blonde hair would not have projected nearly the same visual aura onto black-and-white, soft-focus film. The glow of her hair heightened her sexuality and had the effect of making her unique and effervescent when compared with other actresses. The public's first real look at Harlow was in *Hells Angels* (1930). Audiences were spellbound and watched in amazement as she took delight in lustfully displaying her curves with joyful immodesty. Her archetypal symbol was the alluring immodest woman, particularly fitting for a young woman enamored with her own body—which was not surprising since Harlow was very ill as a child.

Harlow became America's number-one sex symbol by the early 1930s. Cigarette manufacturers, who used her alluring charms in their Lucky Strike ads—such as one where she was titled "Cream of the Crop"— quickly snapped her up. (The public ignored her line from *Hell's Angels* when she tells a male admirer he looks dumb smoking a cigarette.)

Harlow's spoken parts were delivered with warmth and gaiety in an era when silent film was suddenly obsolesced by sound. "Talkies," as the early sound films were often called, didn't need the continuous action required in silent films to keep the story moving. Words smoothed the plot's timing to a more natural pace. Harlow was a gifted natural comedienne, and all she needed to say to capture her audience was, "Would you be shocked if I changed into something more comfortable?" They loved her genuine gift for brazen honesty.

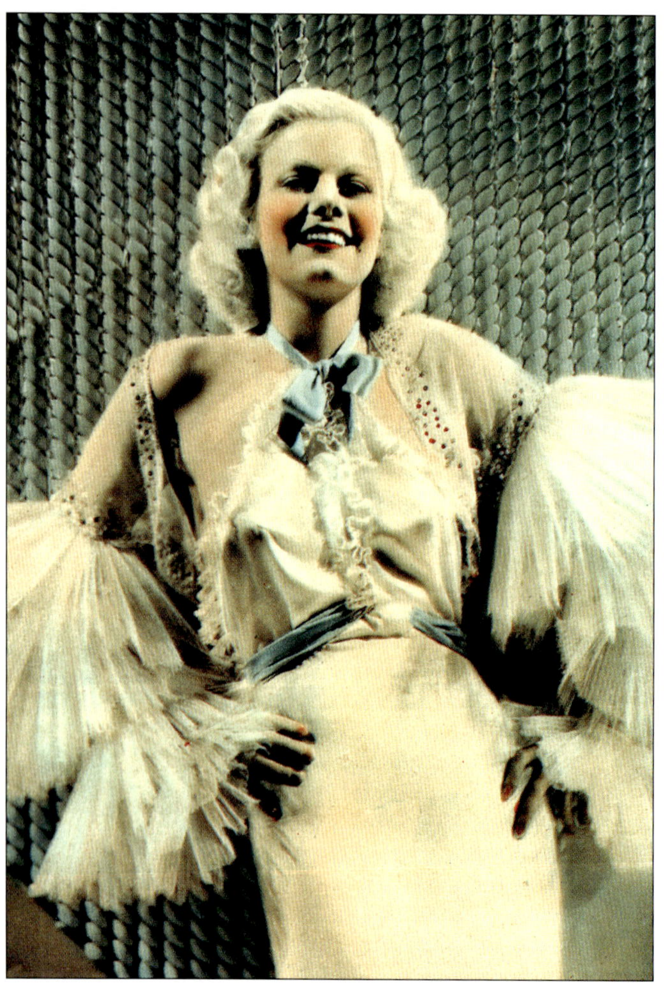

Jean Harlow, hand-colored photograph, postcard © No. 16 in series of 24, placed in larger packages of De Reszke Cigarettes and other Godfrey Phillips Associated Brands, circa 1930s

Had she lived, Harlow would be astonished to know how many women, teenagers, and even young girls have consciously or unconsciously imitated that distinctive American stereotype. By the time Carol Channing and Marilyn Monroe became famous, the Hollywood-blonde stereotype was firmly embedded into the world's psyche.

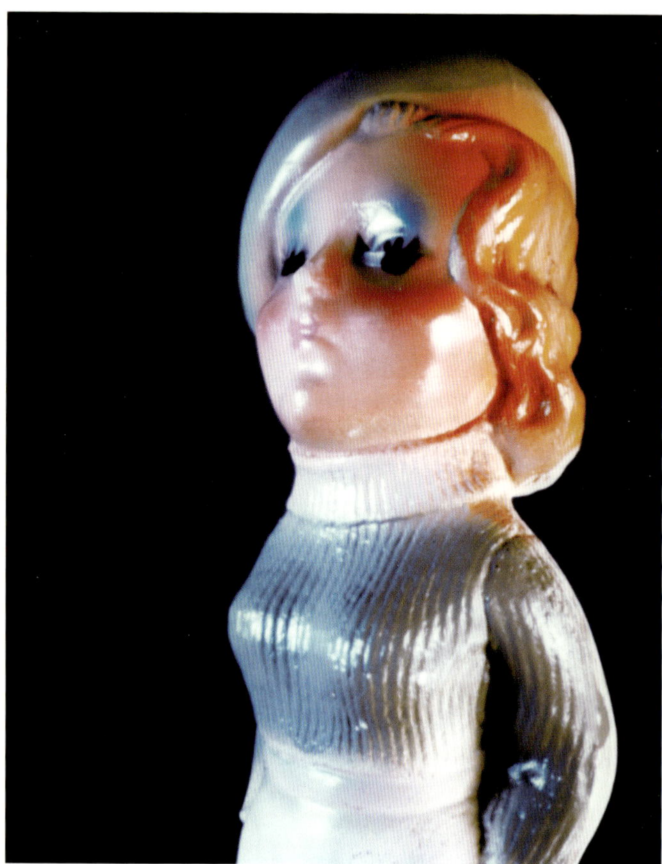

Jean Harlow twelve-inch carnival chalk prize

Jean Harlow was born Harlean Carpentier on March 3, 1911, into an upper-middle-class family in Kansas City, Missouri. Her parents divorced when she was nine. Harlean was enrolled against her wishes in Ferry Hall School in Lake Forest, Illinois, when she was fifteen. A year later, she ran away from school and eloped with Charles McGrew II, who was twenty—and wealthy. They married in January 1928, and after honeymooning on a cruise from New York to Los Angeles via the Panama Canal, bought a house at 618 Linden Drive in Beverly Hills. By that summer, her mother and stepfather also moved to Los Angeles. It was actually her mother, named, appropriately, Mother Jean, who wanted to be the movie star. As luck would have it, it was Harlean who was discovered by smart Hollywood execs, even though she had no designs on being an actress, at least not at first. She started in Hollywood bit parts under the professional name Jean Harlow ("Harlow" was her mother's maiden name). She became pregnant, but Mother Jean forced her to have an abortion. Harlow and McGrew separated in 1929.

Jean Harlow replaced the famed actress and beauty Greta Nissen in Howard Hughes's extravagant aerial war film *Hell's Angels* when she was only eighteen. *Hell's Angels* was a huge box-office success and a year later, she achieved her status as America's number-one sex symbol in *Platinum Blonde*. Next came a series of six films (produced almost yearly) with Harlow starring opposite the handsome Clark Gable (the Harlow/Gable films are her Hollywood legacy). By 1933, her fame was so great that she would parody her own life in the semiautobiographical film *Bombshell*, which initiated the idea that lusty women were an analogue to bombshells.

Her personal life seemed disastrous. She contracted scarlet fever in her youth, leaving her with chronically weak kidneys. The illness probably created the overwhelming codependent relationship she had with Mother Jean and a greedy, abusive, disgusting stepfather whom she despised. Harlow had three brief and difficult marriages. Her only mature love was with William Powell, but they were not destined to be together. Sadly, in 1937, the shocked world learned that Harlow was dead at twenty-six of kidney failure, probably the result of the chronic infection that stayed with her from childhood (and because Christian Scientist Mother Jean waited too long to take her for treatment). A distraught Powell was at her bedside when she died. Hollywood and the world mourned. He could not work for a year.

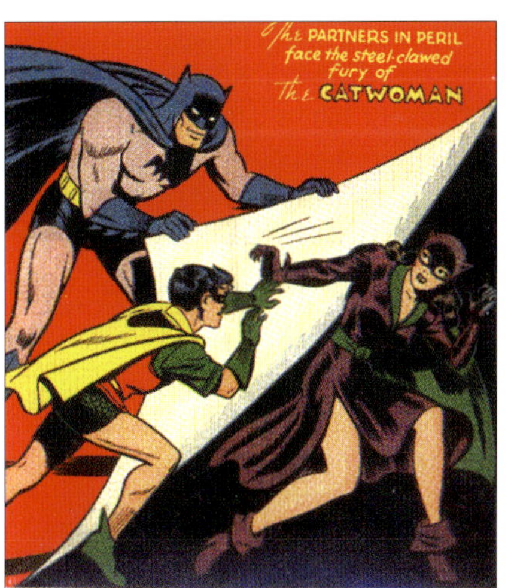

Catwoman, detail, *Batman*, #42 © Action Comics

In the 1940 issue of *BatMan #1*, Harlow was immortalized as Cat-Woman. Her luster and star quality have held throughout the years. Harlow's premature death at twenty-six made her an archetypal symbol for heartfelt remembrance. When Marilyn Monroe entered the Hollywood landscape in the early 1950s (conspicuously resembling the Jean Harlow stereotype), she unconsciously carried that heartfelt remembrance feeling to her admirers. In the grand picture of life, it is not surprising that Monroe also died young. Her tragic, mysterious death added a similar factor into her own enduring icon; connecting her with Harlow more than doubled Monroe's heartfelt remembrance. Monroe's face is better known than any other woman's in the world, and Monroe's and Harlow's youthful images have made both of them timeless. Their glamorous, shining countenances are now classic Greek sculpture chiseled into enduring cinematic and world memory.

In mysterious ways both Harlow and Monroe were liberated outcasts to the social norm; first through abuse and alienation, then through empowered flaunting and flouting. Of Monroe, Arthur Miller wrote:

> She had accepted the role of the outcast years ago, even flaunted it, first as a casualty of puritanical rejection but then with victorious disorder; from her refusal to wear bras to her laughing acknowledgement of calendar photos, her bracing candor—so un-American now in the new empire preparing to lead the war crippled West—was health, the strength of one who has abandoned the illusion of a properly ordered life for herself. With all her concealed pain she was becoming enviable, the astonishing signal of liberation and its joys.[2]

MICKEY MOUSE

(1928-

When I started on Disneyland, my wife used to say, 'But why do you want to build an amusement park? They're so dirty.' I told her that was just the point–mine wouldn't be.
—WALT DISNEY

He still speaks for me and I still for him.
—WALT DISNEY, On Mickey Mouse

There's a sucker born every minute.
—PHINEAS BARNUM

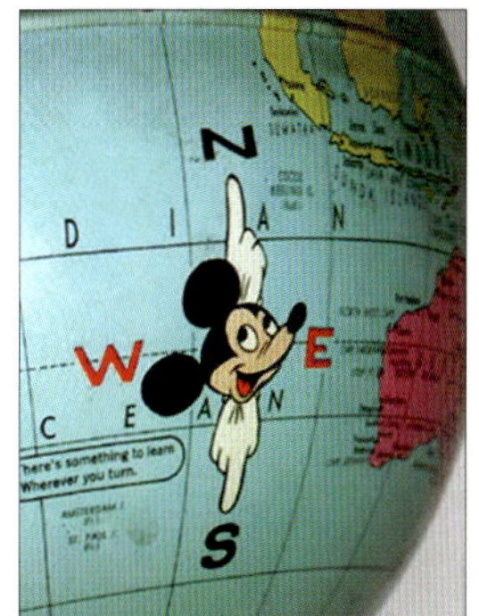

Detail of Mickey Mouse, globe © Rand McNally, circa 1950s-60s

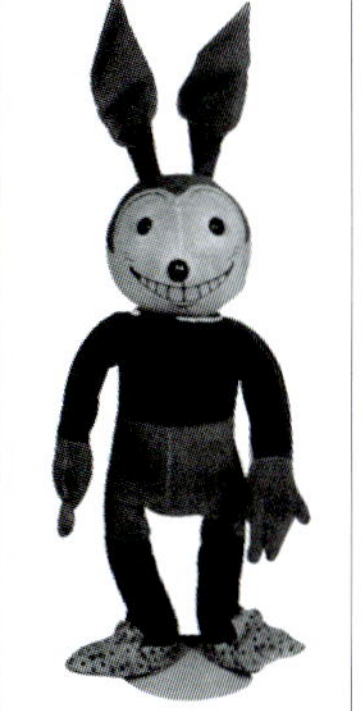

Oswald the Lucky Rabbit Rag Doll © Deans Rag Book Co., 1931. Courtesy: Hake's Americana, Div. of Diamond International Galleries

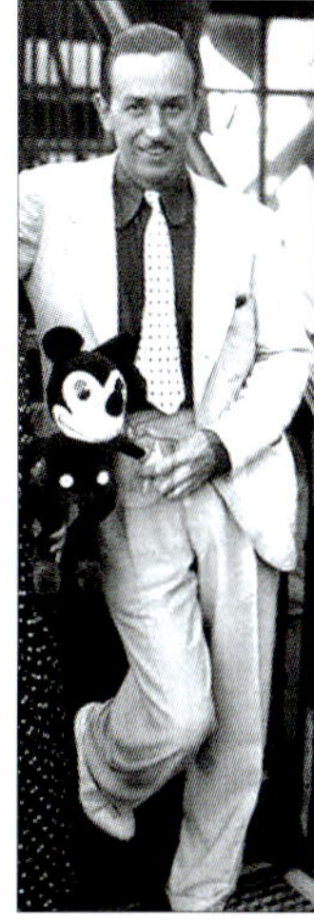

Walt Disney

There are two stories of how Mickey Mouse was created. The most well-known is that Walt Disney was forced to sign away all his rights for his cartoon *Oswald the Lucky Rabbit* to Charles Mintz, head of Snappy Comedies, Disney's distributor for Oswald in 1927. During Disney's train ride back to Hollywood with his wife, Lillian, he realized he had to find a new cartoon character and hit upon the idea of a mouse named Mortimer. Lillian suggested the name Mickey. Disney had created a sketch of the new character by the end of their trip. That constituted the romantic, Disney-gratifying story of Mickey's creation.

The more verifiable story is that Ub Iwerks, an artist and longtime partner who worked with Disney, created Mickey Mouse. This less mythical version was corroborated by the Disney archives. According to Dave Iwerks, Ub's son, when Disney arrived back in Hollywood, he had only a vague idea for a new character. He and Ub independently put their thoughts on paper for a new mouse character based on the idea of Chaplin's tramp. Disney showed Iwerks his drawings of Mickey. Iwerks rejected them because Disney's Mickey looked too much like a self-portrait. Disney admitted he had used the reflection of his own face in a mirror as a model. Iwerks then took one of his own sketches of Oswald, changed the ears and rounded the eyes, and turned Oswald into Mickey. Disney was thrilled to see how easy it was to regain his Oswald the Lucky Rabbit back from Mintz using Iwerk's drawing ability.[1] Later, animators would trace around a quarter to draw Mickey's head and a nickel for his ears.[2] Years later, Disney admitted he never actually drew Mickey.[3]

Disney's first cartoons with Mickey were *Plane Crazy*, homage to Charles Lindbergh, and *Gallopin' Gaucho*—neither were successful. His next try was *Steamboat Willie*, which appropriated liberally from the 1924 Buster Keaton film *The Navigator*. During production, Disney witnessed the premier of Al Jolson's *The Jazz Singer* and realized sound had to be added to his cartoons. On November 18, 1928, the first "sound" cartoon, *Steamboat Willie*, opened at Harry Reichenbach's Colony Theater in New York as the curtain-raiser for the feature film *Gang War*. Reichenbach requested his close friends in the newspaper business attend the opening, so is it any surprise that *Steamboat Willie* received rave reviews in their papers the next day? Disney's fame and fortune grew from then on. He was twenty-seven.

Disney did Mickey's scratchy voice in the early cartoons. With his well-groomed manners and his aw-shucks attitude, Mickey Mouse was not really funny, silly, or foolish; he stereotyped the conscientiously determined, save-the-day good guy warrior. Mickey could accomplish good deeds while under intense pressure, an attitude that exemplified Disney, who was also perjinkety (minutely accurate with prim and proper details). It was Mickey's moments of supernatural heroism that made him extremely popular. Mickey Mouse was a puncher, like Popeye—and like Popeye, he could beat up anyone. Since he was just a mouse, he could be seen by the audience as an archetypal symbol for the unbeatable little guy, a David against Goliath. They cheered him on. Disney disguised Mickey well by giving him favorite sayings that helped out his cute American pie au-shucks stereotype: "Gosh!" "Oh boy!" "That sure is swell!" "Aw, gee!" "See ya soon!"

Part of Mickey Mouse's initial appeal was that Disney's stories were well developed; better yet, Mickey's secondary characters were actually funny. By 1930, Mickey Mouse merchandise was everywhere, proving that if a cartoon character was extremely popular, then successful merchandising was a testimonial to financial security (that was what it was all about), particularly in a time when the Great Depression was taking its toll. That same year, King Features put Mickey Mouse into newspaper comic strips, which brought worldwide attention. Mickey Mouse cartoons were in Technicolor and Mickey Mouse Fan Clubs throughout the United States had a membership totaling a million by 1932. Though Iwerks drew Mickey for the first years, Floyd Gottfredson drew him for the next forty-five. The most important aspect of Mickey Mouse's continued success throughout the mid-1930s was that he was ahead of his time as the first intentionally determined good-guy hero in cartoons. Who could have guessed that the Will Hays Production Code, with its latent potential for bowdlerizing, would revolutionize Hollywood on issues regarding sex, violence, and criminal glorification—even in cartoons. But it did. By 1934, Hollywood's strategy for star eminence was to make the characters as respectable as possible. "Bawdy" Mae West was carefully censored, "teaser" Betty Boop spiraled downward, "pedophilia-prone" Baby

Burlesques were gone, all glorified criminals were outlawed, and a whole lot more. Since Mickey Mouse had been impeccably respectable for many years, he skirted the gambit and won big. He was the upstanding and newly crowned American icon.

The League of Nations presented Disney with a special medal in 1935—Mickey Mouse was a symbol of universal goodwill. By World War II "Mickey Mouse" meant anything that was corny, sentimental, or cheaply insincere. Educational hand-to-hand combat films as well as anti–venereal disease films were considered "Mickey Mouse." In 1944, "Mickey Mouse" was chosen as the code name for the Allied Forces invasion of the European continent under General Dwight D. Eisenhower. Throughout the World War II years, production of Mickey Mouse cartoons was sparse.

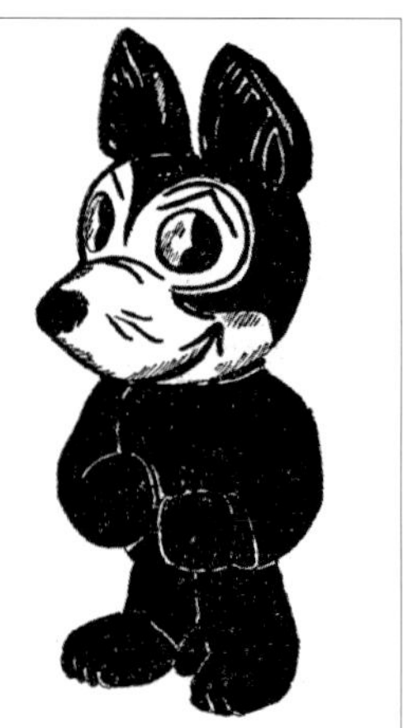

No. 2002—Nick. A very prominent character who is known to everyone. Made of unbreakable composition. Finished in black. Has attractive painted features. Height, 10½ inches.

Each.............25¢
Per dozen.........$2.40

Nick carnival chalk prize © Rodin Novelty Company, 1940–41 catalog

By the 1950s, Mickey had discreetly moved into an upper echelon of cartoon characters. He became the master of ceremonies for the *Mickey Mouse Club* on television. In 1955, when Disney built his first theme park, Disneyland, at Anaheim, Mickey was chosen to be the official host. Because of these corporate promotions, Mickey gradually became America's and Disney's ambassador to every country in the noncommunist world. This meant that Mickey was by then a power archetype—a political force to be reckoned with. His image was almost everywhere. To the children of foreign lands who saw him, he stereotyped a save-the-day good guy, but to those who thought America was becoming too powerful, he represented the big bully, an extension of America's fascination with Manifest Destiny.

Disney animators dramatically altered Mickey Mouse's ears, eyes, nose, facial expressions, body gestures—the whole works—starting in about 1933. By 1940, he looked to be less of a wise-guy.

Walt Disney was born Walter Elias Disney in 1901. Unable to get his parents to write a letter of consent for him to join the military, he forged their signatures and when he was sixteen was accepted as a volunteer into the International Red Cross. He served for the Red Cross in France, but only after the Armistice. To supplement his income, he and a friend bought surplus German helmets and shot them full of holes, after which Disney painted German insignias on them and sold them as souvenirs.[4] He began working as a cartoonist for the Kansas City Film Ad Company in 1920. There he learned the basics of animation. He moved to Hollywood in 1923 and continued his work in animation. He married Lillian Bounds in 1925. Early in 1927, Universal Pictures released his first popular cartoon *Oswald the Lucky Rabbit*; the "lucky" was swiped from popular and lucky Felix the Cat. In 1932, a special Academy Award was given to Disney for the creation of Mickey Mouse. In January 1937, the Junior Chamber of Commerce named Disney "Outstanding Young Man"—Will Hays was on the selection committee.[5] In 1938, Disney received an honorary master of arts degree from Harvard and an honorary master of fine arts from Yale.

Disney workers went on strike on May 28, 1941, for higher wages. Disney was forced to recognize the Cartoonist's Guild and, on September 9, 1941, the strike ended.

On October 24, 1947, after being subpoenaed by the House Un-American Activities Committee, he testified on Communist influences in the motion picture industry. His testimony reaffirmed his well-known disgust with what he considered to be Communist activists who had previously worked for him. Not only did his testimony destroy the careers of several of his artists but Disney further contaminated and influenced the committee's judgment on other Hollywood figures.

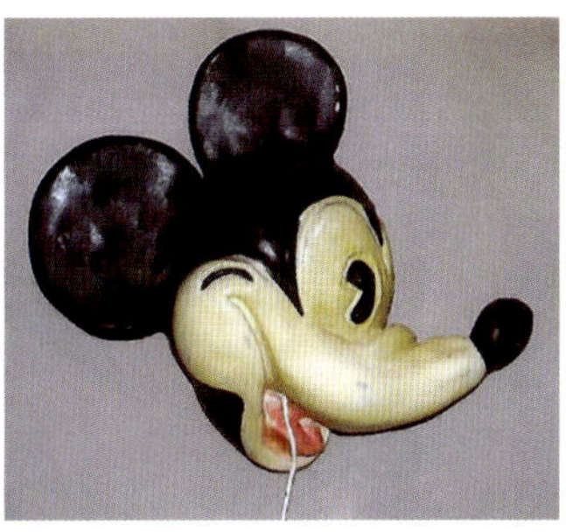

Mickey Mouse carnival chalk string holder prize, 1930s. Courtesy: Larry Pogue. From 1920-1960 chalk string holders were won as carnival prizes—available were Felix the Cat, Betty Boop, Popeye and Howdy Doody.

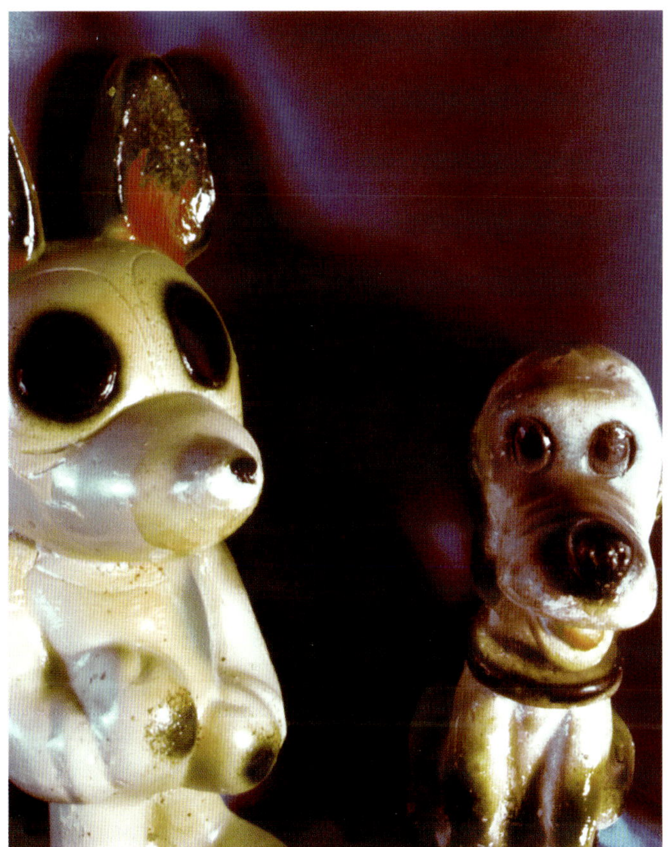

Ten-and-one-half-inch Mickey Mouse and eight-inch Pluto carnival chalk prizes

POPEYE (1919-
OLIVE OYL
WIMPY
SEA HAG
ALICE THE GOON
EUGENE THE JEEP

When asked if he was a sailor, Popeye answered, "Ja think I'm a cowboy?"—a flippant response that would become typical of John Wayne twenty-five years later. That was January 17, 1929, on the eve of the Great Depression. Popeye made his appearance as an add-on character—an extra to Elzie Segar's ten-year-old *Thimble Theatre* cartoon strip. Popeye stuck around, and exactly one week later met his future love, Olive Oyl, who had been in the strip for a long time. Her first words to him were, "Aw, shut up you bilge rat." In just one month, Segar turned Popeye from a sideliner into a first-rate puncher with superhuman recuperative powers. In his first attempt at crime stopping, Popeye was shot sixteen times but still brought down the villain, Jack Snort. Popeye's instinctive boxing rampages against any acknowledged bad guy pushed other *Thimble Theatre* characters to the strip's sidelines—except, of course, beloved Olive Oyl. Certainly Popeye and Olive Oyl represented the archetype of the little man and woman against the big guy. Together they were symbols of indestructibility.

Segar said his inspirations for *Thimble Theater* came from Charlie Chaplin's tramp persona and George Herriman's *Krazy Kat* cartoon strip.[1] For twenty years, Segar and Herriman lived only eighteen miles apart, yet they never met.

To Segar's credit, Popeye was not shown as handsome, nor was Olive beautiful. They were a courageous, creative attempt on the part of Segar to fashion a homely hero and a homelier heroine, ones that represented American's common man and common woman. Segar showed that Popeye and Olive loved each other in a combative way that seemed to work for them. Popeye always represented the little guy, who, if stepped on, surprised everyone with his superhuman punching abilities. Readers of the early strips loved Popeye's violent attacks against bullies more than twice his size. Metaphorically he represented everyone's struggle against the odds of the Depression. He was another archetypal David, of David and Goliath. Popeye's famous line "I yam what I yam" creatively expressed that oft-repeated dilemma that he and Olive faced along with most of the rest of humanity—they were not born rich, beautiful, or handsome.

Eating spinach for increased vitality was extolled by doctors in the late 1920s, almost to fad proportions, so it was natural that Segar added spinach to Popeye's diet—it explained his superhuman strength and recuperative abilities. He was almost a superhero, but not quite. He was disguised as a simple sailor—until the dramatic moment when he ate his spinach. In Popeye's heyday, from 1931 to 1936, spinach consumption in the United States increased by 33 percent.

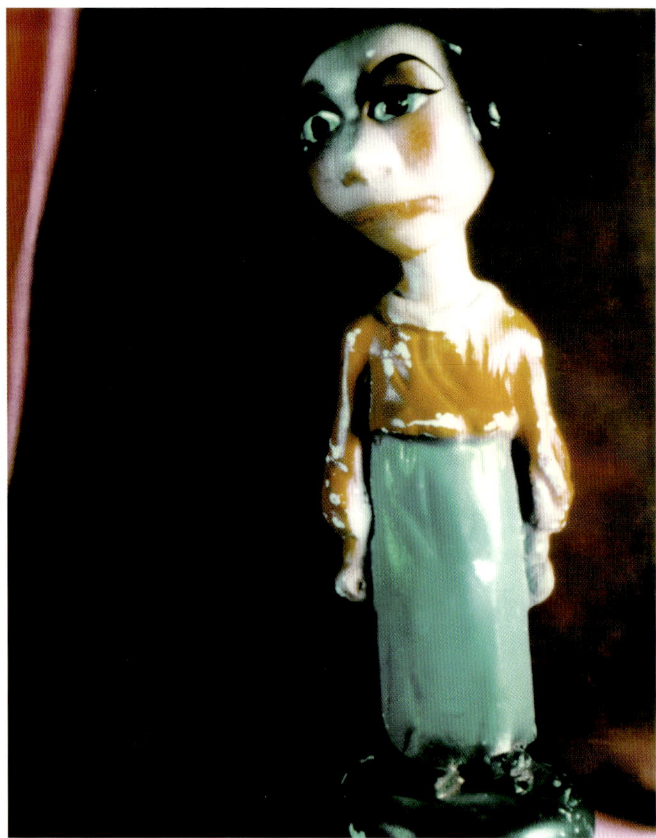
Olive Oyl nine-inch carnival chalk prize

Segar created Olive Oyl in 1919, ten years before Popeye, so fans of the comic strip already knew her fickle, whirlwind, strong-willed personality. Olive's lack of beauty was conspicuous, since the woman as sex symbol stereotype often decorated the comic pages all around her. Popeye might buy a beautiful dress for Olive; she would love it, but of course it wouldn't fit, because she had a flat, straight-as-a-board figure. Whenever necessary, Olive punched as well as Popeye did, and sometimes better. She was almost a superwoman disguised as a homely mortal. She even punched Popeye, but he never punched her back—since she was a woman. Often she occupied the stereotype of a maiden in distress, but when Popeye tried to assist, Olive's strength of character took over. She found her spunk and became the stereotypical new woman with equal rights. Segar deserves additional credit for making her Popeye's equal in a time when most women in comic strips were shown as less equal or simply sexy. Olive did suffer from vanity and irrationality, yet these weaker human characteristics were included as her foil for the ability to assume true equality.

On the day after Christmas in 1929, Popeye's deadly enemy, Sea Hag, first appeared in the strip. Sea Hag was an important addition and cannot be overlooked as the archetypal symbol equated with the Christian witch—a well-empowered anti-God and co-conspirator with the devil. She was the first comic-strip Antichrist. Segar gave her indestructible witch powers—strong enough to defeat Popeye and Olive. Popeye,

once again out of his respect for women, never punched Sea Hag into oblivion; nor could he if he had tried. Olive punched Sea Hag at times, but with little success. Sea Hag as witch/devil was Segar's way to separate right from wrong and good from evil. If Sea Hag wanted to bring piracy back to the high seas, Popeye and Olive fought against piracy. In biblical constructs, the devil has always been God's foil and vice versa. Throughout all the years that Popeye and Olive fought against Sea Hag, she was shown in fixed desperation. She even reached moments of deeper desperation, when she could have destroyed Popeye and Olive, but at those precise moments she realized that if she were to rid herself of them, her life would become drab and less interesting, and she would be useless. As an analogue, the Christian devil is useless unless people believe in God—that belief gives the devil power. Equally, God would become useless if people did not believe in the existence of the devil. Ken Kesey invented a double-reverse God/devil situation in *One Flew Over the Cuckoo's Nest* (1975).

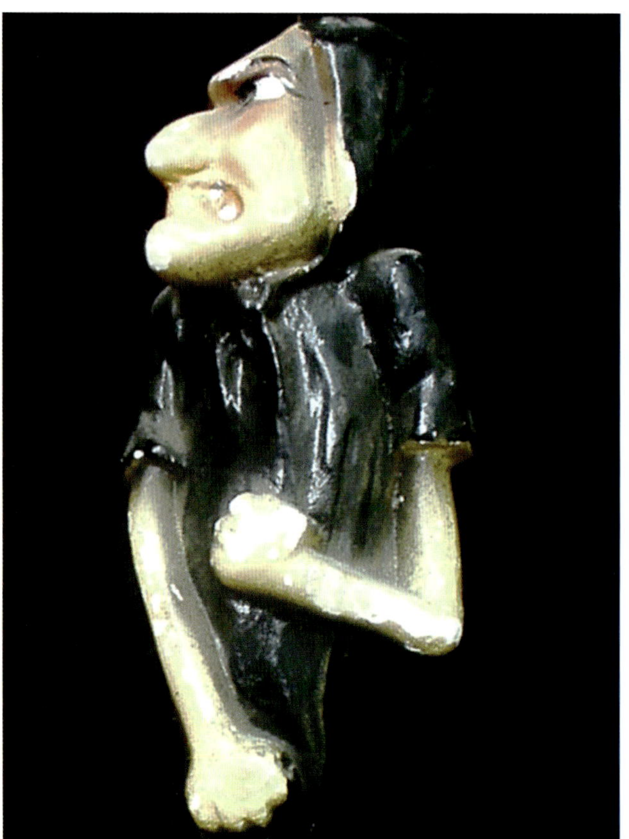
Sea Hag nine-inch carnival chalk prize

In the first comic strips, Popeye always wore a white sailor suit—white being the conventional color sailors wear. Sea Hag was always dressed in black, the traditional color for witches. To white Americans, the color black has for centuries been equated with evil and white equated with good. (One of the few comic-book heroes clothed in black was Batman, although his creator, Bob Kane, was probably not attempting to alter this pejorative color profiling. Because of this analogue, Batman was always considered a dark figure.)

Popeye and Olive adopted a baby in 1933, giving the couple and the strip a special new character: Swee' Pea—not their child from marriage, but their child of fortune—who arrived in a box. Swee' Pea's stereotype was the good-luck child, obviously swiped from lucky Felix the Cat of the previous decade. Swee'Pea instinctively knew the correct number to win the lottery. When Swee'Pea ate spinach, look out—he became the first mini super-puncher, a superbaby, unique to comics at that time.

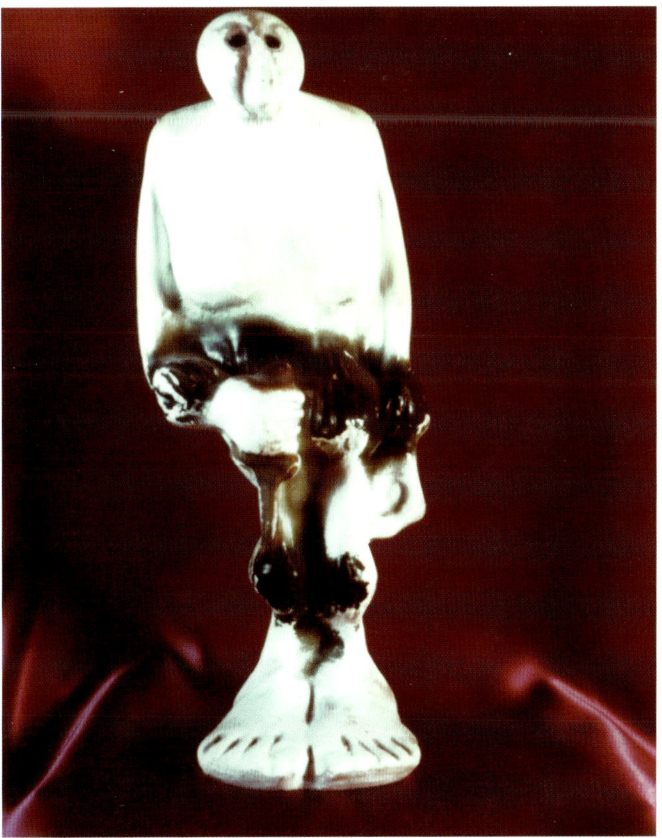
Alice the Goon six-and-one-half-inch carnival chalk prize

Segar created Alice the Goon in 1934 as Sea Hag's slave. She had a bloated, nude body and was hairy in the same places where Popeye was muscled. She spoke no understandable language; squiggles were used in her word balloons. Obviously an alien, she stereotyped the crime boss's scary helper—a goon. And scare she did! Little children felt afraid of her—they immediately recognized that she resembled a plucked chicken. (Segar's word "goon" suggests there was some connection to the gooney bird—a Pacific albatross as well as a fool.) Since art imitates life, Segar received a telegram from his own (scary) boss, the bigger-than-life William Randolph Hearst, telling him to "tone down the strip!" Popeye had to stop swearing, be less brutal, and become more respectable. Alice the Goon had to be warm and fuzzy. No longer could Popeye beat up a horse for no reason, as he did on December 23, 1930, even if it was funny. Hearst's telegram was a call for sanitized resolve, although Olive could still break a chair over a jukebox if it played the wrong song, as she did on June 4, 1944. Segar dramatically changed *Thimble Theatre* by adding a variety of calming and cheery characters. One healthy addition was Eugene the Jeep—a stereotype of a funny, magical fortune-teller—who was just a yellow dog.

No great philosopher, this is how Eugene the Jeep described himself on August 3, 1936:

> A Jeep has magical powers—if asked a question regarding the past, present or future he will answer truthfully by signals—it has been said that a Jeep has a "fourth dimensional brain." When a Jeep bows down like this, the answer is "yes." Ask a question and he doesn't bend down, the answer is "no."[2]

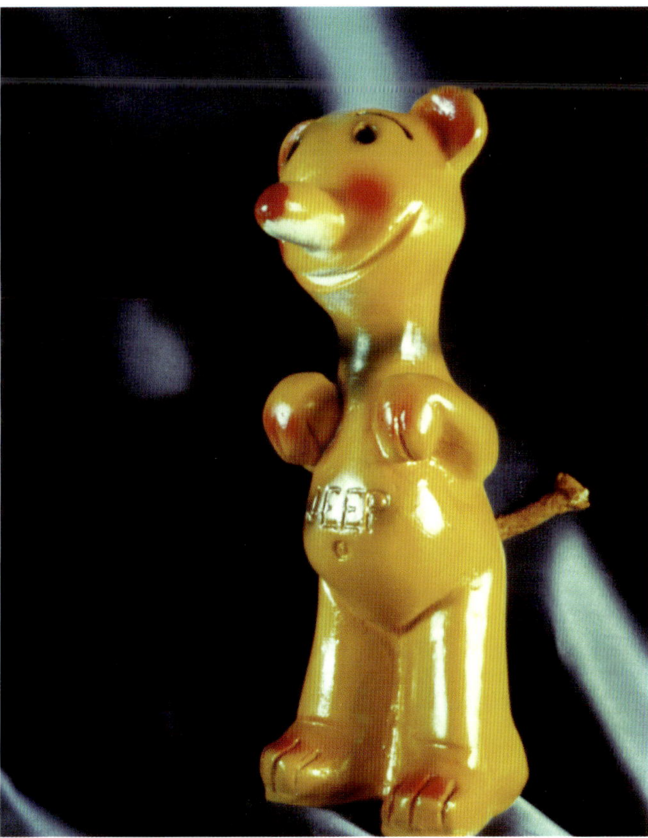
Eugene the Jeep nine-inch carnival chalk prize

Eugene the Jeep always appeared when Popeye or Olive needed a genie archetype. Eugene the Jeep and Shirley Temple were two of the necessary tonics people needed to get through the Great Depression. Segar coined the word "Jeep." Later Jeep was attached to the World War II army vehicle that was supposed to have magical powers.

Popeye's father, the obnoxious Poopdeck Pappy, arrived in 1936. Poopdeck Pappy did everything a father shouldn't do: he punched Olive, was dishonest in business, and if sent to jail, readily enjoyed being a hardened criminal. Poopdeck Pappy gave Segar the freedom he needed to add a violent continuity into the strip while toning down Popeye, who became a babbling sissy when faced with his father's constant immorality. Poopdeck Pappy symbolized the confusion felt by an overwhelmed American populace: How could they get out of the Great Depression? Poopdeck Pappy offered the dishonest criminal approach as one easy option. Popeye and Olive offered the harder, honest struggle. Since everyone knew that Popeye represented an honest-to-goodness fighter for good against evil, Poopdeck Pappy became the foil for Popeye's new shift to a cleaner good-guy role model.

Then there was Wimpy. Segar created him early on in *Thimble Theatre* and then made him more prominent as referee when Popeye became a boxer. Wimpy's famous line "I'll gladly pay you Tuesday for a hamburger today" showed him to be the stereotypical moocher. If people thought a moocher was lazy and foolish, Segar educated them—Wimpy played dumb, but was actually smarter than the person he could mooch from. Wimpy was smarter than Popeye and was fat because he was successful. His stereotype was really the smart manipulative moocher. Wimpy represented Segar's Depression lesson: don't let someone smarter mooch from you!

Max Fleischer convinced Segar that he could put Popeye into film cartoons in 1933. In Popeye's grand entrance, he danced the hula with Betty Boop in *Popeye the Sailor*. Mae Questel's voice was used for Olive Oyl and William Costello's voice for Popeye. The Popeye cartoons followed a strict, formulaic structure that introduced a new cartoon genre. Fleischer simplified Segar's complex personality types into Popeye the underdog versus Bluto the bully, and silly Olive. In every cartoon there was an escalating violent battle that Popeye won at the last minute after eating a can of spinach, of course. But Segar's characters suffered from Fleischer's changes—Olive Oyl the most. She degenerated into a silly, whiny, fickle, coy, manipulative character—all exasperating traits easily blamed on a woman. Fleischer ruined Olive's stereotype; she lost the equality she had gained from Segar.

However, Fleischer's simplistic cartoon structure provided the model for an entire genre that followed—Bugs Bunny, Tom and Jerry, and many other cartoon characters—where the hero always fought the enemy. By 1942, the Fleischer studio changed hands into Paramount and Popeye cartoons became state-of-the-art racist. In *Whotta Knight/ Penny Antics*, the boxing referee was supposed to hit the bell to end the round; instead, he hit the African American guy holding the bell. In *My Artistical Temperature*, Popeye ruined Bluto's masterpiece by squirting his painted sun with black ink—the blackface sun then sang a version of Al Jolson's "Mammy." The Popeye cartoons finally collapsed in 1957.

On September 10, 1935, *Popeye the Sailor* was heard on the radio sponsored by Wheatena—a long way from spinach. The show ended in 1938. In April 1936, a racist King Comics #1 published Popeye on its cover punching an imitation King Kong. When Segar died in 1938, Bud Sagendorf continued the strip. Off and on it has continued to this day.

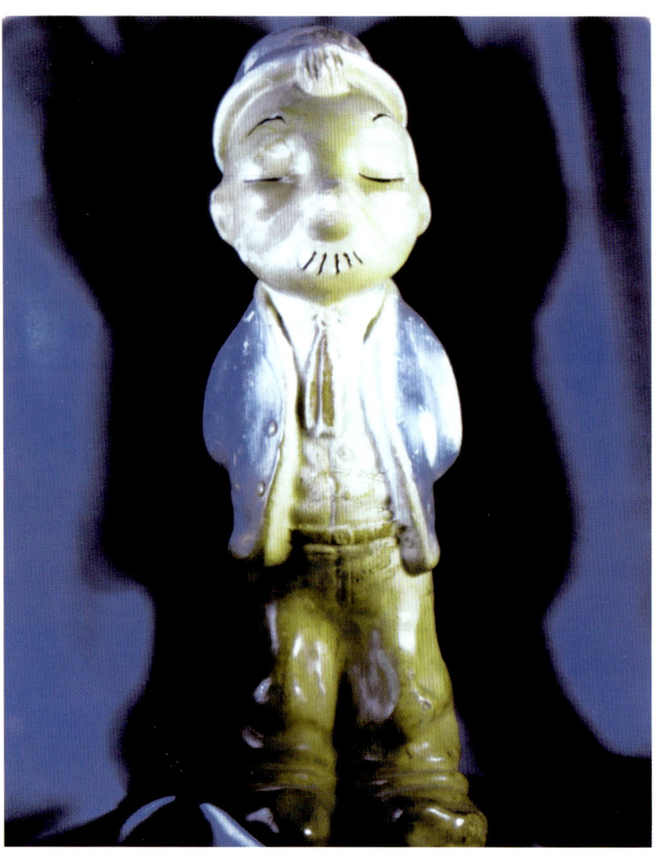

Wimpy fifteen-inch carnival chalk prize

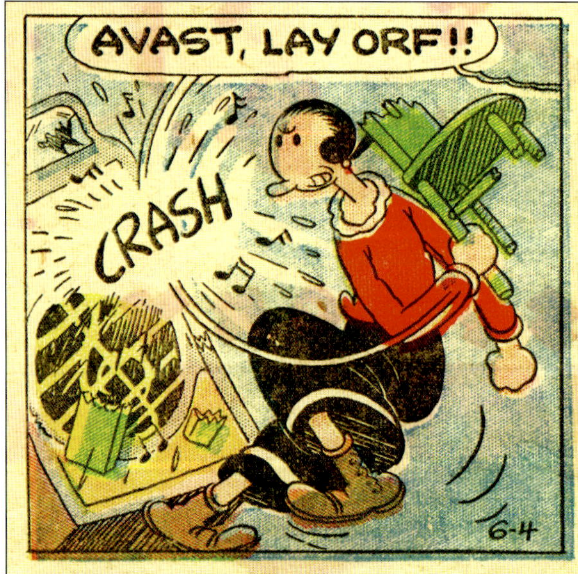

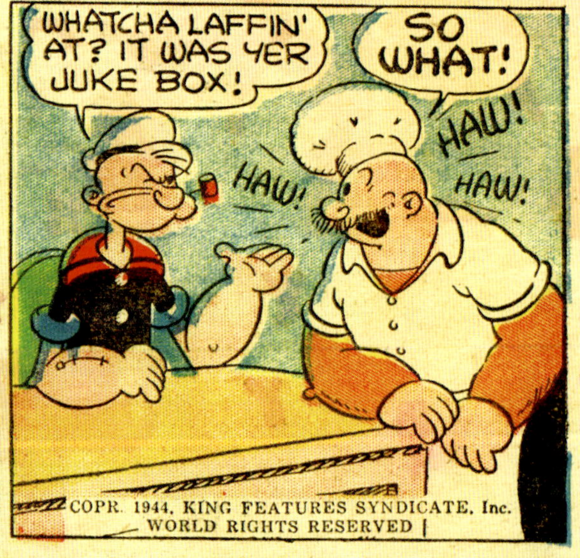

Olive Oyl and Popeye, *Thimble Theatre Starring Popeye*, comic strip detail, Bud Sagendorf, June 4, 1944 © King Features Syndicate, Inc.

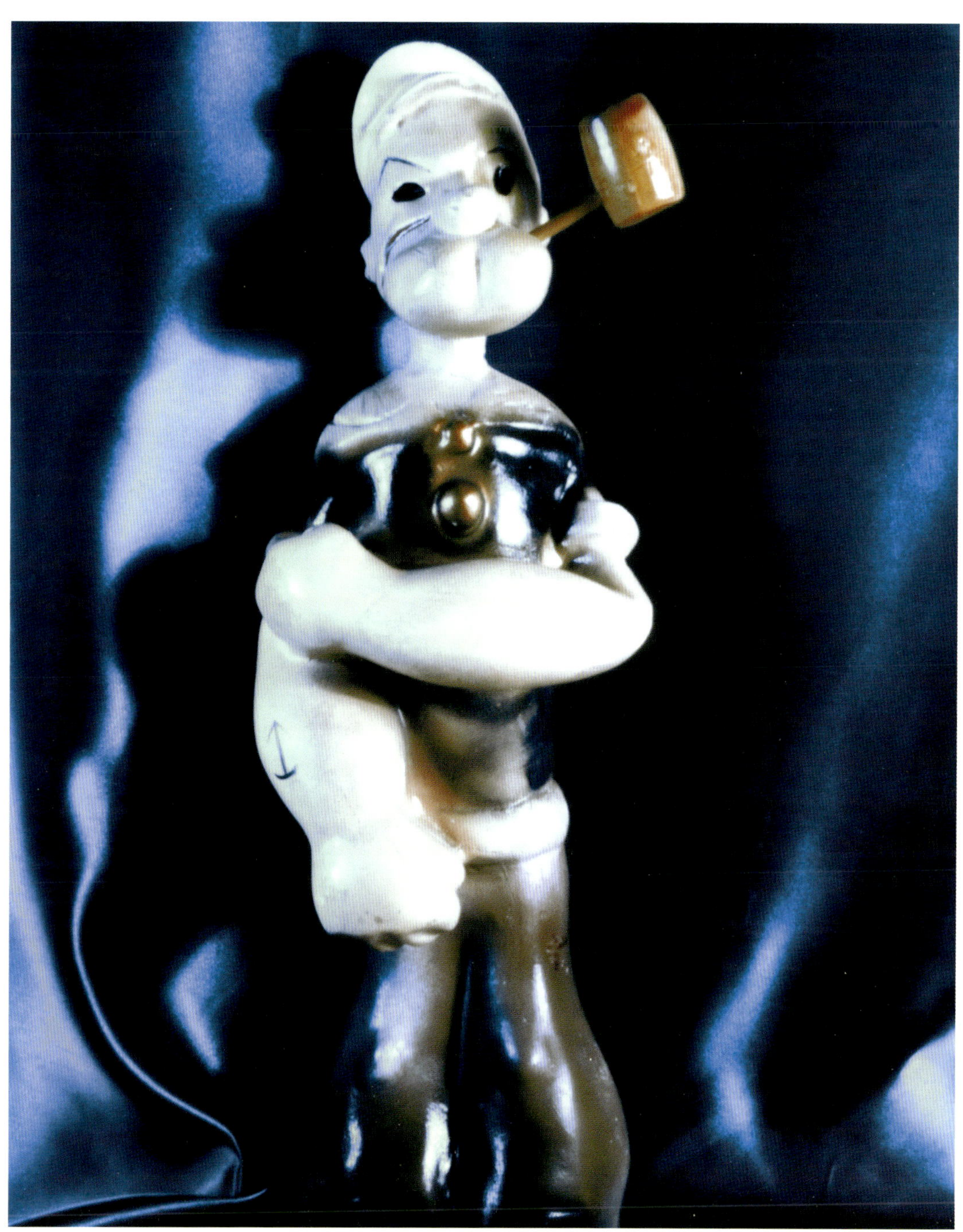

Popeye fifteen-inch carnival chalk prize. Popeye figures were some
of the most varied and popular. For as important as Olive Oyl was to
the story, only a rare few were available.

Amos 'n' Andy (1928-1953)

Then you had people like Clarence Darrow who told us the importance of sociology and other studies rather than law—which he considered to be unimportant. As witness one time, he was trying a case in North Carolina. A Negro beating up a white man. And his whole argument to the jury was, he had never touched the facts of the case, that this was a waste of time for him to stand up there and argue to this all white Southern prejudiced jury; that no way in the world they could give this Negro a chance. They just couldn't do it because they were too prejudiced. And he argued that for two and a half-hours; and the jury went out and came back and proved to him that they weren't prejudiced. And they turned the man loose.
—Thurgood Marshall, *1978*

If a man hasn't discovered something that he would die for, he isn't fit to live.
—Martin Luther King Jr., speech, Detroit, June 23, 1963

I am content to die for God's eternal truth on the scaffold as in any other way.
—John Brown, letter to his children on the day before his execution, 1859

Freeman Gosden was born in Richmond, Virginia, and raised, like many white children in wealthy families, by an African American mammy and her male helper, Snowball. Charles Correll was raised in Peoria, Illinois, where he learned acting and played the piano at a local movie house. Gosden went to Durham, North Carolina, to take acting lessons from Correll and their duo act was born.

The program *Sam 'n' Henry* debuted on radio station WGN on January 12, 1926. Gosden, later to be the voice of Amos, and Correll, who would be Andy, sang and played the ukulele and piano on their local broadcast. Five hundred and eighty-six episodes of their daily ten-minute program were aired over the next two years.

Looking for a national venue, Gosden and Correll moved to WMAQ, and on March 19, 1928, Amos Jones and Andrew Brown were inaugurated as Amos 'n' Andy. The sitcom enjoyed unprecedented and phenomenal success with humor that perfectly fit a white person's idea of the black stereotype. It could be appropriately labeled the Tweedledee and Tweedledum stereotype. Amos was characterized as trusting, simple, and unsophisticated, saying "Ain't dat sumpin?" when he was surprised and "Awa, awa, awa!" when he was frightened. Andy, on the other hand, was cast as domineering, a bit lazy, and always ready to take credit for Amos's brilliant ideas. He was the perfect counterpart for Amos, because Andy was always "restin' his brain," "workin' on the books," and "layin' down to think." The Amos and Andy characters lived in Chicago, after "comin' from Atlanta." They owned the Fresh Air Taxicab Company of America, which consisted of a broken-down topless auto, a swivel chair, a telephone, a soapbox, no pencil, no stationery, and no assets. Amos was in love with Ruby Taylor, the sweet, pretty daughter of a local garage owner. Andy was in love with the Widow Parker, who had survived five financially successful marriages. Sylvester was their loyal friend. His personality was fashioned after Gosden's childhood mammy's young black helper, Snowball.

The other characters were the Kingfish ("good for overdue assessments"), Geranium, and Fred the landlord. Gosden and Correll wrote all the dialogue and supplied the voices for all the characters. The dialogue usually went like this (Amos and Andy figuring up the day's receipts):

> **Amos:** Six and five—'leven.
> **Andy:** Wait a minute heah! Whut is you doin'? Is you mulsiflyin' or revidin'?
> **Amos:** I ain't doin' neitheh one—I'se stackin' 'em up.
> **Andy:** Well, I gits half o'dis money, yo' know.
> **Amos:** You gonna git half of it soon as I figgeh.
> **Andy:** I b'lieve you is deduckin', Amos.
> **Amos:** If I is, de pencil's doin it widout me knowin' it.
> **Andy:** Wait a minute.
> **Amos:** Whut's de matteh?
> **Andy:** Hand me dat paper an' pencil.
> **Amos:** Whut you goin' do?
> **Andy:** I'm goin' times it.[1]

In 1929, Gosden and Correll published the book *All About Amos 'n' Andy*. In it they exhibited ingratiating and self-indulgent unexamined superior race traits, saying:

> The first bit of equipment the boys use in building their story is a thorough understanding of the colored race. For this, Gosden's background has been invaluable. But even today they make frequent contacts with the colored folk in the north, and in the south also when their trips will permit, so that they may keep their characters true to life.[2]

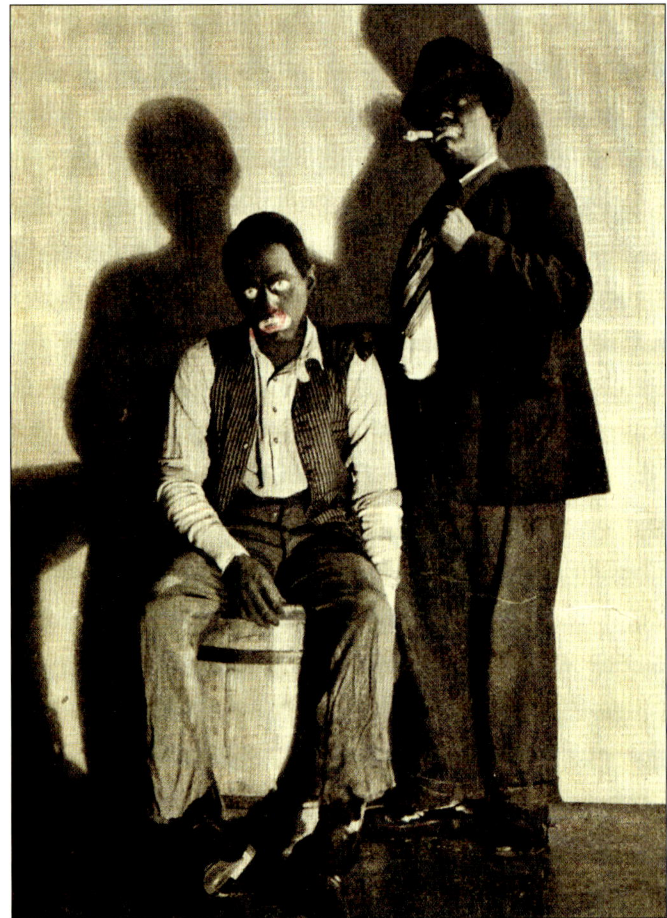

Correll and Gosden in blackface, *All About Amos 'n' Andy* © Rand McNally & Co., 1929

The *Amos 'n' Andy* show was not without its critics. Right from the start, the National Association for the Advancement of Colored People was a bitter foe. Gosden was bothered by the criticism, much more so than Correll. In 1931, a petition begun by the *Pittsburgh Courier* to have it removed from the air received 750,000 signatures, but the show was tremendously popular. The petition lost. The show was so popular that marquees on movie houses announced that films would be stopped at 7:00 PM so *Amos 'n' Andy* could be piped in for the theater audiences. Some Americans still see *Amos 'n' Andy* as an archetype for feeling joy and are unable to (or refuse to) recognize its racist underpinnings.

The series remained on the air for nearly thirty years, although its popularity was at its peak in the 1930s. It was the most popular series in the history of radio. There were daily *Amos 'n' Andy* newspaper cartoons, records of Amos and Andy singing, and they starred in the film *Check and Double Check* (1930).

Unfortunately, the Amos and Andy stereotypical and discriminatory racist humor was contagious. It appeared in a variety of comics, where blacks were always the brunt of jokes. Even Mae West got caught up in it in her film *She Done Him Wrong* (1933), where West, playing the part of Lou, had this exchange with her black maid, Pearl, an Aunt Jemima stereotype:

Pearl: Miss Lou, you're so rich.
Lou: I wasn't always rich.
Pearl: No?
Lou: No. I once was so poor I didn't know where my next husband was coming from.
Pearl: But you ain't been in the circumstances where da wolf was at your door.
Lou: The wolf at my door? Why, I remember when he came into my room and had pups. Pearl! Pearl!
Pearl: I'se cumin'. I'se cumin'.
Lou: You comin', you're head is bendin' low. Get here before winter.
Pearl: Here I is.
Lou: Here you is, here you is. What're you doin,' eight ball, workin' for me, or sleepin' for me?[3]

There were many varieties of the Amos and Andy carnival chalk figures produced around 1931. The most popular was an ashtray with Amos and Andy standing next to an open barrel used for holding cigarettes and a tray for putting them out. The ashtray's edge read "I'se Regusted," a popular Amos and Andy catchphrase. There is a ridiculous misconception that the ashtray was made during the Depression to get black people to register to vote. If anything, it made fun of black people's financial woes during the Depression. Blacks were in a much worse situation than whites and hardly comparable. The Depression was a hopeless time for most African Americans, but not terribly different from earlier hopeless times heavily laden with high rents, joblessness, and segregation. The Depression came at the height of a renewed wave of black lynching, a time in the early 1930s when blacks were more afraid to vote than in the 1920s. By the 1930s many comic strips had racist images of blacks around their edges, Jim Crow merchandise was everywhere, and a new Aunt Jemima was making nationwide appearances.[4]

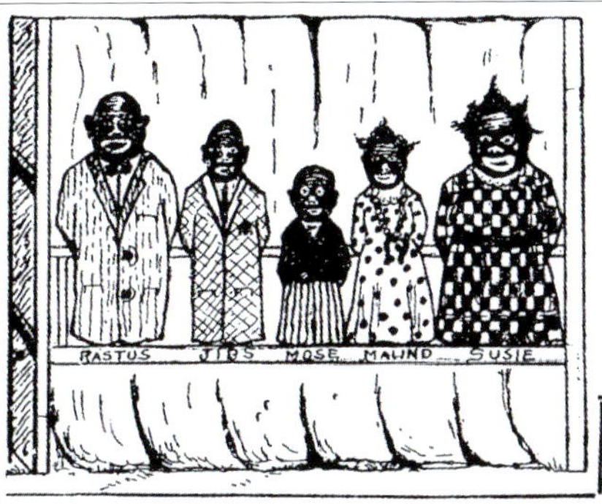

Black Hawk Family, ball-throwing game ad © Slack Manufacturing Company catalog, 1934

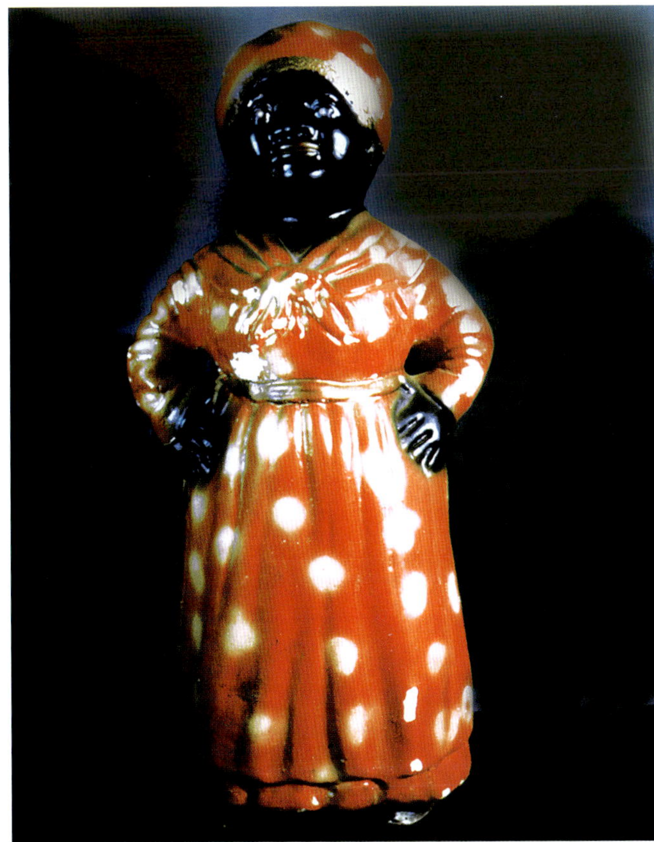

Aunt Jemima twelve-inch carnival chalk prize

Amos 'n' Andy was reinvented for television in 1951. The NAACP sued CBS calling the show a "national disgrace" and issued a bulletin entitled "Why the Amos and Andy Show Should Be Taken Off the Air." Among the reasons given were:

Negroes were shown as lazy, dumb and dishonest . . . that Negro doctors were shown as quacks and thieves . . . that Negro lawyers were shown as slippery cowards, ignorant of their profession . . . that Negro women were cackling screaming shrews . . . and that all Negroes are shown as dodging work of any kind.[5]

By 1953 the show was forced to end. Charles Correll died in 1972 and Freeman Gosden in 1982.

The popularity of the 1930s *Amos 'n' Andy* radio show was the catalyst for the radio soap opera. By 1930, Ima

Phillips wrote and starred in the first one, *Painted Dreams*. It is not a coincidence that soap products would be the sponsor of so many "soaps": Starlight Soap Flakes were used in the first film advertising product placement by Lumiere Brothers in 1896. The soap box was carefully placed in full view, while the audience saw women use it in washtubs.

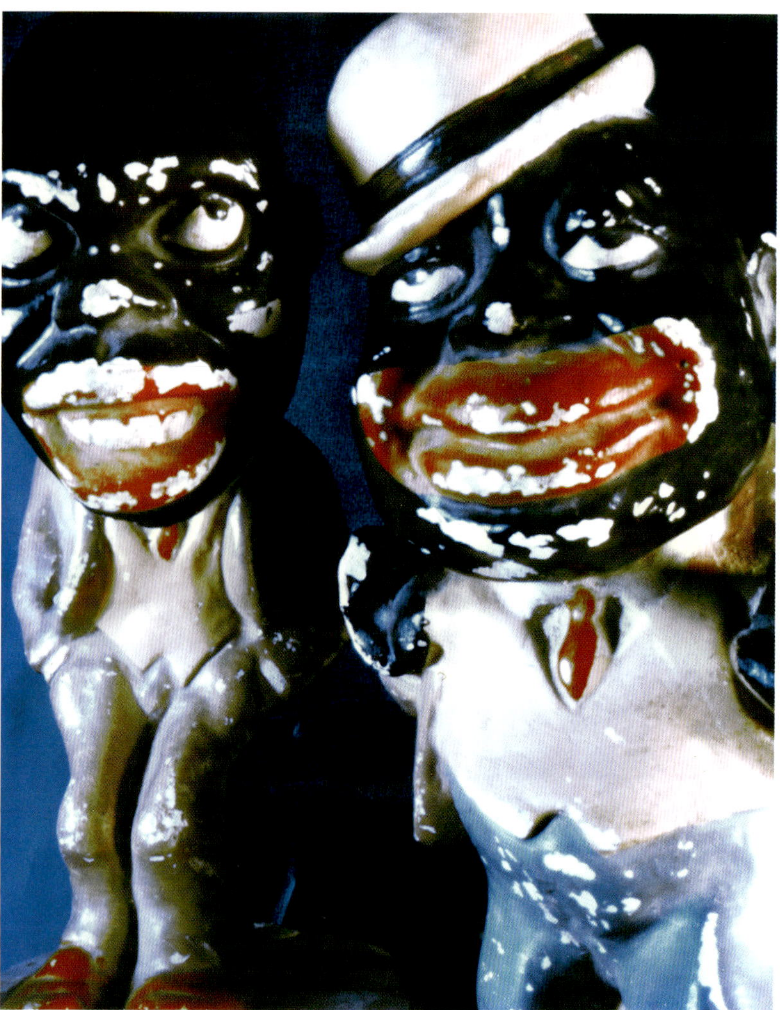
Amos 'n' Andy seven-inch carnival chalk prizes, thirteen-inch prizes were also available

"Zoot" was a common word within the urban jazz culture of the 1920s and early 1930s, meaning something worn or performed extravagantly. Many young African Americans wore suits with overstuffed shoulders and trousers that were extremely tapered at the ankles, so the term "zoot suit" easily passed into everyday usage. Rhyming slang expressions like "zoot suit" and "killer diller" were prevalent in Harlem. A famous white jazz saxophonist Edward Sims attracted the moniker because of his style and became known as Zoot Sims. By 1943, the zoot suiters evolved their stereotypical outfit to the point of representing defiance—never to be confused with subservient. Brutal zoot-suit riots erupted in the United States during the long hot summer of 1943, profoundly affecting a whole generation of America's socially disadvantaged youth—both African American and Latino. That summer, a young zoot suiter unionist and *pachuco* activist by the name of Caesar Chavez learned his first lessons in community politics.

Pachuco was the name given to Mexican zoot suiters, who, like the black zoot suiters, vehemently expressed their dissatisfaction with life in the ghetto (a slur). Octavio Paz wrote:

> The *pachuco* is the prey of society, but instead of hiding he adorns himself to attract the hunter's attention. Persecution redeems him and breaks his solitude: his salvation depends on him becoming part of the very society he appears to deny.[6]

A young pimp named Detroit Red began his political education by participating in the zoot-suit riots in Harlem. Later he became the eloquent and noble African American leader Malcolm X.

In 1955, the civil rights movement was strengthened and civil rights marches began in the south, mobilized by the brutal beating and murder

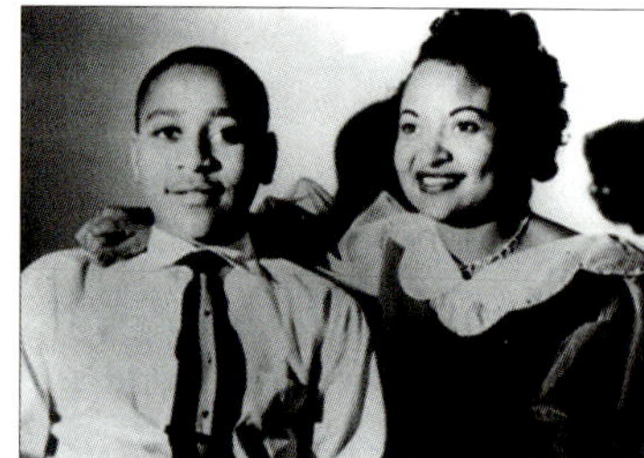
Emmett with his mother Mamie Till

of Emmett Louis Till—a fourteen year-old African American boy from Chicago who had wolf-whistled at a white woman in Money, Mississippi (a state where there had been over 500 lynchings after 1882). He was visiting a cousin over summer vacation and had been warned to be very careful. When his mutilated body was found, it had been wrapped in barbed wire, tied to a fifty pound metal fan, and then thrown into a river. The locals wanted a quick burial, but Emmett's courageous mother, Mamie Till, demanded his body be returned home for burial. He was shipped to Chicago in a large wooden box. When she examined the remains of her son (against the wishes of the funeral home director) and saw how savagely he had been beaten and murdered, she requested an open-casket for viewing—so the world could witness what had been done. Over fifty thousand people viewed the body and the story received national attention. Two white men were put on trial for his kidnapping and murder—crimes which carried the death penalty. Witnesses, who saw them kidnap Emmett Till from his bedroom at night, and others who heard the beatings take place gave testimony, but an all white jury found the men not guilty. The trial was a farce. In 1956, *Look* magazine paid the two proud murderers $4000 to publish their story describing how they kidnapped and murdered Emmett Louis Till. Later,

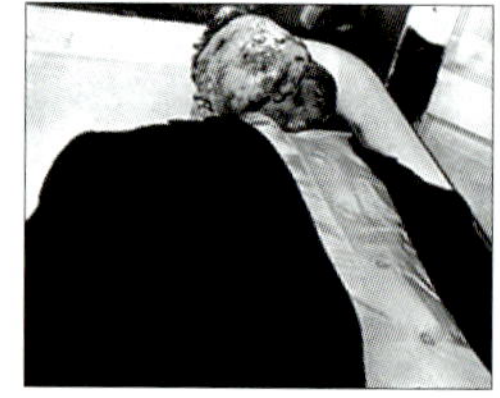
Emmett Till at the funeral home

one of the murderers complained that he had not made as much money as expected from what he had done.

KING KONG (1933)

Better sleep with a sober cannibal than a drunken Christian.
—HERMAN MELVILLE, *Moby Dick*

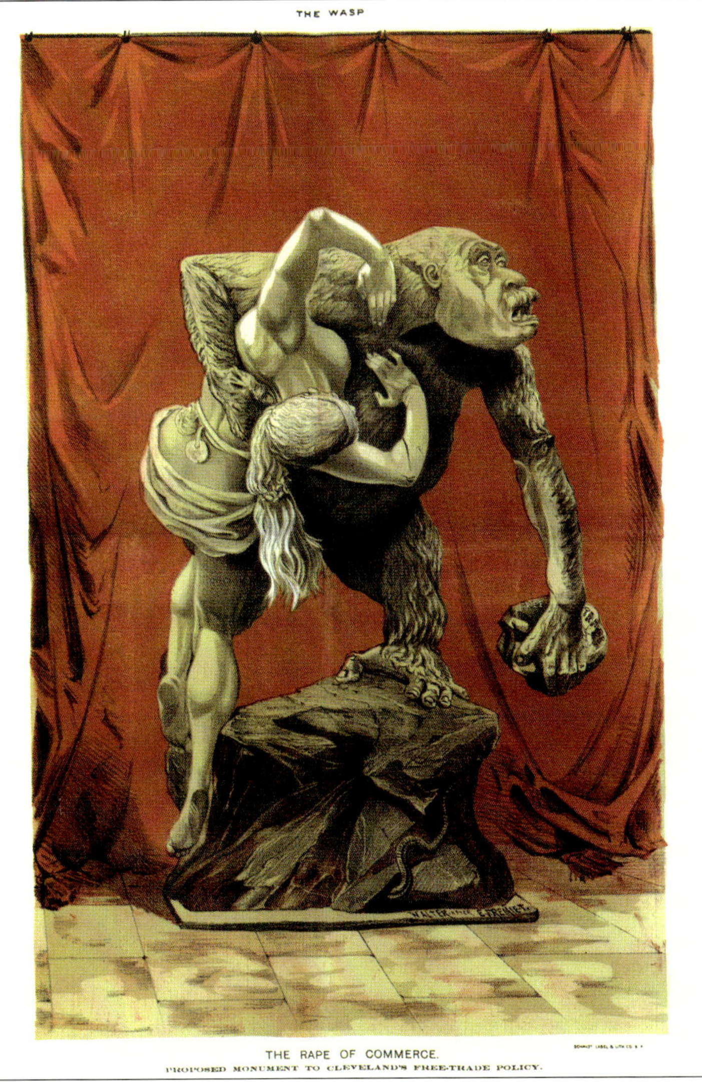

Cartoon on the cover, *The Wasp* newspaper, titled "The Rape of Commerce, Proposed Monument to Cleveland's Free-Trade Policy," March 10, 1888, chromolithograph, cartoonist Solly H. Walter

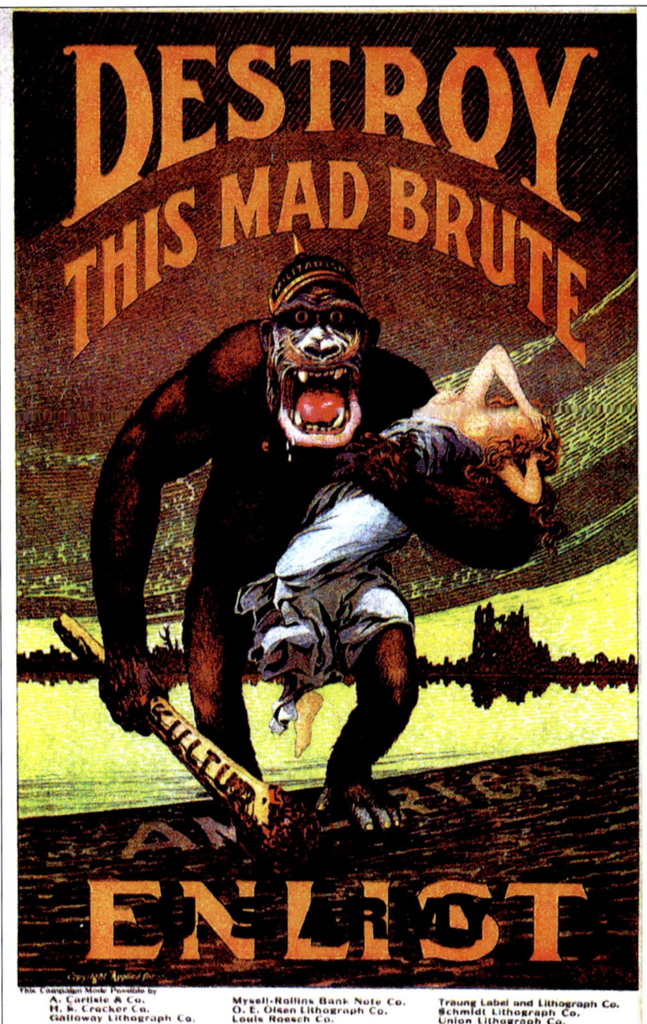

U.S. Army enlistment poster, 1917

The lynching of blacks was on the rise and the Ku Klux Klan could boast of a membership in the millions; this was perfect timing for the film *King Kong* to be released in the Depression year of 1933. The Commission on Interracial Cooperation had met in Atlanta only three years earlier to discuss the resurgence of lynching in the South and what, if anything, white Southern women could do to bring it to a halt.

The Will Hays Production Code censored parts of the original *King Kong.* Removed were the scenes where King Kong strips and peels the clothing completely off the beautiful white heroine (played by Fay Wray), another where he bites a dark-skinned native into pieces, and one where he's attacked by a giant spider. The film's producers and directors were real-life arrivistes, the adventurers Merian C. Cooper and Ernest B. Schoedsack. Not surprisingly, the Hays Code missed the fact that *King Kong* was a racist slur film attacking African Americans and that it overtly promoted indiscriminate God-stealing (the destruction of other culture's icons) by white Americans. An earlier menacing gorilla (a King Kong look-alike) used during World War I on enlistment posters for the U.S. Army in 1917 was not seen as white racism against African Americans rising up and seizing white men's property—it was seen as Germany the monster. For the white population of America the large gorilla was a generic archetype for eliciting fear. An even earlier gorilla gripping a white woman was displayed in *The Wasp,* a San Francisco political newspaper, in 1888. The gorilla's face is President Cleveland's face and he is requesting tariff reform (represented by the woman he is gripping and the rock he is holding). The Republican Party was against tariff reform labelling it "free trade."

King Kong, with his ability to select a beautiful white woman for love, has to be considered for what he truly stereotyped—the gigantic, well-endowed black male. It posed the inherent moral dilemma: What is the right course of action when a black man falls in love with a white woman? It mattered little that King Kong was only a fantasy gorilla; he was truly a symbolic paradigm for a less than human archetype—what white

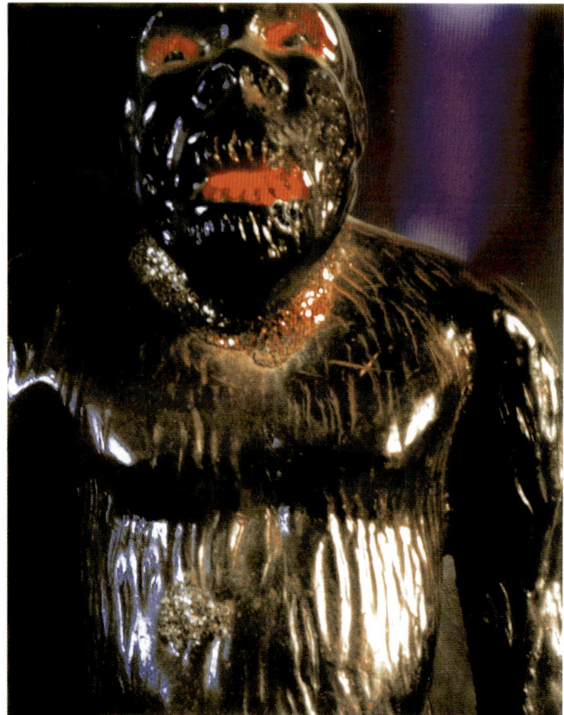

King Kong thirteen-and-a-half-inch carnival chalk prize

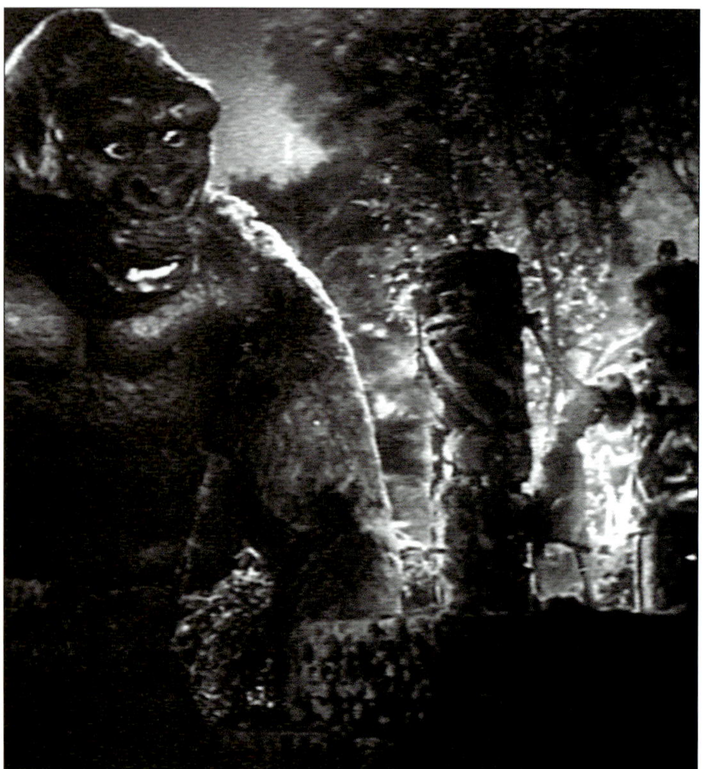

King Kong with Fay Wray, *King Kong*, still, 1933 © RKO

The first scene of *King Kong* shows hard times in depression-ridden Manhattan. A daredevil filmmaker is searching for a beautiful woman to star in his film. He will leave tomorrow on his ship for a distant South Seas isle where natives tend some god or monster that lives behind a giant wall. To find his leading lady, the filmmaker goes to the Woman's Home Mission where women are standing in a bread line, but he sees no potential prospects. He notices a hungry, out-of-work, beautiful young woman nearby. She steals an apple from a fruit market, aha! (Here we have the Old Testament's apple from the Garden of Eden again—sex and Christian morality must certainly play into the film.) The owner is about to call the police, but the filmmaker saves her by paying for the apple. Her name is Ann and she is obviously the ideal woman for his film. She agrees to be his star. Once on board the ship, Ann plays with a little monkey who is the ship's mascot; the men telegraph things to come with the comment, "Beauty and the Beast, eh?"

The ship reaches the island. They hear drums and see a strange tribal ceremony in progress with dark-skinned natives dressed in ceremonial gorilla-ape costumes, chanting "King Kong" and circling a naked, nubile young girl garlanded with marital regalia. She is crouched in fear on the altar. (The natives, through being costumed as gorilla-apes, redrew that age-old parallel—that black people resembled apes and, as such, they were inferior to whites.) The dark-skinned garlanded girl has been selected to be a human offering to their god gorilla, King Kong—she is to be the bride of Kong.

The tribal chief appears and demands that the filmmaker and his crew exchange Ann, the beautiful white girl, for six of his native women. The filmmaker comments, under his breath, "Yeah, blondes are scarce around here." The filmmaker refuses the offer, thinking that the natives may be planning to substitute Ann for the native woman about to be sacrificed to King Kong.

In scenes back on the ship, Ann is shown falling in love with Jack, the ship's first mate. Jack is called to the bridge, leaving Ann on deck, basking in the glow of her newfound love. The determined natives row out to the ship, silently sneak on board, kidnap Ann, and take her back to their village. (Ann is stereotyped throughout the film as a typically beautiful-but-dumb-blonde, hardly smart enough to get away on her own.) The witch doctors prepare to sacrifice Ann to King Kong. They open a tall gate by drawing back a very huge,

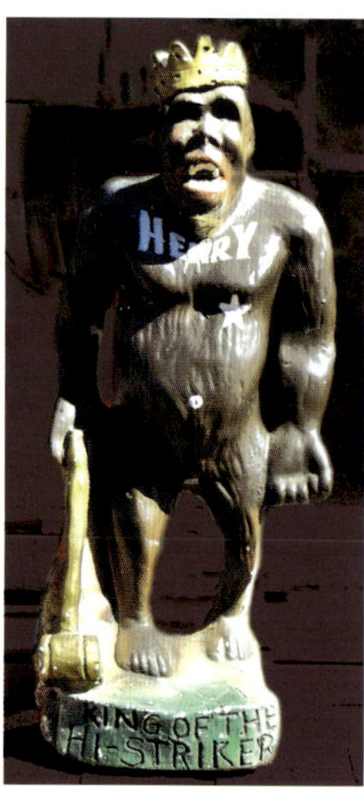

King of the Hi-Strikers thirteen-and-one-half-inch carnival chalk prize, the name Henry painted on it. These were given away in the strongman side shows to any person capable of swinging the heavy mallet hard enough to make the bell ring. For an added incentive your name would be painted onto the King Kong look-alike. Collection: Henry Simpson.

civilization had for centuries thought of blacks: that they were little more than gorillas.

The producers hoped King Kong would subtly and deceptively be disguised as a symbolic monster/beast archetype creating dreaded fear (rather than seen as racist). To accomplish this, the film begins with the old Arabian proverb: "And lo, the beast looked upon the face of beauty. And it stayed its hand from killing. And from that day, it was as one dead."[1]

phalluslike bolt, symbolic of what will be in store for Ann as the bride of Kong. The natives drag her to the top of a high stone altar at the jungle's edge and tie her wrists to two great pillars, each decorated with a human skull. With Ann secured, the witch doctors rush back outside the wall. The gates are closed and resealed. A gong is sounded and King Kong finally emerges, thrashing through the jungle to find his sacrificial bride—he is a massive, thirty-foot-tall gorilla. Ann screams! (So we're expecting her to sing?) King Kong roars! (So we're expecting him to scream?) He unties Ann and takes her from the altar, and after a series of fight-to-the-death scenes with various dinosaurs (which serve to illustrate his strength), Ann and King Kong finally reach a quiet place in the jungle where he fondly caresses her and peels away some of her clothing. King Kong falls in love with Ann. King Kong has an affectionate side, though never does Ann give a hint of returning his affections.

What the audience has witnessed is a reaffirmation of the white American man's fear—that a large black man will fondle a white woman and fall in love with her, even if the white woman doesn't desire and love the black man in return. What's to be done? (Now that the story has unfolded, the Arabian proverb seems to supply the ominous answer.) After lengthy battles in the jungle with the filmmaker and his crew, all-powerful gas explosives predictably subdue King Kong. Ann is saved and the primitive hoards have been bested.

King Kong (getting his first Atlantic cruise, albeit fifth-class cabin) is taken to Broadway to be exhibited. On opening night, the marquee advertising him reads: KING KONG, EIGHTH WONDER OF THE WORLD. The audience—as well as the actual film's audience—now sees King Kong chained and displayed on a metal structure resembling a Christian cross, symbolic of sacrifice. He must die for his sins—for fondling and falling in love with Ann, the white heroine. Shackled to the cross, King Kong, in all his hugeness, also represents the full essence of black slavery—that all slaves were white man's property, that they were dumb and uncivilized and their only worth was their labor used to make a smart and civilized white man rich. (The extras in white hoods and robes are offstage in this scene.)

Flashbulbs blast at King Kong and arouse him from his stupor. He sees Ann being introduced by the filmmaker to the audience as the bravest woman in the world and announcing that she is engaged to marry Jack. Upon hearing this, King Kong goes berserk. He breaks his chains and escapes. He tears down the marquee and throws it at the frightened crowd (a metaphoric gift to those angered and frustrated by the Depression). He looks for Ann, then climbs up the side of her hotel building and sees her in bed. He reaches in the window and grabs her. (This is a very symbolic gesture: this proves King Kong's guilt—showing to the entire world that only a being that is completely deranged or uncivilized would grab a woman from her bed.)

King Kong, with Ann in hand, tears up the snaking tracks of a Third Avenue elevated train, killing many people. He smashes a moving train (which symbolizes prosperous civilization's ingenuity). He clutches Ann. The only way out is up. Still holding the panic-stricken Ann, he climbs to the top of the newly erected Empire State Building (it symbolizes proud white America's prize—the tallest building in the world, a phallic patriarchal symbol completed just two years earlier in 1931). Now that King Kong is on top of America's tallest building, this becomes a fight to the death between the heathen, uncivilized god, King Kong, and America's god, technology, a paradigm for Christianity's civilized God. Never does the film suggest that the filmmaker is guilty of God-stealing!

In a nightmarish display of wartime technology, King Kong is shot over and over again by pilots in attacking warplanes. He finally falls to his brutal death. Jack, now on the Empire State dome, rescues Ann. Again, the audience is reminded of the beautiful-but-dumb-blonde stereotype—she needs a man to get her down from the top of the world's highest building.

In the final street scene, a police officer looks at the dead but still bleeding King Kong. He says to the filmmaker, "Well, the airplanes got him." The filmmaker, who knows better, replies: "Oh, no. It wasn't the airplanes. It was Beauty killed the Beast."

King Kong was considered one of the greatest fantasy/horror films ever made. But hidden within its great animation was the true horror of the film—a black man will die if he falls in love with a white woman. Moreover, America's civilized techno-society and its Christian God will prevail over an uncivilized untechno-society and its heathen god. The director and producers hoped the white audience would fall for their phony disguised "Beauty and the Beast" fairy tale through constant reminders of "See, it's Beauty and the Beast." It worked for white Americans. They loved the film and looked on King Kong as a huge symbol eliciting fear. What, after the Depression, might be in store? They were sensitized to fear.

For African Americans, and those critical of racist propagandist films, the black man/white woman or black slave/white woman archetypal motif was brutally obvious.

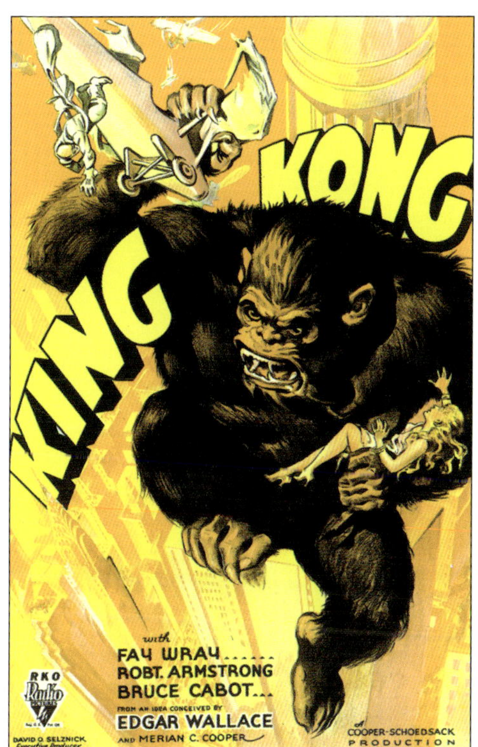

King Kong poster Style "A," illustration S. Barrett McCormick and Bob Sisk, 1933 © RKO

In many ways, King Kong was a fantasy sex replay, redrawn and enlarged from the violent horror/sex scene in D. W. Griffith's *Birth of a Nation* (1915), where a well-dressed but gorilla-like black politician locks a white woman (played by Lillian Gish) in a small room and prepares to marry her.

Loving/stealing forbidden white women was also blamed on monsters (page 70), Native Americans (page 89), Japanese (page 212) and aliens (page 252)—each was an evil Christian Devil motif like the *Au Bon Marché* ad below.

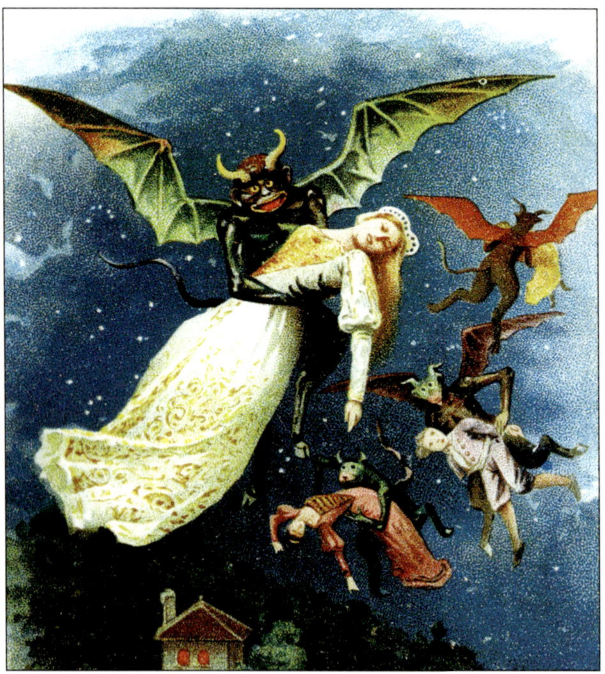

Au Bon Marché, ad, circa 1910s

A number of horror films copied *King Kong*. Possibly the strangest archetypal alteration/denigration statement was created in *Captive Wild Woman* (1943) where a mad scientist attempts to turn a gorilla into a captive woman, played by Acquanetta. The Gorilla/woman then murders another woman.

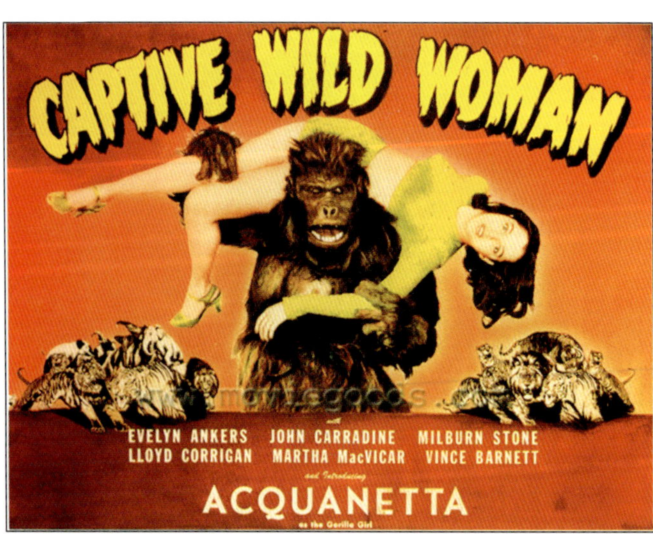

Captive Wild Woman, poster, 1943 © Universal Studios

Betty Boop

(1930-

Betty Boop was the first cartoon film to underscore the portraiture of a full-bodied, aggressively sexy young woman, and was (perhaps predictably) the only female cartoon character ever to attain international notoriety.

She was created during the devil-may-care era of entertainment that was spawned by the need for respite from the gray, weary days of the Great Depression. The emancipative epoch was rather short-lived, however, and a puritanical ethic under the auspices of the Will Hays Production Code soon reclaimed authority over social morality, but the fleeting taste of moral emancipation was sweet indeed for those who chose to take advantage of it.

The Betty Boop character made her first (anonymous) film appearance in *Dizzy Dishes* (1930). In it, she was a cute, curvaceous, anthropomorphic dog with endearing canine physical features who mischievously chortled, "If I want to make whoopee, I have to have boop-oop-a-doop." She had yet to be given the name Betty Boop. The song phrase "boop-oop-a-doop" was made famous by Hollywood actress and singer Helen Kane in her signature song "I Wanna Be Loved by You" from the Broadway play *Good Boy* (1928).

Myron "Grim" Natwick of Fleischer Studios, following the typical animator's habit of appropriation, infused Kane's winsome persona, including her notable facial features, coiffure, and, most significantly, her popularly recognizable ditty, into the Betty Boop personality. Kane's delightful, high-pitched warble was the perfect voice for the boop-oop-a-doop woman-cute-dog character in *Dizzy Dishes*. It wasn't until *Bimbo's Initiation* (1931) that the endearing dog-woman character was given the name Betty and paired with an animated boyfriend dog-man named Bimbo. She acquired her last name Boop in *Betty Boop Limited* (1932). The tenuous disguise using canine features was dropped and she emerged as a full-fledged, very sexy adult woman. (One wonders if the pejorative cliché "she's a dog" may have evolved from the original character.) Natwick then appropriated Mae West's alluring curves and the Betty Boop transformation was complete—a personality that was cute and endearing to children as well as beguiling and sexy to adults. The consummate Betty Boop emerged as a highly marketable persona with broad audience appeal.

Betty Boop's popularity also depended upon riveting, fast-paced action geared to delight children; but she was, in fact, targeted at liberal, nonpuritanical adults. Betty always held her own against obnoxious men, although in a few films, fiercely aggressive men actually touched her body—when a lewd circus master coursed his hand up and down her exposed thighs in *Boop-Oop-a-Doop* (1932), she recoiled in disgust and sang a mock lament to the sympathetic circus audience, "Please don't take my boop-oop-a-doop away" (a subtle double entendre). Betty found herself in impossibly dangerous situations laden with inconceivable monsters at every turn, but our clever cartoon heroine was not to be bested and she invariably won the day.

The early Betty Boop cartoons portrayed the stereotype of an aggressive sex symbol, cheerily showing off a voluptuous, scantily clad, fast-moving, inviting body. Taking advantage of the cartoon venue, free of the inherent decency restraints required of live actors, the Fleischer animators had tremendous fun drawing risqué images of her body. Titillating scenes of her skirt blowing up and exposing her thighs (but not her boop-oop-a-doop) initiated a screen convention destined to be repeated. Multiple skirt shenanigans were included in many of her early cartoons: *Barnacle Bill* (1930), *Dizzy Red Riding Hood* (1931), and *Betty Boop's Ups and Downs* (1932).

The commercial, eye-catching magnetism of the seductive raised skirt skit did not go unnoticed by Hollywood producers and it was quickly assimilated. It became an "oh lucky me" stereotype for wind-blown sex and was written into scenes performed in the 1940s by Betty Grable and in the 1950s by Marilyn Monroe, to name just two of the many stars who usurped it.

Betty staged an inimitable hula in *Betty Boop's Bamboo Isle* (1932), sporting only a lei and a grass skirt. The lei barely covered her breasts and cleavage. She lost the top of her dress to fully reveal a frilly strapless bra in *Any Rags* (1932) and *Poor Cinderella* (1934). She vaulted out of her clothes altogether in *The Old Man of the Mountain* (1933) to reveal frilly undies. Sexual undercurrents in the cartoons could be inventive, as when her dog, Bimbo, became a voyeur and gazed at her back-lighted naked silhouette through gossamer clothing in *Is My Palm Red* (1933). Viewers even caught a glimpse of one of her naked breasts in *Betty Boop's Rise to Fame* (1934). Her double entendres mimicked Mae West's use of similar tableaus.

The early Betty Boop stereotype created by Fleischer animators was much more than a wriggling semi-burlesque star or teaser set against a variety of bizarre backgrounds. All of Betty Boop's films illustrated an emancipated woman who was clever, capable, and embodied power over complicated predicaments. The personality was very similar to the aggressive woman stereotype Mae West perfected through her films. There were some small differences—Betty Boop's flapper clothing was not Mae West's old-fashioned gay nineties style, nor was the more frivolous Betty Boop quite the edgy female impersonator that Mae West often appeared to be. But their similarities were certainly not coincidental. Cartoons usually appropriated, parodied, and made jest of stereotypes of familiar figures of the era as well as drawing on current events. Much of their humor depended on immediately recognizable characters and situations geared to provide their audiences with instant gratification. An astounding number of archetypes and transitory characters flowed through most cartoons, mere bits of flotsam and jetsam inexorably coursing their way to the inevitable rim of Niagara Falls and into the oblivion of the foam below (and to resurface again).

Occasionally the Fleischer animators appropriated surrealist art for their background settings, which added touches of darkness, reminiscent of the Depression, so much so that some early Betty Boop films look like dramatically altered, semigrotesque fairy tales. Her *Minnie the Moocher* (1932) was the first to feature Cab Calloway, one of three big-name jazz stars inserted into her films. (A curious aside: in that film, Betty is portrayed as a Jewish princess and a cocaine user.) Calloway appeared in two other Betty Boop cartoons, *The Old Man of the Mountain* and *Snow White,* both produced in 1933. In *Snow White*, his featured song "St. James Infirmary Blues," remains a semimystery for film buffs. Was Fleischer Studio aware of the true references in the song? When Calloway sings "my baby is stretched out on a long white table," he is referring to the fact that his lover's death was caused by a cocaine overdose. Subtle drug references were tucked innocuously here and there. "Snow White" and "snow" continue as slang terms for cocaine. It has been suggested that animator Roland C. Crandall was quite aware of the references. In *I Heard* (1933), Don Redman sang another narcotics-inspired song, "Chant of the Weed." Another jazz great, Louis Armstrong, was featured in *I'll Be Glad When You're Dead, You Rascal You* (1932).

Mae Questel sang and spoke Betty's lines from 1931 until 1939. Questel was also Betty's voice on the yearlong radio series *Betty Boop Fables Show.*

In 1932, Betty Boop had her own song:

There's a little queen
Of the animated screen;
Wait 'til you, get a view of Sweet Betty!

Made of pen and ink,
She can win you with a wink;
Wait 'til you get a view of Sweet Betty!

Those eyes, that pretty nose,
Although aside from these, she's got so much of those!

If you want to see
Just a perfect little she,
Wait 'til you get a view of Sweet Betty!

There's the moon, 'way up high,
Here are you and here am I,
Oh, do, do, do, something!
Boop-oop-a-doop!

It's been told and explained,
That nothing tried is nothing gained!

Oh, oh, come on, please, do something!
Boop-oop-a-doop!

I've got the time and the place,
And the place and the time, I know,
I've got a bench and a park,
And a park with a bench and all,
Boop-oop-a-doop!

Sitting around seems so dumb,
Hurry, dear, I'm getting numb,

Oh, do, do, do, boop-oop-a-doop-a-doop,

Boop-oop-a-doop!

You can feed me bread and water,
Or a great big bale of hay,
But don't take my boop-oop-a-doop away!

You can say my voice is awful,
Or my songs are too risqué,
Oh, but don't take my boop-oop-a-doop away![1]

Competition arrived in 1933 when Helen Kane published her own comic-strip version of Betty Boop in Hearst newspapers, titling it *Boop-Oop-a-Doop Girl*. Her drawings depicted a much more risqué version of Betty, but Kane's comic strip lasted only a few months. In 1934, Max Fleischer put Betty into comic strips himself, but by this time the Hays Code had inevitably ground her sexuality to a halt and forced a reluctant transition to a family-oriented and therefore less potent presentation. The comic strip did have its high points, as in the 1936 parody of Mae West as a lion tamer, from the Mae West film *I'm No Angel.* In that lampoon, Betty Boop's aunt Tillie combined Popeye's looks with Mae West's carnival clothing as she confronted fierce tigers in a cage. The tigers, of course, were more afraid of Aunt Tillie than she was of them—that fashioned the perfect Mae West counterpart. Fleischer's *Betty Boop* comic strip lasted only three years; by its end, Aunt Tillie had taken over as the lead character.

Betty Boop's animated cartoons, post-1934, were pruned and trimmed and forced into modesty. Her skirt was lengthened and her strapless dress acquired a top and short sleeves. By 1939, the Hays Code had claimed still another victim. It killed Betty Boop—she died a painfully slow five-year death caused by sexual-reference starvation. Betty appeared in approximately 115 film cartoons between 1930 and 1939.

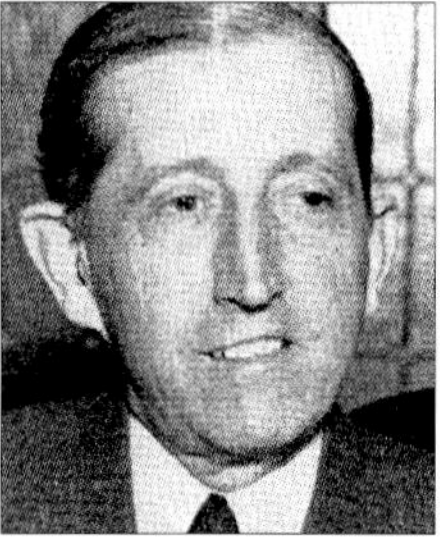
Will Hays, 1930s

The Hays Code was strictly puritanical. Here are a few of the rules as published in the July 18, 1938, *Life* magazine article "The Movies Enter Another Censorship Fight, This Time with a Clean Record":

• Stockings, as a rule, may no longer be taken off by girls themselves, much less by men. Men may not take off their pants, though they may be caught with them off.
• Thighs may not be visible between top of stocking and underclothing. If stockings are not worn, the outside of a woman's thigh is permitted, but the inside is taboo.
• Beds are strictly censored. Unmarried characters may not occupy the same bed nor kiss in a horizontal position.
• The Hays Office forbids nudity and allows seminude or undressing scenes only when essential to plot.
• Prostitutes may be shown only when essential to the plot and must be made unattractive.
• Kisses must not be too long nor too passionate. Must stick to lips, avoid neck, arms, back.
• Drunkenness must not be made attractive. Drunkenness must be followed by a hangover.
• Illicit love may no longer be made attractive.
• Ministers may no longer be used for laughs. If a marriage scene is to be funny the ceremony must be performed by a justice of the peace.
• The human posterior may be freely kicked, but never anything else.
• There will be no mention of striptease and Gypsy Rose Lee must change her name for the screen.
• Hypnotism is all right on the screen if not carried too far.
• Incest is strictly taboo.[2]

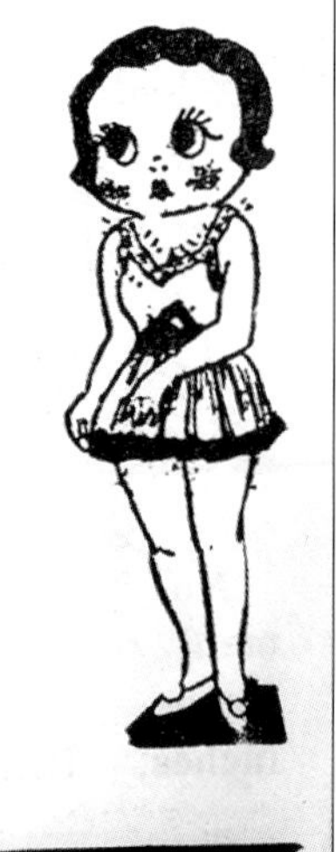

Betty Boop was called "Bathing Girl Beauty," in Optician Bros., *Carnival Goods #37*

Helen Kane, born Helen Schroeder, came from a poor family in the Bronx, New York. Because of her Kewpie-doll looks and her high-pitched voice she became a faddish icon for the 1920s flappers. She made hit recordings and played nightclubs throughout the Great Depression, but her prominence swiftly faded. Kane sued the Fleischers in 1934 for stealing her persona with the Betty Boop character. Unfortunately, the Fleischers won by convincing a judge that Kane had, in turn, copied her popular boop-oop-a-doop from the black singer Baby Esther in 1928.

Kane faded into obscurity, but was briefly rediscovered when Debbie Reynolds portrayed her in *Three Little Words* (1950). Kane was the voice behind Reynolds's dubbed-in vocals in the film's score. Kane was married three times and died of cancer in 1966.

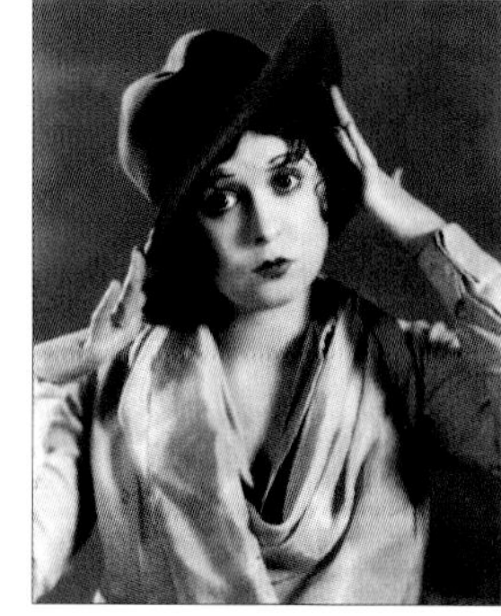
Helen Kane

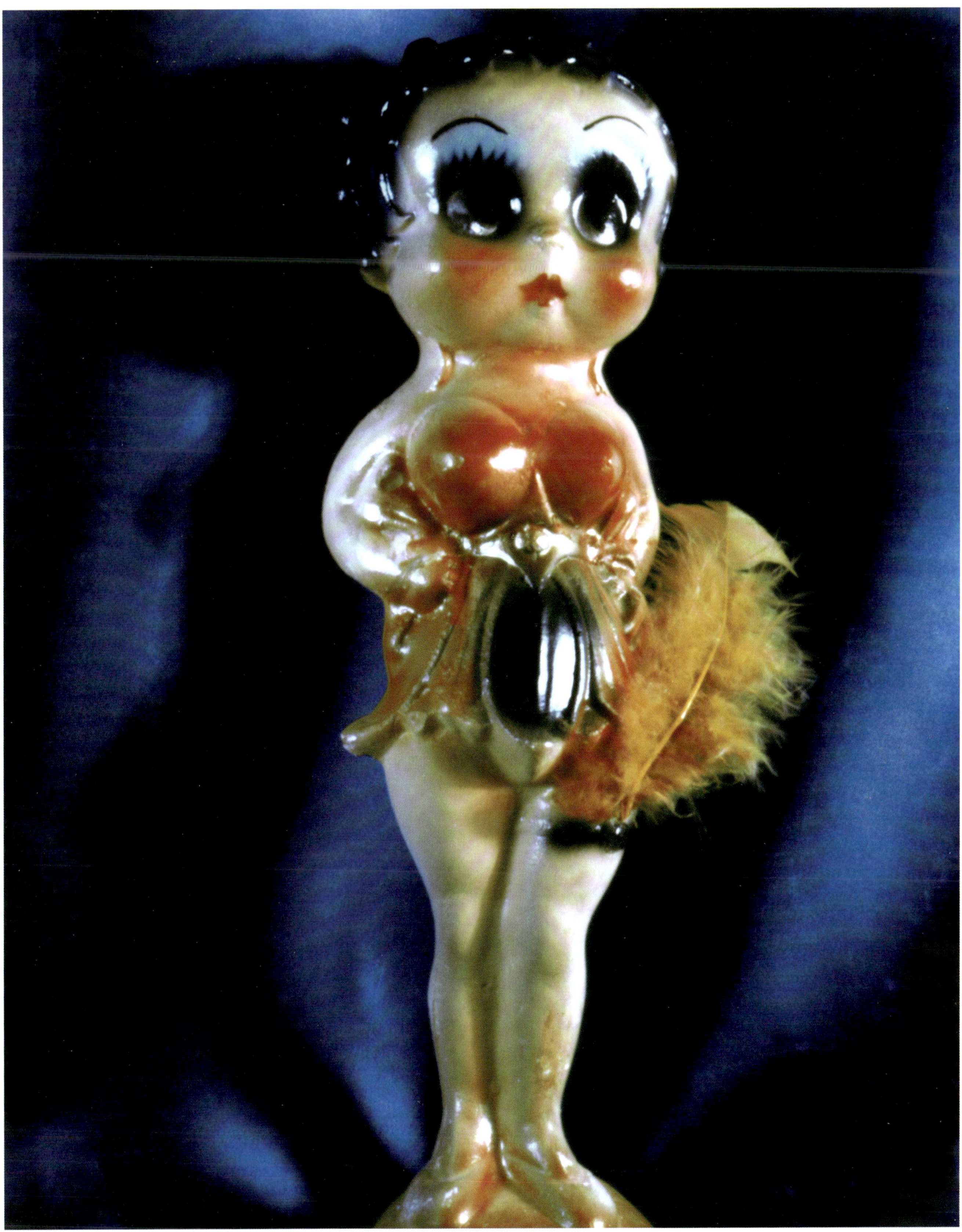

Betty Boop fourteen-and-a-half-inch carnival chalk prize

ASIAN GENTLEMAN

And so, after a strenuous campaign, has another advance been made in the battle with the Japs to keep California white.
—THE GRIZZLY BEAR, a publication of the *Native Sons of the Golden West*, 1924

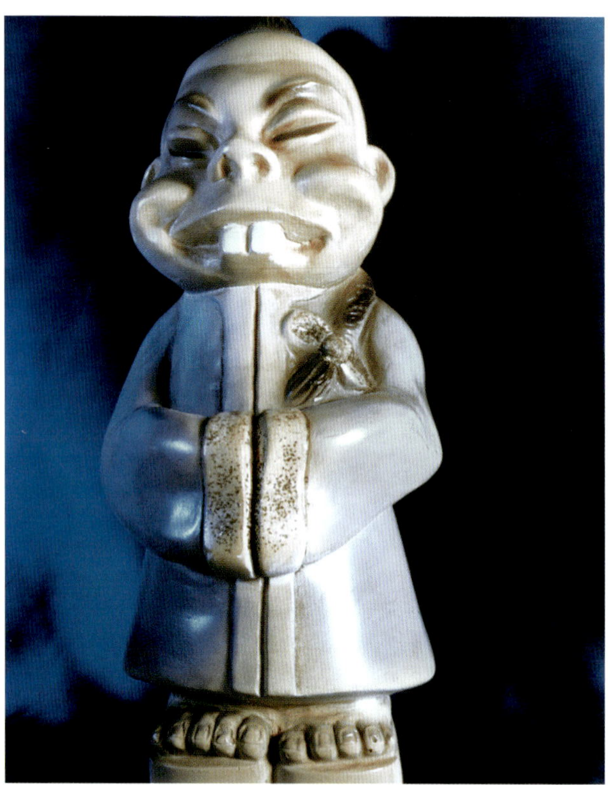

Asian Gentleman thirteen-inch carnival chalk prize, manufacturer's mark R. Nutj. The figure is wearing traditional Japanese geta (wooden shoes with raised platforms) to keep his kimono dry. His kimono, however, is not Japanese but a Mandarin robe worn in China. His hair is braided and tied with a ribbon in a queue, also a style from China. The queue was often an icon of derisive otherness as were clawlike fingernails. Japanese and Chinese were stereotyped with huge buckteeth.

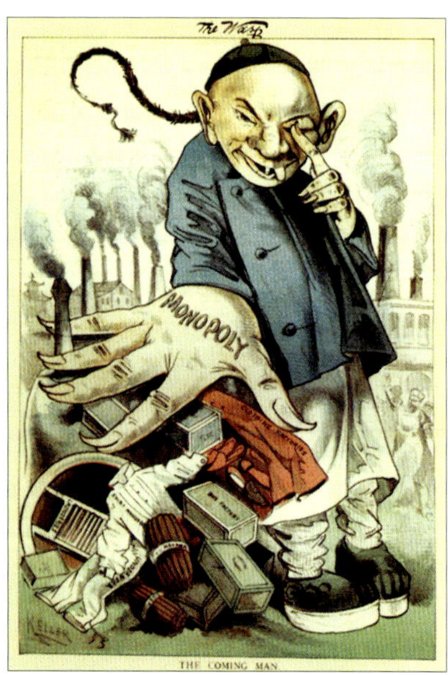

"The Coming Man," illustration G. Frederick Keller, *The San Francisco Wasp* cover, May 21, 1881

One hundred and fifty thousand Japanese immigrated to the United States by 1908. By 1920, the Japanese population was twice that of the Chinese population and U.S. laws purposely stalled immigration. Racism against Asians rose to an even higher pitch in the mid-1920s, culminating with the Immigration Act of 1924, also called the National Origins Act. It stated that any persons automatically denied citizenship, such as Asians, were not allowed to enter the United States as aliens.

The U.S. government had already considered the eventual need to remove American citizens from future war zones in Europe and the Far East before entering World War II. The hostage-exchange program was a little-known agreement, conceived by government officials before the war, whereby the United States would return Japanese nationals to Japan in exchange for white American civilians living there. It proved to be a tricky situation.

Unable to secure Japanese Americans who could be exchanged without facing the legal and international implications of forcibly exchanging American citizens of one race and ancestry for other U.S. citizens who were white, government agencies, the FBI in particular, looked to countries such as Peru and others, where anti-Japanese sentiment was on the rise. Then came Pearl Harbor and America entered World War II. Under secret orders, Peruvian and other Latin American officials, with the assistance of FBI agents, deported 1,200 Japanese Latin Americans without warrants, hearings, indictments, or listening to substantive pleas. Many of the Japanese Latin Americans who found themselves suddenly deported had lived in Peru and other Latin American countries for generations. Even though they had established roots and successful enterprises, their properties and businesses were confiscated, and they were forcibly removed.

The State Department explicitly ordered U.S. consuls not to issue visas to these deportees, and army and navy officials confiscated their passports. Upon their forced entry into the United States, they were labeled "illegal aliens." Now they could legally be sent to Japanese internment camps in the western United States where 127,000 Japanese Americans were being forcibly held; once there the government was free to use them as chattel for trade. The State Department traded more than 860 Japanese Latin Americans for U.S. citizens living in Japan between July of 1942 and September of 1943. As illegal aliens, these Japanese Latin Americans had no recourse against the government, or anyone else for that matter. Many did not even speak Japanese. The government thought it had the last laugh (if you can call it that); they had fooled Japan into thinking they were receiving Japanese American nationals when, in fact, the hapless souls were Japanese Latin Americans.

In 1998, a settlement was reached whereby each Japanese Latin American that was held, bartered, and delivered under this heinous kidnapping scheme was given $5,000 by the American government if they were alive to collect it.

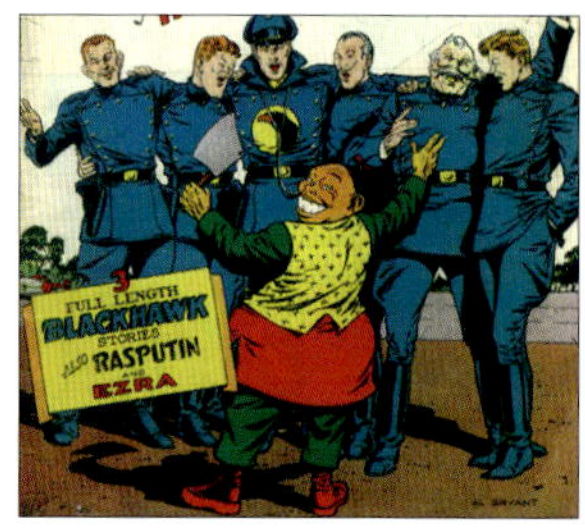

Chop Chop, *Blackhawk*, cover, detail
© Key Comics, 1944

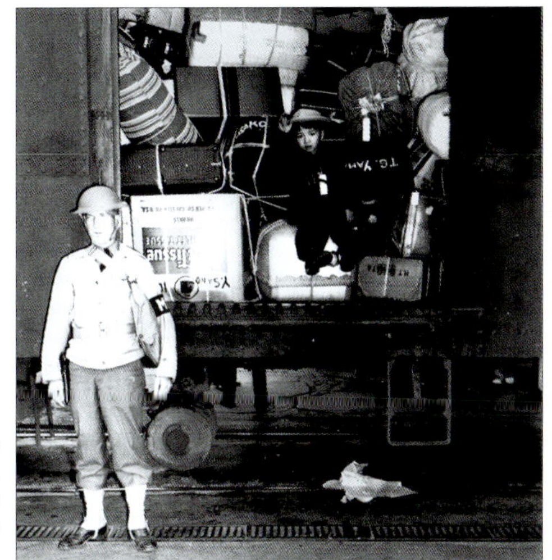

Japanese boy and U.S. soldier, U.S. Relocation Program, 1940s

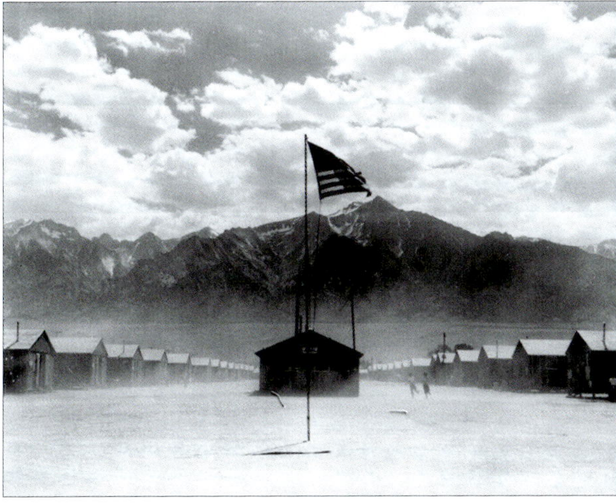

Dust Storm, Japanese Internment Camp, Manzanar, California, 1944, photograph Dorothea Lange. Courtesy: National Archives, Washington, D.C.

In 1944 Key Comics introduced Americans to their racist buffoon/servant Chinese stereotype "Chop Chop" in the comic book *Blackhawk*. Even as late as 1961 the racist Hollywood stereotype of a bucktoothed Japanese man was played by Mickey Rooney in yellowface as Mr. Yunioshi in *Breakfast at Tiffany's* (1961).

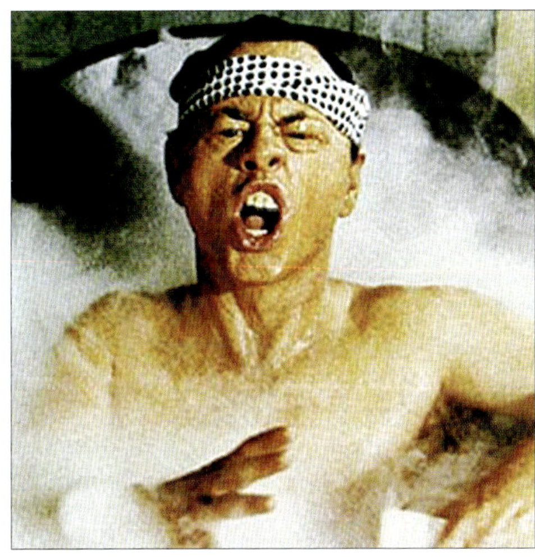

Mickey Rooney in yellowface and buckteeth as Mr. Yunioshi, *Breakfast at Tiffany's,* 1961 © Paramount Pictures

SALLY RAND

(1904-1979)

She was headlining at the Gay Nineties on Hennepin Street in the company of a bevy of strippers of all shapes and sizes and as it turned out, sexes, when Sally came out front to join us, she whispered confidentially in our ears that the sexy, lithe girl on the stage was really a man. 'Yup,' she spicily rendered. 'They cut the cock off!'
—HOLLY KNOX, *Sally Rand: From Fans to Film*

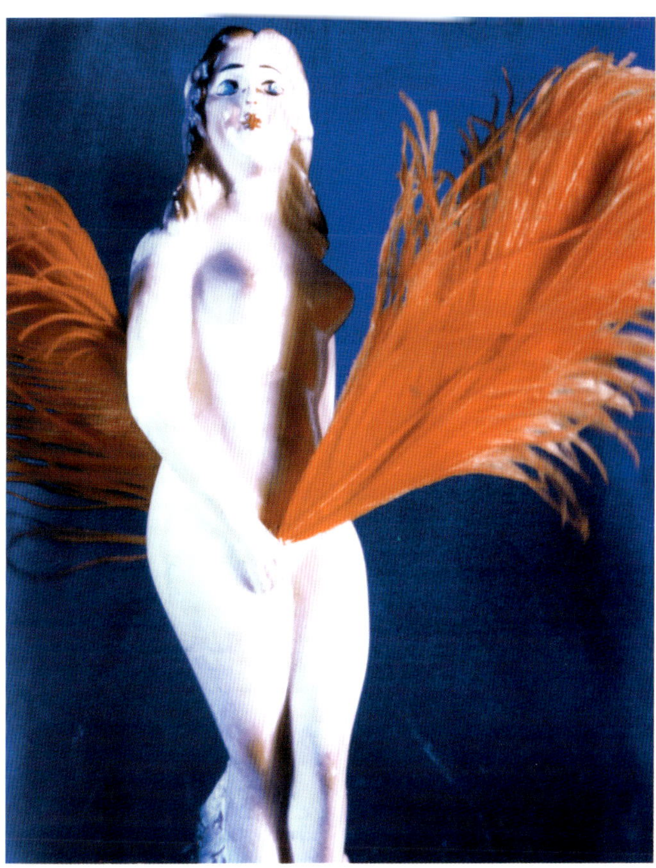

Sally Rand twelve-inch chalk prize, 1933–34 Chicago World's Fair. Rather than a prize in throwing games, this Sally Rand could be yours in a game of chance, by buying a covered punch card for 10 cents—you peeled out the punched area to see if you had won. The entire punch card, with 40 punches to peel out, could be purchased for $4 dollars.

Sally Rand held the position of best-known fan dancer for decades, and her eroticism and sexual dance was constantly surrounded by controversy. Puritans called her lascivious and lewd; less-suppressed people called her sophisticated and elegant. Her beauty, agility, and graceful movement stereotyped her as the fan dancer supreme. For many in her audience, just to say they saw Sally Rand in person was enough to fill scores of future conversations. If one caught a quick glimpse of the person behind the fans, then you knew she really did dance naked—and yep, right there in front of you. Often, at the end of her dance, in a grand finale gesture, she threw the fans into the air.

Sally Rand was born Harriet Helen Beck in 1904 in Elkton, Missouri, a small town in the Ozarks. Her aunt took her to see the great Pavlova dance the *Dying Swan* when Helen was very young. From that thrilling moment onward, she knew she wanted to be a dancer. Her mother found a ballet teacher and Helen walked several miles for dancing lessons. A carnival came to Elkton when she was fourteen, and Helen convinced her mother to allow her to join it. She later returned home, but left again the next year with another carnival—and this time she would not return. She stopped in Chicago and performed with the Adolph Bohm Ballet Company. When the ballet closed for the season, she signed on with the Ringling Circus as a flyer with the famous Flying Ward trapeze act. Next she joined Will Seabury's Repertory Theater Company, studying Chekhov and Ibsen. Onstage in 1925, she played Sadie Thompson, opposite Humphrey Bogart as Reverend Davidson, in *Rain*. Seabury's troupe went to Los Angeles, but disbanded when he became ill. Silent films called next and Helen worked with Hal Roach using the name "Billie Beck." When Cecil B. DeMille saw her, he gave her what would be her final professional name—Sally Rand. Legend claims that DeMille first chose the name Sally, then looked over at a Rand-McNally Atlas and said, "That's it: Sally Rand."

The Western Associated Motion Pictures Advertisers chose her as "Baby Star" in 1927 when she was twenty-three. "Baby" in those times meant "young woman." (As in "Ohhh, Baby" or a "babe"). Previous winners were Bessie Love, Colleen Moore, Fay Wray, and Clara Bow. Although Rand starred in a number of silent films in 1926 and 1927, her movie career was brief. Talking films were the rage by 1929, and to her disappointment, her slight lisp recorded poorly.

By 1932, her fame and fortunes had spiraled downward to the point where she answered a *Chicago Tribune* ad: "Wanted: Exotic Acts and Dancers, Apply Paramount Club." Her tryout, which used two pink ostrich feather fans, purchased for $10 earlier that day, was described by author/actress/burlesque dancer Holly Knox in her glowing biography, *Sally Rand: From Film to Fans*:

> The lights were bright on the tiny stage of the Paramount Club and the piano player was not sober, but the essence of Sally's future was established that night. She manipulated the huge ostrich fans slowly and gracefully to the strains of *Claire de Lune*. She artfully showed only teasing glimpses of her body, caressing the fans as she pirouetted on the small stage. A unity evolved with fans and woman. At times, the fans assumed a lifelike amorosity. Her dance was eight breathtaking minutes long. At the end of it, when she threw up her fans like the Winged Victory statue, even the dancers who were watching from backstage applauded loudly . . . Sally wore net panties on her first show, but she was bare breasted. That would not be the set pattern in all her succeeding performances. Depending on circumstances, she would be stark nude, wearing net panties only, or completely covered by a sheer body stocking.[1]

The 1933 Chicago World's Fair "Century of Progress" looked like a promising place to find work. At the opening-night ceremony, Rand entered through a back gate next to the lake, accessible only by yacht. She was nude, riding sidesaddle on a white horse, dressed only in a flowing, long blonde wig. Although immediately arrested for obscenity, she had made her most famous media debut as Chicago's very own emancipated Lady Godiva. The next day, Rand was on

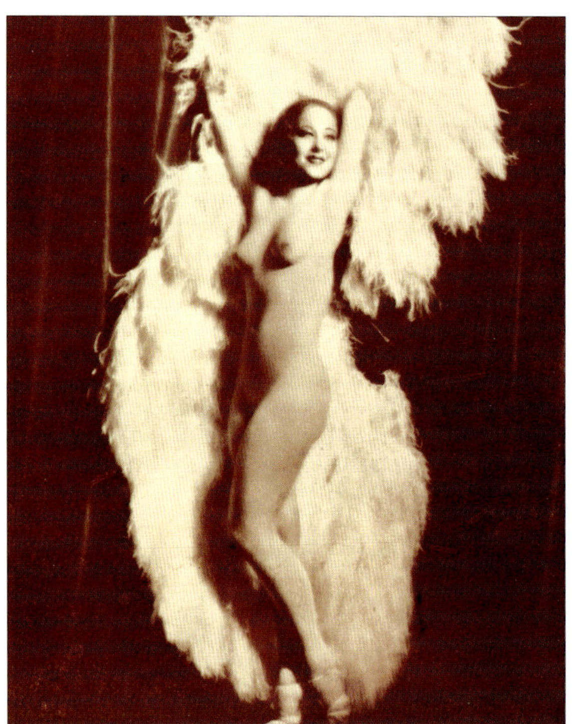

Sally Rand, table ad, Music Box, San Francisco, California, circa 1940s

the front page of all the Chicago newspapers. Rand, not the fair, was all the talk! Her daring piece of bawdy ingenuity supplied her with the overwhelming publicity needed to make her fan dance the most popular spot at the Streets of Paris midway concession. Forty years earlier, the belly dancers and off-limits coochie strippers saved the 1893 Chicago World's Colombian Exposition from financial ruin; in 1933 it was Rand and her ostrich fans that saved the Chicago World's Fair from a similar financial fate. For many who saw her, she was an archetype for the artistically talented/liberated woman, eliciting erotic lust. They loved her. For those who were against striptease and the fan dance, Rand represented an archetypal motif for the corrupting sinner or a tasteless pastiche of classical sensuality. They despised her.

Rand and her fans were engraved on a coin that was available at the fair. She was paid $1,000 a week. Each of her seven-pound fans was made of six or seven male ostrich feathers and measured forty-one inches across, for a total wingspan of eighty-two inches. Rand was only five feet tall. She always danced to Claude Debussy's *Clair de Lune* or Frédéric Chopin's Waltz in C Sharp Minor. Many of the 22 million people who attended the Chicago World's Fair saw Rand and her name became a household word. In the years that followed, she was arrested many times for indecency—one day she was arrested four times—but she continued her fan dance throughout the United States for forty-five years. Her final performance, at age seventy-five, was in her adopted hometown of Glendora, California, on March 17, 1979. She died that same year.

Her ability to squelch women hecklers was legendary. If any woman in the audience felt a wave of Puritanism and called out loud or nasty quips during her act, Rand would stop abruptly and immediately respond: "An acrobat can do a cunning stunt, but you my dear are a stunning cunt—need we go further?" Stories suggest that men rarely heckled her.

M AE WEST
(1893-1980)

Good sex is like good Bridge. If you don't have a good partner, you'd better have a good hand.
—MAE WEST

Long before Paramount signed her for films, Mae West spent nearly three decades inventing and fully developing her unique feminine stereotype. Many Americans knew of her scandalous Broadway play *Sex* because of its highly publicized police shutdown in 1927, but few knew of her years as vaudeville comedienne; her time singing, dancing, and acting on the Broadway stage; or her provocative ideas as an avant-garde playwright and amazing talent as an impersonator. West, even more than Charlie Chaplin, brought a long history of studied movement, gesture, expression, pronunciation, singing, and timing to Hollywood—and moreover, she knew how to work the media. Drawing from her years of professionalism, she made daring Hollywood films during that tortuous period of censorship under the Will Hays Production Code. Although she appropriated much of her persona, she was always a parody, never a pastiche.

The cliché of "starting a new life" must have been what West felt when, at the age of thirty-nine, she was asked to come to Hollywood to star in her first film, *Night After Night*. It was 1932, the year Prohibition ended. She told Paramount executives that either they let her rewrite her part or she would return their $30,000 advance. Fortunately for the history of American film, they agreed. West's comical lines and flamboyant demeanor stole the show. In one famous scene, when a pretty hat-check girl admires West's luscious diamond necklace and remarks, "Goodness, what beautiful diamonds," West follows with, "Goodness has nothing to do with it, dearie." West was superb at double entendre—hers were illicitly suggestive, yet cleverly cryptic. In *She Done Him Wrong* (1933), Cary Grant approaches her with handcuffs, ready to arrest her. West declines, pleading, "Are those absolutely necessary? You know I wasn't born with them." Grant replies, "A lot of men would have been safer if you had." West responds, "I don't know. Hands ain't everything."

Mae West was a free woman in all of her films. She triumphed over difficult circumstances; she survived and prospered in a man's world. Her films were also lavish comical parodies on the bizarre conditions set forth for life's struggles. The loser in most of her films lost because he or she was imprisoned within his or her own weak character or stereotype, while the winner's strength of character was able to turn disadvantage to advantage. West developed her larger-than-life fanfaron (a bragging and bravado) for lust. At the peak of her movie career, she was the paragon of artful titillation. In the photograph from an unknown 1930s newspaper's Sunday magazine section (page 140), Shirley Temple mimics Mae West's come-on. The article was titled "Has He Got a Friend He Can Bring Along?"—blatantly promoting subliminal pedophilia. Obviously, West functioned on many levels, this being the lowest. But there were other levels:

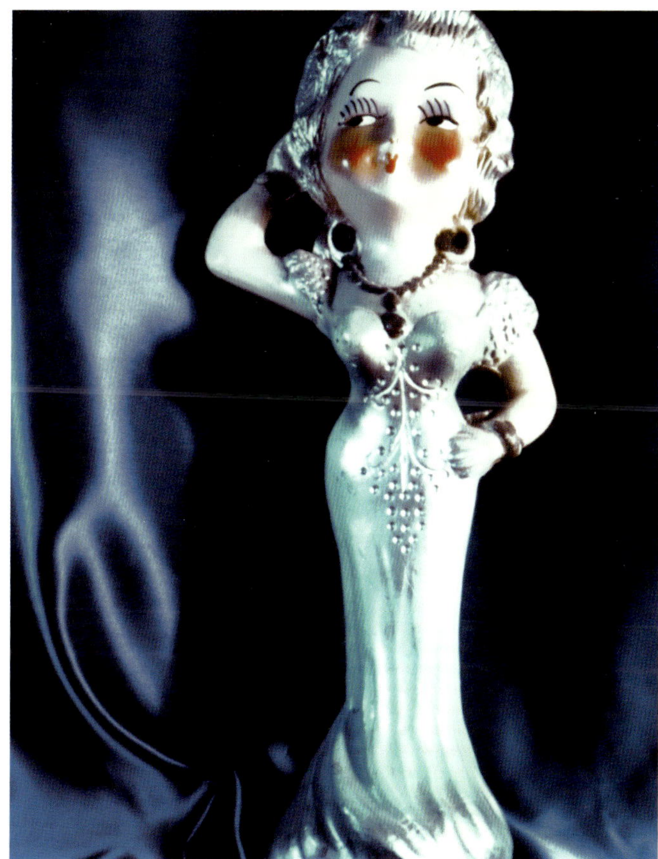

Mae West fifteen-inch carnival chalk prize © Venice Dolls. There were probably fifteen or more versions of the Mae West carnival chalk prize—more than of any other female star.

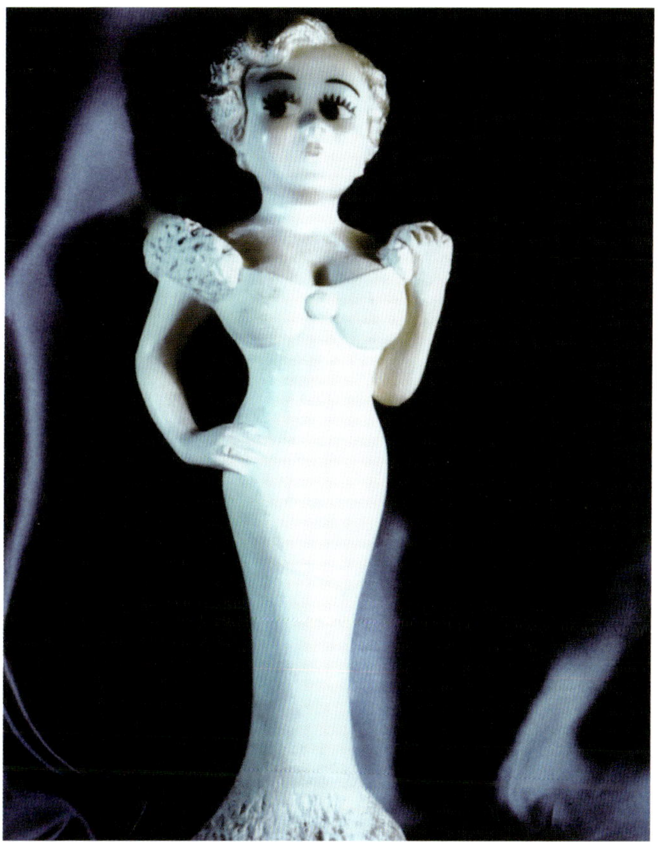

Mae West fifteen-inch carnival chalk prize © William Rainwater, copyrighted as May Doll (original figure carved in wood by Clarence DeWitt)

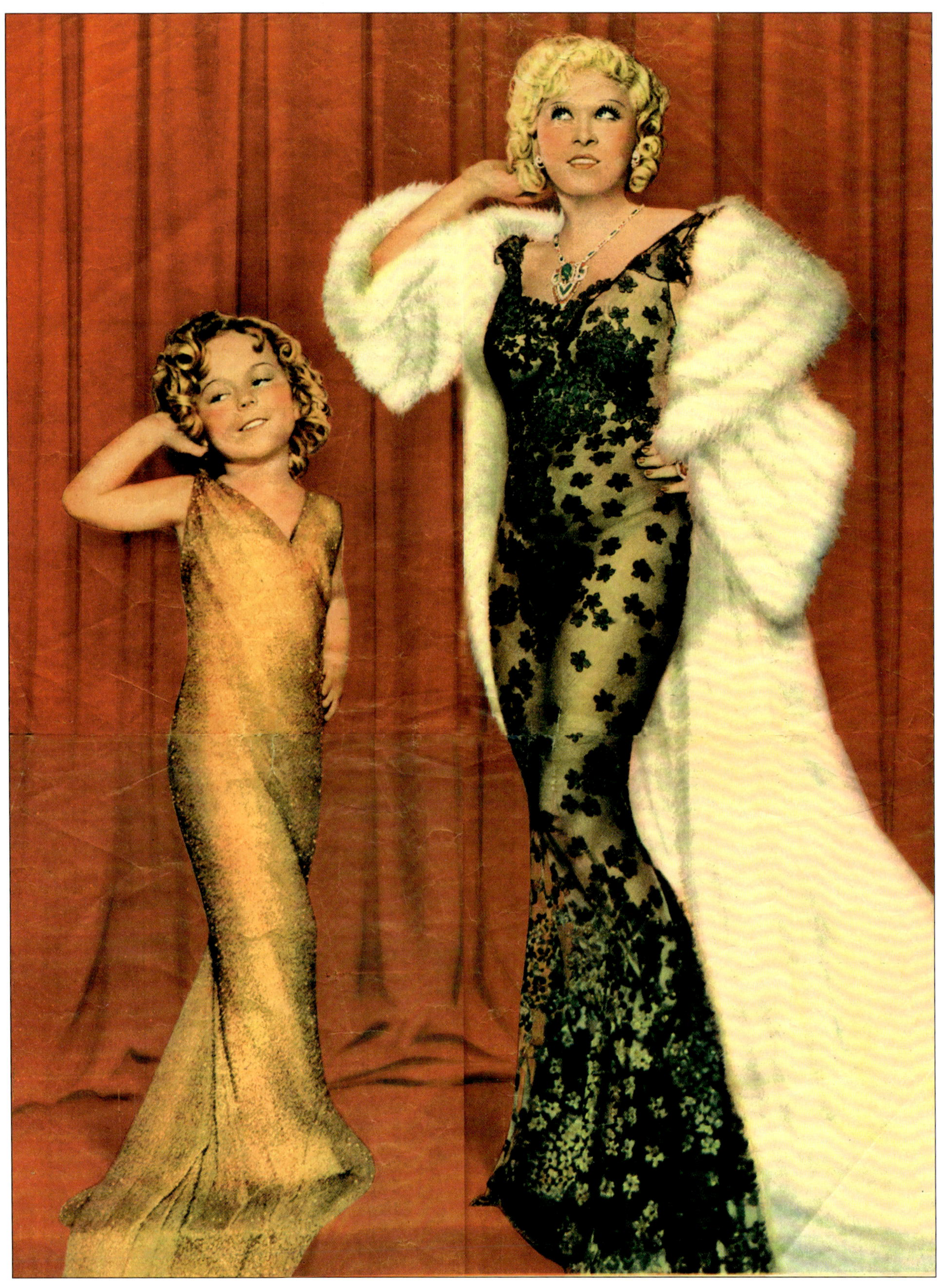

"Has He Got a Friend He Can Bring Along," caption with Shirley Temple and Mae West, newspaper, Sunday magazine section, 1940s

• Most men fantasized West as a Hollywood sex symbol. She parodied an overt, flirtatious, flaunting, and readily available woman. If men perceived and desired West (and other women) to act in that sexy way, then that was what they got—just her desirability and a fantasized knowledge that she was available. However, she knew if a man looked at a woman solely for her sex appeal, then any relationship with a woman would be no more than physical and, therefore, patriarchal.

• On a higher level, as Anaïs Nin has said, "Only the united beat of sex and heart together can create ecstasy." To gain necessary equality, a woman had to feel more than a man's desire—she had to feel her own desire. Since being desired and feeling desire are two very different emotions, when combined they would form a large factor in selecting a partner in a more heartfelt and meaningful relationship. Equally important, both feelings must be there within a man too, if his relationship with a woman is to be balanced and deep. (But that goes against the instinctive feelings that many men hold dear: when they see an archetypal alluring woman they could fall in love with, they fear they might lose their power by loving a woman. "Fall in love" is a cliché, which equates falling with losing power.) Some people realized that West created and exemplified this higher, more evolved level in her films. For those who did, West symbolized a modern-day sex symbol that promoted women's emancipation.

• There was a further, even higher level to West's bravado, which was really her play on her true self. In it, morality was not a presence, which is within the true meaning of traditional burlesque, nor was there a nagging culture, a neighborly busybody, or a Will Hays Production Code. In this heightened situation, a woman or a man was completely free to participate or not to participate in sex. When and if she or he chose to participate, they could be heterosexual, lesbian, tribade (a lesbian with the male role), gay, transgender, or even a woman or a man impersonating their own gender. This highest level of the Mae West symbol created the complete and genuine person. West grew up with female impersonators like Julian Eltinge and Bert Savoy in vaudeville. She admired their playful femininity. Her strut was copied from Savoy's outrageous vamp strut. Everything about West was impersonation: her shimmy came from Gilda Gray, her hair from Jean Harlow, her charm from Clara Bow. To West, impersonation could be a curious paradox: the impersonator could become more real than the person being impersonated. West's most famous line, spoken while she used nictitation (flirting and winking), "Why don't you

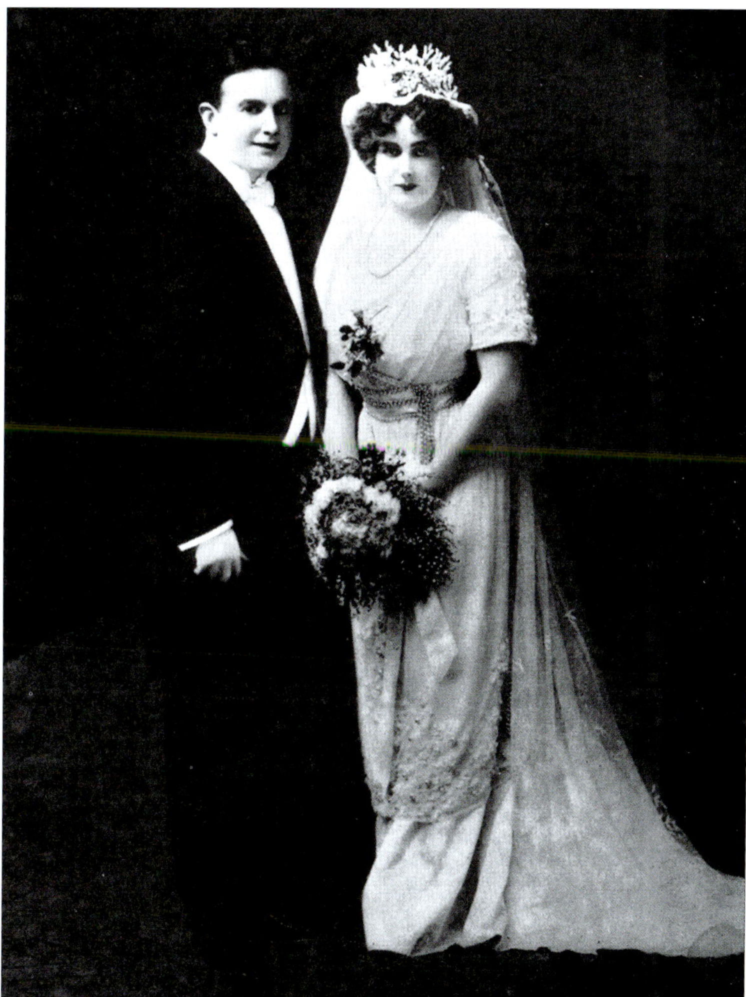

Julian Eltinge marrying himself, circa 1915

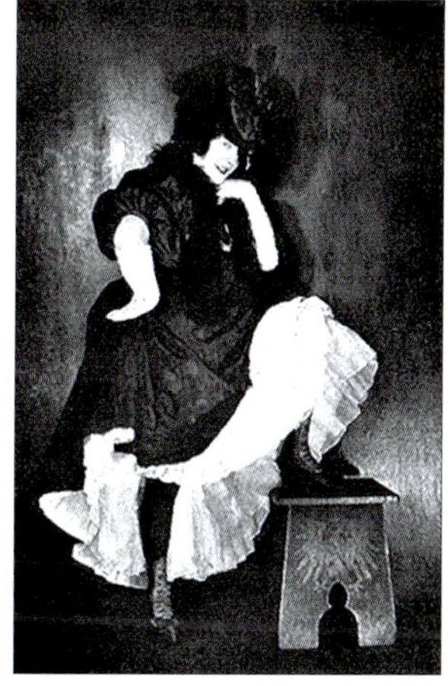

Bert Savoy, circa 1920

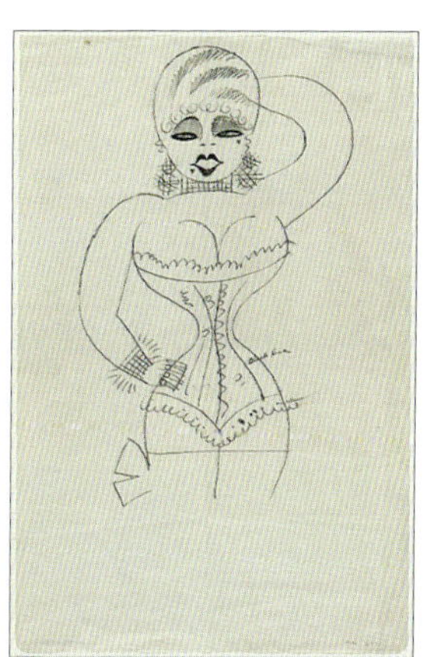

Mae West, sketch Miguel Covarrubias, Courtesy: Library of Congress, circa 1930

come up and see me sometime?" could still be offered and understood in relation to all three of the above sex symbol stereotypes—various meanings and expectations being entirely subjective. West's own exaggerated dress, brash lines, and overt gestures were really a parody of drag queens, so that it could be said that she, as a woman, parodied a man impersonating a woman.

If men desired Mae West as a Hollywood "sex symbol," she certainly had the last laugh—she knew they were falling for one of her many parodies. Much of her success was based on men's archetypal sexual naïveté as the superior man, particularly when it came to understanding lust.

Mae West was a strong willed reactionary railing against the Victorian Age. Her Victorian satires were well ahead of their time, even by the liberated Jazz Age standards of the 1920s. West's staying power only increased with time. Unlike the fate of so many stars, she was never forgotten. Mae West died in 1980.

Shirley Temple

(1928-

. . . as long as our country has Shirley Temple, we will be all right.
—Franklin Delano Roosevelt

Shirley Jane Temple was born in 1928. Six years later, she was the number-one box-office attraction, a position she held for five years. Little did she realize that she single-handedly pulled her studio out of the Depression's red column. Her archetype was easily recognizable as America's little princess. Her singing and dancing made Americans feel hope, joy, and nationalism. She always stole the show, even out-acting her adult co-stars. Unconsciously she epitomized a new moral goodness ushered in by the Will Hays Production Code.

Her tutelage in acting began when she was a mere three years old as her mother pushed her into pedophilia-prone, teaser-type stereotypes in Hollywood's Baby Burlesque Productions—short films in which she mimicked adult sexpot roles. She was one of many delightful, young children, some still in diapers, who parodied adult actors and actresses. In two of her 1932 films, Shirley

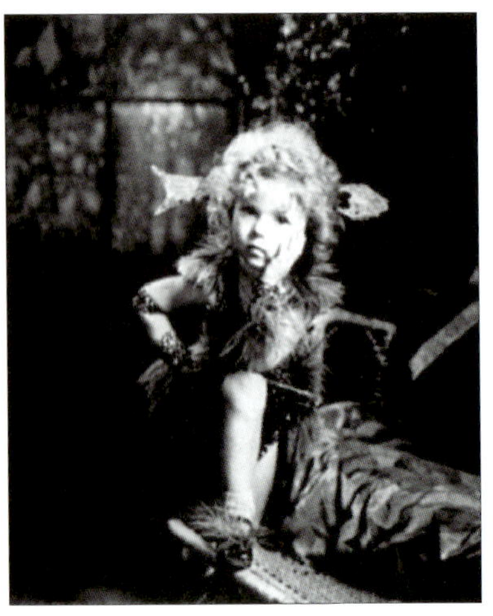

Shirley Temple as Morelegs Sweettricks mimicking Marlene Dietrich, *Kid in Hollywood* (1933)

mimicked Marlene Dietrich as ridiculously sexist Hollywood characters named Morelegs Sweettricks and Madame Cradle-bait. She also played the dimpled Jane to a pint-sized Tarzan, as well as a Wild West femme fatalé to cowboys with guns in their diapers. A year later, the Hays Code stopped Baby Burlesque Productions dead (in its cradle). Did her overly ambitious mother ever realize those films were promoting pedophilia? (Did audiences in general see them that way?) Furthermore, were these films wrecking her childhood forever? In Baby Burlesque Productions, Shirley was not far from a living, breathing fallen woman at the age of three. Even when she was a superstar, Shirley posed as a child sex-pot with Mae West (page 140). What was she to think of that display?

When Fox Studios signed her in 1934, they abandoned her infant sexpot image and let her be what she really was—an energetic, strong-willed, good-natured, and unbelievably talented child. They allowed her to be known for her blonde ringlets, irresistible charm, and ability to sing, tap-dance, and perform stunts—as well as for her incredible acting prowess. No one would have doubted that she was a trained professional by age six, when she first starred in the Fox Studios film *Stand Up and Cheer*. Later that year, Shirley became an icon when she starred in four more films: *Now and Forever*, *Little Miss Marker*, *Baby Take a Bow*, and *Bright Eyes*. She was given a special Academy Award "in grateful recognition of her outstanding contribution." Shirley was one of only a few child stars that Hollywood cast as a child acting as a child and not as a child acting as an adult. Her lines expressed a child's joy, and all of her other abilities played into that.

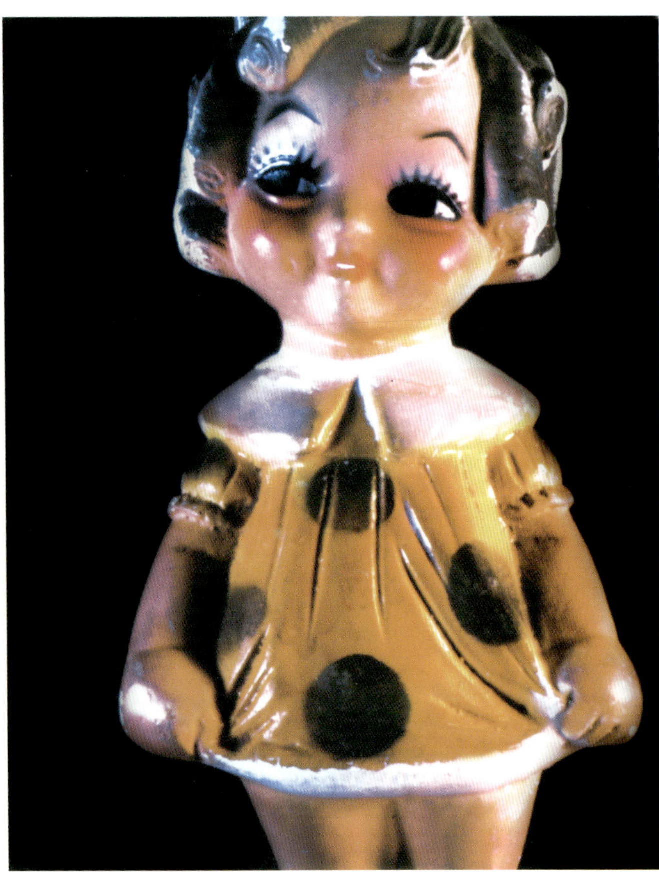

Shirley Temple thirteen-inch carnival chalk prize caricatured from *Baby Takes A Bow* (1934) holding out the edges of her above-the-knee-length skirt

By 1935, Fox Studios became 20th-Century Fox and its dynamic new head, Daryl F. Zanuck, made Shirley his top priority. In that year alone, four of her most memorable films were released. *The Little Colonel* was a Civil War drama with music. It introduced the sweetest, unlikeliest couple in tap-dance history: little Shirley Temple, with the equally incomparable fifty-seven-year-old African American Bill "Bojangles" Robinson. Together, they showed the world how blacks and whites could dance as an incandescent and daring duo. The films *Our Little Girl* and *Curly Top* followed; the latter introduced the classic song "Animal Crackers." The fourth film, *The Littlest Rebel*, teamed Shirley with Robinson again. Most blacks wondered if Shirley and Bojangles were Hollywood's long-awaited, tip-of-the-iceberg token of integration. Shirley outlived her lovable, talented child stereotype and her acting career dwindled. She made her forty-fourth and last film as a child actress in 1940 at twelve years old. Though she made a few teen films from 1940 through 1949, most of her time was spent at Westlake School for Girls, of which she said, "I could hardly wait, catch-up, homework notwithstanding."

The Coogan Act (protecting assets realized by child

actors) was in full effect when Shirley was scheduled to collect her millions. In her memoirs, she confessed that her father, George Temple Sr., had circumvented the law and spent all of her money. She ran, unsuccessfully, as a Republican candidate for Congress in 1967, but since she represented America's goodwill child from years gone by, she was made a member of the U.S. delegation to the United Nations (1969–70), was U.S. ambassador to Ghana (1974–76), and became the first woman in U.S. history to serve as chief of protocol (1976–77) during the administration of President Gerald R. Ford. President George H. W. Bush appointed her ambassador to Czechoslovakia in 1989.

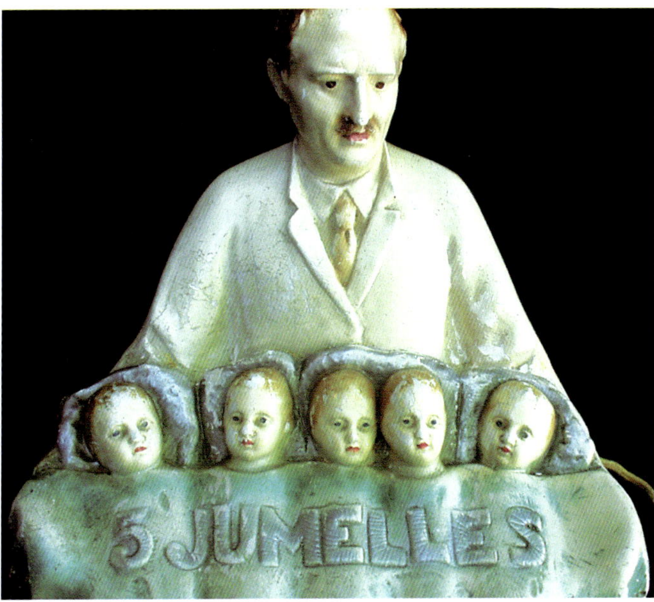

Dionne quintuplets (*5 Jumelles*—5 Twins) with Dr. Allan Roy Dafoe fourteen-inch chalk lamp perfumery souvenir, Montreal, Canada © Brevete, 1934

    The Dionne quintuplets' successful birth was the major media miracle of 1934. Five identical girls were born two months premature; each weighed under two pounds. They were delivered by Dr. Allan Roy Dafoe who became an instant celebrity. The Canadian government made them wards of the state (seeing their $$$$$ potential as early public servants) and placed them in Quintland—a baby theme park across from their parents' home in Corbell, Ontario. Six thousand tourists a day viewed them, confirming their miracle-baby-birth archetype as well as enriching the Depression-laden area with $25 million each year. Through their kindly doctor's entrepreneurship the quints endorsed myriads of products like Baby Ruth candy bars and Quaker Oats cereal. At aged nine their parents regained custody. Their termagant mother immediately took away the quints' Shirley Temple dolls—their most valued possessions—claiming the quints had been spoiled. In the quints' recent book *Family Secrets*, published in 1996, the three who are still alive told how their father had sexually abused all of them—taking one at a time for jaunts in the family car. They had asked their Catholic priest for help— his only suggestion was that they wear heavier coats.[1] *Family Secrets* was written in the hope that unveiling their secret would help others. In a court suit in 1998, the remaining quints were awarded $4 million by the Ontario government.

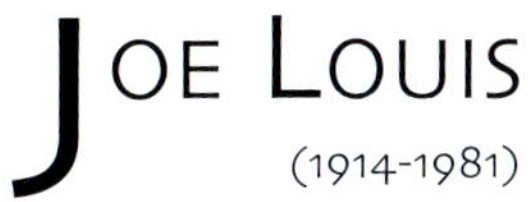

JOE LOUIS
(1914-1981)

He was our Sampson; he was our David. With toughness he destroyed our enemy, with kindness he soothed our wounds and revived our psyche.
—JESSE JACKSON

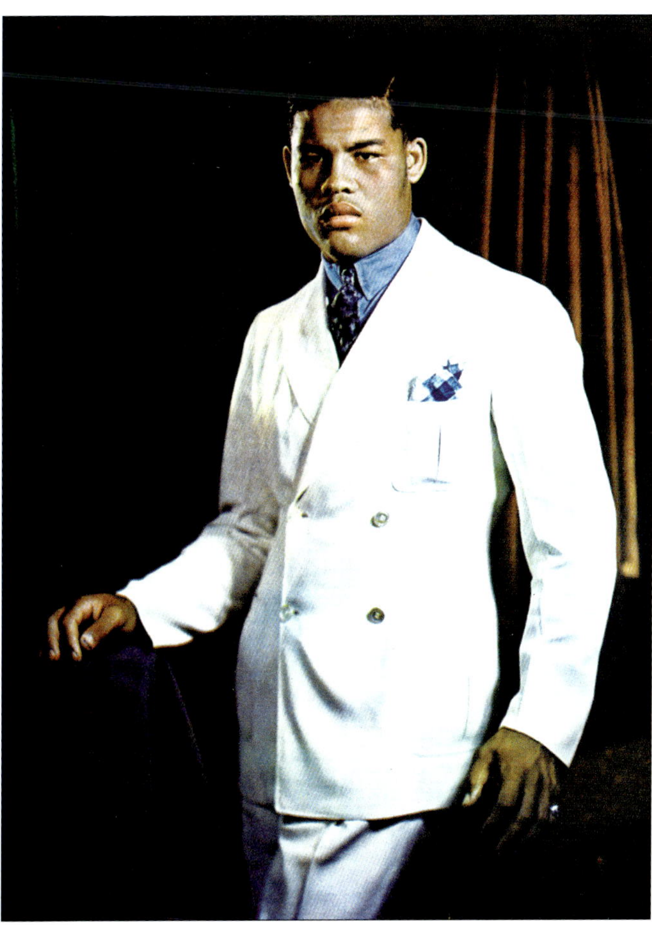

Joe Louis © *Fortune Magazine*, October 1935, photograph White-Redman

    Joe Louis was born Joe Louis Barrow in 1914 on a sharecropper's farm near Lafayette, Alabama, the seventh of eight children. His father, Munroe Barrow, was committed to a psychiatric hospital not long after Joe was born. Somewhat later, the family was told that Munroe had died, but in fact he lived for two more decades. Joe's mother, Lillie, supported the family by taking in washing. When Joe was seven, she remarried Patrick Brooks and combined her eight children with his eight children. Two years later, the large family followed the Great Migration to Detroit, where Joe's stepfather found work. Because of poor schooling in the South, Joe was forced to attend school with much younger students. Humiliated, he developed a stammer. Before school he worked in the Eastern Market, and after school at Pickman and Dean, an ice company. Later he would claim that carrying the fifty-pound blocks of ice helped develop his shoulders and arms. Joe's mother gave him money for weekly violin lessons when he was sixteen, but he used the money to pay for a locker at

Brewster Recreation Center, where amateur boxers gathered and trained. Later he attended a trade school to study carpentry, but his real interest lay in boxing. He left school at seventeen to train on his own. Boxing was the only sport in America that allowed blacks to enter. Why? Because African Americans slaves had always been thought of as an object that wealthy patrons could bet on, much like a rooster in a cockfight, so they were not excluded from a sport that was originally part of Southern men's clubs.

Joe lost his first amateur bout, but then had impressive victories during the next three years, which included more than forty knockouts with only a few losses. In 1934, after he won the national amateur title in the light heavyweight division, he felt ready for professional boxing. John Roxborough and Julian Black, two African American businessmen, agreed to manage him. They encouraged him to drop Barrow from his name, because they thought Joe Louis was easier to remember. They also hired Jack Blackburn, a former lightweight fighter and a well-regarded trainer, who discovered that Louis had very little foot speed. Blackburn taught him to use his flat-footed shuffle and compact punches—which became his signature.

Roxborough and Black were keenly aware of just how much the white public in America despised the first African American heavyweight champion, Jack Johnson, who reigned from 1908 to 1915. Johnson offended white boxing fans by gloating over those he defeated (which were often white opponents) and worse, by having sexual relationships with beautiful white women. Louis's managers counseled him. He needed to be a gentleman in the ring and shy with the press. He was to avoid drinking, smoking, and, most of all, being seen with white women in public. The white man's fear of a large, strong black man could not be overemphasized. He and other African Americans had seen just how popular the film *King Kong* was in 1933. Louis followed his manager's advice. Whites mostly admired him, nicknaming him the "Brown Bomber," and he became widely championed because of his modesty and dignity. Even most white Southerners hailed him as a nonthreatening black man. Privately, although Louis neither drank nor smoked, he enjoyed an active night life with very discreet romances with both black women and white women.

Louis's first professional fight was against Jack Kracken on July 4, 1934, for which he earned $50. In his first year, he won more than twenty fights without a loss, typically against white opponents. In 1935, he knocked out Primo Carnera and earned $60,433. Most African Americans lived vicariously through Louis's punishing blows to whites—after a victory by Louis, entire black neighborhoods were known to burst into spontaneous celebration. In his first year and a half as a professional, his purses added up to $371,645 at a time when the average yearly salary in America was $1,250. On June 19, 1936, Louis met German fighter and former world champion Max Schmeling in Yankee Stadium. At the time, Hitler's fascism was enveloping Europe; the press seized upon the fight to portray Schmeling as a representative of fascism and Louis as a symbol of democracy. To a lesser degree, Louis was also touted as a symbol of racial harmony. Unlike many white American fighters, Schmeling was not afraid to

fight Louis. Schmeling's trainers watched films of Louis's bouts and saw that when Louis jabbed, he kept his left high; when he went for a hook, he set himself ever so slightly and lowered his left hand. Schmeling was advised to step back to evade the jab, and when Louis lowered his guard, to throw a straight right over Louis's left (during the match Schmeling hit Louis with ninety-one right leads). In the twelfth round, Schmeling knocked out the heavily favored Louis, dealing him his first professional defeat. Hitler cited Schmeling's archetypal victory as proof of the superiority of his Aryan race and nationalism for Germany. It was a sad moment for African Americans.

Humiliated, Louis rebounded to seven straight victories and the right to fight heavyweight champion James Braddock on June 22, 1937, in Chicago's Comiskey Park. Braddock, a white man, knocked Louis to the canvas early in the fight, but Louis recovered and won. With that victory, Louis, then only twenty-three years old, became Heavyweight Champion of the World, an archetypal symbol for the best fighting man. Next was a rematch against Schmeling. With the possibility of a European war looming, the Louis–Schmeling rematch took on even greater significance. Louis, a black man, was the Heavyweight Champion of the World, and Schmeling, a white man, the challenger. A replay of the first fight would have been even more humiliating, but in the first round Louis scored a stunning knockout, making him the most popular athlete in America—indeed, throughout much of the world. At that time, he stereotyped for white America a symbol of racial harmony, since he had just won. But for the African Americans, who knew better, he stereotyped a symbol of black triumph within a racist society. He was an archetypal symbol for champion power. And for all Americans he created feelings of nationalism.

After the bombing of Pearl Harbor, Louis gave his entire purse from the next fight to the Navy Relief Fund. Not quite three months later, he repeated the gift, this time to the Army Relief Fund. In 1942, Louis entered the army and boxed in nearly one hundred exhibition matches for the troops (earning $21 dollars a month). Until his time in the service, he had rarely taken on political causes, but when he saw firsthand how segregated the military was he protested; he refused to sit on segregated military buses.

After the war, he resumed his professional career.

Louis's laconic style hid his wit. Before his 1946 rematch with Billy Conn, when reporters asked him how he would deal with that fighter's agility and quickness, Louis coined his most famous remark: "He can run but he can't hide!" He reigned as Heavyweight Champion for eleven years and eight months—still the longest in the heavyweight division's history.

By 1949, Louis had successfully defended his title twenty-five times and retired before turning thirty-five. His finances, however, were in even worse shape than they were in the early 1940s—when his prize money was greatly mishandled. Louis had been a generous champion. He lived simply and gave much of his money away to charities. He helped friends with unsuccessful business ventures. He voluntarily paid back the government the welfare payments that his stepfather had received during the Great Depression, bought a house for an elderly Native American, and purchased much needed uniforms for a group of black army officers. His money problems stemmed from changes in the IRS. In 1931 (the year Louis began boxing seriously), the income tax was so minimal that only 2 percent of Americans even qualified to pay it. But from 1934 on, the top marginal tax rate had soared from 24 to 79 percent. Louis found himself owing the government most of his purse money from each of his fights. During the 1940s, the top marginal rate was hiked to 90 percent, and Louis owed $500,000 to the IRS in back taxes. Unlike later successful athletes, he had no tax shelters or clever accountants. The IRS would not even let him deduct the two fight purses he had donated to the army and navy, nor could he deduct $3,000 worth of tickets that he had bought for soldiers to one of those two fights (nothing new about the IRS). By 1950, badly in need of money, he returned to the ring. Louis compiled several victories but lost twice: to Heavyweight Champion Ezzard Charles and in a knockout to Rocky Marciano. After the Marciano fight, Louis retired for good.

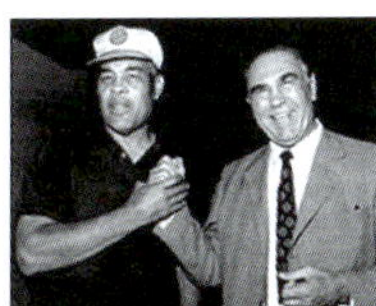

Bitter enemies at first, Louis and Schmeling became great friends. Toward the end of Louis' life, Schmeling helped Louis financially and also paid for part of his funeral expenses.

Louis's personal life was not easy. He divorced three times before marrying Martha Jefferson—the first black woman to practice law in California—in 1959. He died in 1981. Because of his strengths and accomplishments, Joe Louis has remained one of America's most loved heroes.

Modern boxing has its roots in the fairs, pubs, and gambling rooms of early 1700s England. Boxing reinforced English class structure, as only the poor would box for the entertainment of rich patrons. The boxer gambled his life; the patron gambled his money. Who had the most to lose? (Death statistics from boxing show 1,300 boxers have died from ring injuries since 1880). Wealthy Americans from the South learned of its bloody pleasures when they traveled to England, and imported it into impromptu matches between their slaves. Northerners emphasized the moral importance of work and criticized the sport; Southerners enjoyed leisure and viewed boxing as an important aspect of a gentleman's life.

The first important American boxer was Tom Molineau, an ex-slave who in 1810 boxed for the title of World's Best Boxer outside London and lost a controversial match. By the 1830s, organized boxing in America was in its infancy in New Orleans, the only city that would tolerate it as a legitimate professional sport. Boxing has always had its dark criminal side, which has been useful in film noir.

Film noir interprets the human primordial animalistic feelings for top-dog, get-even prowess where a man or woman in their instinctive darkest visceral moods thrill as the depraved criminal. Reason is lost. Violence begets violence. It is the hunter versus the hunted in a world of desperate alienation. This is addictive grist for film noir's hardened viewers and softer voyeurs, stereotyping the watchful chump, the evil crime boss, and anyone macho gun-crazy. For five decades the master-creator of the tough-guy stereotypes was Edward G. Robinson, who first starred in *Little Caesar*

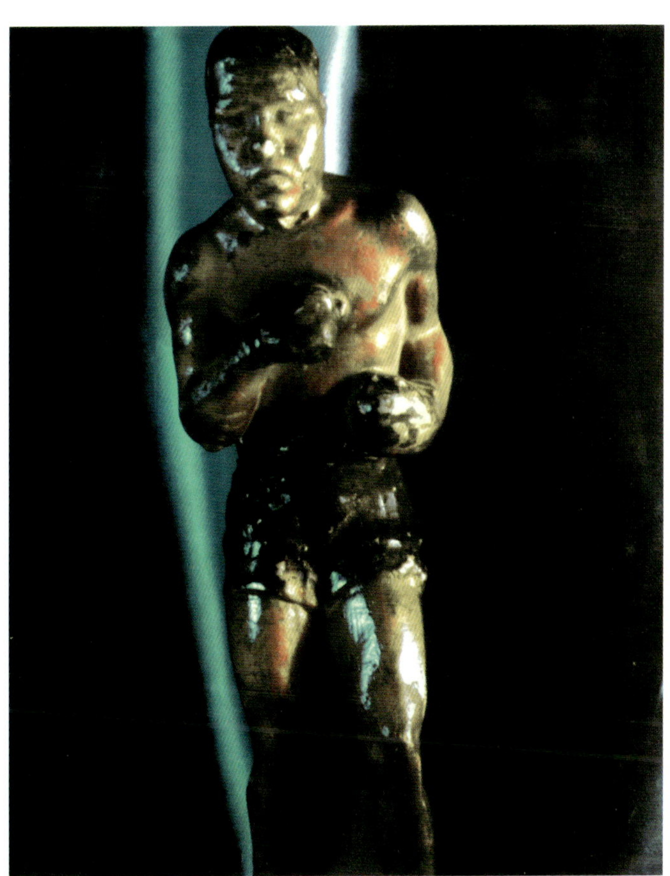

Joe Louis twelve-inch carnival chalk ashtray prize

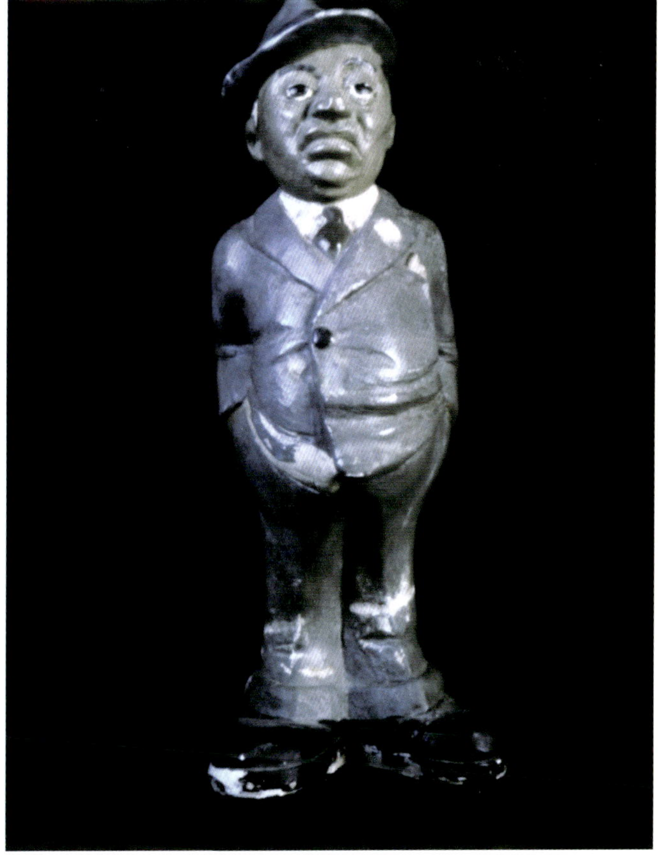

Edward G. Robinson seven-and-one-half-inch carnival chalk prize

(1930). Even his cigar became a stereotype. Crime films were given brutal authenticity by the real-life organized crime boss Scarface Al Capone. Media saturation (propaganda) of Capone's crimes lent legitimacy to the government's need (the FBI's as well as the local's) for law and order in a world of sensationalized gun-crazy mobster violent crime. Easily included into film noir was the femme fatalé. The real-life Bonnie and Clyde gave women the privilege and authenticity to be gun crazy too.

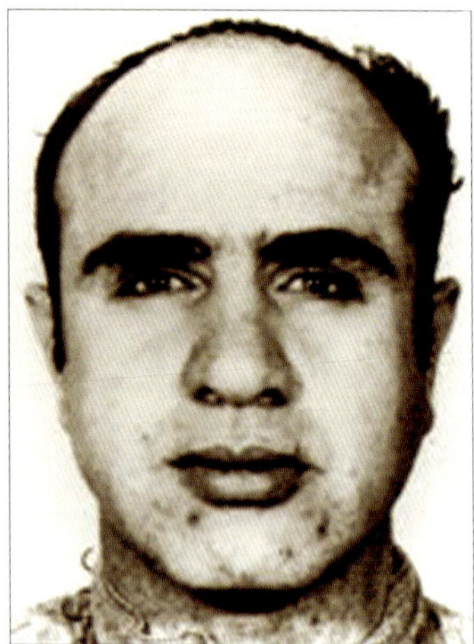
Scarface Al Capone

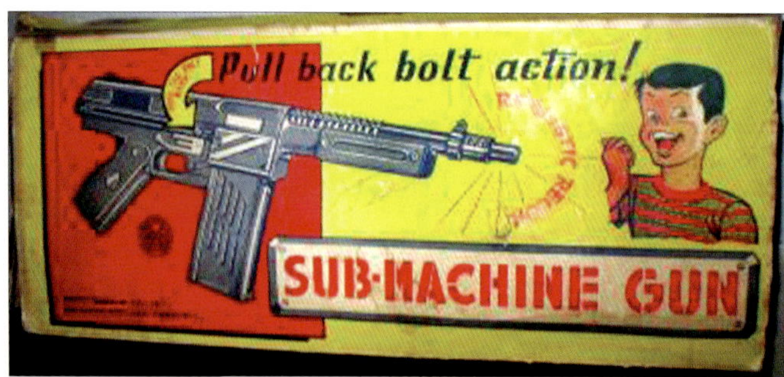

Marx Toy Sub-Machine Cap Gun, 1950s

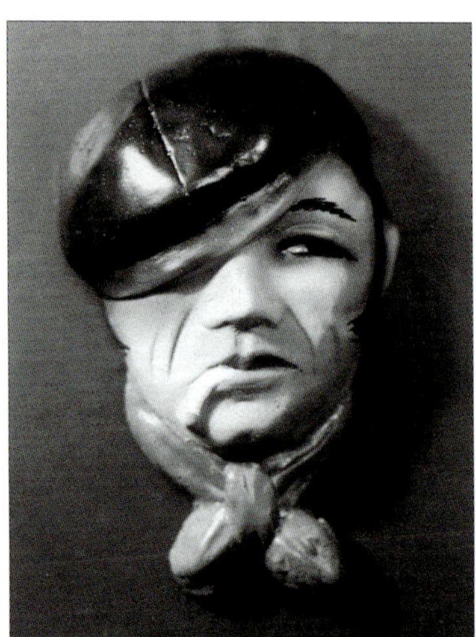
Edward G. Robinson carnival chalk wall prize,
designed by June Yates Jenkins

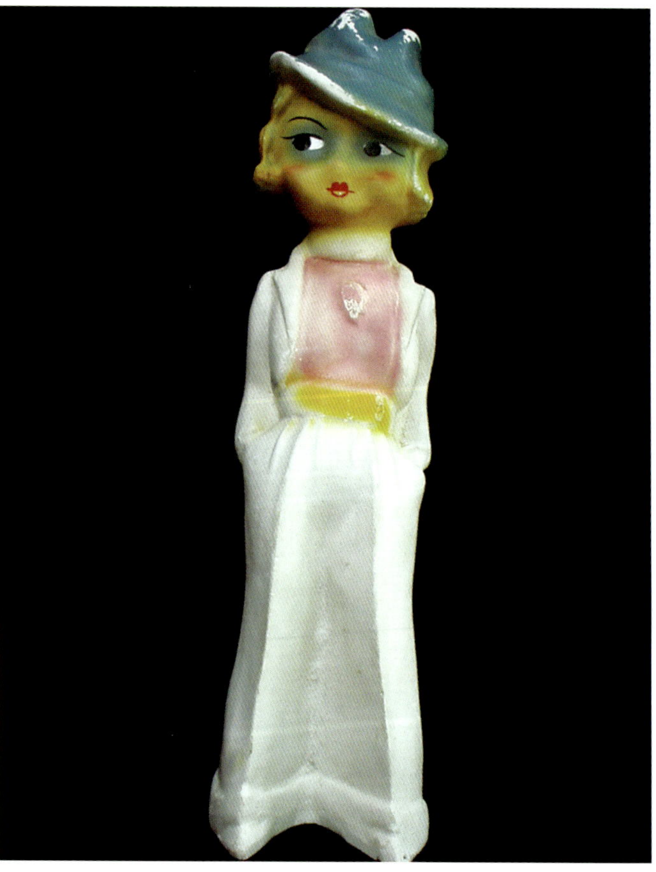

All Shoot Together.

The officers raised up from the weeds at the side of the road. There was a blast of machine and shotgun fire, the automobile careened off the road and crashed into the embankment.

Other bullets crashed into the rear and side of the car. There was a wait of several minutes. No signs of life in the car. . . .

Clyde, with the back of his skull torn away, hung limply from the left side of the car. Across his lap was an automatic rifle. Beside him on the seat was another. Forty bullets from the officers' guns had pierced his body.

Shot in Mouth.

With her head between her knees, a sawed-off shotgun across her lap, lay Bonnie. A bullet had struck her in the mouth, passing completely through her head. This wound caused almost instant death.

Besides this wound, there were approximately fifty others. Her right hand was torn away, the back of he rhead was blasted off and her body and limbs were torn and riddled by the bullets.

Three army automatic rifles were found in the car, along with two automatic shotguns and ten automatic pistols. Approximately 500 rounds of ammunition for the guns and pistols also were in the car.

"All Shoot Together" and "Shot in Mouth," Newspaper article about the death of Bonnie and Clyde, 1934. Their exploits made sensational headlines. Many saw them as the alienated little guy against the cops and big government during the height of the Great Depression when work was not to be found (the David against Goliath archetype). Bonnie had been an honor student in high school, excelling in writing. She had not killed anyone during their robbing and murder spree, so her death by the FBI and police posse has always been disdained. Contrary to the newspaper report, witnesses said she did not die instantly. Before they were taken to the funeral home bystanders took pieces of their clothing and cut locks of their hair to sell as souvenirs—halted by officials when one person tried to cut off Clyde's ear. Over 50,000 curious "mourners" came to the funeral home before they were buried. Their alienation legacy lives on—enshrined in many Hollywood films.

Femme fatalé fourteen-and-one half-inch carnival chalk prize

Sophie Tucker

(1884–1966)

I'm a one-ticket gal, free as the breeze, I go where I like, I do as I please . . . I'm living alone and I like it.
—Sophie Tucker from her song *I'm Living Alone*

Sophie Tucker was born Sophie Kalish in a farmhouse in Russia as her mother was traveling halfway around the world to join her husband, who had already immigrated to the United States. Sophie eventually arrived in Connecticut when she was three, where her family name was changed to the Italian name Abuza in memory of her father's traveling companion, whom he had met while fleeing the tsarist Russian army. Sophie Abuza was singing onstage by the time she was ten. Audiences knew her as "the fat girl"—by the time she was thirteen, Sophie weighed 145 pounds. She married Louis Tuck when she was nineteen and they had a son, Bert. After Sophie and Louis divorced in 1906, she headed for New York, leaving Bert to be raised by her sister. She added the letters "er" to her name in New York to become the familiar Sophie Tucker, singing in amateur shows and later performing as a comic singer in burlesque. Wearing the trademark minstrel's blackface in burlesque shows, she was a popular ragtime "coonshouter"—a slur on singing blackface impersonators. By 1911 (and never again wearing blackface), her booming voice, bawdy songs, and self-effacing humor made her a vaudeville headliner at the Ziegfeld Follies, where she sang Shelton Brooks's "Some of These Days." It was fabulously popular, selling a million copies in sheet music, and becoming her theme song for the next eighteen years. Tucker's sound-film debut was as a nightclub performer in *Honky Tonk* (1929), singing "I Never Want to Get Thin" and "I'm the Last of the Red Hot Mamas"—the latter became her theme song for the rest of her life. Her song "My Yiddische Momme" stirred such emotional pride among European Jews that Hitler eventually forbade the sale of her recordings. Her international fame was perpetuated by her aggressive, mouthy sexuality; hence the carnival chalk prize which honored that side of her bawdy charisma. Tucker also sang about her weight, origins, and liberated lifestyle during an era when being overweight, Jewish, and divorced were not traits generally desired by most American women (and disdained by most American men). Many of her songs promoted undesirability rather than the norms of perfection. Tucker is considered by many to be one of the

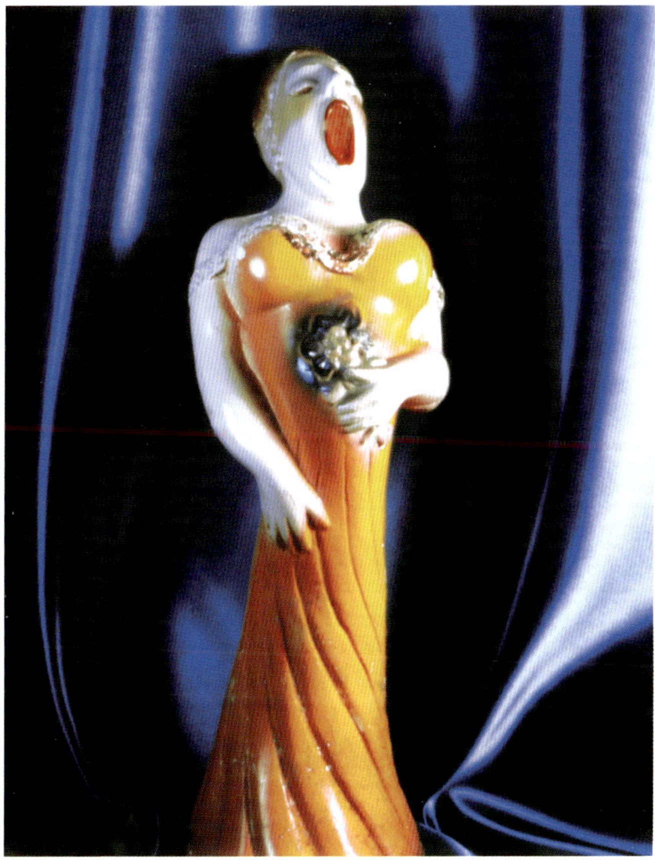

Sophie Tucker thirteen-and-a-half-inch glittered carnival chalk prize

most genuine of early feminists because of her unabashedly honest memoirs presented through her songs (although some of her early songs were racist). She had a bigger-than-life, I-am-who-I-am, foghorn, brassy stereotype. She was often seen as the unstoppable woman—a freight train at full throttle disguised as a woman. She was in truth a freight train of a woman, and it was her lack of disguise and her integrity that was admired and could not be ignored.

Tucker was an individual, one of the few media personalities who didn't just sing about love and the loss of love but had something important to say—yet she was always controversial. For those who disliked her, she was an archetypal symbol for the bawdy woman. People who admired her saw her as a liberated genuine woman.

Tucker, who outlived many of her vaudeville contemporaries, had her own radio show and performed in eight films and, later, on television. She headed the American Federation of Actors, started the Sophie Tucker Foundation, was generous with her money, and raised millions of dollars for servicemen during World War I. She married and divorced two more times. Tucker, who never retired and loved her work, died of lung cancer in 1966.

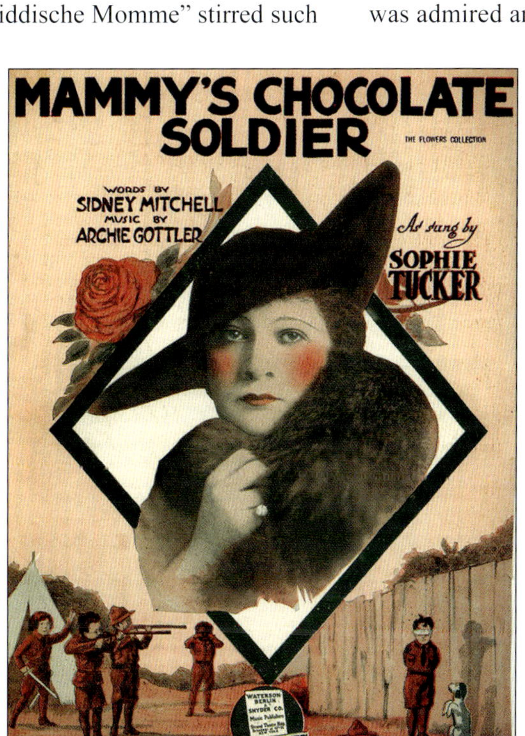

Sophie Tucker, "Mammy's Chocolate Soldier," sheet music cover, words Sidney Mitchell, music Archie Gottler, 1918 © Waterson, Berlin & Snyder Co., NY—a black child's lament—white children would not allow him to play with them and be a soldier

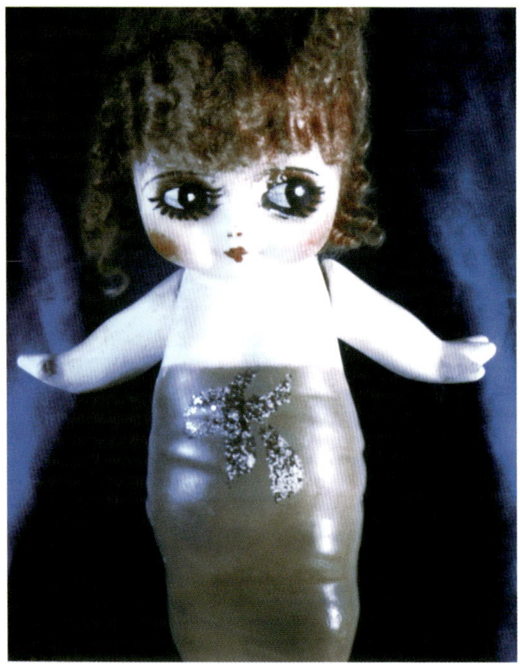

Vamp (?) 1918–20 thirteen-inch carnival chalk prize

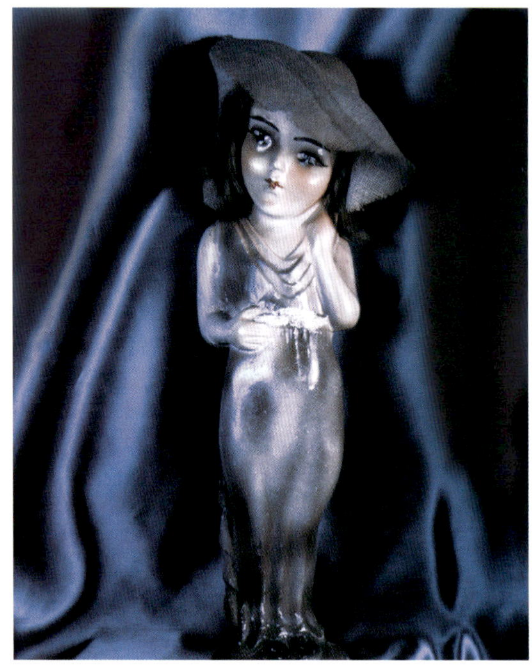

Gloria Swanson (?) 1920-25 fourteen-inch carnival chalk prize

Hollywood Mystery Figures

1920s-1940s

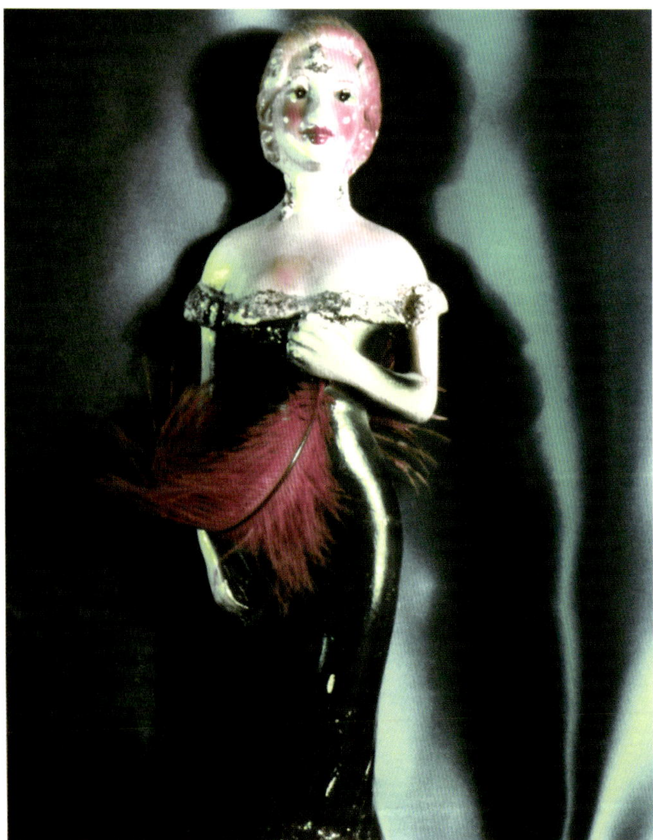

Miss Katy of the Nineties fourteen-inch carnival chalk prize, named by Pacini Statuary Co., 1936, originally the prize had a wide hat—she is probably Mae West from *She Done Him Wrong* (1933)

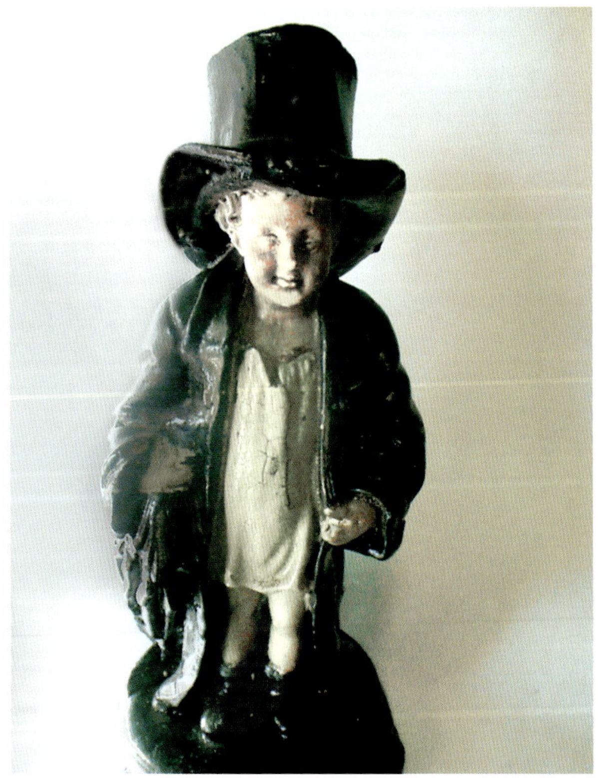

John Darling (?) in a nightshirt, holding an umbrella and wearing an oversize tophat ten-inch carnival chalk prize from the first Hollywood filming of *Peter Pan* (1926)

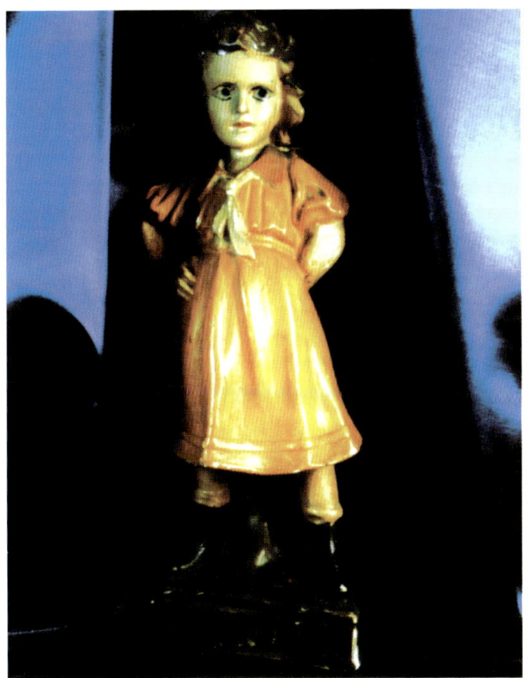

Is this Lillian Gish as Hollywood's archetypal waif or Alice in Wonderland? 1920s twelve-and-one-half-inch carnival chalk prize

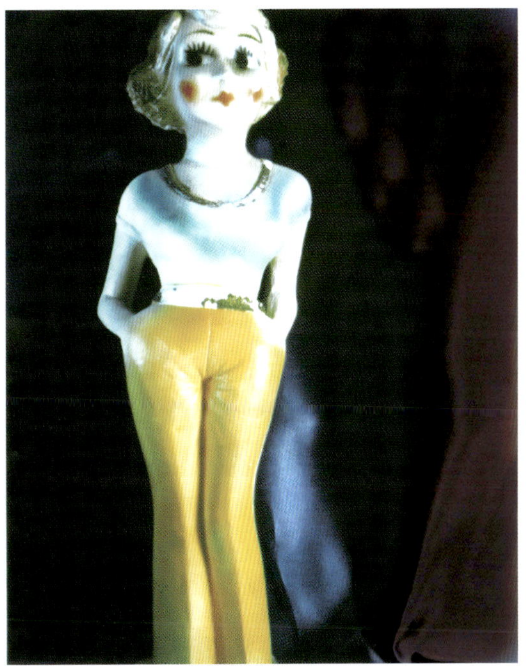

Slack Doll 1930s fifteen-inch carnival chalk prize © William Rainwater (original figure carved in wood by Clarence DeWitt)

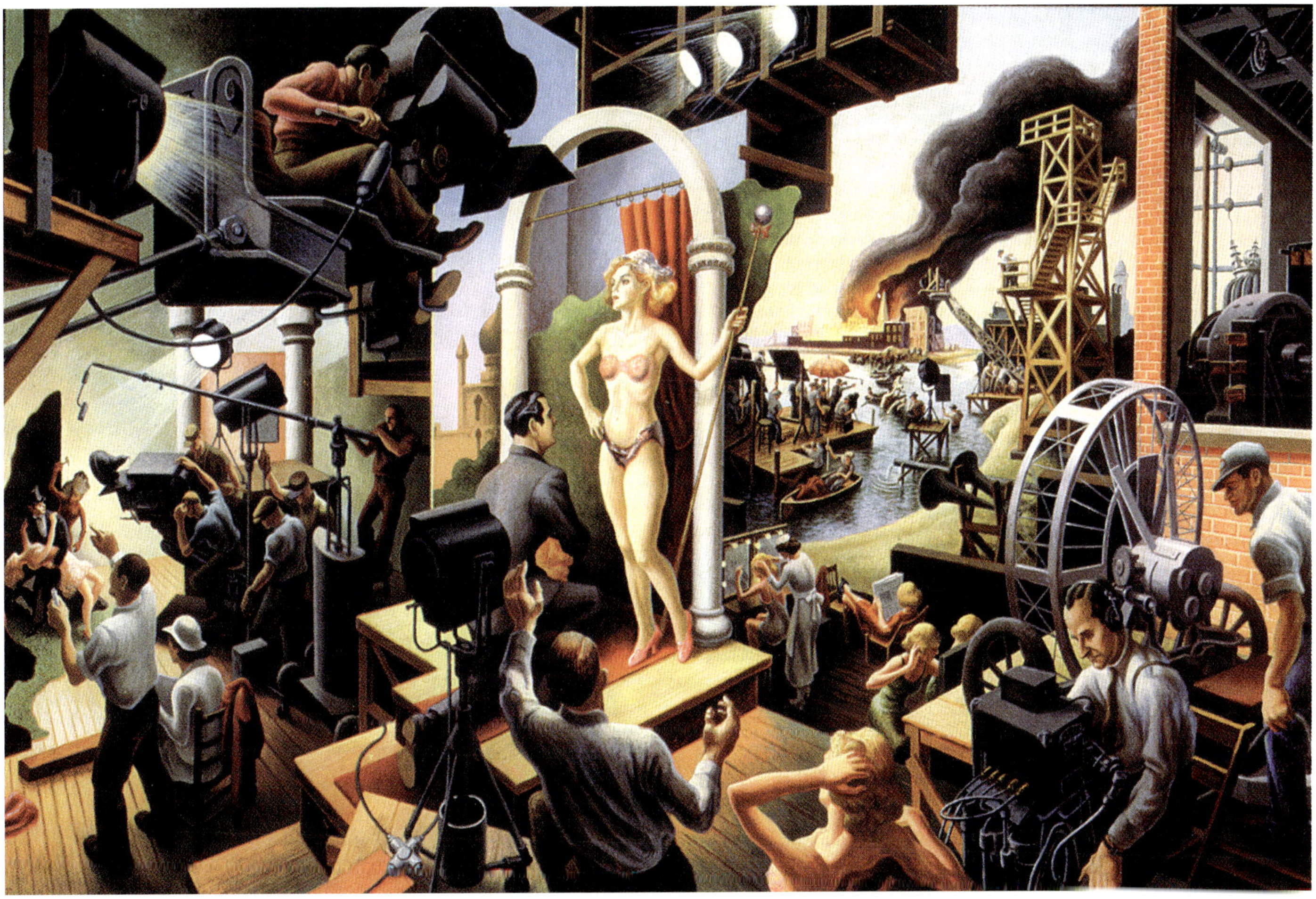

Hollywood, Thomas Hart Benton, 1937. Collection: Nelson-Atkins Museum of Art, bequest of the artist. Benton was commissioned by *Life* magazine in 1937 to paint an image of Hollywood. It was to be a two-page spread; *Life* rejected it as too risque.

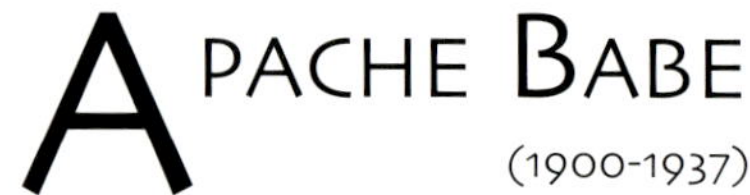 Apache Babe

(1900-1937)

I don't feel dressed without my lipstick.
—LANA TURNER *They Won't Forget,* one of her only lines

Apache Babe was derived from young, tough, lower-class French women who joined Parisian street gangs during the 1870s-1910. This mythic stereotype was spawned by a real-life incident when a domestic quarrel evolved into a knife fight between two men and a woman in front of a Montmartre nightclub in Paris. It is said that the quarrel began over money when a pimp demanded payment from his prostitute. A local news reporter was inadvertently responsible for coining the name "apache" when the newspaper printed his comment: "The fury of a riotous incident between two men and a women rose to the ferocity of savage Apache Indians in battle." After reading about themselves, the proud participants formed gangs called Apaches. They created their own style of dancing that imitated the brutal actions of that night. Their dance, named appropriately the apache dance, was promoted in the world media because it was an evolving empowered stereotype for the feminist movements of the late nineteenth and early twentieth centuries.

In an apache dance there are no real steps, patterns, or routines. Knives are drawn and women are strenuously embraced, lifted, carried, dragged, and thrown about. Women, in their roles in the dance, push and hit the men with great intensity. (It was the first dance where women were equal to men). The entire dance imitates a severe domestic quarrel with music that is much like a tango. Apache dancing was not for everyone and in no way was it a social dance; sometimes bones were broken (some women actually died), and it was usually presented in a breathtaking exhibition. Rudolf Valentino was a trained apache dancer. The apache dance was often billed as "The Dance of the Underworld." It was first presented to the American public in the film *A Tough Dance* (1902) starring Kid Foley and Sailor Lil. Usually the dancers dressed in rags, imitating the poor. It is thought that Willie Hammerstein introduced the apache dance to vaudeville audiences in his Victoria Music Hall in New York around the turn of the century. In an effort to transform the brutal apache dance into a gentler American social dance, it was slowly transformed into the break-a-way in 1919, and continued to be altered. By 1927, it was completely toned down and known as the Lindy Hop, an invention of black dancer Shorty George, in which dancers flew through the air using movements intended to reference the flights of Charles Lindbergh.

The apache dance clearly presented the symbolic archetype of a liberated woman standing up against the strength and brutality of men. Early in the flapper era, young American women saw its possibilities—a display demonstrating toughness and newfound freedom. Many Hollywood films, Broadway productions, and movie magazines portrayed the apache dance. It was performed in *The Apaches of Paris* (1915), a film with Joseph Smith and Laura Hamilton as apache dancers. Rudolph Valentino and Beatrice Dominguez astounded audiences with their apache dance, which was softened to being part tango, in his first major film, *The Four Horsemen of the Apocalypse* (1921). Bela Lugosi, in his American debut on the Broadway stage in 1923, played a male apache dancer in *The Red Poppy*. Clara Bow starred in *Parisian Love* (1925) as a tough apache dancer who thrived on robbing American tourists. When her lover was shot during a robbery, she traded in her ragged trousers for ermine and lace to ably seduce the wealthy culprit. Werner Oland, as the title character, solved the murder of an apache dancer in *Charlie Chan in Paris* (1935), and Ray Milland did a dance similar to an apache dance in *Bolero* (1935). Even the cartoon character Popeye jumped on the apache bandwagon with an animated series of apache dances that ultimately defeated Bluto in the Fleischer's cartoon *Morning, Noon, and Night* (1937).

Some of the early fifteen-inch Apache Babe carnival prizes showed her with a cigarette in her mouth. Hollywood had taken her original persona, as a ragged Paris street tough, and turned her into a glamorous but still tough young American woman. This initiated the analogue that smoking equaled toughness. Hollywood promoted smoking for women during that era and cigarette companies used Hollywood stars, like tough-talking Mae West and bombshell Jean Harlow, in their ads. American men also associated toughness with smoking; by then it was not a gender-specific stereotype. Sly villains like William Powell and handsome heroes like Cary Grant smoked incessantly in films. So popular was the original 1936 Apache Babe carnival chalk figure that throughout the next decade many varieties of her were made. Over time, other of her carnival chalk prize names were Tuffy (she's topless with "Tuffy" inscribed on the base—prize not pictured), Tomboy, Sport Girl, and Sweater Girl. So overproduced were these chalk figures that by the end, they resembled a blancmange, since the stereotype was homogenized into white American culture.

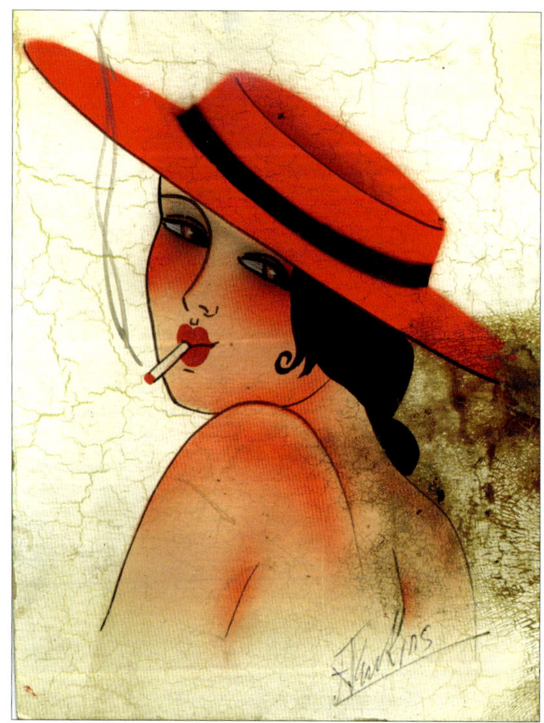

Portrait of a Woman Smoking, painting June Yates Jenkins, circa 1930s. Collection of the author

LANA TURNER (1921-1995)
SWEATER GIRL

—DORY PREVIN, "Mary C. Brown and the Hollywood Sign," 1971

Sweater Girl related to the 1940s sweater-girl craze that was catalyzed by Lana Turner, who at slightly over the age of fifteen was cast in the rare Warner Brothers social-protest drama *They Won't Forget* (1937). Turner's twelve minutes in the film were the first time that a teenager appeared onscreen in a form-fitting sweater and tight-fitting skirt, considered in America to be an intimate view of an immodest teenager. Turner later described what seeing herself for the first time on film on preview night was like:

> . . . out of the darkness and hush of the big theater, a girl came on screen. She walked slowly down the street, then away. She wore a tight sweater and her breasts bounced as she walked. She wore a tight skirt, too, and her buttocks bounced as she walked. She moved sinuously, undulating fore and aft, but with a kind of coltish grace. Mother and I scrooched down in our seats . . . Someone in the audience whistled. There were also some gasps. Then The Thing was gone. I understood later why this girl was there and why she was a Thing. She was the motive for the entire picture. She was the girl who got raped. She had to look like a girl men would like to rape . . . The girl on the screen looked innocent, but also like a blossom waiting to be plucked. She was enough to start a reaction leading up to a murder all right. But she certainly did not seem to be me.[1]

Soon this was Turner's stereotype—tight cashmere sweaters firmly fitted against her breasts—and it became the rage for young American women. It held sway for more than a decade, and Turner was always known as the "sweater girl." By 1948, four and a half million pairs of falsies were sold to fill out some of the sweaters, beginning the evolution toward breast implants and Barbie dolls—with procrustean measurements (brain-washing through fantasy and intimidation) of 36-18-38—invented by Ruth Handler in 1959.

Lana Turner was born in Wallace, Idaho, in 1921 with the name Julia Jean Mildred Frances Turner. Her uneventful birth was a miracle of sorts, since her grandmother had died

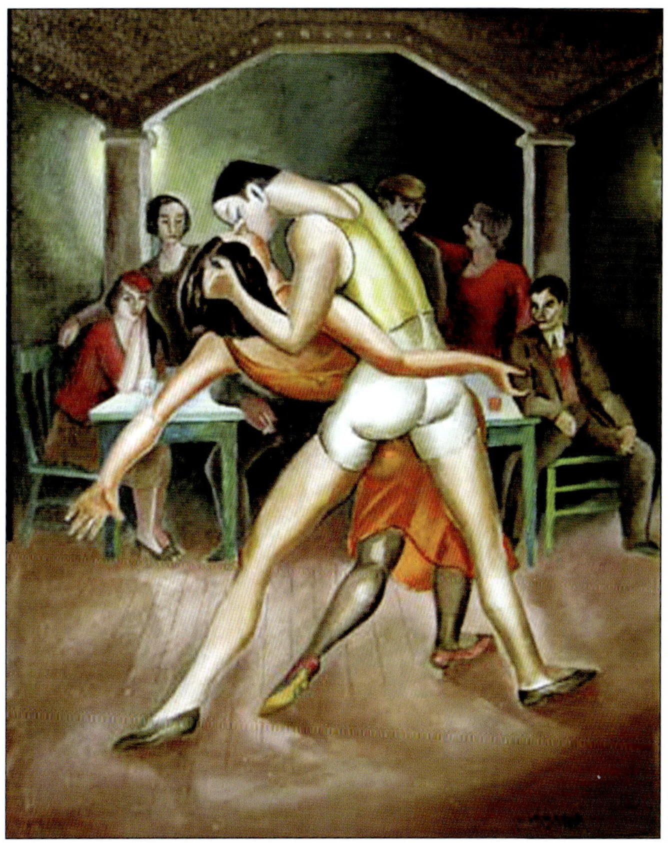

Apache Babe fifteen-inch carnival chalk prize, later known as sweater girl. She was probably the most popular carnival chalk prize of the late-1930s to mid-1940s. Only a few are smoking a cigarette. A beret worn to the side was popular from the 1920s-1940s giving its wearer an empowered look.

Apache Dance, painting Fred Gardner, 1933. Courtesy: Addison Rowe Gallery

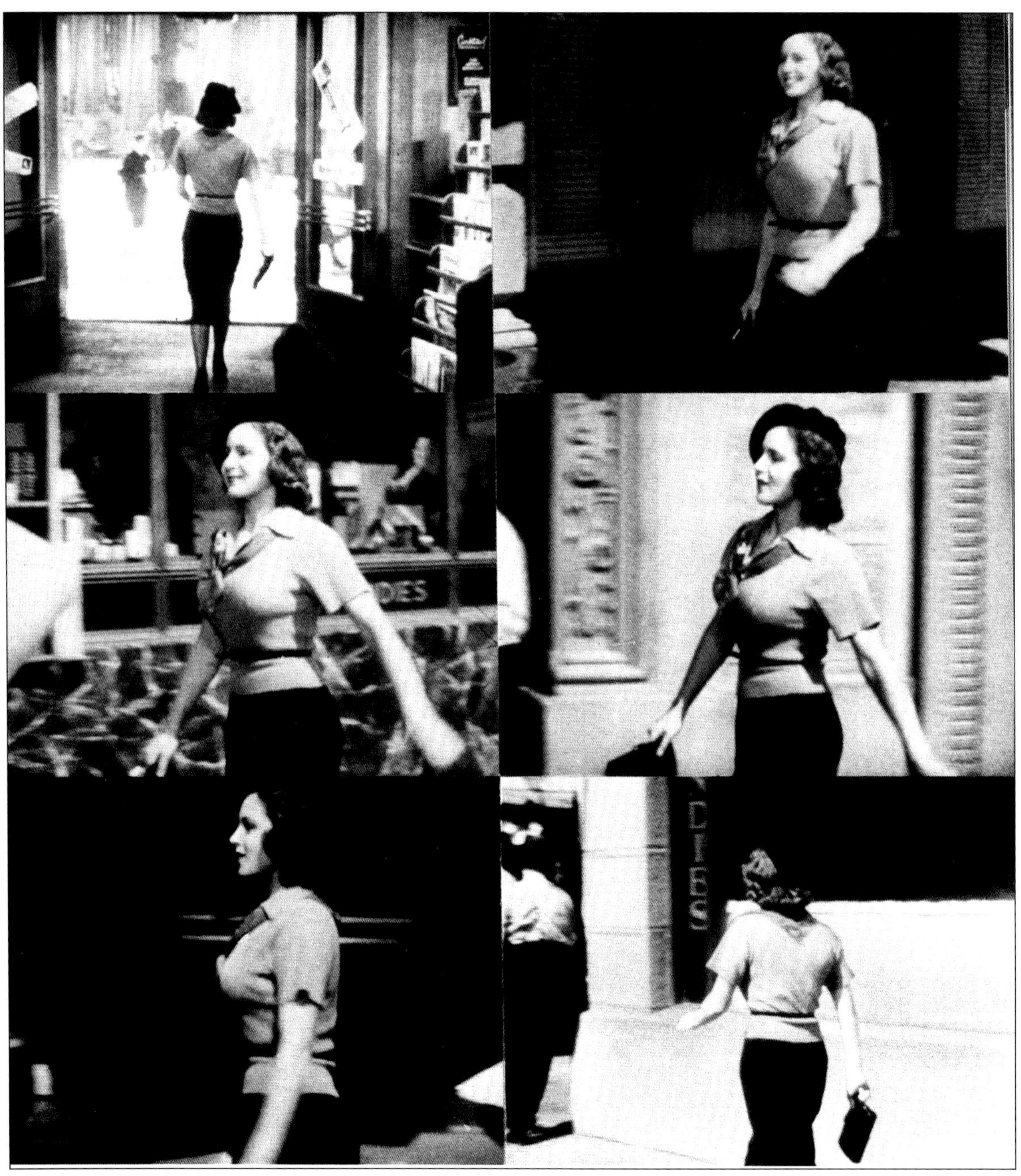

Lana Turner, *They Won't Forget*, stills, 1937 © Warner Bros.

giving birth due to Rh-factor complications, and there was a possibility that the genetic condition had been passed on to Julia Jean's mother. (Turner later discovered that she inherited the disorder. Her one daughter, Cheryl, was saved at birth by a complete blood transfusion.) Julia Jean's father, a coal miner and cardplayer, was murdered during a robbery when she was very young. At fifteen, she and her mother moved to California. One day, shortly after their arrival, Julia Jean went for a Coke after school. Despite the myth, she wasn't at Schwab's Drugstore but at the Top Hat Café, a shop across the street from Hollywood High School, where W. R. Wilkerson, publisher of the *Hollywood Reporter*, discovered her. He introduced himself, gave her his card, and asked her to call a

talent agent named Zeppo Marx. Marx helped team her with director Mervyn LeRoy, who cast her with her new name Lana Turner (from Judy Turner) in *They Won't Forget*, where she wore the infamous sweater and was raped and then murdered. By the age of twenty, Turner was earning $1,500 a week. She was immediately recognizable as a new Hollywood archetypal motif for an alluring liberated teenage woman eliciting extreme instinctual lust (which could cause extreme violence against women, as demonstrated in *They Won't Forget*).

During the filming of *The Adventures of Marco Polo* (1938), her eyebrows were shaved and replaced with fake straight ones—and they never grew back. During the difficult times of World War II, Turner traveled with railroad tours selling war bonds and promised a "sweet kiss" to any man who purchased a bond worth $50,000 or more. Turner later said, "And I kept that promise hundreds of times. I'm told I increased the defense budget by several million dollars."

In 1958, her real life mimicked her film escapades in *Peyton Place* (does this prove that life imitates art?) when it was discovered she had been dating John Steele, an alias for the mobster known as Johnny Stompanato. Turner struggled to end their relationship; Stompanato became abusive and vowed he would disfigure her. During this violent domestic argument, her fourteen-year-old daughter, Cheryl Crane, came upon them, and in fear that Stompanato would kill her mother, attacked and fatally stabbed him with a kitchen carving knife (any knife is an archetypal death symbol—an instrument of power). The murder became an overnight pulp-reality media extravaganza (the sensational famous person sex/murder archetype)—a twist of fate that jump-started box-office receipts from *Peyton Place*.

Stompanato's controversial death was ruled justifiable homicide (even though it was two hours before they called the police, so he bled to death). Ironically and with a strange twist of coincidence, the original domestic quarrel in Paris almost a century earlier that produced the apache gangs and the apache dance (and the Apache Babe stereotype), by then long forgotten, was also fought with a kitchen knife.

Turner, who married seven times, was nominated for an Academy Award for her role in *Peyton Place*. She died of throat cancer in 1995.

Photographs from the article by Bill Becker, "The Short, Happy Life of Johnny Stompanato," in pulp magazine *Rugged Men*, (NY: Stanley Publications, Vol. 1 #6, September, 1958), 38-39. Caption to the image on the right read "A peace officer examines the death knife." Below: "The short happy life......of Johnny Stompanato."

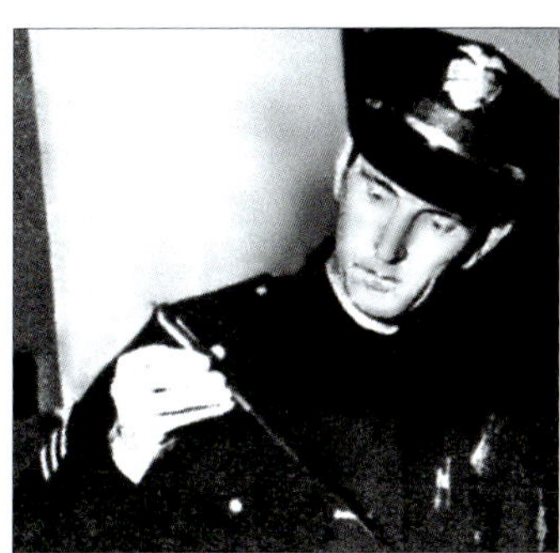

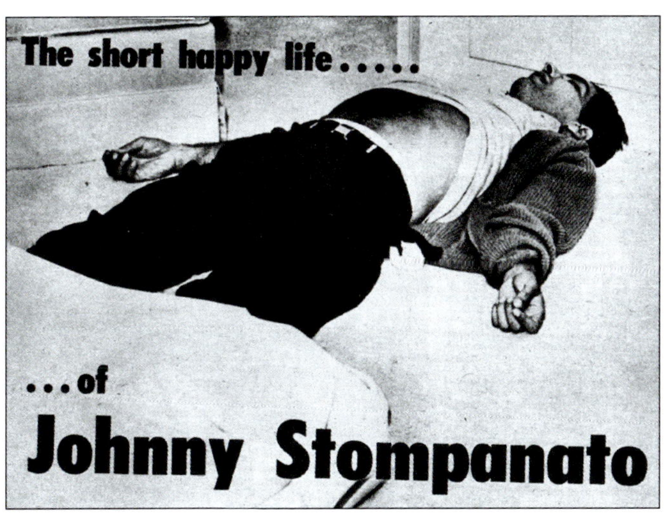

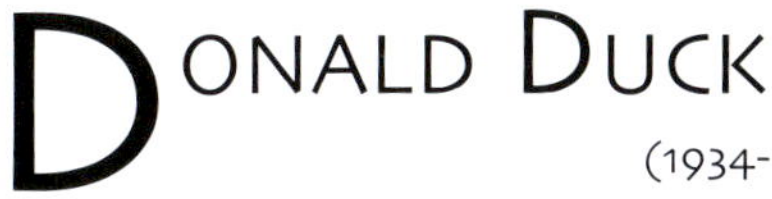

DONALD DUCK

(1934-

They can't collect legal taxes from illegal money.
—AL CAPONE, objecting to the IRS, *Capone*, 1929

We've been swindled, gypped, peeled, cleaned and swamied.
—HUEY, DEWEY, AND LOUIE

The first depiction of Donald Duck was drawn in the book *Mickey Mouse Annual*, where he was an unassuming little winged duckling wearing button-up pants in an illustration accompanying the poem "More HooZoo." The first appearance of the cartoon character resembling the Donald Duck we know emerged in *The Wise Little Hen* (1934). Walt Disney heard the radio voice of Clarence Nash reciting "Mary Had a Little Lamb" (in a falsetto imitation of a kid goat) and immediately hired him for the voice of the soon-to-be-famous Donald Duck.

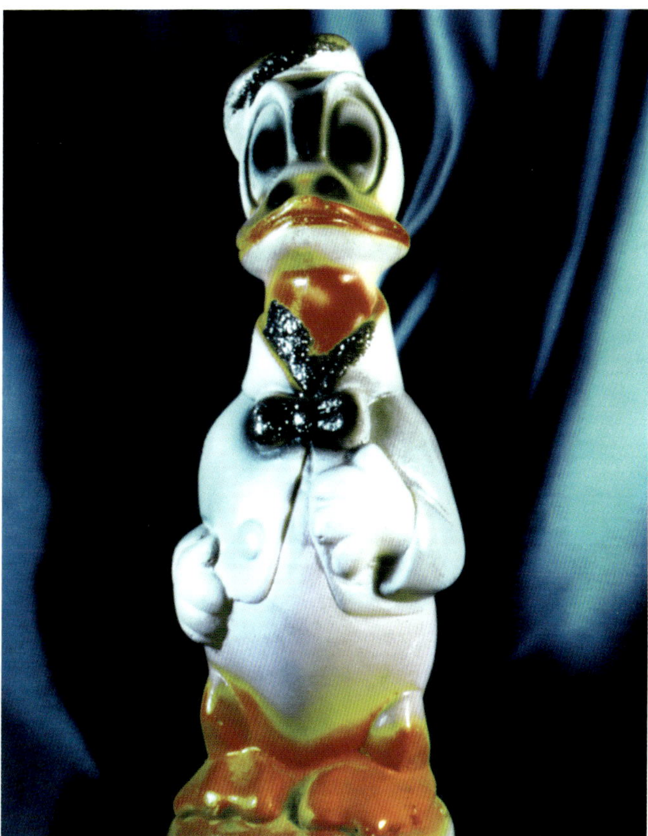

Donald Duck thirteen-and-a-half-inch carnival chalk prize

Donald Duck's rather outlandish personality traits emerged in his second cartoon, *The Orphan's Benefit* (1934). Most viewers and readers saw Donald as a belligerent, temper-tantrum-ridden, compulsive yet happy-go-lucky bumbler who somehow was charmed and blessed. His attitudes were expressed in quirky behavior. Disney was described in that same way by many of his employees. If that was one side of Disney, his other side was finicky and confrontational, much like the personality given to Mickey Mouse. People found Donald Duck funny, but they didn't laugh at Mickey Mouse.

However, control and the ability to always come out on top were the two things Donald and Mickey had in common.

When Donald finally took charge, he collapsed, collided, or crashed, and never calmly—but in the predictable, formulaic slapstick ending, he always came out just fine. Donald was an addict to his own dysfunctional temperamental inabilities. He knew that money or help would fall from the sky into his lap, that providence would prove him right. It didn't matter to Donald that the newfound money would always go back to his Uncle $crooge, whether it belonged to $crooge or not. Donald Duck had a lot of help from the supporting cast of characters in his comic-book world.

• Uncle $crooge: For most people, Uncle $crooge stereotyped the stingy rich uncle (a Disney appropriation of Ebenezer Scrooge from Charles Dickens' *A Christmas Carol*).

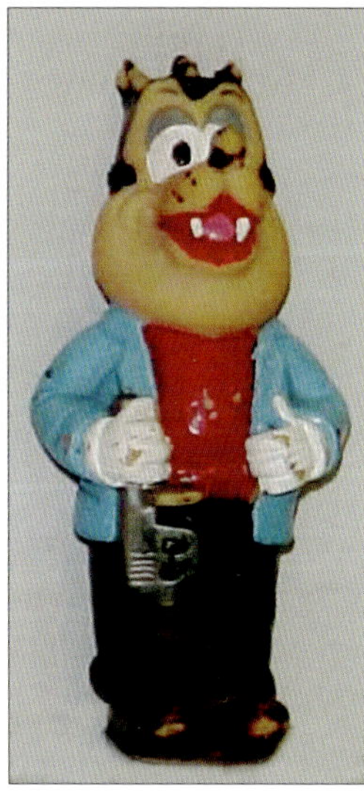
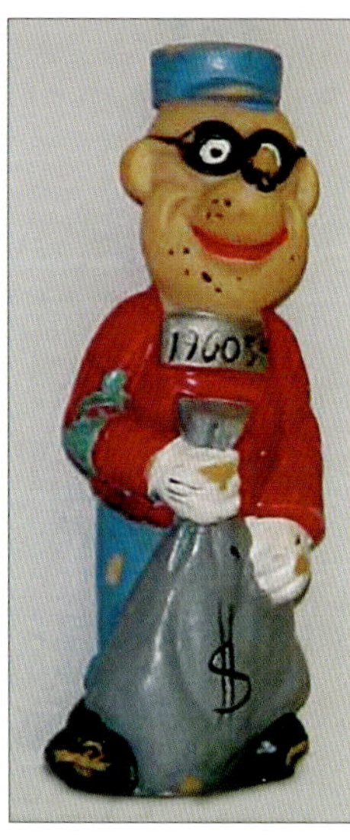
Black Pete (?) holding a machine gun and Beagle Boy #176054 with a money bag, five-inch vinyl squeeze figures, undated, unmarked

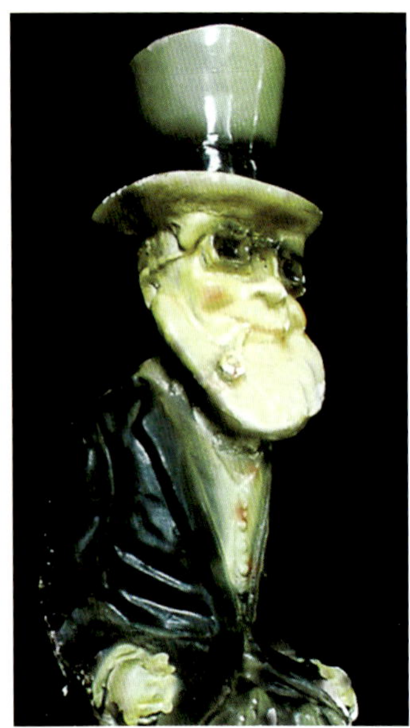
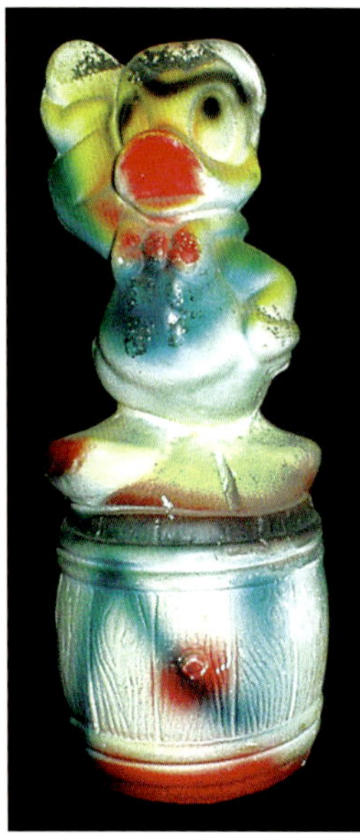
Unkle Eph Thrift Bank thirteen-inch carnival chalk bank prize with "Unkle Eph Thrift Bank" in raised plaster lettering on the back at base, a play on Ebenezer Scrooge from Charles Dickens' *A Christmas Carol*

Donald Duck eleven-inch carnival chalk bank prize

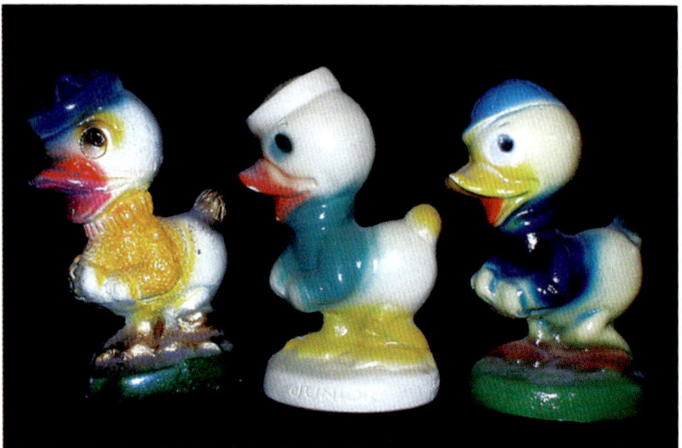
Huey, Dewey and Louie seven-inch carnival chalk prizes (one labeled Junior to avoid copyright infringement)

Uncle $crooge had an entitlement addiction. His actions were an obnoxious formula for an archetypal greedy show-off. He childishly rolled in piles of his money and easily lost money to the Ugly Burglars; but $crooge knew he would always regain his money. $crooge stayed happy—that was his magic.

• The Ugly Burglars: Disney's cartoonists and animators stereotyped many ugly-looking bad guys. Ugly bad guys created a new American bias that stereotyped people with less-than-seemly features, like moles, bumps, scars, or acne (Scarface Al Capone page 146). Might they possess evil intentions and were they to be avoided? In a similar but exaggerated vein, the Dick Tracy comic strips went overboard by creating even uglier bad guys, as in the case of Tracy's arch-enemy, Fly-face. Disney cartoonists continually reinforced the ugly bad-guy stereotype, and new inventions of bad guys, who were out to steal Uncle $crooge's money, were always in demand.

• Huey, Dewey, and Louie: Donald's nephews were the youthful characters in Donald Duck. Artist Carl Barks purposely targeted the children in his audience with the creation of these role models. Huey, Dewey, and Louie always stereotyped good children, embodying an energetic puritan work ethic. They worked hard, strove to help out, and understood, far better than their Uncle Donald, that they could be successful. Barks gave the nephews a comic-book world to live in that allowed them to achieve their goals while managing to fool Uncle Donald at the same time. They fed his narcissistic self and thereby kept him ecstatic. It would be nearly impossible to maintain a work ethic like theirs and keep the boss happy in real life, particularly if the boss had a personality disorder like Donald's, with his tendency toward colossal temper tantrums. Donald Duck was mentally abusive! Such a scenario would only be possible if you accepted the idea that children are basically slaves.

• Daisy Duck: As Donald's sometime lover, she stereotyped the frivolous, attentive, silly female. When Donald performed challenging feats to gain her attention, she responded with adoring eyes. Otherwise, she tended to play the field. Daisy was the pert, teasing female trapped by a shallow idea of romance, and the best show-off or the flashiest dresser could win her affections. Gladstone Gander took a good stab at it. Disney never really dealt with issues of gender equality; for the most part, she was just an enabler who dared Donald and Gladstone to try anything, and everything, to obtain her approval. Her only role seemed to be to create situations in which Donald appeared funny. In real life, what woman would give someone with Donald's personality the time of day?

Al Taliaferro was Donald Duck's first comic-strip artist from 1934 until his death in 1969. Bob Karp wrote for the strip from 1934 to 1974. But Carl Barks became Donald's best-known artist and storyteller in the *Donald Duck* comic books, hence Barks was dubbed "Duck Man." He created Uncle $crooge, Gyro Gearloose, Gladstone Gander, and the city named Duckburg. Huey, Dewey, and Louie first appeared in a comic strip in 1937 and then reappeared in the animated film *Donald Duck's Nephews* (1938), directed by Jack King. Daisy Duck first appeared in comic strips in 1940 and in the animated film *Mr. Duck Steps Out*. In 1937, she was known only as Donna in the animated cartoon *Don Donald*.

Was there a bigger picture that Disney, Taliaferro, Karp, and Barks were trying to convey? Was there a hidden reason for these convoluted personality traits, particularly obvious in Donald Duck and Uncle $crooge, with their unenviable codependent relationship. Were they disguised? Was Uncle $crooge a metaphor for the IRS vis-à-vis the U.S. government? Was Donald a metaphor for all U.S. men and Daisy a metaphor for all U.S. women? Were Huey, Dewey, and Louie metaphors for all U.S. children?

By simple addition and, in a strangely diabolic way, by combining these major characters in Donald Duck, did they sum up the entire U.S. population and U.S. government? Because no matter where the money comes from, some of it will go back to the government by way of the IRS. It could be said that the government ($crooge) prospers because of its money on the way. (At least back then it could depend on money coming its way. Can it now, considering the massive deficits? Are they a disguise by neoconservatives to alter social issues?)

Why did so many Donald Duck stories have a capitalist undercurrent? Oftentimes Donald, Huey, Dewey, Louie, and Uncle $crooge went blindly into an exotic, untouched place in the world, where they looked upon the natives as oddly alien and in need of help, and where they wound up proselytizing the natives with worldly capitalist ideas while lifting them out of their primitive, uncivilized, heathen lifestyle. Does this sound familiar? But in real life, worldly capitalist ideas do not always work. Forays into foreign lands are often a metaphor for culture change or, at the very minimum, what John F. Kennedy had in mind when he created the Peace Corps. Making Donald Duck an archetypal symbol for an explorer of foreign lands and proselytizer of know-how to the natives added one more psychological attribute to his already lengthy and bothersome personality—that being his not-so-accidental American arrogance and feelings of superiority.

Could Donald Duck have been an analogue for a missionary who brings Christian morality to the natives? Could this complete production of Donald Duck have been an analogue for Disney himself, as the explorer/missionary (Uncle Walt) bringing Christian morality to those who viewed his films throughout the world—both Christian and heathen?

Snow White

Actually, if you could see close in my eyes, the American flag is waving in both of them and up my spine is growing this red, white and blue stripe.
—Walt Disney

It took Walt Disney three years to produce *Snow White and the Seven Dwarfs*. Over two million drawings were created and the entire project cost $1.5 million—the most expensive film up until that time. Premiering in 1937, its eighty-three-minute length made it the first feature-length color and sound cartoon in America.[1] Most of the world was entranced by its vivid animation, made by multi-plane-camera filming techniques. They loved beautiful young Snow White, the handsome heroic Prince Charming, and the cute pint-size dwarfs; they hated the wicked stepmother, Queen. The film made Disney an estimated $8 million during the dark days of the Depression.

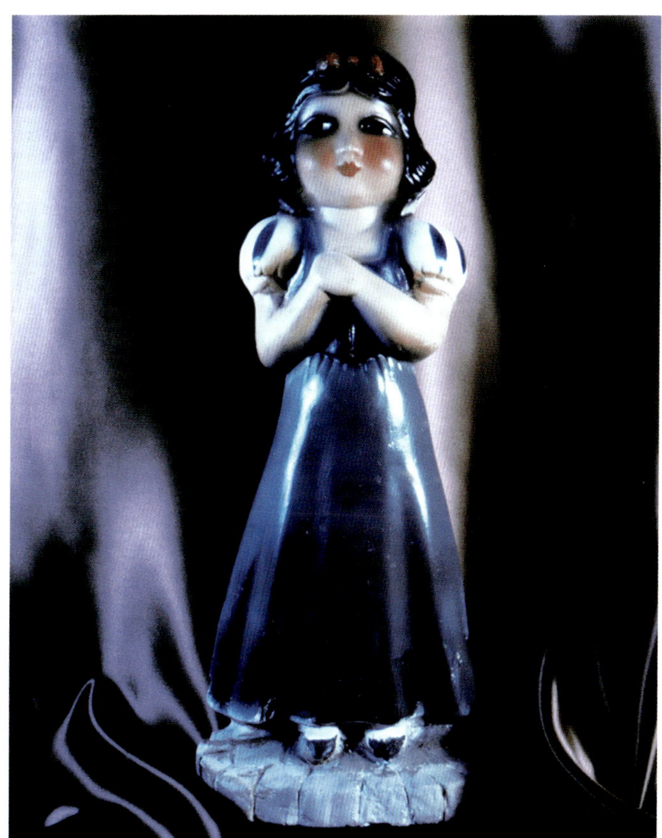

Snow White fourteen-inch carnival chalk prize © June Yates Jenkins

Disney deftly repackaged *Snow White and the Seven Dwarfs* from a Grimm brothers fairy tale. The stepmother, Queen, was vainly hoping to attain eternal beauty by way of catoptromancy (divination by mirror). As everyone knows, she asked her magic mirror, "Mirror, mirror on the wall, who's the fairest of them all?" The mirror, much like the supposedly impartial judges in the Miss America Pageant, selected the fantasized young woman of perfection—the Queen's lovely stepdaughter. In many ways, Snow White and Miss America are interchangeable archetypes/stereotypes. Disney's Snow White was reinforced by the existence of the Miss America archetypal motif, started seventeen years earlier in 1921; the winners were usually aged fifteen to seventeen, and always white.

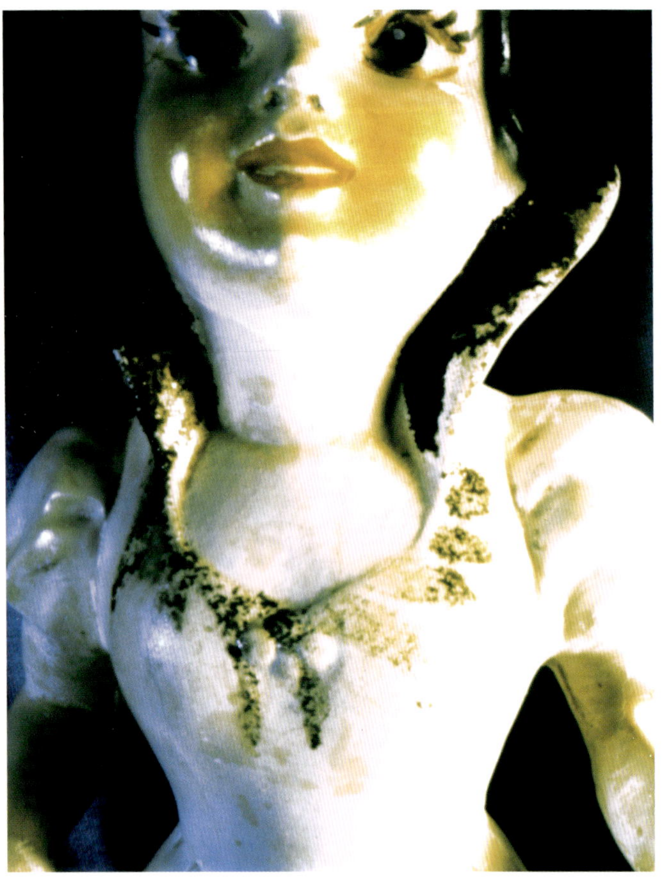

Snow White fourteen-inch carnival chalk prize, one of the most popular of the late 1930s

Disney was a moralist, as demonstrated by his choice of fairy-tale remakes. *Snow White and the Seven Dwarfs* subliminally transported the viewer back into iconographic Christian metaphors and archetypes that taught life lessons and religious values to both children and adults. Between 1810 and 1815, more than a century before Disney, the Grimm brothers had updated hundreds of handed-down fairy tales for moralist reasons. Strangely enough, by the end of World War II, Allied commanders banned the publication of the Grimm brothers' fairy tales in Germany, believing that they had contributed to Nazi savagery. The Grimm brothers' modifications were actually less savage than the earlier tales. For instance, in the end of a pre–Grimm brothers *Snow White and the Seven Dwarfs*, the wicked Queen was forced to put on red-hot iron slippers and dance until she died, an ending not too far removed from actual events during the Holocaust.

Some of the metaphors, archetypes, and stereotypes in *Snow White and the Seven Dwarfs*:

• **Snow White's name implied that she was a virgin.** In the Disney cartoon, she definitely has the figure of a young woman, making it apparent that although she had gone through puberty, she was undoubtedly a pure, white-as-snow

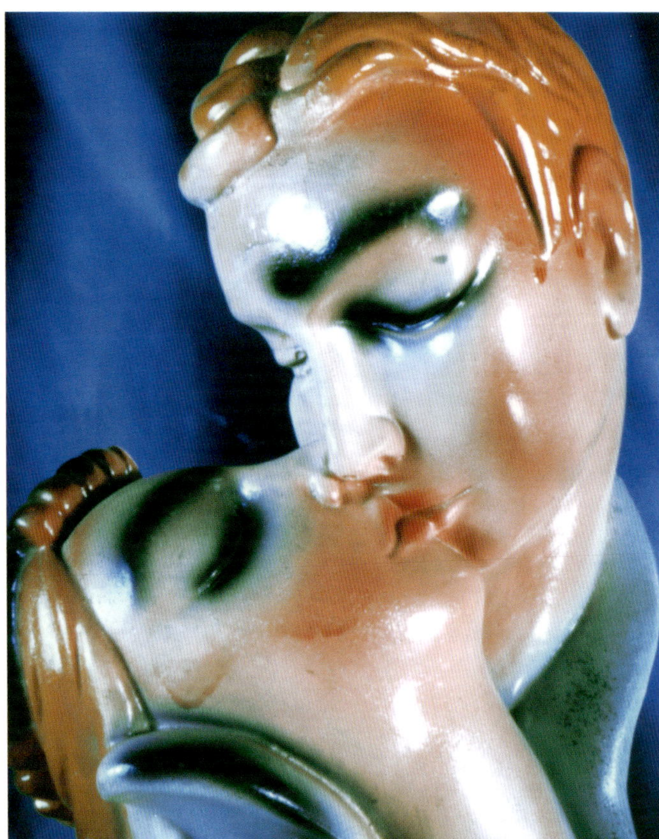

Snow White and Prince Charming eleven-inch carnival chalk prize. His head leans down to kiss the almost horizontally placed Snow White. Its curving art-deco design is unusual for carnival chalk.

virgin. In most cultures that read the fairy tales of the Grimm brothers, virginity was the most prized possession for every young woman of promise to retain, by necessity, until married, otherwise she was dammed to suffer as a fallen woman. John Gay's lurid poem from Act 1 in *The Beggar's Opera* (1728) said so:

> Virgins are like the fair Flower in its Lustre,
> Which in the Garden enamels the Ground;
> Near it the Bees in play flutter and cluster,
> And gaudy Butterflies frolic around.
> But, when once pluck'd, 'tis no longer alluring,
> To Covent-Garden 'tis sent as yet sweet,
> There fades, and shrinks, and grows past all enduring
> Rots, stinks, and dies, and is trod under feet.

"Convent-Garden" referred to a London flower garden frequented by prostitutes—in Gay's time, "flower" was a smear word for "prostitute." The term "deflowered," meaning loss of one's virginity, evolved from this reference.

• **At the point where Snow White was handed the apple, the tale became a replay of Christian morality.** The apple illustrated, with certainty, that Snow White was still a virgin. She would not have been offered it unless she had something to lose (her virginity). The Queen, now with ugly moles on her face and disguised as the beldam (old hag), was actually the devil incarnate (someone who was corrupt), ready to hand Snow White the poisoned apple. This was similar to the serpent in Genesis, who was the devil incarnate from the story of Adam and Eve in the Garden of Eden, ready to hand Eve the apple—who also had something to lose. In Disney's film, the dialogue goes:

Old Hag: And because you've been so good to poor old granny, I'll share a secret with you. This is no ordinary apple. It's a magic wishing apple.
Snow White: A wishing apple?
Old Hag: Yes! One bite and all your dreams will come true.
Snow White: Really?
Old Hag: Yes, girlie. Now, make a wish and take a bite. There must be something your little heart desires. Perhaps there's someone you love.
Snow White: Well, there is someone.
Old Hag: I thought so. I thought so. [laughter] Old granny knows a young girl's heart. Now take the apple dearie, and make a wish. [placing the apple in Snow White's hands]
Snow White [holding up the apple with her eyes closed]: I wish, I wish . . .
Old Hag: That's it. Go on, go on.
Snow White: And that he will carry me away to his castle where we will live happily ever after.
Old Hag: Fine! Fine! Now, take a bite! . . . Don't let the wish grow cold!
Snow White [after biting into the apple]: Oh, I feel strange, oh, oh . . .
Old Hag [expectantly rubbing her hands together]: Her breath will still. Her blood congeal.

The Old Hag offered wish fulfillment; the serpent offered wisdom—metaphors for love and knowledge. Eating the apple would result in death for Snow White. Eve was blamed for sin from sex and for death. It says in Genesis III:

Now the serpent was more subtle than any beast of the field which the Lord God had made:
and he said unto the woman,
Serpent: Yea, hath God said, Ye shall not eat of every tree of the garden?
And the woman said unto the serpent,
Eve: We may eat of the fruit of the trees of the garden: But of the fruit of the tree which is in the midst of the garden, God hath said, Ye shall not eat of it, neither shall ye touch it, lest ye die.
And the serpent said unto the woman,
Serpent: Ye shall not surely die: For God doth know, that in the day ye eat thereof, then your eyes shall be opened; and ye shall be as gods, knowing good and evil.
And when the woman saw that the tree was good for food, and that it was pleasant to the eyes, and a tree to be desired to make one wise; she took of the fruit thereof, and did eat; and gave also unto her husband with her, and he did eat.

Nothing ever written has done more harm toward women (and snakes) than this legerdemain (doublespeak), other than possibly the following line from the Roman Catholic Bible, Ecclesiasticus 25:33: "Sin began with a woman, and thanks to her we all must die." Only the entire *Malleus Maleficarum*, which was the judges' guide used during the Inquisition, was more deadly specific. Just like Eve in the Old Testament, Snow White ate the apple. Had it not been poisoned, she would have found her Prince Charming and lived happily ever after—but there were no moral lessons to be learned in that rendition.

• The point of the Snow White fairy tale was to teach Christian girls purity and a belief in God and the devil. Don't take the apple offered by a devil. Don't commit the sin of sex before marriage. Remain pure. Ever since Eve took the apple, women have been blamed whenever sex gets out of hand. It's always the woman who has fallen, never the man. Blaming women fit well into the patriarchal Christian guilt system, which is designed to immobilize every Christian woman's sexuality and mentality. If you were a Catholic, the Snow White fairy tale moved you into the Virgin Mary story—if you were a virgin you were fine, but once you had sex, you were left impure in both body and mind. Disney knew the obvious archetypal implications of purity versus impurity—good versus evil.

• Prince Charming could not be anything less than a real Prince Charming, since Snow White was the fairest of them all. As Prince Charming he would be not only rich and handsome but also heir to a throne. Prince Charming was a fantasy archetype for both boys and girls. At first glance, the archetype looked like a worthwhile project for any boy to duplicate and any girl to desire—be a Prince Charming, be rich, be handsome. Achieve those goals and you'll get the Snow White of your dreams. But every man was not rich and handsome. Even if they were, very few men were heir to a throne. At best, only a few of the richest in all the land could even be considered a Prince Charming. America has never believed in a succession of kings, but somehow the Prince Charming archetype was, and remains, viable for determining superiority.

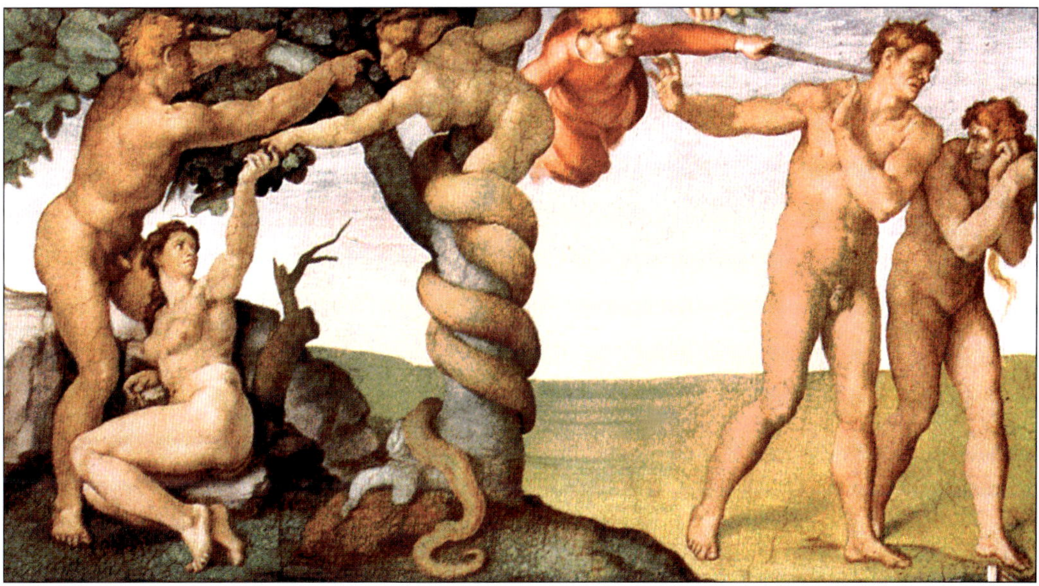
Expulsion, Michelangelo Buonarroti, Sistine Chapel, 1510. On the left Adam and Eve are a picture of health; on the right they are a picture of deceit. The snake offering the apple has a head and body of a woman.

(When he was running for president, George W. Bush fit the Grimm brothers' fairy-tale Prince Charming archetype perfectly, more so than any other presidential candidate in the last forty years—he was rich, handsome, and, most important, was an heir to his father's presidential throne. John F. Kennedy's brother Bobby was the last presidential candidate to fit the profile, but he was grievously assassinated. Had George H. W. Bush not been president, young Bush would never have been selected as a candidate for governor of Texas or for president of the United States. This got him the presidency, along with a big shove from a conservative Supreme Court and a phony, disguised Fox News report that he had won Florida—his cousin was the reporter. Was this all a well-planned setup?)

• Only Prince Charming's kiss could break the wicked Old Hag's devil-like spell. The kiss was a metaphor for one of Christianity's most valued projections: because Snow White was in a deathlike state, Prince Charming's kiss performed an archetypal God-like miracle. His kiss made her feel magically inspired; thereby she was raised her from the dead. It destroyed the devil's spell: no more Old Hag! Christianity works only if there are miracles to claim, because miracles evoke the existence of God as well as the existence of the devil. Christianity's devil can be in anyone—specifically it is in a witch. In Disney's film we were shown that the wicked stepmother was actually a witch when she went down into the cellar and read her witch's brew book. When she disguised herself as the Old Hag, she became a stereotype of the evil witch of the Christian Inquisition—a hideous replica of the devil—and she had to die. Disney's animators made her look like the perfect archetypal witch inspiring feelings of fear and hatred. (So much did she look like a witch that countless witches in later Hollywood films resembled her.) The Old Hag did die at the end of *Snow White and the Seven Dwarfs* when the dwarfs chased her over a cliff.

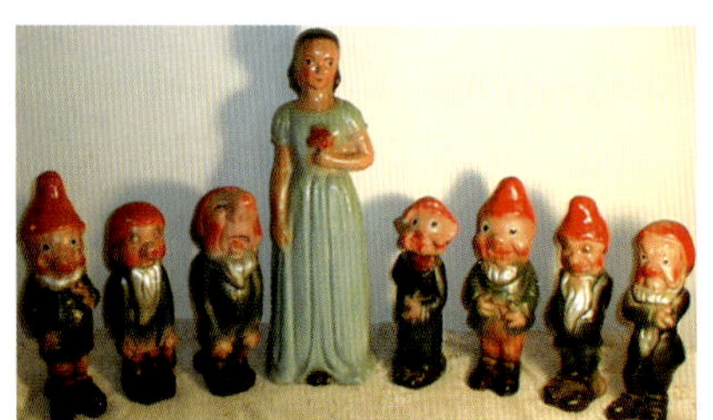

Snow White and Seven Dwarfs fifteen-inch and seven-to-ten-inch carnival chalk prizes

• The Seven Dwarfs had a subtle but major role in the story, even though they cared for Snow White, worked hard, and seemed harmless enough. They were disguised—their real job was ridding the kingdom of the devil. Hidden behind their simpleton-like, joyful cuteness, they stereotyped a band of seven white vigilante executioners like the *Malleus Maleficarum*, they were the secular locals who executed the wicked stepmother/Old Hag, who was an archetypal devil witch. (During the Inquisition the church never performed the execution—the locals did.) Here's the real mind twist: the film's audience gets to be the church's inquisitor. Didn't most viewers think the Old Hag was an evil witch, and weren't they glad to see her die (no need to put her on trial)? Here's an even bigger mind twist: Don't all Hollywood evil bad-guy films push the audience to hope the bad guy will die in the most awful way possible? And he never gets a trial because the audience fills the expectation to be the vigilante jury.

Gypsy Rose Lee

(1914-1970)

Praying is like a rocking chair—it'll give you something to do, but it won't get you anywhere.
—Gypsy Rose Lee

We looked over the chick's music in the cloakroom during our break. She didn't sing, or hum—just showed us the cuts and endings. When we went back on, we started with an up-tempo, "There's No Business Like Show Business," and the M.C. bounded onto the stage and started telling jokes the likes of which I had never known existed. (I couldn't wait to bring them back to my school buddies.) Finally, he announced, "And now, ladies and gentlemen . . . introducing the Marilyn Monroe of Burlesque (his exact words), Miss (Whatever Her Name Was)." We started her first tune. It was called Blue Violins. I'll never forget it and I can still play it, although I've never played it on a gig since that night. It was a dragging, bump and grind blues. I was busy reading the music, trying not to make any mistakes. Hell, I was a kid with a big gig, right? I listened for her to start singing, but she never did. A red cape flew over my music stand. I looked up, gasped, and thought, "Bolek, screw the music, the time has come for you to use your ears and learn how to improvise." I consider that stripper's act my first jazz lesson and The Marilyn Monroe of Burlesque was a highly motivating instructor.
—Bolek Peplowski, jazz musician, on playing for a striptease act when he was fourteen

There are two definitions for burlesque and both offer concepts to be considered:

1. A form of entertainment differing from comedy or farce in that it achieves its effects through caricature, ridicule, and distortion, and differs from satire in that it is devoid of any ethical element.
2. A literary or dramatic work that makes a subject appear ridiculous by treating it in an incongruous way, as by presenting a lofty subject with vulgarity or an inconsequential one with mock dignity.

The most famous woman in American burlesque was Gypsy Rose Lee; she was known as "the most publicized woman in the world." (Yet her international fame was not as great as the 1920s African American dancer Josephine Baker who found freedom and fame in Europe.) When Gypsy was very young, she started working in vaudeville alongside her more beautiful sister, June, in an act that was directed by their overly ambitious, burlesque-dancer mother, Rose Hovick. The duo was called Madame Rose's Dancing Daughters. June left the act to become a Hollywood star while Gypsy reinvented herself as a solo act and starred at Minsky's Burlesque in New York during the 1930s. Mayor Fiorello La Guardia shut Minsky's down in 1937 when Margie Hart removed her G-string (named after the violin's thinnest string). With Minsky's closed, Gypsy went to Hollywood and working under her real name, Louise Hovick (the Will Hays Production Code had forced the name change), starred in six films. Mike Todd became her manager and lover. She returned to New York to perform at the 1939–40 New York World's Fair, then at Todd's Theater Café in Chicago where 16,000

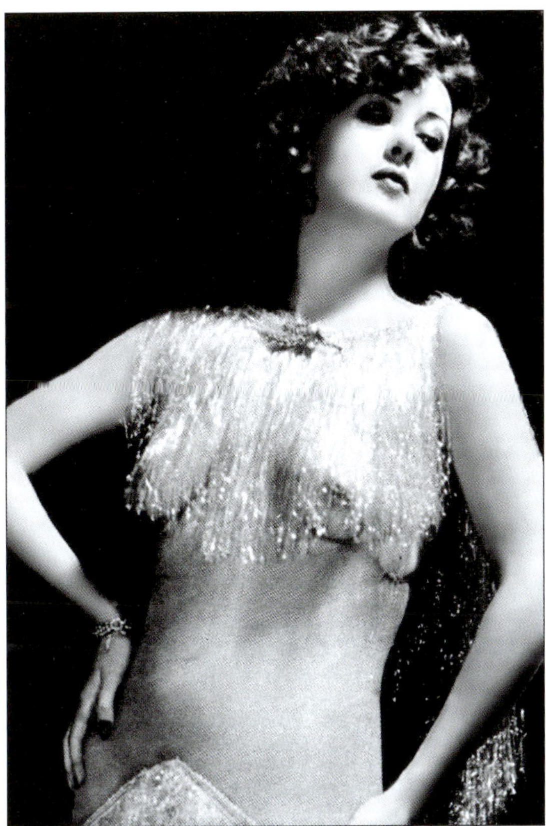

Gypsy Rose Lee, circa 1930s. Courtesy: Culver Pictures

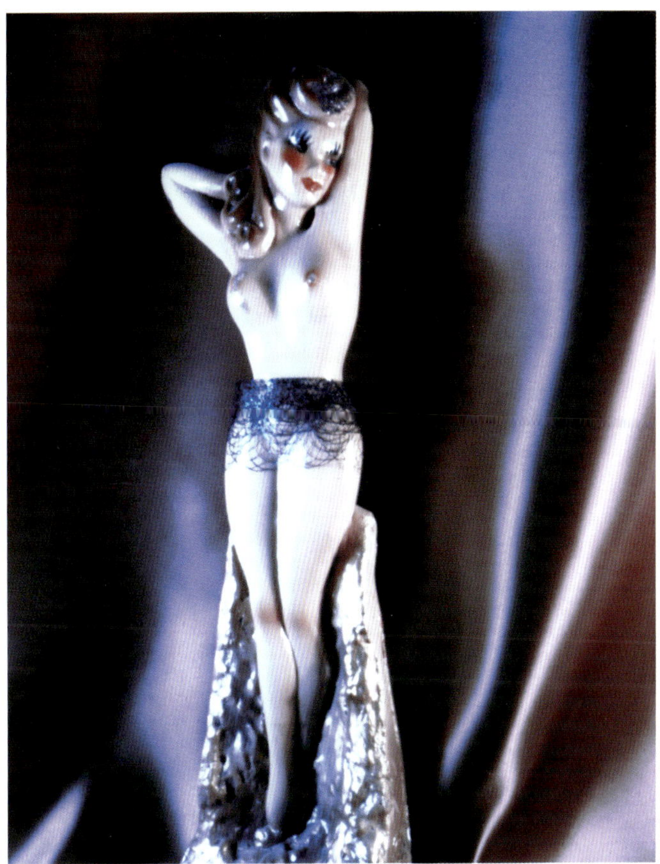

Gypsy Rose Lee thirteen-and-a-half-inch carnival chalkware prize, black lace cover

people came to see her the first day. Her trademarks were black lace, black garters, and black fishnet stockings.

By 1943, she changed her Hollywood name back to Gypsy Rose Lee (she was a superstar—the Queen of Burlesque—so Will Hays couldn't demean her as just another stripper) and toured the carnival circuit with Royal American Shows from 1948 to 1955. Her talent for enticingly removing just a very few netted, see-through outer coverings, while offering clever and witty dialogues, had become world renowned. Taking forever to expose that which the audience had come to see, she put the tease into striptease. As an archetype, Gypsy represented, for those who admired her, the number-one erotic woman, eliciting the freedom of feeling sexual desire. For those who rallied against her, she represented devil trash and was a living testimony to the puritanical idea that the world was most certainly made up of opposites like good and evil—and they despised her. Characteristically, most pictures of her seem to purposely make her look like a glorified, oversexed housewife (not like the image shown above), reflecting the real meaning of burlesque. Her success as the most famous American striptease artist was more a matter of serious study than of happenstance. She knew more about herself, her clothing, sexual arousal, and the medium in which she worked than any other striptease star. Other strippers removed more clothing in less time, but Gypsy realized that simply stripping was not the point, not the hook, and certainly not the show. Using sexual innuendo and wittiness, Gypsy is partly credited with creating the unusual idea of the intellectual stripteaser, which for some was a delightful oxymoron. She died in 1970.

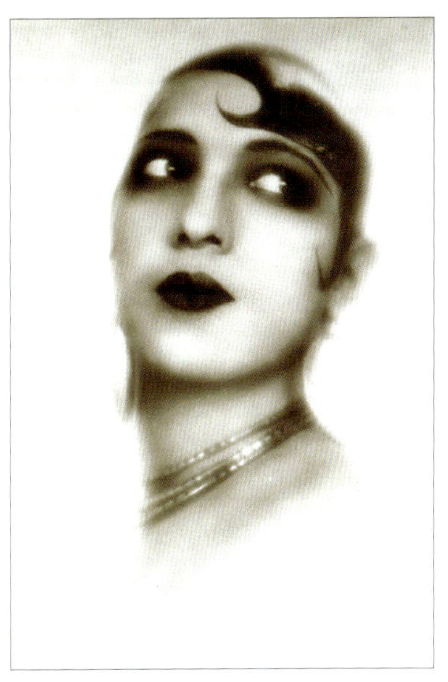

Josephine Baker, postcard, photograph, performance at Prince Edward Theatre, October, 1933

Family-oriented vaudeville shows started in 1885 and replaced many of the minstrel shows. By the mid-1890s, burlesque became a risqué part of vaudeville due to its scantily clad women, exotic stage sets, and comedy routines with titillating sexual (and overtly racist) overtones. There were nine hundred vaudeville theaters in the United States by 1920, but by 1930, all of the larger vaudeville theaters had been converted into movie houses, except for the Palace Theatre in New York. The risqué women of burlesque, hungry for work, or just plain hungry, either scampered off to traveling carnivals or continued in the few burlesque theaters, like Minsky's in New York—not really family entertainment, although that was how it was billed. Burlesque theaters of the 1930s slid into the barely legal realm of striptease, meaning G-strings and pasties. The police generally left them alone if the ladies retained these scant, token coverings.

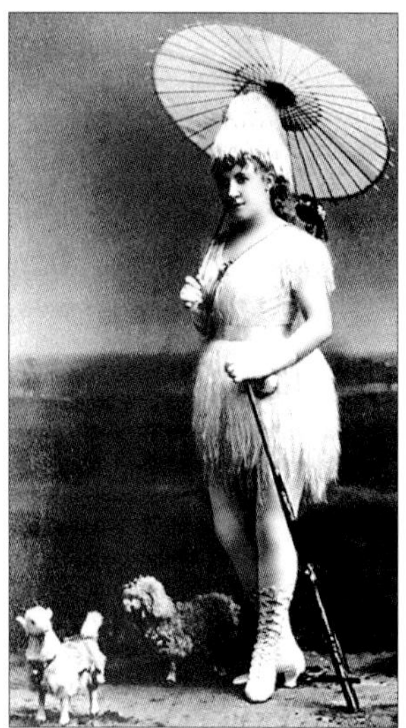

Lydia Thompson brought her troupe *Lydia Thompson and the British Blondes* to New York in 1869, setting the stage for American burlesque

Burlesque dancers were often called Sugar Babies, and certain ones became famous for their acts. Carrie Finnell was known for her DC-8, where she wore a tassel pasted to each nipple and a tassel on each of her rear cheeks and when she got all the tassels revved up and spinning she resembled a DC-8 in flight. She could spin one breast at a time, or spin one breast in one direction and the other breast in the opposite direction, or she could vary their speeds individually. She could even perform these feats while lying on her back. (Ignoring the erotic elements, one could say that she had perfected quite a refined juggling act.) Rosita Royce was famous in the 1930s for her Dance of the Doves—thirty-nine white doves were trained to alight and flutter on her arms, shoulders, and head. Their flight and motions effectively hid her breasts, which were completely naked while she danced. Yvette Dare had a trained parrot that plucked off her garments one by one. Ann Corio, second in fame to Gypsy, invented Ladies Night at burlesque theaters. Many of America's best-known comedians from 1920 to 1950 also came from burlesque: W. C. Fields was a juggler, Fanny Brice and Joe E. Brown were acrobats, Sophie Tucker and Al Jolson were comic singers in blackface. Eddie Cantor began as a juggler's assistant. Bert Lahr, Buster Keaton, Ed Wynn, Will Rogers, Jackie Gleason, Red Skelton, and Danny Thomas all launched stage careers as burlesque comedians.

Burlesque performers developed a unique backstage language all their own:

blisters: a stripper's breasts
cheeks: a stripper's backside
gadget: a G-string
quiver: shake the bust
shimmy: shake the posterior
bump: swing the hips forward
grind: full-circle swing of the pelvis
trailer: the strut taken before a strip
Boston version: a cleaned-up routine
jerk: audience member
skull: make a funny face
talking woman: delivers lines in comedy skits
cover: perform someone's scenes for them
the asbestos is down: the audience is ignoring the jokes
from hunger: a lousy performer
mountaineer: a new comic, fresh from the Catskill circuit[1]

Burlesque theaters limped along until the 1960s. They finally closed forever when pornography became widely available.

Mt. Rushmore (1927-

I will say, then, that I am not, nor ever have been, in favor of bringing about in any way the social and political equality of the white and black races—that I am not, nor ever have been, in favor of making voters or jurors of Negroes, nor of qualifying them to hold office, nor to intermarry with white people; and I will say in addition to this that there is a physical difference between the white and black races from living together on terms of social and political equality. And inasmuch as they cannot so live, while they do remain together there must be the position of superior and inferior, and I as much as any other man, am in favor of having the superior position assigned to the white race.
—Abraham Lincoln, fourth Lincoln-Douglas Debate, Charleston, IL, *Abraham Lincoln Speeches and Writings 1832-1858*, Ed. by Roy P. Basler, (New York: The Library of America, Penguin Books, 1989), 636

In 1845 John L. O'Sullivan wrote the following in the *United States Magazine and Democratic Review*:

The American claim is by the right of our manifest destiny to overspread and to possess the whole of the continent which Providence has given us for the development of the great experiment of liberty and federative self-government entrusted to us. It is a right such as that of the tree to the space of air and earth suitable for the full expansion of its principle and destiny of growth.

This statement, later to be called Manifest Destiny, was exactly the metaphor that sculptor Gutzon Borglum's monumental Mount Rushmore represented. It still does. Displaying those four male presidential faces together exemplified that the country had grown from its revolutionary phase, through the Civil War, and even past Roosevelt's huge immigration moment—America had fulfilled a part of its Manifest Destiny. The four faces embody the archetype of a nation's greatest leaders. Most Americans feel nationalistic reverence and see them as powerful, sacred icons—much like the flag. History books teach devout reverence to them, although books like *Lies My Teacher Told Me* by James W. Loewen[1] have begun to open the crack in the liberty bell, a blatant pun for showing that history is not always how it is taught.

The implications behind Manifest Destiny are not that different from morality issues of colonizers and Christians, whose motives and actions could always be explained in the cosmogony (origin theory) of Genesis:

1:27 So God created man in his own image, in the image of God he created him; male and female he created them. 1:28 God blessed them and said to them, "Be fruitful and increase in number; fill the earth and subdue it. Rule over the fish of the sea and the birds of the air and over every living creature that moves on the ground."

In 1927, President Calvin Coolidge dedicated America's "Shrine of Democracy," the government's name for Mount Rushmore. Borglum began drilling and blasting into its upper elevations (with his early-American figurative earthworks), five hundred feet up. Washington was completed and dedicated in 1930, Jefferson in 1936, Lincoln in 1937, and Roosevelt in 1939. They presently overlook a setting of pine, spruce, birch, aspen, a parking structure, amphitheater, museum and theater complex, visitor orientation center, Presidential Trail, and the AmFac restaurant and gift shop.

The four exalted presidents carved into Mount Rushmore were not always consistent in matching their deeds with their stated ideals of democracy. The following lines written by Thomas Jefferson, and later deleted from the final draft of the Declaration of Independence, prove clearly that he thought slaves had their own rights of life and liberty, which were violated by the slave traders and the King of England who profited by slave trading. Had these lines not been deleted, the history of civil rights may well have been different. (The first word "He" in the following statement referred to the King of England), Jefferson wrote:

> He has waged cruel war against human nature itself, violating its most sacred rights of life and liberty in the persons of distant people who never offended him, captivating & carrying them into slavery in another hemisphere, or to incur miserable death in their transportation thither . . . Determined to keep open a market where MEN should be bought & sold, he has prostituted his negative for suppressing every legislative attempt to prohibit or to restrain this execrable commerce.[2]

Those who helped finalize the Declaration of Independence were aware of the deeper meaning that these lines represented: that slaves were human beings with feelings, who deserved life, liberty, and the pursuit of happiness. Jefferson, who owned slaves, suggested that the only way to solve this difficult issue, since he considered amalgamation impossible, was to send slaves either back to Africa or to a colony in Central America. Three-quarters of a century later, Lincoln expressed a similar idea. Explaining the excuse and justification for slavery, Sylviane A. Diouf decried:

> Medieval Europe traded in European slaves on a large scale. Slavs, Irish, Welsh, Greeks, Scandinavians, Russians, and Turks furnished the bulk of the slave population across Europe up to the middle of the fifteenth century . . . what became unique was that by the sixteenth century Europeans reserved slavery for the Africans, and the enslavement of whites totally disappeared from the countries they controlled. Slavery and color were linked for the first time, and adherence to Christianity on the part of the Africans did not make any difference. Their evangelization was a priority as a religious duty but served primarily as a justification for the slave trade.[3]

George Washington also was born into a world in which slavery was commonplace. He became a slave owner at the tender age of eleven, when his father died and left him ten slaves and five hundred acres of land. When he began farming Mount Vernon at the age of twenty-two, he had a workforce of about thirty-six slaves. With his marriage to Martha Custis in 1759, twenty of her slaves came to Mount Vernon. Washington later purchased even more slaves. By 1799, when he died, there were 316 slaves living on his beautifully manicured Virginia estate.

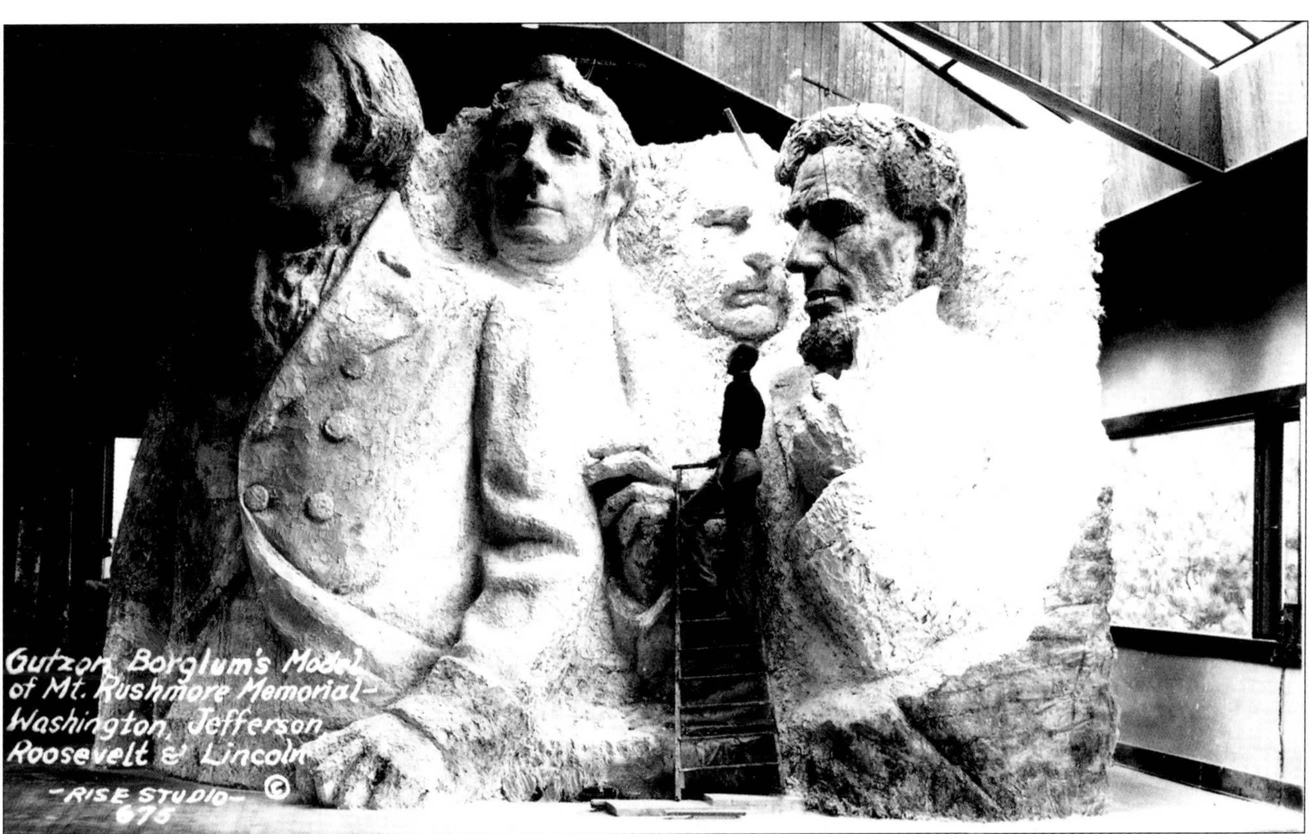

Gutzon Borglum's Model of Mount Rushmore, postcard © Rise Studio, circa 1925

Lincoln stated many times that he despised slavery, yet he was not able to visualize amalgamation and equality. In an address given at Springfield, Illinois, on June 26, 1857, he said:

> A separation of the races is the only perfect preventive of amalgamation, but as immediate separation is impossible the next best thing is to keep them apart where they are not already together. Such separation, if ever affected at all, must be effected by colonization. The enterprise is a difficult one, but "where there is a will there is a way," and what colonization needs now is a hearty will. Will springs from the two elements of moral and self-interest. Let us be brought to believe it is morally right, and at the same time, favorable to, or at least not against our interest, to transfer the African to his native clime, and we shall find a way to do it, however great the task may be.[4]

By the time Theodore Roosevelt became president, the issues of slavery were supposedly over—but the issues of civil rights were not. Roosevelt had his own ideas about how this country and its colonizers had lived up to the ideal of Manifest Destiny. He loved to repeat the proverb "Speak softly and carry a big stick." It was Roosevelt who said, regarding the extermination of most of the Native Americans and the expropriation of their lands, "it was as ultimately beneficial as it was inevitable. Such conquests are sure to come when a masterful people, still in its raw barbarian prime, finds itself face to face with the weaker and wholly alien race which holds a coveted prize in its feeble grasp." Roosevelt also glibly remarked: "I don't go so far as to think that the only good Indians are dead Indians, but I believe nine out of ten are, and I shouldn't like to inquire too closely into the case of the tenth."[5]

Roosevelt believed that the better classes of America were being overwhelmed by immigration. He spoke of immigrants as degenerates, criminals, feebleminded, and said that "all these peoples should be forbidden offspring."[6] From these pronouncements and similar views held by the powers that be, the field of eugenics developed. The Office of the Department of Genetics of the Carnegie Institute of Washington, D.C., was started in 1910, and until 1939, its superintendent was Harry Hamilton Laughlin, who also served as eugenics expert for the Committee on Immigration and Naturalization. Sterilization became acceptable as a means to control offspring.

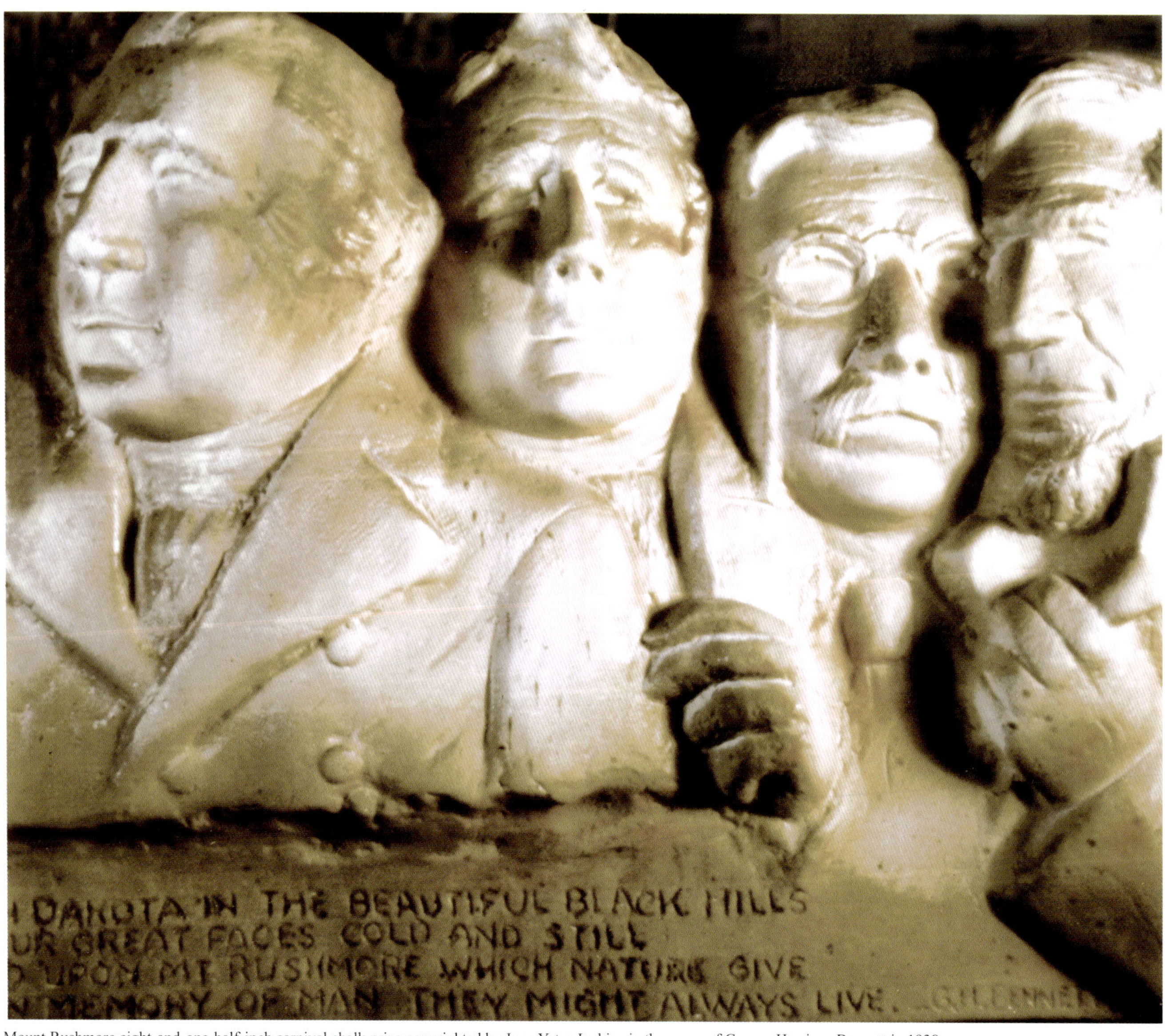

Mount Rushmore eight-and-one-half-inch carnival chalk prize copyrighted by June Yates Jenkins in the name of George Harrison Bennett in 1938

In stricter cases, castration or ovariotomies were performed; in milder cases, vasectomy or salpingectomy. In 1914, Laughlin published his Model Eugenic Sterilization Law. It proposed to authorize sterilization of the "socially inadequate"—

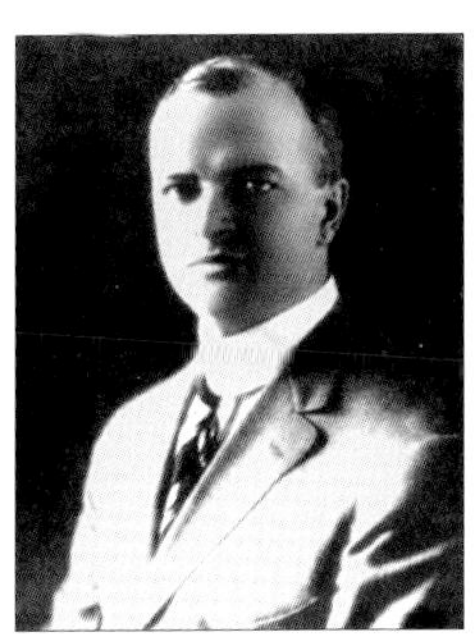

Harry Hamilton Laughlin

people who were supported in institutions or "maintained wholly or in part by public expense." His model sterilization laws were passed by thirty states, and his studies led to harsh immigration quotas as well as the Racial Integrity Acts of 1924. Those people he deemed in need of sterilization included the "feeble-minded, insane, criminalistic, epileptic, inebriate, diseased, blind, deaf, deformed, and dependent"—including "orphans, ne'er-do-wells, tramps, (how did he miss getting Charlie Chaplin?) the homeless and paupers." (He had no children from his marriage.) Margaret Sanger, a stern figure in eugenics and the founder of Planned Parenthood in 1921 calculated that 47.3 percent of Americans were morons, therefore they should be sterilized.[6]

The Model Eugenic Sterilization Law was passed in 1924. It stated that sterilization could not be used as punishment for a crime but was to be administered for "general racial welfare" regardless of the criminal tendencies of the persons operated upon. To be sterilized by the state a person needed to be affected by hereditary insanity or incurable chronic mania. Any minor, idiot, or fool under the care of the state; an inmate of prison for life; anyone showing signs of sexual perversion or who had been committed three times for other crimes could be sterilized (an early "three strikes and you're out"—really out). Some states sterilized gay men convicted of sodomy, labeling them sexual perverts. Between 1909 and 1925, there were 6,244 people sterilized in the United States, most of them in California (2,624 men and 2,012 women). Virginia enacted the Eugenic Sterilization Act in 1924, which led to the eventual sterilization of 8,300 people. By 1928, 376 colleges nationwide were teaching eugenics.

Hitler's 1933 sterilization laws were fashioned after Laughlin's model. Laughlin proudly published a translation of the "German Law for the Prevention of Defective Progeny" in *The Eugenic News*. This led to Germany's legalized sterilization of between 350,000 people and 3.5 million people from 1933 to 1945. In 1936, Laughlin was awarded an honorary degree from the University of Heidelberg as a tribute for his work in the "science of racial cleansing." (Did they hold a ball afterward?) Laughlin also devoted considerable time to developing ideas toward a common world government (a Fascist world). By the time the Model Eugenic Sterilization Law was struck down by the Supreme Court in the 1970s, more than 60,000 Americans had been sterilized—20,000 were from California.

John Gutzon de la Mothe Borglum was born in Idaho into a physician's ranching family in 1867. At seventeen he moved to California with his family, determined to become an artist. He studied at the San Francisco Art Academy and in Paris at Académie Julian and the École des Beaux-Arts, and with Auguste Rodin. He soon realized that enterprising sculptors could make a reputation and a good living by working on the numerous public monuments being erected. During Borglum's time there was an emergence of civic and nationalist pride. This trend—known first as the American Renaissance, later as the Civil Works Era, and finally as the City Beautiful movement—started shortly after the Civil War and coincided with the concentration of great fortunes in the hands of a few individuals who could gain social recognition by sponsoring public monuments. Borglum's first commission, after his return to New York in 1901, was the statue of Lincoln that stands in the Capitol rotunda. He initially helped organize the Armory Show of 1913, which brought Europe's avant-garde artists to New York, but he resigned when he realized that traditional artists were not going to receive much attention.

In 1915, Borglum was asked to design a monument to the bravery of the Southern soldier. This ideologically charged monument, originally a seventy-foot statue of Robert E. Lee, was to be carved into a steep mountainside in Georgia that would be named Stone Mountain Confederate Memorial. The federal government agreed to help sponsor the project through the minting of a special Stone Mountain half-dollar coin. Originally sponsored by the United Daughters of the Confederacy, the site soon became one of the main rallying centers of the newly energized Ku Klux Klan. Borglum designed and began blasting the monument in 1916, but the work was interrupted by World War I and was not resumed until 1924. His idea was to have a 750-soldier army spread across the mountain, which differed considerably from the original intent of just Robert E. Lee. After fund-raising, controversy, and the completion of Lee's head, Borglum ceased work, smashed his models, fled Georgia, and set up a studio in San Antonio, Texas, where he designed Mount Rushmore. (Later, Lee's carved head was destroyed by Augustus Lukeman, Borglum's successor on the Stone Mountain project.)

By 1939, Borglum had carved 90 percent of Mount Rushmore using dynamite. It had taken twelve years at a cost of $1 million. He became so proficient in his blasting technique that he could carve out the monument to within inches of his desired finished surface. He enlisted miners to drill and set charges at precise locations previously determined by a system he called "pointing." With this system, the clever Borglum crafted a one-twelfth scale model on which he mounted circular plates on the presidents' heads. A plumb bob was dropped until it touched the model's heads. The measurements were then multiplied by twelve and transferred to the mountain. Borglum always considered his Mount Rushmore sculpture as artist-specific—that it incorporated his own particular view of what the United States of America meant to him. Borglum died in 1941, after only the president's heads were finished.

Borglum held another dream: to create an enormous memorial to the Sioux in Pine Ridge, Nebraska. He wanted the Native Americans to be memorialized equally. To accomplish this, he would haul to the site leftover granite boulders from the Mount Rushmore memorial, in pieces weighing up to eighty tons. Borglum proposed to sculpt a twenty-foot-high scene of Lakota Sioux high on a sun-lit hill, but he died well before his dream could be realized.

T HE PINUP

Some consider Austrian-born illustrator Raphael Kirchner to be the father of the pinup. His erotic postcards (not called pinups at the time) were extremely popular during World War I. Kirchner worked mostly in Paris until the outbreak of war in 1914, when he moved to the United States.

The first issue of *Esquire* in 1933 included an air-brushed drawing-cartoon by George Petty, and he is generally thought to have founded the American pinup stereotype; his imagery, however, was based on Kirchner's work. Petty's lusty, sexist drawings were much in demand. Calendar manufacturers, always on the lookout for archetypal sex symbols, found sales dramatically increased when they had a variety of aggressively teasing pinups drawn by artists such as Billy De Vorss, Rolf Armstrong, and Gil Evgren. Pinup calendars were concentrated in bars, workplaces, and garages, which further reinforced the idea of the alluring woman archetype—that it was to be shared by everyone (a pre-*Playboy* mentality), friends and sweethearts alike. It proved that a free calendar could provide feelings of momentary visceral, escapist lust (not to mention a multimillion-dollar industry for calendar makers). As archetypal symbols, pinups are not yet out of style—they're just kitschy and politically incorrect, constantly reinforcing misogyny and unexamined feelings of superiority.

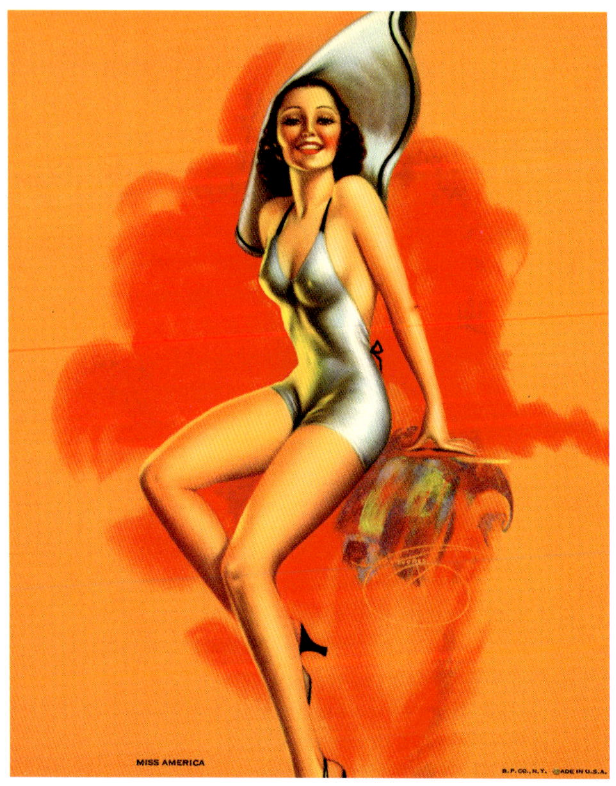

Miss America, pinup, Billy De Vorss © B. P. & Company, 1938

The 1939 issue of *Esquire* included the first foldout pinup, a thirty-inch George Petty drawing. *Life* magazine claimed to have coined the term "pinup" in its July 7, 1941, issue on national defense, and anointed Dorothy Lamour as the first official pinup girl. *Life* was savvy enough about archetypes to combine national defense with the pinup. During World War II, Betty Grable, Rita Hayworth, and Lana Turner well surpassed *Life*'s expectations. For servicemen, a pinup was the constant reminder of what was missing and what made life worth living.

During war years it was the servicemen's God-given right to visit brothels. Prostitution has always had an inherent connection to war, as has rape. Countries and leaders, who use young men in their sexual prime to fight their horrid wars, traditionally look the other way when it comes to prostitution and their warriors.

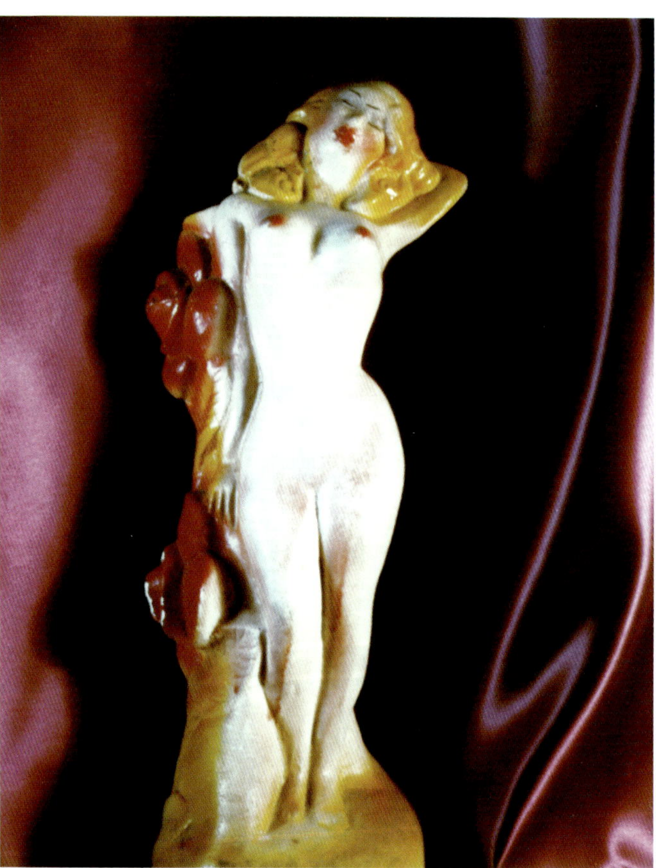

Carnival chalk prize suppliers were quick to make pinup-style nude figures, particularly since nudity was part of the carnival side shows. This thirteen inch candle holder was one of several. Is she a caricature of Marilyn Monroe?

What would later become the most famous pinup was the 1948 nude calendar pose by Marilyn Monroe. She was paid $50 for that session. In 1952, RKO cast Monroe in a lead role in the Barbara Stanwyck film *Clash by Night*, a performance that brought Monroe significant attention. Soon after the film, the publication of the nude calendar photograph brought even more momentous publicity. It was a promotion disguised as a scandal that whisked her into celebrity status and catapulted her career. Monroe easily surpassed Betty Grable to become the number-one sex symbol. With Monroe, lust could be full-bodied. *Playboy* used the same calendar pinup for the centerfold of its premiere issue in 1953. It was the first time that nudity somewhat acceptably entered into the average American home.

If ever there was a specious argument over the right to publish nudity, *Playboy* invented it. *Playboy* stated that a beautiful woman's body deserved to be seen, that their nude women not only were clearly pleased to share their bodies with all viewers but were happy with their lives and career

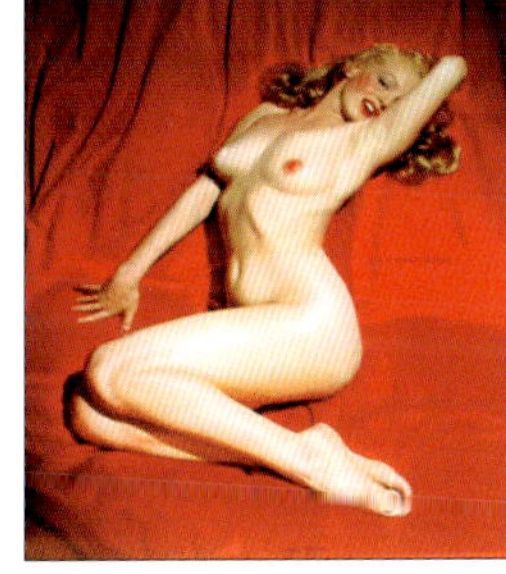

Marilyn Monroe calendar, probably the most famous image of the 1950s

choices. Never did *Playboy* tell of the poverty and hardships that generally accompanied women who wound up posing nude. Monroe was the perfect example of a poverty-stricken and psychologically entrapped child who suffered from problematic traumas throughout her life. Her first seven years were spent in a foster home. From 1935 to 1937, she lived in an orphanage in a bedroom shared with twenty-seven other children. She was shuffled through many more foster homes until, at age sixteen, she was placed into an arranged marriage, simply to avoid being returned to the orphanage. By the time she was paid for her *Playboy* spread, she was a Hollywood superstar and her poverty, family trauma, and abuse were an issue *Playboy* never wanted to discuss. *Playboy*'s desire was to be thought of as a high-class, glitzy, quasi-intellectual liberating magazine. The Playboy bunny was an alluring woman placed on Hugh Heffner's pedestal for financial greed and power.

Playboy did help to break some of the puritan ethics that gripped America, which certainly needed to be altered. Yet in doing so, it promoted the well-endowed, cosmetically enhanced, surgically altered, mentally fantasized, smoothed, oiled, suntanned stereotypical look, and a demeaning sexism that men enjoyed having over women. The *Playboy* look was an evolutionary leap from the Lana Turner sweater-girl stereotype, but there was nothing natural in it. Their airbrush-altered pictures were testimony to the falsity of it all. The *Playboy* mentality held women hostage to what they weren't, rather than allowing them to be what they were.

Through intimidation, *Playboy* challenged every woman, and it subtly stated that every woman had her price to take her clothes off. *Playboy* was democratic—every woman, no matter if she were Marilyn Monroe or the local ticket taker at the movie theater, could, for money, beautify their pages. Through its specious argument for glamorous paid-for beauty, *Playboy* deceptively used paid-for sex as a vicarious form of visual prostitution. It replaced the 1950s suburbanite's fear of prostitutes, brothels, gonorrhea, and syphilis with glitzy, readily available, printed-page, Marshall McLuhanesque fantasy sex.

In the bigger picture, their bunny was simply one more motif for misogyny, while their cartoons playfully exemplified negative attitudes toward marriage (misogamy). *Playboy* was all about male baby-boomer escape, lust, and safety.

Scarlett O'Hara (1936- Vivien Leigh (1913-1967)

The former field hands found themselves suddenly elevated to the seats of the mighty. There they conducted themselves as creatures of small intelligence might naturally he expected to do. Like monkeys or small children turned loose among treasured objects whose value is beyond their comprehension, they ran wild—either from perverse pleasure in destruction or simply because of their ignorance.
—MARGARET MITCHELL, *Gone With The Wind*

David O. Selznick's epic film *Gone With the Wind* (1939) was adapted from Margaret Mitchell's 1936 book, which was second in sales only to the Bible. It took her ten years to write and won both a Pulitzer Prize and the National Book Award in 1937. The book and the film studied the inner workings of Scarlett O'Hara, a young Southern belle of marriageable age (played by Vivien Leigh in the film). She is seen as childish in the film's initial scenes: giddy, shrewd, self-serving, patronizing, temperamental, energetic, manipulative, false, histrionic, strong-willed, a tease, and, of course, a beautiful woman. Scarlett's many character qualities appear to collectively combine as weaknesses (aside from her beauty) in scenarios portrayed before the onset of the Civil War. Fitting perfectly into dresses seems to make her the happiest, along with fussing with her slave, Mammy (played by Hattie McDaniel). She is in love with Ashley Wilkes (played by Leslie Howard). But is she just in love with herself? When Ashley Wilkes announces he will marry Melanie Hamilton (played by Olivia De Havilland), Scarlett is childishly upset and (as childishly) vows to love Ashley forever.

Ashley's choice for a mate, Melanie, stereotyped the ideal planter-class wife: modest, religious, well-mannered, passive, docile, nurturing, devoted to her husband and their fine home (submissively and conventionally genteel). During that era, many marriages in the South were constructed with the continuance of that traditional ideal in mind. The foundations of power in the South came from land use and slavery rather than from business growth and capitalism, as in the north. The Southern wife's role was to have as many children as possible; consequently many women died from the excessive strain placed on their health and bodies. It is obvious that Ashley cares for Scarlett, but marriage with her is out of the question and Melanie is the model choice for this Southern patriot. Scarlett meets Rhett Butler (played by Clark Gable) while she is in the middle of a temper tantrum. The aloof, gallant Rhett confuses and intrigues her by saying he wants her, not for marrying but for love, because they share the same rogue qualities. Rhett is unconventional, worldly, and clever enough to know that mere honor is not worth dying for, as all Southern planter-class men seem prepared to do in the ensuing war. Rhett is a self-proclaimed scoundrel of a different ilk. He pragmatically explains to a roomful of aristocratic men that the South will lose the war simply because it has no cannon factories. He should know, he is a goods procurer. Rich, savvy, and, of course, handsome (good looks also being the ultimate proof of intelligence), the scoundrel-hero Rhett has a psyche that contradicts all other Southern men who fall

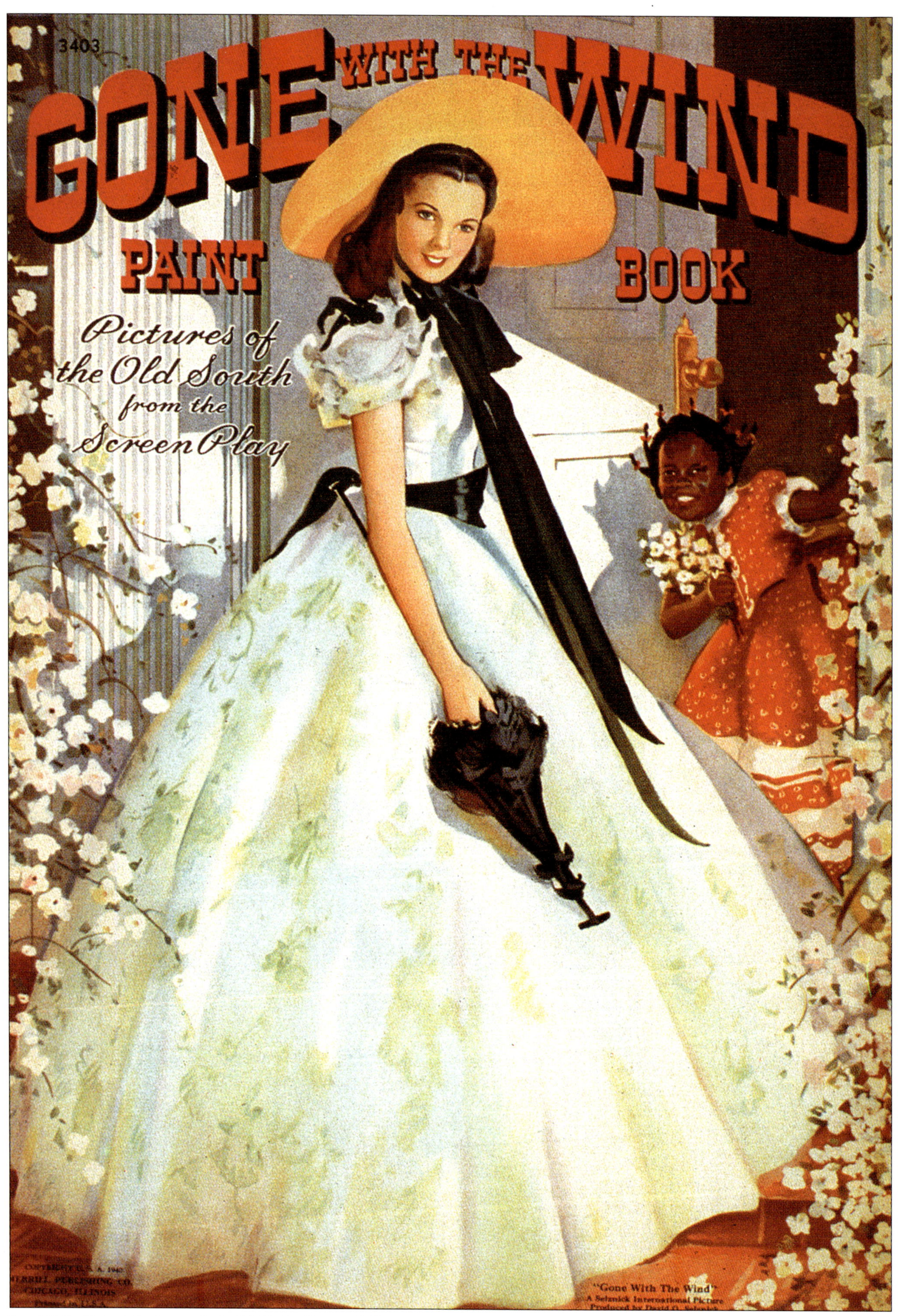

Gone With the Wind, paint book, cover © Merrill Publishing Company, 1940

prey to the instinctive warrior archetype of feeling honor and valor. Because of Rhett's unconventional character, *Gone With the Wind* is an epic antiwar myth. It illustrates that any man, even if he does not choose honor, bravery, and possible death in war, can still be a hero.

The film realistically depicts the brutal consequences of the South under siege in the Civil War. Finally, under the stress of fleeing battle zones, Scarlett learns to use her energy and transform her multitudinous personality flaws into strengths. (This mastery of subtle characterization was the ingredient that catapulted *Gone With the Wind* to fame, in both book and movie form.) After the heinous war is over, she reinvigorates her plantation home, Tara. Recognizing their similar character traits, and forgoing her need to cling to romantic illusion and maintain the Southern wife's expected stereotype, Scarlett marries the realist Rhett. She has matured, yet she has managed to be unconventional and strong. She is an emancipated woman well before her time. Because of Scarlett, *Gone With the Wind* is an epic self-help adaptation myth, metaphorically honoring women's changing role in the twentieth century.

Unlike Rhett, the one thing that eludes Scarlett is an understanding of true love. It is her insurmountable nemesis, a by-product of the turmoil and battle she fights between false romantic traditions and the ability to drop barriers and find tender honest love. It hurts Rhett who by necessity projects his love toward their lovely doll-like daughter, Bonnie Blue. In time, Ashley's wife, Melanie, dies. Scarlett had nursed the sickly Melanie back to health, but those days were in the past. With Melanie gone, Scarlett tries to remind Ashley of his love for her (still tenaciously clinging to the Southern norm she almost abandoned), but Ashley has been destroyed by the South's defeat and subsequent loss of honor, and he finds it impossible to summon love when he has no honor. The only man left for Scarlett to attempt to love is her husband, Rhett, but he has finally given up loving her, especially after discovering Scarlett and Ashley in an embrace. Tragedy strikes when Bonnie Blue falls from her horse and dies. Grief-stricken Rhett and Scarlett are given heartfelt support by Mammy. The film ends with Rhett's famous Hemingwayesque line delivered to Scarlett as he walks out of her life: "Frankly, my dear, I don't give a damn." This is his last hurrah.

When Scarlett and Rhett struggle against each other's strengths, they both lose. It is still ambiguous as to whether Scarlett has fully understood his love, much less her own, although at the end, she vows to somehow get Rhett back. (Are we led to believe it may simply be desperation on her part? Do we ever really believe she is capable of loving anyone?) They are tragically paired as heroine and hero in an opulent, racist South that is no more. Scarlett and Rhett have survived by being unconventional, but their love cannot survive when their weaknesses are piqued. If there was a lesson to be learned, it was to tell the viewer that Scarlett and Rhett are just human. This same humanistic idea was aptly demonstrated in Belle, the film's white prostitute, who had valuable qualities of caring and courage, balancing her stereotypical fallen-woman status.

The harsh realities of slavery were not shown. Slaves who worked for Scarlett and her family were always adoring

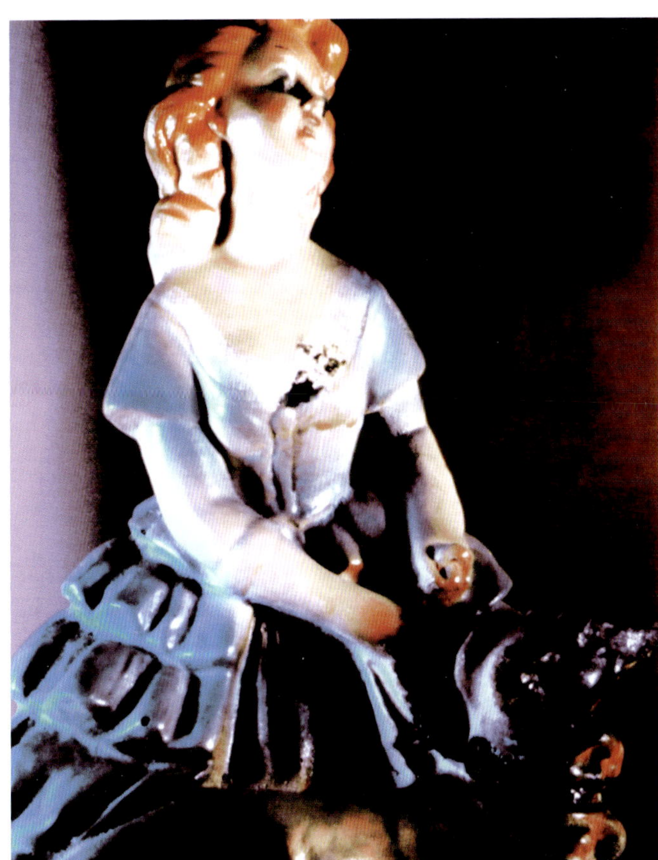

Scarlett O'Hara ten-and-one-half-inch carnival chalk prize, stereotyping her in the opulent white dress worn in the film's first scenes. Similar to the Snow White prizes, where the manufacturers must have rushed to the plaster-casting rooms, most of the Scarlett O'Hara figures are also of inferior quality.

in their subservient positions, both before and after the Civil War. The bowdlerist Will Hays Production Code warned Selznick that white people should not use the slur word nigger in his film. In response, Selznick showed the barest of white's mistreatment of slaves and very little of the disgust that slaves felt. Black actresses Hattie McDaniel and Butterfly McQueen were glad to get their parts in *Gone With the Wind*. In fact, McDaniel was chosen for the part of Mammy over Elizabeth McDuffie, who was Eleanor Roosevelt's maid. Selznick did hire blacks to play black parts rather than having whites in blackface, but that was a very small step forward, particularly for a film that was supposed to show an accurate portrayal of history. Mammy is the sensible sage and the reliable support, but her wise Mammy stereotype is one of overindulgence on Selznick's part. Prissy is an older black Topsy stereotype, a remnant from *Uncle Tom's Cabin* and nineteenth-century Jim Crow stereotypes—which were usually cast into many films showing less-educated slaves as untruthful, afraid of the dark, and half stupid. Prissy was a necessary character reinforcement of slavery humor, but there was no pity as with Stowe's earlier Topsy. Selznick would have known that most whites in the audience would laugh at Prissy rather than pity her because, unfortunately, she only added racist comic relief to the film, particularly when she admits to the exaggeration of her abilities: "Lordy, we got to have a doctor! I don't know nuthin' 'bout birthin' babies!" For all of its redeeming qualities, Selznick's depiction of slavery was a farce.

When *Gone With the Wind* premiered in Atlanta in

1939, many of the white stars were present for its unveiling, but none of the African American performers had been invited to the gala in still-segregated Atlanta. When Hattie McDaniel's picture appeared on the back of the movie programs, it proved to be an archetypal insult to Atlanta society. Wealthy white Atlanta citizens ordered the programs destroyed and new ones printed.

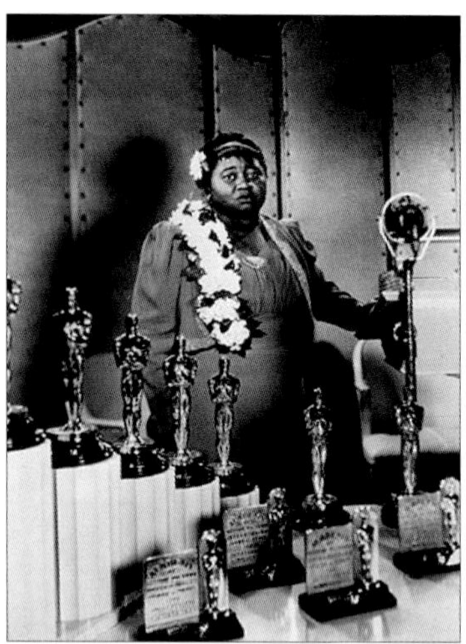

Hattie McDaniel, 1940

Hattie McDaniel previously played the stereotypical black mammy in other Hollywood films. Between films, she took odd jobs as a domestic housemaid just to get by. When blacks criticized her for continuing the mammy stereotype, her response was that she preferred the wages of a Hollywood screen housemaid to those of a real one. "What was the real difference?" she quipped. "The wardrobe was the same."

McDaniel won the Oscar for Best Supporting Actress in 1940. It was a leap year, and an enormous step for black actors.

Al Capp, America's favorite satirist of the era, mercilessly attacked Margaret Mitchell for her book. After the film premiered, Capp said it was overly sentimental to the point of being mawkish and disgusting. Mawkish, disgusting, brilliant, or lacking, *Gone With the Wind* has proven to be the most profitable film in Hollywood's history.

Vivian Mary Hartley was born in Darjeeling, India, in 1913. She enrolled at the Royal Academy of Dramatic Art and married Leigh Holman in 1932. Vivian Leigh became an overnight sensation in the play *The Mask of Virtue* in 1935. Leigh possessed a complex manic-depressive personality, which she periodically subdued with temporarily successful shock treatments. Another aspect of her personality was a focused drive to achieve targeted goals, one of which was to marry Lawrence Olivier. They became romantically involved in 1936 and were married in 1940. Leigh also set her sights on getting the part of Scarlett O'Hara after reading *Gone With the Wind*. Selznick was impressed with her performance in a London theater, and she then lobbied privately and publicly to get the part that would lead her to her first Oscar. Leigh announced she was pregnant in 1944 and began filming *Caesar and Cleopatra*; tragically, while on the set, she fell and suffered a miscarriage. The next year Selznick took legal action to stop her from appearing in the play *The Skin of Our Teeth*, citing her for breach of contract. He lost the court battle and Leigh appeared in the play to great success. She played Blanche DuBois in Tennessee Williams's *A Streetcar Named Desire* in 1949, a role she identified with to such an extent that she would shake uncontrollably after each performance. The film version of *A Streetcar Named Desire* was released in 1951 and Leigh won her second Oscar. Olivier divorced her in 1960. She died of tuberculosis in 1967.

L i'l Abner, Daisy Mae

(1934-1977)

Abstract Art: A product of the untalented, sold by the unprincipled to the utterly bewildered.
—Al Capp

Painting is a blind man's profession. He paints not what he sees, but what he feels, what he tells himself about what he has seen.
—Pablo Picasso, *Journals* (Jean Cocteau), 'Childhood'

Cartoonist-satirist Al Capp invented hulking Li'l Abner and love-struck Daisy Mae as the Depression's paradoxical lovers in the 1934 cartoon strip *Li'l Abner*. Li'l Abner was uninhibited in exhibiting his towering, backwoods, godlike physique. He was a paragon of virtue, continually reinforced by his charismatic but childlike naïveté. In many instances he was the stereotype of a lout, particularly when it came to serious love with Daisy Mae. In typical archetypal superior male fashion he couldn't afford the feelings of a loss of power to a woman who loved him, nor did he want to lose her. Li'l Abner was a member of the Yocum family, which could well have been Yokel, and he satirically stereotyped the male country bumpkin and his struggle with life's worries of love, money, and position while living within a society run by the snooty upper class, deceptive intellectual frauds, city slickers, greedy capitalists, and phony politicians.

As an eye-catcher, Daisy Mae Scragg unabashedly exhibited her goddesslike physique (copied by Dolly Parton). She was curvaceous and voluptuous, while attired in only her abbreviated backwoods scanties, and like Li'l Abner, she too was a paragon of virtue. But she came from the Scragg family, who were the paragon of evil. Unlike Li'l Abner, she constantly did all the work. Daisy Mae satirically stereotyped the female country bumpkin who was dedicated in her struggle to gain romantic love while having to counter against Li'l Abner's ho-hum attitude. Her persona can be simplified into loving dedication.

In a larger sense, Li'l Abner and Daisy Mae were a metaphor for America's class struggles against mega-capitalists, upper-class snobbery, finger-pointing warmongers, fake icons, and specious ideas. They were symbolic stereotypes of the country folk against the city slickers, or better yet the simple folk against the insider-government, corporate-industrial mega-system. They just wanted to live happily ever after. (Isn't that what the Constitution promised?)

In 1936 Li'l Abner had his own comic and in 1940 his own film; the cartoon strip was a tough satire. Capp's brother Elliott Caplin, in his book *Al Capp Remembered*, put it this way:

> For the whole of his professional life, Alfred had reveled in taking aim at targets he loathed for their perfidy and hypocrisy. In *Li'l Abner* he splayed victims with such lustful revulsion, there was no room for compassion . . . Captains of industry, politicians, poseurs, super salesmen of worthless chattels, intellectual frauds, cheats, fools and con artists were all scourged by Alfred. He ridiculed, satirized relentlessly the fakery he found rampant in public and private life . . . Margaret Mitchell (via her lawyers) threatened Alfred

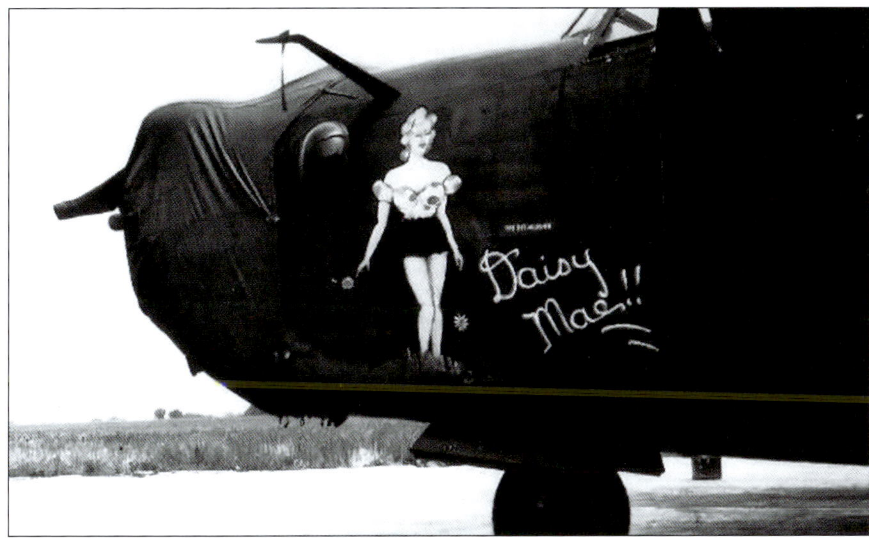
Daisy Mae nose art, World War II bomber, photograph G. Warden Clark, 1940s

with a law suit that would have resulted in his paying damages roughly equivalent to the cost of building the Panama Canal. *Li'l Abner* had parodied Miss Mitchell's sensational book *Gone With the Wind* with a pitiless attack on the specious and mawkish sentiments of Rhett, Scarlett, Melanie et al. . . . So when Alfred in later years, shifted his range of attack from the stuffed icons of the right to what he considered to be the fakes, the deceivers, the malingerers of the liberal left, he did so with a firm conviction that he hadn't changed, "they had."[1]

Al Capp was born Alfred Caplin in New Haven, Connecticut, in 1909. At the age of nine, he lost a leg when a trolley car ran over him. In some ways both Li'l Abner and Daisy Mae represented a personal antithesis for Capp; it was as if he used them to write a reverse autobiography. In real life he was physically impaired but never mentally impaired. As country bumpkins, Li'l Abner and Daisy Mae were fantasized as being mentally impaired, but when it came to their physiques and dealing with a larger world beyond Dogpatch, they were never physically impaired. At the youthful age of thirteen, Capp passionately read Charles Dickens, George Bernard Shaw, Mark Twain, and the works of "the great iconoclast," William Cowper Brann. In 1932 he worked as a ghosting assistant to Ham Fisher of *Joe Palooka* fame (Capp did the work—Fisher signed it). By 1934 Capp had matured, changed his name from Caplin and started *Li'l Abner* on his own terms.

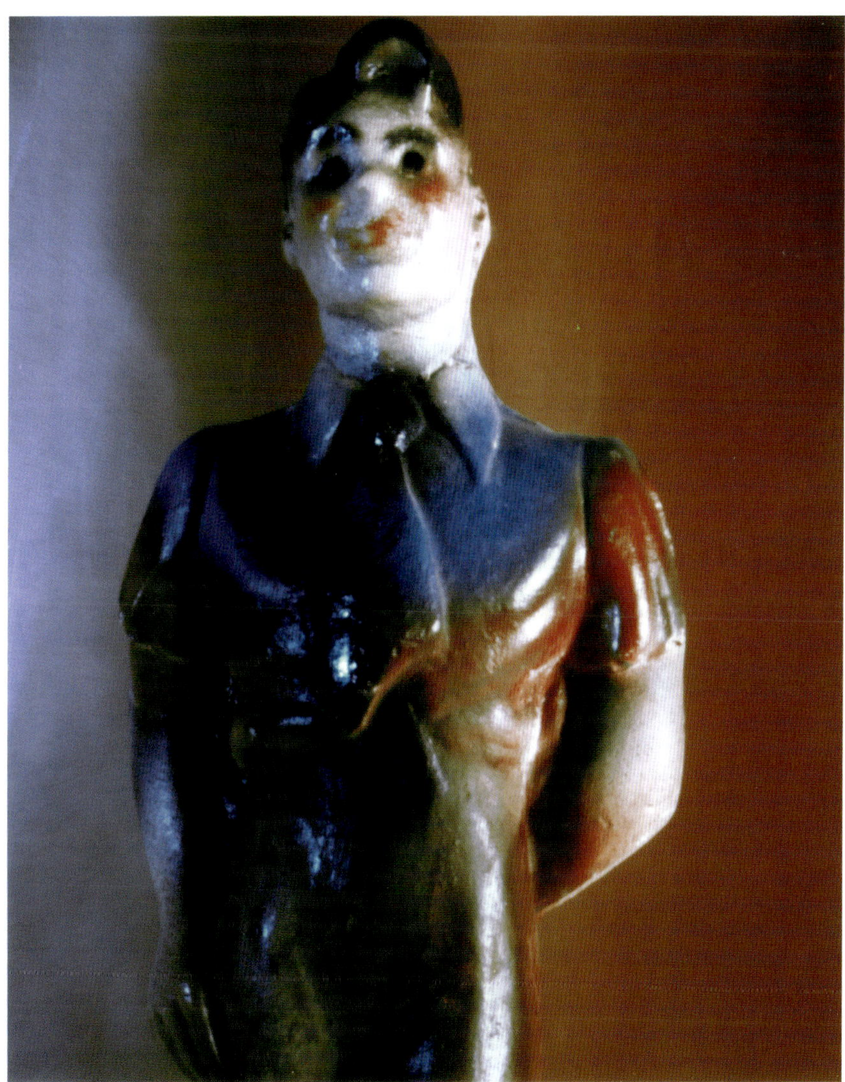
Li'l Abner sixteen-inch carnival chalk prize—somewhere there must be a Daisy Mae

Through parody, Capp used Li'l Abner and Daisy Mae to confront what he thought were the world's finest and greatest frauds (it must have been a challenge to figure out who was the most worthy). John Steinbeck admired him to the point of saying: "I think that Capp may possibly be the best writer in the world today."[2] Capp contributed words such as "druthers" and "irregardless" to the English language. The comic strip *Li'l Abner* ran for forty-three years. Capp died of emphysema in 1979.

Santa Claus

Scholars believe Saint Nicholas was derived from ancient pagan deities that became Christianized. Each Saint Nicholas eidolon (idealized apparition, idol) had archetypal similarities. One source of Saint Nicholas was the Germanic God of Thunder, known as the white-bearded Thor, who rode through the air in a chariot drawn by two goats. His palace was in the north, and he wore red and came down chimneys into his special element of fire, giving gifts at Yuletide. Another was the Norse God Woden, who rode his horse through the sky at the winter solstice bringing gifts to humans. Early Romans celebrated Saturnalia, a festival dedicated to Saturn, the god of peace and plenty, which ran from December 17 to 24. On December 25, they celebrated the birth of the ancient pagan sun god Attis in Phrygia and of the Persian savior, Mithra.

The basis for the Christian-era Santa Claus was the Byzantine bishop of Myra named Nicholas, who was born in Patara, now named Turkey, in 280 AD. It is said that as an infant he mostly fasted, only suckling one of his mother's breasts on Wednesdays and Fridays (now that's a special baby!). He became a priest at age nineteen and later was a bishop. He performed many miracles, such as resurrecting the dead from a magical cauldron. Christians said that by the year 300, he was jailed and tortured under the Roman emperor Diocletian for refusing to accept the divine heritage of kings. Scholars have noted that early Christians greatly exaggerated Diocletian's persecutions, and in all fairness to Roman history, Diocletian had far more tolerance of Rome's many religions than early zealot Christians did. In actuality, Diocletian attempted to stop radical Christian sects from fighting against one another. Three Christian eunuchs set fire to Diocletian's palace at Nicomedia and he had them executed—later the three became canonized martyrs as Saint Dorotheus, Saint Gorgonius, and Saint Peter. Other priests were arrested, but most were released. Scholars assume that these halfhearted attempts at Christian persecution actually helped Christianity become widespread.

Constantine became the first Christian emperor of the Roman Empire in 324. He reinstated Nicholas as bishop of Myra and set December 6 as Saint Nicholas's official name day. A church was built in his honor. It is thought that Saint Nicholas died in 342 and was buried in Myra. It is also thought that even after death Saint Nicholas's miraculous bones exuded a fountainlike panacea of holy oil that was capable of curing all diseases. The Roman Catholic Church honored Saint Nicholas as helper of the poor. He was also the patron saint of seafaring men—in one of his miracles, he stopped a storm, saving many sailors. At that point Saint Nicholas was considered a multi-tasking miracle worker. By 354, the Church of Rome set the celebration of Jesus Christ's birthday on December 25, to specifically counteract the Mithraic religion and Mithra's December 25 birthday (page 104), eventually turning Rome's followers of Mithra into

Christians. This was, of course, a political determination.

By 1087, Italians had secretly excavated relics from Myra, which were said to be Saint Nicholas's bones (grave robbing is okay if we do it to them). The bones were taken to Bari, Italy, where they were dedicated in a shrine—one that had earlier been dedicated to the Grandmother, or Pasqua Epiphania (thereby lessening women's stature once again). Previously, the Grandmother filled children's stockings with presents.

Most Christian faiths throughout Europe celebrated Saint Nicholas. Russia's oldest Orthodox church was named in his honor. In England he was called Father Christmas.

When the Puritans arrived in America in 1620, they did not celebrate Christmas because they believed it was pagan. (Who'd want all those nasty presents anyway?)

The Sinter Klaas (Saint Nicholas) legend was brought to America slightly later by Dutch settlers who founded their own colony of New Amsterdam, which became New York. They celebrated Sinter Klaas on December 5. The famous Dutch American writer Washington Irving gave Dutch Americans one of their first detailed descriptions of Saint Nicholas in his *History of New York*, published in 1809. Irving described a dark-robed stern saint who arrived on a flying horse on December 4 (the Eve of St. Nicholas) to give gifts to children. A year later, John Pintard, the Dutch founder of the New York Historical Society, chose Saint Nicholas as the society's patron saint. Pintard later illustrated a Christmas poem that portrayed the harsh, slim Saint Nicholas as an all-seeing stern enforcer (somewhat similar to a low-flying hawk-eyed J. Edgar Hoover of the nineteenth century). Pintard's poem emphasized children being good, promoting fear, because Saint Nicholas brought along a rod—those who had been bad were severely beaten.

A more joyful Saint Nicholas was fully realized in 1823 with the publication of the famous poem "A Visit from Saint Nicholas," more commonly known as "The Night Before Christmas," supposedly written by Clement Clarke Moore but recently attributed to Henry Livingston. At this point the legend gets more interesting, because Saint Nicholas was promoted and propagandized for Dutch American political purposes. Here is how this occurred. Irving, Pintard, and Moore were wealthy Dutch patrician landowners who, because of their aristocrat status, could vote. The three were also members of the New York Historical Society, and the society was opposed to any attempts by non-landowners to get the privilege to vote (that's democracy in action!). But Christmas was the one time of year that extreme rowdiness in New York City could prevail, because non-landowners went "a wassailing"—which meant getting drunk and breaking into the houses of the wealthier patrician landowners. As a political ruse against wassailing, Moore apparently published Livingston's poem, hoping to keep the non-landowners home, patiently waiting for Saint Nicholas while celebrating inside their own houses. The ruse eventually worked. "The Night Before Christmas" was so overwhelmingly popular in America that it enmeshed Saint Nicholas and Santa Claus, and established December 24 as the one and only Christmas Eve. In Livingston's poem, Santa was elf-size, more capable of going down and back up chimneys. Approximately fifty years later,

Santa's image was further defined by political cartoonist (and anti-immigrant, anti–Irish Catholic) Thomas Nast, who depicted a slightly demonic human-size Santa for Christmas issues of *Harper's Weekly* from the 1860s to the 1880s. Nast included details of Santa's workshop at the North Pole and made Santa a jolly note-keeper and gift-giver—he had the list of the good and bad children. No longer did he carry a rod for discipline.

In ads that began in 1931, Santa went corporate when the Coca Cola Company featured him drinking Coke and being jolly. Coke subtly took his image for their own needs, attempting to create a disguised stereotype of being

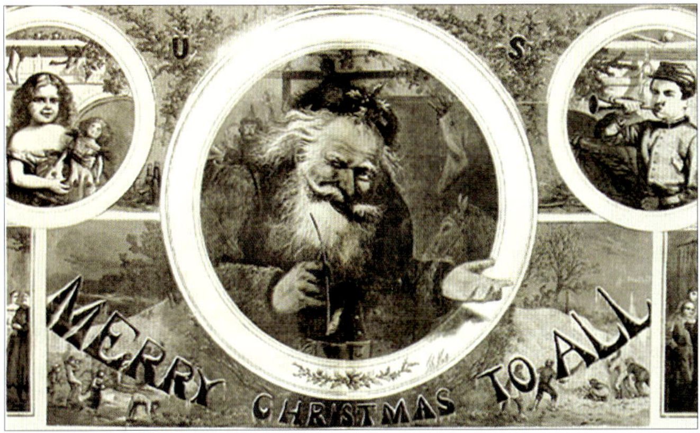

"Merry Christmas to All," Santa Claus, illustration detail, Thomas Nast, *Harper's Weekly*, 1865

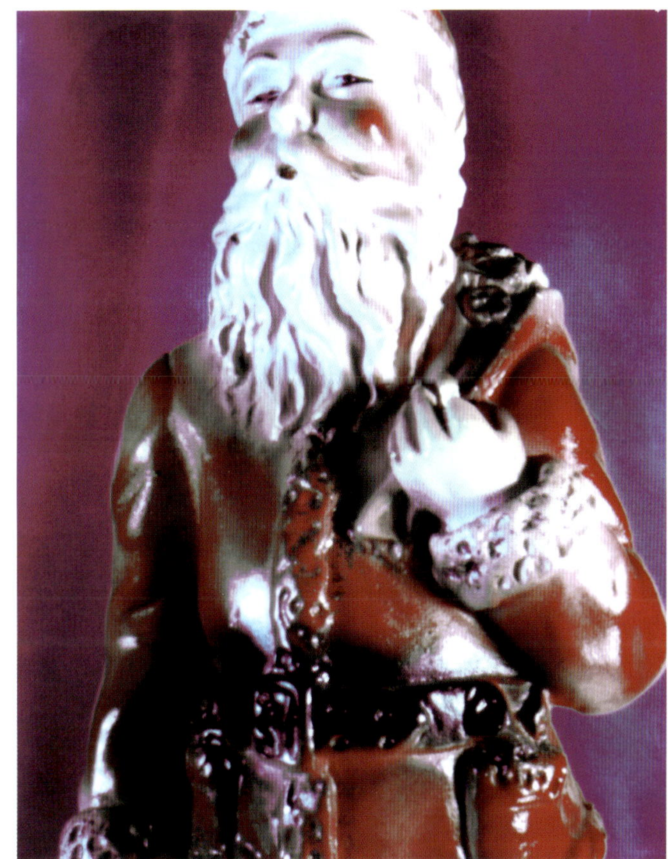

Santa Claus twelve-inch carnival chalk prize, 1930s—he was not as rotund then, having been fashioned after an earlier, skinnier Santa

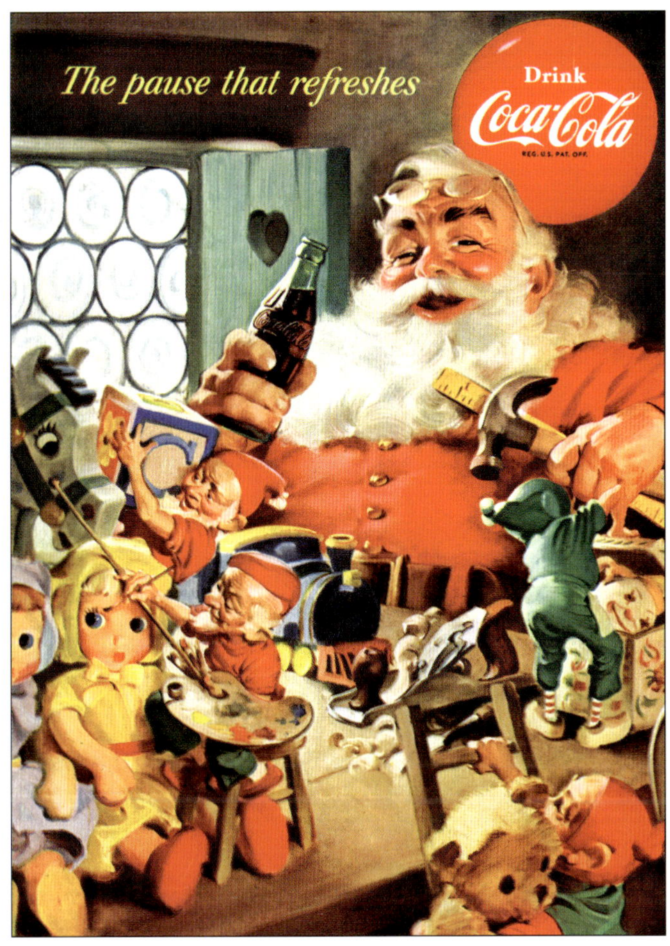

Coca Cola, ad, 1940s © Coca Cola Inc.

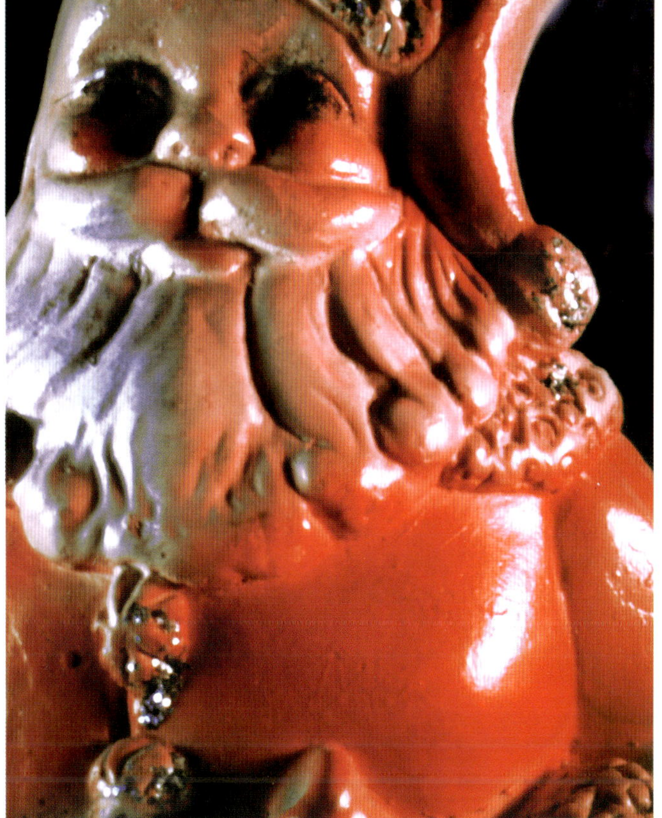

Santa Claus eleven-inch carnival chalk bank prize, 1950s—caricatured to full girth

jolly from drinking Coke while gaining weight. For the next thirty-five years the Coca Cola Company progressively bulked up Santa's body size to an exceedingly rotund person—this identified and stereotyped Coke as a jolly drink. (Back then overweight people were thought of as jolly—like Hollywood comedians John Bunny, Fatty Arbuckle, Oliver Hardy, etc.)

Could there be a correlation between Coca Cola's decades-long ad campaign of jolly equals rotund and recent statistics on Americans' gradual increase in body weight? Is the Coca Cola Company partially responsible for America's current problem with obesity?

By 1955, it was fairly easy to be cynical about Santa Claus—since he was pictured in mega-corporate advertising selling almost everything, not just Coke. In the United States, his highly secular archetype became capitalism's joyful feeling, the Ho-Ho-Ho jolly present-giver.

Other parts of Christmas, which are generally taken for granted, have symbolic roots. The Christmas tree has pagan roots, ascribed to the return of increased daylight and life's renewal—a symbolic need, because the deepest, darkest hours of winter are past. German Lutherans began to have Christmas trees in the late 1500s and they brought the custom to America. But Christmas trees were not widely used in America until the 1850s, when President Franklin Pierce arranged to have the first Christmas tree in the White House. The first glass ornaments, named kugels, were glass balls intended to protect houses against evil spirits. They were produced at Lauscha, Germany, in 1830. Those of spherical design were meant to remind German Christians of the apple that had tempted Eve in Paradise. The circular Christmas wreath was Mithraic, a paean to the sun.

New additions to Christmas symbols continually appear—for instance, Rudolph, the ninth reindeer. He was invented in a Chicago Montgomery Ward's by their copywriter Robert May, who put Rudolph in a giveaway booklet in 1939. May's brother-in-law, composer Johnny Marks, wrote the popular 1949 song "Rudolph the Red-Nosed Reindeer" (all in the name of Christmas spirit, not merchandising)—sung by Gene Autry as he galloped through verdant hills of newly planted Christmas trees.

Pancho
(1930-1950s)

Pancho was the 1940s "laughable" sidekick of the Cisco Kid in films of that same name. Each film was a low budget cowboy/romance story based on the formulaic slick handsome Mexican cowboy (Cisco) who had help from a humorous, but goofy, overweight sidekick (Pancho) versus any obnoxious bandits. An attractive girlfriend (always for Cisco) was added into the mix. Many of the "Mexican style" antics in the show played upon the otherness stereotype/slur for anything Mexican.

The 1940s jolly-good Pancho was played by Martin Garralaga. In earlier 1930s film versions of *The Cisco Kid* Pancho was named "Gordita" and played by jolly-rotund Chris-Pin Martin, whose real name was Ysabel Ponciana Paiz.

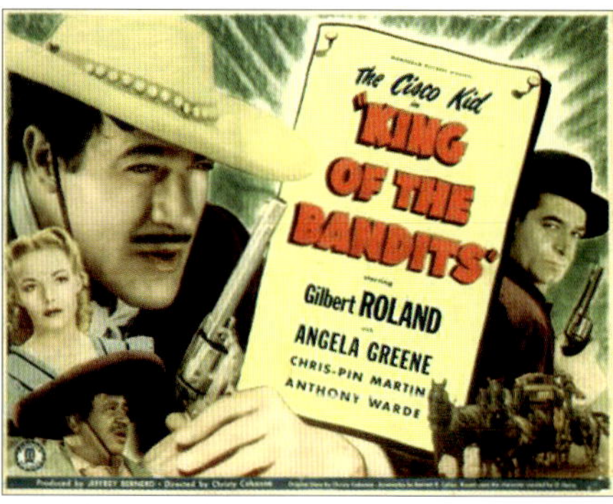
Pancho in lower left in *King of the Bandits* poster, 1930s

The 1950s Cisco Kid was Duncan Renaldo with Leo Carillo as the most famous Pancho. They were paired by United Artists in five features before making the popular network television show of the early 1950s which lasted for one hundred and fifty-six episodes (made in color so they would appeal later when color TVs were available).

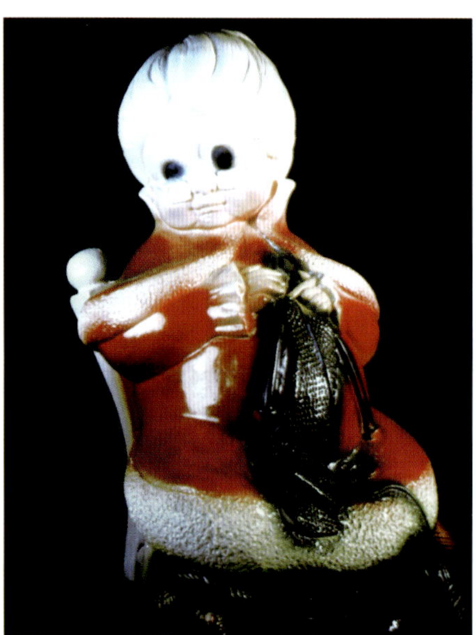
Mrs. Claus fifteen-inch carnival chalk prize

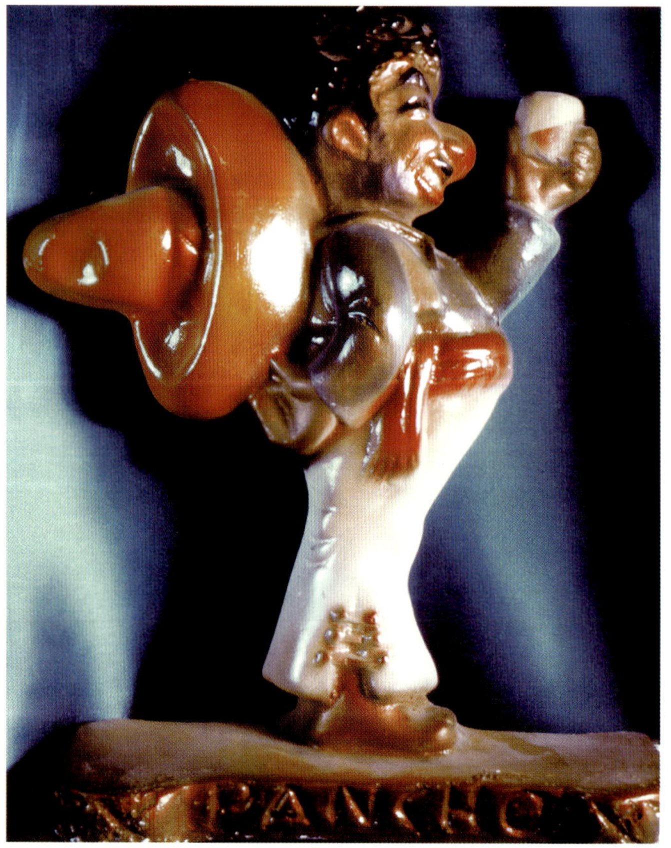
Pancho twelve-inch carnival chalk prize

On January 1, 2006 the state of California Senate Bill 670 became law, titled *Apology Act for the 1930s Mexican Repatriation Program.* No money was involved, just an apology for the little known fact that two million (!) Mexicans were deported to Mexico through the offer of free train rides or—if that was not acceptable, then they were forcibly removed. Many were farm laborers in the southwestern states (mostly California) during the 1931 Hoover administration. It was thought that anyone of Mexican heritage living in America was holding a job that could have been performed by an Anglo-American during the Great Depression's hard times. Sixty percent of the two million deported were U.S. citizens (at least four hundred thousand deported Latinos in California were U.S. citizens). Over one million of those deported were born in the U.S. and only a relatively small percentage spoke Spanish. Some who looked Latino, but were not of Mexican heritage, went too.

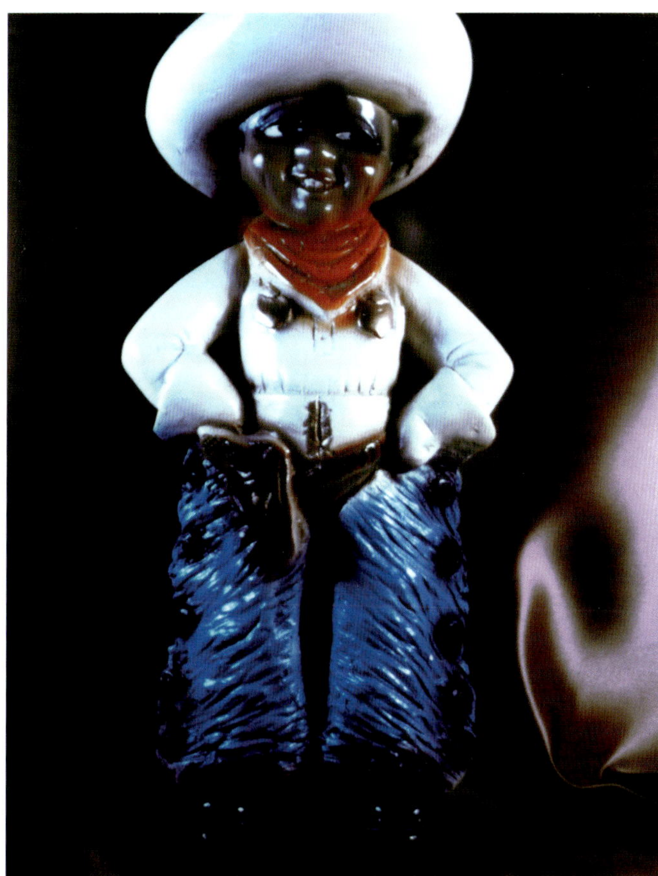

Mexican Cowboy fifteen-inch carnival chalk prize, "Yippee" written on front base
© 1943 June Yates Jenkins

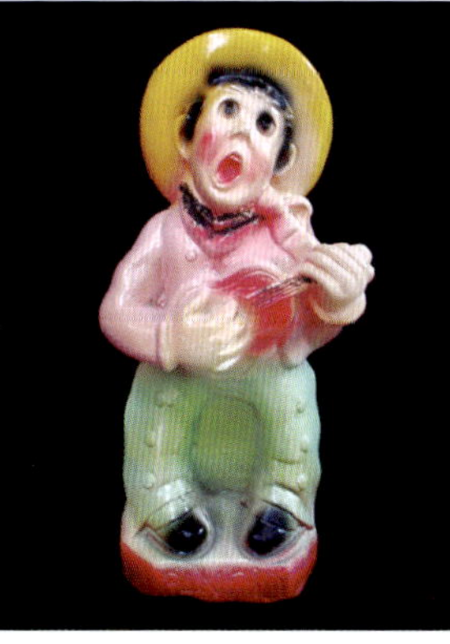

Singing Cowboy rare fourteen-inch carnival chalk prize, "Pancio," written on front base

WILLIAM POWELL (1892-1984)

They claim to be he-men, but the hair from their combined chests wouldn't have made a wig for a grape.
— ROBERT BENCHLEY

William Powell shaved his trademark mustache, dressed in a woman's suit, and wore a monocle for a faux-drag scene in the film *Love Crazy* (1941). By that time, Powell was extremely famous in films, as was his mustache. Together they created the sly stylish sleuth stereotype in his Thin Man series, begun in 1934. More to the point, he was the lover of some of the most beautiful Hollywood stars. The public did wonder who the real William Powell was. How did he manage it? Not because he tried to stay out of the gossip columns, but because in the early 1930s he was the lover of Hollywood's number-one sex symbol—Jean Harlow. After Harlow's premature death, he married and then later divorced the young, beautiful Carole Lombard. He and the starlet Diana Lewis were married in 1940—he was forty-seven and she was twenty-one—after knowing each other for one month. These romantic escapades made him the "Good Time Willie" stereotype. His public actually knew very little of him—they didn't know about his near fatal colon cancer and the operations he barely survived in 1940.

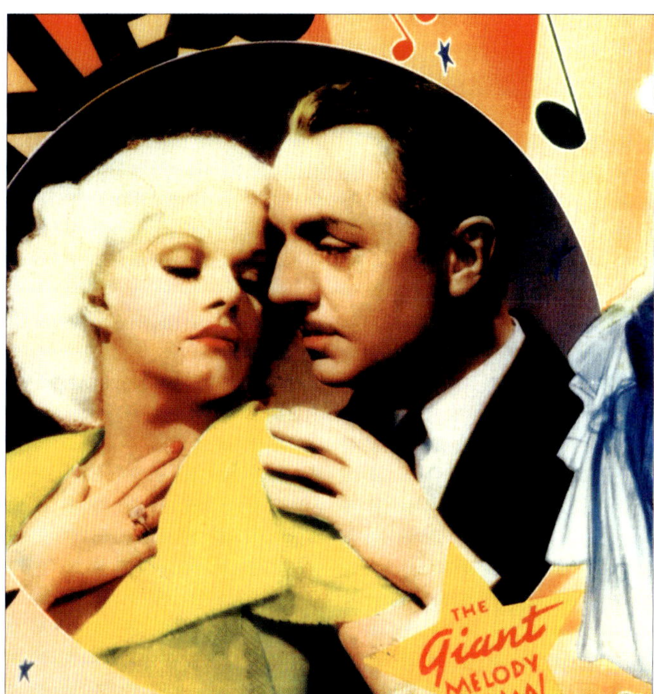

Jean Harlow and William Powell, *Reckless*, lobby card detail, 1935 © M-G-M Studios

In the Thin Man mystery series, Powell was teamed with Myrna Loy. Their cheerful chemistry was just what a Depression-era American public needed in the mid-1930s. In those films, Powell played a role described in David Thomson's *The Biographical Dictionary of Film* as "the patron saint of those politically incorrect, but very cinematic habits—

smoking and drinking." His tuxedo gave him the dapper Dan stereotype.

Powell always played the extremely sly villain part in his earlier years on Broadway and silent films. His superb renditions of evilness were often more popular than the good-guy actors whose played the handsome hero. Powell's looks were never thought to be either heroesque or handsome by his producers, but he proved them wrong. So well did he play the villain (with felicitous words and actions) that his fan mail from adoring women increased when he played those roles. It became obvious that he was very attractive to many women in an inspired sort of way.

He explained the "why" of his sex appeal in October, 1926, in the *New York Telegram*:

> To begin with, women admire suavity, poise, cleverness, flattery, qualities with which the modern dramatist—happily for us who play the parts—endows his villains. Women are apt to be less severe in their condemnation of his villainy when it involves a woman, than men, because consciously or unconsciously they attribute weakness to the victim which, in themselves, under similar circumstances would surely be strength. As many men relish the stimulant of physical danger, so many women are fascinated by the presence of moral danger. This fascination is likely to attach itself to the embodiment of the danger, which is the villain, and he becomes an object of absorbing interest. If his offense is not too heinous and he is allowed to show the smallest fraction of repentance, his faults become positive virtues. After all—he has lost everything in the pursuit of his object—that object being a woman. While the hero—well, his role has been quite passive in comparison. The noble, conventional fellow has simply sought to protect the lady—a time honored service which has grown irksome in many feminine eyes.[1]

William Powell was born in Pittsburgh, Pennsylvania; his family moved to Kansas City when he was nine. Determined to be an actor, he attended the American Academy of Academic Arts in New York City and graduated in 1912. Ten years of struggling on Broadway brought him almost no money and little fame—the movie industry seemed a logical next step. His professional abilities, as well as his meticulously trained voice, prepared him for the transition from silent to sound films. The Thin Man series with Myrna Loy carried them as film partners from 1934 to 1947. One of his finest performances was in *Life with Father* (1947). He was nominated for Best Actor three times, but never won. He was always known as a gentleman in the finest meaning of the word. His very private, personal life was as intense a drama as anything he ever played onscreen. He was married three times; his final marriage lasted forty-four years, until he died in 1984.

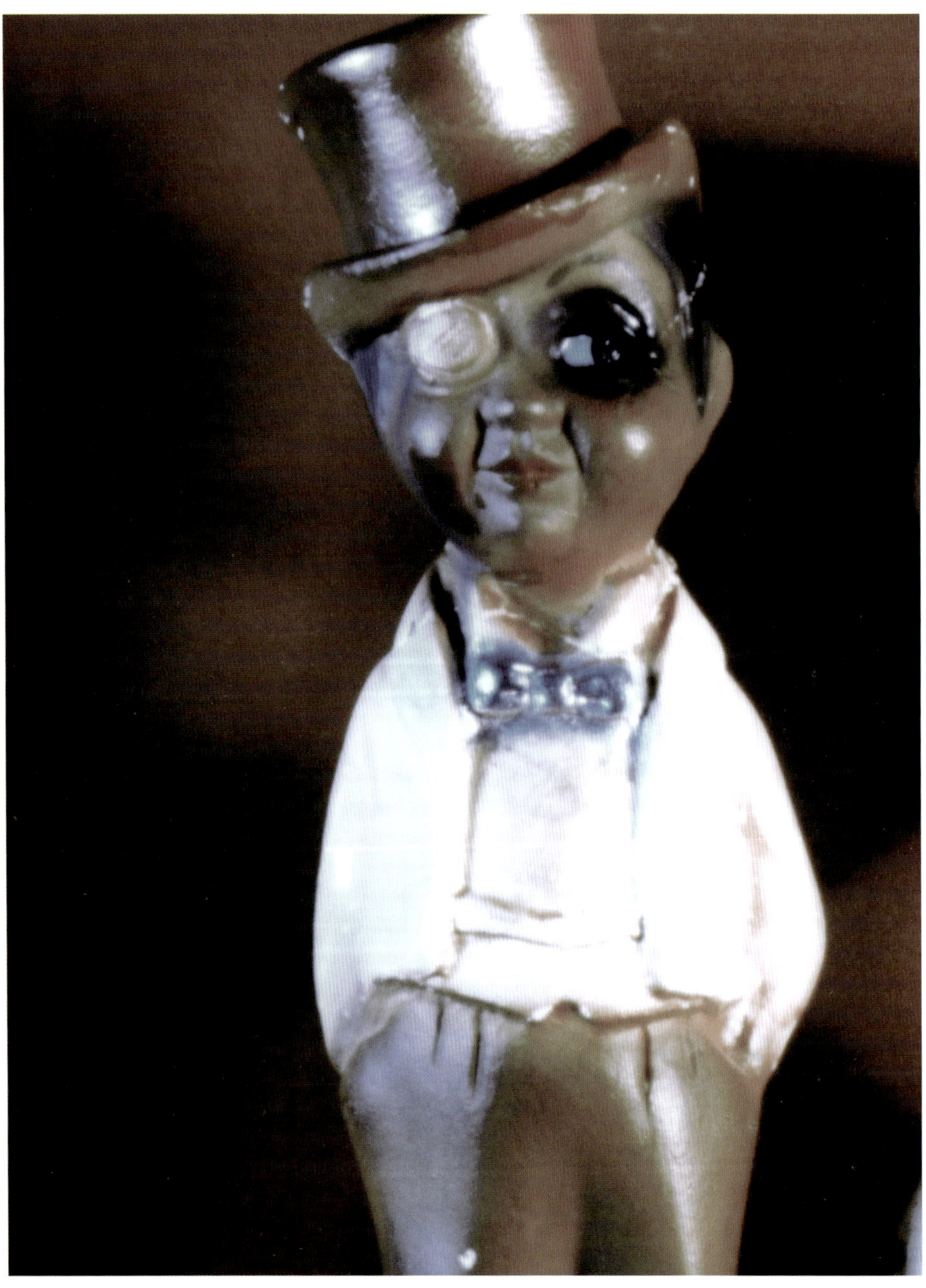

William Powell nine-inch carnival chalk prize inscribed "Good Time Willie" on the back

SUPERMAN

(1938-

*I figured that the character would be so advanced that he would be
invulnerable in other ways than physically. Secretly, I kind of enjoyed
the thought that women, who just didn't care at all about somebody
like Clark Kent, would go ape over somebody like Superman. I enjoyed
the fact that he wasn't that affected by all their admiration. When you
come down to it, some of the greatest lovers of all time simply aren't
that crazy about women: It's the women who are crazy about them.*
—JERRY SIEGEL, co-inventor of *Superman*

Jerry Siegel's statement is, unfortunately, a very sad
select male archetype—that men are afraid to give their power
to women. With those words, Siegel unknowingly shed a lot
of light on his Superman in just one short paragraph. This
archetype also provides an explanation for super bodybuilder
and movie star turned politician Arnold Schwarzenegger's odd
Valentine to Maria Shriver, which said, "I love you because
you love me."[1] Schwarzenegger's not giving away any of his
power, but she has to love him. He's the ultimate male superior
narcissist archetype.

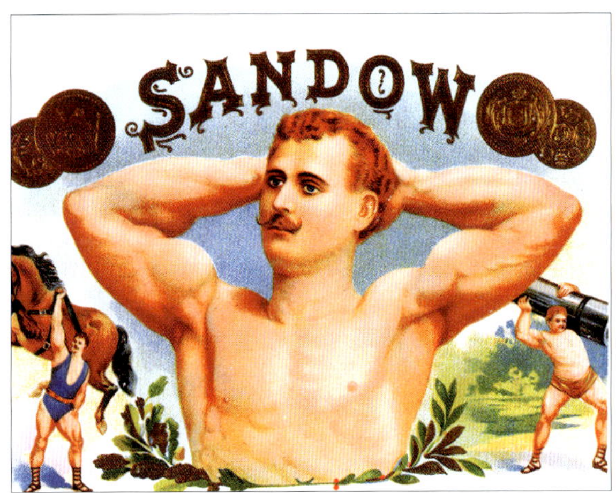

Eugen Sandow, cigar box label (lifting a horse and a huge weight), circa 1900s

The superman ideal is a mythological fantasy
archetype, one that is replayed century after century. It was
replayed in the early twentieth century by the muscleman,
weight lifter, and showman Eugen Sandow, whose physique
made him a star attraction of *Sandow Trocadero Vaudevilles*,
produced by Florenz Ziegfeld in Chicago. Sandow also performed at the 1893 World's Columbia Exposition, where for
$300 (which went to charity) the public could come back-
stage and feel his muscles (men preferred seeing Little Egypt,
women preferred Sandow—the beginnings of equality[2]). He
was considered the father of modern-day bodybuilders, and his
extraordinary feats and muscle size were eventually recorded

into twentieth-century medical books, giving him further
legitimacy as a superman. Ziegfeld billed Sandow as the
"world's most perfectly developed man."

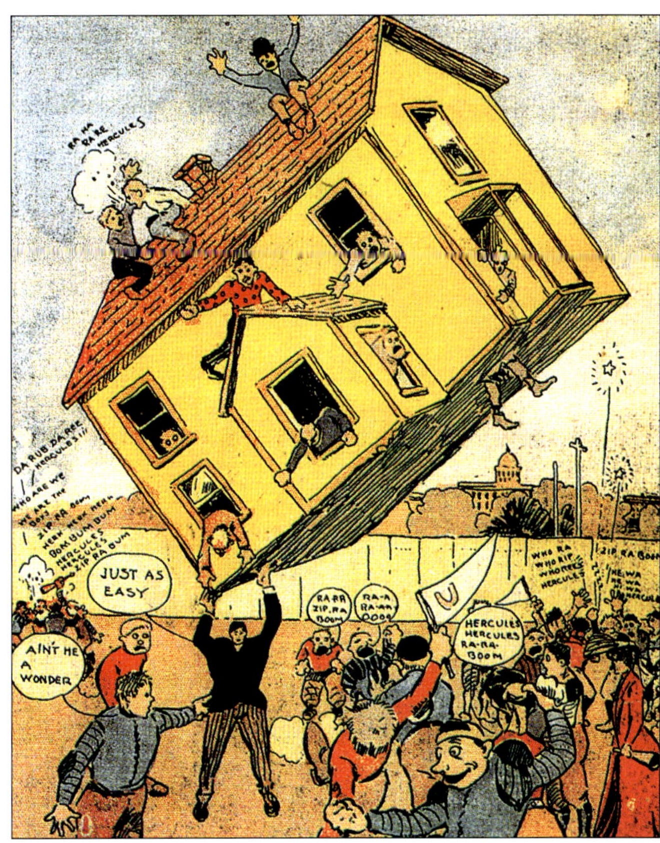

"Hugo Hercules Misses the Football, But" detail, *Hugo Hercules*, J. Koerner © *Chicago Tribune*, 1902

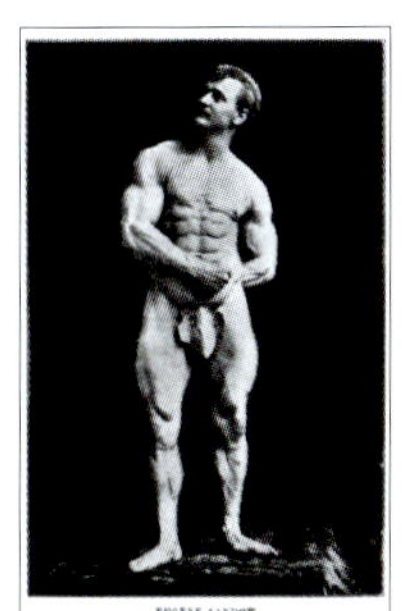

Eugen Sandow, medical book illustration, circa 1900s

J. Koerner created the first super-
strongman (a Sandow type—not a superhero) comic strip titled *Hugo Hercules* for
the Chicago Tribune in 1902-03.

Bodybuilder Bernarr Macfadden
sponsored the first physique contest in
1903 at Madison Square Garden. The
$1,000 prizewinner in Macfadden's 1921
contest for the "Most Perfectly Developed Man in America" was Angelo
Siciliano, an Italian immigrant, later
known to the world as Charles Atlas.
The idea for a super-physique came to
Atlas after seeing the imposing statue of
the muscular Hercules in the Brooklyn Museum. It was Atlas
who made a merchandising coup by mythologizing his autobiographical story about a Coney Island teenage bully kicking
sand in his face. In one year, Atlas had gone from a ninety-
seven-pound weakling to a strongman in the carnival on
Coney Island, bending 1,500 railroad spikes with his bare
hands! Men who were eager to face down bullies subscribed
to Atlas' Dynamic Tension, a mail order course advertised
in the back pages of many male-oriented comics. Atlas invented the "Hey Skinny—yer ribs are showing!" intimidation technique directed at anyone whose self-image was poor
enough to be the wimp on the beach—a cruel stereotype aimed
at teenage boys whose bare chests looked skimpy.

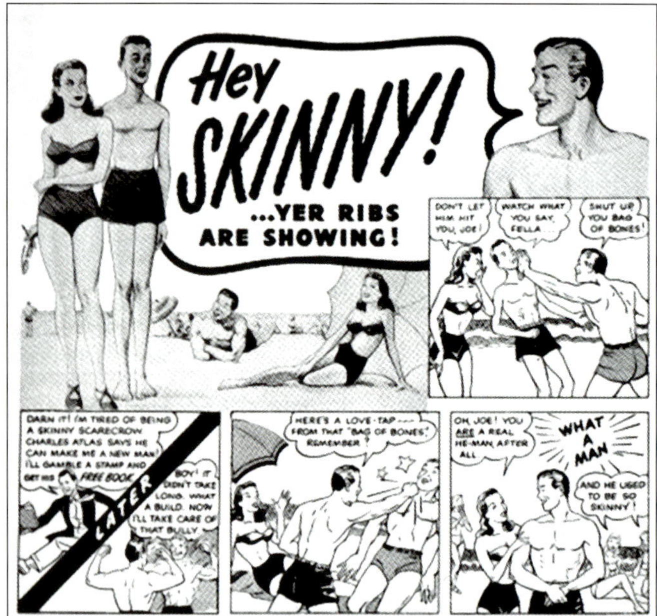

Charles Atlas, magazine ad, circa 1940s

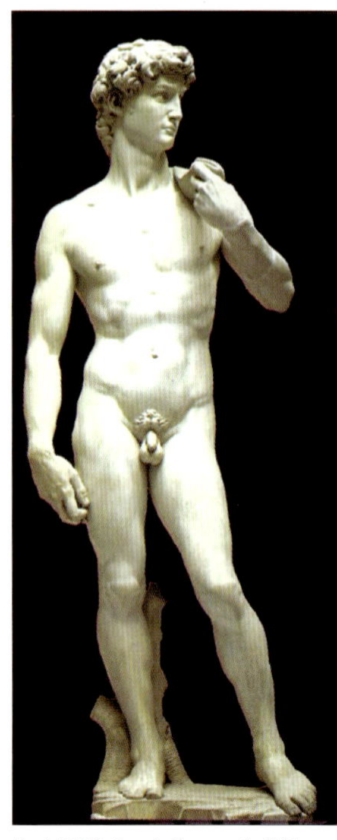

As the immigrant's recipient of the American dream, millionaire Atlas was also sought after by artists who used him as a muscular model for sculptures of fearless great Americans—he posed for the statue of George Washington, sculpted by James Earle Fraser in Washington Square, New York.

Six million pupils took Atlas' course (his most famous students were Rocky Marciano and Joe DiMaggio). The obvious earlier archetype for a muscular invincible man would be David (of David and Goliath fame), sculpted by Michelangelo during the Italian renaissance.

David, Michelangelo Buonarroti, 1501

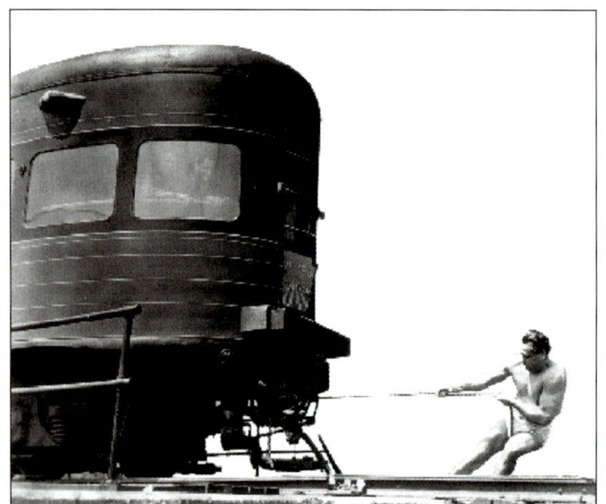
Charles Atlas pulling a seventy-two-ton locomotive for 112 feet, Sunnyside, Long Island, 1920s

Superman, the comic-book fantasy replay personality, continues to be an American superhero. His meteoric rise in popularity from 1938 paralleled the rise of interest in comic books. His popularity also inspired the creation of four hundred other attempts to create a superhero superstar.

We all know that Superman came from another planet, resided here on Earth disguised as the well-dressed, mild-mannered newspaper reporter Clark Kent. He could transform himself into Superman at will. Superman captured criminals, saved people in distress, destroyed warmongers, and defended good countries like the United States (thereby preserving life, liberty, and the pursuit of happiness for all deserving, honest, law-abiding American citizens). Superman was a flying, bulletproof analogue of and enforcer for the Declaration of Independence. His super-abilities increased over time: at first he could leap tall buildings, but he couldn't fly; then he could fly, but no faster than a speeding train; ultimately, he could fly as fast as the speed of light. He also became more bulletproof: at first shells shot at him could penetrate his skin, but they were bouncing off him by World War II. At first he could not see through buildings, then he gained super-senses. He went from criminal to supercop. When first introduced, he was wanted by the police because he took the law into his own hands, but not for long; he soon began working with the police. Lois Lane and Superman were married in 1952, but that turned out to be only a comic-book dream—(although it did increase sales).

Once Superman's powers were fully realized, his stereotype could have been viewed several ways. At the lowest level, Superman's stereotype was the perfect good guy fighting for truth, justice, and the American way—always ridding the world of the criminal mind. On a higher level, he was the great indestructible protector, an archetypal godlike symbol to make Americans feel safe when their very lives were in danger, particularly during World War II. His role then was the invincible protector of the United States. He supplied readers with an empowered patriotism that embodied the notion that America's war effort was indomitable— Americans were right and would win. Furthermore, didn't the Japanese attack America first? Those others were killer cowards—that was Japan's archetype for the American public.

Superman never fully dealt with interpersonal relationships. Lois Lane was a mentally tortured lover, so much so that Superman should have been charged with confusing and disturbing the minds of his readers. Combining the God-like quality of Superman with the nerd quality of Clark Kent proved to be a twisted role model for anyone trying to understand love and trust. Superman and Clark played one monstrous mind game on Lois. She was in love with Superman, although she disdained Clark. Readers knew Clark was not supposed to reveal his true identity to Lois, even though he was apparently in love with her. Well, if you can't communicate with the woman who is in love with you and whom you love, then who can you communicate with? (Maybe the whole story was a parody on the inability of men to communicate with women, but I doubt it.) As it was, Clark's communication skills with Lois provided boys and men who read the comic nothing but inarticulate babbling abilities when

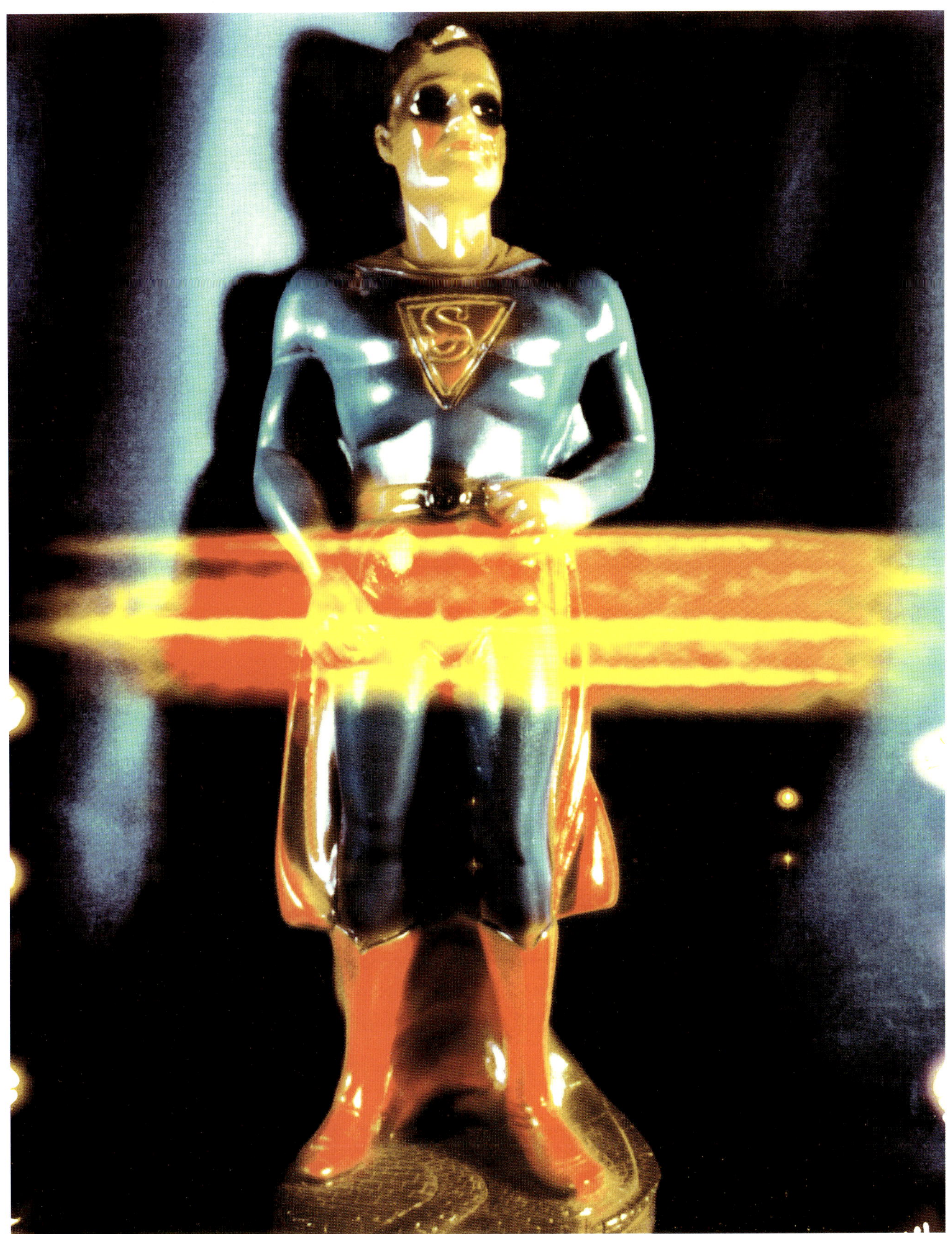

Superman fifteen-and-one-half-inch carnival chalk prize, similar to the Captain
Marvel prize, except for the glittered or cast in relief *S* added onto Superman's chest.
His facial expression seems to imitate Tom Tyler's from *The Adventures of Captain
Marvel* in Hollywood's serialized films.

it came to speaking with women. Certainly the reverse was also true; if a hero like Superman could not communicate fairly with Lois, why should women even try communicating with regular men? The entire relationship left Lois and Clark unfulfilled. Even though it was, on the surface, only two people supposedly in love, it became one of the strangest ménage-a-trois relationships in all of twentieth-century fiction.

Clark's nerd stereotype was unfortunate and grievous—it was simply because of his eyeglasses. His glasses were a perfect opportune otherness stereotype that most children automatically accepted: it designated every bespectacled young person of Superman's era during the 1940s and early 1950s as being physically challenged and unathletic, and it was torture for those who needed to wear eyeglasses. (I know. I wore them.) When projected onto a girl who wore glasses, the image implied that she was incapable of achieving beauty. (Was there ever a Miss America who wore glasses?) In my childhood, almost everyone watched Superman—we were all under the influence of the ill-conceived, glasses-wearing stereotype.

Superman did take the side of civil rights and religious tolerance for a very short time in the radio serial *The Adventures of Superman* (1946). He even fought against the Ku Klux Klan. Clayton Bud Collyer, the radio voice of Superman, in an interview with *Time* magazine spoke about Superman's campaign against racism; however, his campaign was short-lived at best because it was unpopular. (Or can we more accurately say because racism was popular?)

Superman's main competition in comic-book sales was Captain Marvel, created by C. C. Beck and Bill Parker in 1940. Captain Marvel stories were more lighthearted. For all of the 1940s, Captain Marvel was more popular than Superman, mainly because his was a fantasy story particularly suited for children. By saying "Shazam" newsboy Billy Batson could transform himself into Captain Marvel. Superman ran in comic strips from 1939 to 1966. *Superboy* was added to compete for children's love of Captain Marvel. In his earliest comic strips, Superman was harsh and violent; he might spank a woman and tell her she deserved it, or he might let criminals die without any sign of remorse.

Prior to *Superman*, Lee Falk's *The Phantom* comic books appeared in 1938, but they never achieved popularity. Action Comics #1 in 1938 initiated the appearance of America's new icon—*Superman.*

Superman was created by two college students, Jerry Siegel and Joe Shuster. During a hot night in 1933, Siegel, unable to sleep, got up and invented Superman. The next morning, Siegel raced twelve blocks to see his friend Shuster, who then drew the artwork for Superman's costume on the first try. The word "superman," from the German *ubermensch*, was coined by philosopher Friedrich Nietzsche in his book *Thus Spake Zarathustra* (1891). Zarathustra was superior in his morals and virtues—he would uplift everyone in the world. Siegel later stated that he had read the title of an American pulp-fiction book *Superman Doc Savage—Man of Master Mind and Body* and took some of his inspiration from that, but he was also inspired by Philip Wylie's novel *Gladiator* (1930), as well as Nietzsche's superman.

United Features refused Siegel and Shuster's first Superman story, saying "It was a rather immature piece of work." Five years later, in 1938, Siegel and Shuster finally found a publisher and sold their rights to Superman to Harry Donenfield of DC Comics for $10 a page for their thirteen-page story. To everyone's surprise, the Action Comics *Superman* became a huge success. Paul Sassienie, in his book *The Comic Book*, states:

> It is impossible to overestimate the significance or importance of Superman. He is indisputably the most imitated character in comics. It is likely that without him we would never have seen the likes of Spiderman, Wonder-Woman, X-Men and more specifically, Batman or, as he was known in 1938, the 'Bat-Man.'[3]

The radio show *Superman* made its debut in February of 1940. The Fleischers (of Betty Boop cartoons) introduced Superman animated cartoons in 1941; they were extravagant and lavish, enjoying immediate success. These cartoons introduced the "Look! Up in the sky! It's a bird! It's a plane! It's Superman!" and the "Faster than a speeding bullet" phrases spoken through Collyer's overdubbed voice.

The Adventures of Superman was broadcast weekly on national television to an even wider audience by 1951. The show ran until 1957 and starred George Reeves as Superman. Two years after the TV serial stopped running, Reeves was found dead in his home from a handgun wound, his death an apparent suicide caused by depression over being unable to find suitable work because he had been typecast as Superman. Conflicting circumstances surrounded his death and many believed he was murdered. Christopher Reeve began his Superman films in 1978. He was more successful at finding other film roles and was able to "escape the cape," as he put it.

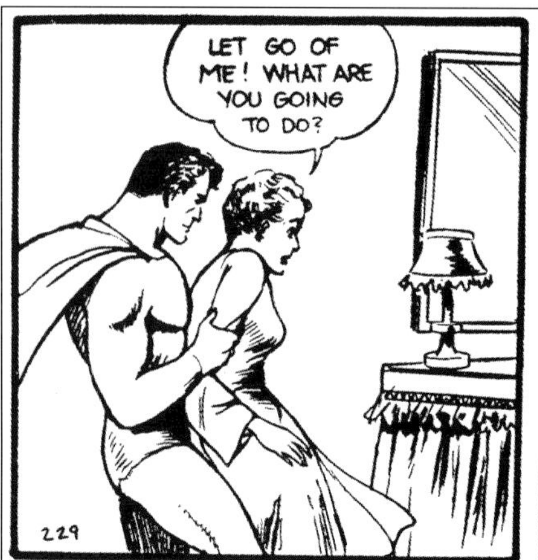

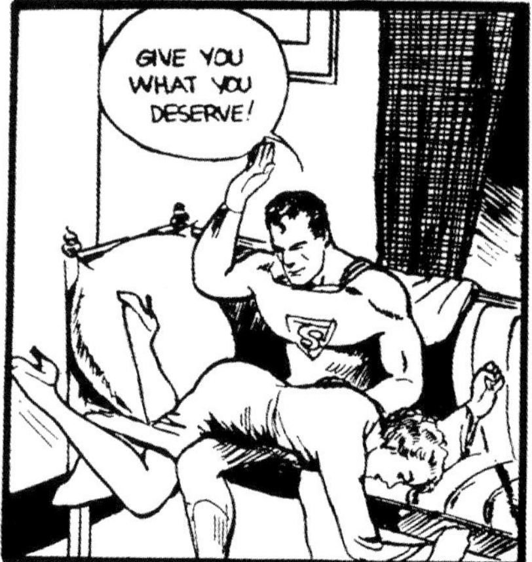

Superman, comic strip detail, Jerry Siegel and Joe Shuster, *Royal Death Plot*, 1939 © DC Comics

LUKE APPLING

(1907-1991)

OR IS IT BABE RUTH?

I swear, that park must have been built on a junk yard!
—LUKE APPLING, *commenting on Comiskey Park*

Voted the greatest living Chicago White Sox player in a 1969 fan poll, shortstop Luke Appling started with the Atlanta Crackers in the Southern Association. He was sold to the Chicago Cubs late in the 1930 season and then traded to the Chicago White Sox. At first, Appling was a less than remarkable player: his throws were highly inaccurate, sometimes winding up in the stands, and he was prone to muff just about any routine ground ball. After manager Jimmy Dykes took him under his wing in 1934, Appling learned how to throw accurately and to field ground balls. He adjusted his batting stance and became one of the most productive hitters and walk producers of his era. On one occasion, to wear down the opposing pitcher, Appling fouled off seventeen straight pitches before hitting a triple. In 1936, his greatest year, Appling led the American League with a .388 average. It was the first batting title won by a White Sox player. In 1943, at age thirty-five, he won his second batting title. The next year he enlisted in the service and entered World War II, missing most of the 1945 season. He established the Major League shortstop record for games played and double plays, and the American League record for putouts and assists. He acquired the nickname "Old Aches and Pains" for twenty years of griping about his physical ailments, the condition of the infield, or his salary. Appling was promised a $5,000 bonus if he won the batting title in 1936. He won it—the offer was rescinded, so he tore up his 1937 contract. When he agreed to play again, he was forced to accept a reduction in salary. Appling hit over .300 for fourteen years and was elected to the Hall of Fame in 1964.

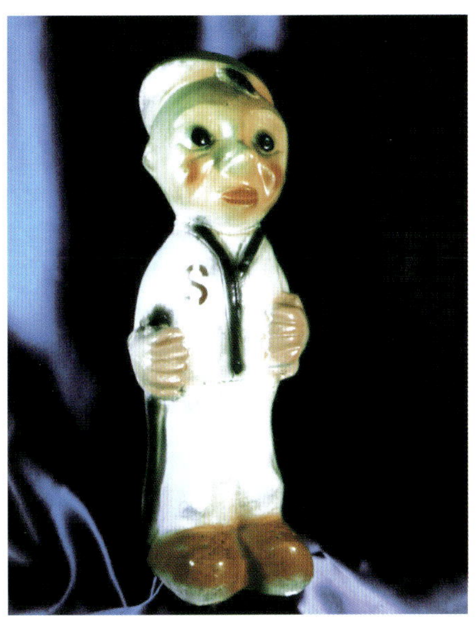

Chicago White Sox (?) fourteen-inch carnival chalk prize Or is it a "Why me?" caricature of Babe Ruth as a Boston Red Sox player? Ruth was traded from the Boston Red Sox to the Yankees in 1920 for $125,000.

Professional sports rely upon fans' archetypal need for escapism, thrills, winning and almost primordial patriotism to a local team and its turf. Baseball fans dream of their local team winning the World Series (which rarely happens), or they root for the NY Yankees, the nationalistic winner archetype.

PINOCCHIO

(1882-

Contrary to rumors that persist to this day, Walt Disney wasn't frozen. Sick jokes about it percolated through the studio for weeks after his death. One animator recalled a running gag at the time that freezing was Walt's attempt to make himself a warmer human being. In fact his body was cremated.
—MARC ELIOT, *Walt Disney: Hollywood's Dark Prince*

Walt Disney's *Pinocchio* opened in February of 1940. The most expensive animated film ever made, it retold the fairy tale originally created by Carlo Lorenzini (pen name C. Colodi), first published in 1882. So dissimilar was Disney's version that the author's surviving nephew, Paolo Lorenzini, sued Walt Disney Studio but lost the suit.

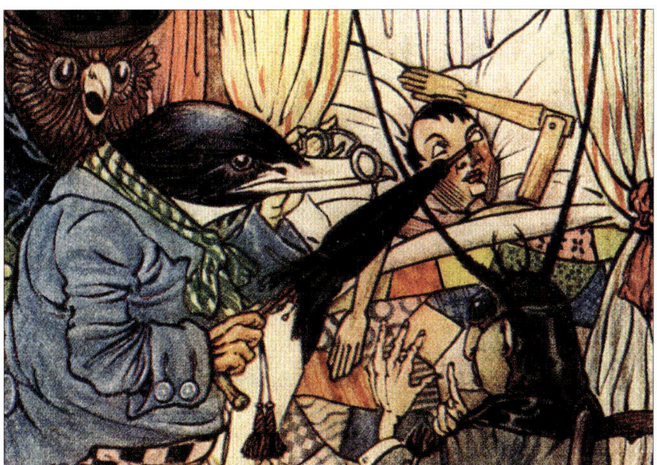

"The Doctors came immediately . . . " *Pinocchio*, C. Colodi, illustration detail, Charles Folkard © Grosset & Dunlap, 1910

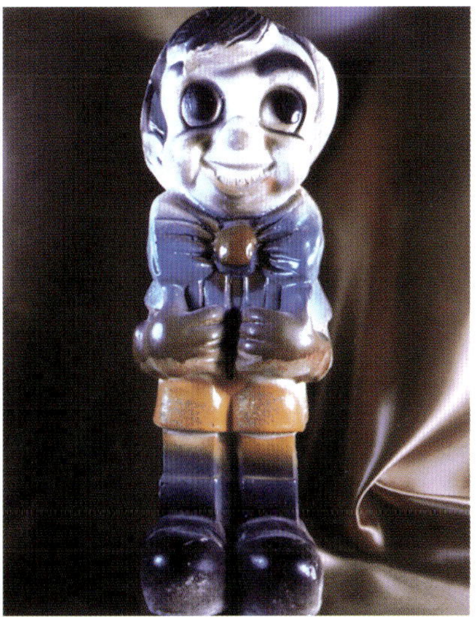

Pinocchio fourteen-inch carnival chalk prize

As in *Snow White and the Seven Dwarfs*, where good was attached to Snow White and evil was attached to the Old Hag, in *Pinocchio* good was attached to the puppet maker Gepetto and evil to the puppeteer Stromboli. Disney's

Pinocchio puppet was the vehicle through which Christian morality of good and evil was aptly demonstrated. It also provided a symbolic look at heaven and hell.

In Disney's allegorical film, Gepetto constructed Pinocchio, who simply wishes to be real. The Blue Fairy grants Pinocchio's wish, but only partially. Pinocchio moves, Pinocchio thinks, but he has no soul. (At this point he is something slightly less than the stereotypical heathen, who could be converted and has a soul.) She tells him that if he works hard, goes to school, and behaves, he will receive a soul. (Ah—conditions: there's the catch.) Disney disguised the Blue Fairy—she may look like the stereotype of a charming magical fairy or even a surrogate mother making requests of her son Pinocchio, which seems simple enough. But what does she really ask of him? In exchange for Pinocchio receiving a soul, she tells him to work hard (a promotion of the puritan work ethic), go to school (which means conform and learn), and behave (which means not to sin, a fundamentalist analogue for Christian morality). Although she looks sweet and glittery, the Blue Fairy is really a stereotype of the stern Sunday school teacher. After all, receiving a soul is not to be taken lightly. She is really threatening Pinocchio: if you work, learn, and behave, you will get a soul, otherwise you will remain soulless—meaning you have been bad. The real meaning is: those without a soul are heathens, they are bad and they burn in hell, but if you truly behave and receive a soul because you have not sinned, then you will go to heaven. Her catchword was "behave."

Disney then shows us what "behave" means, because Pinocchio is soon led astray by a variety of evil characters, including Stromboli. Pinocchio descends deeper into misbehaving, that is, into the valley of the shadow of death—a replay of the twenty-third Psalm. Romans 6:23 says "for the wages of sin is death." Pinocchio is approaching his cartoon hell. The narrator of the story is Jiminy Cricket—not quite playing Dante, though he does take the audience through a little of Disney's own idea of animated hell.

At the end, Pinocchio rescues Gepetto, who was swallowed by a great whale—an obvious analogue for the Jonah and the whale. For saving Gepetto, Pinocchio finally receives his soul from the Blue Fairy. As soul giver, she switches from Sunday school teacher to Christian minister, performing Pinocchio's baptism. The entire film is disguised to look like a cute birthday present come true, but the subliminal message underneath the present's wrapping is the stereotypical fundamentalist lesson of good equals heaven and sin equals hell.

The Blue Fairy is a surrogate for Walt Disney, who was the most important twentieth-century master of disguise. He wanted to be thought of as the kindhearted, upstanding, giving American, part of everyone's family known as Dear Uncle Walt—the gift giver of wonderful animated cartoon stories made especially for everyday America. Also like the Blue Fairy, he was an unforgiving, ever-righteous moralist and, because of his influence and wealth, he did indeed possess the potent powers of a controlling fairy—and affected many people's lives.

What about Walt Disney, a major figure in the Hollywood media of that era? What was on Disney's mind on the afternoon of November 29, 1938, in the midst of the production of *Pinocchio*, when he heard that his mother, Flora

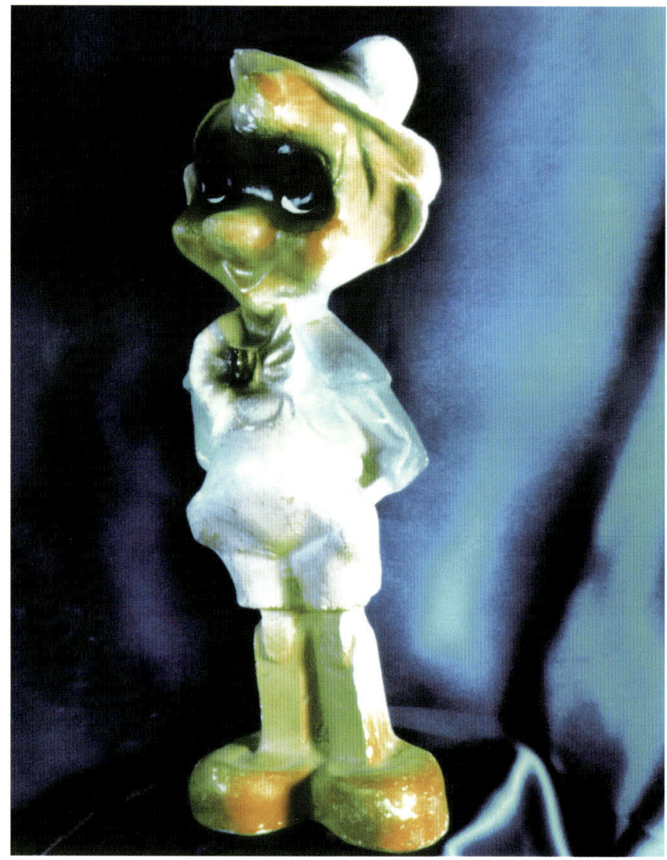

Pinocchio eleven-and-one-half-inch carnival chalk prize

Disney, had died, apparently from the fumes of a defective water boiler? He had always questioned whether she was his real mother, from the time when as a teenager he wanted to enlist in 1918 and couldn't get a valid birth certificate. The Department of Vital Statistics could only produce a certificate for a person named Walter Disney born on January 8, 1891, to Elis [*sic*] and Flora Disney, which of course was impossible, since he believed he was born in 1901. Mystery surrounded dates and documentation and a birth certificate could not be found. Without it, he could not enlist. Was he an illegitimate child?

When Disney heard of Flora's death, he was seized with grief. He refused to see anyone, including his wife, Lillian, until it was time to attend Flora's funeral several days later. For those miserable days he hid in his studio office. Oddly, Disney had recently selected and purchased the house that his parents moved into; his mother had become increasingly depressed under Elias's constant and unstable dominance. The cause of her death was listed as accidental asphyxiation, though there was one unanswered question: Elias had just set up his workshop in the basement, so why had no one else smelled fumes upstairs in the kitchen where she had died, particularly since the water boiler was in the basement?

After the funeral, Disney returned to the production of *Pinocchio*. He ordered all of the completed footage discarded and a new script written. The rewritten script left out the puppet maker's wife. Marc Eliot in *Walt Disney: Hollywood's Dark Prince*, suggests that the remake of *Pinocchio* was a traumatically projected self-examination:

Indeed, when projected through the lens of Disney's psyche, Pinocchio reveals a powerful Fundamentalist underpinning: the quest for self-redemption and the hellish fate that awaits those who lack the inner strength to resist the inherent evils of pleasure. Ultimately, the film becomes a journey through Disney's inner terrain over the involved question of his own parentage and, therefore, his "real" self. When Pinocchio lies to the Blue Fairy, for example, his "mother," his nose grows longer. Later he pays a penalty for this shameful display of moral imperfection, dramatized with striking Oedipal overtones, when, ironically, he "dies" and is placed in a coffin like environs. This tragic moment is followed, as it was in Snow White when she "died," by a miraculous rebirth, a symbolic passage to a far better life than the one left behind.[1]

Did he have a different mother? Possibly some of the answers are in the following: Elias and Flora Disney were married in the spring of 1888 and Elias took a job as hotel manager in Daytona Beach, Florida. Later that year, their first child, Herbert, was born, which suggests Flora was pregnant when they married. Elias enlisted to fight in the Spanish-American War in 1889. After seven days of basic training, he received a medical discharge. The family moved to Chicago. That same year, their second son, Raymond, was born. A third son, Roy, was born in 1893. Elias, a Fundamentalist Christian, worked for his minister, Walter Parr of the Christian Fundamentalist St. Paul Church. Elias declared that when he had another son he would name him Walter, after his minister and boss. He kept that promise. In 1901, Walter Elias Disney was supposedly born. Two years later, in debt from drinking and gambling, the sinner Elias moved the family to a farm in Marceline, Missouri. Elias became an active member of the American Social Democratic Party. He began holding evening diatribes, raging against the exploitation of the working class by wealthy Jews who ran the world's banks. By 1909, Herbert and Raymond left the farm, leaving sixteen-year-old Roy and eight-year-old Walt behind. The two boys worked hard on the farm, but to insure that the rules were kept, Roy and Walt suffered many beatings from Elias's heavy belt. Flora never interfered, nor apparently did she care. Roy was the only other human there for Walt's comfort. It was during this time that Walt began to draw pictures of the farm animals using a piece of coal on toilet paper, since the family was too poor for anything else. Farm animals became his most important friends, other than Roy. Of the daily beatings, Eliot explained:

It was in his brother's comforting arms that Walt found both the protective warmth he longed for from his mother and the feel of father's brute strength. Often he would fall asleep huddled close to Roy, then wake up suddenly in the middle of the night and urinate on his brother. Other times during the day, Walt would sneak into his mother's bedroom and put her clothes on and her makeup. Afterward, he would stand in front of her full-length mirror to admire his reflection. He knew this version of his mother, unlike the real one, would always be there when he needed her.[2]

By July 1936, with Disney's unparalleled fame and reputation as an upstanding American, J. Edgar Hoover sent Disney a recruitment letter asking him to act as an informant for the FBI. In 1940, Disney finally agreed, apparently in exchange for the FBI's continuing assistance in locating his mother's true identity. That same year, two FBI men went to the village of Mojacar, Spain, in search of information about Isabelle Zamora Ascensio, who may well have been Disney's real mother. Disney may have been her son, christened José Guirao.[3] In 1900, both Elias and Isabelle were in California. Was an extramarital tryst possible? Was a child born as a result of it? Many journalists have researched this story, including investigators under the Disney Studio's employ after Disney died. It has been suggested that whatever evidence Disney's investigators found was destroyed, perhaps to let sleeping dogs lie without tarnishing the Disney myth.

Elias died in 1941. It was the year *Fantasia* flopped and the studio went on strike. Most film scholars agree that Disney's creative genius for animated films ended at that time. He gave forceful testimony to the House Un-American Activities Committee in 1947. In 1954, Disney was promoted by J. Edgar Hoover and the FBI to Special Agent in Charge, which meant other agents below him now reported to him.[4] Disney sent their reports directly to Hoover.

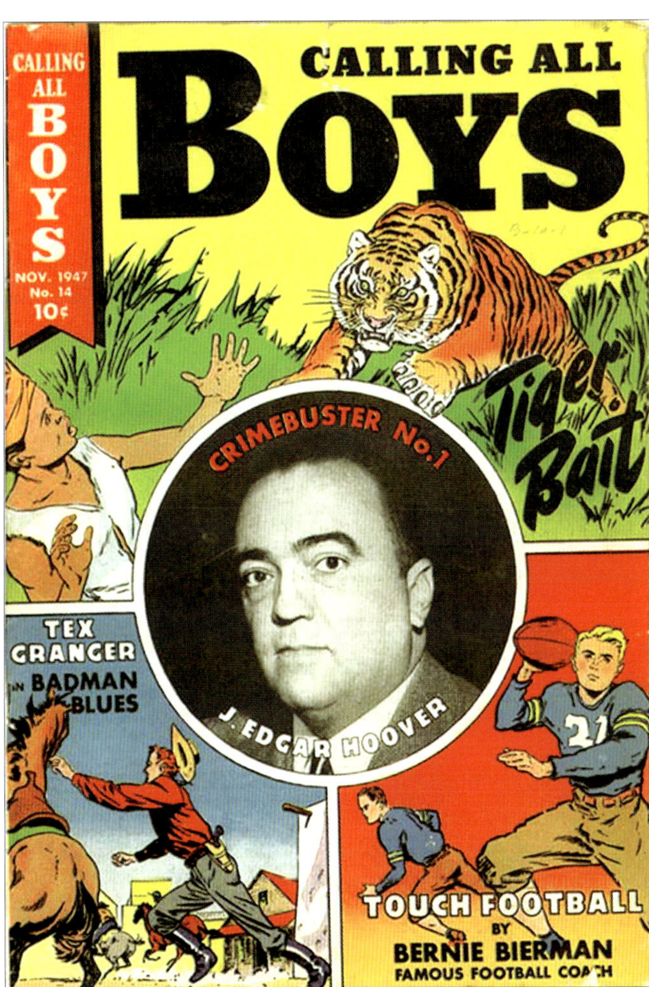

Cover, *Calling All Boys* comic, No. 14, November, 1947

L OUIS ARMSTRONG

(1901-1971)

*The way they are treating my people in the South, the government can
go to hell.*
—LOUIS ARMSTRONG

*I believe that today more than ever a book should be sought after
even if it has only one great page in it: we must search for fragments,
splinters, toenails, anything that has ore in it, anything that is capable
of resuscitating the body and soul. It may be that we are doomed,
that there is no hope for us, any of us, but if that is so then let us
set up a last agonizing, bloodcurdling howl, a screech of defiance,
a war whoop! Away with lamentation! Away with elegies and dirges!
Away with biographies and histories, and libraries and museums!
Let the dead eat the dead. Let us living ones dance about the rim of
the crater, a last expiring dance. But a dance!*
—HENRY MILLER, *Tropic of Cancer*

Cold empty bed...springs hurt my head
Feels like ole ned...wished I was dead
What did I do...to be so black and blue?

Even the mouse...ran from my house
They laugh at you...and all that you do
What did I do...to be so black and blue?

I'm white...inside...but, that don't help my case
That's life...can't hide...what is in my face?

How would it end...ain't got a friend
My only sin...is in my skin
What did I do...to be so black and blue?
—BLACK AND BLUE, jazz tune written by Andy Razaf and Fats Waller,
lyrics interpreted by Louis Armstrong, 1928-29.

*Always keep a white man behind you that'll put his hand on you and
say 'That's my nigger.'*
—LOUIS ARMSTRONG

Music has power—without a doubt, intense or gentle
sounds made by musical instruments and the human voice,
and various rhythms are among the strongest of archetypes.
Human instincts can be so influenced by music as to start
revolutions. Music is the most basic and intrinsic ingredient of all the cultures of the world. Sounds and rhythms are
stylized and fashioned to celebrate and induce love (most
commonly lamenting the lack of love), rally a nation to war or
revolution, bewail death, exuberate marriage, and so on. Media would be dull without music. So prevalent is music in all
its varieties that it is almost taken for granted. Like breathing,
it is part of our nature and seems to be an inherent ingredient
of our very survival.

No history of American jazz can be written without the inclusion of Louis Armstrong—the most important
jazz musician in the first half of the twentieth century. Born
in 1901 into an era of extreme racism, his natural showmanship played well to white audiences. His exuberant invented
vocals and exhilarating abilities on the trumpet made him a
favorite. He hid his anger about racism, paving the way for
other jazz musicians who came later, like Miles Davis, who
never hid his disgust for whitey. By the 1930s, Armstrong was
thought of as the world's greatest trumpet player. Later his
immense international fame made him America's "Ambassador of Goodwill." That became his stereotype. To many
African Americans, Armstrong's stage presence was, by necessity, in large part a play on the Jim Crow Uncle Tomness
that was apparent in his Hollywood films. Billie Holiday put it
best when she said Armstrong was "Tomming with his whole
heart," meaning that they both knew in the end it was the music that counted and you did what you did just to survive in the
white man's world.

Armstrong grew up in the era of minstrel shows and
blackface. His tragically honest song "Black and Blue"
thoroughly describes the multitude of horrid contradictions
any black had to face and tolerate just to exist. Marijuana was
his extension. He once explained to John Hammond, a record
producer who disapproved of marijuana, "It relaxes you,
makes you forget all the bad things that happen to a Negro.
It makes you feel wanted, and when you're with another tea
smoker it makes you feel a special kinship." He was proud to
be a "Viper"—a member of the fraternal order of the weed.[1]
The Ku Klux Klan was reinvigorated when Louis was fourteen years old; ten years later, in 1925, there were upward of 9
million Klan members. Civil rights was a distant dream and
hardly a coming reality. Armstrong's fame had grown, first
through live music, then through sound recordings, and finally
through Hollywood films. An example of him having to play
the part of the black fool—as well as Bing Crosby the white
racist—comes from Laurence Bergreen's biography, *Louis
Armstrong: An Extravagant Life*:

> In the film, *Pennies from Heaven* (1936), Crosby plays a
> wandering troubadour who resolves the difficulties of the
> less fortunate and, later on, inherits a haunted mansion that
> he converts into a nightclub. At this point Louis appears,
> casually dressed, and the two of them launch into some
> banter dwelling on black inferiority and subservience when
> Bing invites Louis to perform at the new club for a salary of
> ten percent of the business.
> "Is that enough?" Bing asks.
> "Well, yes. And, no," Louis replies. "There's seven
> men in the band. And none of us knows how to divide ten
> percent up by seven. So if you could make it only seven
> percent."
> Bing laughs his hail-fellow-well-met laugh, and agrees.
> Louis exclaims, "I told them cats you'd do the right
> thing."[2]

By 1957, an aging Armstrong could finally show his
years of pent-up frustration and anger when he called Dwight
Eisenhower a hypocrite because an African American girl
in Little Rock, Arkansas, was spit on and refused entry to
her local school due to the color of her skin. His statement,
"The way they are treating my people in the South, the
government can go to hell," surprised African Americans.
He refused to go on a Soviet tour and be America's goodwill
ambassador. He refused to work for any country that was in
conflict with its own people. Fortunately, his outspoken
honestly did not injure his career.

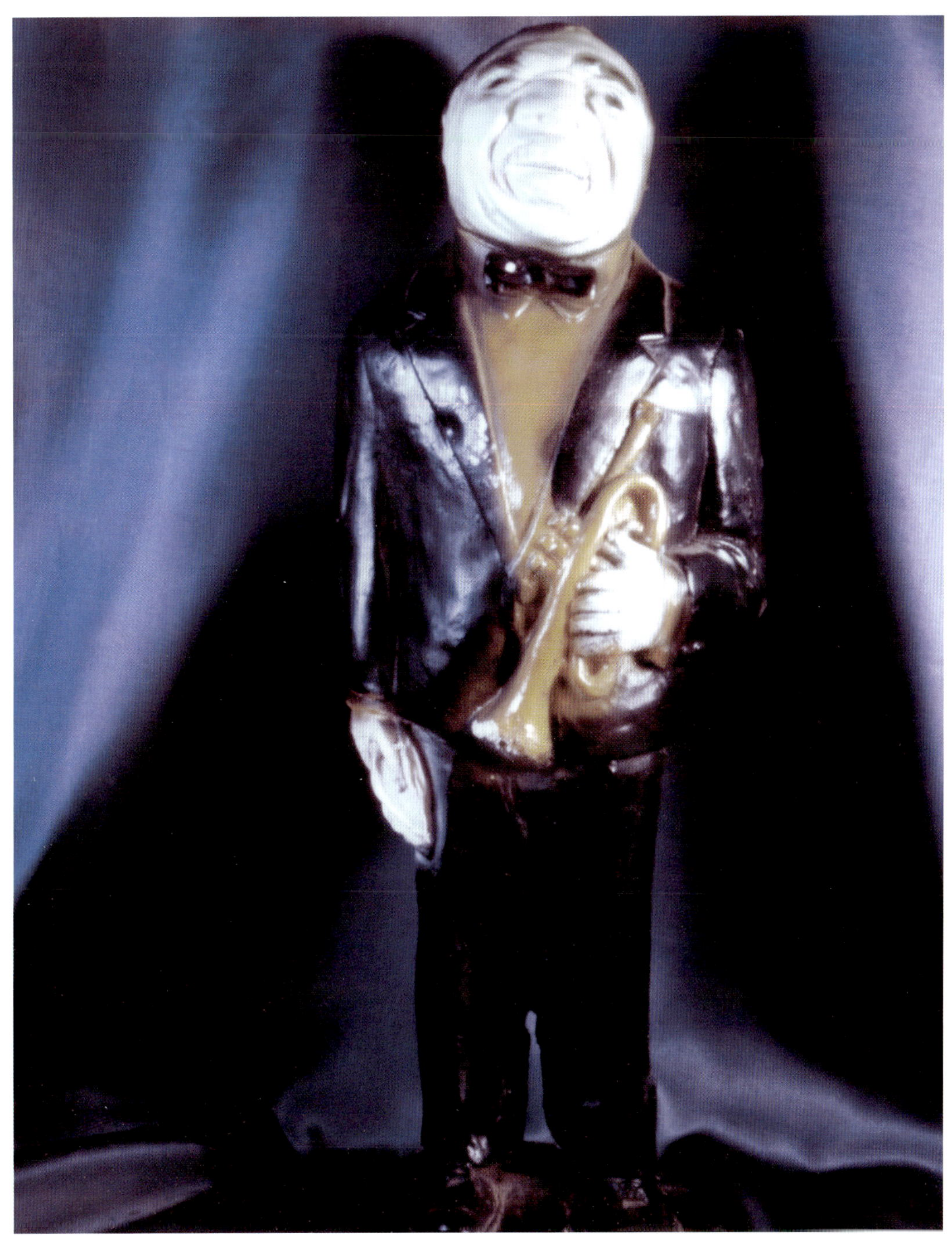

Louis Armstrong in whiteface fourteen-inch carnival chalk prize,
the most telling of all prizes. It embodies the irony of ironies: his
skin has been painted white! The carnival chalk manufacturer must
have loved him so much that they just couldn't bring themselves to
paint him black, so they painted him white. (Impossible for them
to revere a totally, totally, totally black man, after all.)

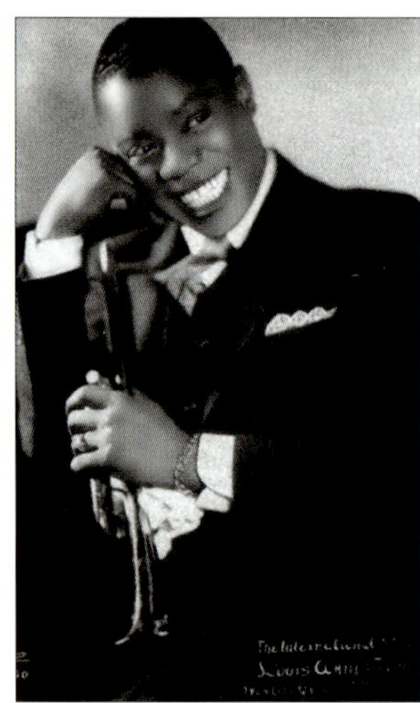

Louis Armstrong © Chicago 1933. Courtesy: Louis Armstrong House and Archives at Queens College/CUNY

Born into the most extreme poverty in Storyville, the prostitution and party area of New Orleans, Armstrong was surrounded by thieves, gamblers, pimps, prostitutes, and murderers. African Americans, like Armstrong, with the darkest skin coloring had the least chance of surviving and were thought of as on the bottom rung of a rickety ladder. Yet the desperate, colorful life that surrounded him in many ways matched his vibrant personality, and he never turned his back on that part of his early struggle. Luckily, he somehow lived through it. Many didn't. In 1913, at age twelve, Armstrong was sentenced to the Colored Waif's Home for firing a pistol in the air during a New Year's celebration. After proving he was not really a troublemaker, he was given a bugle to play, then the cornet. He had actually played a cornet before. The Waif's Home provided an environment where he could concentrate and focus on achieving skills on the horn. Strict discipline from the band leader, including the use of the lash, became part of his forced routine; eventually, he became the leader of the band. Later, after being released due to his parent's pleas, he hauled coal to the prostitutes, played music in the brothels and on the streets, and worked as an unsuccessful pimp from age thirteen to seventeen. In later years, Armstrong kept an active journal and of the period when he delivered coal to the prostitutes wrote:

> Since the Red Light District were Strictly All White—we Negroes were not Allowed to buy Anything Sexy. Some of those Girls who were Standing in the doorway of those Cribs, they looked just like a bunch of Girls who had just finished High School, or just received their Diplomas from College, they looked so young. They all had pimps to give their money to. As long as I was working for the white man—I could witness all this. Even the tough cops didn't bother me. And believe me they were really Tough. They were known to whip heads so fast until one would think that they had an Electric Stick. The whores had to have heat. So that's where I came in, and was safe and nobody bothered me.[3]

The trumpeter Joe Oliver, also known as "King" Oliver, became Armstrong's mentor and surrogate father. Armstrong called him "Papa Joe." After Storyville was destroyed, Oliver moved to Chicago. Slightly later, Armstrong received the famous telegram from Papa Joe asking him to join the band in Chicago—a dramatic move that altered Armstrong's life forever. It was in Chicago that he used an indoor bathtub for the first time!

By 1923, sound recordings were being produced and Armstrong's as well as Oliver's chance came to record for Gennett Records, a company that also recorded promotional songs for the KKK—songs like, "Johnny, Join the Klan."[4]

In the sad, often-repeated irony of a jazz musician's life, Oliver's popularity faded; he ran out of money and moved to Georgia, where he worked as a janitor in a poolroom until his unheralded death in 1938.

Over time, Armstrong's name would emerge as the most influential jazz musician from 1925 to 1955. Most notable jazz musicians of today still recognize him as the first father and preeminent genius of jazz and pay homage to his ever-fresh musical inventions and interpretations. He was married four times; his final marriage in 1940 was to Lucille Wilson, a chorus girl at the Cotton Club and Armstrong's "Brown Sugar." They were together until his death in 1971, when he suffered a major heart attack and died in his sleep. Armstrong was, and still is, a genius musician—"still is" because the gift of his genius lives forever in his recordings. He patronized and survived whitey's world because that was the framework he found himself in and one he had to tolerate in order to vent his passion for his art form. It took guts not so much to enter the antagonist's world and play the part but to follow his passion and genius in the face of it. One wonders how many downtrodden, racially ostracized geniuses who lacked Armstrong's special courage the world has been deprived of over the centuries and what has been lost to everyone because of it. Armstrong became an archetypal symbol for the genuine man.

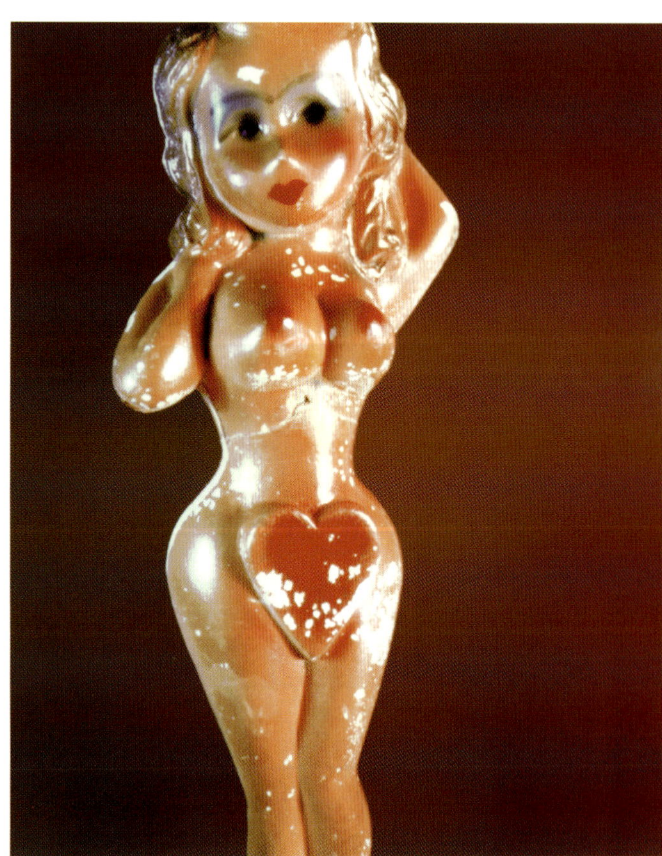

Stripper Heart thirteen-inch carnival chalk prize

Carnival Stripper Prostitute

See, saw, Margery Daw,
Sold her bed and lay upon
straw.
Was she not a dirty slut,
To sell her bed and live in
dirt?
—Mother Goose Rhyme, 1898

The despair among the loveless is that they must narcotize themselves
before they can touch any human being at all.
—James Baldwin

The carnival chalk figure of a busty naked woman with a heart over her genital area was not intended as a Valentine's Day doll. It was most likely a double entendre— a humorous representation of a heart-shaped G-string on a carnival stripper, who through circumstance did double duty as a carnival prostitute. The heart shape typically symbolizes love and instills the warm feeling derived from the shape's archetypal motif, but the wicked heart on this chalk figure metaphorically directs men's desire toward her erogenous zone and the misplaced, patriarchal mind twist that equates love with lust. The strategically placed heart's function was also intended to suggest that sex with the carnival stripper was readily available—for a price. (Perhaps it would not have been as tasteless and nasty, and more to the point, if her pubic area had been covered with a dollar sign.) A carnival stripper's value was easily calculated; if she performed well, the boss could see that the people in the audience were sexually aroused.

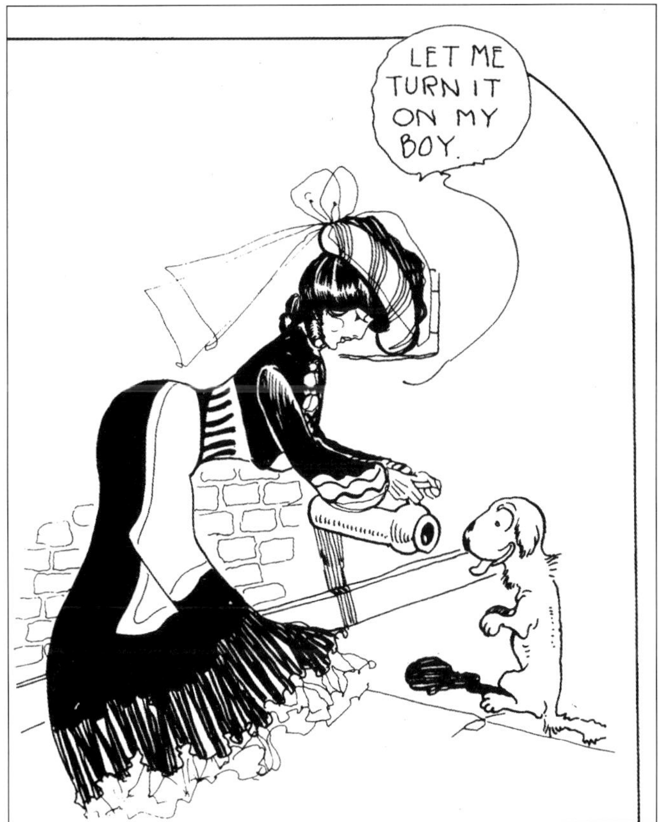

Lady Bountiful, comic strip detail, circa 1910 © *New York Herald*

Prostitution depends on similar instincts; it is generated by a need for purchased lust, which is embodied in the prostitute's archetypal motif. Unfortunately the prostitute is also a symbol for feeling violence against women, or violence against men if the prostitute is a man. The accompanying photo of carnival strippers' backsides lustfully satisfied some viewers

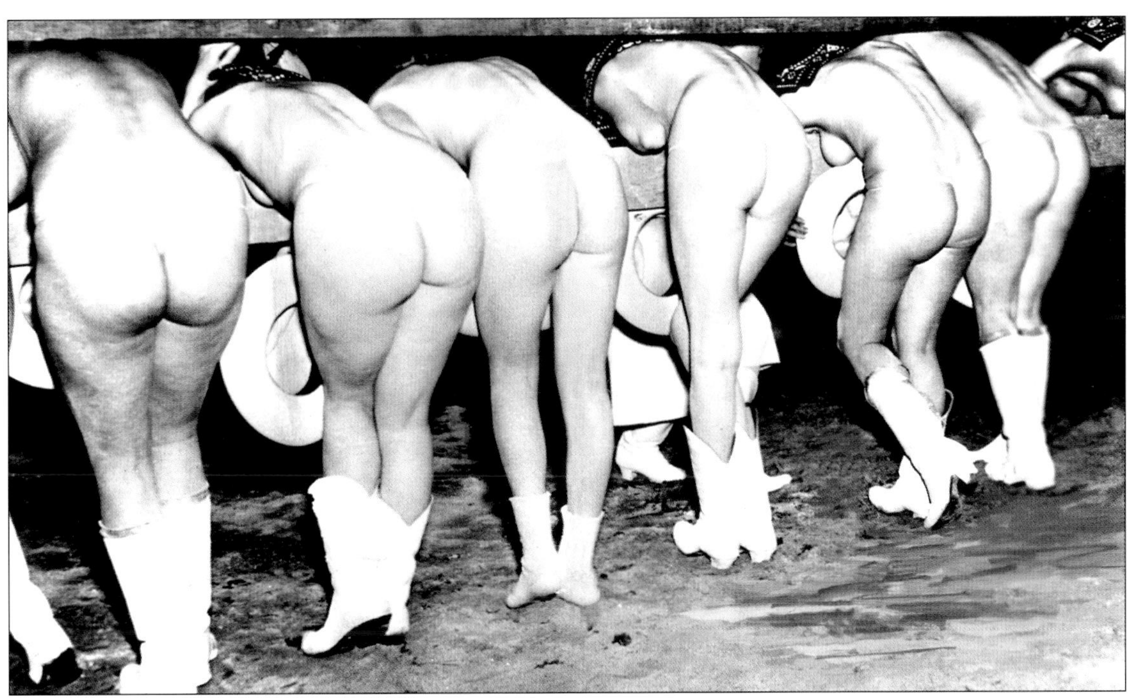

Carnival strippers, Harry G. Seber of California Revue, circa 1940s

but could be repulsively disgusting to others. Both are instinctive responses. Calling prostitution "the oldest profession" is a sexist slur against women. But because it is so familiarly embedded in our clichés, it is not as obvious a slur as one might expect and its implications generally pass unnoticed. Most people simply agree with it without giving it a thought. Prostitution arrived in America with colonization. It was part of a patriarchal system that gave men dominion over women in a situation of culturally enforced violence against women. Colonial women had almost no rights and were confined to their gender role in both the North and the South. The puritanism in the North proffered that men were capable of understanding logic, reason, and spirituality, while women were not. Southern women were also dependent on men, not through puritanism but through the decorum and constraints of family stature. Prostitution in the North started simply as a means of survival. Many women lacked clothing and food, so sex was bartered for these necessities. This was especially true of the workers who arrived in the New World prior to 1820, when 60 percent of the white immigrants were indentured for a minimum of seven or eight years. This New World type of prostitution, defined by early colonial standards, was neither an occupation nor a commercial vice; it was only a temporary sin. Black female slaves were forced to comply with their masters' sexual needs and money did not change hands. Rape was not illegal. This constituted patriarchal violence against women and was rampant in both the North and the South.

The first laws against streetwalker prostitution were passed in 1699 in New Amsterdam, Boston, and Philadelphia. Prostitution as a commercial enterprise mushroomed in tandem with increased industrialization and population growth in the 1800s. Sex was big business, but it was also a moral issue. Leviticus 19:29 stated "Do not prostitute thy daughter to cause her to be a whore, lest the land fall to whoredom, and the land become full of wickedness." This infamous invective is a slur against parents and daughters, and women in general. Every unmarried woman who lost her virginity through any circumstance, whether for pay, through rape, or for love, was considered a fallen woman. Naturally this was not the case for men. Unmarried women who found themselves in this untenable situation were often forced to turn to prostitution because they were generally deemed unfit for marriage. Exchanging sex for money was consistently blamed on women, when the blame should have been more accurately placed on the patriarchal system that forced them into those humiliating straits.

The first anti-prostitution organizations in northeastern American cities were founded in the 1820s and attempts were made to eradicate prostitution and forcibly shut down brothels. This Sisyphean task had little success. By the 1860s, prostitution was an intrinsic part of mining and ranching life in the West. Some mining towns designated one side of their street for brothels and prostitutes, while the other side was reserved for respectable family women. In cities like San Francisco, 85 percent of the Chinese women were prostitute slaves, having been brought to America for that singular purpose (page 71).

The 1870s brought another wave of anti-prostitution

attempts in the northeast. A more reasonable acceptance of prostitution became the standard, and specific red light districts were created and deemed within the law. However, by the 1880s and 1890s, puritanical standards rose to the forefront once again and female reformers advocated minimum wage laws to help working women (but not women working as prostitutes). They sought punishment for men who used the services of prostitutes and provided instructions in proper morals for prostitutes. But control of prostitution was not an easy matter in the eastern cities, since minimum wage laws were counterproductive, particularly with immigration numbers soaring during those decades. It was impossible to shut down the brothels in the red light districts. Corrupt officials and the police had developed strong and profitable liaisons with the madams, pimps, and prostitutes within their domains.

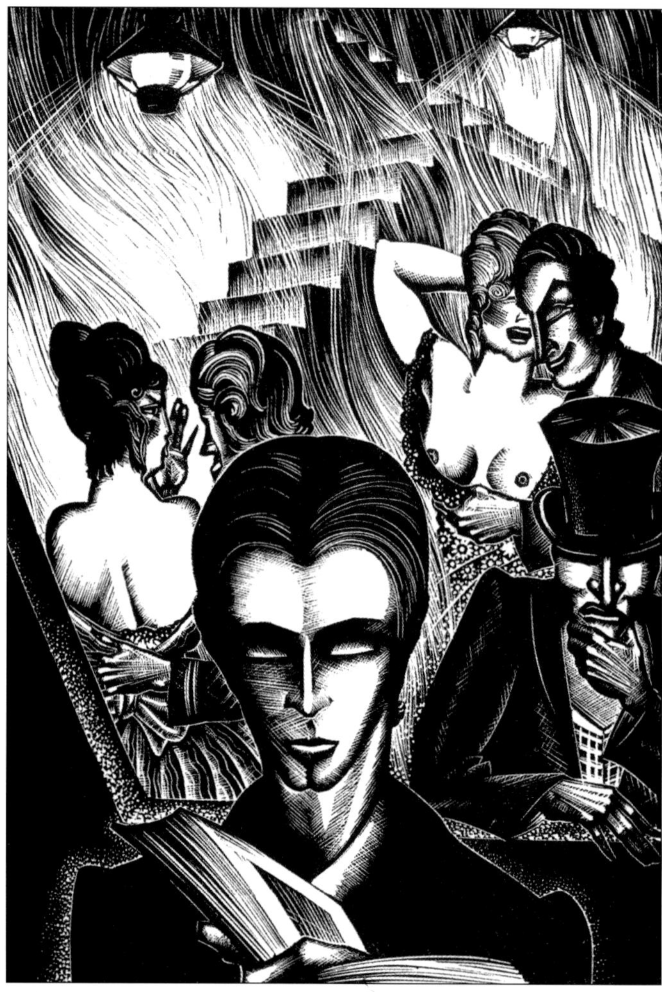

Mad Man's Drum, woodcut Lynd Ward © Jonathan Cape and Harrison Smith Inc., 1930

By 1910, Congress had passed the Mann Act, which prevented interstate transportation of women for immoral reasons, and the May Act, which prohibited prostitution on military bases. Both laws were fairly unenforceable. How, and by what means, could interstate transportation be monitored? As for the May Act, prostitutes simply moved off the military bases and into the surrounding neighborhoods. To illustrate the May Act's ineffectiveness, during World War I more American men left the service disabled due to venereal disease than war wounds. In a weak effort to appease the gnatlike reformers, prostitutes were fined when caught in the act but not jailed, and probation was mandatory. Young prostitutes continued to be subjected to instructions in morality. This system eventually failed and degenerated further into individual state's criminal systems through which prostitutes were jailed. Once prostitution was elevated to a criminal act, and was no longer simply a moral offense, the foundations were laid for the endless cycle of jail, release, poverty, prostitution—followed in turn by jail, release, poverty, drugs, prostitution—a sad and destructive cycle that persists to this day.

The urban ghetto of the 1920s and 1930s was the womb of the African American pimp. The roots of pimping ran deep and emergence from the ghetto during the civil rights era gave the African American pimp a top-dollar trade. "Sugar Daddy" was the street name for pimp, both white and African American. "Sugar" referred to a prostitute, regardless of ethnicity. Explaining the derivation of these terms, John Kendrick wrote:

> It's a common slang term from at least the early 20th Century—possibly earlier. The phrase stems from the use of "sugar" as a slang equivalent for both "sex" and "money"— it not only referred to prostitutes and pimps, but to rich men and their kept women. Examples of the popular use for "Daddy"—1938—Mary Martin's character in *Leave It to Me* sang "My Heart Belongs to Daddy." 1949—Carol Channing's Lorelei Lee in *Gentlemen Prefer Blondes* explained that she learned "the one you call your Daddy ain't your Pa."[1]

Money, mind control, and power are seen to be reason enough for the exploitative profession of pimping, although some women think they need their pimp's protection, direction, and connection. Another compelling factor (one that hasn't disappeared) was that there were few employment opportunities for intelligent African Americans. Malcolm X is a good example—in his youthful, pimping years he was known as Detroit Red. Another is writer Maya Angelou, who at eighteen was a prostitute. She wrote: "I answer the heroic question 'Death, where is thy sting?' with 'It is here in my heart and mind and memories.' "

Iceberg Slim, one of the most famous African American pimps of the 1940s, wrote in *Pimp*:

> A pimp is the loneliest bastard on Earth. He's gotta know his whores. He can't let them know him. He's gotta be God all the way. A pimp is happy when his whores giggle. He knows they are still asleep . . . all whores have one thing in common just like the chumps humping for the white boss. It thrills 'em when the pimp makes mistakes. They watch and wait for his downfall.[2]

Early in his book he explained his first encounter being abused for someone else's sexual pleasure (his slang term for this is "Georgied"):

> Her name was Maude and she "Georgied" me around 1921. I was only three years old. Mama told me about it, and always when she did her rage and indignation would be as

strong and as emotional perhaps as at the time when she [Mama] had surprised her [Maude] panting and moaning at the point of orgasm with my tiny head wedged between her ebony thighs, her massive hands viselike around my head. Mama worked long hours in a hand laundry and Maude had been hired as a baby sitter at fifty cents a day. Maude was a young widow. Strangely, she had a reputation in Indianapolis, Indiana as a devout Holy Roller. I have tried through the years to remember her face, but all I can remember is the funky ritual. I vaguely remember not her words, but her excitement when we were alone. I remember more vividly the moist, odorous darkness and the bristle-like hairs tickling my face and most vividly I can remember my panic, when in the wild moment of her climax, she would savagely jerk my head even tighter into the hairy maw.[3]

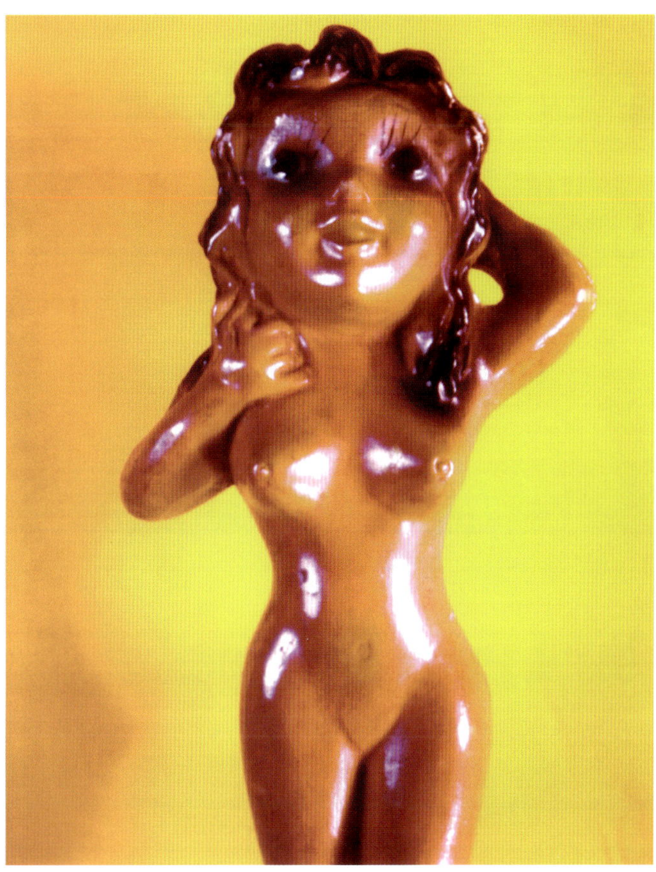

Nude fifteen-inch carnival chalk prize

Presently, average prostitution arrest numbers break down to 70 percent female prostitutes, 20 percent male prostitutes, and 10 percent customers. A minority of prostitutes are women of color; however, an inordinate majority of prostitutes sentenced to jail are women of color. Of those arrested, 85 to 90 percent work on the street, even though street work accounts for just about 20 percent of prostitution. The Department of Health consistently reports that only 3 to 5 percent of sexually transmitted diseases in this country are related to prostitution, compared with 30 to 35 percent among teenagers.

Violence is one of the major problems for prostitutes. Though figures vary, one report states that 60 percent of the abuse against street prostitutes is perpetrated by clients, 20 percent by police, and another 20 percent from within their domestic situation. Research suggests that prostitutes in general suffer from negative identities or lack of self-esteem, although a 1986 study by Diane Prince found that 97 percent of call girls and brothel workers had higher self-esteem after they became prostitutes. According to Kinsey's report, 70 percent of adult men have engaged in prostitution at least once.

In 1973, the US National Organization for Women passed a resolution supporting the decriminalization of prostitution. Twenty years earlier, in 1949, the United Nations adopted a resolution in favor of the decriminalization of prostitution. It was ratified by fifty countries, but not by the United States (where prostitution is legal only in parts of Nevada). Many countries complied by decriminalizing prostitution per se, but leaving all related activities, such as soliciting and advertising, illegal. Even where prostitution is legalized, equality and human rights are compromised.

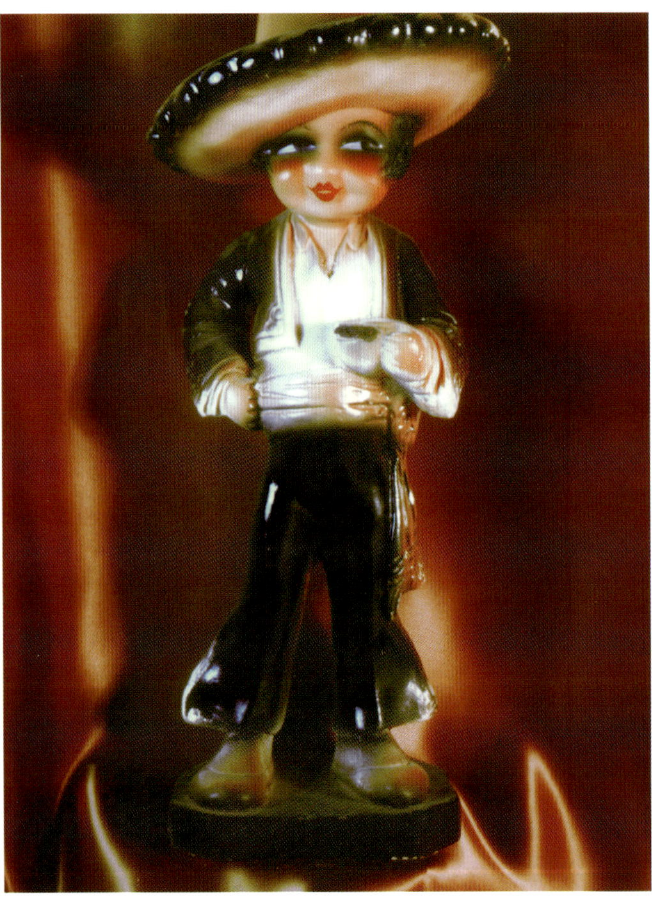

Mexican girl fifteen-inch carnival chalk prize © June Yates Jenkins.

Unfortunately, Mexico has long been thought of as an easy place to find a special friend; border cities like Tijuana and Juarez are notorious for prostitution, including child prostitution (as always the prostitute takes the slur and not the purveyor). The United Nations presently lists Mexico as the North American center of pedophile organizations. An estimated 10,000 Mexican children are currently involved in prostitution, pornography, and sex tourism. There are no laws in Mexico that define child prostitution and child pornography as criminal, although sex workers are expected to be at least eighteen years old.

L ITTLE GENEVIEVE (1940-1950)

the way to hump a cow is not
to get yourself a stool
but draw a line around the spot
and call it beautifool

to multiply because and why
dividing thens by nows
and adding and (i understand)
is hows to hump a cows

the way to hump a cow is not
to elevate your tool
but drop a penny in the slot
and bellow like a bool

to lay a wreath from ancient greath
on insulated brows
while tossing boms at uncle toms
is hows to hump a cows

the way to hump a cow is not
to push and then to pull
but practicing the art of swot
to preach the golden rull

to vote for me (all decent mem
and wonens will allows
which if they don't to hell with them)
is hows to hump a cows
—e. e. cummings

Little Genevieve was played by Ted Morse on the 1940s radio show *National Barn Dance* on WLS in Chicago, which competed for country listenership with the *Grand Old Opry*. *National Barn Dance* had a live studio audience of around 2,000, so Morse got plenty of laughs dressed in Little Genevieve's ruffled baby dress and bonnet. Little Genevieve was a crybaby; she cried on every show. Morse, at 250 pounds, was also a trumpet player in the instrumental group known as the Virginia Hams, as well as Otto in Otto and the Novelodeons, but he was most famous as humorously cross-dressed Little Genevieve. The carnival chalk prize of Little Genevieve shows Morse with a pleased little pig held between

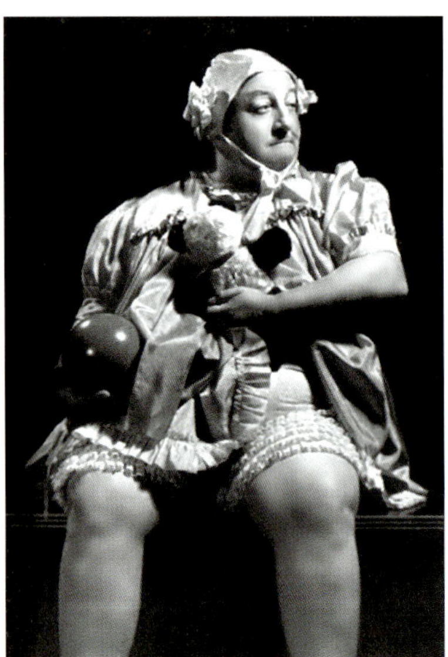

Ted Morse as Little Genevieve. Courtesy: Jack French

his large baby legs. During the late 1940s and early 1950s,

Alfred Kinsey's research revealed that 50 percent of rural men stated they had sex with animals, so it is not unlikely that rural humor would appreciate the archetypal motif of the happy pig.

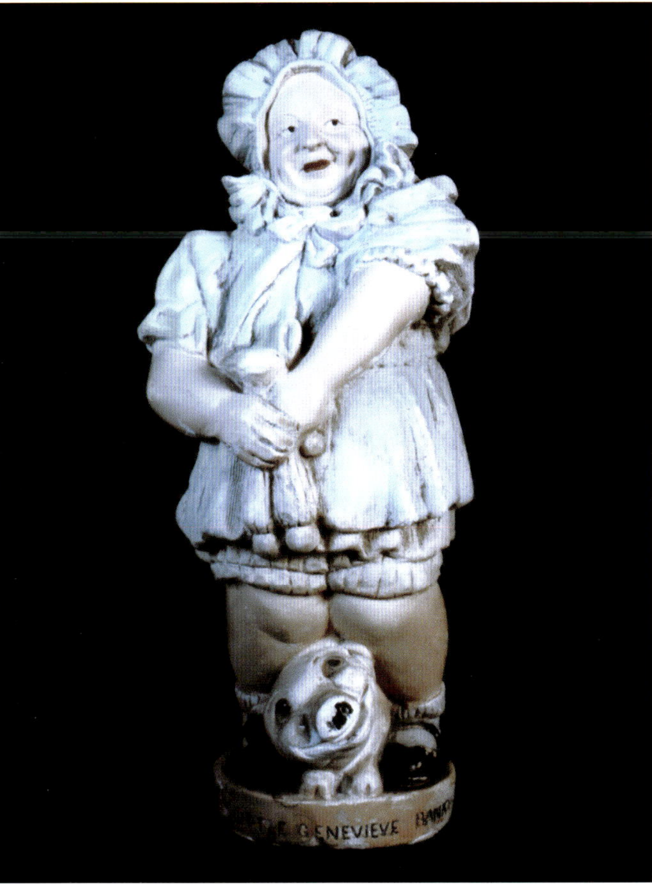

Little Genevieve ten-inch carnival chalk bank prize

Animals have always been alluring archetypal symbols for people whose instinctive sexual urges required various satisfaction remedies beyond relations with a human, although the subject is usually hushed. An early writing about bestiality comes from Procopius in his *Secret History* who tells of Empress Theodora, wife of emperor Justinian, ruler of the Byzantine Empire (527 AD). From early childhood Theodora had performed on revue stages. When Justinian fell in love with her she was very young and a comic in the, "Leda burlesque where she performed with a goose that was trained to pick out grains of corn from between her thighs whilst she writhed in transports of delight."[1] The erotic allure of an sensual Leda with her devoted swan has fascinated visual artists for centuries.

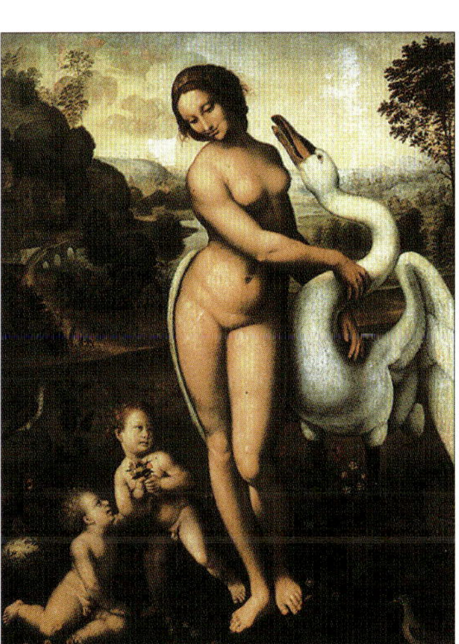

Leda and the Swan, copy, original Leonardo da Vinci painting lost, circa 1510-15, Galleria Borghese, Rome

MICKEY ROONEY
AS ANDY HARDY (1937-1958)

No, no, no, judge! You don't understand; she don't understand, either. Oh, she don't mean no harm to us, but . . . we're not her kind of people —or yours, either. We belong in show business. We gotta start young so we can get some steel in our backbone. Well, gee, we're developing. You couldn't teach us a trade: we've GOT one. And you couldn't do without it . . . Oh, we're only kids now, but someday we're gonna be the guys that make ya laugh and cry and think that there's a little stardust left on life's dirty old pan. Oh, she don't understand: she'd put butterflies to work makin' rubber tires!
—MICKEY ROONEY, *Babes in Arms*, 1939

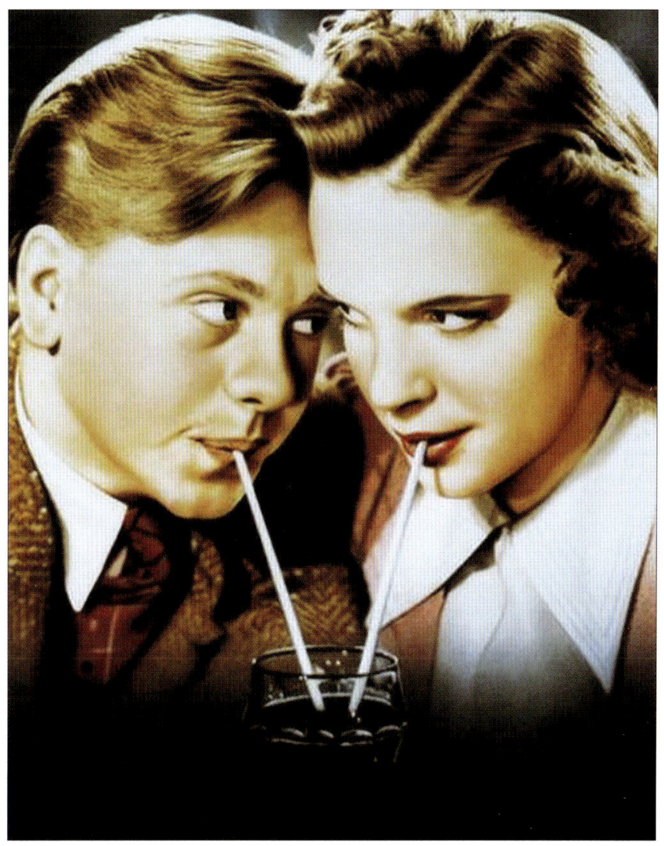

Detail, Lobby poster, Mickey Rooney and Judy Garland, *Love Finds Andy Hardy*, 1938 © M-G-M. This glowing archetypal image of love—eyes transfixed, sucking on straws sharing a soda—perfectly defines that 1938 moment when Hollywood promoted the purity and innocence of a boy and girl attempting to find togetherness for their first time.

Hollywood's eternally bouncy, energetic boyish, save-the-day teenage human equivalent to Disney's cartoon Mickey Mouse was a well-mannered Mickey Rooney in his sixteen Andy Hardy films. (Mickey Rooney claimed to have sat on Disney's knee and helped Walt name Mickey Mouse, making Rooney's lengthy life story an odd fantasy-quest.) Somehow five foot tall Mickey Rooney performed the miracle of entertaining most Americans through those tormented and anxious years prior to World War II—as well as into the maelstrom and madness after Pearl Harbor. He had lots of help from Ann Rutherford, who played across from him, as well as Andy Hardy series guests Lana Turner and Judy Garland. Usually falling in love was as easy as learning the a-b-c's.

If you count the low budget *A Family Affair* (1937) as the first Andy Hardy film, then nineteen years later *Andy Hardy Comes Home* (1958) ended the series (on a sour note). *A Family Affair* was based on the 1928 play *Skidding* by Aurania Rouverol, wisely purchased by M-G-M. The series was continued when the first Andy Hardy film was so popular, well beyond M-G-M's expectations. Andy Hardy films were happy and sappy family oriented fun reinforcing wholesome family values taught by family patriarch Judge Hardy, played by Lionel Barrymore in the first episode.

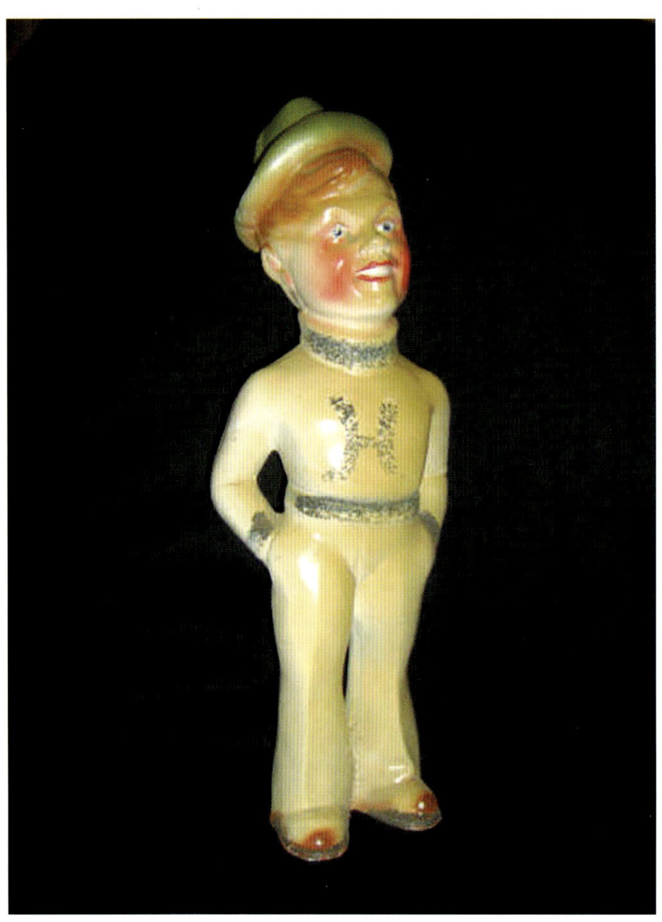

Mickey Rooney fourteen-inch carnival chalk prize. Collection: Kathie and Lanny Patrick

Andy Hardy is fantasy. Mickey Rooney's life has not been that easy. His acting career began at seventeen months wearing a pint-size tuxedo and reciting speeches as part of his parent's vaudeville act. Did he ever really have a life as a child, teenager or adult? By 1926, (at six) he played the midget in *Not to be Trusted*. His demonic performance as Puck in *A Midsummer Night's Dream* (1935) is considered his most artistic. With the Andy Hardy series, Rooney was the #1 box office draw from 1939-1941. But, starting in 1949, and no longer a child or teenage actor, his films became tawdry and without praise. In *Baby Face Nelson* (1957) he is the archetypal David against Goliath, but this David is a demented runt sporting a Tommy gun and hating humanity. With eight marriages and two hundred films to his credit, his need to make Rooneyesque appearances has not diminished. He is still acting.

Johnny Appleseed

(1774-1845)

I like pretty things the best.
—Grandma Moses

One does not sell the land paeople walk on.
—Crazy Horse, September 23, 1875

Johnny Appleseed was America's renowned wilderness wandering folk hero of the post–Revolutionary War era. Rather than an archetypal symbol for a macho warrior (a Davy Crockett type) whose symbols of advanced weaponry were the gun or Conestoga wagon, Johnny Appleseed represented the gentle warrior, a more ethereal but necessary bountiful civilizer whose weaponry was simply seeds to plant—helping turn the untamed wilderness into civilized, cultivated garden plots, homes, and prettified villages. Both the gun and the apple seed were equally important if America was to fulfill its quest for Manifest Destiny.

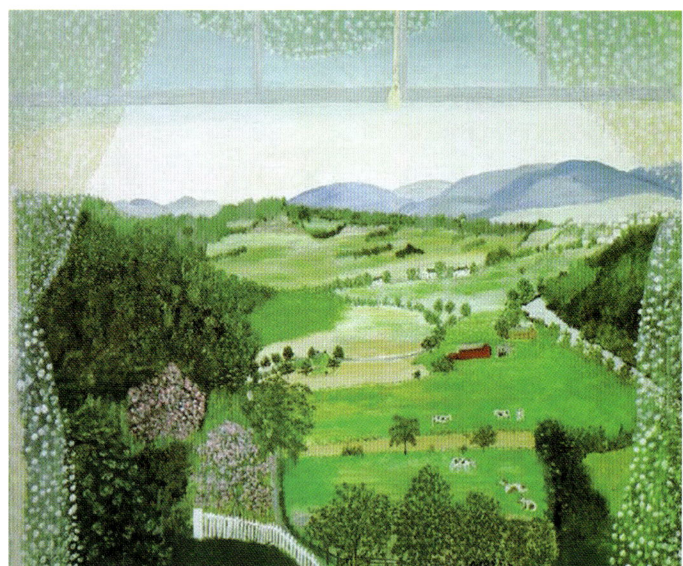

Hoosick Valley from the Window, Grandma Moses, oil, 1946, private collection

Johnny Appleseed supplied apple seeds and Swedenborgian religious tenets to the myriad of homesteaders who were required to "plant fifty apple or pear trees" per allotment—a law intended to insure that the land was actually being used by its recipients and not just held as land speculation. The legendary Johnny Appleseed displayed the unusual blending of a gentle, loving, sharing yet puritanlike Saint Francis; a poor, suffering, self-denying mystic; and a caring-for-others trumpeter sounding the alarm. Who he really was is not known, other than that his religious fervor pushed him to the far reaches of the frontier. Mythological stories like "Johnny Appleseed—A Pioneer Hero" were published in the 1871 *Harper's New Monthly Magazine*. This widely read article conveyed various aspects of his personality, sketched from life by W. D. Haley. Johnny Appleseed was a real person, but Haley's story is more

190

a work of fiction than fact, meant to elicit feelings of awe, an archetypal god of the wilderness, forest, and plain. Haley wrote:

> . . . but Johnny would shoulder his bag of apple seeds, and with bare feet penetrate to some remote spot that combined picturesqueness and fertility of soil and there he would plant his seeds, place a slight enclosure around the place, and leave them to grow until the trees would be large enough to be transplanted by the settlers, who, in the mean time, would have made their clearings in the vicinity.
>
> . . . He was a most earnest disciple of the faith taught by Emmanuel Swedenborg, and himself claimed to have frequent conversations with angels and spirits; two of the latter, of the feminine gender, he asserted, had revealed to him that they were to be his wives in a future state if he abstained from a matrimonial alliance on earth. He entertained a profound reverence for the Swedish seer, and always carried a few old volumes with him.
>
> . . . Our informant refers to one of these [instances] when the news of Hull's surrender came like a thunderbolt upon the frontier. Large bands of Indians and British were destroying everything before them and murdering defenseless women and children, and even the blockhouses were not always a sufficient protection. At this time Johnny traveled day and night, warning the people of the approaching danger. He visited every cabin and delivered this message: "The spirit of the Lord is upon me, and he hath anointed me to blow the trumpet in the wilderness, and sound an alarm in the forest; for, behold, the tribes of the heathen are round about your doors, and a devouring flame followeth after them."
>
> . . . The Indians also treated Johnny with the greatest kindness. By these wild and sanguinary savages he was regarded as a "great medicine man," on account of his strange appearance, eccentric actions, and especially the fortitude with which he could endure pain, in proof of which he would often thrust pins and needles into his flesh. His nervous sensibilities seem to have been less acute than those of ordinary people, for his method of treating the cuts and sores that were the consequences of his barefooted wanderings through briars and thorns was to scar the wound with a red-hot iron and then cure the burn.[1]

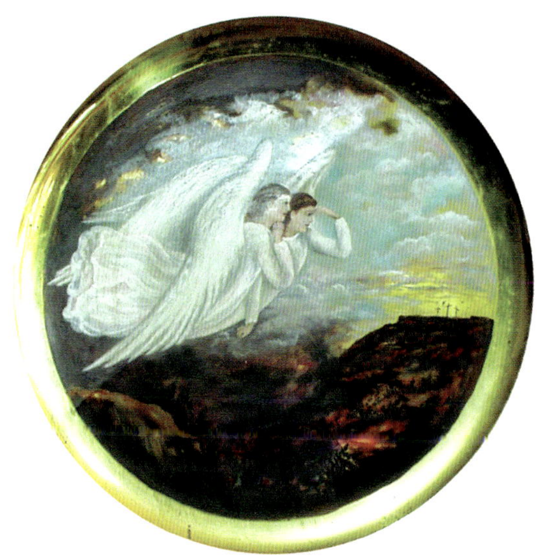

Angels, folk art, oil on tin plate, circa 1890s

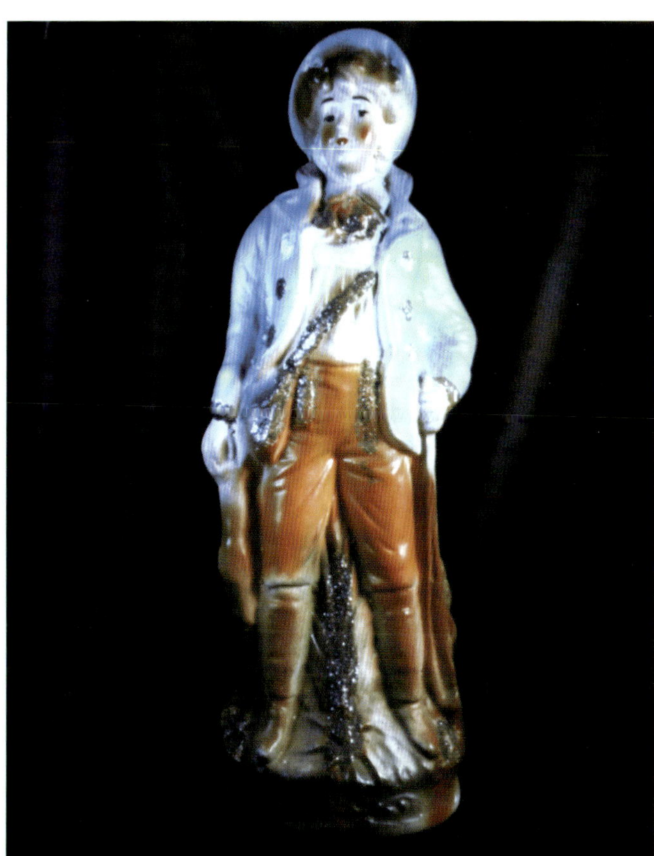

Johnny Appleseed fourteen-inch carnival chalk prize, caricatured with his legendary seed bag and walking stick, but his attire is more akin to Gainsborough's *Blue Boy* than the image of a barefoot man wearing torn rags and a pot on his head for a hat. Undoubtedly the carnival chalkware manufacturer wanted a romanticized version of Johnny Appleseed; otherwise he would have resembled the immigrant-looking comic Happy Hooligan (page 29), who had a tin can on his head and whose clothes never came close to an up-to-date fashion statement.

John Chapman, otherwise known as Johnny Appleseed, was born in Leominister, Massachusetts, on September 26, 1774. Information about his childhood is not known. He traveled from western Pennsylvania through Ohio, Indiana, and Illinois, planting orchards as the settlers moved westward, from 1797 until his death in 1845. He eventually owned about 1,200 acres of orchards. He lived along French Creek in Venango County, Pennsylvania, between 1797 and 1804. Records indicate he had a nursery there as well as one near Warren, Pennsylvania. He never married and was a dedicated Swedenborgian colporteur (peddler of religious literature).

Johnny Appleseed's visions of angels as future wives were in a similar vein to those of his mentor, the scientist turned spiritual explorer Emmanuel Swedenborg who wrote lengthy, detailed descriptions of the many angels that he had witnessed. (A person does not have to be "spiritual" to have a supernatural experience—like seeing halos— nor should religions claim that seeing the supernatural belongs within their territory only.)

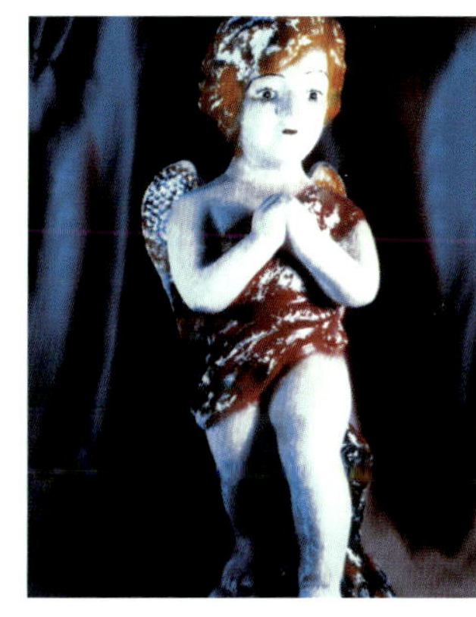

Winged Angel twenty-eight-inch carnival chalk prize, possibly the tallest prize

BUGS BUNNY

(1938-1970)

Brer Rabbit keep on axin' 'im, en de Tar-Baby, she keep on sayin'
nothin', twel present'y Brer Rabbit draw back wid his fis', he did, en
blip he tuck'er side er de head. Right dar's whar he broke his mer-
lasses jug. His fis' stuck, en he can't pull loose. De tar hilt' im.
But Tar-Baby, she stay still, en Brer Fox, he lay low.
—JOEL CHANDLER HARRIS, *Uncle Remus*

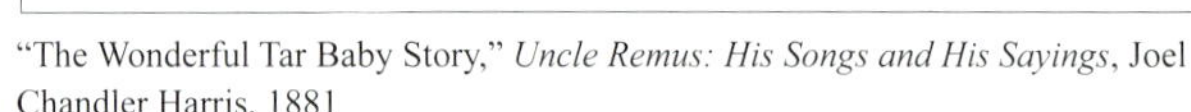

"The Wonderful Tar Baby Story," *Uncle Remus: His Songs and His Sayings*, Joel
Chandler Harris, 1881

Bugs Bunny's original name was Plotwise, and he
made his first silver-screen appearance in the Warner Brothers cartoon *Porky's Hare Hunt* (1938), directed by Cal Dalton
and Ben "Bugs" Hardaway. The dashing, devil-may-care,
winsome rabbit's antagonist in that film was not the befud-
dled Elmer Fudd but none other than Porky Pig. The Bugs
Bunny and Elmer Fudd characters first appeared together
one year later in *Hare-um Scare-um* (1939), but neither had
their final names or shapes. In that film, Bugs looked like
Daffy Duck in a rabbit suit and Elmer was much thinner and
resembled Egghead. Tex Avery created what would become
carrot-munching Bugs Bunny's signature phrase (using Mel
Blanc's crossover Brooklyn-Bronx accent), "Eh, what's up,
Doc?" in *A Wild Hare* (1940). (And, as if this factlet is
important, that film also saw Bugs kiss hunter/foil Elmer for
the first time.) His name was "Bug's Bunny" for three years
and he didn't lose his apostrophe until *Elmer's Pet Rabbit*
(1941), directed by Chuck Jones. It was a fussy little difference, but not when it came to crediting who Bugs's true
creator was. Director and cartoon animator Chuck Jones
usually receives credit for Bugs, but the truth is that Bugs
was a collaborative effort of a number of great minds and
animators hunkered over their drawing tables in a rundown,
back-lot Warner Brothers shack nicknamed "Termite Ter-
race."

Bugs got a new look to go along with his final name
and became more attractive and expressive, while Elmer
morphed into a rotund, diminished, almost gnomelike fellow,
as first seen in *Wabbit Twouble* (1941).[1] Bugs's stereotype
reflected the cool, collected, cocky, freethinking critter,
and, as described by Elmer, he could be summed up with
a singularly, stereotypical word: "wascal." Bugs was a cool
and cocky rapscallion, and one who could not be bested. He
was a wily winner archetype, a great-grandchild (maybe, great
great) evolved from Joel Chandler Harris's derogatory tale
"The Tar Baby Story."

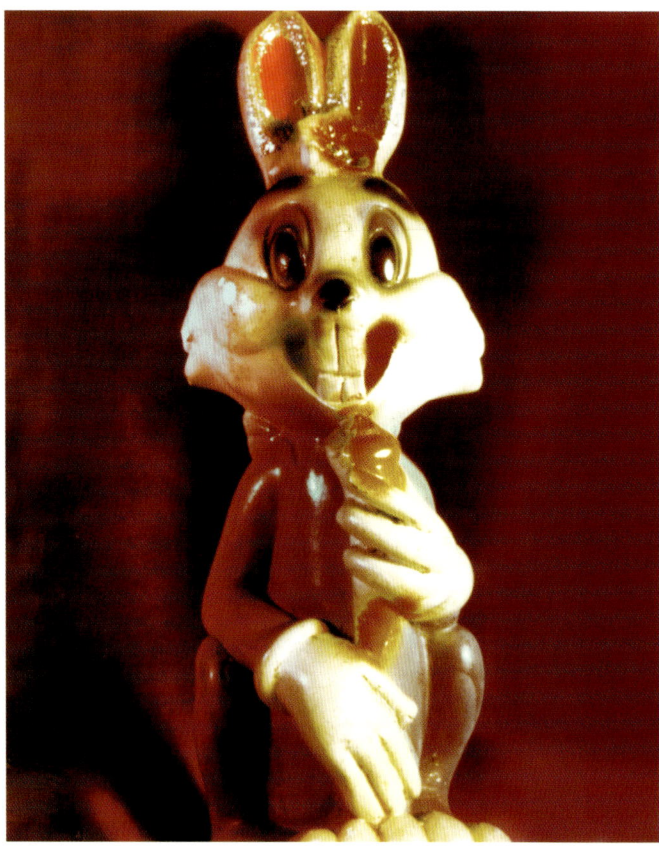

Bugs Bunny fourteen-inch carnival chalk prize, similar in design to a larger twenty-one-
inch chalk bank distributed later by Warner Bros.

Elmer typified the conservative, determined,
never-gonna-give-up macho warrior archetype, but against
Bugs, Elmer is always the antagonist loser. Most times he
was a role reversal for the stereotypical American hunter.
Elmer never got his game. The popularity of hunting, as
well as the visually enticing weapons for the sport (how can
an enterprise in which the end result is killing something be
called a sport?), demonstrated that sneaking through the great
outdoors is an insatiable, oftentimes dominant part of many
American male's macho warrior appetite—a survival archetype. Hunting relies upon the hunter's need to feel praise from
others (or simply from oneself). "Look what I got!" It is a
pitiful way to build self-image at the expense of other living
beings. Warner Brothers poked fun at Elmer as a hunter, (but
not at the NRA nor the idea of hunting). They understood
that for Bugs to remain funny, he also always needed to
be the winner and Elmer the loser. Winning turned out to
be the key ingredient that shuffled Bugs to the top of the
cartoon deck. He was number one on the pop charts for many

years. Popeye usually held the number-two spot and Mickey Mouse was a distant number three.

Quite a few of Bugs's 1940s cartoons depended on ethnic humor (to soften reality phrases, such as racist humor). But many of the cartoons embodied true racist tenets. In *All This and Rabbit Stew* (1941), Bugs outwitted a shuffling, drawling black hunter who said threateningly, "Ah'm gonna ketch me a ra-a-a-bbit." Bugs eventually won all the hunter's clothes in a game of craps. The cartoon *Fresh Hare* (1942) ends with Elmer and a chorus of Mounties, made up in blackface, playing "Dixie" on their banjos. Not unexpectedly, anti Japanese humor was prevalent in the plots presented during the war years, as in *Bugs Bunny Nips the Nips*, when Bugs gives "Good Rumor" bars containing hand grenades to Japanese soldiers and calls out, "There ya go, Monkey Face. Don't push, Slant Eyes."

Dell Comics published *Bugs Bunny* from 1953 to 1962 and he appeared in comic strips between 1940 and 1970.

Monuments dedicated to animals are few. If in your travels you see a sign for the White Buffalo Monument in Snyder, Texas, don't be confused. It's not a monument dedicated to the rare white buffalo cherished by Native Americans. It *is* a bronze monument of a white buffalo, but, it is dedicated to hunter J. Wright Mooar, who shot the rare white buffalo. The monument's hyped text reads:

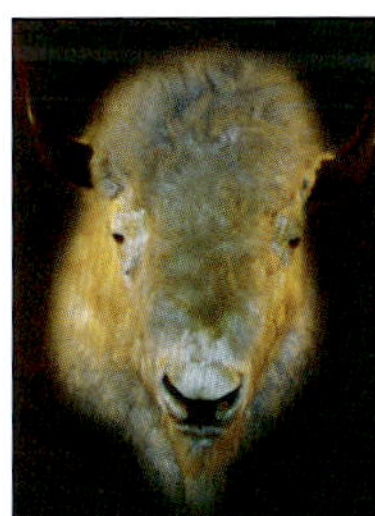

white buffalo trophy

J. Wright Mooar: Champion hunter of buffalo—largest game animal in North America. Born in Vermont; came west at 19. Began hunting in 1870 to supply hides for market. In partnership with his brother, John W. Mooar, in 1873 established first buffalo hunting camp in the Texas Panhandle. On Oct. 7, 1876, at his first hunting camp in Scurry County, killed a rare albino buffalo—one of two known to have been killed in Texas. The hide of that albino, afterward shown in 1904 St. Louis Fair and many other occasions, is now preserved here in Scurry County by Mooar's descendants. Hunted regularly until 1879; in 1881 helped furnish game and hay to feed construction men and animals building Texas & Pacific Railroad in West Texas. During his career, he shot about 22,000 buffalo—a record probably unsurpassed. His ability to hit a vital spot at a distance of 1,000 feet or farther won the respect of such Indians as Comanche Chief Quanah Parker, who became his friend in later life. Began ranching with his brother in 1877. Also had a business in Colorado City, 1881–1905. Highly esteemed. Site of killing of white buffalo (10 mi. NW of here) is near the Old Mooar Ranch headquarters, where his hand-dug water well is now surrounded by oil wells.

To get a closer look at the American frontier macho-warrior mentality archetype (a cosmetic name for killing or packing away Native Americans, destroying the buffalo that was their movable feast, appropriating their land, then overgrazing through cattle ranching, and profiteering in the 1920s oil boom), study the town of Snyder. It is a perfect historic case study—Texas style. Even more ironic (tragic), there still exists an "exotic" hunting ranch in the U.S. where great white hunters can shoot white buffalo.

THE LONE RANGER

(1933-1957)

Striker was a writing machine—the greatest hack writer who ever lived . . . Striker was writing 60,000 words a week, the equivalent of the Bible every three months.
—JOHN DUNNING, *The Encyclopedia of Old Time Radio*

Fran Striker created the radio program *Covered Wagon Days*, which later became *The Lone Ranger*. It began in 1930 as a half hour drama airing on WEBR in Buffalo, New York. The program's hero acquired the name The Lone Ranger in 1933 when Detroit radio station WXYZ, owned by George W. Trendle, began carrying the show. Striker sold Trendle his rights to *The Lone Ranger* that same year. The Lone Ranger's cavalier attitude (like laughing after he shot someone) was too harsh for Trendle's taste, so Striker was forced to tone him down—a character change that would eventually pay off. *The Lone Ranger* began with the resonant musical strains of "The William Tell Overture" playing gallantly under these swaggering lines:

A fiery horse with the speed of light, a cloud of dust and a hearty "Hi Yo Silver!" The Lone Ranger rides again. With his faithful Indian companion Tonto, the daring and resourceful masked rider of the plains led the fight for law and order in the early western United States. Return with us now to those thrilling days of yesteryear. Out of the past come the thundering hoof beats of the great horse Silver. The Lone Ranger rides again!

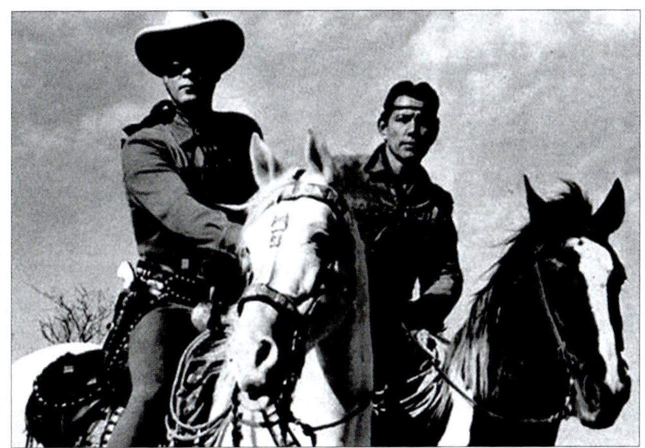

The Lone Ranger and Tonto © *The Lone Ranger,* ABC TV, circa 1950s

The Native American sidekick Tonto appeared in broadcast number ten. Striker wrote a booklet describing Tonto's role as well as various traits of his masked hero.

On racial tolerance: The Lone Ranger's friend is Tonto, a Comanche Indian. If The Lone Ranger accepts the Indian as his closest companion, it is obvious to the child listener that great men have no racial or religious prejudice. On religion: The Lone Ranger is shown not to be a member of any specific church, but he is definitely a respecter of all creeds, and the only man besides Tonto who knows him is a Catholic Padre of a mission. On morality: The Lone Ranger is to never kill anyone.[1]

The Lone Ranger played to all ages. He embodied the perfect good-guy stereotype, with a big twist of mystery because of his mask. Striker gave him an interesting history that could only be pieced together bit by bit. The fragments were gleaned by fans from the various books, radio broadcasts, and television shows. These added to his aura of obscurity.

The legend of his life could eventually be mapped in this way: the Lone Ranger's older brother, Dan Reid, was born around 1842 in Texas and John Reid (The Lone Ranger) was born around 1850. Tonto was born in 1854. Ten-year-old John saved Tonto's life from a band of outlaws, but lost his own parents during the horrible battle. John was then adopted by Tonto's tribe as a blood-brother to Tonto. Dan eventually found his brother and sent him to live in Detroit with their Aunt Martha. Dan met his future wife, Linda, during the Civil War. John, who was too young to be in the war, studied to be a lawyer. After the war, Dan and Linda, now married, went to Texas and met John. Prospecting together, they discovered a silver mine, which they kept secret. This mine would later supply The Lone Ranger's silver bullets (never-miss firepower) and silver horseshoes for his horse, Silver. Dan became a Texas Ranger in 1872 and John became a lawyer. Dan Jr. was born. Dan was now a captain in the Texas Rangers. Then John also joined the Rangers, but quit after learning about the massacre of Native Americans by a crooked white sheriff. Unbeknownst to John, Tonto's wife, child, and sister were killed in that massacre. Captain Dan Reid and his troop of Texas Rangers, accompanied by John, rode out to capture the killers. They were ambushed and all were killed except John, who barely survived and was then nursed back to health by Tonto. John fashioned a mask from his dead brother's vest and vowed to wear it always as The Lone Ranger. He avenged his brother's death, and helped others in distress. His mask hid his face and, through a most clever ploy, very little more of his history was ever given.

The construction of The Lone Ranger idol displayed masterful storytelling craftsmanship and he was exactly the right hero for the time, striking sentiments in vital areas for both children and adults. On the one hand, he represented the religious belief that goodness prevails over evil and is delivered through a mysterious entity identified only through his good deeds. (Americans also saw themselves in that light after saving the world during the two world wars and then withdrawing to their hidden fortress, America.) On the other hand, the character also represented the morality lesson that one should do good deeds for others without expecting anything in return—a rare human trait indeed. The Lone Ranger offered munificent moral preciosity for the masses, and they soaked it up and basked in it.

The Lone Ranger was an earthbound archetypal superhero, a God, a cowboy superman. Characteristically he appeared out of nowhere just in the nick of time to save those in distress. As silently as The Lone Ranger appeared, he disappeared. Those who wondered about his provenance uttered the questioning line: "Who was that masked man?" It was understood that he left because all was now well and there were others to help mop things up. Obviously he left before he could be complimented. He and Tonto were always poker-faced, presenting to American men of the era two role models with zero emotions and feelings that might give away who they were underneath. Tonto gave the series an authenticity with his Native American abilities, such as tracking, intuition, and bravery. (Why Striker named him "Tonto" is unknown. Translated into Spanish, it means "foolish" or "stupid.") The Lone Ranger never swore, drank, used poor grammar, or killed anyone, nor did he have romantic ties with women, so gender equality was never an issue. He operated in a West where there were no laws; as a past Texas Ranger and a lawyer, he had the credentials of ultimate authority. He always recognized right from wrong and knew how to deal with injustice. The Lone Ranger's creed was a glorified political speech:

I believe that to have a friend, a man must be one. That all men are created equal and that everyone has within himself the power to make this a better world. That God put the firewood there but that every man must gather and light it himself. In being prepared physically, mentally, and morally to fight when necessary for that which is right. That a man should make the most of what equipment he has. That "This government, of the people, by the people and for the people" shall live always. That men should live by the rule of what is best for the greatest number. That sooner or later . . . somewhere . . . somehow . . . we must settle with the world and make payment for what we have taken. That all things change but truth, and that truth alone, lives on forever. In my Creator, my country, my fellow man.[2]

It has been estimated that The Lone Ranger was more popular in his time than all other cowboys combined. In a larger sense, he was and still is a paradigm for any person, group, or institution that assumes it has jurisdiction over anyone or everyone (similar to the Patriot Act enacted after 9/11). The Lone Ranger was in control and in charge wherever he went, even convincing those who were suspicious of his mask—telling them gently that they had nothing to fear for he was the paragon of goodness, honesty, and right action. The mask (really a disguise covering feelings, as if he were beyond such insignificant humanness) said: "I am a white God: don't ever question my authority, for I am ultimately the best for you." His mask also represented an empowered force eons stronger than simply human. Silver, his famous stallion, is white and The Lone Ranger is dressed in white, so together they automatically instill the great, white God of justice into their archetype. No other cowboy could even attempt to get higher than that.

Tonto operated as a primary reinforcement character for The Lone Ranger. He was disguised as a stereotypical believer—a convert to Christian morality (he's going to heaven). America, in the 1800s, placed Native Americans on reservations and surrounded them by populations of whites and a government that knew what was best for them. They had no choice. Religions did a coin toss, as to which one would put their churches on whose reservations.

By 1953, *The Lone Ranger* was broadcast three times each week to a listening audience of 12 million people, and the television program (which had premiered in 1949) was telecast on ninety television stations with 5 million viewers—the highest-rated western on TV. *The Lone Ranger* also appeared in 177 daily newspapers, 119 Sunday newspapers, and was read by 71 million people in comic strips. Striker published eighteen Lone Ranger books from 1936 to 1956, and comic books, under various publishers, ran from 1936 to 1977.

Clayton Moore was The Lone Ranger of television fame, replaced by John Hart in 1952 after a salary dispute, but at the end of that year, Moore returned and was from then on: The Lone Ranger. In real life, Moore was a circus acrobat as well as an actor. He was inducted into the Stuntman's Hall of Fame in 1982. Jay Silverheels, who played Tonto, was part Mohawk. The last television broadcast of *The Lone Ranger* was June 6, 1957.

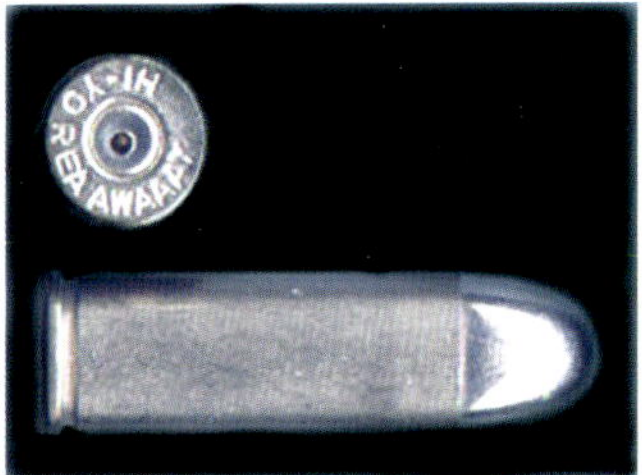

Remington Colt 45 nickel plated spent primer Silver Bullet, circa 1960s, made as an advertising gimmick for promoting the Railway Express Agency. Embossed on the casing was HI-YO REA AWAAAY. So legendary was the right, might and power of The Lone Ranger's "silver bullet" that it became a new motif for the "never fail" cliché archetype—the answer to solving a specific problem—finding the "silver bullet." Recently Silver Bullet became the name for a line of miniature vibrators—their end is bullet-shaped.

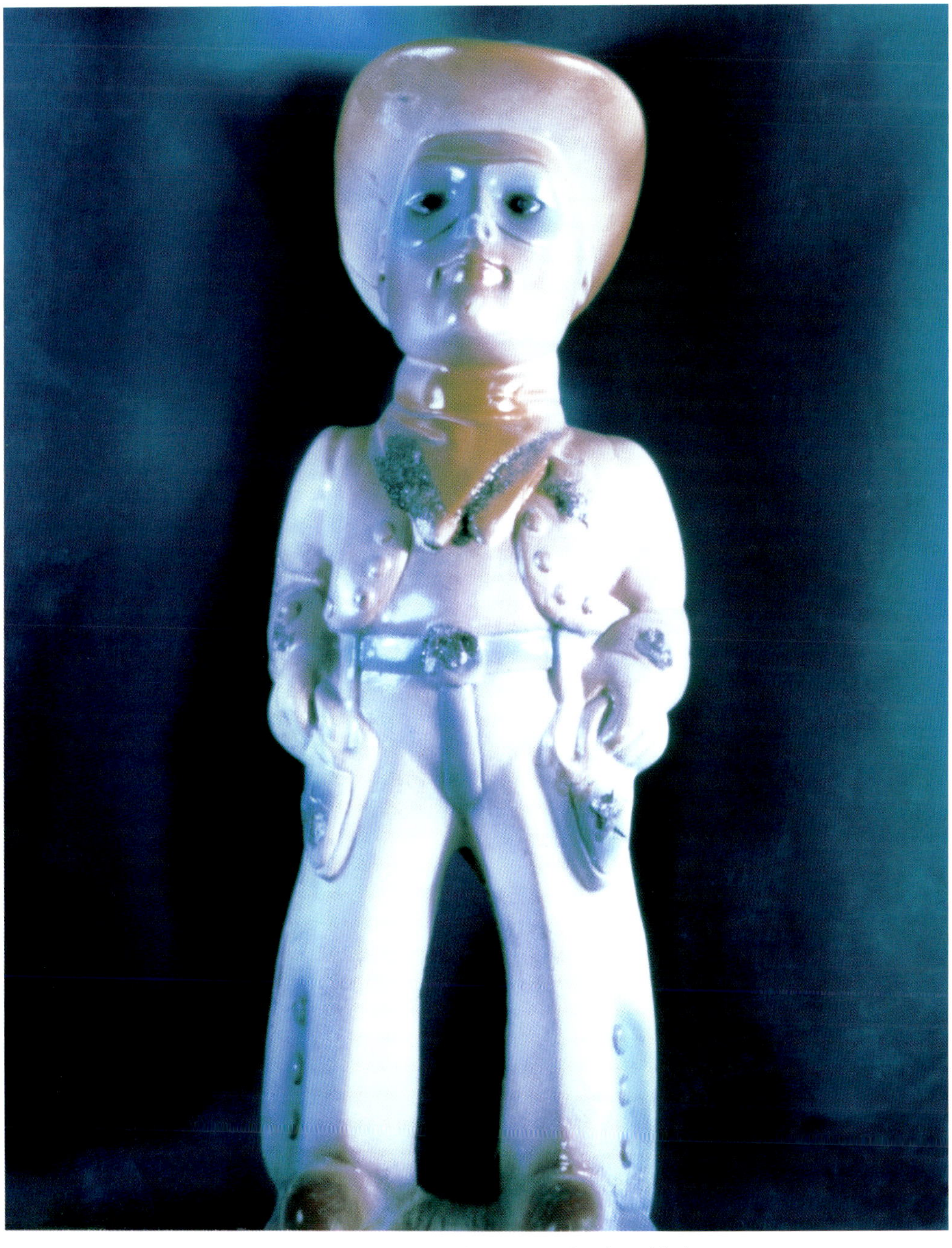

Lone Ranger fourteen-and-a-half-inch carnival chalk prize, one of the most popular prizes of the late 1940s and early 1950s, this particular one has a subtly painted mask—most were black

BATMAN (1939-

Bob Kane (1916-1998) conceived *Batman* in 1934, but it wasn't until the 1939 success of the comic book, *Superman*, that he sat down to fully create his own SuperHero, *The Batman* (his original name in the May, 1939 issue of *Detective Comics*).

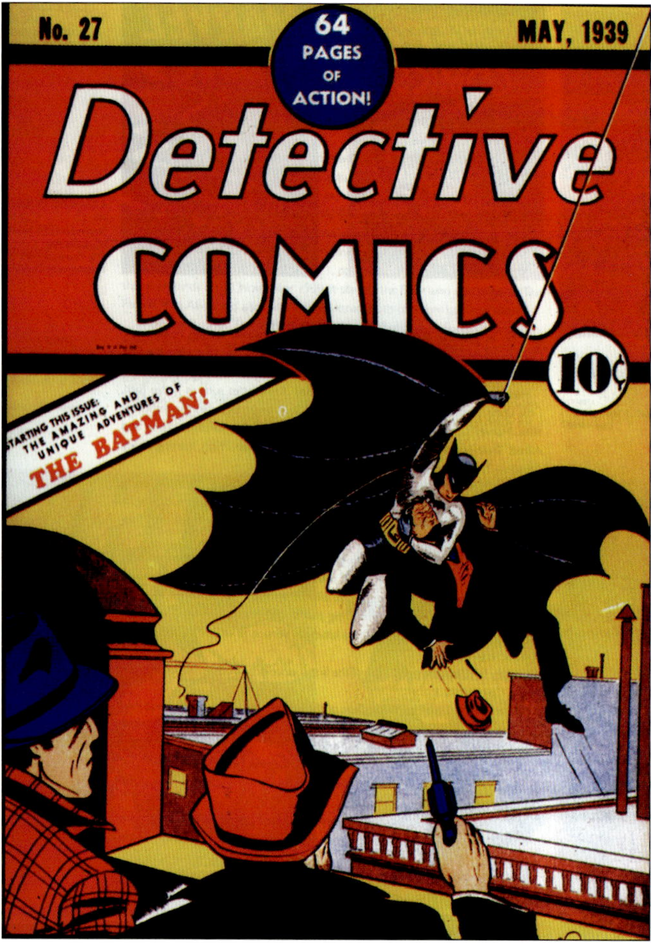

"The Batman," cover, Bob Kane © Detective Comics #27, May, 1939

Kane said that Batman came from a variety of inspirations: Leonardo da Vinci's drawings of flying machines; the masked figure of Douglas Fairbanks in *The Mark of Zorro* (1920); the films *The Bat* (1926) and *The Bat Whispers* (1930); and the 1930s radio show *The Shadow.*

Bruce Wayne, aka Batman, was cruelly orphaned as a child: numb with panic, he had watched as a thug murdered his parents. This brutal event mapped the course and mission of his life and the still-traumatized adult Bruce Wayne transformed himself into the vengeful Batman whenever he discovered crimes in progress. From human to bat is a scary transformation for any human to undergo, particularly when the end product becomes a self-styled, masked, empowered, superhuman vigilante.

Through daring captures, Batman became Gotham City's most famous (and infamous) crime fighter. He usually worked at night, preferring the intimate cover of darkness.

His motives appeared justifiable, but at the same time darkly revengeful. Although Batman fought for law and order, as did Superman and Captain Marvel, his temperament was dissimilar, bearing more of a resemblance to the reflective, dark-sided crime fighter, one who used the utmost human intelligence to prevail against his enemies. Shadows lurked beneath his surface and Batman never came close to achieving the good-guy stereotypes exhibited by Superman and Captain Marvel. He didn't possess superhero body powers, bullets didn't bounce off him, and he didn't fly at the speed of light. In many respects Batman's darkness was medieval—right out of a Hieronymus Bosch hellscape. Since he was a bat-human, he could easily have reflected the devil, which has often been represented with batlike wings, but by making his enemy the Joker represent a maniacal evil clown-devil (page 260), Batman could represent good. Batman's technical abilities required quite a leap of faith on the part of the reader—faith that a human could actually perform these feats and was capable of inventing seemingly unlimited techno-extensions. Once having taken that leap, however, the reader accepted that Batman's archetypal psyche celebrated brains over brawn (a notion consistent with Leonardo's drawings of war machines). Batman was, moreover, a reconstruction of the dark-hero image and he emerged as a new role model who used the demonic, imaginative side of his intellect.

Of Batman, Chip Kidd writes:

> The themes at the heart of the Batman mythology are eternal: tragedy, loss of innocence, redemption and the unending crusade. But what makes it compelling is its reversal of form and content. Batman is a figure that performs good works in the guise of an evil being, a demon. The Joker, his nemesis, dispenses horror and mayhem while assuming the form of someone meant to make us forget our cares, a clown. This message—that things are not what they seem, and therefore one must judge actions, not appearances—has a sense of irony that is closer to classic dramatic traditions than it is to the stereotypes of popular culture.[1]

The comic entitled *Batman* flowered in the spring of 1940. It sported Batman's new sidekick Robin, functionally, Bruce Wayne's surrogate son; the crime queen Catwoman, styled after sex symbol Jean Harlow, who had died four years earlier; and the Joker, fashioned after the image of Conrad Veidt in the 1928 film *The Man Who Laughs.* The Joker was the perfect archetypal schadenfreude (one who derives pleasure from the misfortunes of others—a joker-devil). Batman's formidable enemy Penguin appeared in December 1941 (inspired by an article Kane had read in *The Saturday Evening Post* about emperor penguins).

Throughout his crime-fighting career, Batman struggled against a variety of unusual criminal minds. His enemies were mostly archetypal symbols for the psychologically corrupt, intertwining feelings of greed with power. When Batman was pitted against Catwoman, they seemed almost to fall in love, but her love came from an obviously irreparably damaged criminal mind. They always remained on opposite sides of the law and shared a wistful but distant unfulfilled love. Her character represented an archetypal,

heavily disguised, very beautiful she-monster psychopath.
When pitted against the Joker, Batman was really fighting
against the archetypal he-monster psychopath. Both enemies
supplied feelings of fear of the unknown in a world of psycho
chaos.

Batman became the star of his own newspaper strip
in 1943 and leapt into Hollywood in two fifteen-part serialized
films, *Batman* and *The New Adventures of Batman and Robin.*
It was in these movies that Alfred the Butler first appeared.
Alfred was the stereotype of a secret helper or inside man.
Another comic-book regular was Vicki Vale, who appeared in
1948 as Bruce Wayne's steady girlfriend. She remained with
him until 1963. Batman made appearances on radio during the
late forties, but only as a guest star on *Superman.* Later the superheroes appeared together in the comics in *Superman #76*
(1952). They were never popular together. Batman's mere
human powers always played a weak second to Superman's
superpowers.

Although women as lovers were generally left
out of Batman's plotlines (except for lover–not lover Catwoman—his doomed love, and Vicki Vale—his destined
love), it seemed more natural that Batman, the traumatized
orphan, would not be ready to fall completely in love until
his psychological trauma had healed. Gender equality
issues were not a part of the Batman sagas until the late
1940s. Catwoman's powers equaled Batman's, so there was
a certain amount of shared gender equality, but his attach-
ment to her manifested itself more as desperate, momentary
infatuations with the sinister and incorrigible.

The dark-sided human duo of Bruce Wayne vis-à-vis
Batman never performed psychologically in the same fashion
as that of the superhuman alter-ego duo of Clark Kent vis-à-
vis Superman, or the alter ego, human/superhuman duo Billy
Batson vis-à-vis Captain Marvel. Bruce Wayne's dark psyche,
even though he was a wealthy socialite, was exactly like Batman's dark psyche and presented a two-sided mirror with
different visual images and parallel souls. Clark Kent's
psyche, because he was forced to act as if he were human, was
never anything like Superman's superhero psyche. And Billy
Batson's psyche as a human boy never came close to matching
Captain Marvel's psyche as an adult superhero.

In 1954, psychiatrist Frederick Wertham's damning
book *The Seduction of the Innocent* was published. It created
a fury against comic books by connecting violence in comic
books with juvenile crime. That same year, Wertham gave
twenty-five minutes of testimony to the U.S. Senate. In
the beginning of the hearing he stated: "The difference
between surreptitious pornographic literature for adults and
children's comic books is this: one is a question of attracting
perverts, in the other of making them." In the middle of his
testimony he drew conclusions about increasing homosexuality
and comics, citing Batman and Robin in his statement: "They
live in sumptuous quarters, with beautiful flowers in large
vases, and have a butler, Alfred. Batman is sometimes shown
in a dressing gown. As they sit by the fireplace the young boy
sometimes worries about his partner: 'Something's wrong with
Bruce. He hasn't been himself these last few days.' It is like a
wish dream of two homosexuals living together."[2] Fortunately,
they survived Wertham's slur (and his homophobia).

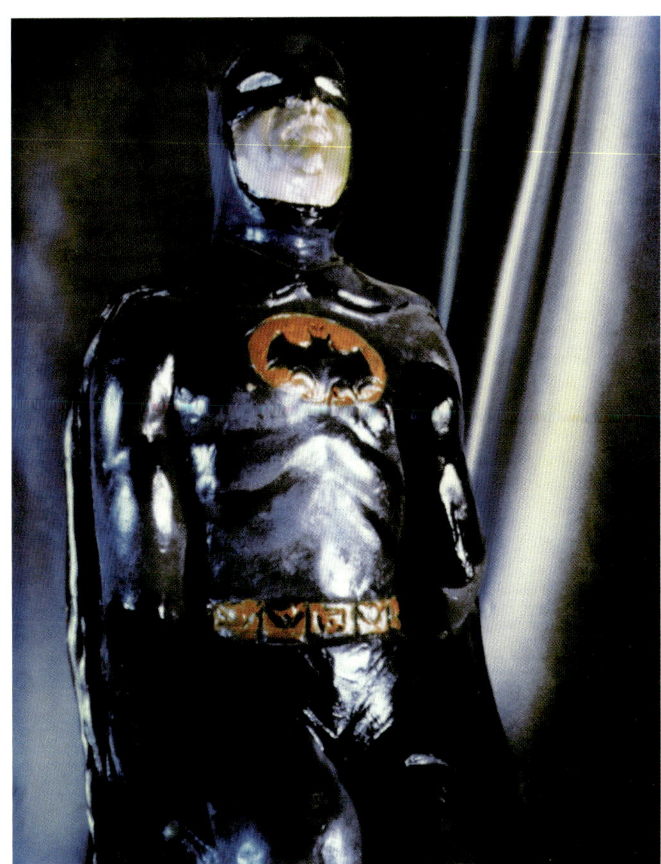

Batman eleven-inch carnival chalk prize (?), similar body size to the Superman/Captain
Marvel carnival prize. Its unique difference is the odd bended-knee stance, as if Batman
were about to leap upward, caricatured from Bob Kane's drawings using visually
stimulating cinematic angles. The above prize is after 1960—that's when Batman first
wore an insignia on his chest.

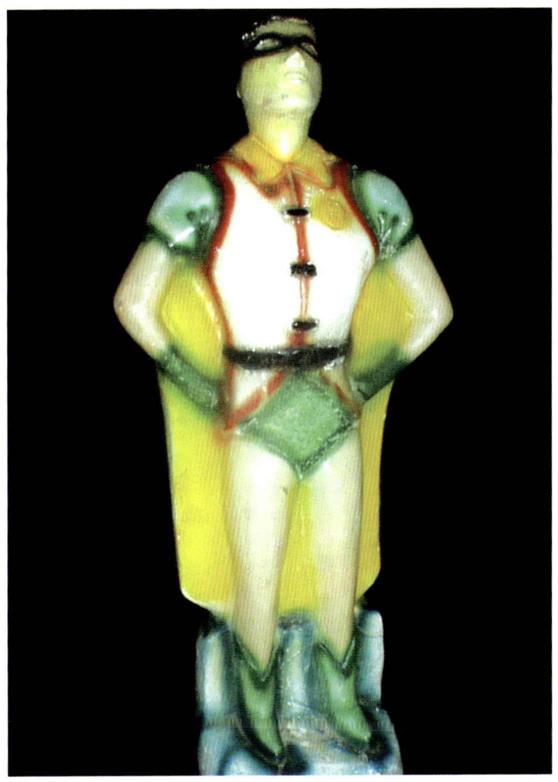

Robin eighteen-inch carnival chalk bank prize, 1940s. A similar prize is
shown on page 36 in *Batman Collected* by Chip Kidd.

Captain Marvel

(1940-1953)

To keep readers from having their attention drawn away from the stories, I deliberately used characters, settings and props that would be instantly recognized by everyone everywhere, in other words, stereotypes. If the story called for a stuffy corporation head or a conservative banker, I drew a pompous man wearing a high, stiff collar and sporting a small mustache. If he was a crook I gave him a big cigar and a bigger mustache.

When characters fought, they fought each other; when they talked, they faced each other; when they ran, they ran across the stage, not out of it and into the laps of the audience. This kind of presentation was in such contrast to the superhero comics of the time that it caught on immediately and made Captain Marvel the biggest-selling comics of the Golden Age. He was a comic-strip character, as plain and simple as Harold Teen, Daddy Warbucks or Offissa Pup. He was not—I repeat, not—a superhero.

—Charles Clarence Beck in an interview by Tom Heintjes

I think it would be a good idea.

—Mahatma Gandhi, reply on being asked for his view on Western civilization

a mysterious stranger into an abandoned subway tunnel, where he met the wise old wizard Shazam. Shazam bestowed little Billy with a very special power—whenever Billy spoke the wizard's name, his physique miraculously expanded and he was transformed into the astoundingly powerful Captain Marvel. That was hardly surprising, since Shazam was an acronym for Solomon, Hercules, Atlas, Zeus, Achilles, and Mercury, and the transformed Captain Marvel acquired all of their powers. Regardless of the fact that his creators did not see Captain Marvel as a superhero stereotype, that was how readers inevitably perceived him.

Captain Marvel was an instant hit, probably because of the lighthearted stories and the psychological charm of a child being able to say a magic word and instantly become the strongest super-adult in the world. He also had the ability to reverse the procedure and go back to being a child. Children who read the stories could easily fantasize the condition of being two different people at the same time—particularly if they possessed a strong alter ego. (Unfortunately, the notion, as compelling as it was, also subliminally projected the concept that physical weakness was a flaw and superior physical prowess was a goal.) As an archetypal motif, Billy Batson

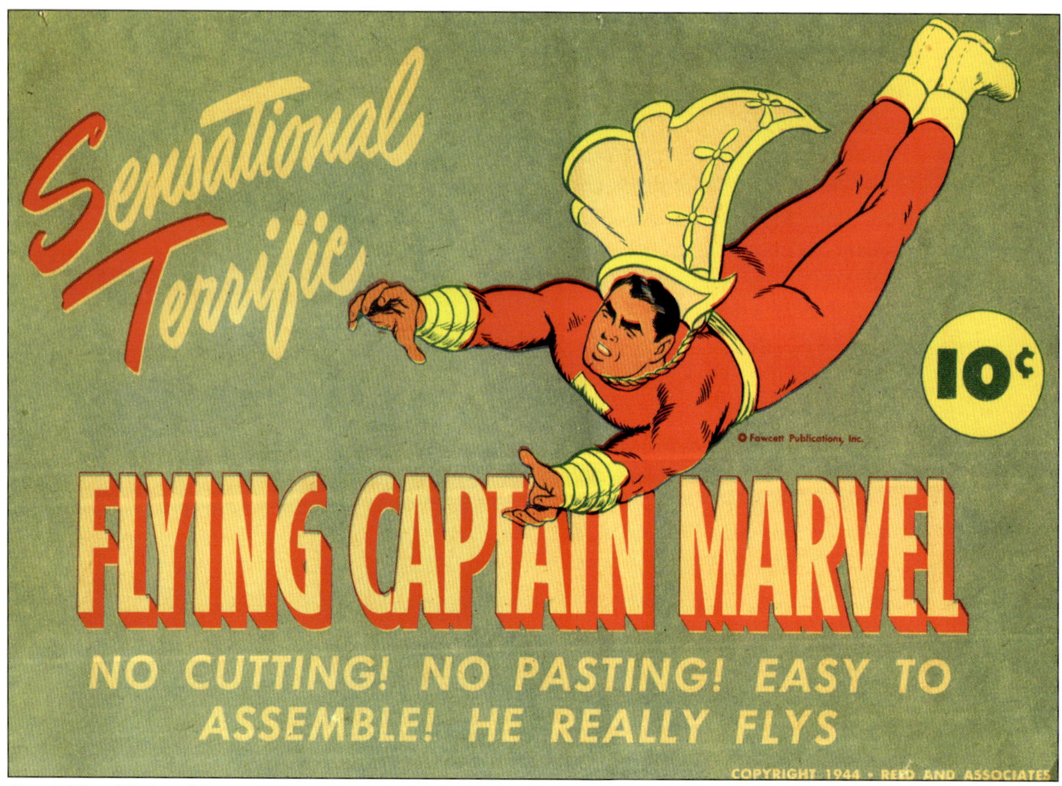

Captain Marvel, flying glider toy ad © Fawcett Publications Inc., Reed & Associates, 1944

Writer Bill Parker and artist Charles Clarence Beck created Captain Marvel in 1940. Their brainchild was published by Whiz Comics, owned by Fawcett Publications, publishers of the slick lovelorn *True Confessions* as well as that bastion of home engineering *Mechanics Illustrated*.

The grit of the Captain Marvel story was centered on an endearing, homeless newsboy, Billy Batson, who followed

vis-à-vis Captain Marvel was a child's projected self-fulfilling God-like escapist's dream hero, a thrilling fantasy in which he, or she, could perpetually create a perfect world and one which they could control, if only through a fairy tale or myth where every problem is surmountable. It was not possible to manipulate such problems in the imperfect real world, where a child might be subject to mental or physical abuse (or just having to attend school), and where difficult situations were patently inescapable, especially when perpetrated by an adult.

Republic Films introduced *The Adventures of Captain Marvel* in 1941, with Tom Tyler, bedecked in a red skin-tight suit and flourishing a white cape with gold trim, starring in twelve serialized films. Tyler had previously performed in almost one hundred cowboy films and, as the illustrious Captain Marvel, enjoyed resurgence into stardom in super-flying fashion.

Unfortunately, as Tyler ascended into stardom, DC Comics, publisher of *Superman*, launched a lawsuit against Fawcett Publications, accusing them of fashioning the popular Captain Marvel character after their own blue-suited, red-caped hero. The lawsuit dragged on for years—a particularly irritating time for DC Comics, because Captain Marvel continued to maintain the popular edge over Superman. By 1946, the *Captain Marvel* comic book was selling 1.4 million issues every month. The case finally came to trial in 1948 and the court decided in Fawcett's favor. The court stated that some of Superman's physical images were published without the correct copyright notations, but also recognized that there were similarities between the two characters. DC Comics appealed the decision and received a new trial. The fogs of legalese enshrouded the case until, in 1951, the court decided that the

DC Comics copyright was valid despite their earlier errors in publishing copyright notices and that it was obvious that DC had no intention of abandoning the Superman character. The case was finally settled out of court in 1953. Fawcett paid DC Comics $400,000 and agreed to stop publishing *Captain Marvel* comics.

After the 1954 U.S. Senate hearings, when comic books received such bad press, only the strongest sellers, like *Superman*, were able to survive the vigilante onslaught. *Captain Marvel* would have also survived, but he and Billy Batson were legally forced out of the superhero fray. Toward the end of that Senate hearing, Dr. Frederick Wertham answered a question by Senator Kefauver by stating: "I think Hitler was a beginner compared to the comic book industry. They get the children much younger. They teach them race hatred at the age of four before they can read."[1]

Prior to Captain Marvel's departure from the superhero scene, he stereotyped the super-strong good guy—a fighter for truth, justice, and the American way—while his alter ego, Billy Batson, stereotyped the American child, fantasizing magical strength (like the Charles Atlas ads in the back pages of the comics promised) in a complicated and difficult adult world. One, being two, how could they lose.

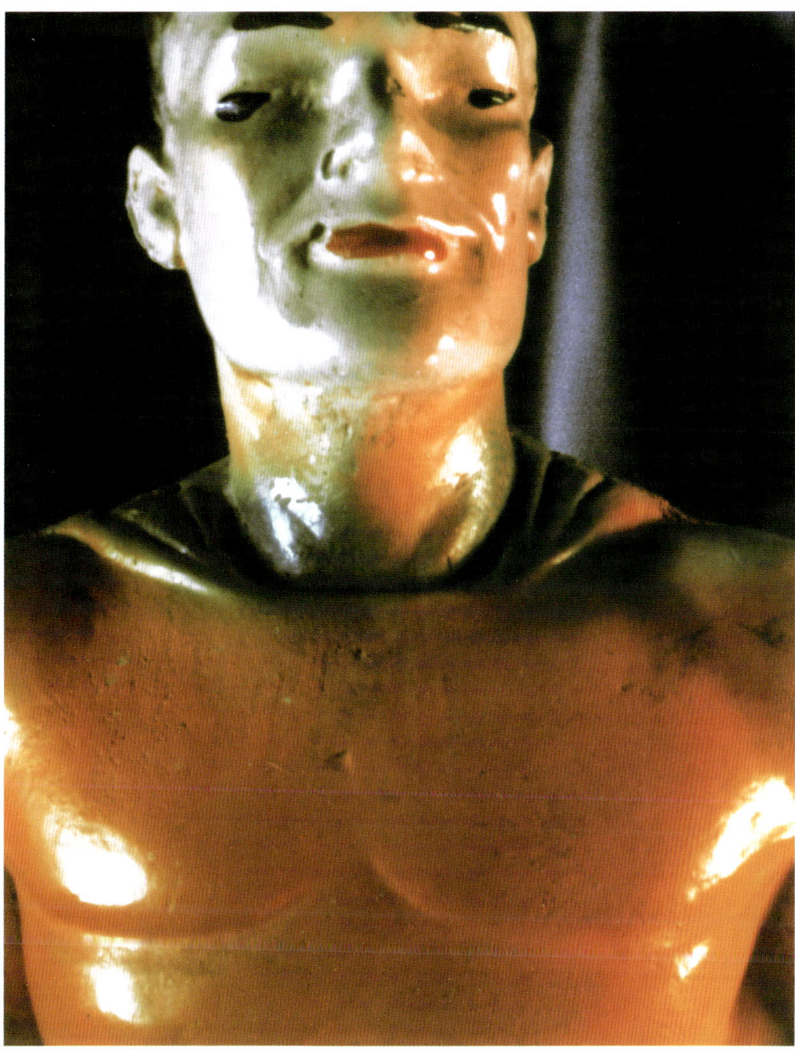

Captain Marvel fifteen-inch carnival chalk prize

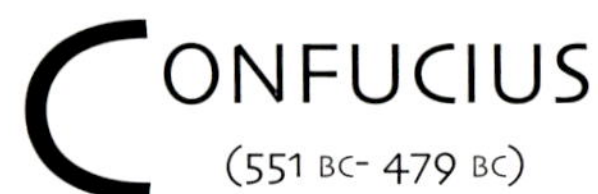

CONFUCIUS
(551 BC– 479 BC)

Do not be concerned about others not appreciating you. Be concerned about your not appreciating others.
Learning without thought is useless. Thought without learning is dangerous.
Recompense injury with justice, and kindness with kindness.
Knowledge is not equal to devotion. Devotion is not equal to joy.
It is only the very wisest and the very stupidest who never change.
—CONFUCIUS, *Analects*, 500 BC

Confucius is considered to be one of the greatest educators of practical and ethical morality in world history. His life span closely approximates that of the Buddha. Confucius was born into a meager, deposed royal family in 551 BC, in the vassal kingdom of Lu. His father died when he was three. Confucius invented fantasylike temple rituals when he was a child and later, in his early years, worked as a servant for a wealthy family, where he quickly earned a reputation for fairness, politeness, and a love of learning. At seventeen he was married and became an inspector of corn markets. He had two daughters and a son. Confucius began teaching when he was twenty-two and his mother died shortly thereafter. He created an ancestral shrine of mourning and prayer at his parents' resting place—a practice not known in Chinese antiquity, but one now steeped in tradition and ritual.

Confucius was granted interviews with Lao-tze, the founder of Taoism,[1] in 517 BC. At age fifty-two, he was made chief magistrate for the city of Chung-too. The reformations that his educational principles affected were so striking that he was subsequently appointed minister of justice. In time, he resigned from this post, a decision precipitated by the intolerable debauchery of the marquis. He traveled in poverty for thirteen years with his disciples—all of them living harshly and at great personal sacrifice.

His teachings were presented through informal conversations. Discourses covered family life, classics, philosophy, political reform, the revival of ancient ceremonies, poetry, and music. Confucius spoke about living life as a true gentleman, a loving part of the family, offering respect to all—including deceased ancestors. In philosophies similar to those of Socrates, he stated that vice sprang from ignorance and knowledge could lead to virtue. Through his travels, he collected the songs of the people and used them in his teaching. They were later edited into a collection known as *The Book of Songs*. Three thousand young men studied under Confucius and of those, seventy-two were his closest disciples. Confucius was never considered a religious leader during his lifetime, although after his death, his ethical tenets formed the basis for the religion of Confucianism and to many he is an archetypal man-as-god symbol.

Confucianism does not have supernatural elements; its basis is in the practical and in ethical education. His most important thoughts were collected into *Analects of Confucius*, which became the Chinese bible[2] and was later translated by various authors into many languages, including English. The complexities of thought found in his writings are equaled by the variance in translations.

The racist, fear-driven American populist invention called the "yellow peril" was piqued by the numerous Charlie Chan films, wherein Chan often supplied homilies to define solutions to mystifying situations. Through seemingly complete ignorance, as well as ignominious nationalistic instincts, Americans demeaned the esteemed educator using crude humor. His brilliant proverbs became raunchy "Confucius say" jokes, debasing the Chinese. On examination, the jokes serve to point out the childish stupidity, crass vulgarity, and extensive sexual repression found in America. "Confucius say" jokes are the perfect example of monocultural racism—America was the only country that degraded Confucian thought.

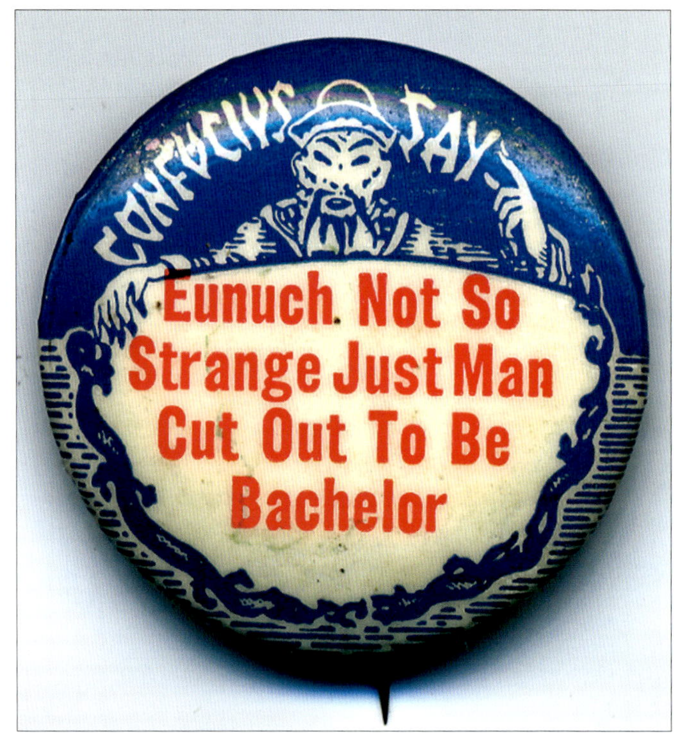

Confucius Say, pinback button, circa 1940s

"Confucius say" jokes were common inanities by the mid-1950s. Like knock-knock jokes, they relied upon the use of a double entendre for their humor. They also relied upon an uninformed American educational system, one in which the only thing students were taught about Confucius was that he was Chinese. "Confucius say" jokes demonstrated the decades-long absence of a worldview in the education of schoolchildren during the lengthy nationalistic, isolationist, era in America's development (a condition that has hardly improved). Sadly, these racist jokes clearly italicize the world's notion of the ugly American stereotype. The jokes were purposely weighted toward horrible misogyny as well as constant slurs on sex. Some of these mean-spirited sayings were:

- Confucius say: Woman who cooks carrots and peas in same pot unsanitary.
- Confucius say: Man who go to bed with hard problem wake up with solution in hand.

• Confucius say: Stenographer not permanent fixture till
screwed on desk.
• Confucius say: Woman who marry detective must kiss
dick.
• Confucius say: Woman is like swing music, 3/4 jazz time,
1/4 rag time.
• Confucius say: Wife who put husband in doghouse soon
find him in cat house.
• Confucius say: Woman not bowlegged, just pleasure bent.
• Confucius say: Man who lays prostitute puts stomach "on
the bum."
• Confucius say: Man have more hair on chest than woman,
but on whole woman have more.

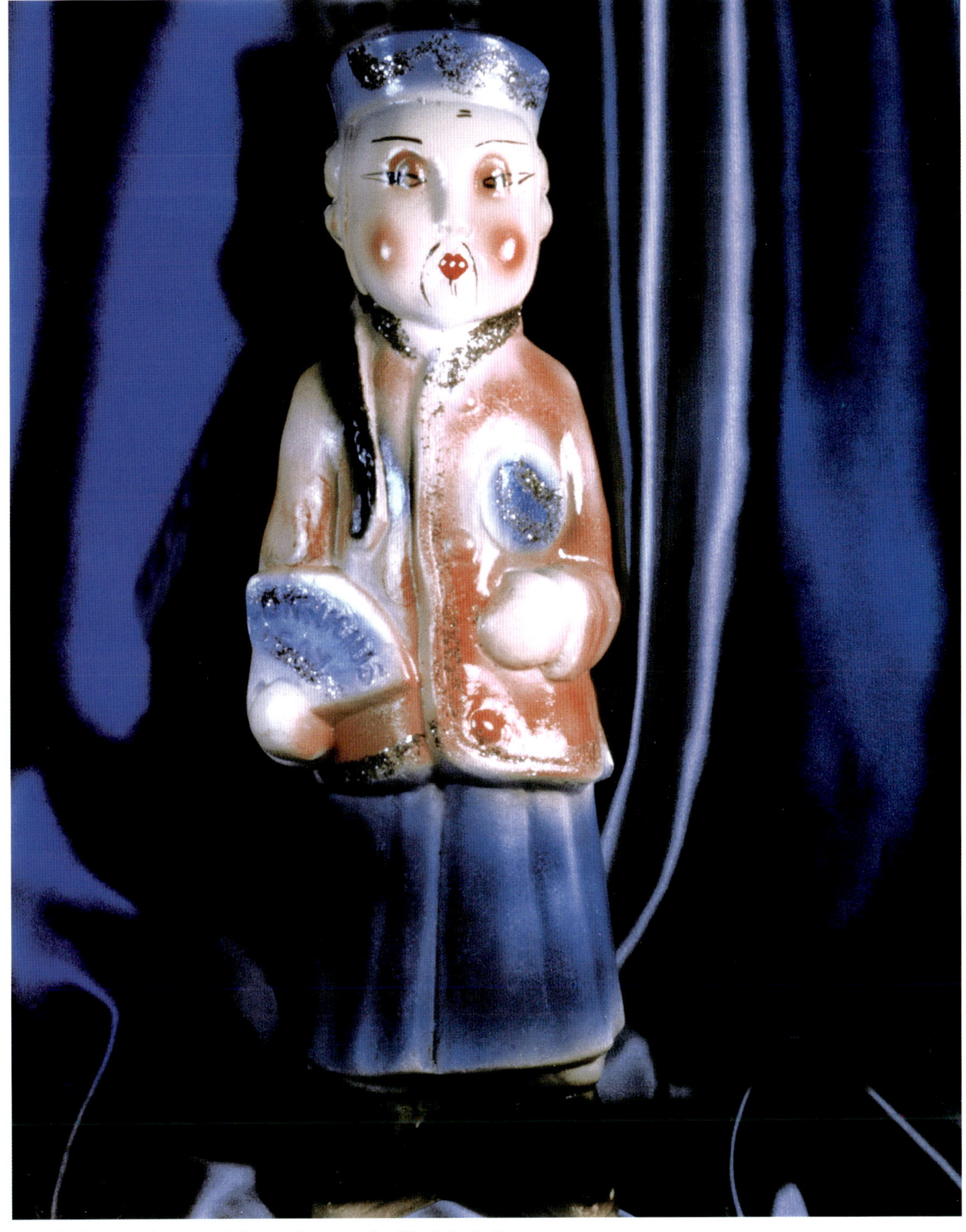

Confucius fourteen-inch carnival chalkware prize, text on fan: "Confucius Say"

BETTY GRABLE

(1916-1973)

There are two reasons why I'm in show business, and I'm standing on both of them.
— BETTY GRABLE

I want a girl just like the girl that married Harry James.
— G.I. SLOGAN, World War II

Betty Grable stereotyped the World War II pinup girl. It was estimated that her bathing-suit picture was pinned up, or at least owned, by one out of five U.S. servicemen during World War II, more than any other Hollywood star. Two million pinups of her were given away in 1943. She wore a Betty Boop–style garter on one leg in the original photo, but censors removed it by retouching the photograph. Postmaster General Frank C. Walker banned her pinup image from being sent through the mail system in 1944—a restriction that had the effect of making it even more delicious contraband and a hotter item in the barracks.[1] Eisenhower called her the "girl who helped us win the war," and he was right. She raised millions by auctioning her nylons at war bond rallies and worked tirelessly at the Hollywood Canteen, which opened its doors in October 1942. Many GIs on their way overseas, some never to return home, were afforded the rare opportunity to dance and talk with their favorite pinup queen, who also served them crullers and coffee, as well as entertaining them with a cheerful song.[2]

The Betty Grable pinup poster was a mild sex fantasy, especially when compared with the measure and availability of the pornography that followed, but a more essential function during World War II was its message to the soldiers that home, country, style, and the girl next door were causes worth fighting for—worth giving up their lives for. This was perhaps the subtle essence of Eisenhower's accolade for Grable's contribution. Her image helped to impart values to the soldier's horrific notion of being killed in a battle far from home. For a general engaged in deadly combat, having troops who are dedicated to the cause is perhaps more essential than weapons and rations. If a sweet smile and sexy legs can help to instill that allegiance, all the better. Grable was Hollywood's number-one sex symbol of the 1940s, so much so that by 1943 her legs were insured for $1,250,000, adding a great deal to her media hype. She was placed in numerous romantic musicals developed specifically for her sweet singing voice and glamorous dancing. She pleasantly lit up the wartime screen with her stereotypical white bread charm, a warm smile, blonde hair, and, of course, those shapely legs. Hollywood thought America needed her as a clean, positive sex symbol as a reminder that an overly talented apple-pie girl did live right next door. When superstar fame arrived, she demanded to always be filmed in bright Technicolor— good down-home state-of-the-art ra-ra-ra, sis-boom-ba. She wanted to be glistening with a wholesome perfect-woman archetype, supported by sappy big-band music and the over-the-counter bottled-blonde stereotype. Grable was living proof that the Will Hays Production Code had titivated (tidied up the decor) Hollywood.

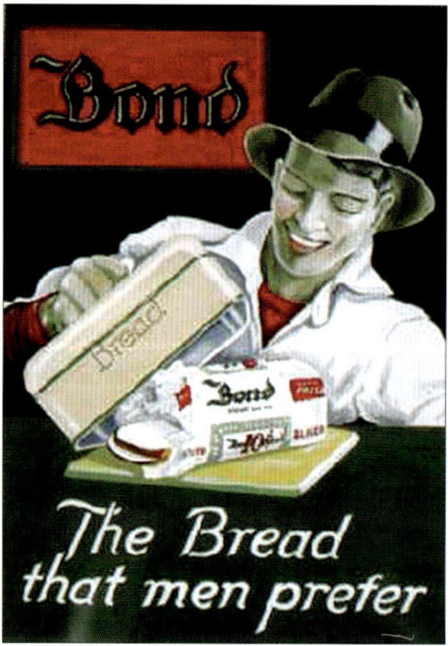

"The Bread that men prefer," Bond Bread ad, illustration Walter L. Mayo, 1938

Ruth Elizabeth Grable was born in St. Louis in 1916. Her overly ambitious mother enrolled her in dancing school at age three. In 1929, at thirteen, she secured a blackface part in *Let's Go Places*. She did go places! She married Jackie Coogan in 1937. Daryl Zanuck discovered her star qualities and whisked her away from chorine bit parts to give her the major dancing and singing roles that would make her legs famous. Her first starring roles had college and football themes—she starred as a cheerleader in *Million Dollar Legs* (1939) and the name became her trademark. That same year, Coogan began to suffer from depression—he could not obtain the money he had made as a child star—and they divorced. In 1940, *Down Argentine Way* became her biggest box-office hit, although it alienated many South Americans. *Life* displayed her skirt-lifting antics and glorious legs on their December 11, 1940, cover, swiping Betty Boop's cartoon antics from a decade earlier. Grable married band leader and trumpeter Harry James in 1943. She was one of the highest paid Hollywood stars, but in her contract with Fox Studios she was limited to singing only on film sound tracks.[3] Many of her films were formulaic: love, followed by misunderstanding and breakup, then a final audience-pleasing reconciliation. Her career collapsed when she began being

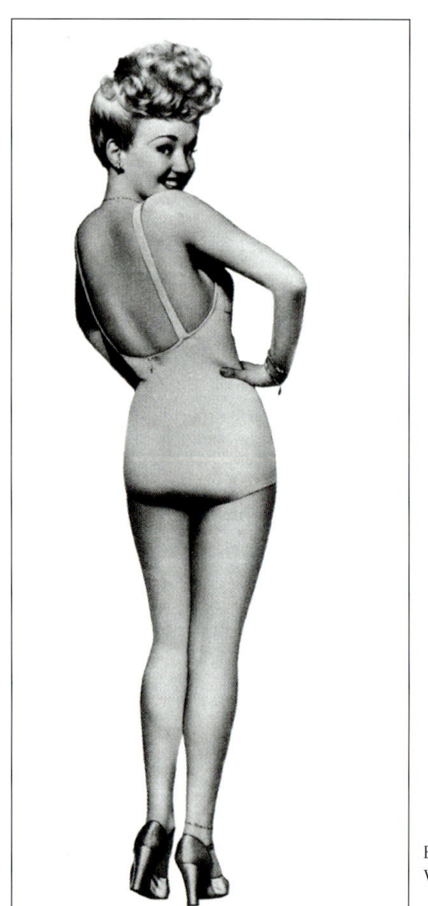

Betty Grable, pinup,
World War II

compared to a rising star named Marilyn Monroe. She already knew it on the set of *How to Marry a Millionaire* and told Marilyn, "It's your turn honey. I've had it."

A restricted, repressed, overly diligent war-torn white America had vicariously lived through her glitz, like a jeweled opaque curtain that hid them from their Rosie the Riveter, nose-to-the-grindstone era. Grable divorced James in 1965, and she died of cancer in 1973.

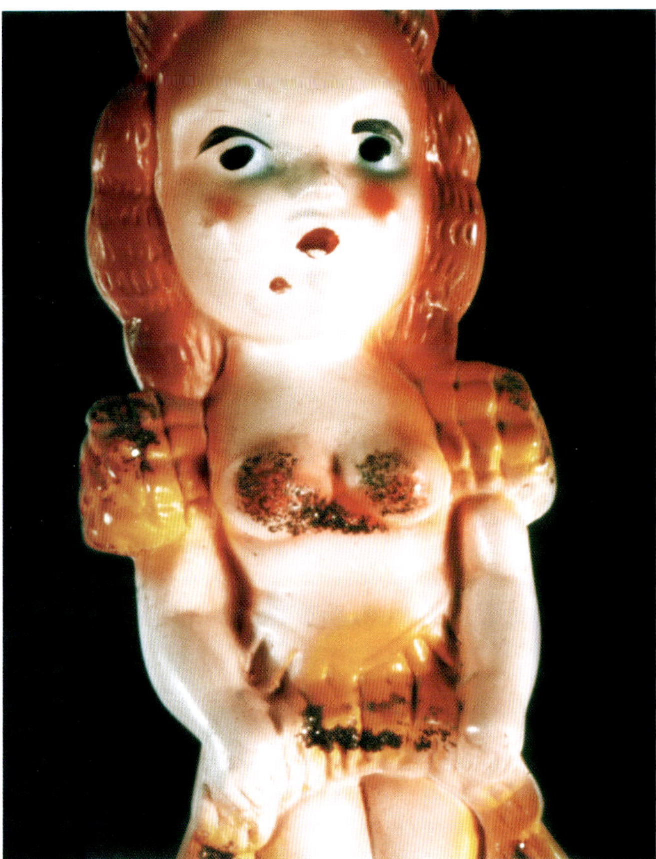

Betty Grable thirteen-and-a-half-inch carnival chalk prize, from the film *Down Argentine Way* (1940). Some of the multitudes of majorette carnival chalk prizes were probably meant to be a high-strutting, short-skirted Betty Grable from *Million Dollar Legs* (1939).

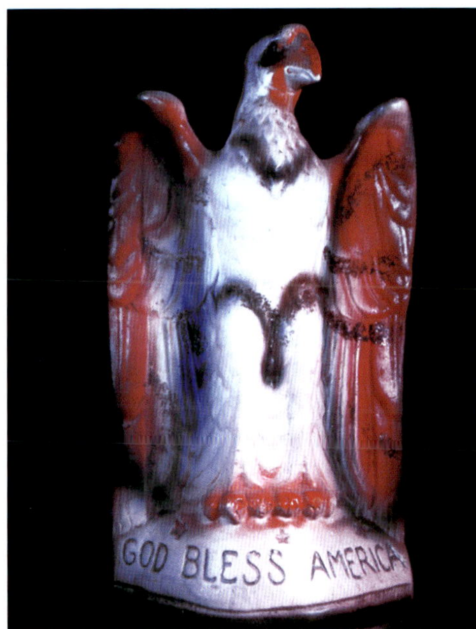

God Bless America, twelve-inch carnival chalk prize, World War II

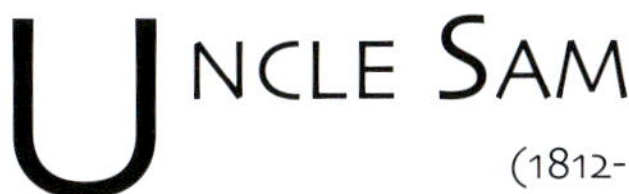

UNCLE SAM

(1812-

We must play a great part in the world, and especially perform those deeds of blood and valor, which above everything else bring national renown.
—THEODORE ROOSEVELT

You can go a long way with a smile. You can go a lot farther with a smile and a gun.
—AL CAPONE

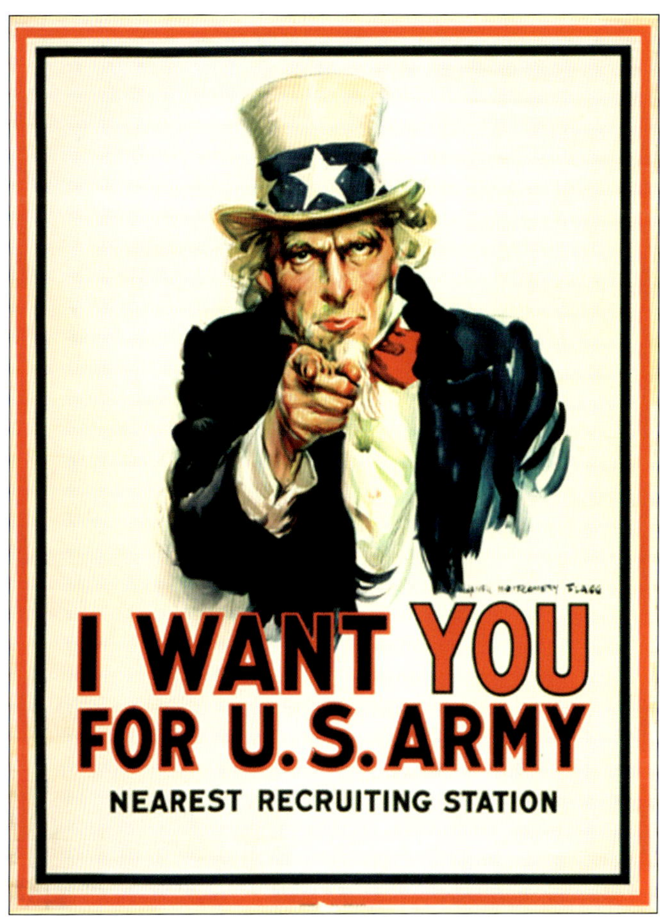

"I Want You," U.S. Army poster, James Montgomery Flagg, World War I

Giving legitimacy to one of America's most symbolic icons and nationalistic archetypes, the 87th Congress of the United States adopted the following resolution on September 15, 1961: "Resolved by the Senate and the House of Representatives that the Congress salutes Uncle Sam Wilson of Troy, New York, as the progenitor of America's National symbol of Uncle Sam." Samuel Wilson of Massachusetts served first as a drummer boy and then as a soldier in the Revolutionary War. He moved to Troy, New York, in 1789, where he ran a meatpacking business. His friendly attitude, fair dealing, and knowledgeable business manner earned him the affectionate nickname "Uncle Sam." In the War of 1812, Wilson provided pork and beef to the army troops in barrels labeled "US." That abbreviation was not in general use, so when a federal inspection team visited Wilson's plant in 1812 and asked a workman what the "US" on the pork barrels signified, the worker replied, "Uncle Sam"—the derivation of both "pork barrel" and "Uncle Sam." Soon soldiers and civilians alike transferred the nickname from their real-life Uncle Sam Wilson to the federal government. The earliest surviving use of the term is from the *Troy Post* of September 3, 1813: "Loss upon loss, and no luck stirring but what lights upon Uncle Sam's shoulders, exclaim the Government editors, in every part of the Country."

Though the original Sam Wilson was tall and thin, the first imaginary Uncle Sam was caricatured as a portly man in a black top hat and tails. Later he was dressed patriotically in red, white, and blue—the colors in the American flag. Finally he became tall, gaunt, and bearded when imagined by Thomas Nast and other nineteenth-century political cartoonists who modeled him after deified president Abraham Lincoln. Throughout the twentieth century, Uncle Sam has continued to represent the government and patriotic spirit—as well as the draft and taxes. In images connected to war Uncle Sam is always an archetypal symbol motif for winning.

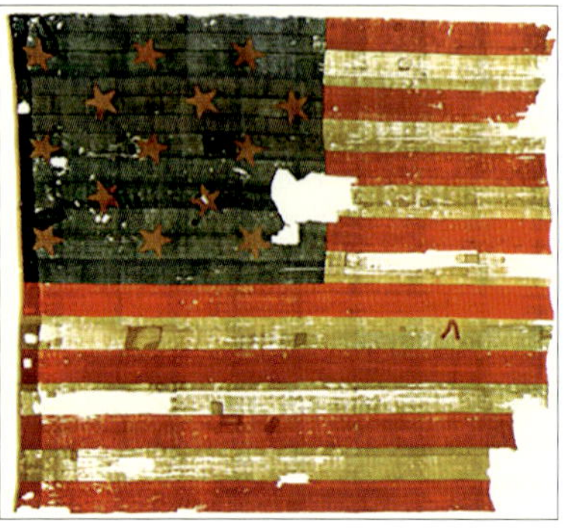

U.S. Victory Flag flown on September 14, 1814, over Fort McHenry that Francis Scott Key celebrated in his poem "Star Spangled Banner." The original flag measured 30 feet by 42 feet. Three weeks earlier on August 24, 1814, British troops burned the U.S. Capitol and the President's Mansion in Washington. President James Madison and his wife Dolly barely escaped. Presently the flag measures 30 feet by 34 feet because 200 square feet of it were given away in small pieces as souvenirs, including one of the stars (an archetypal prize motif). Collection: Smithsonian Institution

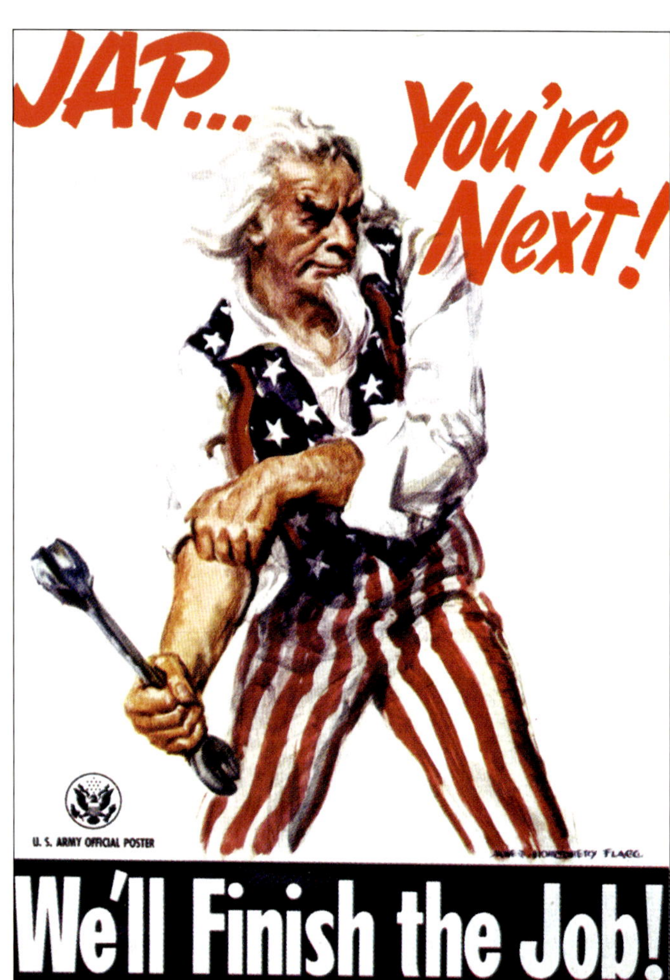

"Jap, You're Next!," U.S. Army poster, James Montgomery Flagg, World War II

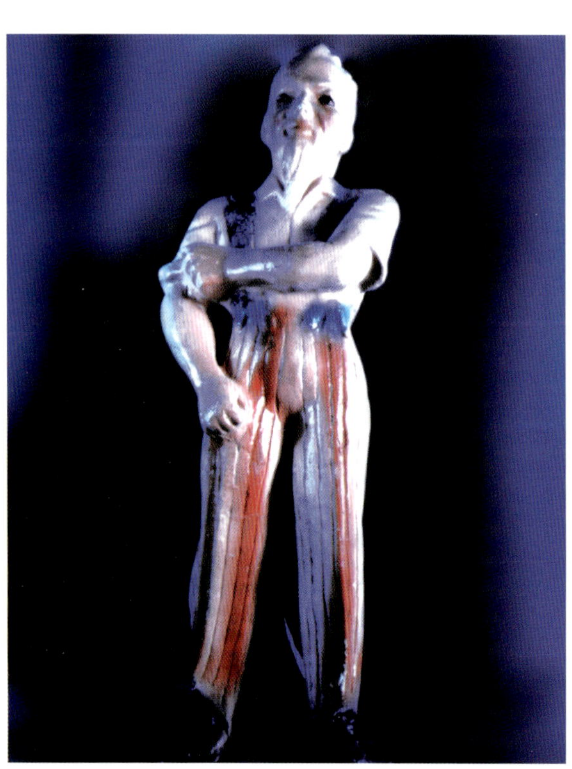

Uncle Sam fifteen-inch carnival chalk prize, World War II

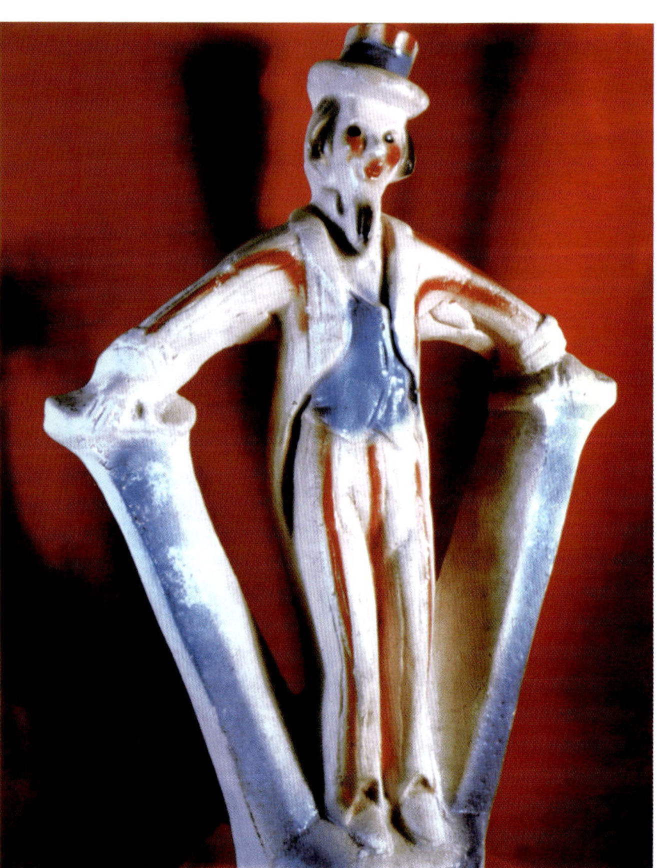

Uncle Sam thirteen-inch carnval chalk prize, the V is for Victory, an archetypal motif for feeling hope and the thrill of victory

F RANKLIN DELANO ROOSEVELT (1882-1945)

The average man won't really do a day's work unless he is caught and cannot get out of it. There is plenty of work to do if people would do it.
—HENRY FORD, March 1931—a few weeks after making this statement, Ford Motor Company laid off 75,000 workers

Let me assert my firm belief that the only thing we have to fear is fear itself.
—FRANKLIN DELANO ROOSEVELT, speech, July 2, 1932

Born into a privileged family in 1882, Franklin Delano Roosevelt was schooled by governesses and private tutors until he was fourteen. The following four years, he attended Groton School in Massachusetts, where he was considered superficial by his classmates who nicknamed him "Featherduster." Groton School did, however, teach him that those born of privilege have a duty to serve. He attended Harvard and became infatuated with his cousin Eleanor. They married in 1905, when he was twenty-three. Eleanor and Franklin's uncle Teddy gave the bride away. Politics became FDR's social venture—through name recognition and the Roosevelt fortune, he was elected to the New York State Senate in 1910. He was the archetypal Prince Charming, entrusted and favored nephew of the popular Spanish-American War hero-celebrity Theodore Roosevelt.

FDR became assistant secretary of the navy in 1913 and gained wider name recognition when he ran for vice president in 1920. He lost the 1920 election, but expanded his political savvy through his years in Washington. Two years earlier, in 1918, as World War I was ending, Eleanor, who had borne him six children by then, discovered that FDR was having an affair with her personal social secretary, Lucy Mercer. Eleanor did not divorce him; on the contrary, she became his strong emotional anchor, particularly when he contracted polio in 1921 and his legs were paralyzed. Eleanor continually infused him with energy and they gradually created a strong partnership in the world of politics.

FDR was elected governor of New York in 1928. In 1930, after the stock market crash, he began giving inspired radio addresses. Later, when he became president, these talks were known as fireside chats. The French reporter Amaury de Riencourt described these radio talks as "a remarkable exercise in mass hypnotism." FDR's heartfelt radio moments made him masterful, immensely popular, and even more charismatic. In reality his speeches contained sophisticated world superiority archetypes. Unlike Hitler and Mussolini, who took advantage of the new medium of radio to expound their views through bombastic speeches made against a background of mass hysteria, FDR preferred a more homely approach. He spoke calmly, purring his thoughts and ideas into the aspirations and fears of American families. Many felt he was talking to them personally and that he understood their problems.

When accepting his party's nomination for president in 1932, FDR said:

> I pledge you, I pledge myself, to a new deal for the American people. Let all of us here assembled constitute ourselves prophets of a new order of competence and of courage. This is more than a political campaign; it is a call to arms. Give me your help, not to win votes alone, but to win in this crusade to restore America to its own greatness.

The words "new deal" stuck with the electorate. During the Depression, these chats helped his New Deal, "this socialist measure" as a hostile Congress often called it.[1]

FDR went on to win an unprecedented four terms as president, seeing the country through controversial social programs devised to end the Depression and later through World War II. After Pearl Harbor, FDR ended his radio address of December 9, 1941, by saying:

> The true goal we seek is far above and beyond the ugly field of battle. When we resort to force, as now we must, we are determined that this force shall be directed toward ultimate good as well as against immediate evil. We Americans are not destroyers; we are builders.
>
> We are now in the midst of a war, not for conquest, not for vengeance, but for a world in which this Nation, and all that this Nation represents, will be safe for our children. We expect to eliminate the danger from Japan, but it would serve us ill if we accomplished that and found that the rest of the world was dominated by Hitler and Mussolini.
>
> We are going to win the war, and we are going to win the peace that follows.
>
> And in the dark hours of this day, and through dark days that may be yet to come, we will know that the vast majority of the members of the human race are on our side. Many of them are fighting with us. All of them are praying for us. For, in representing our cause, we represent theirs as well, our hope and their hope for liberty under God.[2]

Some found FDR politically tricky and wanting, particularly H. L. Mencken, who thought FDR stereotyped a "quack doctor" who "carried out his job with an ingratiating grin upon his face, like that of a snake-oil vendor at a village carnival." Many historians felt that FDR's inflexible and obdurate policies toward Japan forced that empire into a war with the United States and seeded their subsequent attack on Pearl Harbor. Historians felt that America had no right to meddle in Indo-Chinese policies, which clearly lay outside America's interests, particularly at a time when war with Germany was ready to ignite. Many Americans did wonder why FDR had placed so much of the U.S. Navy in one spot.

World War II pulled America out of the Depression by making use of mass produced goods, much of which was sold to the Allies. The United States had only three aircraft carriers in the fall of 1942. A year later there were fifty, all due to an unstoppable female stereotype named Rosie the Riveter. Wars produce profits for some, but a sad truth of history that echoes through the hearts of common folk is that people are not as precious as wealth, power, territory, and possessions.

By the time FDR was reelected for his fourth term

in 1944, his doctors knew he suffered from hypertension
and heart disease. That same year, he met again with his
former lover, Lucy Mercer, who was with him when he died
in 1945 at Warm Springs, Georgia.

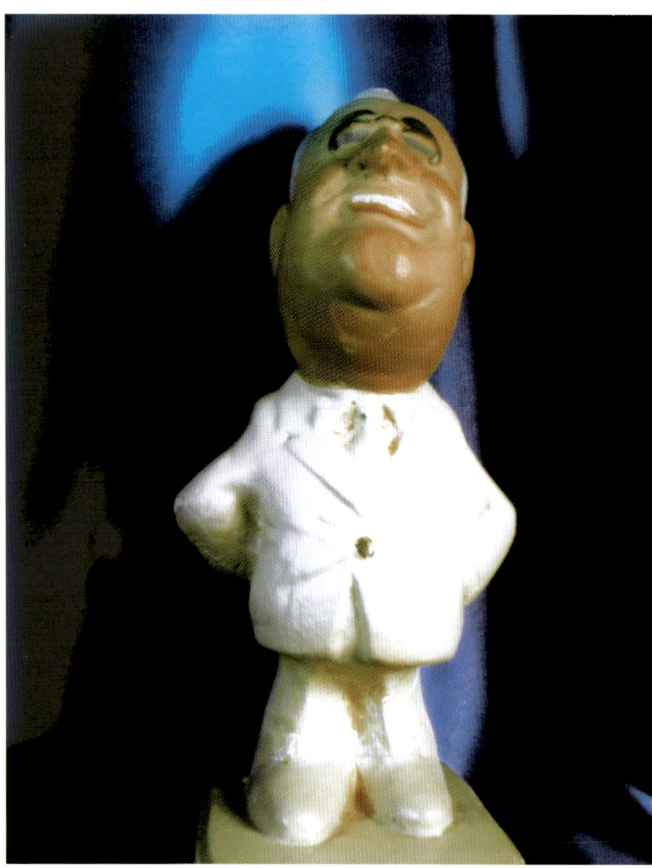

Franklin Delano Roosevelt eight-and-a-half-inch carnival chalkware prize, part of a set of
three Allied WWII figures including Churchill and Stalin

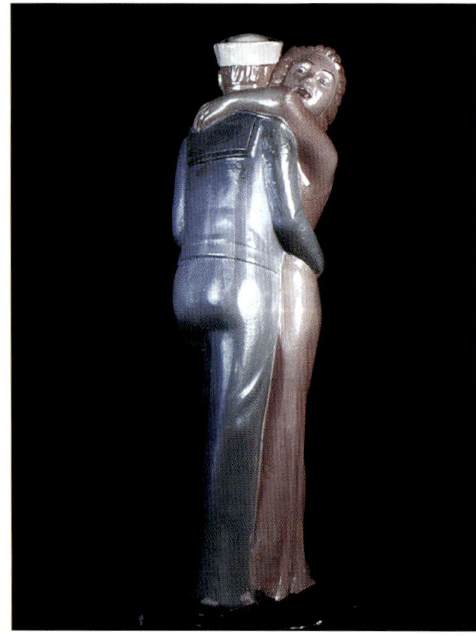

World War II dancers fourteen-inch carnival chalk prize
© Alexander Kahn Products, 1942

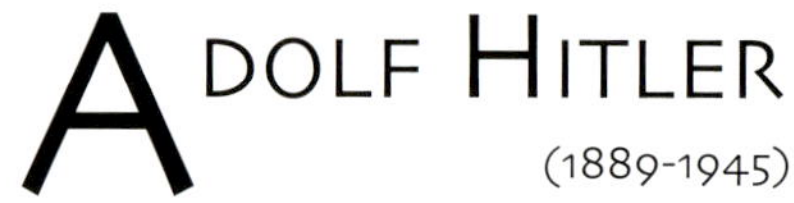

Adolf Hitler

(1889-1945)

All those who are not racially pure are mere chaff.
—Adolf Hitler, *Mein Kampf*

*. . . from maggots up to man, the universal law is the violent destruc-
tion of human beings. The whole earth, continually steeped in blood,
is nothing but an immense altar on which every living thing must be
sacrificed without end, without restraint, without respite until the
consummation of the world, the extinction of evil, the death of death.*
—Joseph de Maistre (1753-1821), the Jesuit Catholic reactionary
who influenced European fascism

*A certain sense of cruelty towards oneself and others is Christian;
hatred of those who think differently; the will to persecute. Hatred
of mind, of pride, courage, freedom, libertinage of mind, is Christian; hatred of the sense, of the joy of the senses, of joy in general is
Christian. . .*
—Friedrich Nietzsche

Adolf Hitler has always presented a volatile embarrassment to Christianity. Many have tried to assert that he was
not a Christian. But he was raised a Roman Catholic and
due to his fanaticism, became an extremist militant Christian.
Through an intentional rewriting of history, Hitler has been
assigned to the stereotype of Fascist Nazi madman.

Hitler repeatedly revealed his Christian convic-
tions in many speeches. The following was part of a speech
he gave on April 12, 1922:

> My feelings as a Christian points me to my Lord and Savior
> as a fighter. It points me to the man who once in loneliness,
> surrounded only by a few followers, recognized these Jews
> for what they were and summoned men to fight against
> them and who, God's truth!, was greatest not as a sufferer
> but as a fighter. In boundless love as a Christian and as
> a man I read through the passage which tells us how the
> Lord at last rose in His might and seized the scourge to
> drive out of the Temple the brood of vipers and adders [the
> Jews as moneylenders]. How terrific was His fight for the
> world against the Jewish poison. Today, after two thousand
> years, with deepest emotion I recognize more profoundly
> than ever before in the fact that it was for this that He had
> to shed His blood upon the Cross. As a Christian I have no
> duty to allow myself to be cheated, but I have the duty to be
> a fighter for truth and justice.[1]

This speech reinforces the archetypal imagery
of Jesus throwing the dirty, evil moneylenders, the Jews,
out of the temple. This archetypal cliché is unknowingly
reflected contemporaneously when we use the term "dirty
money."

Here is part of a speech Hitler gave in Munich on
February 24, 1939, the same year Germany invaded Poland:

> If positive Christianity means love of one's neighbor, i.e.
> the tending of the sick, the clothing of the poor, the feeding
> of the hungry, the giving of drink to those who are thirsty,

then it is we who are the more positive Christians. For in these spheres the community of the people of National Socialist Germany has accomplished a prodigious work . . .[2]

In thought and action, Hitler assessed himself as a Christian fighter recast in a role similar to that of Jesus as a lone fighter. Monster that he was, Hitler's murderous programs were no more extreme than those of Pope Urban II, who started the first People's Crusade in 1095. The Crusades—which were continued by certain subsequent popes—continually strove toward the same goals that Hitler later attempted to achieve. Those who fought on the side of the early popes in the Crusades were offered "forgiveness from all their sins" and "guaranteed eternal bliss in their secured place in heaven." But because Hitler also promoted his master race ideals, it is easy to see how the rest of the Christian world stereotyped him as a Nazi madman and cast aside any connections he had to Christianity. For most Americans, Hitler epitomized the archetypal motif of the ultimate enemy. That he was.

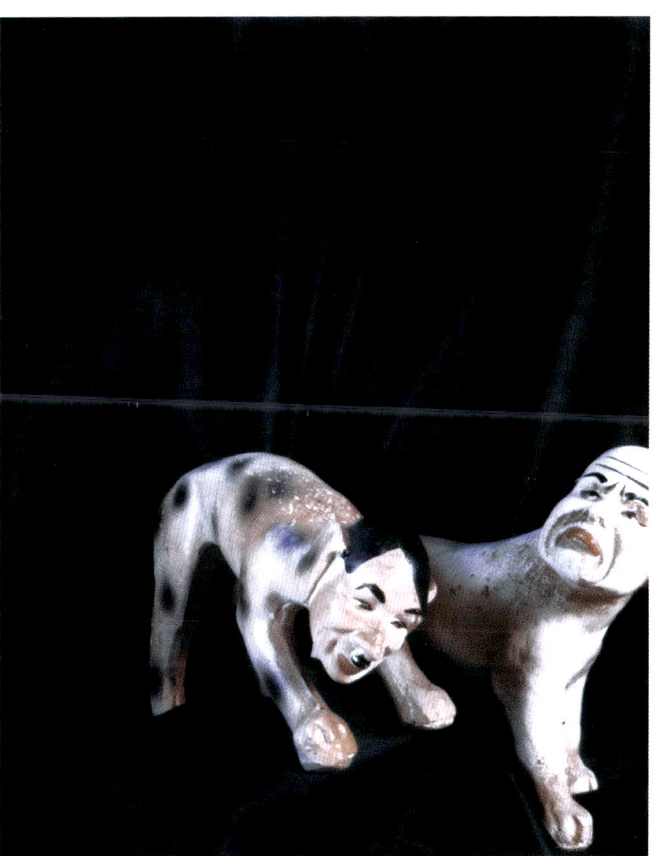
Five-inch Hitler jackal and five-and-one-half-inch Mussolini dog carnival chalk prizes

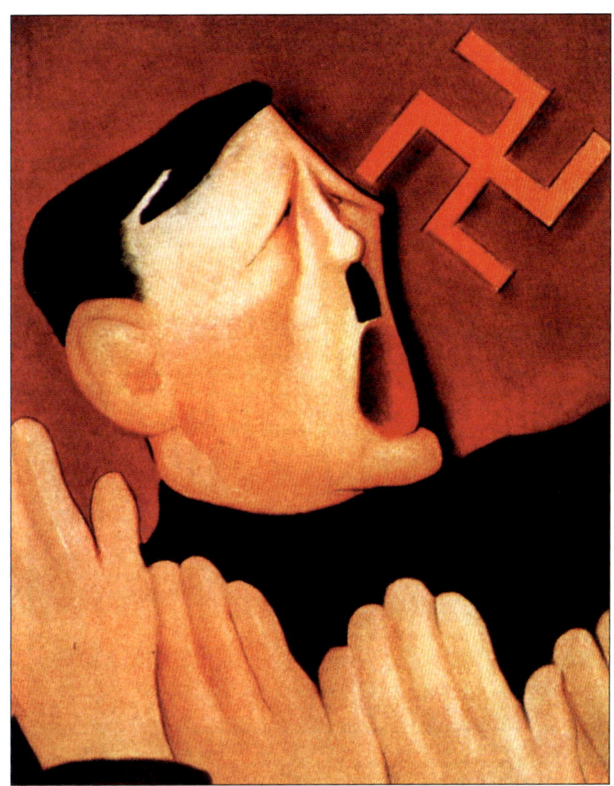
Adolf Hitler —Napoleon Jr., magazine illustration W. Cotton, 1933

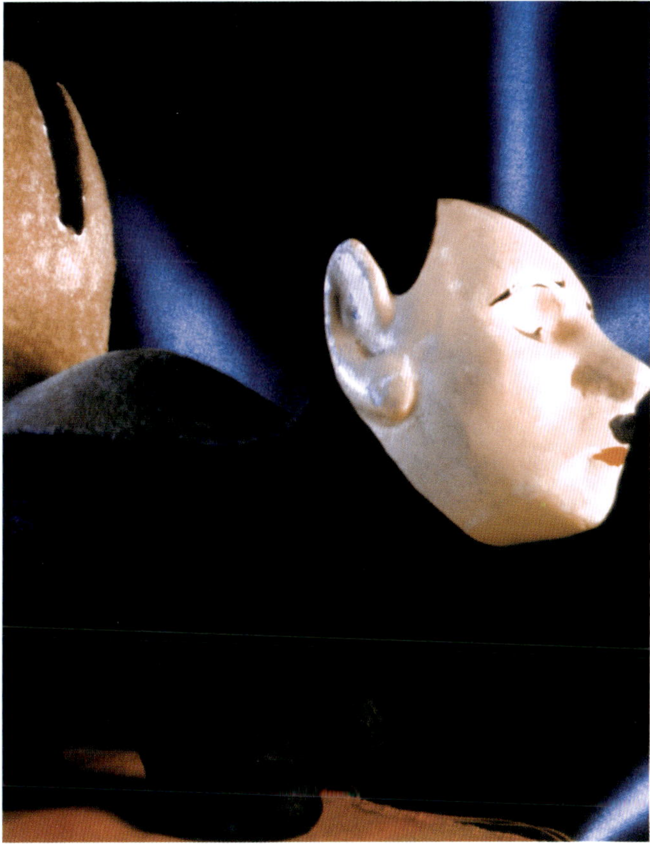
Hitler skunk five-inch carnival chalk prize, Wisconsin Deluxe, designed by Ned Torti, a 1940s caricature of the despised Hitler with tail up—spewing his stinking ideas

Helena Petrovna Blavatsky, the Russian-born occultist and founder of the Theosophical Society, published *The Secret Doctrine* in 1888. In it she wrote that each cycle of creation has seven stages of evolution emanating from what she called "root races." One of these root races she named Aryan, although none of her races were seen as superior to any other. Three years later, Friedrich Nietzsche gave his "superman" or "overman" the name Zarathustra in *Thus Spake Zarathustra*. In the late nineteenth century, Austrian mystic Guido von List took Blavatsky's term "Aryan" for the name of his Aryan-Germanic master race movement, known as Ariosophy, which was heavily anti-Jewish. List adopted the swastika as his group's emblem and wrote a series of occult essays known as *Die Religio der Ario-Germanen*. By 1911, Hitler had studied philosophy, Oriental mysticism, astrology, hypnotism, and Germanic mythology. One of his mentors, Lanz von Liebenfels, was editor and publisher of the anti-Jewish magazine *Ostara*, which also used the swastika as its symbol. Another of Hitler's influential mentors was the occultist Ernst Pretzsche, a Viennese bookstore owner and devotee of Wolfram von Eschenbach's *Parzival*, in which initiates acquired the mystic's art of reading from the cosmic chronicle of human destiny—a past, present, and future united into one uncoiling ribbon of time. Pretzsche indoctrinated Hitler in Germanic mysticism and successfully encouraged him to use the hallucinogenic drug peyote as a tool for achieving mystical enlightenment. For a time, Pretzsche lived in a German colony in Mexico, where the peyote cactus is native; his father was the local apothecary. Earlier research on peyote by German pharmacologist Ludwig Lewin had been published in 1888; he received peyote samples from Parke-Davis Pharmaceutical Company of Detroit (mescaline was isolated in 1895 and synthesized in 1919). In his drug-induced trance, Hitler found himself, both as an earlier villainous spirit and as a prophet for Aryan master race events that would take place later in his lifetime. He used drugs to reinforce his belief that his was the God-chosen way and that he was the God-chosen leader of a superior race of Christian fighters descended from a previous superrace, all archetypes for God-Messiah-power.

became closely associated with the secret occult organization Thule, a group that believed in List's Aryan master race and preached the coming of a German Messiah—a chosen one who would lead Germany to glory and a new Aryan civilization. Thule was financed by some of the same industrialists who supported the Army District Command, and was believed by its followers to be a legendary island in the far north, similar to Atlantis, supposedly the center of a lost, higher-level civilization. Not all secrets of that civilization had been completely destroyed, and those that remained were guarded by ancient, highly intelligent beings. The truly initiated could establish contact with these beings by means of mystical rituals and, in turn, the ancients endowed the initiated with supernatural strength and energy. With the help of these energies, the goal of the initiated was to create a race of supermen of Aryan stock who would exterminate all inferior races. Jews topped the list.

At the end of 1919, Hitler met Dietrich Eckart, publisher and editor of the extreme right-wing anti-Jewish journal *In Plain German*. Eckart was a committed occultist and a master of magic. He belonged to the inner circle of Thule and, like Hitler, first achieved transcendence through peyote rituals in Berlin. Eckart trained Hitler in techniques of self-confidence, self-projection, persuasive oratory, body language, and discursive sophistry. With these powerful new skills, Hitler was able to move his obscure workers party from its beer-hall atmosphere into a mass movement in a short

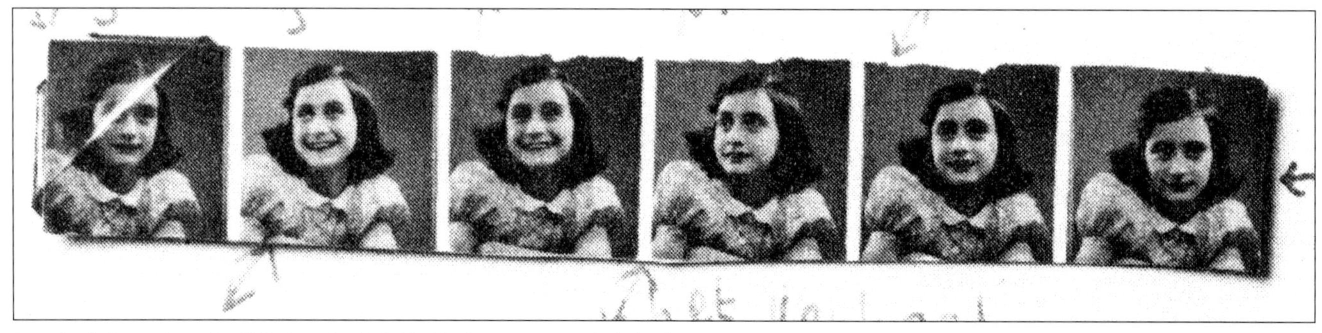

Anne Frank, *Diary*, September 1942. Anne Frank died in March 1945, two months before liberation.

Hitler enlisted in the army during World War I and narrowly escaped death several times. He received the Iron Cross in 1918, two months before he was blinded by mustard gas. While recuperating at Pasewalk military hospital in northern Germany, he was diagnosed as suffering from psychopathic hysteria. According to Hitler, during his hospital stay he experienced a powerful vision in which he was told he must restore his sight in order to lead Germany back to glory. Now in a more fanaticized state, Hitler rejoined the military after World War I and identified pro-Communist soldiers to be executed, a service that earned him a promotion and an assignment to the highly secret Political Department of the Army District Command.

Hitler's new unit was an intelligence operation that engaged in acts of domestic terrorism. Refusing to accept Germany's defeat in World War I, the unit assassinated a number of the German leaders who had negotiated the surrender. By joining the Army District Command, Hitler

period of time. He became an expert orator and rodomontade (someone capable of mesmerizing vast audiences). He dedicated *Mein Kampf* to Eckart, who by 1923 had died from a weakened heart and body, as a derelict heroin addict.

When Hitler came to power in the 1930s, he chose the swastika as the emblem for his Nazi Party, thinking that it already symbolized identity against the Jews—but he turned the swastika backward. Occultists thought his turning the swastika backwards was a bad omen.

In 1932, the Nazi Party received 40 percent of the German vote. A year later Hitler became chancellor of Germany. The worldwide depression had been hard for Germany's reconstruction after World War I, and in his uncompromising election speeches, Hitler protested against paying the war debt and said that Jews and Communists were the cause for Germany's defeat in World War I. He promised to rid Germany of Jews and Communists and to reunite the German-speaking part of Europe. Hitler enacted sterilization laws in 1933, modeled after the American eugenics expert Harry Hamilton Laughlin's Model Eugenical Sterilization Law, written in 1914 and passed in the United States in 1924. Laughlin was awarded an honorary degree from the University of Heidelberg in 1936 for his work in the "science of racial cleansing." The word "cleansing" is important to understand, as it has pertinent implications to many archetypal symbols of unclean or polluted, thereby unworthy of life. Robert Jay Lifton, in *The Nazi Doctors*, explained:

> Pollution imagery is associated with many forms of victimization involving class and caste as well as color and race. The traditional Japanese group of outcasts bear the name "Eta," whose literal meaning is "full of pollution," "full of filth," or "abundant defilement."[3]

A crude, yet contemporary archetypal motif for this slur would be to label someone "full of shit." Lifton goes on to explain the hatred of Jews and the reasoning behind the wholesale destruction of Jews in the Holocaust, by saying:

> Jews have also been frequently associated with death and defilement, but in ways even more dangerous to others: accusations of being well-poisoners and plague spreaders, of practicing necromancy and in ceremonial drinking of blood or ritual murder of Christian children as sacrifices for a black mass. Jews have also over the course of their history been confined to the same defiling professions in which the Eta engage, as well as forced to associate with money or "usury," the term meaning "lending money with interest" but conveying a sense of dishonesty, ugliness, and taboo very close to defilement. The symbolism of money as "filthy lucre," "evil excrescence," and also "immortal stuff" (mystical and magical) suggests its relation both to feces and death on the one hand, and to an immortalizing mode on the other. But by becoming bound up with what was generally perceived as an illegitimate and tainted mode of immortality, the Jews became further vulnerable to victimization . . . Nazi genocide can, in fact, be understood as a fierce purification procedure.[4]

By 1934, Hitler had declared himself Führer, or dictator. Many of Germany's leading scholars, intellectuals, industrialists, and political consultants were Jews. German Jews had fought in World War I and considered themselves as German as anyone else. Under Hitler's government, the Third Reich, most German people (other than the German Jews), through government propaganda, were fanaticized into believing his agenda, "The Final Solution," which would create the perfect Aryan race. On January 2, 1939, Hitler was named *Time* magazine's "Man of the Year" for 1938. He invaded Poland in 1939, and began his unification of Germanic-speaking peoples.

Hitler devised a system that placed Nazi doctors at the top of the hierarchy of selectors of Jews and others who were put to death in concentration camps. Generally, the Jews who were killed first were those shown to have any unclean areas on their body, such as scabs or lesions of any kind. In order to heal the Nordic race, Nazi doctors worked within a terrible paradox of healer/killer and medical experimenter/

killer. Susanne K. Langer explains:

> The Auschwitz self was the means by which the Nazi doctor could bring to his killing the mana [supernatural force] of a shaman, a priest, a magician. For in the case of such an ancient healer, "there is no cleavage between the domain of fantasy in which he acts and the world of affairs wherein his mystic acts are efficacious." . . . In that way, the Auschwitz doctor-shaman becomes "loaded up with powers."[5]

And Lifton adds:

> He is a recognized healer with special powers; his killing is legitimated by, and at the same time further legitimates, the regime's overall healing-killing reversals. Thus it became quite natural to use a vehicle marked with a red cross to transport gas, gassing personnel, and sometimes victims, to the gas chambers.[6]

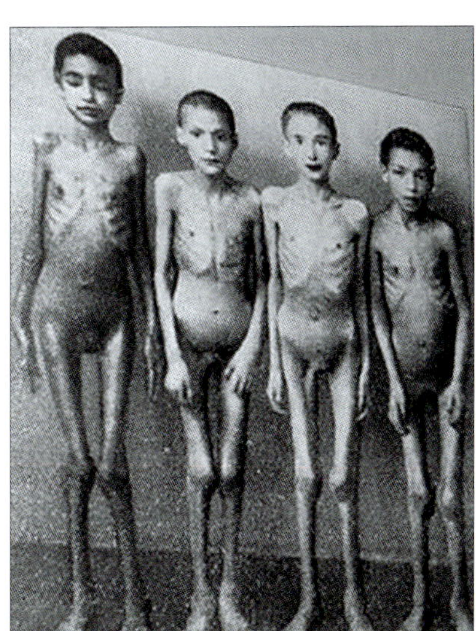

Deported concentration camp children photographed during use for medical research. Courtesy: Auschwitz Museum

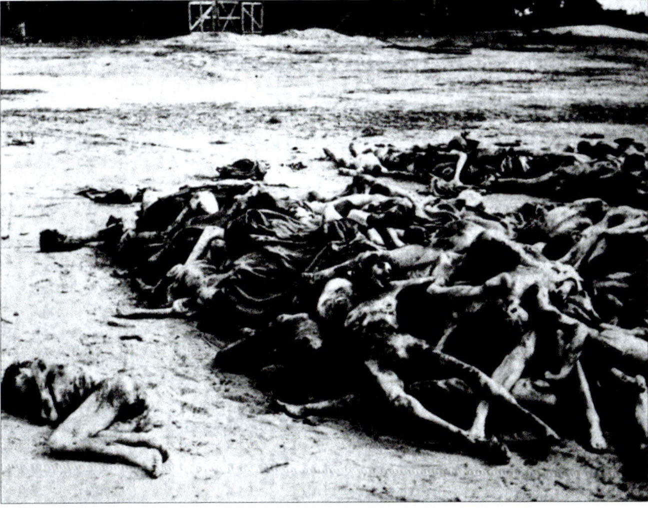

Bergen-Belsen Concentration Camp, at the time of British troop arrival. Courtesy: Netherlands State Institute of War Documentation

It wasn't until the end of the war that Americans would learn the full extent of the Holocaust, although many scholars suggest that it would have been impossible for Churchill and FDR not to know, at least to some degree, what was happening.

BENITO MUSSOLINI

(1883-1945)

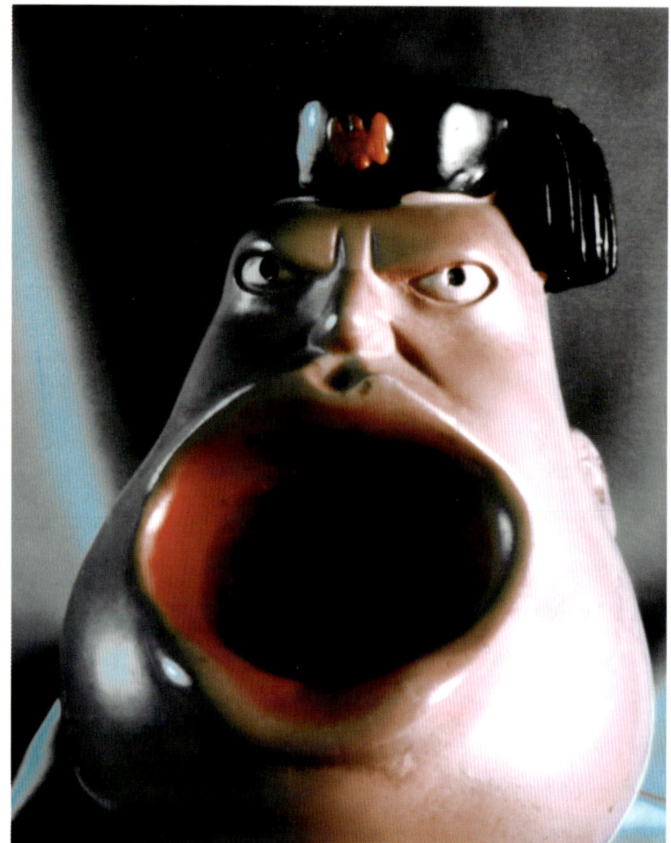

Mussolini five-inch carnival chalk ashtray prize

I glory in the fact that I am Latin, and I recognize a barbarian in every man of non-Latin blood.
—GABRIELE D'ANNUNZIO, the Father of 20th century Italian Fascism

Throughout history, it has been the inaction of those who could have acted; the indifference of those who should have known better; the silence of the voice of justice when it mattered most; that has made it possible for evil to triumph.
—HAILE SELASSIE

Fascism should rightly be called Corporatism as it is a merging of state and corporate power.
—BENITO MUSSOLINI

Mussolini for all his aspirations to exercise power . . . turned out to be no more than an ambitious intellectual from the provinces who believed that his will mattered, and who thought, as did others, that he was a Duce and could lead a state like Italy. He was a 'Sawdust Caesar,' no more than a buffoon.
—R. J. B. BOSWORTH, *Mussolini*

Someone who murdered hundreds of thousands of his Communist-leaning countrymen and was responsible for at least a million deaths during World War II should not get off merely being labeled as a buffoon, yet many still think of Benito Mussolini with that grandiose clown stereotype in mind. Replacing the heinous with the historically absurd might make history more palatable, but no one should be fooled. Wartime Americans stereotyped Mussolini as a loudmouthed buffoon, but underneath they knew he was the archetypal motif for the hostile brethren—a monster in partnership with madman Hitler and coward Tojo.

Benito Mussolini was born in rural Predappio, Italy, in 1883. His father was a Socialist and a blacksmith; his mother a schoolteacher. Mussolini immigrated to Switzerland in 1902. Unable to find work, he was arrested for vagrancy and deported to Italy to perform military service. By 1908 he had moved to Trento, Austria, working as a news reporter and writing the novel *The Cardinal's Mistress*. Deported to Italy once again, he became the editor of *La Lotta di Classe* (The Class Struggle). By 1911, he spoke of himself as a pacifist anti-imperialist and became editor of the important magazine *Avanti* (Forward) in Milan. Mussolini was badly injured by a grenade in a training accident in 1914, during World War I. He read political-social theory and spoke three languages. His brother, Arnoldo, became an important Fascist theorist.

Mussolini organized the *Fasci Italiani di Combattimento* (Italian Combat Veteran's League) at a gathering of war veterans, revolutionary Socialists, and futurists in 1919, which created a powerful force in Italian politics and brought the word "fascism" into the public arena. Fascism came from the Italian word *fascio*, meaning "union," and referred to the ancient Roman symbol of discipline and authority; the fasces was a standard—made of a bundle of rods and an ax—carried by Roman officials. By 1921, at age thirty-eight, Mussolini headed the Italian Fascist Party, which rallied against communism.

It was designed to bind all classes together under a capitalist system, but with major industries controlled by the state. To accomplish his rise in power, the black-shirted "Sawdust Caesar" (a slur from that era) had turned his political views 180 degrees to the ruthless right. A year later, King Victor Immanuel III made Mussolini the head of the Italian government. After 1922, Mussolini headed the ministries of interior, foreign affairs, colonies, corporations, army, and public works—as well as being premier. By 1925, he had dissolved all other political parties. His ability to propagandize was his talent and also his ruin.

Mussolini controlled the press and proclaimed himself to be Il Duce: "the man of absolute rightness, the true leader." Teachers in Italian schools and universities had to swear an oath to defend Mussolini's Fascist regime. All journalists were required to possess a certificate of approval from the Fascist Party. Trade unions became the corporative system, with no independent power. Under Mussolini, Italy became a total police state and was later imitated by Hitler (who also became Mussolini's close friend). Much of Mussolini's time was spent organizing labor, propagandizing about himself, bullying, and when necessary committing murder. He did bring stability to the economy and made the trains run on time. To project the necessary machismo charisma, Mussolini would give his passionate speeches at political gatherings with his chest bared. To those who rose against him, obsessive inflated narcissism became his stereotype. When Italy invaded unarmed Ethiopia in 1935 using chemical warfare (poison gas), world opinion turned against Mussolini. Particularly angered were the British and the French. Hitler

210

was to be his ally. Mussolini coined the term "Axis Powers" in 1936, connecting himself to Hitler in Germany and Franco in Spain, which further turned world opinion against him.

Even after Fascist Germany attacked France, Italy was still at peace and not part of Hitler's war against the French and British, but by 1940, Mussolini chose to fully align himself with Hitler and declared war on France. Italy's army was ill prepared and was defeated on all fronts, as were their navy and air force, whose biplanes were obsolete. With the British-American landing in Sicily in 1943, many of Mussolini's colleagues turned against him, including Count Galeazzo Ciano, who was his foreign minister and son-in-law. With Italy's defeat in the dismal future picture, the king of Italy dismissed and arrested Mussolini. However, in a daring and much publicized glider rescue designed by Hitler's commando Otto Skorzeny, Mussolini escaped from his mountain imprisonment. This allowed him to set up a Fascist, albeit puppet, state for Hitler in northern Italy. Mussolini had Count Ciano executed.

By 1945, with Hitler's fall imminent, Mussolini saw the end nearing and wrote his memoirs, *My Rise and Fall*. He attempted to flee to Switzerland with his mistress, but Italian partisans captured the couple. They were killed and then displayed hung upside down in a Milan square. The pictures of their hung, defamed corpses were reproduced worldwide—a retribution symbol for the hundreds of thousands of humans killed in the name of the inhumane and the self-serving ideology that Mussolini as a big-mouth macho enemy created. Americans despised him. The scholar R. J. B. Bosworth notes that those who want fast food in Milan "can appease their appetites at a McDonald's overseeing the site."[1]

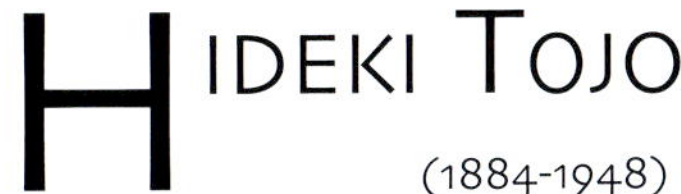

HIDEKI TOJO

(1884-1948)

Further, at the end of July 1939, the United States suddenly applied economic pressure, principally by rescinding its trade and commerce treaty with Japan. This, together with the outrageous act of economic blockade by means of the freezing of Japanese assets by the United States, Britain, and Holland, was a mortal threat to Japan, whose economic activities depended on foreign trade. This kind of economic blockade by nations with which Japan was not in a state of war was felt as an enemy act that was little different from war. From a military point of view, the US-British side openly increased its support of the Chungking forces, thus causing the war to continue. Moreover, the United States, Britain, and Holland, in concert with the Chungking government, concentrated troops in the Philippines, Malaya, Burma, and Dutch Indochina, and strengthened their military preparations by such means as increasing air base facilities. A great American fleet was assembled in Hawaii and readied so as to be able to start operations at a moment's notice. Such were the threats that faced Japan. Moreover, at the same time, according to reports, on October 3, 1941, British and American leaders met in Manila to discuss operations. Further, on October 9, a U.S. military delegation was received at a meeting in Hong Kong, at which support for China and the continued resistance of Chungking were discussed. Like-wise, a certain American admiral [Commander of the Pacific fleet, Husband E. Kimmel] threatened Japan with his famous statement to the effect that if there were war with Japan, the entire Japanese fleet could probably be sunk in a few weeks. Further, on Nov. 10, 1941, the British Prime Minister, at a luncheon for the installation of the [lord] mayor of London, said that if there were war between Japan and the United States, Britain was prepared to declare war on Japan

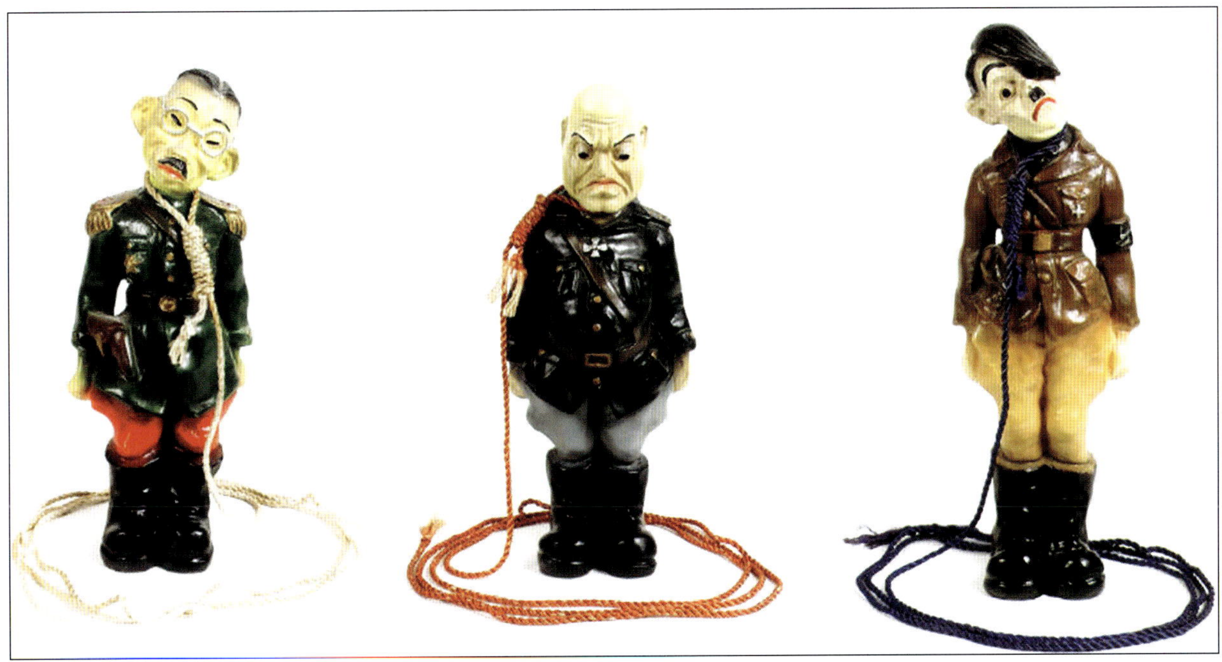

Tojo, Mussolini, and Hitler twelve-inch carnival chalk prizes, without manufacturing marks.
Courtesy: Hake's Americana, Division of Diamond International Galleries

—HIDEKI TOJO, *Prison Diary*

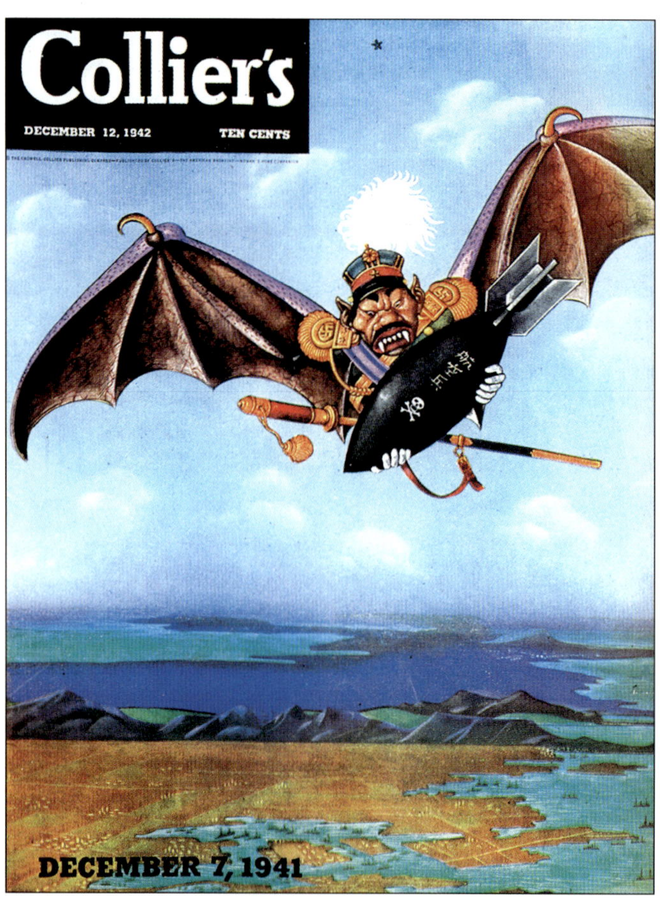

Tojo-Bat-Devil © Colliers, illustration Arthur Szyk, December 7, 1941

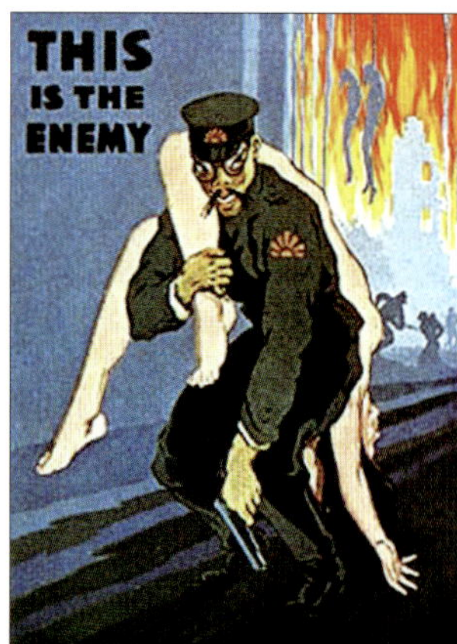

Poster, World War II,
Anonymous

Saipan in the Mariana, Tojo was relieved of his command of
the general staff; two days later, his entire cabinet resigned.
Tojo's leadership officially ended on July 19, 1944.

In August 1945, Tojo shot himself in the chest, but
was nursed back to health to stand trial for war crimes. While
in prison, he wrote lengthy documents to defend his political
war motives. Upon conviction, he refused to allow an appeal of his death sentence and preferred to die as a traditional
Japanese warrior. Hideki Tojo was hanged on December 22,
1948. To patriotic Americans, he stereotyped a lethal rat
or malicious coward, one who would prepare and deliver a
sneak attack. His archetype for Americans was somewhat
similar to Hitler's: the ultimate despised enemy. Tojo,
because of Pearl Harbor, had the coward thrown in, so he was
the ultimate cowardly despised enemy.

Hideki Tojo, nicknamed "Kamisori" (which trans-
lates to "The Razor," for being brutally sharp and hard on
his enemies), was a lifelong military man born into a minor
Samurai family. He attended Japan's prestigious War College
in 1912, graduated with honor, and was sent to Switzerland in
1919, then to Germany in 1921. Before returning to Japan, he
visited the United States and found the American flapper era
to be wholly decadent. He considered hedonist, flamboyant
Americans a threat to no one—an archetypal foofaraw (much
ado about nothing). Gradually, Tojo moved up in the Japanese
military ranks.

Even before he became prime minister in 1941,
he was advocating formation of the Tripartite Pact with the
Third Reich and Italy. As prime minister, Tojo proposed the
creation of the Greater East Asia Co-prosperity Sphere under
Japanese leadership. He assumed responsibility for the Pearl
Harbor sneak attack, although later he said that war with the
United States was supposed to have been announced beforehand. By the Battle of Midway in June 1942, when Japan's
military began to see its first reverses, Tojo had assumed
supreme dictatorial powers over Japan. He was viewed as
much more important than Emperor Hirohito.

In the ensuing two years, Japan increasingly lost its
foothold in the Pacific and, on July 16, 1944, after the loss of

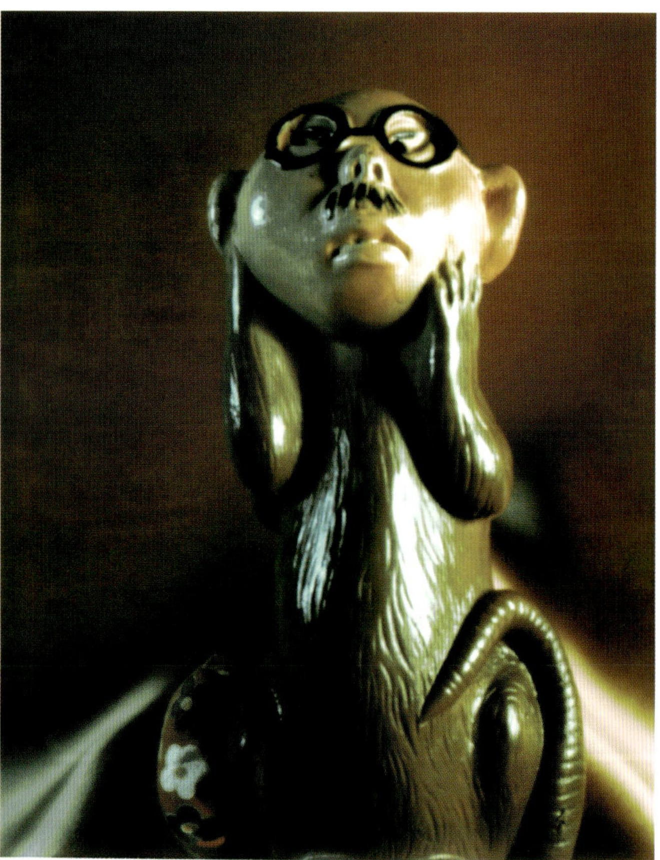

Tojo Rat pincushion five-inch carnival chalk prize, pincushion is attached at lower left,
Hitler's face appears on the back of Tojo's head

WINSTON CHURCHILL

(1874-1965)

I want to be alone.
—GRETA GARBO

Alone, alone, about the dreadful wood
Of conscious evil runs a lost mankind,
Dreading to find its Father.
—W. H. AUDEN, *For the Time Being*

Ah, horrible war, amazing medley of the glorious and the squalid, the
pitiful and the sublime, if modern men of light and leading saw your
face closer, simple folk would see it hardly ever.
—WINSTON CHURCHILL

Fa, Fe, Fi, Fo, Fum!
I smell the blood of an Englishman;
Be he alive or be he dead,
I'll grind his bones to make my bread.
—MOTHER GOOSE RHYME, 1898

Winston Churchill, in his first statement as prime minister to the British House of Commons, declared, "I have nothing to offer but blood, toil, tears and sweat." Less than a month later, on June 4, 1940, referring to the colossal military disaster that Britain suffered at Dunkirk, Churchill ended his speech with this:

> Even though large tracts of Europe and many old and famous States have fallen or may fall into the grip of the Gestapo and all the odious apparatus of Nazi rule, we shall not flag or fail. We shall go on to the end, we shall fight in France, we shall fight on the seas and oceans, we shall fight with growing confidence and growing strength in the air, we shall defend our Island, whatever the cost may be, we shall fight on the beaches, we shall fight on the landing grounds, we shall fight in the fields and in the streets, we shall fight in the hills; we shall never surrender, and even if, which I do not for a moment believe, this Island or a large part of it were subjugated and starving, then our Empire beyond the seas, armed and guarded by the British Fleet, would carry on the struggle, until, in God's good time, the New World, with all its power and might, steps forth to the rescue and the liberation of the old.[1]

England stood very much alone after all the other European democracies had fallen to Hitler's armies. Churchill made grand use of this steadfast and defiant leader archetype. Britain was David; Germany was Goliath. Churchill promised the citizens of England that he would "wage war against a monstrous tyranny, never surpassed in the dark, lamentable catalogue of human crime."[2] This was his rallying cry for patriotism: to die preserving one's country—the most tragic archetypal scream of all. Churchill raised two fingers in an archetypal V for victory—a symbol destined to stay in our vocabulary of hand gestures with different but similar meanings—and that V became Britain's international symbol for determination and hope, a portable war poster and rallying cry

that could be carried and displayed by all. The struggle against Germany was left to Britain and Russia. Churchill attempted to align himself with Stalin, even though communism and Stalin's previous misdeeds were not in the least bit agreeable to him. Britain lost almost 400,000 lives in the war; Russia lost more than 21 million.

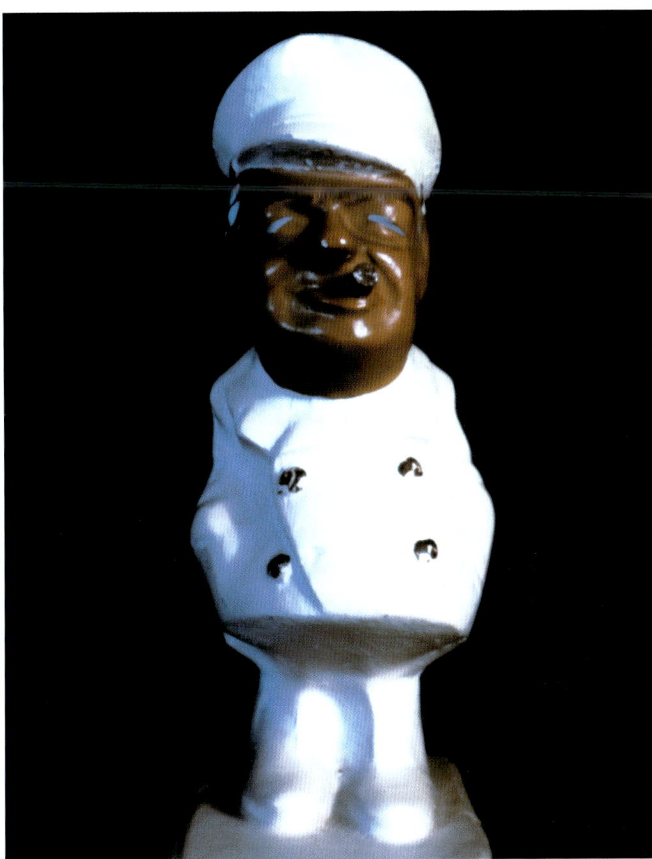

Winston Churchill eight-and-a-half-inch carnival chalkware prize

Winston Churchill was born in 1874. His great-great-grandmother was Native American. His mother, Blanche Ogilvie, was American and his father British. When he was a child, Churchill owned 1,500 toy soldiers from the Napoleonic era, which he used to devise war strategies and march into mock battles. Churchill was of undistinguished academic accomplishment: after failing in his first two attempts, he was admitted to Sandhurst, the Royal Military College. He was not a towering man, standing only five foot six. Churchill received his commission in 1895 and entered the army at a time when the vast British Empire covered one-quarter of the earth's land surface and its 380 million inhabitants lived on every continent and on islands in every ocean. Churchill survived three military campaigns: Spain's struggle in Cuba in 1895; the Northwest Frontier campaign in India in 1897; and the Sudan campaign of 1898—often described as the British Army's last cavalry charge at Omdurman—where he was one of the 21st Lancers.

Churchill received the Nobel Prize in Literature for *The History of the Second World War*. Writing never fully engaged his energies, but politics consumed him. He entered Parliament in 1901 at the age of twenty-six. He left

213

the Conservative Party in 1904 to join the Liberals. It was, in part, a calculated new affiliation, as he correctly deduced that the Liberals were the up-and-coming political party. He soon achieved a fine reputation and then a high office within the party. He became Home Secretary in 1910 and First Lord of the Admiralty in 1911. He was at the helm of the Royal Navy at the outbreak of World War I in 1914, but was forced to resign in 1915 because he was blamed for the failed Dardanelles Campaign. In 1916 Lloyd George appointed him Minister of Munitions, a post in which he developed the use of the tank in warfare. Churchill was in and out of politics for the next twenty years. He was the only British politician to espouse strong, anti-Nazi policies between 1933 and 1939. It was a determined stance, which ensured that when the inevitable moment of confrontation between Britain and Germany arrived, Churchill would stand out as the strongest politician in which the nation could place its trust. He could most legitimately say, "I told you so." Churchill decried the prewar appeasement policies of the conservatives Baldwin and Chamberlain. When Chamberlain lost the confidence of Parliament in 1940, Churchill was installed as prime minister. No individual better personified the will and guts of English-speaking peoples to resist the Nazi juggernaut during World War II than Churchill. Because of his unflagging sinew, he grew in stature to become the most important free-world politician of the century. It was Churchill who coined the term "Iron Curtain" when referring to the approaching cold war with Russia in his famous speech at Fulton, Missouri, in 1946. President Kennedy made him an honorary citizen of the United States in 1963.

JOSEF STALIN

Archetypal symbols of patriotism and nationalism can be shrouded, disguised, and abused by any politician willing to indoctrinate and to exploit—to bind their nation's people to their own ill devices. An example might be the 1919 Red Scare—that communism would control the world—brought on by the 1917 triumph of the Bolsheviks in Russia and the establishment of the Soviet Union. Terror was instilled in the United States on June 2, 1919, when a number of bombs were detonated in eight American cities, including one by the home of A. Mitchell Palmer, attorney general under Woodrow Wilson. In response, Palmer and his newly appointed special assistant J. Edgar Hoover orchestrated well-publicized raids against radicals and World War I pacifists under the Espionage Act of 1917 and the Sedition Act of 1918. Beginning on November 7, 1919, Palmer's men raided labor union offices and the headquarters of Communist and Socialist organizations without search warrants, concentrating on foreigners. They arrested more than 10,000 people. A month later 249 of the those arrested were placed on the *Buford* (the press nicknamed it "Soviet Ark") bound for the Soviet Union. By January 1920, another 6,000 were arrested (4,000 in a single night), mostly members of the anarcho-syndicalist union Industrial Workers of the World. Many were held for a long period. The U.S. Government, along with other governments, were afraid that the workers of the world would unite with the Bolsheviks. Palmer predicted that May 1, 1920, would be a day of massive anti democracy demonstrations, but his predictions proved false. Palmer's credibility waned due to the widespread belief that he had manufactured the Red Scare to gain the 1920 presidential nomination.

Stalin relied on class struggle, Russian nationalism, gains in World War II, and his police state to build an empire—turning Russia's peasant farm society into a world superpower. Death surrounded the cataclysmic change, leaving the Russian people in a stranglehold. In the process Stalin rose from being a behind-the-scenes bureaucrat into one the most powerful totalitarian dictators of the twentieth century.

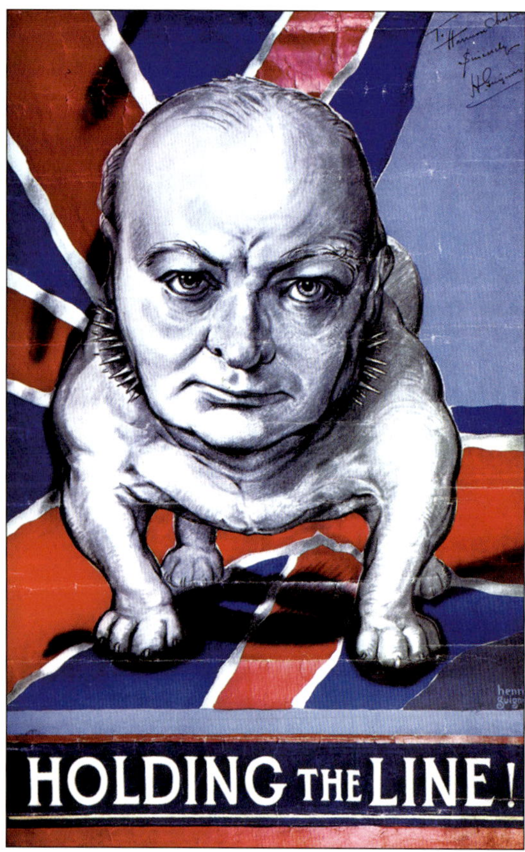

"Holding the Line!," U.S. war poster, illustration Henri Guignon, 1942

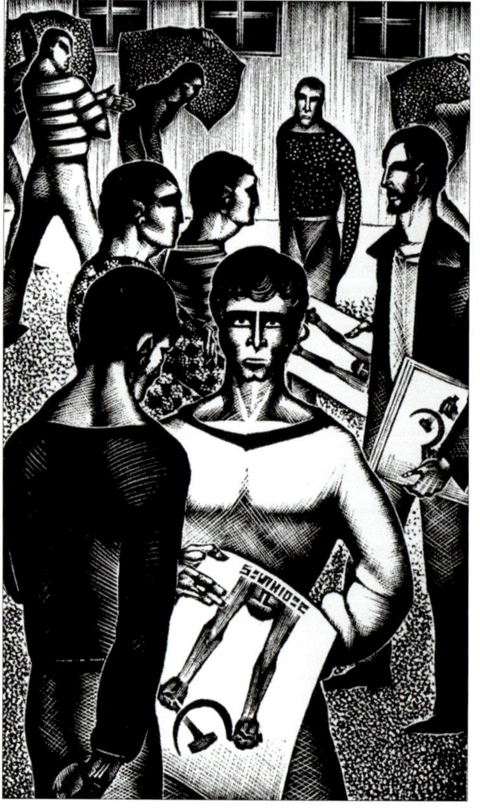

Mad Man's Drum, woodcut Lynd Ward © Jonathan Cape and Harrison Smith Inc., 1930

For Americans, Stalin symbolized the ruthless manipulative killer-dictator. Stalin and communism—iconized by the hammer and sickle—were propagandized as the threatening hostile brethren archetype against a safer freedom-loving world constructed of democracy and capitalism (which by then were inseparable from Christianity). By the 1950s, another feverish Red Scare known as the cold war was fanned by politicians and the media in the United States. Churchill's concept of an Iron Curtain became a reality, but by that time Stalin was dead—murdered in 1953 because he was about to pursue another of his purges. Four days after his death, his embalmed body was entombed in Moscow alongside that of Lenin's in Red Square.

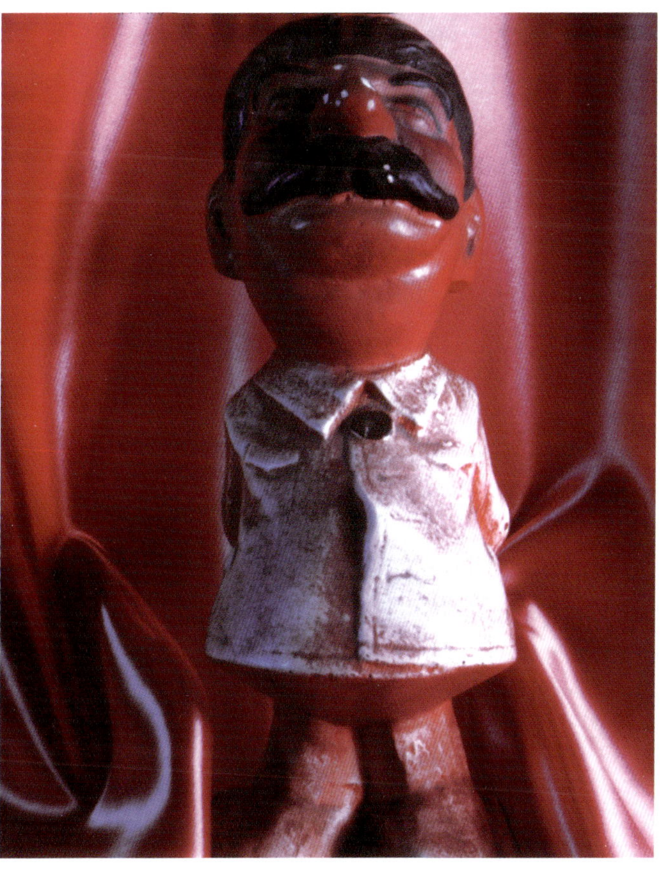

Josef Stalin carnival chalk prize. Stalin's era of domination, 1925 to 1953, coincides with carnival chalk prizes; he was part of the Churchill and Roosevelt set shown on pages 206 and 213.

Iosif Vissarionovich Djugashvili (Josef Stalin) was born in southern Russia in 1879, an only child. Three sisters, born earlier, died while very young. Apparently both of his parents treated Iosif cruelly. His father was an unsuccessful, usually drunk, shoemaker who left his family to work in a factory in Tiflis. He died in 1890 from wounds received in a brawl. His mother, Yekaterina, took in washing and sewing, and hired out for housework. Iosif contracted smallpox at an early age and the disease permanently scarred his face. He also contracted septicemia, which slightly crippled his left arm for life. He started schooling at eleven and by age fifteen had received a scholarship to the religious seminary in Tbilisi—hoping to become a priest in the Georgian Orthodox Church. It was the year that Tzar Nicholas II began his reign.

The Tbilisi seminary, like many Russian schools of that era, circulated forbidden revolutionary ideas. It was there that Iosif read Karl Marx. By 1898, Iosif joined a secret Marxist revolutionary group called *Mesame Dasi*. He was expelled just before his graduation in 1899; his contumacious (rebellious) attitude prompted his dismissal.

Iosif joined the Social Democratic Party in September of 1901. He began to write illegal pamphlets for the Georgian Marxist journal *Brdzola* (The Struggle). He lived and wrote agitprops under a succession of pseudonyms; his favorites were Koba, the name of a legendary Georgian folk hero meaning "The Indomitable," and Stalin, meaning "The Man of Steel." He began reading Vladimir Lenin and joined the Bolshevik Party. He was arrested for the first time in Batum in 1902 and exiled to Siberia in 1903, only to escape and reappear in Tiflis in 1904. He met Lenin in 1905. Over the next ten years, he was imprisoned or exiled six times, escaped five times, and was released once. He changed his last name to Stalin in 1913.

By 1917, Josef Stalin was the editor of the Bolshevik newspaper *Pravda* and was a behind-the-scenes administrator in the Bolsheviks' seizure of power. He became general secretary of the Communist Party Central Committee in 1922, a position that allowed him to place his supporters in various party positions in the newly named Soviet Union, behind the back of the committee. Lenin died in 1924 and Stalin overthrew most of his political rivals in the following six years and became dictator in 1928. He eventually forced Trotsky, his main rival, to leave Russia in 1929. All of his other rivals were systematically murdered.

Stalin ruled and held the Soviet Union in a terror death grip, forcing the poorest peasants onto massive collective farms. Five million modestly wealthier Kulak peasants, who would not work collectively for the state, were murdered or starved during his first major purge. Other laborers were forced into gulags, where brutally long work hours with little food became the standard. Millions of workers died in these hostile environments and factory managers were executed if production was not increased. By 1932, as a result of his ruthlessness, Stalin could trust no one, and sooner or later many who were part of his government organization were purged, including comrades, close friends, and even relatives who fell victim to his growing paranoia. His major purge years were 1937 and 1938; millions were executed or exiled to Siberia to die. Death statistics from Stalin's twenty-five years of purges ranged from 20 million to 80 million. Aleksandr Solzhenitsyn estimated it to be 66 million.

In a speech he delivered at a meeting of voters of the Stalin Electoral District, Moscow, December 11, 1937, Stalin explains why his form of democracy is best:

> Further, comrades, I would like to congratulate you on the occasion of the forthcoming national holiday, the day of the elections to the Supreme Soviet of the Soviet Union. (Loud applause.) The forthcoming elections are not merely elections, comrades, they are really a national holiday of our workers, our peasants and our intelligentsia. (Loud applause.) Never in the history of the world have there been such really free and really democratic elections—never! History knows no other example like it. (Applause.) The

point is not that our elections will be universal, equal, secret
and direct, although that fact in itself is of great importance.
The point is that our universal elections will be carried out
as the freest elections and the most democratic compared
with elections in any other country in the world.

Universal elections exist and are also held in some
capitalist countries, so-called democratic countries. But in
what atmosphere are elections held there? In an atmosphere
of class conflicts, in an atmosphere of class enmity, in an atmosphere of pressure brought to bear on the electors by the
capitalists, landlords, bankers and other capitalist sharks.
Such elections, even if they are universal, equal, secret
and direct, cannot be called altogether free and altogether
democratic elections.

Here, in our country, on the contrary, elections are
held in an entirely different atmosphere. Here there are no
capitalists and no landlords and, consequently, no pressure
is exerted by propertied classes on non-propertied classes.
Here elections are held in an atmosphere of collaboration
between the workers, the peasants and the intelligentsia, in
an atmosphere of mutual confidence between them, in an atmosphere, I would, say, of mutual friendship; because there
are no capitalists in our country, no landlords, no exploitation, and nobody, in fact, to bring pressure to
bear on people in order to distort their will . . .[1]

In August 1939, Stalin startled the world when he
brought the Soviet Union into a nonaggression pact with
Nazi Germany. One month later, Germany invaded Poland,
starting World War II. The nonaggression pact permitted the
Soviets to seize eastern Poland, attack Finland, and absorb
the Romanian provinces of Bessarabia and Bukovina without
German opposition. However, in June 1941, the Soviet
Union was attacked by Germany. Hitler greatly miscalculated
Russia and Stalin; that miscalculation became Hitler's hamartia
(a tragic flaw in one's judgment that creates a downfall). Hitler
underestimated Russia's patriotic strength and willingness to
sacrifice, and, perhaps most of all, the brutal Russian winters.
Stalin stood firm and Russia lost 21 million lives. Hitler lost
the war; this became Stalin's gain and he happily increased
the overall size of the USSR, swallowing a number of Slavic
countries in one gulp.

Little is known of Stalin's personal life. He lived
mostly in secrecy. Yekaterina Svanidze and Stalin married
in 1904; she died in 1907 of tuberculosis. They had a son,
Yakov, who was captured by the Germans in 1941 and
died of a gunshot wound in the Sachsenhausen death camp
in 1943—an apparent suicide. Stalin had refused an offer
to exchange Yakov for a German prisoner—Stalin (ever in
the throes of ideological mania) believed that all Russian
POWs were traitors, including his own son. He thought they
should have died fighting. Stalin also had Yakov's Jewish
wife arrested. Later he had relatives of his first wife shot.
Allilujewa-Stalina Nadezhda Sergejevna and Stalin married
in 1919 when she was only eighteen. She was the mother
of Vasily and Svetlana. Allilujewa never fit into Stalin's
political environment; she became an unhappy outsider. In
1932, she was found dead in her sleeping room, a revolver
in her hand. Her death was attributed to appendicitis, yet
many facts pointed to murder. (Although an appendectomy
executed with a pistol would have made medical history.)

In February 1956, Nikita Khrushchev addressed the
20th Soviet Communist Party Congress in secret. He devoted
three hours to the systematic destruction of Stalin's image
as a public hero, placing Stalin well on his way to ignominy.
Among other charges, Stalin was now accused of wanton
slaughter during the prewar purge trials, of being abnormally
suspicious of associates, and of causing thousands of unnecessary casualties during World War II by incompetently interfer-
ing with Red Army campaigns. Above all he was denounced
for having paraded himself as a messiah, an archetype.

At the 22nd Soviet Communist Party Congress
in 1961, the denunciation of Stalin was resumed. Before
the session adjourned, Stalin's body had been removed from
Red Square and reburied within the Kremlin walls among the
graves of lesser Soviet heroes as a lasting oubliette. His name
was removed from public buildings, streets, and factories.
Stalingrad was renamed Volgograd.

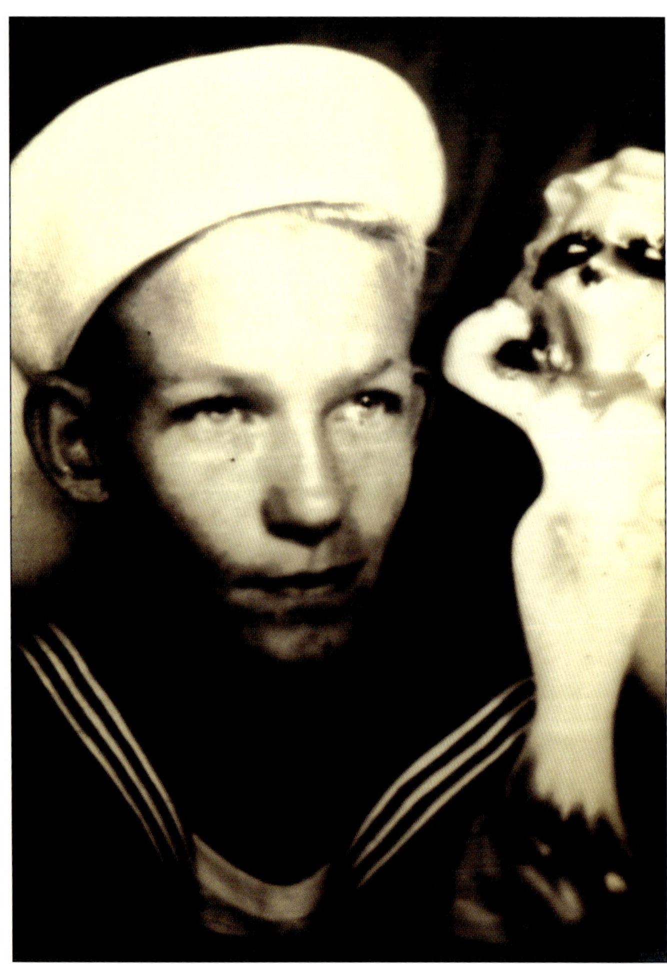

U.S. sailor with Mae West carnival chalk prize

U S SERVICEMEN
SERVICEWOMEN
WORLD WAR II (1941-1945)

If only I had known, I should have become a watchmaker.
—ALBERT EINSTEIN, *New Statesman*, April, 16, 1965

Every gun that is made, every warship launched, every rocket fired, signifies in the final sense, a theft from those who hunger and are not fed, those who are cold and are not clothed. This world in arms is not spending money alone. It is spending the sweat of its laborers, the genius of its scientists, the hopes of its children. This is not a way of life at all in any true sense. Under the clouds of war, it is humanity hanging on a cross of iron.
—DWIGHT EISENHOWER, April 16, 1953

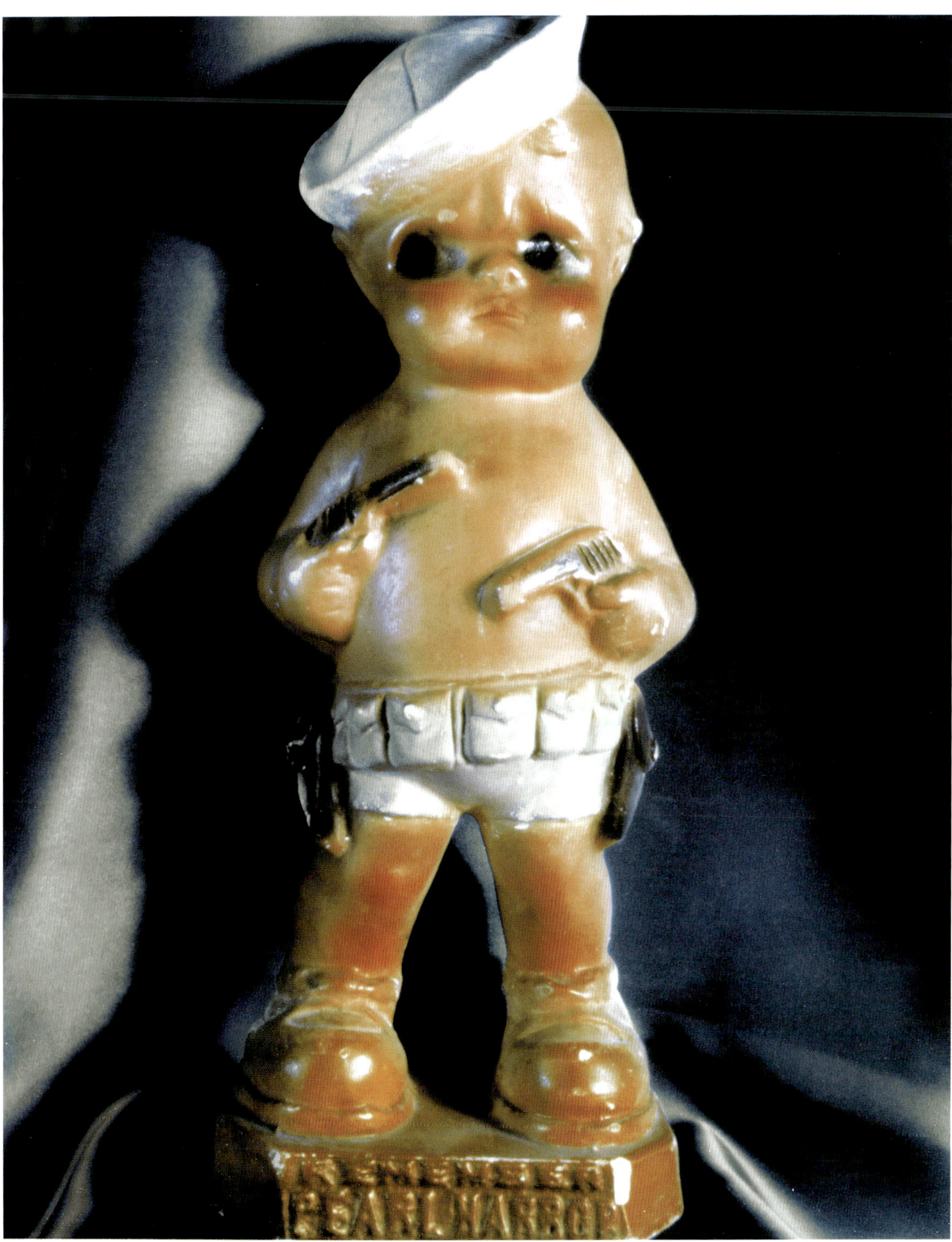

"Remember Pearl Harbor," U.S. sailor thirteen-inch carnival chalk prize, there is a similar U.S. army prize

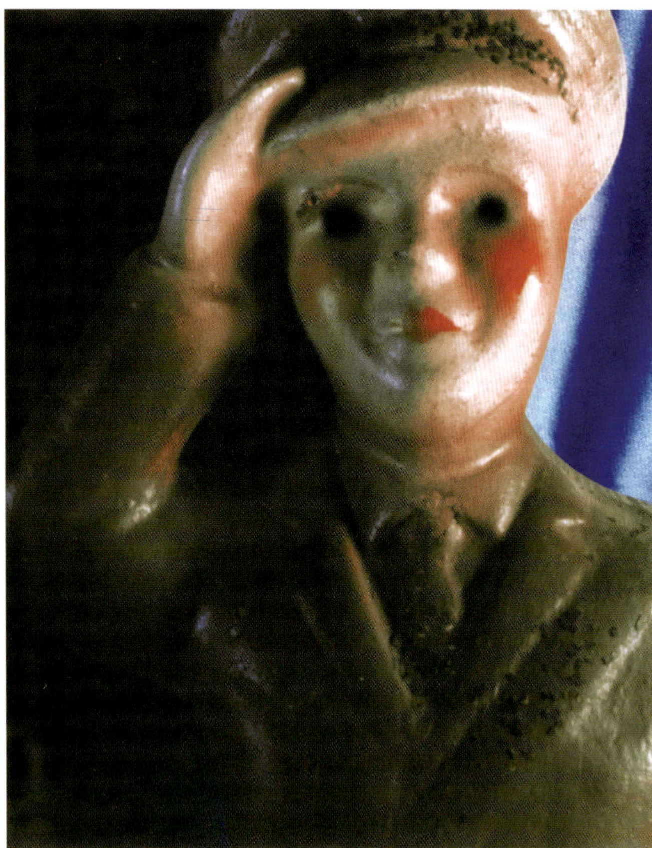

U.S. soldier fifteen-inch carnival chalk prize

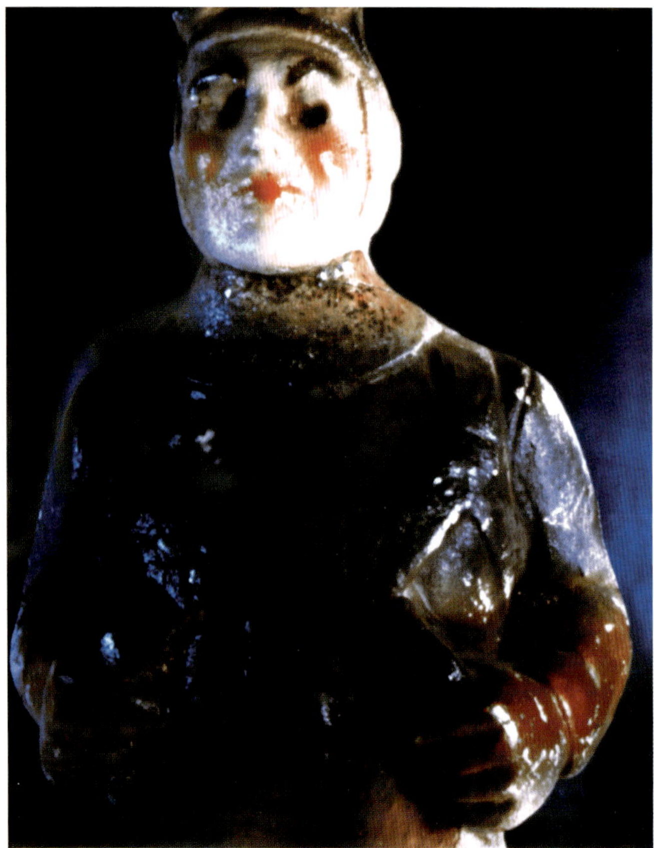

U.S. airman sixteen-inch carnival chalk prize

—MARK TWAIN, *Prayer of War*, 1904-05, found in his unpublished manuscripts after his death

—ERNEST HEMINGWAY

Political leaders have always counted on the gathering of forces—those ready to join the military as an instinctive reaction against a common enemy who has declared war on the homeland. It must be one of the strongest of knee-jerk archetypal responses: to defend your country as a war hero. Included is a vain hope that somehow you will survive. The young and poor go first. They have not been educated to understand the most basic of archetypal nationalistic propaganda. Through the centuries, politicians have unfairly taken advantage of the young's self-sacrificing hero and heroine instincts. If politicians were asked to die for their country, would they readily sacrifice? Most of them hide behind the transparent camouflage of leadership, often the same leadership responsible for providing the self-serving ideologies leading to war.

Politicians suffer from their own archetypal knee-jerk responses: their need to see themselves as the best and most powerful, unaware that it is an archetypal response for feelings of greed and superiority.

Casualties from World War II should cry out, but they do not. They are dead. In death, they are archetypal war heroes and heroines. But in vain—the path they have blazed leads to a continuum not of peace but of more war. The dead, as always, become mere statistics, useful only for rallying emotional responses for the next wave of heroes.

Being ready to fight is a lot easier than embracing logic. Until reaction instincts are brought within the realm of an evolved educational system there will never be peace. Why not create programs that nurture people in Instinctive-Feelings Control and Understanding Propaganda?

Here are statistics of the human losses, both military and civilian, during World War II. Seeing these deaths as numbers makes them readable; but hearing their pain in sum total would be a deafening scream heard to the distant edges of our solar system.

World War II Casualties[1]

Country	Military	Civilian	Total
Soviet Union	13,600,000	7,700,000	21,300,000
China	3,500,000	10,000,000	13,500,000
Germany	3,250,000	3,810,000	7,060,000
Jewish Holocaust			6,000,000
Poland	850,000	6,000,000	6,850,000
Japan	1,506,000	300,000	1,806,000
Yugoslavia	300,000	1,400,000	1,700,000
Rumania	520,000	465,000	985,000
France	340,000	470,000	810,000
Hungary			750,000
Austria	380,000	145,000	525,000
Greece			520,000
Italy	330,000	80,000	410,000
Czechoslovakia			400,000
Great Britain	326,000	62,000	388,000
United States	295,000	115,000	410,000
Totals:	25+ million	30+ million	63+ million

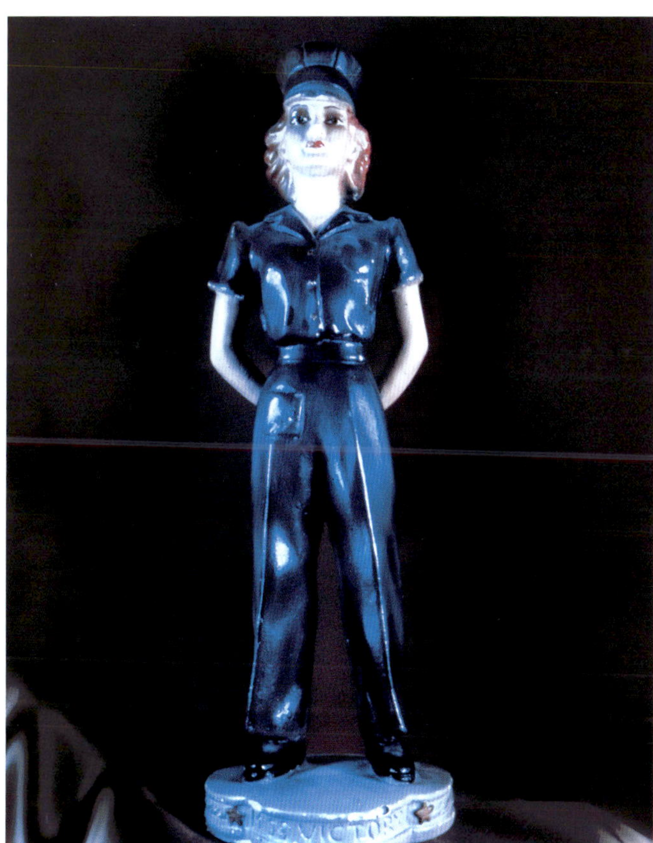
Miss Victory thirteen-inch carnival chalk prize, text on base is Miss Victory

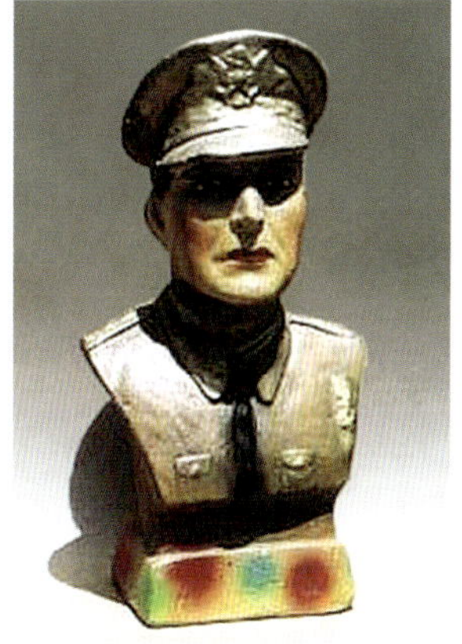
General Douglas McArthur carnival chalk prize

The statistics from World War II qualify it as by far the largest war in the history of the world in terms of human and material resources expended. In all, sixty-one countries totaling 1.7 billion people, three-fourths of the world's population, participated. Some 110 million persons were mobilized for military service, more than half of those by three countries: USSR (22 to 30 million), Germany (17 million), and the United States (16 million). The largest number of troops on duty from the major participants at any one time were 12,500,000 from the USSR, 10,938,000 from Germany, 12,245,000 from the United States, 8,720,000 from the British Empire and Commonwealth, 7,193,000 from Japan, and 5,000,000 from China.

Many of those who died in China were civilians bombed by Japan. While the rest of the world was occupied with war, 3 million people died of famine in India in 1943.

After the bombing of Nagasaki and Hiroshima, many more died from radiation than shown in the above statistics and an incalculable number of those listed as Japanese were actually Korean men kidnapped to work on Japanese bomb shelters and Korean women kidnapped to work as prostitutes.

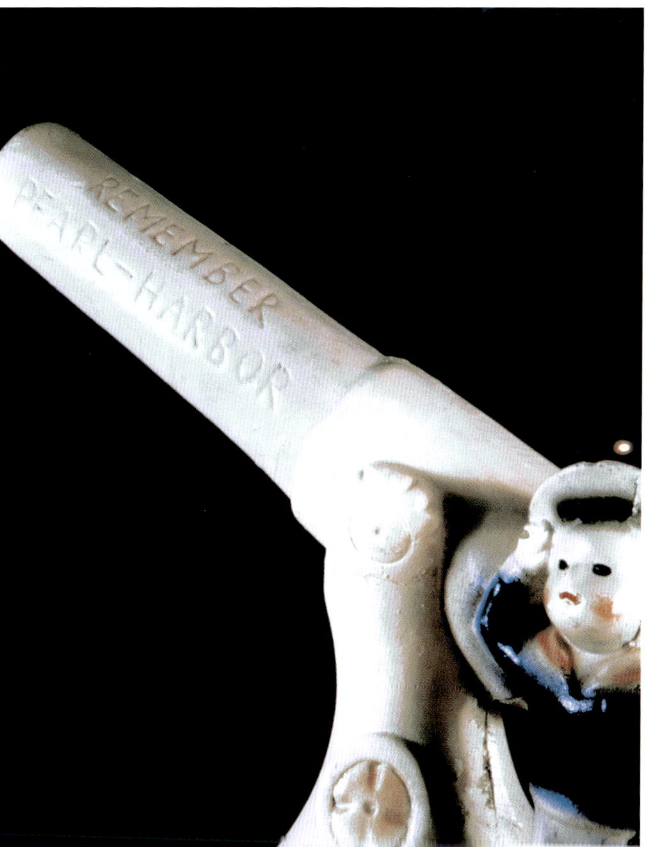

"Remember Pearl Harbor," U.S. sailor and cannon eleven-inch carnival chalk prize

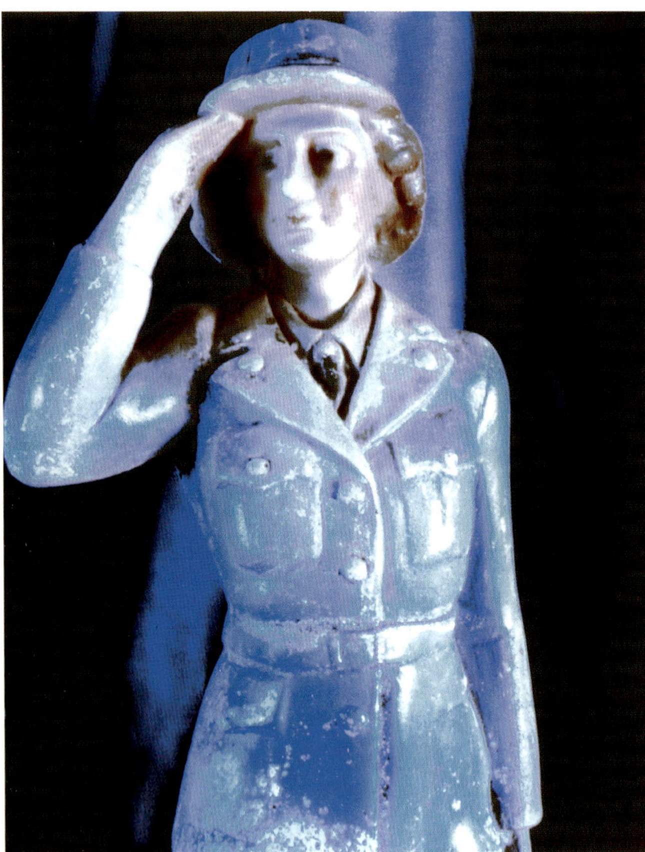

WAAC sixteen-inch carnival chalk prize

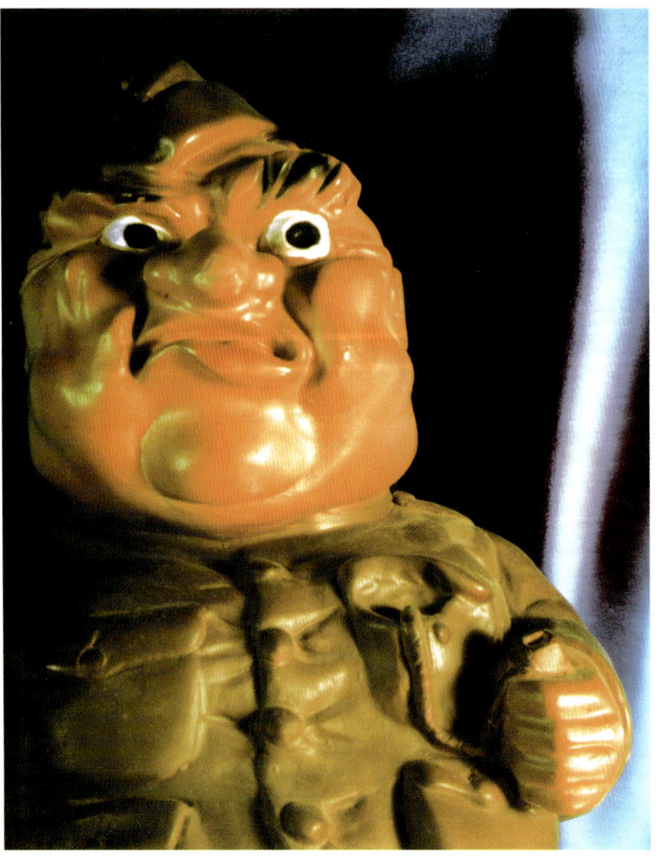

U.S. sergeant thirteen-inch carnival chalk prize

In an ironic side note: cigarettes were given away at a nominal cost to U.S. servicemen and women; deaths caused by lung cancer later on are estimated to be much higher than the figure for war casualties. The same held true for women who worked in factories where asbestos was used. Furthermore, the National Association of Radiation Survivors states that 400,000 veterans were exposed to radiation in atmospheric tests or as occupational forces.[2]

American factories devoted only to wartime production turned out some 295,000 aircraft, 71,000 ships, and 86,000 tanks. Sixteen million American women worked on assembly lines producing these wartime products, many of which went to Allies.

The United States spent an estimated $341 billion, including $50 billion for lend-lease supplies, of which $31 billion went to Britain, $11 billion to the Soviet Union, $5 billion to China, and $3 billion to thirty-five other countries. Germany's expenditures were $272 billion, the Soviet Union $192 billion, Britain $120 billion, Italy $94 billion, and Japan $56 billion. Except for the United States and some of the less militarily active Allies, the money spent does not come close to being the war's true cost. The Soviet government has calculated that the USSR lost 30 percent of its national wealth, while Nazi exaction and looting were of incalculable amounts in the countries they occupied. Bombing and shelling produced 5 billion cubic yards of rubble in Germany.

During World War II, American minorities, like African Americans and Native Americans, were segregated into their own units. Ostensibly all army jobs were open to black soldiers, but in reality most black soldiers were assigned to support units clustered in the quartermaster, engineering, and transportation units. Only a small percentage of African American soldiers saw combat. In 1941, controversy erupted over the discovery that the Red Cross had established racially segregated blood banks. The Red Cross admitted that it had no scientific justification for the racial separation of blood and blamed the armed services for the decision. Despite scientific evidence and the risk of demoralizing the black community, the army's surgeon general defended the controversial practice as necessary to insure the acceptance of a potentially unpopular program. Ignoring constant criticism from the NAACP and elements of the black press, the armed forces continued to demand segregated blood banks. Blacks appreciated the irony of the situation, for they were well aware that a black doctor, Charles R. Drew, had been a pioneer researcher in the plasma extraction process and had directed the first Red Cross blood bank. The World War II segregation issues became a building block for the civil rights movement that followed.

About 300,000 U.S. women served and many of them were in combat zones. Of the more than 59,000 American nurses who were in the Army Nurse Corps, 200 died. More U.S. servicemen died in the Air Corps than in the Marine Corps. While completing the required thirty air missions, an airman's chance of being killed was 71 percent.

The youngest U.S. serviceman was twelve-year-old Calvin Graham, USN, who was wounded and given a dishonorable discharge for lying about his age. An act of Congress later restored his benefits.

Expenditures on items purchased by United States defense included 86,027 tanks; 676,433 two-and-a-half-ton six-wheel-drive trucks; 1,054 eight-inch howitzers; 476,628 2.36-inch bazookas; 4,014,731 Garand rifles; 4,072,000,000 rounds of .45-caliber ammunition; 206,753 Handie-Talkie radio sets; 7,570 locomotives; 23,510,030 military gas masks; 3,898 B-29 Superfortresses; 500,754 bottles of influenza virus vaccine; 57,488,000 wool undershirts; and 116,000,000 pounds of peanut butter.

At the height of World War II, volunteer air raid wardens were posted throughout America as archetypal feelings of fear and insecurity were brought on by the heinous visions of another Pearl Harbor. Battle footage, flags, and civil defense symbols were among the media's omnipresent reminders. Air raid wardens wore specially designed civil defense helmets and carried batons, making sure everything was readied in air raid shelters, lights were turned out, and the many drills were properly conducted. In Hawaii, there were small-aperture black covers for car headlights to keep the lights dim. The top half of headlights on American cars were painted black. The most likely symbols that might have created unwarranted archetypal rage or hysteria were the 120,000 Japanese American citizens who were torn from their homes and placed in ten internment camps, supposedly for their own safety—the justification was that other Americans would vilify them for Japan's war deeds. People with as little as one-sixteenth ancestry were considered Japanese. Camp conditions were supposed to be humane; after a three-year internment, the deleterious effects on Japanese American families and their former communities were immeasurably damaging, both psychologically and financially. Some Italians and Germans were also interned.

As with all wars, sex slavery was rampant. Hawaii, not yet elevated to state status, was infamous for its brothels for American soldiers. Prostitutes even moved to Hawaii from cities like San Francisco.

In *A Moveable Feast*, Hemingway had this to say about living through war:

> For luck you carried a horse chestnut and a rabbit's foot in your right pocket. The fur had been worn off the rabbit's foot long ago and the bones and the sinews were polished by the wear. The claws scratched in the lining of your pocket and you knew your luck was still there.

Many scholars have pondered humanity's propensity for making war and illogically killing its own species over the centuries. Is it possible that humanity is destined to live in this bubble of self-destruction until we completely annihilate ourselves? Will an educated moment descend, when all our destructive instincts of power, greed, and ideological proselytizing can be seen in a new light of understanding? When will we realize that we are manipulated by our own archetypal symbols? Propagandizing will not stop until the mass of humanity gains the understanding to make war end. Killing in the name of ideology or religion is still murder.

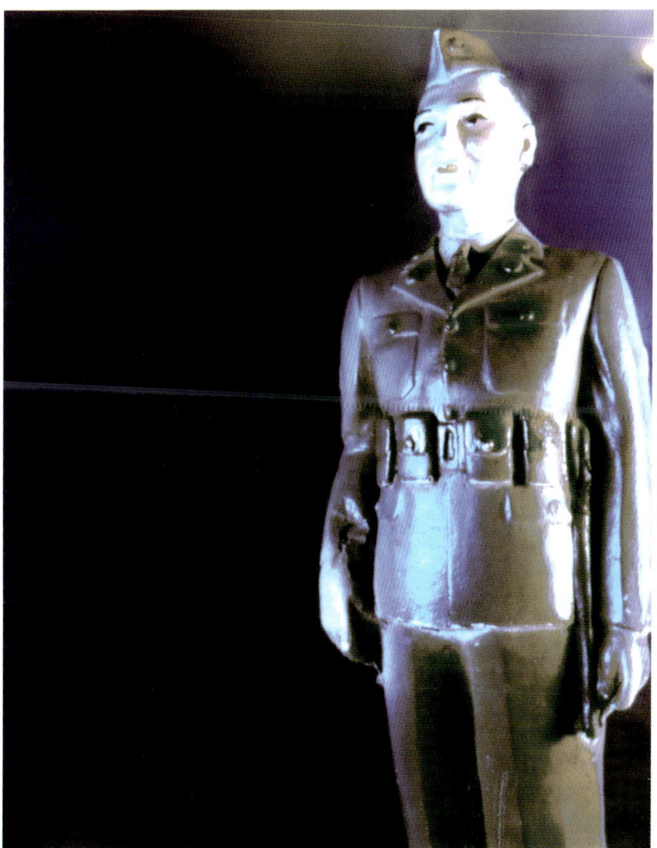

U.S. soldier fifteen-inch carnival chalk prize

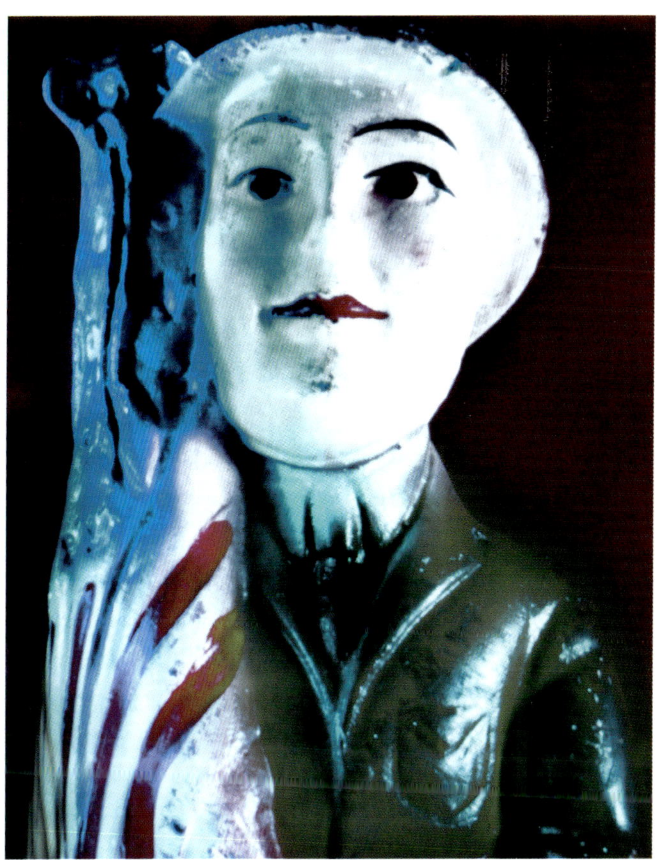

U.S. civil defense soldier fourteen-and-one-half-inch carnival chalk prize

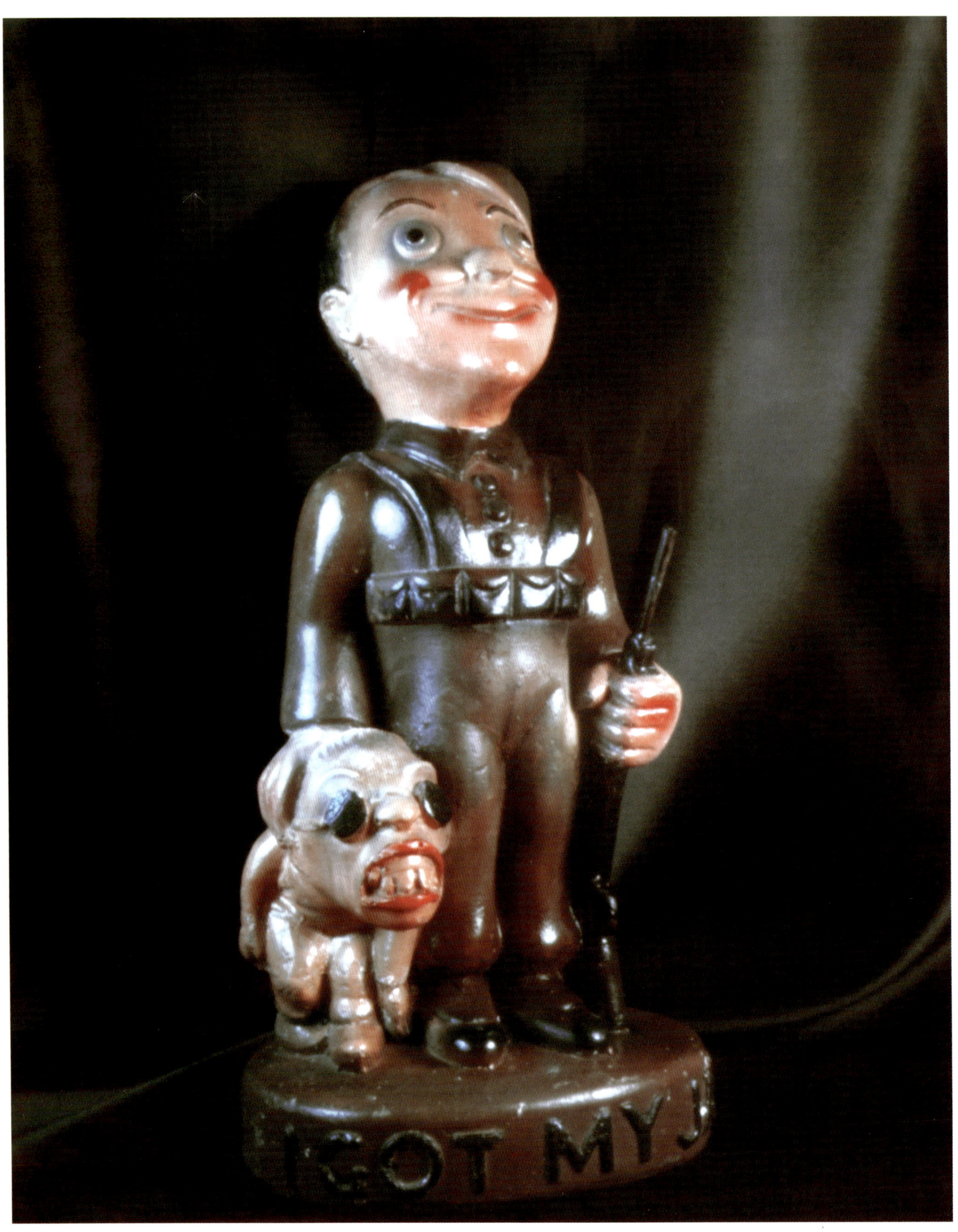

Soldier eleven-and-one-half-inch carnival chalk prize, gun barrel is plastic, text "I Got My Jap" in raised letters on the base

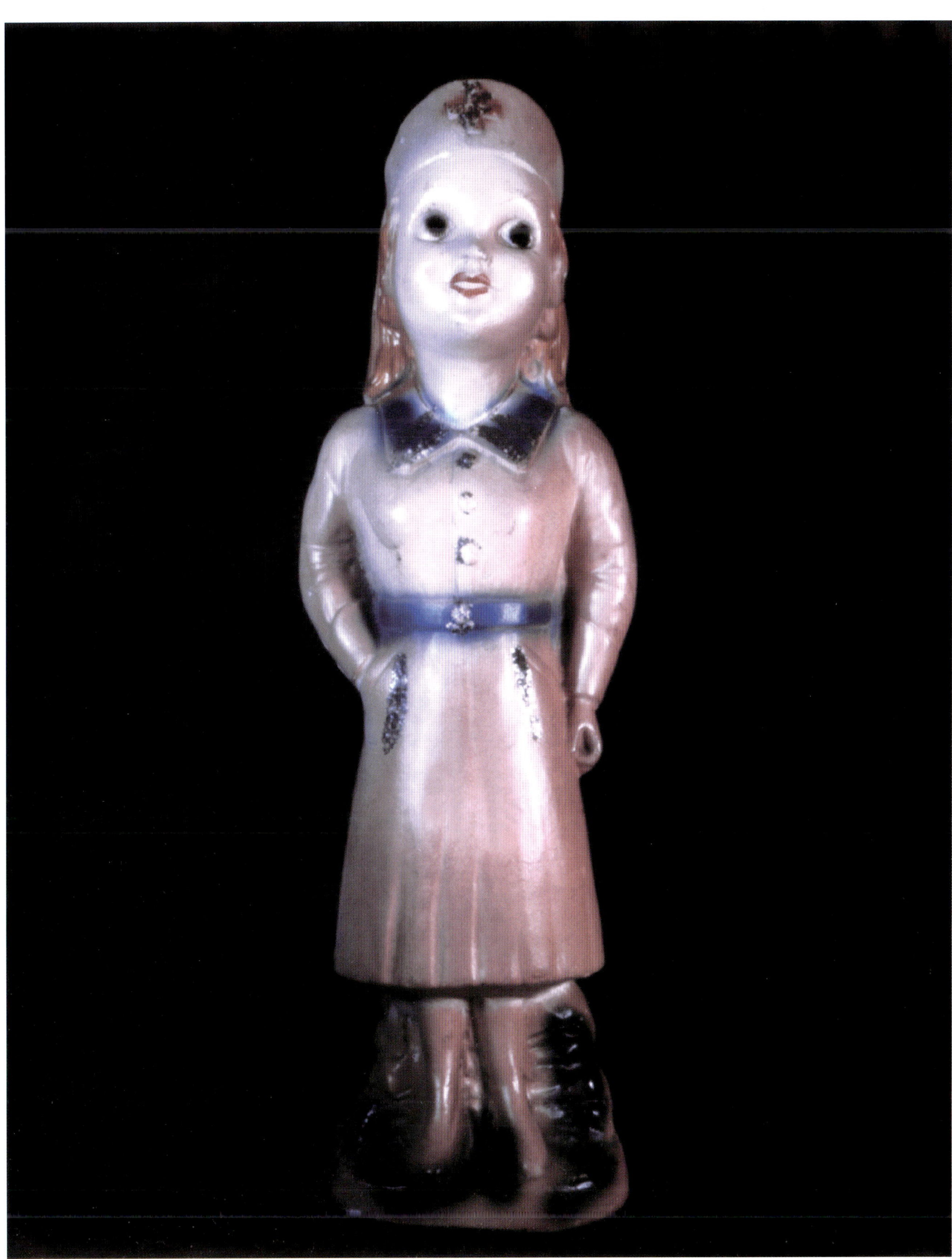

World War II Red Cross Nurse fifteen-inch carnival chalk prize

Skull and Rattlesnake

Everybody wants to go to heaven, but nobody wants to die.
—Joe Louis

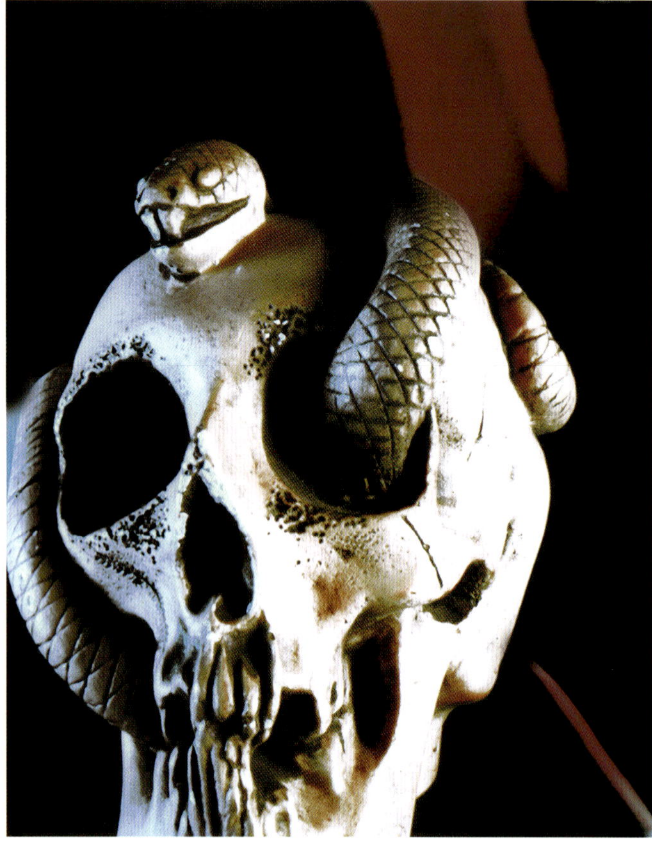

Skull and rattlesnake seven-inch carnival chalk prize, an archetypal symbol for dreaded feelings of fear of death. A skull would have done just as well, but the rattlesnake indicated just how temporal time on earth could be, and, equally important, the snake subliminally connected to Eve. The rattlesnake acted as necromancer, announcing that death was quick and permanent.

Religions owe their existence to the unique ability of the human animal to understand that he or she must die.[1] Similarly, humans are probably the only animals to understand that they were born. Paganism did not shrink and tremble at the thought of death; it fostered the idea of growth and decline, rebirth and renewal. Romans believed that death should be kept in mind at all times, especially at the peak of life when one might forget about death—both aspects, life and death, being equally necessary as a part of the complete cycle. When a military hero entered Rome in a triumphal procession, riding in a golden chariot, he was hailed as a god. Standing to the side of him was a person wearing the mask and costume of death, and preserving the hero from the sins of feeling excessive pride—repeating over and over in his ear, "Man, remember you will die."[2]

On the other hand, Hollywood often showed youthful military heroism as morally good red-blooded fun—death was not an issue. Many film posters have acted in the place of U.S. military enlistment posters.

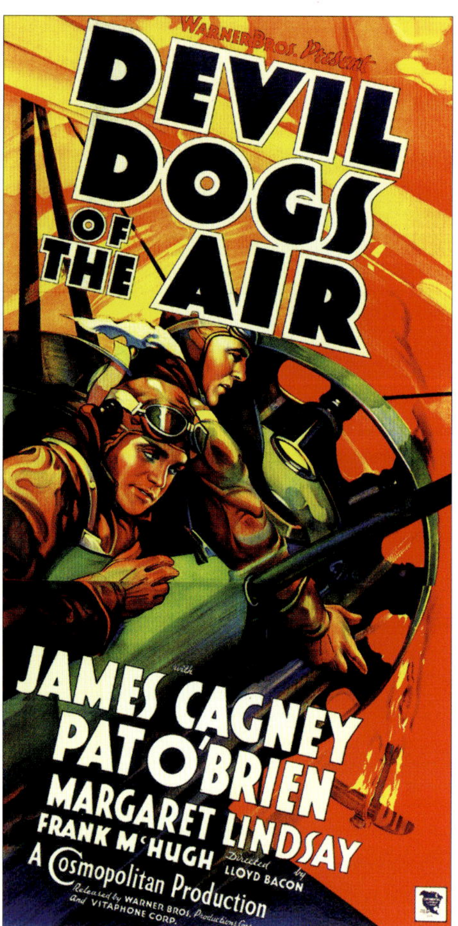

Devil Dogs of the Air, lobby poster, 1935 © Warner Bros.

Early Christianity denied that members of its sect could die, and those who did were said to have fallen asleep, soon to awaken with the second coming of Christ. A morbid anxiety accompanied this ritual denial. As Frank Kermode says in *The Sense of an Ending*: "Christianity of all the great religions is the most anxious; it is the one which laid the most emphasis on the terror of death."[3]

Catholics have a symbolic fear of damnation unless they are buried in sacred ground, which was particularly disturbing during World War II, when many Catholic soldiers lost their lives on remote islands in the South Pacific or in scattered areas of Europe. In the 1944 poem "The Dead in Europe," Robert Lowell is asking for the intercession of Mother Mary at the day of Resurrection, which was expressed in the refrains "Raise us, Mother" and "Our sacred earth." At the age of thirty, Lowell won the 1947 Pulitzer Prize for his war poems.

> After the planes unloaded, we fell down
> Buried together, unmarried men and women;
> Not crown of thorns, not iron, not Lombard crown,
> Not grilled and spindle spires pointing to Heaven
> Could save us. Raise us, Mother, we fell down
> Here hugger-mugger in the jellied fire;
> Our sacred earth in our day was our curse.
>
> Our Mother, shall we rise on Mary's day
> In Maryland, where corpses married
> Under the rubble, bundled together? Pray

For us whom the blockbusters marred and buried;
When Satan scatters us on Rising-day,
O Mother, snatch our bodies from the fire:
Our sacred earth in our day was our curse.

Mother, my bones are trembling and I hear
The earth's reverberations and the trumpet
Bleating into my shambles. Shall I bear,
(O Mary!) unmarried man and powder-puppet,
Witness to the Devil? Mary, hear,
O Mary, marry earth, sea, air and fire;
Our sacred earth in our day is our curse.[4]

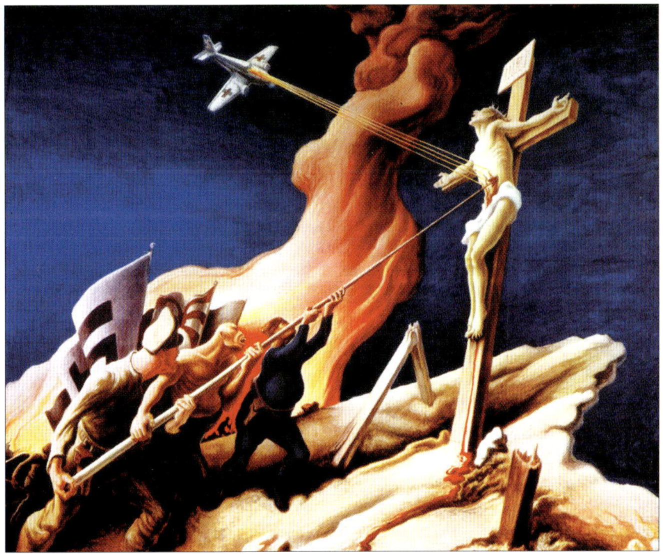

Again © Thomas Hart Benton, 1943

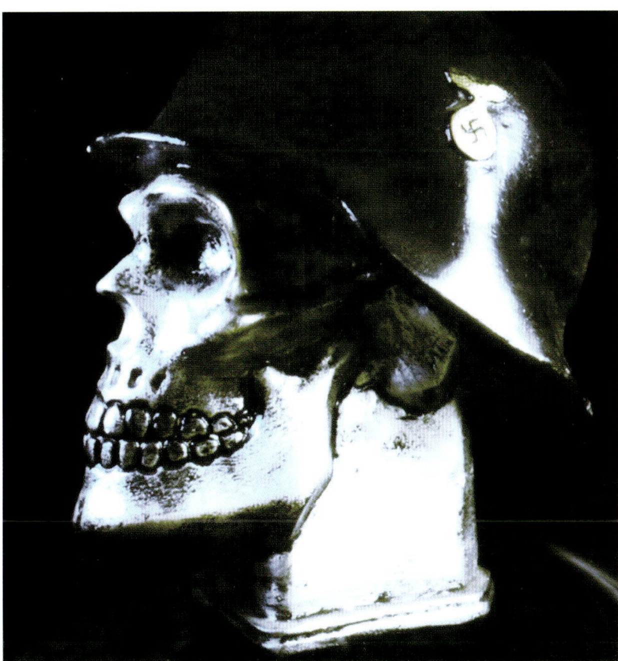

Nazi skull and helmet eleven-inch carnival chalk bank prize, available to the hardened war-minded patriot (quite a place to store your spare change)

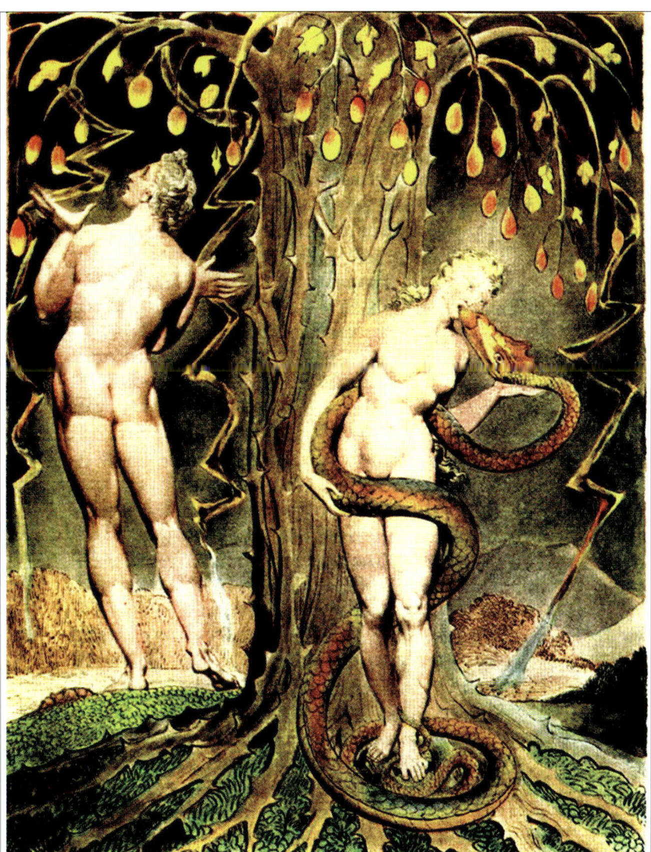

Paradise Lost, William Blake, 1808, the apple being transferred from the snake's mouth

In the New Testament, Saint Paul blames only Eve for the phenomenon of death, effectively absolving Adam from all blame in the apple-eating incident.[5] The presiding opinion was that Eve disobeyed God's instructions—death was the result. If not for her transgression, the condition of death would not have been set in motion. The Roman Catholic Bible states in Ecclesiacticus 25:33 that "Sin began with a woman, and thanks to her we all must die." This was the origin of the church fathers' fear and hatred of women.[6] A woman's ability to give birth did not act as a logical counterbalance.

By the Middle Ages, theologians described how Christ descended into Hell to rescue Adam and take him to heaven. But Eve was not forgiven and remained in Hell. By pulling Adam into a superior position, Eve remained below and inferior. Adam was stereotyped as the good man. He was, and still is, a symbol for men are good. Eve was stereotyped as the bad woman, which she continues to be. If women could be blamed for death, then the sinister stereotype of woman as witch easily followed. At least 6 million women (and men), were burned at the stake because of the *Malleus Maleficarum* (The Witch Hammer, 1486), which contained deadly labels and evil stereotypes that were mental and physical traps set by the authors into which the accused fell. Defining a woman as a witch separated her from other women, who were not necessarily thought of as good.

STATUE OF LIBERTY

(1886-

Not like the brazen giant of Greek fame,
With conquering limbs astride from land to land;
Here at our sea-washed, sunset gates shall stand
A mighty woman with a torch, whose flame
Is the imprisoned lightning, and her name
Mother of Exiles. From her beacon-hand
Glows world-wide welcome; her mild eyes command
The air-bridged harbor that twin cities frame.
'Keep, ancient lands, your storied pomp!' cries she
With silent lips. 'Give me your tired, your poor,
Your huddled masses yearning to breathe free,
The wretched refuse of your teeming shore.
Send these, the homeless, tempest-tost to me,
I lift my lamp beside the golden door!'
—EMMA LAZARUS, *The New Colossus*, 1883

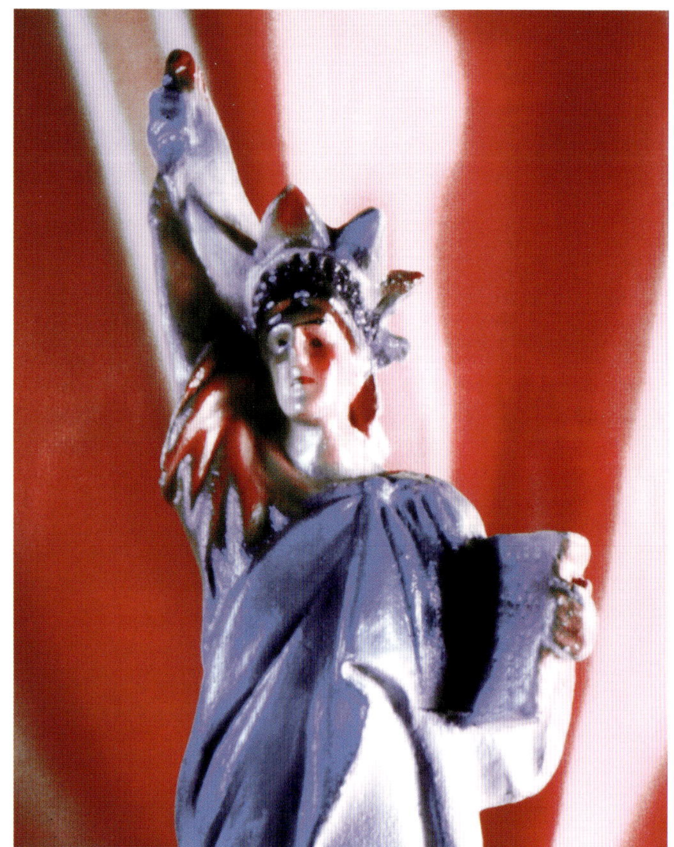

Statue of Liberty thirteen-and-one-half-inch carnival chalk prize

At a dinner party in 1865, while America's Civil War was ending, the Frenchman, Edouard Laboulaye, chairman of the French Anti-Slavery Society, proposed a monument be designed commemorating U.S. freedom and independence. In 1867, French sculptor Frederic-Auguste Bartholdi, with Laboulaye's idea in mind, proposed a statue of a robed woman holding a torch, entitled *Egypt Bringing the Light to Asia*, to commemorate the opening of the Suez Canal; the idea did not generate enough interest and was unsuccessful. Four years later, Bartholdi arrived in New York and proposed a similar Franco-American monument for Bedloe's Island in New York Harbor. When the Franco-American Union was created in France in 1875, fund-raising began for the statue and Laboulaye formally presented the idea to President Ulysses S. Grant. Finally, in the 1880s, design and construction began on Bartholdi's statue *Liberty Enlightening the World*. It's concept was similar to the 110-foot Colossus of Rhodes, built circa 282 BC and destroyed in an earthquake around 226 BC.

Bartholdi's huge statue is composed of three hundred copper sheets, assembled onto a framework of steel supports. Liberty's index finger is eight feet long; the length of her hand is sixteen feet. The statue's construction was engineered by Eugene-Emmanuel Viollet-le-Duc and Alexandre-Gustave Eiffel of Eiffel Tower fame. The copper plates were completed in 1881. The 151 foot statue was completed in 1884, then disassembled into 350 pieces and packed into 214 crates for transit to the United States. The ship carrying the crates almost sank in stormy seas. The statue was finally reassembled on Bedloe's Island and placed on a huge pedestal base, making it 300 feet high. It is thought that her face was modeled after Charlotte Bartholdi, the sculptor's mother; the arms and body were modeled after Jeanne-Emilie, Bartholdi's African girlfriend.

As everyone knows, it is now called the Statue of Liberty—a gift of international friendship from the people of France to the people of the United States. The Statue of Liberty was officially dedicated in 1886 and designated a National Monument in 1924. Originally intended to commemorate the centennial anniversary of America's Declaration of Independence, it arrived ten years late. Joseph Pulitzer was fund-raiser for its pedestal base. The poem "The New Colossus" by Emma Lazarus, who was of Russian-Jewish origin, is on a tablet set within its pedestal.

The statue immediately became a symbolic nationalistic archetype connected to instinctive feelings about the United States of America. To people who immigrated to this melting pot hoping to realize their dream, it represented feelings of freedom. Within recent decades, to those who have questioned America's role and actions throughout the world, it represents disgust as an analogue for unbridled capitalist aggression, as demonstrated by the 10,000 people in the city of Solo, Java, on April 5, 2003, who burned a mock Statue of Liberty in protest of George W. Bush's war with Iraq.

Unquestionably, the Statue of Liberty—along with the American flag—remains one of the most recognizable of all U.S. icons. Uncle Sam is the other well-known nationalistic archetype, but usually he is thought to represent the draft, taxes, and the power of government. Mount Rushmore represents America's growth from its Revolutionary times.

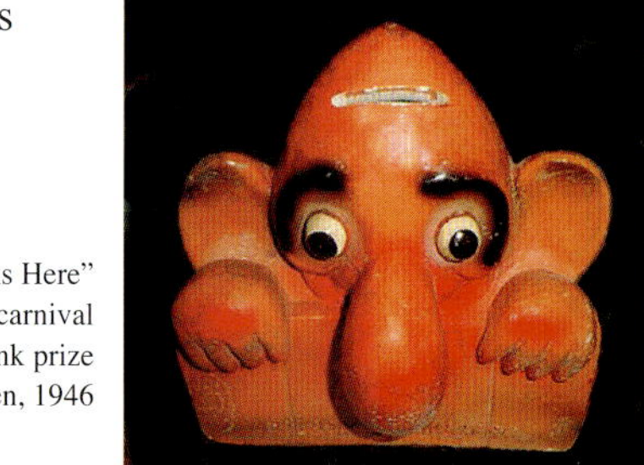

"Kilroy Banks Here"
six-inch carnival
chalk bank prize
© Hansen, 1946

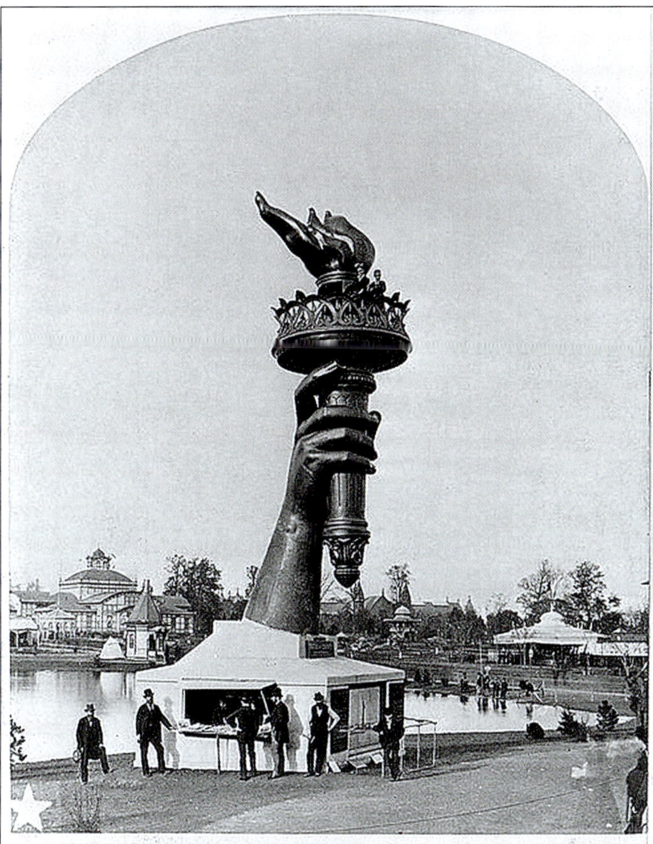

Display model of the arm and torch in Philadelphia, 1876

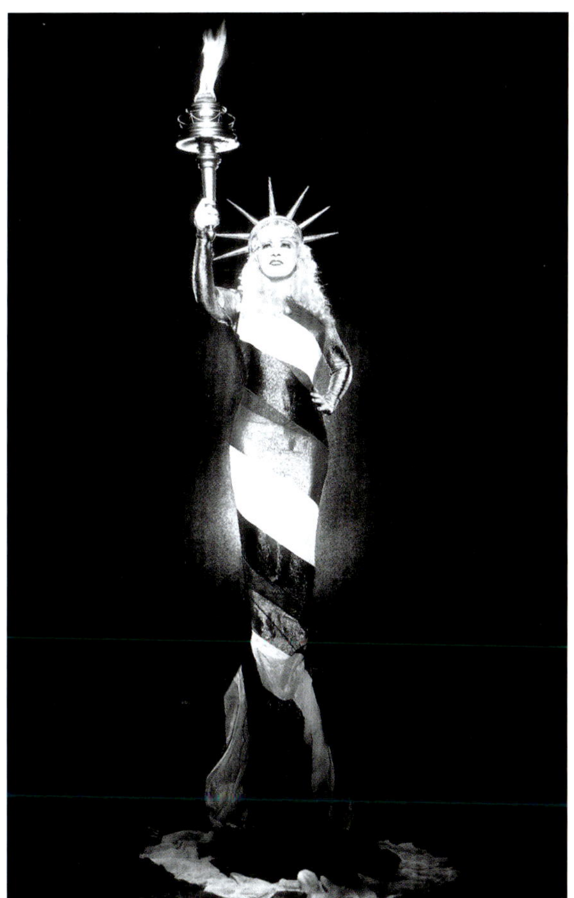

Mae West posed as the subtly flag-draped Statue of Liberty in *Belle of the Nineties*, 1934 © 20th Century Fox Film Corp., (page 24, an image update with Pamela Anderson)

KILROY WAS HERE
(1942-1945)

Man is by nature a political animal.
—ARISTOTLE, *Politics*, Book I

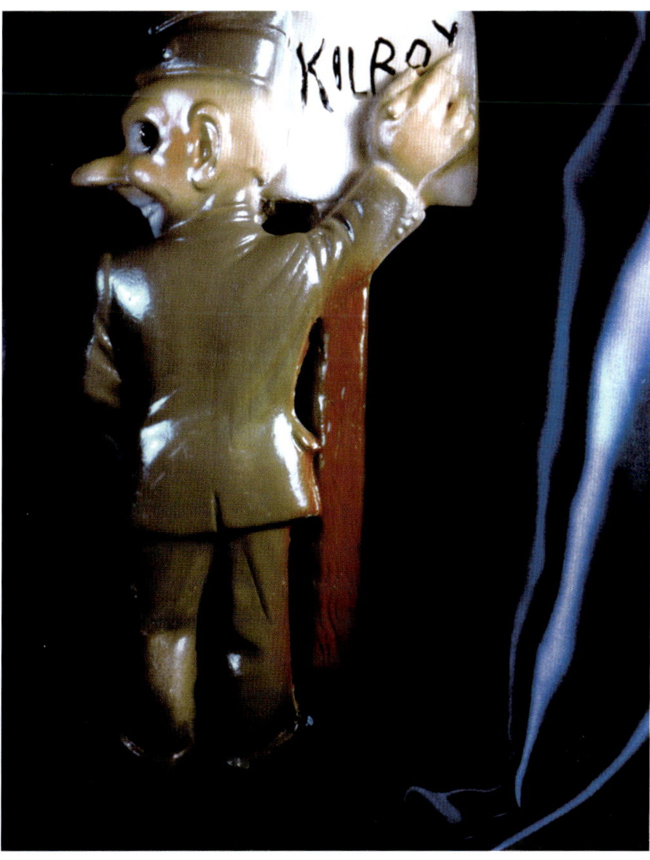

Kilroy was Here thirteen-and-a-half-inch carnival chalk prize, design W. E. Heaberlin, 1946. The soldier is the mysterious Kilroy himself, peeing on someone else's country while in the act of marking graffiti about himself.

Much like an intrusive pictograph belonging to unknown persons painted on walls in foreign places, the mysterious American phrase (or picture) "Kilroy Was Here" became symbolic graffiti that appeared wherever U.S. troops passed during World War II. An observant GI who found one, knew some other GI had gotten there first. Most often "Kilroy Was Here" decorated those highly visible places above urinals or on the walls of toilet stalls. As the war wore on, it became a game as well as a physical challenge to find the most unlikely places that Kilroy had been. If one was not already drawn in an exotic spot, the searching GI was apt to draw one of his own.

"Kilroy Was Here" is a nationalistic identity archetypal symbol portraying American passage. It is not quite as serious an intrusion as Christian crosses, which were pecked into rock faces by exploring Catholic missionaries who discovered Native American petroglyph sites in what would later become the western United States. The zealot proselytizers thought their highly civilized Christian identity symbol would negate heathen power.[1]

The words "Kilroy Was Here" were usually accompanied by the cartoon-style image of a simplistic face with a long drooping nose, two biggish round eyes, and dot-sized eyeballs humorously peeking over a wall. Sometimes Kilroy's fingers were shown gripping the wall's edge, or just a line could be drawn representing the top of the wall. The rest of Kilroy was hidden behind the wall. Kilroy's nose was patently phallic. The American Transit Association, on the *Speak to America* radio program in 1946, sponsored a nationwide contest in an attempt to discover the origins of Kilroy. The answer seems to have been one James J. Kilroy, a ship inspector who worked at the Fore River Shipyard in Quincy, Massachusetts. He was responsible for checking the holes riveters closed each day as the ship's hulls were being built. He used a yellow marker and wrote "Kilroy Was Here" so that other inspectors would not count the same rivets twice. Troops, travelling to the war front, saw his "Kilroy Was Here" markings on the hulls.

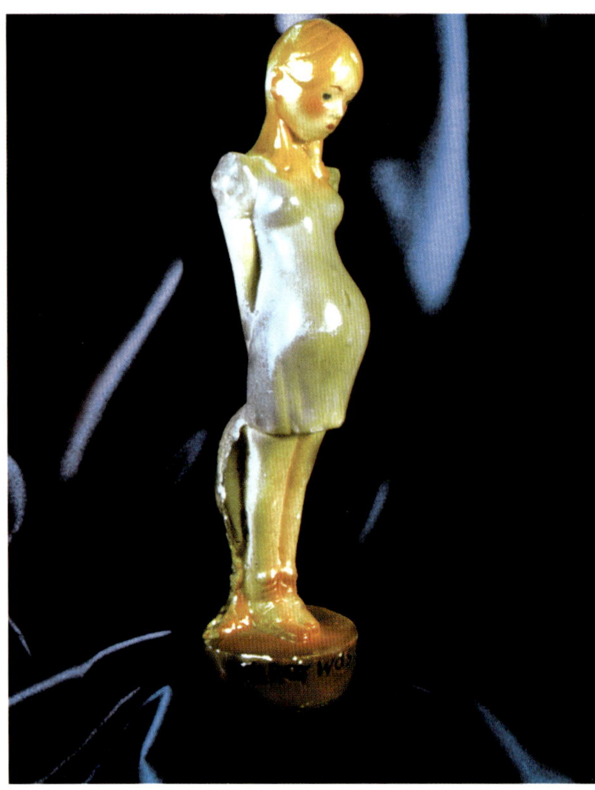

Kilroy Was Here ten-inch carnival chalk prize

After the war, "Kilroy Was Here" met greater challenges. According to Charles Panati, "Kilroy Was Here" made it to the moon, to the top of Mount Everest, to the torch of the Statue of Liberty, and to the Marco Polo Bridge in China.[2] Even during peacetime, "Kilroy Was Here" became an underground symbol, reflective of an archetypal U.S. identity, instinctively filling a need that certain Americans had to visually mark where they had traveled. It was apparently meant in jest, although politically incorrect. When "Kilroy Was Here" was placed on the moon, it must surely have been a proclamation of U.S. identity—as in "We got here first!"

GEORGE WASHINGTON AND THE CHERRY TREE STORY
(1800-

Yankee Doodle came to town,
riding on a pony;
He stuck a feather in his cap
And called it macaroni.
—BRITISH TROOP SONG, ridiculing Americans, to which Americans added new verses telling of their victories in the Revolutionary War

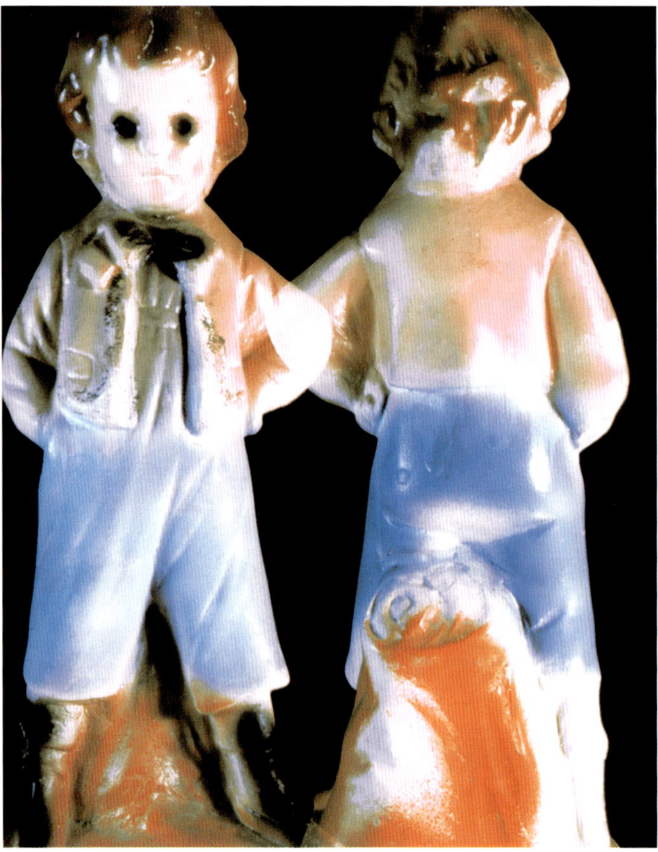

George Washington twelve-and-a-half-inch carnival chalk prize, standing with legs apart, in a thoughtful pose in front of what was left of the chopped-off tree trunk. Double exposure

Mason Locke Weems, known as Parson Weems, invented and promulgated the "Little George Washington and the Cherry Tree" honesty fable in his book *Life of George Washington*. His much-cherished Christian book was first published in 1800—by 1850 it was in its fifty-ninth edition. After having studied medicine and theology, Weems became a writer and traveling bookseller, and in 1784 was ordained as a minister in the Church of England. Weems wrote Christian self-help books, including *The Philanthropist, or a Good Twenty-Five Cents Worth of Political Love-Powder*; *God's Revenge Against Dueling*; *God's Revenge Against Gambling*; and *God's Revenge Against Adultery*.

Washington was of Deist faith, which stressed a belief in God, morality, and reason, rejecting the orthodox Christian view of the divinity of Jesus Christ, often viewing Christ as merely a sublime teacher of morality. Weems, the ever thoughtful parson, did his best to add exaggerated Christian morality into his George Washington myth.

228

"Little George Washington and the Cherry Tree" did not appear until Weems' fifth edition, published in 1806. Here is the tale, exactly as told by Weems:

> When George was about 6 years old, he was made the wealthy owner of a hatchet! of which, like most little boys, he was immoderately fond; and was constantly going about chopping every thing which came in his way. One day, in the garden, where he often amused himself by hacking his mother's pea-sticks, he unluckily tried the edge of his hatchet on the body of a beautiful young English cherry tree, which he barked so terribly, that I don't believe the tree ever got the better of it. The next morning, the old gentleman, finding out what had befallen his tree, which, by the by, was a great favorite, came into the house; and with much warmth asked for the mischievous author, declaring at the same time, that he would not have taken 5 guineas for his tree. Nobody would tell him anything about it. Presently George and his hatchet made their appearance. "George," said his father, "do you know who killed that beautiful little cherry tree yonder in the garden?" This was a tough question; and George staggered under it for a moment; but quickly recovered himself; and looking at his father, with the sweet face of youth brightened with the inexpressible charm of all-conquering truth, he bravely cried out, "I can't tell a lie, Pa; you know, I can't tell a lie. I did cut it with my hatchet."—"Run to my arms, you dearest boy," cried his father in transports, "run to my arms; glad am I, George, that you killed my tree, for you have paid me for it a thousand fold. Such an act of heroism in my son is worth more than a thousand trees, though blossomed with silver and their fruits of purest gold."[1]

Weems' tale was debunked in 1926 in W. E. Woodward's *George Washington: The Image and the Man*. But to this day, the honest-leader legend is still told and retold in most grade schools throughout the United States as if it were true. It is a symbolic mythomania (a compulsion to embroider the truth) archetype for nationalism—that American presidents are indisputably honest, and if you are honest, you too can be president.

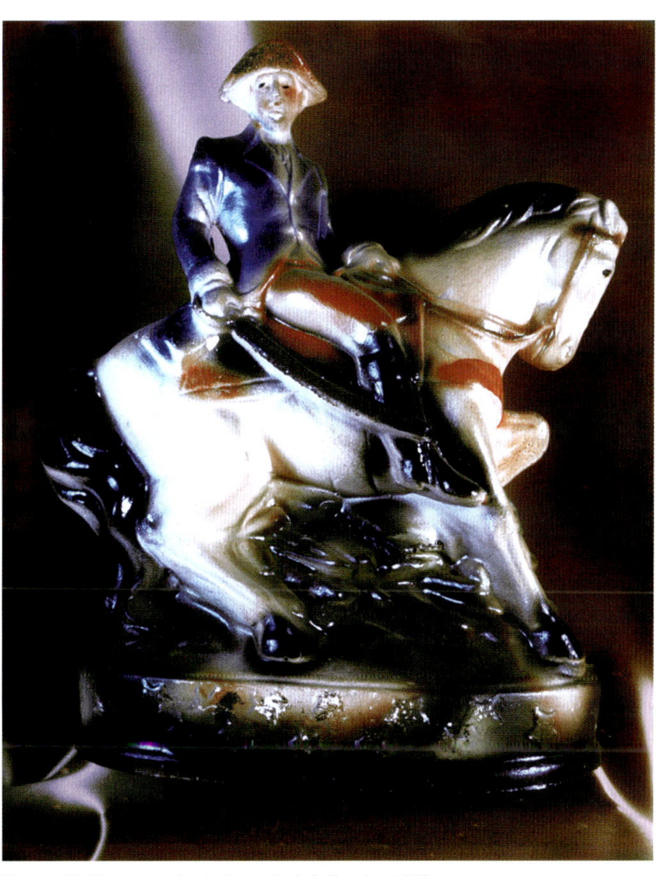

George Washington twelve-inch carnival chalk prize, 1940s

PAUL REVERE

THE MINUTEMAN

Listen my children and you shall hear
Of the midnight ride of Paul Revere,
On the eighteenth of April, in Seventy-five;
Hardly a man is now alive
Who remembers that famous day and year.
He said to his friend, 'If the British march
By land or sea from the town to-night,

Hang a lantern aloft in the belfry arch
Of the North Church tower as a signal light,--
One if by land, and two if by sea;
And I on the opposite shore will be,
Ready to ride and spread the alarm
Through every Middlesex village and farm,
For the country folk to be up and to arm.

—FIRST TWO STANZAS: *Paul Revere's Ride*, Henry Wadsworth Longfellow, published in 1861 as a prelude to the Civil War

It is little known that Paul Revere's ride was supposed to extend to Concord. On that leg of the ride there were three riders—only one of them got through to Concord, and it wasn't Revere, it was Dr. Samuel Prescott. Prior to his famous ride of April 18, 1775, Revere's reputation as an express rider and intelligence agent extended from Boston to New York to Philadelphia, and he was even known in London.[1] Revere was one of many in the Sons of Liberty movement who organized aggressively against the British. General Thomas Gage, commander in chief of British forces in North America and governor of Massachusetts, arrived in Boston on May 13, 1774, only to be greeted with unceremonious defiance. Some months earlier, on December 16, 1773, the patriots had struck against the Tea Act, a tax imposed to help the failing East India Company sell its "baneful, detested, dutied Article tea," which had been boycotted by the colonies for three years. Disguised as Native Americans, the patriots overtook three ships in the Boston Harbor and threw 342 chests of tea overboard during the famous Boston

Tea Party. Revere was one of them.

In rebuttal, on March 31, 1774, Massachusetts Parliament passed the Boston Port Act, which stated that the port would be closed on June 1 and would remain closed until the citizens of Boston repaid the East India Company for the destroyed tea. Meetings had been held and patriots expected a confrontation at any time. On April 16, under orders from Dr. Joseph Warren, Revere was sent to Lexington to alert John Hancock and Samuel Adams that the British were about to seize military armaments in Concord and arrest citizens who had committed acts of treason. On his return, Revere stopped in Charlestown, where the lantern signal was devised: two if by sea, one if by land, to be placed in the church steeple. Two nights later, Revere and William Dawes rode again, attempting to go as far as Concord. Jayne E. Triber, in *A True Republican*, describes the night that catapulted Revere into everlasting glory:

> On Tuesday evening, April 18, 1775, Dr. Warren received word from several sources that British soldiers were marching to Boston Common, "where was a number of Boats to receive them." About ten o'clock, Dr. Warren "Sent in great haste" for Revere "and beged [*sic*] that I would immediately Set off for Lexington" to warn John Hancock and Samuel Adams of the movements of the soldiers. Revere, after learning that Warren had already sent another express, William Dawes, by a longer route over Boston Neck, "called upon a friend" to hang the prearranged lantern signals from Christ Church. In his letter to Jeremy Belknap, Revere poetically recalled the scene as two friends rowed him across Charles River to Charlestown, past the British warship Somerset: "It was then young flood, the Ship was winding, and the moon was rising."
> . . . In Charlestown, Colonel Conant "and several others" told Revere they had seen the lantern signals, and Richard Devens of the Committee of Safety informed him that he had observed nine or ten British officers "all well mounted, and armed" on the road to Concord. Revere set off for Lexington about eleven o'clock, riding "a very good Horse" borrowed from Deacon Larkin of Charlestown. He had "almost got over" Charlestown Common when two British officers spotted him. Revere "turned my horse short, about, and rid upon a full Gallop" toward Medford with one of the officers in pursuit. He "got clear" of the officer, who got stuck in a clay pond, awakened the captain of the Medford Minutemen, and "alarmed almost every House, till I got to Lexington."[2]

Later that evening, on their way to Concord, Revere and Dawes were joined by another Son of Liberty, Dr. Samuel Prescott. British soldiers stopped all three about halfway between Lexington and Concord. Dawes eluded capture by leading two pursuing soldiers to a local farmhouse where the British were afraid to attack. He then returned to Lexington. Prescott escaped by jumping his horse over a low stone wall, then rode through to Concord. Revere put up a good verbal fight, but was escorted back to Lexington, where his horse was taken.[3] There he joined Adams and Hancock, who fled to safety in Burlington. When the British arrived on April 19, the Minutemen were waiting for them. Revere returned to rescue valuable papers in Hancock's trunk.

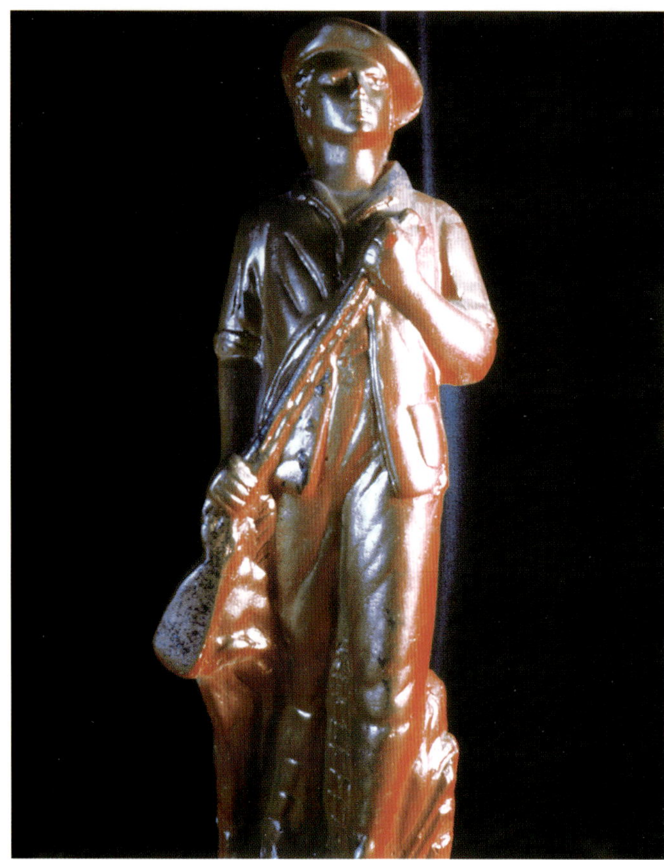

Paul Revere, Minuteman fifteen-inch carnival chalk prize

Paul Revere was born on January 1, 1735, in Boston, Massachusetts. He studied at the North Grammar School in Boston. His formal schooling completed at thirteen, he entered his father's silver and goldsmith business. Revere married Sara Orne in 1757. On May 3, 1773, Sara died at age thirty-seven, just five months after the birth of their eighth child, six lived. On October 10, 1773, Revere married Rachel Walker, aged twenty-seven. This was his courtship poem:

> Take three fourths of a Paine that make Traitors confess
> (Rac)
> With three parts of a place which the Wicked don't Bless
> (Hel)
> Joyne four sevenths of an Exercise which shop-keepers use
> (Walk)
> And what Bad men do, when they good actions refuse
> (Er)
> These four added together with great care and Art
> Will point out the Fair One nearest my Heart.[4]

Revere's military career was undistinguished. In 1778 and 1779, Lieutenant Colonel Paul Revere commanded a garrison at Castle Island. On the ill-fated expedition to Penobscot Bay, Maine, he disobeyed an order from Brigadier General Peleg Wadsworth, though a court-martial later acquitted Revere of the charge. Wadsworth had asked Revere to give up his boat in order to save the crew of an American schooner, which was drifting toward the enemy. Revere refused because his private baggage was at stake, although he did later agree. At the court-martial he admitted to his first refusal. Ironically, Henry Wadsworth Longfellow was the grandson of Brigadier General Wadsworth.

Longfellow's epic poem made Revere's fame as a hero equal to that of the Founding Fathers. It was hawkish chest-pounding—propagandism meant for war——a poetic archetype for feeling bravery and honor:

> So through the night rode Paul Revere;
> And so through the night went his cry of alarm
> To every Middlesex village and farm,
> A cry of defiance, and not of fear,
> A voice in the darkness, a knock at the door,
> And a word that shall echo for evermore!
> For, borne on the night-wind of the Past,
> Through all our history, to the last,
> In the hour of darkness and peril and need,
> The people will waken and listen to hear
> The hurrying hoof-beats of that steed,
> And the midnight message of Paul Revere.

Immigrating to America was not easy from the 1600s to the 1820s. Shipping agents accepted indigents who signed an indenture paper agreeing to work for three to seven years to pay for their passage. If a family member died while on passage, which frequently happened, the remaining family members had to add to their indentured years. It is estimated one-half to two-thirds of all immigrants coming to America before 1820 were indentured; this does not include Africans brought against their will as slaves. Indentured servants could be sold. Often children from one family ended up with different masters. Children traveling alone were indentured until the age of twenty-one. Ship owners regarded their indentured passengers as freight; as such, space between decks was limited to five feet in height. Immigrants, regardless of sex or marital relation, slept three to a berth in a space allotment of two feet wide by six feet long. Dependent upon weather and destination, voyages lasted from six weeks to six months. Stormy days forced passengers below deck and portholes for light and air were nonexistent. In 1752, a ship from the Netherlands arrived in Philadelphia with only twenty-one survivors out of the 340 who began the journey; the rest had starved. Food was always scarce and disease plentiful on board the ships. Rather than jailing convicts, Britain sent 50,000 of them to the colonies from 1718 to 1775. Depending upon his or her crime, each convict was banished for seven to fourteen years.[5] Despite the hardships, tens of thousands of immigrants survived. Many of the survivors lived in poverty in cramped ethnic enclaves.

Prejudice was rampant in the colonies from the outset. Roman Catholics were the most despised and constituted less than one-percent of all the colonists. Catholics were not allowed to carry arms, were prohibited from serving in the militia, and paid double taxes. Jews, Catholics, and women were not allowed to vote. In most colonies, Jews were not allowed to become physicians or lawyers. By 1760, the population soared to 2 million. By the 1770s, Britain's hold on the colonies was tenuous and revolution was imminent, setting the stage for Paul Revere and the Minutemen.

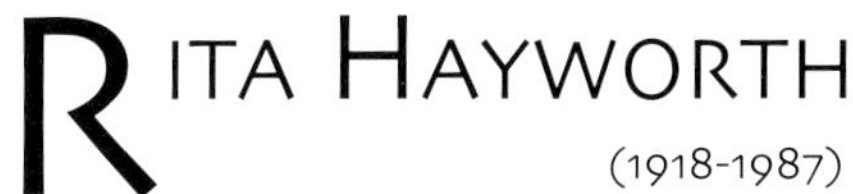

R ITA HAYWORTH

(1918-1987)

We are all tied to our destiny and there is no way we can liberate ourselves.
—Rita Hayworth

Now we are all sons of bitches.
—Kenneth Bainbridge, U.S. Physicist after the first atomic test

During the mid-1930s, the gifted Latina dancer Rita Cansino played her parts quite naturally in Hollywood films like *Dante's Inferno* (1935). A few years later, Cansino would appear completely transformed. Gone was her Latina look. From then on she would be a cosmetically altered, cosmopolitan, Anglo star. Through the use of electrolysis, hair was removed from her forehead and eyebrows, and her hair color was changed first to auburn and later to red. To complete the disguised metamorphosis, she also had a new name: Rita Hayworth. Her obvious Anglicization was hidden within the media for as long as possible (a slur on the Latino-Mexican look, but done for commercial gain).

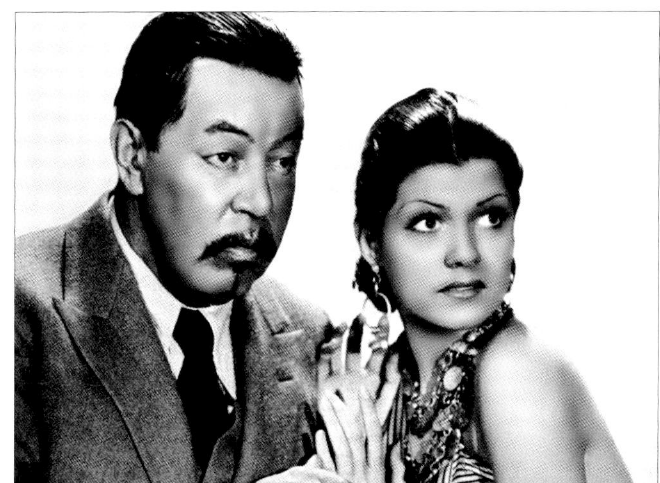

Warner Oland and Rita Cansino, *Charlie Chan in Egypt*, 1935 © Fox Film Corporation

Her new name, along with her performance with Cary Grant in *Only Angels Have Wings* (1939), began the rise to star billing for the newly discovered, talented Rita Hayworth. By 1940, 3,800 publicity stories were printed promoting her as an American beauty and saying she would be Hollywood's new sex symbol. *Strawberry Blond* (1941) gave her that desired status.

During World War II, she became the U.S. servicemen's second most popular pinup when she appeared in a two-piece bathing suit on the cover of the August 11, 1941, issue of *Life* magazine, although it was the picture of her kneeling on a bed, inside the magazine, that was pinned up. She was exotic. Betty Grable, the number-one pinup, was the apple-pie, all-American girl next door. These two very different archetypal symbols both offered a rare moment for escapist lust.

Winthrop Sargent, a *Life* magazine writer, dubbed

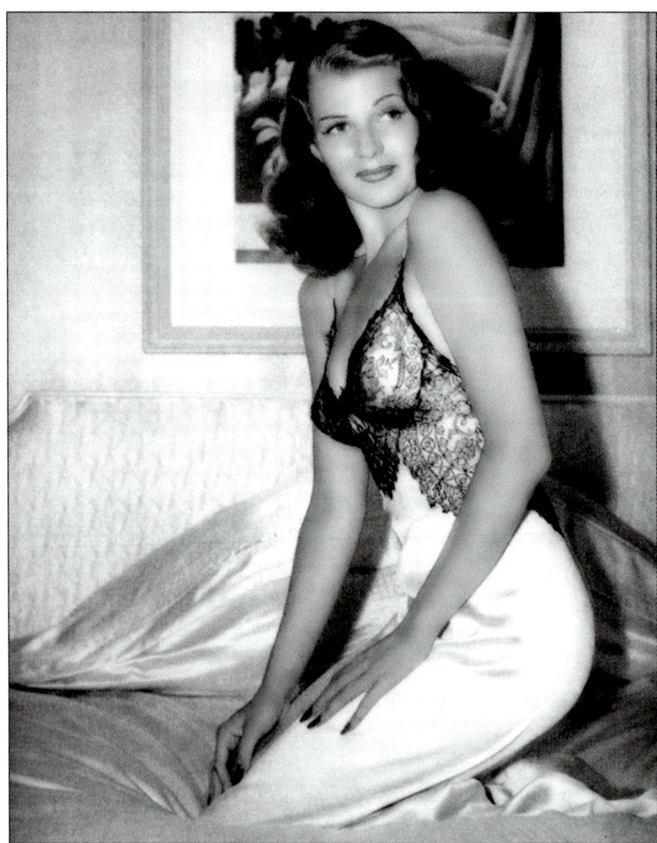

Rita Hayworth © *Life* magazine, August 11, 1941

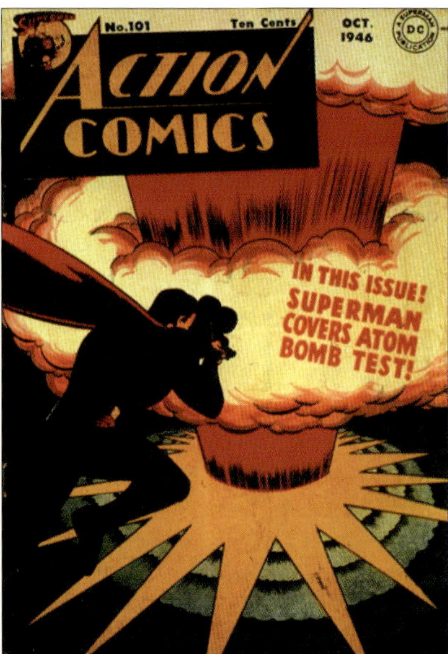

Action Comics cover, No. 101, October, 1946
© DC Comics

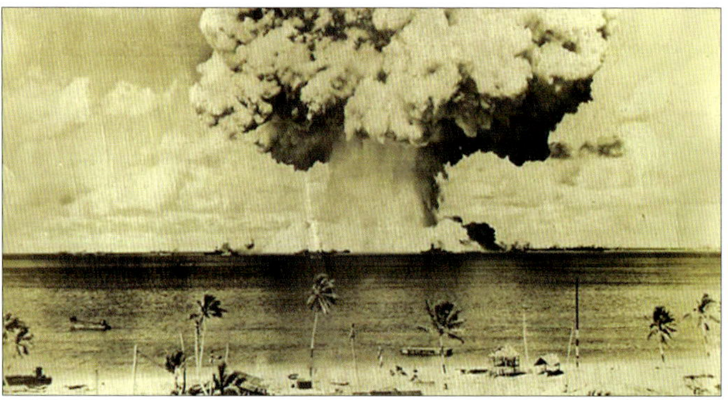

Project Able, atomic bomb named "Gilda," after Rita Hayworth in the film *Gilda*, 1946

Hayworth the "Great American Love Goddess," which became shortened over time to "Love Goddess." In *Gilda* (1946), the film that elevated her to superstardom, she became the tempestuous lover. She created an enduring Hollywood moment with her memorable archetypal striptease, where only her long black gloves were removed. She achieved a heightened sensuality, one rarely seen on the 1940s movie screen.

The name "Gilda" easily connected back to Gilda Gray, whose sensual shimmy was all the rage of the flapper era twenty years earlier. Gray sued Columbia Pictures, stating that their 1946 film copied her life. It didn't exactly, and Columbia was likely to win the case, but to keep Hayworth's value on track, Gray was given an out-of-court settlement.

The timing of Hayworth achieving superstardom in *Gilda* had strange repercussions. Since the film was released within a year of the conclusion of World War II, scientists who were working on the Able atomic project decided to name their first non-war, atomic test bomb "Gilda" in her honor—a dubious honor at best. Earlier bombs dropped on Hiroshima and Nagasaki had been given the cryptic masculine appellations "Fat Man" and "Little Boy." The pinup picture of Hayworth was painted on the bomb casing.[1] As the world watched, most in horror (and a few with praise, intrigued by the twentieth century's "weapon of mass destruction," archetypal symbol), many felt an instinctive fascination with death and fear. Most Americans felt superiority. "Gilda" was dropped and exploded in midair near the Bikini atoll on July 1, 1946. Part of Bikini Island was named "Rita," also in her honor. The idea of naming a deadly bomb "Gilda" upset Hayworth enormously.

Some 242 navy ships, 156 aircraft, 25,000 radiation recording devices, 5,400 experimental rats, goats, and pigs, and half of the world's supply of movie film were involved in the tests. More than 42,000 U.S. military and civilian personnel were also involved. Ten percent of the test animals died instantly from the impact of the blast. Photographs showed one of the goats munching hay without interruption as the shock wave struck and the debris fell all around. The heroine of the test was a female rat that gave birth to three baby rats, which were promptly named Alpha, Beta, and Gamma. By July 23, a quarter of the animals were dead, including the three baby rats. A second atomic bomb test, known as the Baker test, was exploded underwater in the same area on July 25, 1946. That bomb was named "Helen of Bikini." The third test, Project Charlie, with an unnamed bomb, was canceled, mostly due to concerns that America was depleting its arsenal of atomic weapons. After the cancellation, a reception was held in honor of Vice Admiral Blandy, commander of the Bikini Task Force. The next day, a photograph appeared in newspapers showing the admiral and his wife cutting a large cake topped by a mushroom cloud. Infuriated by the photograph, the Reverend A. Powell Davis of a Washington, D.C., church thundered to his audience: "If I had the authority of a priest of the Middle Ages, I would call down the wrath of

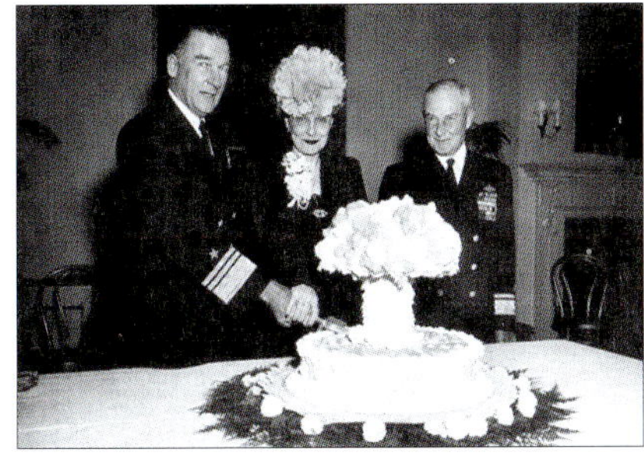

Vice Admiral W. H. P. (Spike) Blandy and his wife cutting
the replica atomic bomb angel food cake, 1946

God upon such an obscenity. I would damn to hell these people of callous conscience, these traitors to humanity."[2]

It is explainable only within the context of man versus woman gender bias, firmly rooted within archetypal symbols (Jean Harlow was nicknamed "Bombshell"), that the wartime atomic bombs were given male names while the peacetime atomic bombs were given female names. Four days after "Gilda" was exploded, French auto engineer Louis Reard named his new bathing suit "bikini," after the atom, as it was smaller than competing french swimsuits named "Atome."

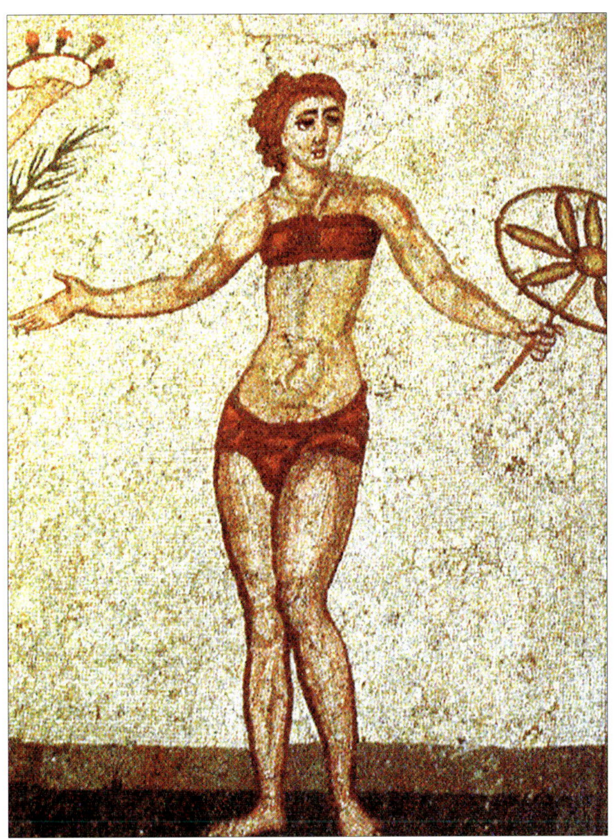

Mosaic detail, *Bikini Room*, Villa of Casale, Piazza Armerina, Sicily, 400 AD

The bikini was new for the twentieth century, but not new historically. Sixteen centuries earlier, mosaics in Sicily had depictions of women wearing bikini-type suits during athletic contests. Reard's bikini was simply a more recent archetypal motif for feeling lust for a scantily clad woman. By 1951, bikinis had been banned as too lascivious to be worn in American beauty pageants and did not reach acceptance in the United States until the 1960s. But by then, a strange

primal bond had begun to form between Bikini Island, the bomb, the swimsuit, and the archetypal feelings of liberation, promoted first by a scandalous X-rated Brigitte Bardot wearing a bikini and less in *And God Created Woman* (1956); then by Ursula Andress, who came from the sea in a space-age /cave-woman bikini, accessorized with hunting knife in hip holster, in the first James Bond film, *Dr. No* (1962); and next by Raquel Welch, who wore a Stone Age fur bikini in *One Million Years* BC (1966). These three films fantasized an wildly exotic, Bikini Island, stone-age immodesty that a

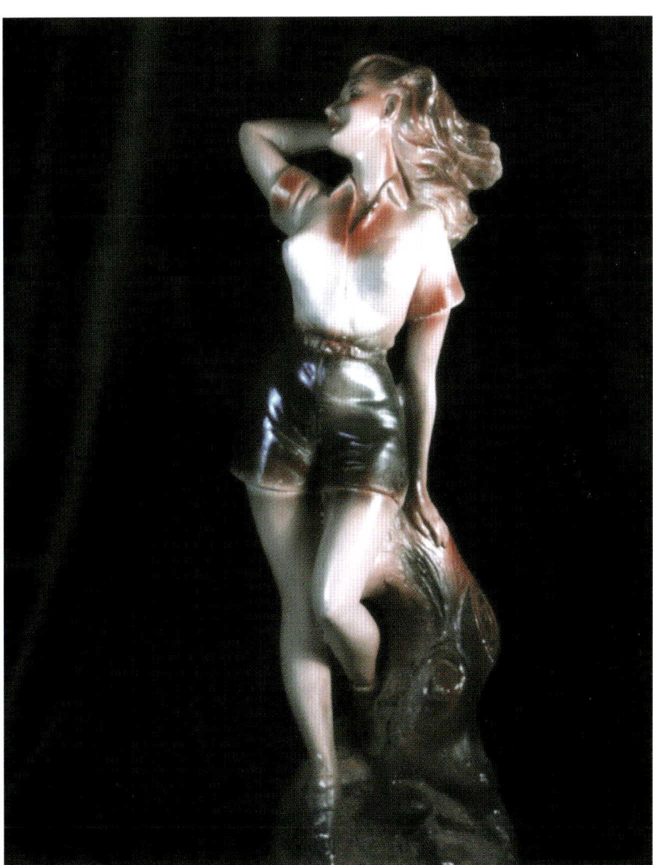

Rita Hayworth fourteen-inch carnival chalk prize

media-ridden, war-torn humanity found comforting to return to. Reverting to a phony liberated Stone Age sounds odd, but the power of even larger bombs, such as the mammoth Bravo test, demonstrated that Earth was probably on a collision course with its own linear time—and its time was running out. Escaping back to the Stone Age felt like a good idea.

Although she was trained as a flamboyant dancer almost from birth, the real Rita Hayworth was shy, unassuming, and quiet. It was hardly known that she was, in truth, the antithesis of her stereotype. Her father was the famous Spanish dancer Eduardo Cansino, who with his sister, Elsa, came to America in 1914. A year later, while dancing with the Ziegfeld Follies, Eduardo and dancer/showgirl Volga Hayworth (also spelled Haworth) met; they married in 1917. Their Brooklyn-born daughter, Margarita Carmen Cansino, danced professionally, and by age four had appeared with her father and aunt in a recital at Carnegie Hall. The Dancing Cansinos can be seen in *Anna Case* and *La Fiesta* (silent films from 1926) with then eight-year-old Margarita. Her family relocated to Los Angeles, where Margarita went to school through the ninth grade. At age thirteen, she began dancing at the Caliente Club in Tijuana, and it was there that she was discovered by Winfield Sheehan, vice president of production at Fox Film Corporation, when she was sixteen. Her early films included *Human Cargo*, and *Meet Nero Wolfe*. She married Edward Judson, her Hollywood publicity agent, in 1937, and he pushed her to change her Latina appearance. By the 1940s, Hayworth became a major leading lady to most of the big stars, including Orson Welles—her second, and soon to be ex, husband—in *Lady from Shanghai* (1948).

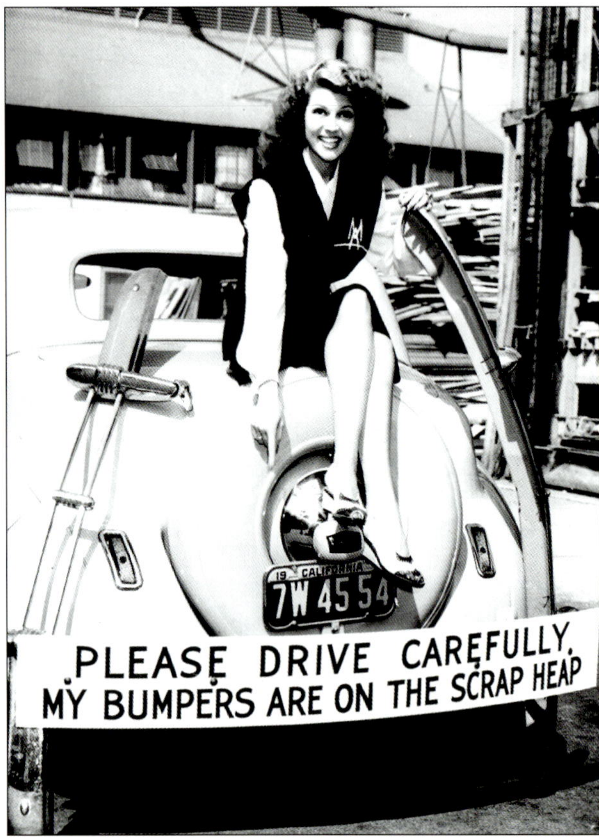

"Please Drive Carefully, My Bumpers Are on the Scrap Heap," World War II photograph of Hayworth promoting metal for use in the war effort. Courtesy: National Archives, Washington, D.C.

She intrigued some of the American public with her tempestuous and adulterous romance with Aly Khan, son of a Muslim leader, but disgusted the Hollywood powers that had structured the racially defined Will Hays Production Code. Church groups condemned her amorous affair with a "colored man."[3] Khan and Hayworth were married in 1949, but divorced in 1951. By then the public had tired of her romantic disasters and the gossipy headlines. Her Love Goddess title had boomeranged. She married two more times. Her superstardom in *Gilda* remained with her, as well as her famous quote, "Every man I have known has fallen in love with Gilda and awakened with me." She was diagnosed with Alzheimer's in 1980 and spent her declining years being cared for by her second daughter, Yasmin Aga Khan. Hayworth died peacefully in her sleep in 1987.

Smokey Bear
(1944

Few Americans know that in the spring of 1942 a Japanese submarine surfaced near the coast of Southern California and fired a salvo of shells that hit the mainland—they exploded in an oil field near Santa Barbara, extremely close to the Los Padres National Forest. Fear-struck Americans were shocked that the war could be brought directly onto American soil. What if the shells hit the timber stands of the Pacific Coast, setting off raging forest fires with no one left to fight them other than old or disabled men, working women, and children? Experienced firefighters and able-bodied men were off at war. Protection of America's forests became a matter of national importance. Early posters gave warnings of imminent fire and enemy takeover.

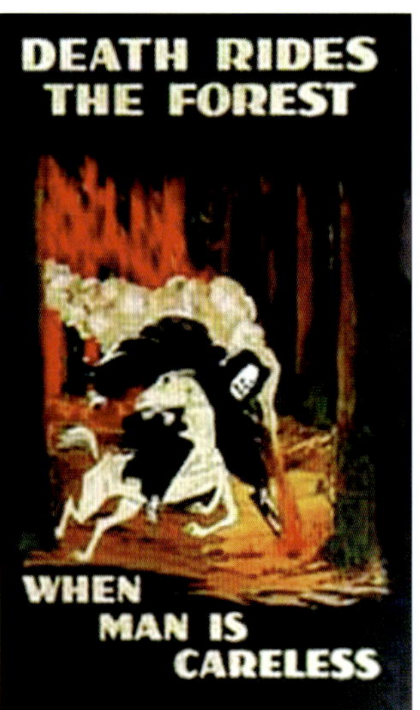

"Death Rides the Forest," U.S. Forest Service poster, 1940

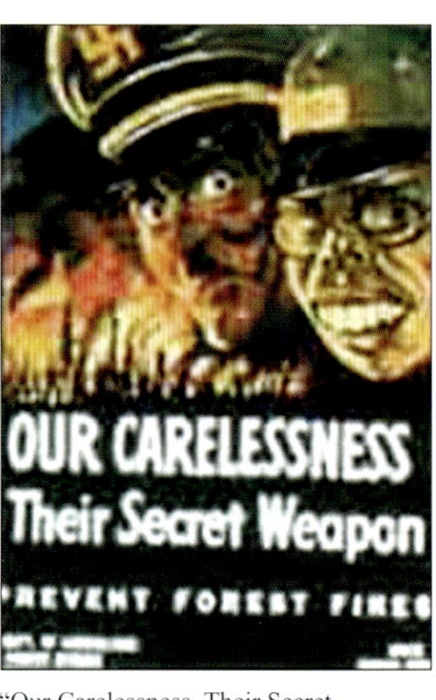

"Our Carelessness, Their Secret Weapon," U.S. Forest Service poster, 1943

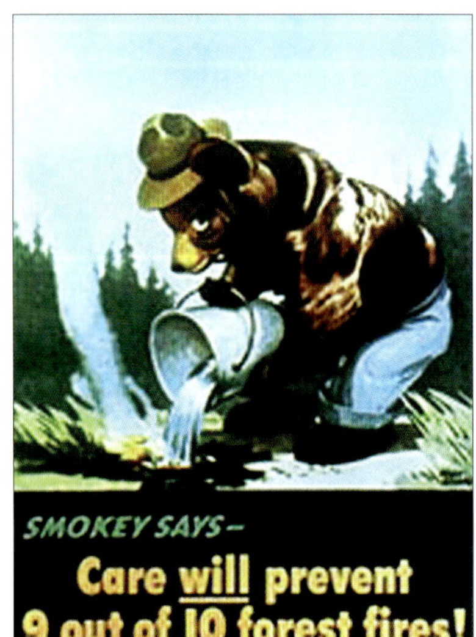

"Smokey Says," U.S. Forest Service poster, 1944, illustration Albert Staehle

The U.S. government decided an icon needed to be invented that would alert people to be very careful to prevent forest fires. Bureaucracy took over. The Forest Service organized the Cooperative Forest Fire Prevention Campaign

with the help of the Wartime Advertising Council. At first Walt
Disney's Bambi was used, but a cute little fawn could not be
used in future campaigns because Bambi was on loan from
Disney Studios for only one year (where was Uncle Walt's
patriotic spirit?). The Forest Service needed a new four-legged
replacement. Enter Smokey Bear (not Smokey *the* Bear, as
most people think), created by Rudolph Wendel. His Smokey
Bear had a bit of a bare bear beer belly—a tad bit too much
bare bear showing. By August 9, 1944, the first poster was
designed by Albert Staehle, with Smokey Bear (minus the
bare bear beer belly) fashionably dressed in a Forest Ranger's
hat and belted blue jeans. He was hunched over, pouring a
bucket of water on a campfire.

In May of 1950, a human-caused fire ravaged
17,000 acres of forest near Capitan, New Mexico. During
the fire, a tiny bear cub climbed up a tree and was found
by a fire crew. They named him Hotfoot, probably because
he had been burned on his feet and bottom. People quickly
realized Hotfoot was a living symbol of Smokey Bear, and
his name officially became Smokey Bear. He was flown by
Game Warden Ray Bell to a veterinary hospital in Santa Fe.
After his burns healed, Bell took him home, but Smokey Bear
dominated the family pets. Too bad. So Smokey Bear was
transferred to the National Zoo in Washington, D.C. Through
media exposure (a nice name for media inundation), he was
presented to schoolchildren to encourage them not to play
with matches or fire. He became a bear superstar—luckily for
him the zoo didn't dress him in the Forest Ranger hat and blue
jeans. He was an animal hero symbol for vigilant care.

By 1952, a much-loved Smokey Bear was being
heavily merchandised, so an act of Congress took the Smokey
Bear symbol out of the public domain and placed him under
the control of the Secretary of Agriculture. This meant the
government collected fees and royalties for any commercial
use of Smokey. Later, Smokey Bear even got his own zip
code, 20252, because so many people wrote to him. (Did he
ever write them back? Did he even get to read their letters?)

Smokey Bear died in 1976 and is buried in Smokey
Bear Park, Capitan, New Mexico.

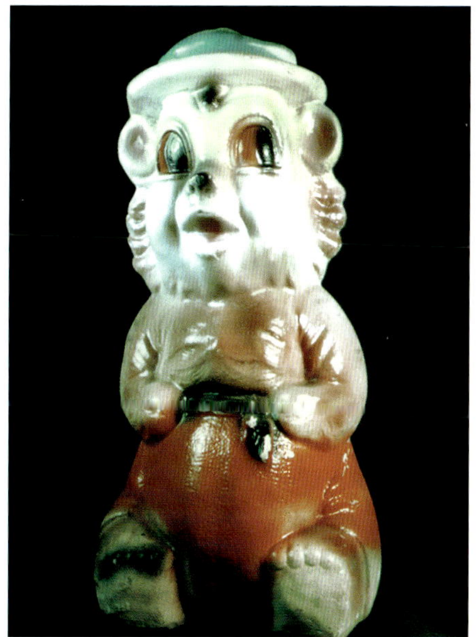

Smokey Bear eleven-inch
carnival chalk bank prize

Bing Crosby
(1903-1977)

Man, if you gotta ask you'll never know.
—Louis Armstrong

It was a great game.
—Bing Crosby

Bing Crosby's early idol was the acclaimed blackface
minstrel protagonist Al Jolson, the most illustrious singer of
the early twentieth century. Jolson's career was on the decline in
the early 1930s, while Crosby's career was soaring. Crosby's
initial radio success stemmed from his seemingly unlimited
vocal talent and his ability to adapt it to various musical
environments. His voice was utilized as an athletic, jazzy com-
ponent in Paul Whiteman's Orchestra, the most popular band
of the 1920s, and didn't resemble the familiar, easily identifiable
singing style of the intimate, sappy crooner in his famous
rendition of *White Christmas*. Twenty of his songs swept to
the top of the record charts between 1931 and 1936. Crosby
started his meteoric rise in Hollywood with his role in *The Big
Broadcast* (1932).

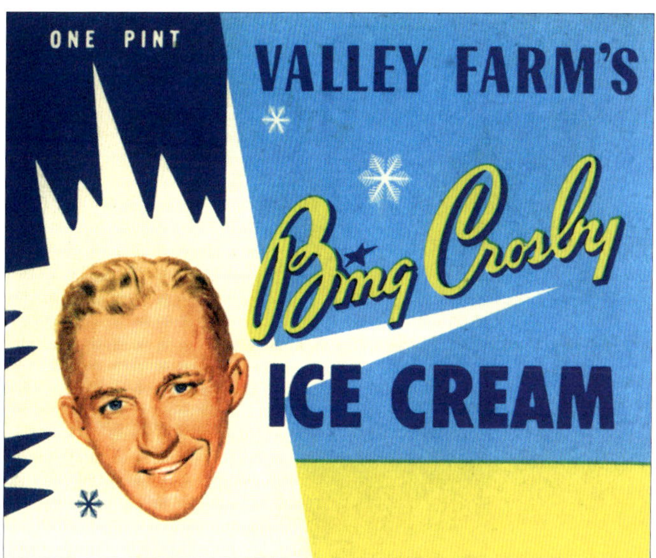

Valley Farm's Bing Crosby ice-cream box, circa 1940s–50s

Crosby films were predominantly agreeable comedies,
in which he was cast as a singer or songwriter. His stage image
provided the stereotypical unblemished good-guy next door,
a model the public delightedly embraced in an era fighting its
way out of the Depression and later the horrors of World War II.
Crosby crooned and sparkled in those otherwise dark days.
He was the thoroughly charming male and he wooed many
equally charming females in his films. As the quintessential
clean-living, talented, traditional swell guy, he represented
the consummate dream from which to sip romance and forget
one's woes. Crosby may have inherited Jolson's title as the
World's Greatest Entertainer, but he expanded the boundaries.
And despite their stylistic differences, their lyrics shared the
same sappy qualities. To pull off the gambit, Crosby disguised

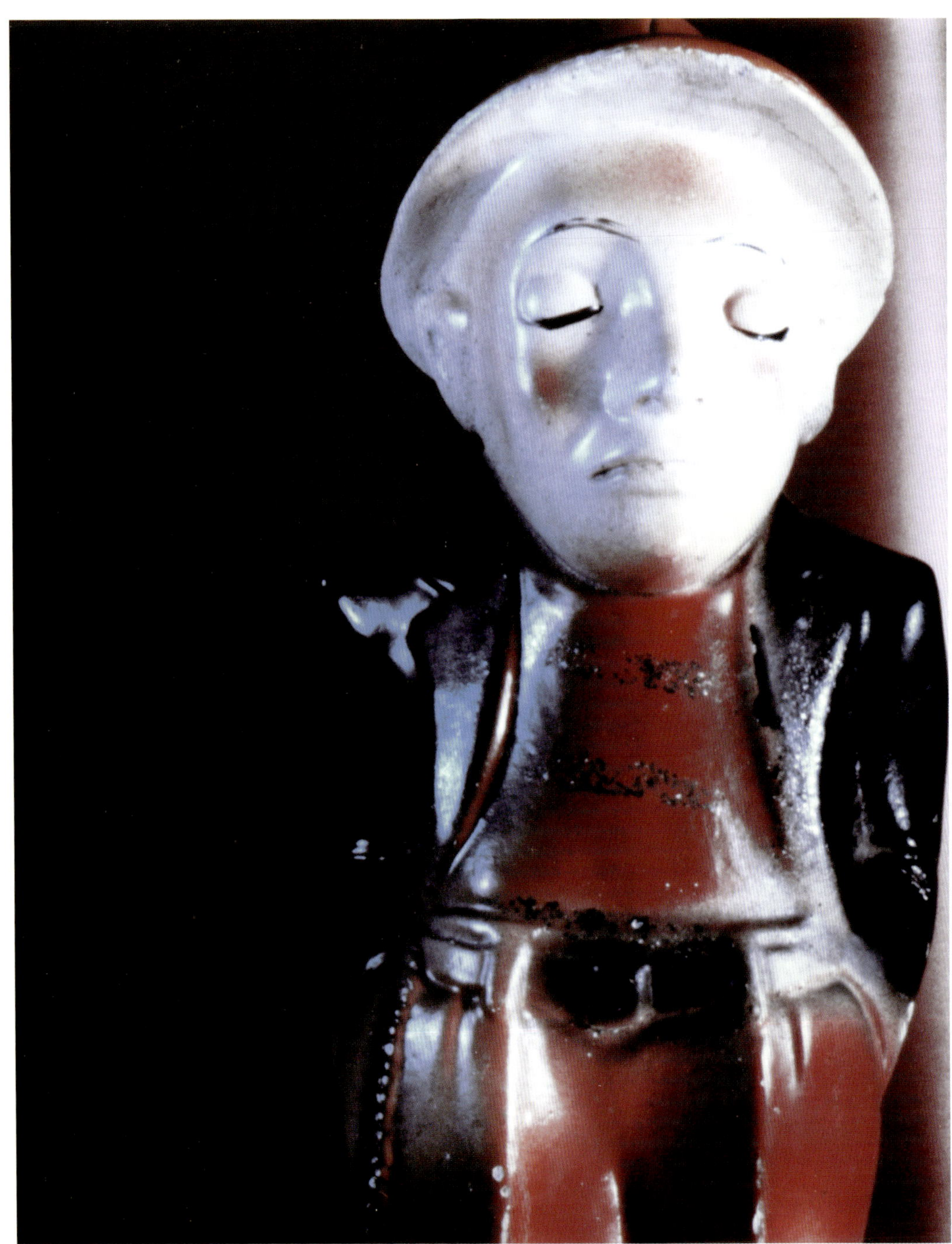
Bing Crosby thirteen-inch carnival chalk prize

himself as the pipe-smoking, calm, perfect-guy stereotype (not just a good guy but one who embraced an entirely different romantic persona than Jolson). Crosby was perceived as being well mannered and pleasantly joyful; Jolson was squawky, begging, crawly, an overly demonstrative blackface minstrel. Crosby also enjoyed the advantage of an important and opportune technological development—the microphone. He crooned softly and easily into the newly invented amplification device, while Jolson had been forced to practically scream at his audiences for them to hear his lyrics.

Crosby could sometimes be labeled as an archetypal symbol for the 1940s, an unassuming, swell, aw-shucks human analogue to Disney's pleasantly romantic and seriously helpful anthropomorphic Mickey Mouse. Interestingly, Crosby also served as a male analogue to Betty Grable. His ingratiating lyrics to "Swinging on a Star," from his film *Going My Way* (1944), sum up the persona:

> Would you like to swing on a star
> Carry moonbeams home in a jar
> And be better off than you are
> Or would you rather be a mule?
>
> A mule is an animal with long funny ears
> Kicks up at anything he hears
> His back is brawny but his brain is weak
> He's just plain stupid with a stubborn streak
> And by the way, if you hate to go to school
> You may grow up to be a mule.
>
> Or would you like to swing on a star
> Carry moonbeams home in a jar
> And be better off than you are
> Or would you rather be a pig?
>
> A pig is an animal with dirt on his face
> His shoes are a terrible disgrace
> He has no manners when he eats his food
> He's fat and lazy and extremely rude
> But if you don't care a feather or a fig
> You may grow up to be a pig.
>
> Or would you like to swing on a star
> Carry moonbeams home in a jar
> And be better off than you are
> Or would you rather be a fish?
>
> A fish won't do anything, but swim in a brook
> He can't write his name or read a book
> To fool the people is his only thought
> And though he's slippery, he still gets caught
> But then if that sort of life is what you wish
> You may grow up to be a fish
> A new kind of jumped-up slippery fish
> And all the monkeys aren't in the zoo
> Every day you meet quite a few
> So you see it's all up to you
> You can be better than you are
> You could be swingin' on a star.

Harry Lillis Crosby was born in 1903 in Tacoma, Washington, the fourth of seven children. He received the nickname "Bing" from a friend who shared his enthusiasm for the comic strip *The Bingville Bugle*. While studying law at the Jesuit-run Gonzaga University, he met Al Rinker, with whom he formed a musical act in Los Angeles. Paul Whiteman discovered them and they joined his orchestra in 1926. Whiteman added Harry Barris, and the new trio was known as the Rhythm Boys. Crosby was suspended from the Whiteman Orchestra in 1931 after not showing up for a solo performance in a Whiteman film—he was in jail for drunk driving. He signed a contract with Brunswick Records the following year, and Brunswick producer Jack Capp cleverly insisted that Crosby should smooth out his jazzy vocals and develop a more nonchalant crooner's delivery. Bing-o . . . the new sound was magic for his career.

Crosby made recordings every year of his fifty-one-year career—some 2,000 titles. He is considered the most successful recording artist of the twentieth century, with more than 300 hits and twenty-two Gold Records. He was also one of Hollywood's most successful movie stars, among the top-ten box-office draws for fifteen years, and he held the number-one spot from 1944 to 1949. He won the Academy Award for Best Actor in 1944 for his portrayal of Father Chuck O'Malley in the film *Going My Way*. As his fame began to languish in the 1950s, he was cast in more dramatic roles.

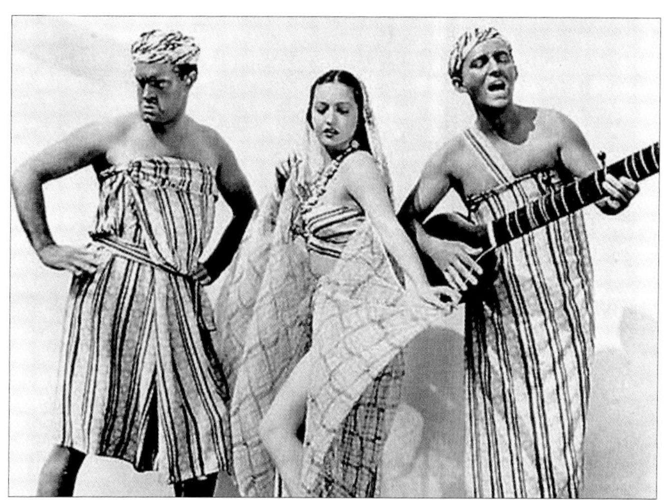

Bob Hope, Dorothy Lamour and Bing Crosby, still, *Road to Singapore,* 1940
© Paramount Pictures

To his own chagrin, Crosby was most remembered for his seven shallow, faux-zany road films with Bob Hope and Dorothy Lamour—beginning with *Road to Singapore* (1940)—which spanned an unbelievable twenty-two years. His seventh, and last, was *Road to Hong Kong,* in 1962. The first of many Bing Crosby television appearances was on December 19, 1948, when he sang "Silent Night" with the Mitchell Boy's Choir (Crosby remains analogous to the Christmas season to this day). He was married twice and was reportedly a harsh disciplinarian to his sons, a trait not quite in keeping with the comfy cardigan sweater and nonchalant pipe-smoking image he projected onstage.

Crosby died of a heart attack on a golf course in 1977, as he finished playing the eighteenth hole. As he was dying, he bowed and uttered his last, witty words: "It was a great game."

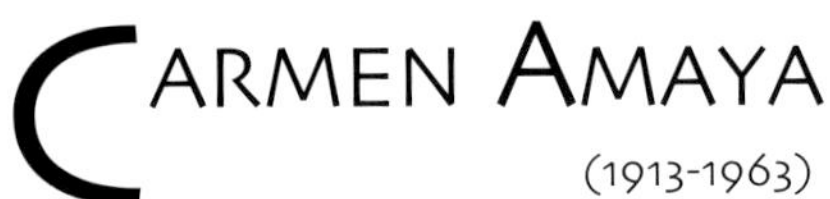

CARMEN AMAYA

(1913-1963)

I have never in my life seen an artist with as much rhythm and fire as you!
—ARTURO TOSCANINI

All human beings are born free and equal in dignity and rights.
—ANONYMOUS, Article 1, *Universal Declaration of Human Rights*, 1948

The Romani, also called Roma, are a distinct ethnic minority originally thought to have migrated from Egypt, but now believed to have left India in the eleventh century to escape oppression. The Roma have been persecuted throughout the centuries and continue to be, especially in the Eastern European countries of the former Soviet bloc. They are commonly known as Gypsies, derived from their earlier label "Gyptians" and the supposed Egypt connection. The word "Gypsy" is often thought of as a pejorative and remains a lingual reminder of their plight through history. The common word "gyp," meaning "to cheat," also comes from Gypsy. The Romani are often associated with a nomadic lifestyle and wily methods of surviving (without the benefit of a homeland), but they are perhaps best known for their music and dance.

Carmen Amaya was the most acclaimed Romani flamenco dancer of all time. Her flair and fiery approach changed the traditional Roma genre forever. Her father accompanied her on guitar for most of her early years, and she upheld the Roma tradition of traveling and performing with her family throughout her life. During the peak of her career, in the 1940s to the 1950s, she was an internationally admired cultural icon and the quintessential representative of the wild, exotic flamenco. Her extraordinary dancing intermingled fierce Spanish pride with a roaming, vagrant Roma's soul, and its integrity and authority were unmistakable.

Amaya left Spain at the outbreak of the Spanish Civil War and expanded her fame to both North and South America. She mesmerized audiences in Argentina, Brazil, Cuba, Mexico, and the United States. She made films in Hollywood, appeared before an audience of 20,000 at the Hollywood Bowl in 1943, appeared on the Broadway stage, danced for Franklin Delano Roosevelt and Winston Churchill, and toured the world—often accompanied by Sabicas, one of the greatest flamenco guitar virtuosos of all time. Amaya remained true to her Roma heritage and was its formidable ambassador. The authority of her dances and the power of the culture that spawned her dazzled audiences. During the World War II years of 1940 to 1945, she lived in New York and Hollywood. Amaya embodied the archetypal symbol motif for an exotic woman of power.

Amaya pushed the boundaries of flamenco by teaching herself the fast and furious footwork traditionally reserved for male dancers. She often performed in men's clothing to skillfully combine the elegance and grace of the feminine with the ferocity and high-impact footwork of the male. Her dance became the fieriest in all flamenco and effectively altered the future of the dance. She had a prodigious sense of rhythm, an absolutely unrelenting tempo, and it has been said her beat was like a hammer hitting steel. No other dancer has ever performed her most famous whirlwind turn, the "broken-turn backward."

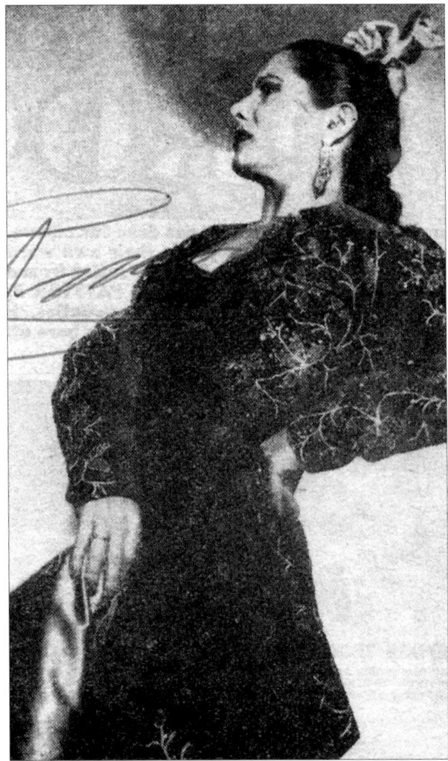

Carmen Amaya, autographed newspaper clipping, circa 1940s

Carmen Amaya was born in Barcelona in 1913. Accompanied by her father on the guitar, she danced flamenco from the age of four, appeared in Paris at the age of eight, and began performing regularly with the Raquel Meller Company in Paris at the age of ten. Amaya and guitarist Sabicas were lovers throughout the early 1940s. In 1947, she returned to Spain. In 1952, she married Juan Antonio Agüero, a guitarist from her company. She was awarded Spain's highest honor, the Grand Cross of Isabella, just before her untimely death from kidney failure in 1963, at the age of fifty.

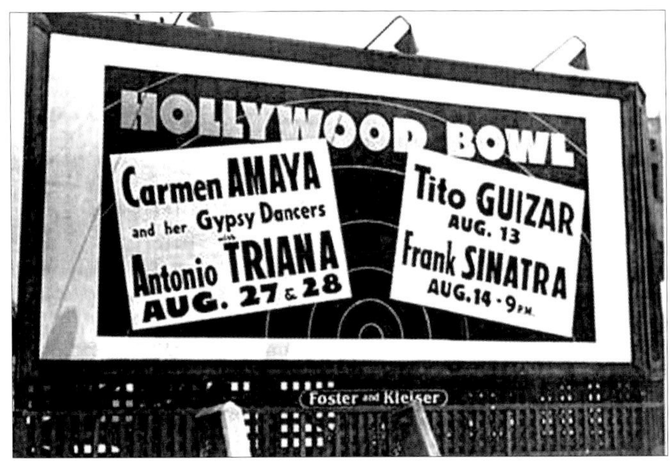

Carmen Amaya and her Gypsy Dancers, Hollywood Bowl, billboard ad, 1943

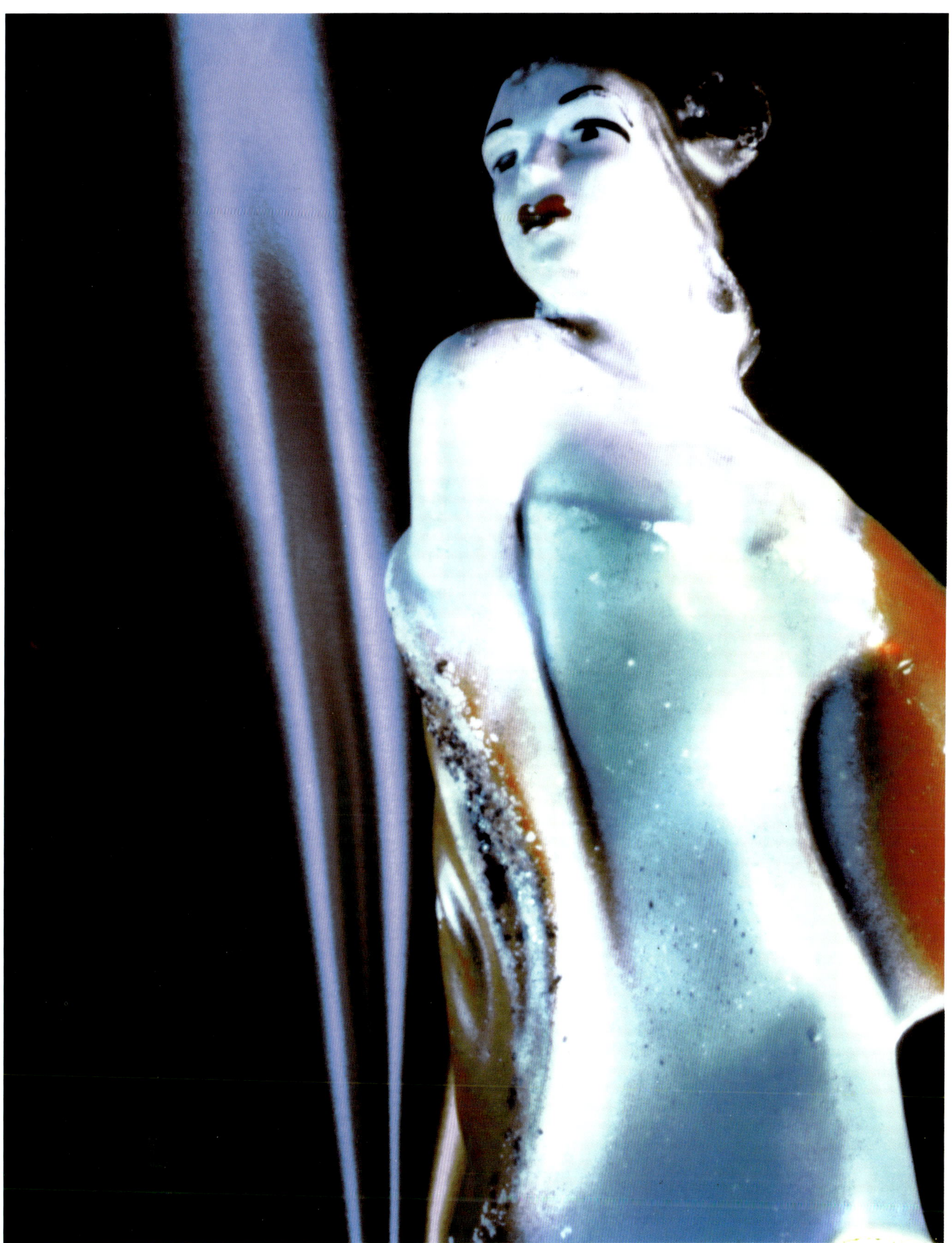

Carman Amaya fourteen-inch carnival chalk prize, 1940s, possibly from her film *Panama Hattie* (1942), or *Knickerbocker Holiday* (1944). It caricatured the strength reflected in her uplifted chin and the fascinating whirl of her dance. Amaya was the first performer to popularize the art of flamenco to American film audiences.

Esther Williams

(1922–

Well, baby, I told you I was gonna kiss me a mermaid today.
—Clark Gable to Carole Lombard, at Esther Williams' M-G-M screen test, 1941

This morning, one of our companie looking over board saw a mermaid, and calling up some of the companie to see her, one more came up, and by that time shee was close to the ship's side, looking earnestly upon the men: a little after, a Sea came and overturned her: From the Navill upward, her backe and breasts were like a woman's.., her body as big as one of us; her skin very white; and long haire hanging down behinde, of colour blacke; in her going down they saw her tayle, which was like the tayle of a Porposse, and speckled like a Macrell.
—Henry Hudson, polar navigator, 1608

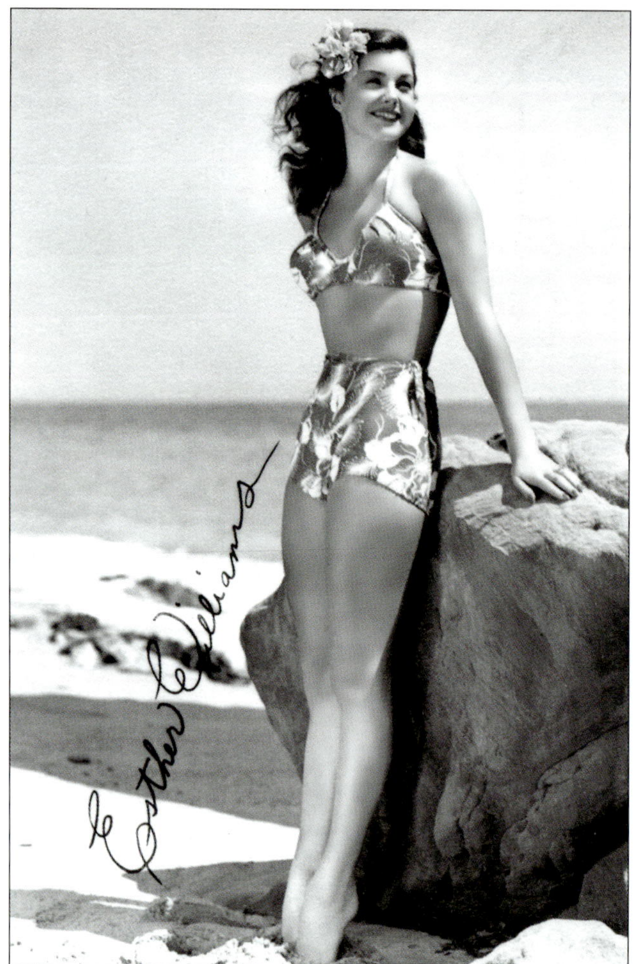

Esther Williams, fan club card, circa 1940s

Esther Williams was born in Los Angeles and spent her childhood swimming at local pools. Her older brother, Stanton, a child film star, died suddenly from a kinked intestine when he was only sixteen. She was eight. When Williams was thirteen, her obsessed foster brother, Buddy, raped her repeatedly. She explained the trauma in her autobiography:

> I didn't realize I could prove what happened with physical evidence. But even if I could, something more powerful sealed my lips: embarrassment, shame, guilt. Rape is such a horrible word, and the stigma hangs over a victim until she dies. "She acted provocatively. She asked for it." In the 1930s these were the prevailing sentiments. And I heard my mother's words echo in my head, words that she had said to all of us when something out of control happened: "What part of the problem are you?"[1]

Williams had earned three national swimming championships in both the breaststroke and freestyle by the time she was sixteen. At eighteen, she was on the 1940 Olympic team headed for Tokyo. World War II intervened, canceling the games and dashing her hopes. All was not completely lost, however, and that year she starred opposite Olympic swimmer and famous screen star Johnny Weismuller (known to the world as Tarzan) in *San Francisco Aquacade*—a Broadway musical in the wet. Williams was featured as Aqua-Belle #1, performing duets with Aqua-Adonis #1.

Her Hollywood film debut was opposite Mickey Rooney in *Andy Hardy's Double Life* (1942) when she was twenty. After the success of that film, she performed in *Bathing Beauty* (1944), Hollywood's first aquatic movie and the one that would begin a swimming rage. The combination of Williams's acting skills and swimming abilities laid the groundwork for a new film genre, one that was perfectly suited to bathing suits and, in particular, to the muscular and beautiful swimming star. She found ready, eager fans in the easily infatuated, intellectually uninterested, escapist, macho, and feel-good beach-boy audience. They loved seeing a smiling, busty woman in a bathing suit. She became an overdone sensation of that era, very similar to the sexy, short-shorts-clad ice-skater Sonja Henie.

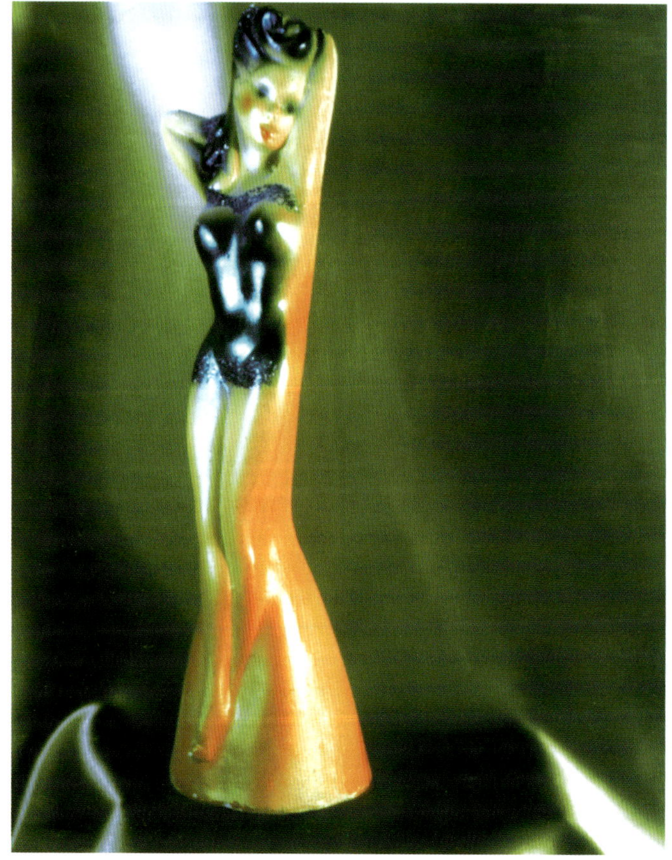

Esther Williams twelve-and-a-half-inch carnival chalk prize

Williams's racy autobiographical exposé, *The Million Dollar Mermaid*, was published in 2000. She was completely aware of her stereotype—the swimming goddess, a living, breathing, sexy, smiling mermaid. In it, she provides many details of a deeper life that were never known publicly. In 1959, she had taken LSD under the guidance of her therapist Dr. Mortimer Hartman to help her understand her feelings about the loss of her brother. She explained one of her most positive insights:

> After dinner, I gently ushered my parents into the guest house for the night. Then I rushed back to my bedroom and locked the door. I needed to be alone. I went into the bathroom and looked at my face in the mirror. I couldn't see myself clearly. I scrubbed away all of my makeup. I splashed water on my hair and slicked it back because I couldn't stand to have anything soft around my face. I stripped off my clothes. When I looked in the mirror again, I was startled by a split image: One half of my face, the right half, was me; the other half was the face of a sixteen-year-old boy. The left side of my upper body was flat and muscular, like the chest of a boy. I reached up with my boy's large, clumsy hand to touch my right breast and felt my penis stirring. It was a hermaphroditic phantasm that held me entranced as I discovered my divided body. I don't know how long I stood there touching and exploring, but I was not afraid. Finally, I understood perfectly: when Stanton had died, I had taken him into my life so completely that he became a part of me.

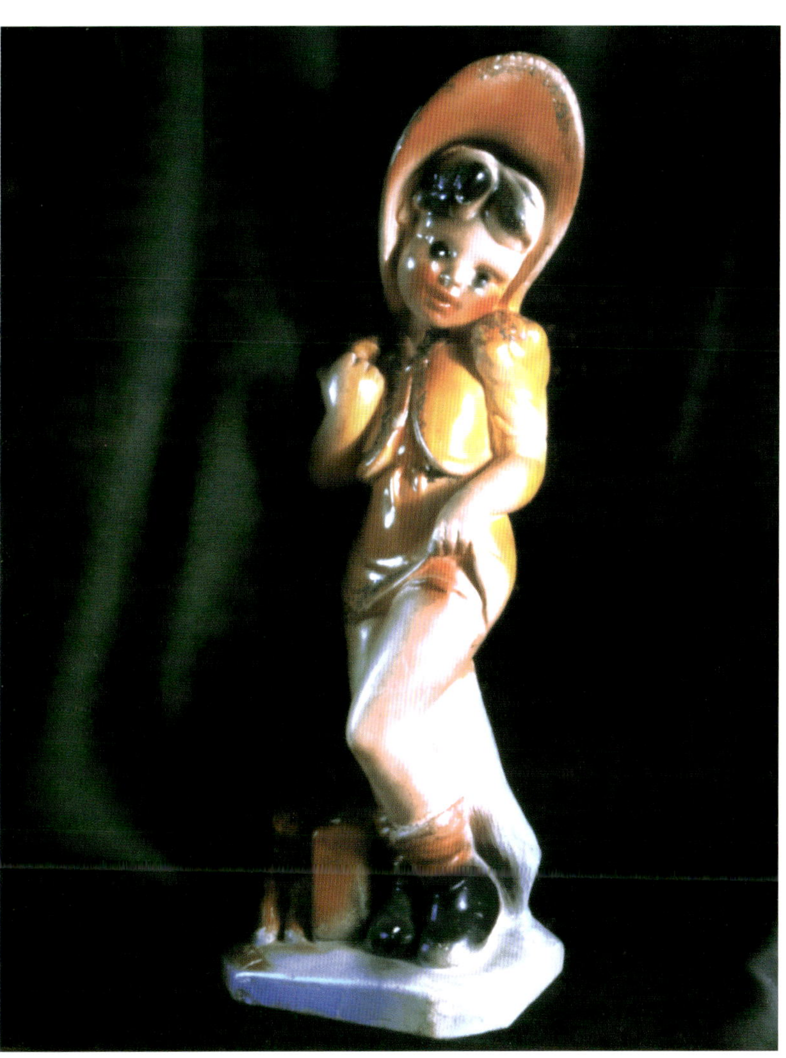

Devil Mermaid with Ears, etching, circa 1790s

A seminude mermaid offered a symbolic archetype for the unknown woman. She would evoke lust but also fear. What creatures, other than monsters, lay under the watery depths? Were they of benefit to sailors, or of evil intent?

The existence of mermaids has been written about since Pliny the Elder in the first century AD. Even Columbus reported he saw three mermaids on January 4, 1493.[3] Pictures of lusty mermaids were included in most medieval travel accounts, inspiring the lonely at sea to look forward to that joyous and fearful sight. Numerous accounts of mermaid sightings claimed to be true.

Many religious scribes attempted to impart mermaids with evil intent—slurring anything that even half-resembled a woman as being a succubus (an evil spirit that descends upon men to have sex with them). One of these works, *De Propietatibus Rerum* by Bartholomew Angelicus, made the mermaid a lethal seductress disguised as a swimming goddess. Angelicus stated that mermaids charmed seamen through sweet music. "But the truth is that they are strong whores" who lead men "to poverty and to mischief." Typically, a mermaid lulled a crew to sleep, kidnapped a sailor, and took him to "a dry place" for sex. If he refused, "she slayeth him and eateth his flesh."[4] Scribes built upon the she-monster archetype, and violent actions against a mermaid's seductions were the only remedy.

Once every three minutes a female is raped in the United States. Carnival chalk prizes like the young girl with her suitcase and friendly dog, thumb out and skirt lifted, fantasize the hitchhiker as someone who is there for the taking. Prizes like this were overtly suggestive of the Lolita archetype/stereotype eliciting violence against women—and are only too real in light of rape statistics. In Esther Williams's words, many people still think "She asked for it."

Hitchhiker twelve-and-one-half-inch carnival chalk prize

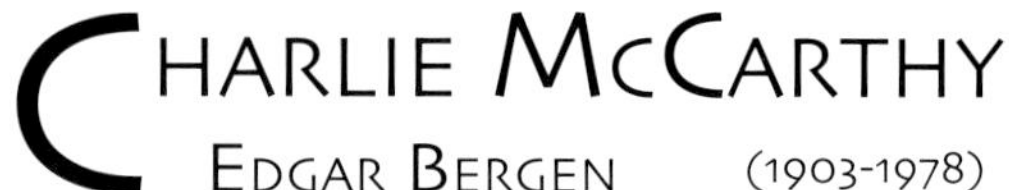

CHARLIE McCARTHY

EDGAR BERGEN   (1903-1978)

Facts are ventriloquists' dummies. Sitting on a wise man's knee they may be made to utter words of wisdom; elsewhere they say nothing or say nonsense.
—ALDOUS HUXLEY, *Time Must Have A Stop*

We often use an imitative slight of voice when quoting people whose regional or ethnic characters are markedly different than our own. Descriptive illusion is an integral part of our communication skills and nowhere do we find it more refined than in the ventriloquist's art. The engastrimyth (ventriloquist) and his (not so dumb) dummy play off each other with the ventriloquist cast as the straight man in an odd sort of double entendre. The obvious reality is that while both characters are the same person, if the ventriloquist is skilled and his script well crafted, the audience assimilates the notion that there are indeed two different personalities onstage.

Edgar John Berggren was born in Chicago and later altered his name slightly to Edgar Bergen. His Swedish parents returned to Sweden when he was four, where young Edgar learned Swedish, a language Charlie McCarthy would later speak from time to time. The family came back to Chicago when he was eleven and he began teaching himself magic and the art of ventriloquism. When he was fifteen, Bergen saw a performance by the famous ventriloquist Harry Lester, known as "The Great Lester." After the performance, Lester listened to Bergen's youthful attempts at ventriloquism, was impressed, and, recognizing his potential, generously gave Bergen free daily lessons in "belly talk" (as it's called) for three months. A year later, Bergen invented the famous alter ego, who would be his dummy partner for life. Local bartender/carpenter Theodore Mack modeled the animated face after Charlie, a quick-witted Irish newsboy from the neighborhood. He carved the face from a piece of pine for $35 and made the backbone from a nine-inch broomstick. Bergen named his forty-pound dummy after both the newsboy and the carpenter—Charlie McCarthy.

Bergen began studies in premed at Northwestern University and paid for his education with the income from gigs with Charlie. But the lure of vaudeville was too great and Bergen never completed his degree. Instead, he took up the life of a traveling performer, touring across America, playing wherever he could, and then going to Europe and South America. By the 1930s, during vaudeville's dying moments, Bergen played the Palace Theater in New York; he was the first ventriloquist ever to occupy that stage. One of his best routines was drawn from an experience during his premed studies. He called it "The Operation." Charlie was the patient; Bergen the surgeon. As a counterpoint to society's ragged look, created by the Depression, Charlie was the Dapper Dan stereotype—outfitted with a monocle, top hat, and tails, as was Edgar, minus the monocle.

Throughout their fifty-eight-year career, Bergen played the part of the corrective, stern, moralistic father, while Charlie was his nonchalant, mischievous scamp. Because of Prohibition, skits about drinking always produced the most laughter. Their routine went:

Bergen: Don't you know, young man, that alcohol is slow poison?
Charlie: Is what?
Bergen: It's slow poison.
Charlie: Is that so?
Bergen: Yes.
Charlie: Slow poison, eh?
Bergen: Yes.
Charlie: Well, I'm in no hurry.[1]

As a media stereotype, Edgar Bergen and Charlie McCarthy represented a unique dualistic projection—a two-for-one psychological persona. All options were left open; that was the point of their double being. They could be bawdy, sexist, outrageous, macho, patriotic, insulting, or moralistic. In many ways they created a moral plurality (good and not so good) that easily transferred to stereotypes of people (good and not so good). Radio listeners found the act humorous because they could easily identify with either character. The audience usually sided with Charlie and loved his wry innuendoes, a ploy that was cleverly calculated by Bergen, who realized early on that he could make outrageous statements through Charlie, which he could not have gotten away with if they came from him. Charlie was the comedian's perfectly disguised foil, because Charlie the dummy wasn't thought of as fully human, even though he was the conduit for human sentiments. Charlie could say all sorts of things that, had he been human, would have been censored. He was the disguised ruse for sidestepping the Will Hays Production Code. People loved Charlie because he was their projected outrageous, liberated, childlike self in an era of puritanical Draconian turmoil.

Bergen was an unstoppable, elusive comedian and through his genius was able to project his humor, and Charlie's, over the airwaves. The duo's first radio performance was in 1936 as guests on Rudy Vallee's *The Royal Gelatin Hour*, an appearance for which they were paid $150. By 1937, they had their own show, which ran until 1955 with a variety of sponsors. In their early radio years, Bergen wisely selected famous Hollywood personalities to join them on the show, W. C. Fields, Joan Blondell, Dorothy Lamour, Don Ameche, and Mae West.

On December 12, 1937, Mae West delivered her prewritten dialogue to their "Adam and Eve" skit from a script that had already passed the NBC censors. Her dialogue did not, however, get past the censorship of America's religious goodie-goodies, who were regular listeners of the program. When the serpent in the Garden of Eden got itself stuck while trying to slither through the fence that surrounded the tree, West seductively cheered him on: "Oh, shake your hips! Yeah. You're doin' all right. Get me a big one, I feel like I'm doin' a big apple. Nice goin', swivel-hips. Like women are gonna feed men for the rest of time—applesauce!"[2] (Whatever that meant!)

Apparently listeners thought these lines radiated

enough raunchy, sacrilegious overtones to damn the show. It caught the producers by surprise. Thousands of letters poured in, and Christian moralists had their long-awaited heyday. Who had they been waiting for? Not Edgar Bergen and Charlie McCarthy, but the one and only sexy renegade Mae West, of course. The Reverend Dr. Maurice S. Sheehy of Catholic University labeled the show "the most indecent, scurrilous, and religiously irreverent program that it has ever been my misfortune to hear."

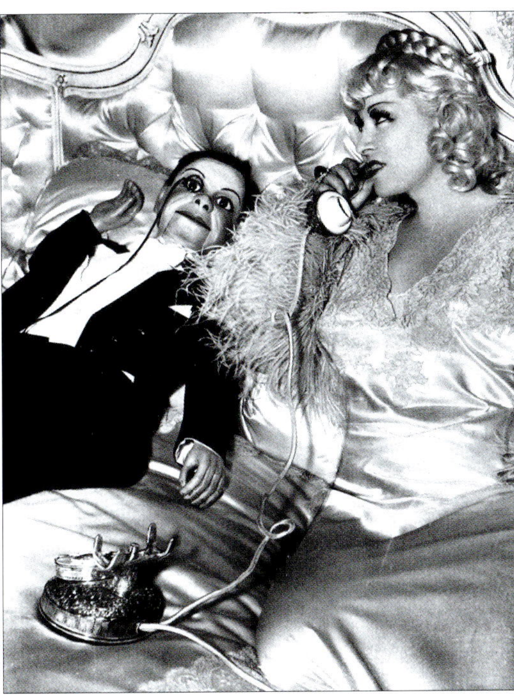
Charlie McCarthy and Mae West, 1930s

The religious goodie-goodies hadn't minded the sexual innuendoes uttered earlier in the show in lines like these:

Mae: So good-time Charlie's gonna play hard to get. Well yuh can't kid me. You're afraid of women. Your Casanova stuff is just a front, a false front.
Charlie: Not so loud, Mae, not so loud! All my girlfriends are listening.
Mae: Oh, yeah! You're all wood and a yard long.
Charlie: Yeah.
Mae: Yuh weren't so nervous and backward when yuh came up to see me at my apartment. In fact, yuh didn't need any encouragement to kiss me.
Charlie: Did I do that?
Mae: Why, yuh certainly did. I got marks to prove it. An' splinters, too.[3]

The FCC was called in, and things got so out of hand that chairman Frank McNinch implicitly reminded NBC chairman Lenox Lohr that the "Federal Communications Act of 1934 provides that no person shall utter any obscene, inde-cent, or profane language by means of radio communication. The Commission is charged by law with the enforcement of that provision."[4] Rival broadcasting companies got into the act and also condemned NBC. The *Chicago Tribune* said the show was "vomitus." The sponsor, Chase and Sanborn,

apologized over the air the following week. In January 1938, in a self-regulatory act, NBC stated that any use or utterance of Mae West's name was prohibited on the radio.

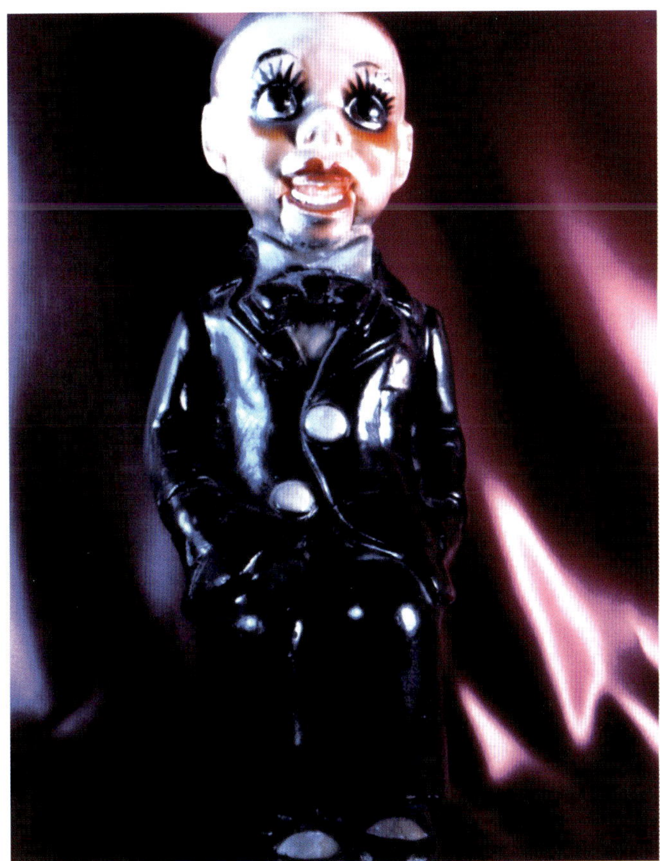
Charlie McCarthy fourteen-inch hatless carnival chalk prize

The prohibition remained in effect for fifteen years, and West was permanently banned from the radio. Of course, Bergen and Charlie got a little slap on their sullied hands.

The Mae West–fundamentalist skirmish confirmed to many liberals that the government had more control over radio censorship than it did over Hollywood. Many felt that the government had gone too far and was seriously censoring freedom of expression on the radio. They suggested that Chase and Sanborn had exploited West; had been insulted by the advertising agency J. Walter Thompson, who had a lot of input in creating the script; and had been subsequently made into a scapegoat by the government and NBC. More than anything, West had fallen victim to her liberated woman Antichrist archetype. In her autobiography, she proclaimed that she had been set up.

Bergen and Charlie also starred in twenty-five Holly-wood films, and the movies helped radio audiences visualize the characters who had made them laugh. Charlie promoted enlistment in the armed services during World War II. Bergen married in 1946. He was making TV guest appearances in the 1950s, but by then his age was showing, while Charlie's, of course, remained the same. Bergen announced his retirement in 1978, stating he would only do a few more shows and then donate Charlie to the Smithsonian. One of them died a week later in his sleep.

T HE S HMOO

(1948-1955)

Twelve voices were shouting in anger and they were all alike. No question, now, what had happened to the faces of the pigs. The creatures outside looked from pig to man, and from man to pig, and from pig to man again; but already it was impossible to say which was which.

—G EORGE O RWELL, the final paragraph, *Animal Farm*, 1946

The year 1948 brought the shmoo craze. Al Capp's rare invention was a bright new member in the cartoon-animal kingdom. The shmoo was not given a human face, nor did it speak like so many other anthropomorphic cartoon characters (Bugs Bunny, Mickey Mouse, etc.). Throughout his career, Capp invented words that sounded and were spelled almost like other words: yocum for yokel (a gullible rustic), schmooze for snooze (what an idle person does), or shmoo for moo (what a cow does).

The shmoo—joyful millions of them were on Capp's every page as a peacetime symbol of the postwar era—symbolized economic peace and prosperity, an archetype for feeling hopeful, making lots of sense (but not politically): no need to worry any longer between capitalism or communism because the shmoo provided for everyone. Upon request, a shmoo happily keeled over and died to provide food. The shmoo was Capp's contribution to America's baby-boomer crisis, Red baiting, the cold war, nuclear weapons, and the threat of worldwide famine. Yet there was more to shmoos than food: they supplied entertainment, helped with chores—whatever humans needed any shmoo gladly offered. Humanity could just sit back and schmooze watching their new media—TV, (or was the shmoo a TV?)

Capp made it apparent that the shmoo mated and supplied offspring quicker than the proverbial rabbit. In *The Life and Times of the Shmoo*, one happy pair of shmoos could make a million cute little ones in no time flat, and on the next page, those little ones made trillions more. Nor did they overgraze the land. Here Capp played the shmoo as an analogue for the nineteenth-century American buffalo, long since departed, which had provided amply for Native Americans (buffalo didn't overgraze either). Capp found only one problem with the shmoo—they altered price structure. So greedy businessmen—those who charged exorbitant prices for their goods—were made obsolete, and their lingering greed turned to gang warfare. Evil businessmen attempted to gun down all the shmoos they could find. Witnessing shmoo genocide made everyone in Dogpatch feel disheartened. Li'l Abner saved a pair. Daisy Mae educated him to the fact that they needed to be male and female.

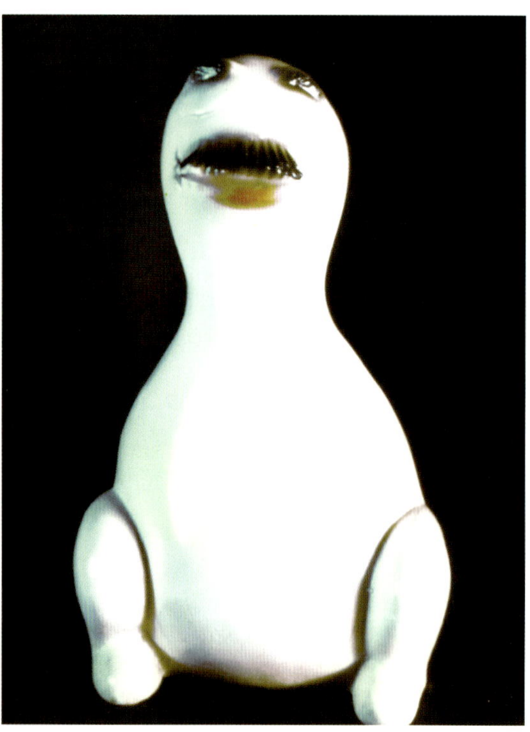

Shmoo six-and-one-half-inch carnival chalk prize

Animals were the lifeblood of the ancient order of Roman soothsayers, known as the haruspex, whose job it was to make prophesies from careful examination of the entrails of sacrificed animals. This specialized practice of showmanship, inherited from ancient Etruscans, was like present-day horoscope readings, using instinctive feelings and well-crafted intuitions for divining the future. In many ancient cultures, shamans were granted great power, well beyond that ascribed to most members of their community. Their abilities were in healing and in prophesying through use of ceremony, prescribing medicinal curing agents, and specialized sacrifice of animals. Their feelings were tinged with emotions that came directly from within their own being as a pathway, as well as through an all-enveloping Earth as the guiding force.

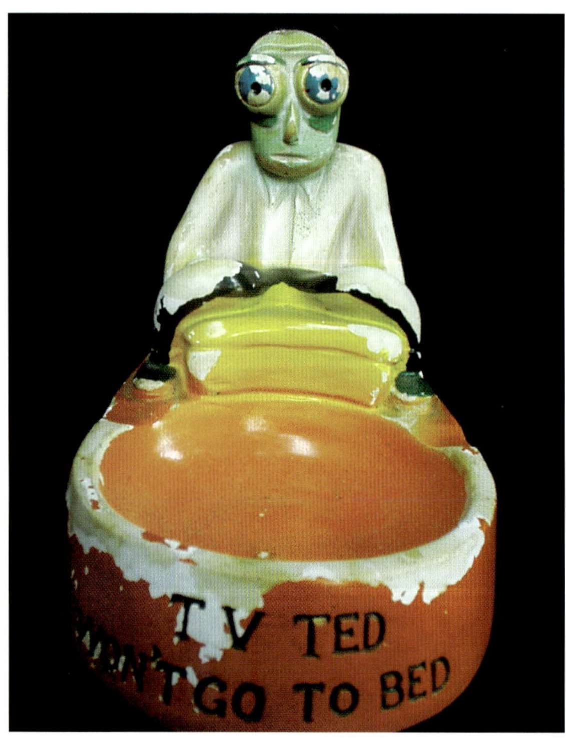

"TV Ted Won't Go To Bed" five-inch carnival chalk ashtray prize

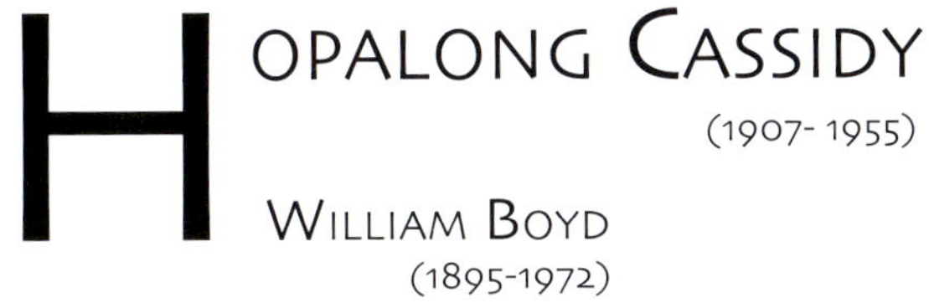

HOPALONG CASSIDY
(1907- 1955)
WILLIAM BOYD
(1895-1972)

Pies like mother used to make . . . An' pills like popper used to take.
—HOPALONG CASSIDY, *Bar-20*, 1907

Clarence E. Mulford, a Brooklyn City Hall clerk, created the cowboy idol Hopalong Cassidy as the principal character in twenty-eight of his popular novels that were published between 1907 and 1941. The character bore little resemblance to the Hopalong Cassidy made famous onscreen.

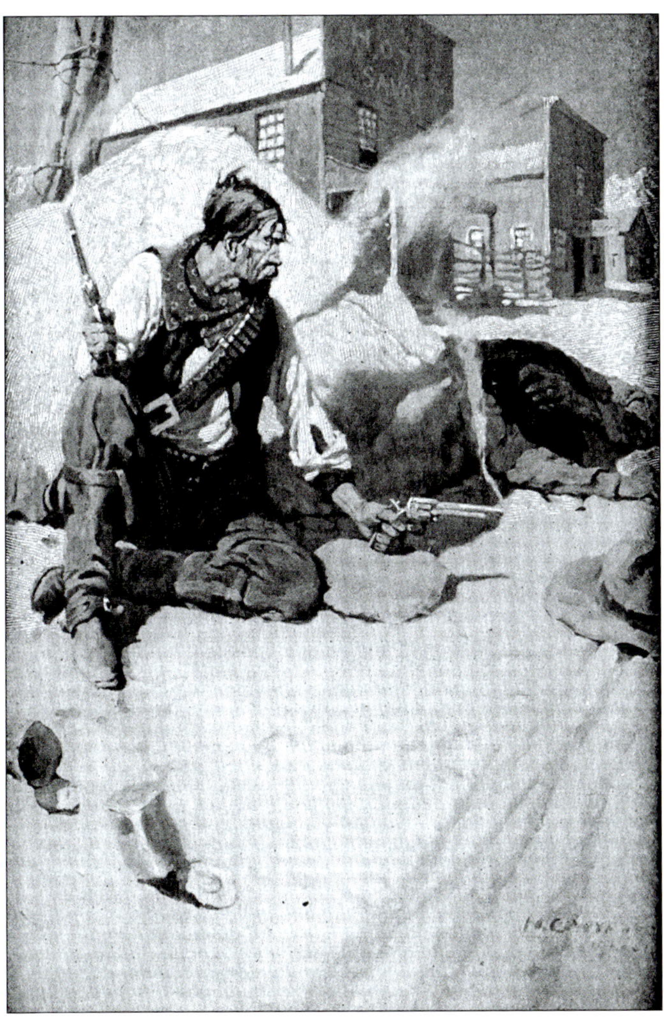

"Setting up cross-legged, with each hand holding a gun," Hopalong Cassidy, illustration N. C. Wyeth and F. E. Schoonover, *Bar-20* © A. L. Burt Company, 1907

In Mulford's first Cassidy book, *Bar-20*, Hopalong debuts on page 10, struggling with a mouthful of beef. His first word is "Gu," short for "Good." He was attempting to talk with his mouth full, unable to get the entire word out. Mulford's first depiction of Hopalong cleverly set up the characterization for the rough-and-tumble, patently ungenteel cowboy protagonist who would dominate his novels. We next see Hopalong fourteen pages later, glibly shooting his initial, "H," into a door with a pistol, mischievously trying to kill an unknown enemy who is standing behind it. The Mulford story reads:

> Hopalong bit off a chew of tobacco and drowned a green fly that was crawling up the side of the barn. The yellow liquid streaked downward a short distance and was eagerly sucked up by the warped boards.
>
> A spurt of smoke leaped from the battered door and the bored Hopalong promptly tumbled back inside. He felt of his arm, and then, delighted at the notice taken of his artistic efforts, shot several times from a crack on his right. "This yer's shore gittin' like home," he gravely remarked to the splinter that whizzed past his head. He shot again at the door and it sagged outward, accompanied by the thud of a falling body. "Pies like mother used to make," he announced to the empty loft as he slipped the magazine full of .45s. "An' pills like popper used to take," he continued when he lowered the level of the liquor in his flask.
>
> He rolled a cigarette and tossed the match into the air, extinguishing it by a shot from his Colt.[1]

Mulford's 1907 Hopalong Cassidy persona was a long shot from the 1935 Hopalong Cassidy persona created by producer Harry Sherman and actor William Boyd in their first super-cleaned-up Hollywood film. Mulford's book cowboy was authentic and typified the Western tough. He was the limpin', drinkin', smokin', shootin', and showin'-off kind of cowboy slob named Hopalong Cassidy. Sherman and Boyd turned Mulford's Bubba Hopalong into a silver-haired, absolutely decent, law-and-order cowboy. Their Hoppy (a gentler, kinder nickname) never smoked, drank, kissed a lady, swore, or even used bad grammar onscreen. Furthermore, he was the best and ultimate judge of honesty and justice. He could access any situation and always managed to ferret out corruption and the bad guys behind it. He tried to catch his villains without the use of gunplay—if a shoot-out became unavoidable, the bad guys always pulled their triggers first, and, of course, missed. Hoppy didn't miss, but as a somewhat nonviolent hero, he never tried to kill his enemies; instead, he wounded them, after which they were carted off to jail limping or holding a gun arm with a bullet hole in it. He dressed in black, an unconventional color choice at that time, considering its dark racial overtones. His contrasting white horse was named Topper. Sherman produced fifty-four of the popular grade-B Westerns.

Hoppy trailed in popularity behind Hollywood's crooner cowboys Gene Autry and Roy Rogers. All three of them lagged well behind The Lone Ranger. Boyd wisely bought the rights to Hoppy from Mulford and produced another twelve films himself. Mulford despised the way Hollywood had changed his original, authentic Bubba Hopalong, but he knew he would never realize as much money from the novels as he would from Boyd. The sale of the rights to Hopalong made Mulford rich and Boyd almost poor, but it paid off for Boyd in the long run.

There were sixty-six Hoppy films made by 1948. Never in Hollywood's history has one man played the same character in so many features. Audiences came to view Boyd and Hopalong Cassidy as synonymous. For most, only Hopalong existed. People never thought of Boyd, the actor, when he made public appearances; he had been completely taken over by the persona of Hopalong Cassidy. Boyd starred in forty half-hour episodes of *Hopalong Cassidy* on television from 1952 to 1954, and licensed fifty-two of his films to NBC to be broadcast as one-hour programs. TV made Hoppy an international cowboy star; he received 15,000 fan letters a week. Hoppy had a personal responsibility creed:

Hopalong Cassidy's Creed for American Boys and Girls
1. The highest badge of honor a person can wear is honesty. Be truthful at all times.
2. Your parents are the best friends you have. Listen to them and obey their instructions.
3. If you want to be respected, you must respect others. Show good manners in every way.
4. Only through hard work and study can you succeed. Don't be lazy.
5. Your good deeds always come to light. So don't boast or be a show off.
6. If you waste time or money today, you will regret it tomorrow. Practice thrift in all ways.
7. Many animals are good and loyal companions. Be friendly and kind to them.
8. A strong, healthy body is a precious gift. Be neat and clean.
9. Our country's laws are made for your protection. Observe them carefully.
10. Children in many foreign lands are less fortunate than you. Be glad and proud you are an American.[2]

Sounds like Disney's Blue Fairy in *Pinocchio*. The silver screen (and other mediums) can impart and reinforce ideals and lessons about morality through the use of good verses evil—a disguise that often fits over the framework of religion. Whether executed knowingly (as in Boyd's pros- elytizing moralities) or accidentally, moviemakers frequently take advantage of their temporarily engrossed audiences by instilling idyllic, dogmatic notions that are far removed from the realities of day-to-day life. The magic of cinema is close to the magic of religious ceremony; both offer hope and refuge to those who embrace their tenets—tenets founded in ideals rather than realities. The era through which Hoppy galloped is the time of Mom's apple pie, the girl next door, Dad who brought home the bacon, the brother who went gallantly off to war, and the righteous cowboy who always got his man. Social issues were ghosts in the swamp and Hollywood did its best to keep them there. This was the disguise and the ruse of Hoppy. It was this shunning of the truth that Mulford objected to. Times change, the pendulum swings, and now Hollywood tends to exaggerate injustices in a sensational and bloody manner. Where filmmakers once dished out pabulum, they now sell fear.

When Boyd reached the age of sixty, he realized his star was too old to continue, so he retired Hoppy and Topper, and turned his television crew over to a new TV series called *Gunsmoke*.

Boyd played on the idea that a cowboy could rep- resent America's symbol, the archetypal perfect hero, as role model and good guy to the young children who were his principal fans. They would participate in the joys and thrills of the cowboy life. His own clean living exemplified that he was the ideal model for this part. His keen ability to recognize the criminal and the corrupt made him a protector of the innocent and moral judge of right and wrong (a superior vigilante). Hoppy ruled his world in every way, but without a badge. He did not stereotype the sheriff, even though his actions were often imitative of policemen. He upheld the law of moral right and wrong in the stereotypical lawless old West. Sexuality and gender equality were never issues. Hoppy, along with his idealist views, ruled in an unreal film, radio, comic-book, and TV old West.

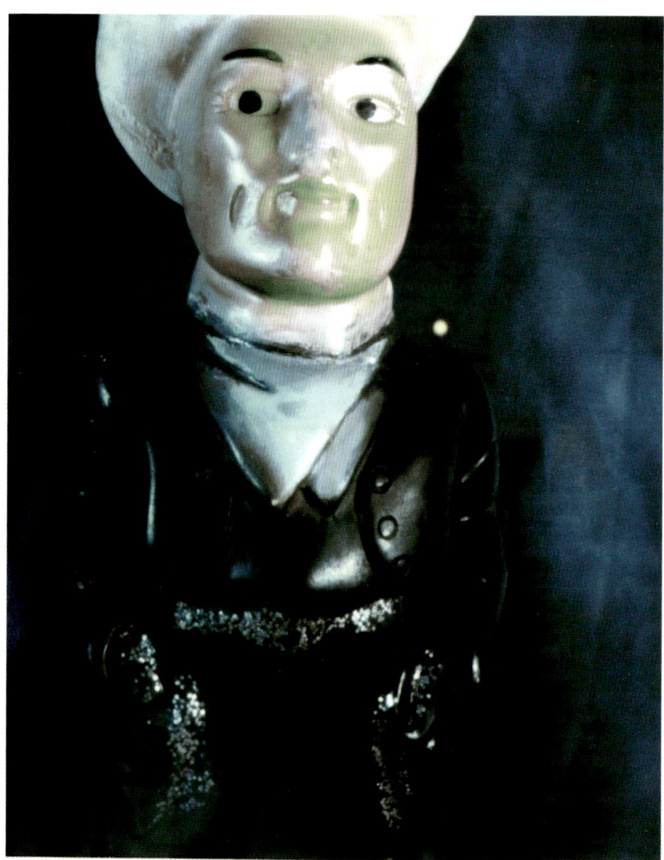

Hopalong Cassidy fifteen-inch carnival chalk prize. The figure dates from the early 1950s when Hopalong's popularity increased on television. To make the Hoppy figure, the carnival chalk manufacturers used the Lone Ranger carnival chalk mold and removed the mask. The Lone Ranger carnival chalk figure was much more popular.

William Lawrence Boyd was born in Oklahoma in 1885, the son of a day laborer. Both of his parents died when he was in his early teens. At eighteen, he took odd jobs, worked his way west to Los Angeles, and landed a bit part in Cecil B. DeMille's silent film *Why Change Your Wife?* (1920). He co-starred as the handsome hero in many silent films in the mid-1920s. By 1930, his film career seemed to dim. *Hopalong Cassidy Enters* (1935) changed his life. Up until then, Boyd was known in private as a wild character: a drinker and carouser who loved the ladies. He had married four times. When he became famous as Hopalong Cassidy, he changed completely. He seemed to imitate Hoppy's good- guy characteristics—he didn't drink, smoke, or carouse. His son died of pneumonia in the early 1920s, perhaps prompting Boyd's benevolent custom of giving money to children's chari- ties. Shortly after he became good-guy Hoppy, he married his fifth wife, actress Grace Bradley. The marriage lasted thirty-five years. He has the rare distinction of having starred in silent films in the 1920s, sound films in the 1930s and 1940s, and on television in the 1950s. *Hopalong Cassidy* was a radio program from 1948 to 1952. Hopalong Cassidy comics arrived in 1943 and were published by a variety of companies, ending in 1958. When Boyd died in 1972 many obituaries listed him simply as "Hopalong Cassidy."

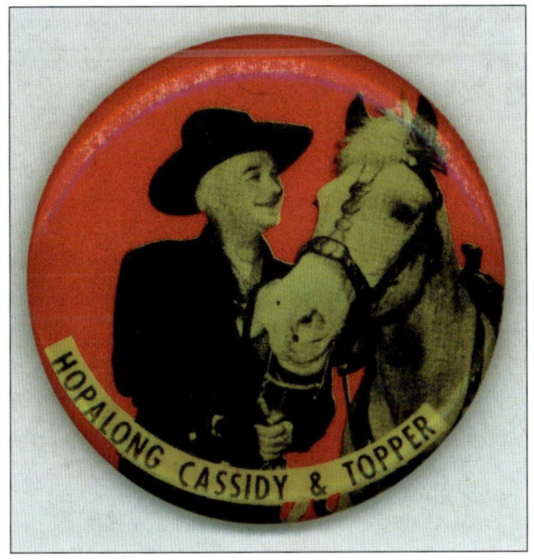

Hopalong Cassidy and Topper pinback, circa 1950s.
Collection: Donna Samuels

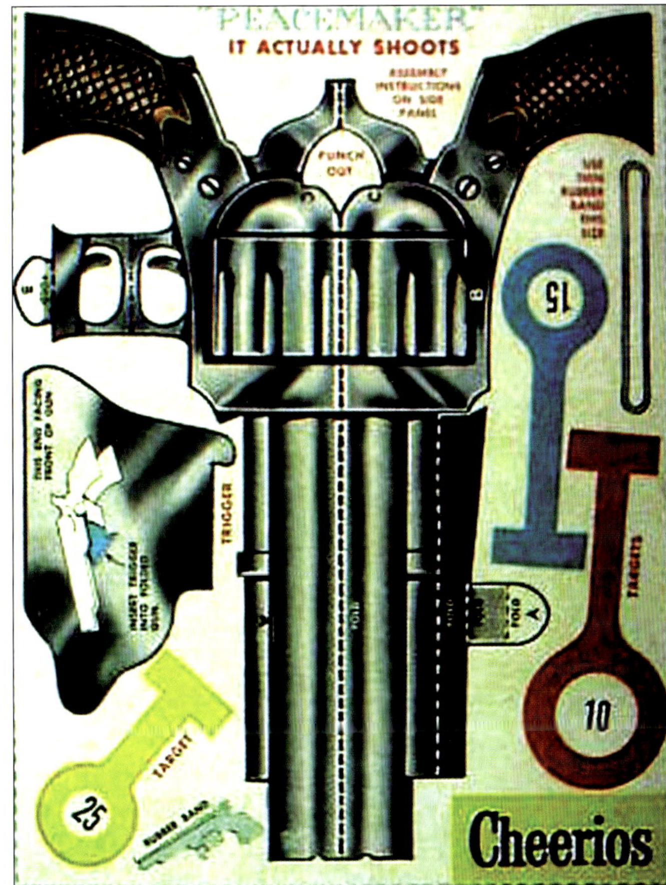

Colt Peacemaker cutout fold-up, Cheerios box back, 1950s

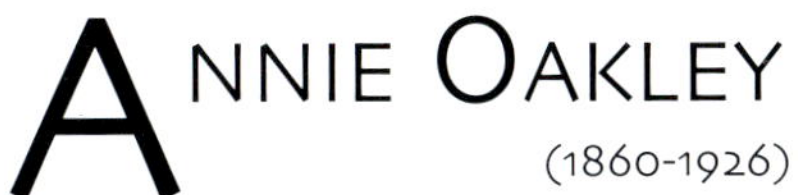

ANNIE OAKLEY

(1860-1926)

Over increasingly large areas of the United States, spring now comes unheralded by the return of the birds, and the early mornings are strangely silent where once they were filled with the beauty of bird song.
—RACHEL CARSON, *The Silent Spring*

It is personalities, not principles, that move an age.
—OSCAR WILDE

Annie Oakley was only sixteen years old when Sitting Bull and Custer's Last Stand was reported in the newspapers on July 5, 1876, the day after the glorious July 4th Centennial celebration in Philadelphia. Custer's death stunned the country and dampened the celebration's finale. Five days later, Walt Whitman published his "Death Sonnet for Custer" in the *New York Tribune*. Its first stanzas read:

> From far Dakota's canons,
> Lands of the wild ravine, the dusky Sioux, the lonesome
> stretch, the silence,
> Haply to-day a mournful wail, haply a trumpet-note
> for heroes.
>
> The battle-bulletin,
> The Indian ambuscade, the craft, the fatal environment,
> The calvary companies fighting to the last in sternest
> heroism,
> In the midst of their little circle with their
> slaughter'd horses for breastworks,
> The fall of Custer and all his horses and men.
>
> Continues yet the old, old legend of our race,
> The loftiest of life upheld by death,
> The ancient banner perfectly maintained,
> O lesson, opportune, O how I welcome thee![1]

Whitman's line "The fall of Custer and all his horses and men" referenced Humpty Dumpty's fall: "All the King's horses and all the King's men couldn't put Humpty Dumpty together again." Custer's fall became a sacrifice, and he became a genuine American martyr—an archetypal symbol for a death-hero martyr, someone who creates deep sympathy. Custer's death epitomized the Wild West as an untamed place where myths were born. It demonstrated that Native Americans could massacre Custer and his troops, which gave the West its authentic savage motif. Paradoxically, only nine years later, when Oakley was getting top billing in Buffalo Bill's Wild West Show, she befriended another member of the troupe, Sitting Bull, one of Custer's mortal enemies.

Oakley was famous as the greatest late-nineteenth-century markswoman. Some of her formidable records with a rifle include breaking 945 out of 1,000 tossed balls; 96 of 100 small clay pigeons; 50 straight double clays; and 49 of 50 live birds. It was also recorded that she broke 4,772 of 5,000 glass balls in one day of shooting. She shot a dime from between her husband's thumb and forefinger with a .22 rifle from a distance of thirty paces. Because of her shooting abilities, thrilling tales about her reached mythic proportions. Through myth she represented a woman of magical superpower. As a woman, she was an atypical analogue to the gun, the supreme force that settled the West.

Phoebe Ann Moses was the sixth child born to a Quaker family that lived in a cabin in Darke County, Ohio. Her father died when she was six years old. Her mother remarried, but her new stepfather died shortly thereafter. Subsequently, Phoebe Ann went to live with the superintendent's family at the Darke County Infirmary for the Elderly, the Orphaned, and the Insane. During her stay, she was loaned out to a local farm family as a servant. According to her autobiography, this family abused her, both mentally and physically.

When she was twelve years old, Phoebe Ann was given her own rifle and taught herself to shoot. She ran away when she was thirteen and returned to her mother, who had remarried again. But Phoebe Ann found her family still living in desperate financial straits. Using her newfound shooting ability, she supplied small game to hotels and restaurants in Ohio, earning enough to pay off the family mortgage. Her fame as a markswoman grew.

Ann against Frank Butler, a well-known twenty-five-year-old professional marksman. It was reported that Butler laughed when he learned that this small young woman was to be his local competition. The match was held on the shooting grounds at Oakley, now a part of suburban Cincinnati. Phoebe Ann won the close match by hitting 25 out of 25 while Butler 24 out of 25.[2] Although he lost the competition, Butler won Phoebe Ann's young heart ("if you can't beat-um join-um"). They married in 1876, and she stayed at home continuing her education while he toured.

Seven years later, Phoebe Ann, under the name of Annie Oakley, replaced Butler's shooting partner who was ill. She took the professional name Oakley after the name of the town where their first match was held. She was known to be shy, modest, kind, and only a meager five feet tall.

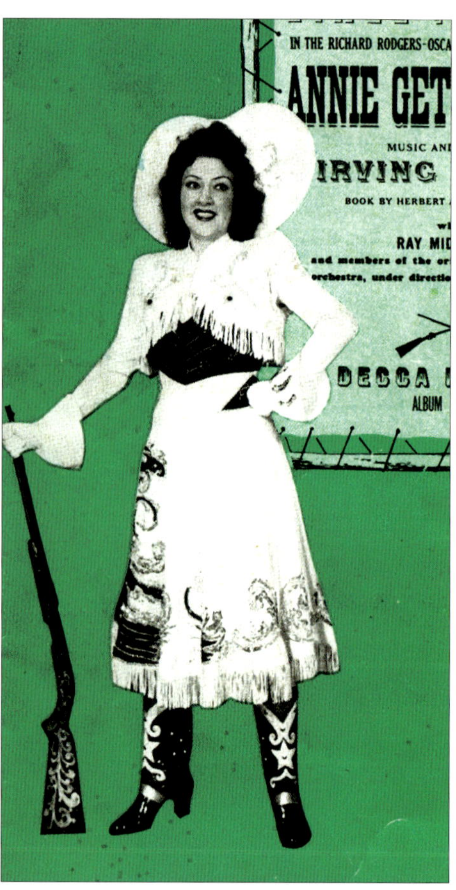

Ethyl Merman, *Annie Get Your Gun*, 1946

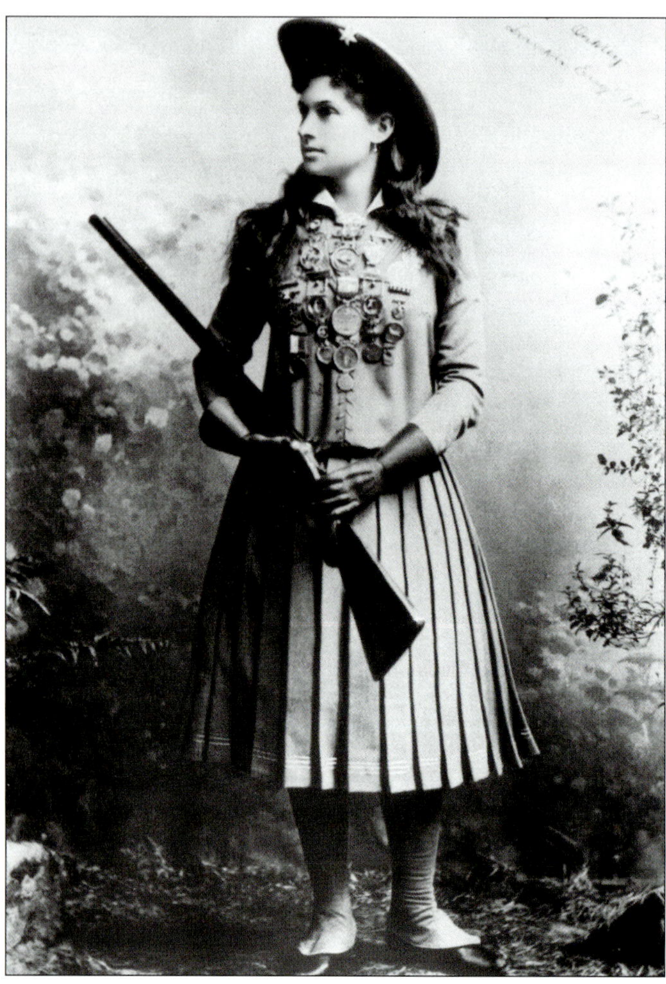

Annie Oakley © Denver Public Library, circa 1880s

In the spring of 1875, the Baughman and Butler Shooting Act was to perform in Cincinnati. To build local interest, a hotel owner entered fifteen-year-old Phoebe

Oakley met Sitting Bull, the great Hunkpapa Lakota Sioux medicine man and chief, after a shooting performance in 1884 in St. Paul, Minnesota. Sitting Bull was elevated to be a great war chief by General Sheridan, who called Custer's battle "Sitting Bull's War," but actually other Sioux chiefs, such as Crazy Horse and Chief Galla, were more important at the battle.

By 1885, Butler and Oakley joined Buffalo Bill's Wild West Show, but Oakley was now the star. In her autobiographical notes, written years later, she was to describe Colonel Cody's introduction of her to his troupe:

My husband and I were introduced as one of them—the first

white woman to stand and travel with what society then
might have thought impossible. Every head bowed. I felt
something like a wild gooseberry sticking in my throat
as the friendly, rough hands covered mine, one at a time,
as they passed with a "How! Waste!" meaning an "all is
good." A crowned Queen was never treated by her courtiers
with more reverence than I by those whole-souled Western
boys.[3]

Oakley's name appeared on the advertising posters
and marquees as "Champion Markswoman." Butler moved
to the background and their roles were reversed. Butler was
Oakley's manager, assistant, and gun cleaner. Because of her
association with the Wild West show, it was generally thought
that Oakley stereotyped a true Western markswoman, trained
from daily hardships experienced while settling the West. The
myth surrounding her epitomized the spirit of the last frontier—in the manner of Davy Crockett almost a hundred years
earlier—but it was only a popular misconception. Oakley's
frontier never went farther west than Ohio. Her struggle with
family poverty had taught her to shoot and it was her seemingly miraculous ability that made her an archetypal motif.

Sitting Bull was transferred from the Sioux Reserva-
tion to become a paid performer in Buffalo Bill's Wild West
Show in 1885. It has been widely speculated that this transfer was favorable to government Indian policy. Moving the
agitator Sitting Bull quietly away from his desperate people
kept the Sioux in a state of despondent peacefulness (it's no
different today—first he was made to look like an important
human being who should be respected, then . . .). In time,
Sitting Bull and Oakley became friends. She reminded him
of one of his daughters who was killed after the Battle of
Little Big Horn. Sitting Bull adopted Oakley, referring to her
fondly as Little Sure Shot, a name that stuck and was later
used on advertising posters. During 1886, the show toured
Europe and Oakley achieved an international reputation.
She returned to Europe again in 1889, but Sitting Bull was
not allowed to travel. In fact, due to the strength of Wavoka's
ghost dance prophecies (that the white man would fade
away), and now fearing a Sioux uprising, the government
wanted Sitting Bull arrested. During his arrest a gunfight
erupted, and Sitting Bull and twelve others were accidentally killed. The U.S. Army had killed him (. . . he was no longer
needed, so he was eliminated).

Oakley and Butler stayed with the Wild West show
until 1901. They retired from public performances in 1913,
but remained active sharpshooters. When the United States
was drawn into World War I, Oakley offered to raise a regi-
ment of women volunteers. She had made the same offer earlier, during the Spanish-American War. Neither of her offers
were accepted. In later years, she spoke for women's right's,
explaining how she had risen to the top in a field dominated
by men. She also explained that in dress and manner she had
not associated with the carnival's risqué side—a side that was
often stereotyped as an entertainer's sinful lifestyle. Oakley
and Butler both died in 1926, eighteen days apart.

In 1935, Barbara Stanwyck played Annie Oakley in
the popular Hollywood film *Annie Oakley*. Oakley was celebrated again in the 1946 Herbert and Dorothy Field's Broadway musical *Annie Get Your Gun*, starring Ethel Merman, with

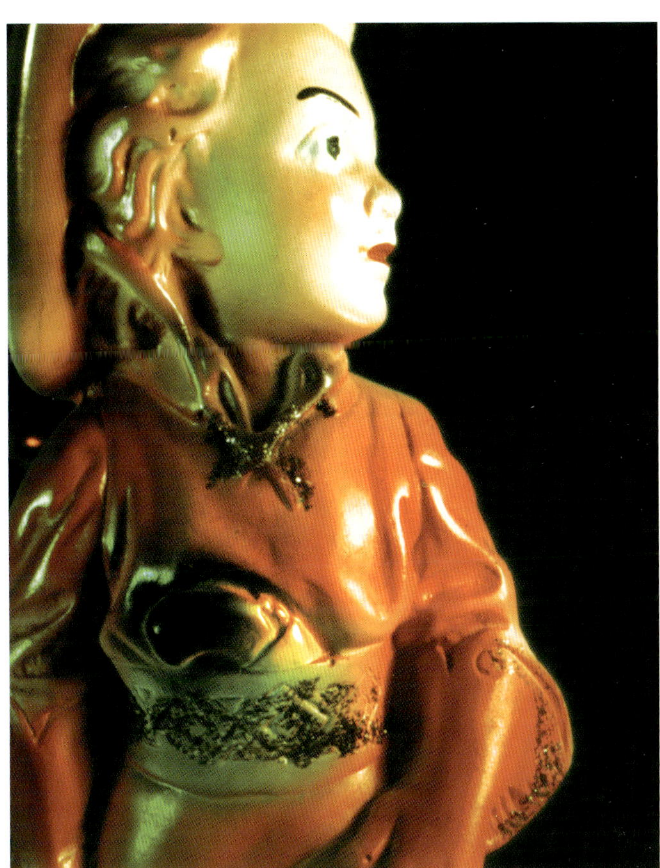

Annie Oakley fourteen-inch carnival chalk prize, early 1950s. She appears to be a
composite image from nineteenth-century photographs of Oakley, Ethyl Merman in the
1946 play *Annie Get Your Gun*, and Betty Hutton in the 1950s film of the same name.
For her clothing, Oakley's simple, frontierlike nineteenth-century clothes were updated,
her skirt was given an added flamboyant flair by being shortened and glittered. The
original Oakley would never have worn that costume—glitter was not her style!

music composed by the inventively patriotic composer Irving
Berlin (eight years earlier he had resurrected "God Bless America"
for Kate Smith). *Annie Get Your Gun* was the biggest hit in
Merman's career. It ran for 1,147 performances and was the
third-longest running musical of the 1940s. Two deprecating
verses in Irving Berlin's song "I'm an Indian Too" from the
musical went:

With my chief in his tepee
We'll raise an Indian family,
And I'll be busy night and day,
Looking like a flour sack
With two papooses on my back
And three papooses on the way.

Like the Chipp-e-wa
Iroquois, Omaha;
I'm an Indian Too—
A Sioux-ooh, a Sioux-ooh,
Just like Rising-Moon,
Falling Pants, Running-Nose,
Like those Indians,
I'm an Indian Too—
A Sioux-ooh, a Sioux-ooh.[4]

In 1950, Betty Hutton and Howard Keel starred in a screen adaptation of *Annie Get Your Gun.* The first Annie Oakley comic was published by Marvel in 1948; later it was continued by Dell Comics (1953–59), renamed *Annie Oakley and Tagg,* and was published concurrently with eighty-one television episodes entitled *Annie Oakley,* starring the blond, pigtailed Gail Davis. Davis, whose face and flashy cowgirl blouse were always on the cover of the comic, had worked with Gene Autry in twenty of his movies and was an excellent rider and markswoman in her own right. The *Annie Oakley* television show ran from 1953-56. It had a family-oriented clean twist—everyone in it had a popular horse. When asked about her work, Davis replied, "So far as I'm concerned, I'm going to be Annie Oakley for the rest of my born days."

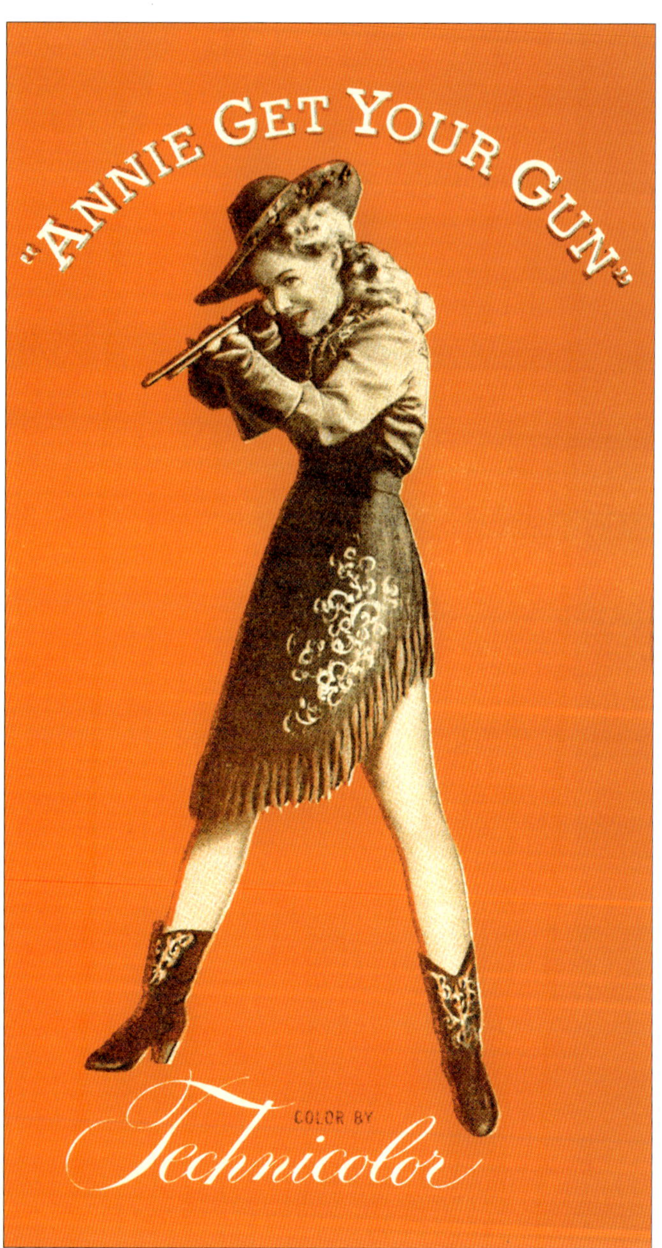

Betty Hutton, *Annie Get Your Gun,* magazine ad, 1950 © M-G-M Studios

Lucille Ball
(1911-1989)

Whatta honk of a woman!
—DESI ARNAZ, the first words he spoke upon seeing Lucille Ball. She was in costume for the film *Dance, Girl, Dance* wearing a gold lamé dress, sporting a fake black eye, playing a tough, wisecracking stripteaser (he had actually met her earlier, but, didn't realize she was the same person).

Here's what I advise any young struggling actress today: The important thing is to develop as a woman first, and a performer second. You wouldn't prostitute yourself to get a part, not if you're in your right mind. You won't be happy, whatever you do, unless you're comfortable with your own conscience. Keep your head up, keep your shoulders back, keep your self-respect, be nice, be smart. And remember that there are practically no 'overnight' successes. Before that brilliant hit performance came ten, fifteen, sometimes twenty years in the salt mines, sweating it out.
—LUCILLE BALL, *Love Lucy*

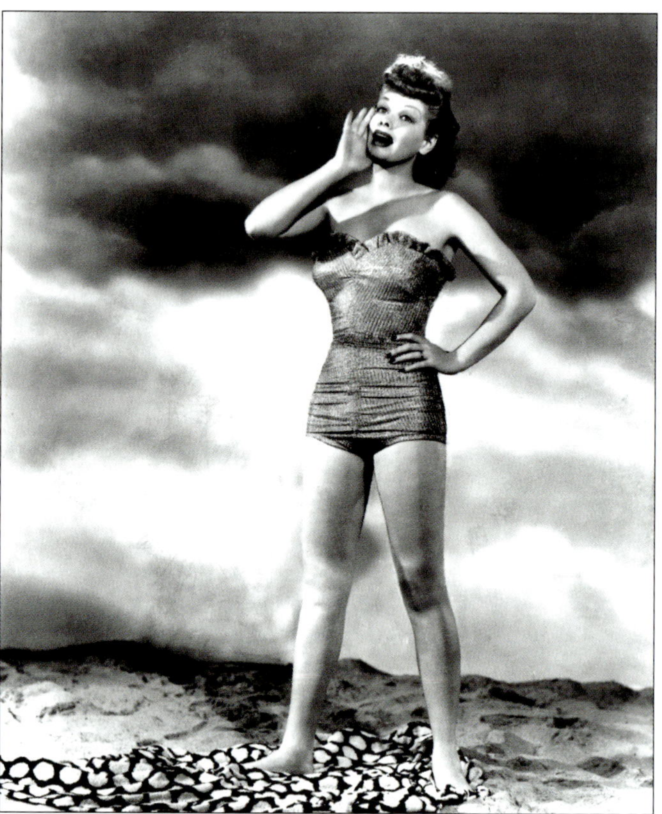

Lucille Ball, 1940s

Lucille Ball is a testament to hard work, perseverance, and creativity. Her father died when she was four and she was raised mostly by her grandparents (her mother was working full time, and at one point had left). The family lived next to Celoron Amusement Park by Lake Chautauqua, New York. Of this experience she said: "I appreciated the magic of the place and the spell of make-believe it cast, it's hard to develop a real sense of values growing up next to a commercial carnival."[1] When she was sixteen, and a sophomore in high school, her grandfather (she called him Daddy), purchased a .22-caliber rifle for her twelve-year-old brother. Early the next morning, while shooting tin-can targets, her brother's friend accidentally shot an eight-year-old neighbor boy who had surprised them by running in front of the targets. He was paralyzed for life. The boy's father sued Lucille's grandfather for negligence and by 1928 the family had lost everything—the house and the savings—right on the eve of the Great Depression. Ball went to New York City, where she failed at theater school. She humbly admitted: "In short they discovered that I couldn't sing, I couldn't dance, I couldn't control my body or my voice properly. Both students and teachers ignored me, which almost seemed fitting. To me everyone was head and shoulders above me in every way."[2] She was fired from a play (many times she was told that she couldn't act).

Then unable to move her legs—and not knowing why the pain was so great or what the illness really was—Ball went back home, where she was bedridden for many months. She survived, returned to New York, and worked as a model for commercial illustrators and also modeled clothes. A painting of her was sold to Chesterfield cigarettes for billboards around the city. As a Chesterfield Girl, she was asked to perform along with seven other Chesterfield Girls as the "eight slave girls" in an Eddie Cantor film being made in Hollywood. There she began her years of playing bit parts. Slowly she realized that she could not compete as a dramatic actress (nor did Hollywood see her that way), and decided to concentrate on her natural talent for comedy. Ball knew she could play the goofy fool and make people laugh (a female Chaplin). By 1938, she found her way onto radio as a comedienne on Jack Haley's weekly *The Wonder Show* and Phil Baker's *Hollywood*. She gradually got larger parts in Hollywood films. Finally she was in so many that she became known as the "Queen of the B's."

In her autobiography, published after her death, Ball writes that when success came in 1939, she bought her first fur coat and hired a personal maid, an African American named Harriet McCain, who worked for her for decades.

Ball met musician and band leader Desi Arnaz when she was twenty-eight while working as the wisecracking stripper across from Maureen O'Hara in *Dance, Girl, Dance*. Ball and Arnaz married, but their conflicting schedules led to marital problems. Ball filed for divorce in 1944; somehow they resolved their differences one day before the divorce was to be finalized. They realized they needed to act together—so they pitched the idea to CBS about a sitcom starring Ball as the wacky wild redhead married to Arnaz the goofy Cuban band leader. CBS passed on it, claiming the American public would never accept an interracial couple. They formed their own production company, Desilu, and turned their sitcom into an imitation vaudeville act—a funny parody on gender stereotypes (who does what?) and marriage archetypes. On July 17, 1951, their daughter, Lucie, was born. In October they made the pilot episode of *I Love Lucy* using their own money. It instantly became the most popular television show in America. Now CBS wanted it. Little by little the show became a copy of their life (art imitates life), particularly when Ball was pregnant with Ricky. At his long-awaited birth, 44 million Americans watched in awe. Eisenhower was inaugurated as president the same week and on that Sunday night Walter Winchell said over the radio: "This was a banner week: the nation got a man and Lucy got a boy."[3] By 1957, Ball and Arnaz bought RKO Studios. On March 3, 1960, they filed for divorce on the grounds of extreme mental cruelty. No one on the show had been speaking to one another for ages—it all ended. *I Love Lucy* had run successfully for six years. The first four years *I Love Lucy* was number one in the Neilsen ratings. In the era of civil rights it was the first popular show that featured an interracial marriage. Ball eventually remarried, and she died in 1989.

Lucille Ball eight-and-one-half-inch tatooed carnival chalk prize (some are named "I Love Lucy"). Apparently the carnival chalk manufacturer thought she should be caricatured in something tight-fitting from her "Queen of the B's" era, when she wore cheesy bathing suits and frivolous costumes. She might not have been amused by the prize, nor found it overly complimentary—maybe that was the intention, to poke fun at the various roles she had played.

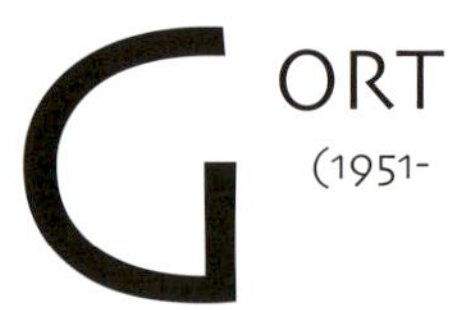

GORT (1951–

In the first space-odyssey film, *A Trip to the Moon* (1902), the man in the moon grimaced when an Earth rocket hit the moon (appropriate! a still from the film, page 38). This classic was created by French filmmaker Georges Méliès. Its fourteen minutes of science fiction celebrated authors like H. G. Wells and Jules Verne. Méliès' films first appeared in the United States in 1896.

By 1928, American spaceman Buck Rogers appeared in the novelette *Armageddon-2419 A.D.* by Philip Francis Nowlan. Then *Buck Rogers in the Twenty-Fifth Century* appeared in daily newspaper comic strips in 1929, with a string of sensational characters named Wilma Deering, Dr. Huer, and Killer Kane. Their disintegrators, jumping belts, inertrons, and paralysis rays were symbolic death weapons, and as archetypes were more fascinating than the characters who used them. Buck Rogers was so popular that in 1934 a Virginia department store, rather than dredging up a boring old Santa Claus at Christmas, suited up an actor as Buck Rogers.

Then came competition for outer space. *Flash Gordon* first appeared in comic strips in 1934, written by Don Moore and drawn by Alex Raymond. Raymond's beautifully crafted drawings made the series much more popular than *Buck Rogers*, who quietly soared out of view.

Hollywood actor Buster Crabbe lifted off as Flash Gordon in *Atomic Rocket Ship* (1936). Flash's companion was the tantalizing Dale Arden, played by Jean Rogers, who delighted her audiences in tight-fitting two-piece outfits, perfect for deep-sex space travel and more appropriate for Sunset Strip than Mars. It was not until the Roswell Incident that Americans realized that an alien craft might have actually crashed to Earth. The U.S. Air Force issued a press release, then a retraction. Their initial report told of an alien "craft" that had crashed northwest of Corona, New Mexico (oddly enough, not far from the Trinity Site, where two years earlier Los Alamos scientists and the government exploded their first test atomic bomb). Five little bodies were collected by some unknown task force. Debris from the flying saucer was recovered—it could not be cut.

Buck Rogers, Flash Gordon, and the many other fantasy spacemen of that era reinforced the superior attitude/archetype that American spacemen were the best techno-warriors for fighting against the best alien adversaries that outer space had to offer. Their spacesuits resembled the heavy metal duds Christopher Columbus wore when he arrived as Spain's best techno-warrior pitted against the unknown (the natives turned out to be friendly). Not so with the natives in Washington,

D.C., when Klaatu and Gort arrived in the film *The Day the Earth Stood Still* (1951). With no real provocation, a U.S. soldier shoots the space hero/alien Klaatu as he attempts to give a present to earthlings after landing near the nation's capital. His mission is to tell all of the world leaders that their countries should not conduct any more atomic research. If they continue, it would be too dangerous for other space civilizations. The film was a brilliant antiwar, anti–nuclear research idea. Its message was simple: "Stop, before it's too late!" Klaatu's all-powerful robot, Gort, steps off the spaceship and demonstrates his indestructible power.

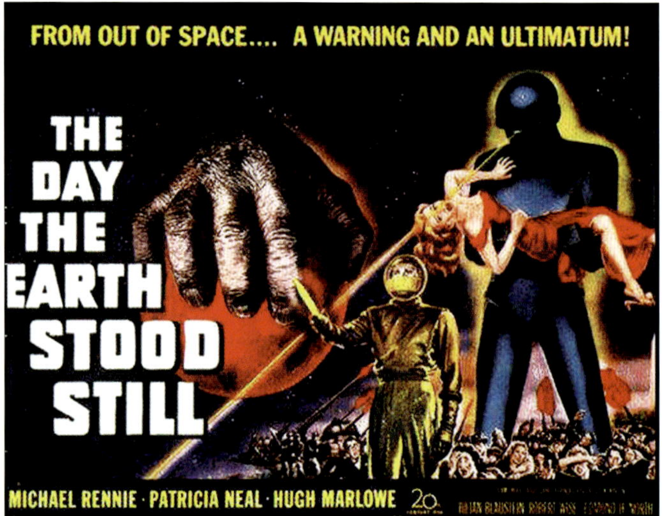

The Day the Earth Stood Still, lobby card, 1951 © 20th Century Fox. The lobby card gives a false impression of the film—Gort never attempts to kidnap the white heroine.

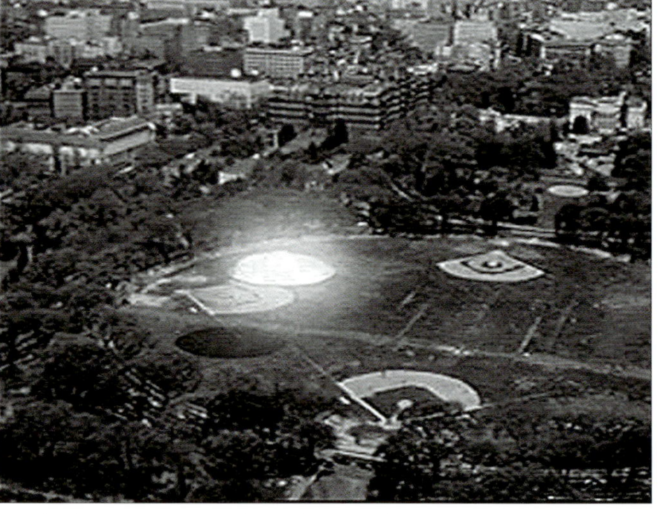

Hovering flying saucer, *The Day the Earth Stood Still*, still, 1951 © 20th Century Fox

A shocked America pondered its future on October 4, 1957, when the USSR successfully launched *Sputnik I*. The world's first artificial satellite was about the size of a basketball, weighed only 183 pounds, and took approximately 98 minutes to orbit the Earth on its elliptical path. The launch ushered in new political, military, technological, scientific, and propagandist developments in the cold war.

That was the start of the space age and the U.S.–USSR space race. The Soviets won again a month later, when *Sputnik II* was launched, carrying a much heavier payload, including a dog named Laika. Americans were afraid that the Soviets' ability to launch satellites translated into the capability to launch ballistic missiles carrying nuclear weapons. On April 12, 1961, a further dismayed American public heard in disbelief that Yuri Gagarin was the first human to fly in space aboard *Vostok 1*. He orbited Earth once, but one orbit was enough to start a war of attrition between the capitalist United States and the communist USSR, in which imponderable amounts of money were spent by both countries trying to outdo each other in a space propaganda race. It is completely bizarre that two men from Hollywood decided the all-consuming issue: George Lucas with his *Star Wars Episode 1: A New Hope* (1977), and actor/President Ronald Reagan, who blamed the USSR for escalation in his Star Wars speech of March 23, 1983. In it he proclaimed the United States would meet the challenge. This planned response invigorated the antagonism and upped the ante. Everything he said built upon the politicized fear as the USSR now was the dreaded enemy archetype. Reagan said:

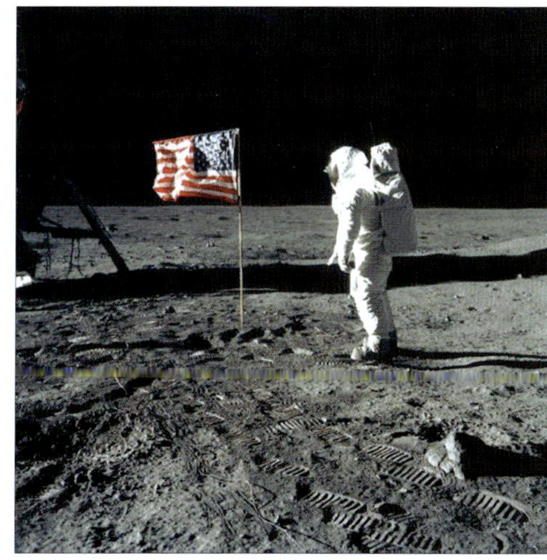

The archetypal motif for winning, July 20, 1969 when Neil Armstrong was photographed on the moon with the U.S. flag, Apollo II. Courtesy: NASA

> Tonight, consistent with our obligations of the ABM treaty and recognizing the need for closer consultation with our allies, I'm taking an important first step. I am directing a comprehensive and intensive effort to define a long-term research and development program to begin to achieve our ultimate goal of eliminating the threat posed by strategic nuclear missiles.[1]

Ironically, every single studio in Hollywood had refused Lucas's *Star Wars* except for 20th Century Fox, which gave him a measly $10 million to make what was probably the most politically influential film in the history of cinema. More important, Reagan's speech made it obvious that humankind, for the first time in its history, had the capability (and the willingness) to destroy its own planet—much more completely than fantasized aliens like Gort. In the words of Klaatu, "Klaato baruda nikto," which translates as: "STOP."

Hollywood's unsuspecting stars John Wayne and Susan Hayward would have agreed with Klaatu, but by the time of Reagan's speech they were dead from cancer as a result of nuclear testing in Nevada where they filmed *The Conqueror* on a hot spot in 1954.[2]

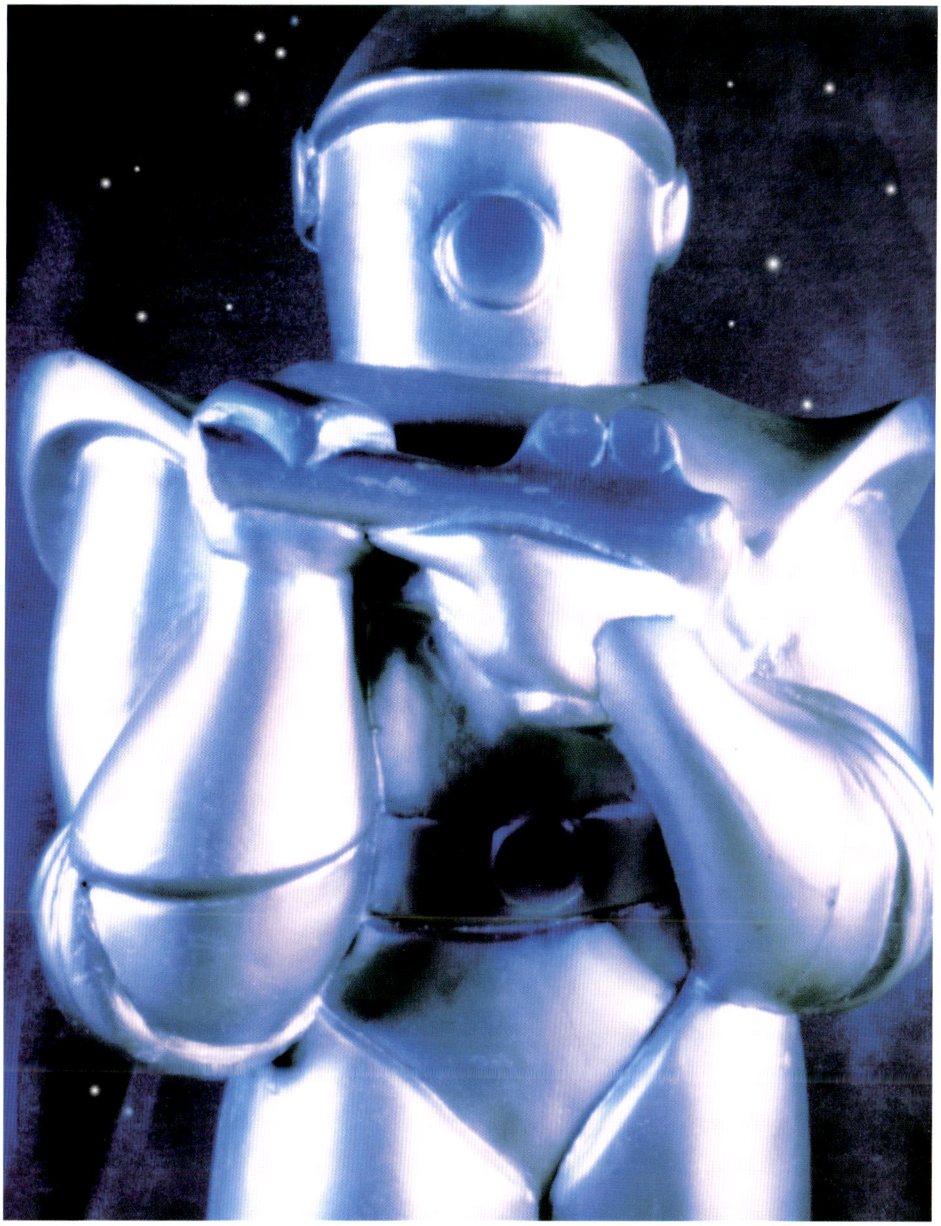

Gort thirteen-inch carnival chalk prize © M. J. Golden & Company. Gort did not need a ray gun in his film *The Day the Earth Stood Still.* It was the first science-fiction film to be taken seriously, to the credit of director Robert Wise.

253

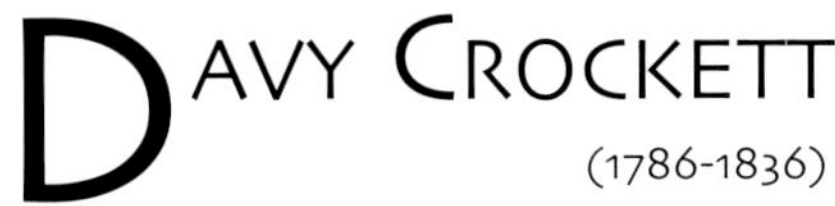

DAVY CROCKETT

(1786-1836)

Why should you wish to shorten my life by taking from me my shadow?
—CRAZY HORSE

The Davy Crockett figure was one of the last carnival chalk figures to be mass produced, and one of the few directly linked with television. It was part of the great, Disneyesque, media-merchandising moment during the mid-1950s Crockett craze, which included comics, books, records, coonskin caps, guitars, and just about anything that could be given a Davy Crockett look. Even President Eisenhower wore a Davy Crockett tie (a flashy media archetype). Five thousand Davy Crockett coonskin caps were sold every day. Prior to introducing the TV show, and betting on the success of Crockettmania, Disney had purchased thousands of raccoon tails at five cents each. (Crockett's original hat was made of bobcat.)

The Hollywood frontiersman stereotype wore fringed buckskin. Native Americans wore fringed buckskins because they were strong, practical, and functional garments. They shed rain, provisions could be tied to them, and the swishing movement of the fringe shooed insects away. Fringed buckskins were popularized as frontier wear in the nineteenth century and worn by Buffalo Bill in his Wild West show.

The first episode of Walt Disney's television Davy Crockett trilogy, *Davy Crockett Indian Fighter*, aired on Wednesday, December 15, 1954, starring Fess Parker. Just about every boy I knew (including myself) sported a coonskin cap before the January 26, 1955, telecast of the second episode, *Davy Crockett Goes to Congress*. The last episode, *Davy Crockett at the Alamo*, was aired on February 23, 1955. The craze spawned an incessant bombardment of the banal *Davy Crockett* theme song, which most folks thought was a treatment of an old, authentic country ballad. The truth of the matter was that Disney scriptwriter Tom Blackburn and Disney songwriter George Bruns composed the ditty in twenty minutes. The record sold 10 million copies, equaling the sales of coonskin caps. The song went:

> Born on a mountaintop in Tennessee,
> Greenest state in the land of the free,
> Raised in the woods so he knew every tree,
> Kilt him a b'ar when he was only three.
> Davy, Davy Crockett,
> King of the wild frontier!

That was only the first of twenty verses! Forty-one different singers recorded the song. Of the craze, Walt Disney lamented:

> We had no idea what was going to happen on Crockett. Why, by the time the first show finally got on the air, we were already shooting the third one and calmly killing Davy off at the Alamo. It became one of the biggest overnight hits in TV history, and there we were with just three films and a dead hero![1]

It was obvious that Disney made a vast amount of money on Davy Crockett, so his faux lament was simply playing at rich man's pity. Meanwhile, a judge in Baltimore decreed that the name "Davy Crockett" was in the public domain. As a result, 3,000 different merchandising items were produced and store shelves were inundated with Crockett merchandise. The craze abruptly collapsed in early 1956.

The re-created, fantasized, cleaned-up, made-for-TV version of Davy Crockett sported a glittered layer, just like the phony 1955 carnival prize. Disney stereotyped Crockett as the epitome of the American frontier spirit—the friendly, sharp-shooting, backwoods hunter and Indian fighter, with morals decent enough and humor ready enough to be a politician. He had a "always be sure you're right, then go ahead," simile aimed at Congress, or anyone else for that matter. Crockett represented frontier freedom—American freedom! He was nationalism personified. Killing Native Americans and/or Mexicans was his God-given right as an American. No examination of conscience was necessary and no consideration was given to the fact that Native Americans and later Mexicans inhabited the continent earlier. Crockett, just by virtue of his existence, was the good guy and anyone he fought against was the bad guy. Disney's dramatization of Crockett's glorious death at the Alamo projected an image of Christlike brotherly love and unshakable patriotic courage. He died a martyr for his cause and his America! The timing of making Crockett into a great American icon in 1955—at a time when Americans felt extremely patriotic, vis-à-vis the Korean War—was the perfection of corporate enterprise. It was an example of marketing and commerce taking advantage of the public sentiment that traditionally follows disasters, similar to the introduction of a patriotic toothpaste that came out of its tube in red, white, and blue squirts of American flags just after 9/11.

Disney's fascination with resurrecting specific fantasy heroes from the scrap heap of American history was not an accident. Underlying the frontier-freedom and Crockett archetype were urgings and instinctive feelings that gave credibility (thus approval) to America's continued Manifest Destiny to light the torch of Democracy over the world. During the propaganda-ridden cold war era, if war became necessary, its acceptance by the American people was guaranteed. Uncle Walt knew the Crockett image gave America what it thought it needed: an allegorical macho hero who not only protected America's boundaries and promoted American superiority but also gave America the right to stamp out the spread of the ugly disease known as communism. In return, Americans gave their consent and wallets to Walt Disney—democracy and capitalism. The Davy Crockett films were propaganda— the government, vis-à-vis the all-powerful J. Edgar Hoover, could not have asked for more—and the American public was a readily receptive, propagandized audience.

But who was the flesh-and-blood Davy Crockett? He was born in a small frontier cabin near Limestone, Tennessee. His father's mill and their home were washed away in a flood when Davy was eight years old. At age twelve, he was contracted out by his father to herd cattle three hundred miles away in hilly, hardscrabble Rockbridge County, Virginia. A year later, to avoid punishment for skipping school, young Davy contracted himself out to drive cattle to Fort Royal,

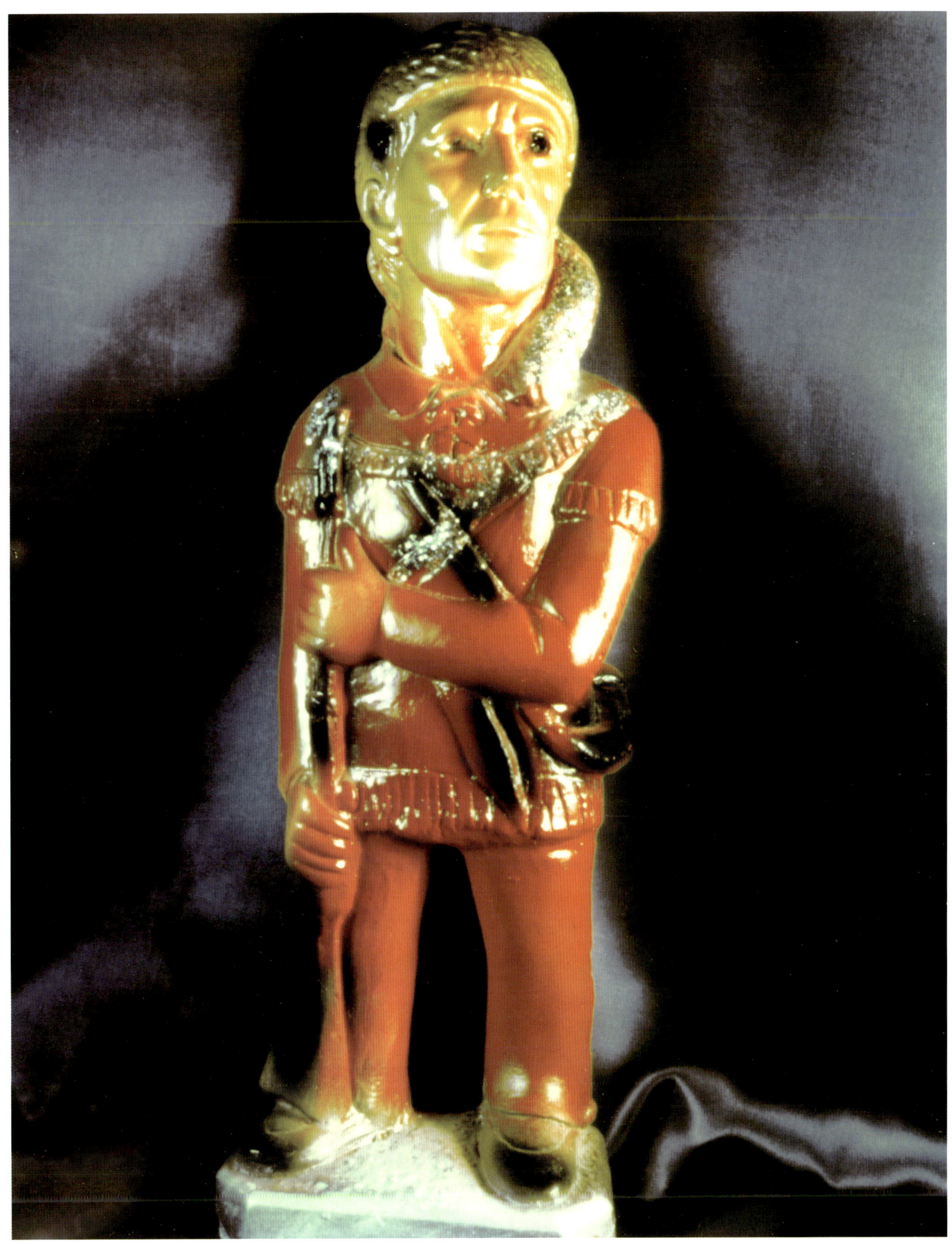

Davy Crockett fifteen-inch carnival chalk prize, an extremely rare version has Daniel Boone inscribed onto the base plate

Virginia. He returned home when he was sixteen and was schooled part time for six months—as he said, "in this time I learned to read a little in my primer, to write my own name, and to cypher some in the three first rules in figures"[2]

Just after his twentieth birthday, after being spurned by Margaret Elder, to whom he was engaged for some months, he married Polly Finley. He earned enough to buy his own rifle and horse and started winning local shooting contests. In 1813, he joined the Tennessee Volunteer Militia and fought in the Creek Indian War. Later he participated in the Battle of Tallussahatchee. A son was born during those years, but after the birth of the second son in 1815, Polly died. Of her death he lamented: "Death, that cruel leveler of all distinctions entered my humble cottage, and tore from my children an affectionate good mother, and from me a tender and loving wife."[3]

He then married Elizabeth Patton, a widow with three children. His rise in politics began in the early 1820s, when he was thirty-five. In his first election into the Tennessee State Legislature, he gained attention with a roorback (a political smear) when he labeled his opponent an aristocrat, then memorized his opponent's campaign speech and was able to parody it—delivering the entire speech word for word. This bit of political stagecraft gave him his victory. He was defeated in his first bid for Representative to the U.S. Congress in 1825, but his notoriety rose when, in that same year, he killed 105 bears in just six months (a David against Goliath archetype).

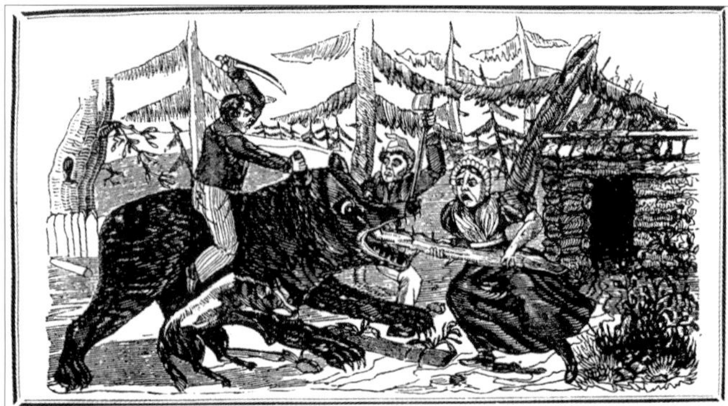

"A Desperate Contest with a Great Black Bear," *Davy Crockett's Almanack of Wild Sports of the West*, vol. 1, no. 3, 1837

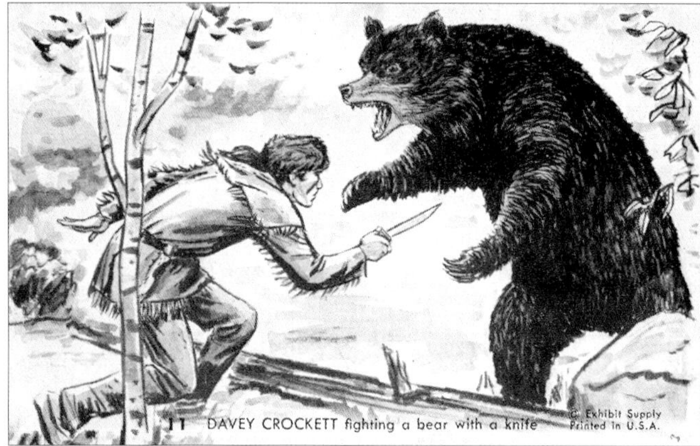

"Davey Crockett Fighting a Bear with a Knife," card © Exhibit Supply Company, 1950s

Running for congressional Representative again in 1827, his winning campaign was highlighted by an incident where guinea hens interrupted his opponent's speech. Davy,

with ready stage wit, claimed they were calling "Crockett! Crockett! Crockett!"

While serving in Congress, he championed the Land Bill, which allowed homesteaders in the west to buy land at a very low cost, rather than allowing it to be sold for profit in order to raise money for each state's education programs. This stance set him against President Andrew Jackson and brought about Crockett's defeat in the 1830 congressional election. In his concession statement, Crockett emphatically stated:

> I would rather be beaton [*sic*] and be a man, than to be elected and be a little puppy dog. I have always supported measures and principles and not men. I have acted fearless and independent and I never will regret my course. I would rather be politically buried than to be hypocritically immortalized.[4]

Reelected in 1832, he joined the Whig party in opposition to Jackson, but lost the election in 1834. Acknowledging defeat in his final congressional statement, Crockett said: "Since you have chosen to elect a man with a timber toe to succeed me, you may all go to hell and I will go to Texas."[5] And that's what he did, hoping that Texas would soon be an independent territory where he could once more run for office. Two years later, on March 6, 1836, Crockett died at the Alamo, along with 182 other staunch defenders who had sided with the anti-Jackson faction in the divided Texas government. They had disobeyed Sam Houston, who had ordered them to destroy the mission-fort and retreat a month earlier. It is said they fought against an army of 5,000 Mexicans. No one knows where Crockett was laid to rest. A tombstone over a false grave near Limestone, Tennessee, reads:

> Davy Crockett, Pioneer, Patriot, Soldier, Trapper, Explorer, State Legislator, Congressman, Martyred at The Alamo.
> 1786–1836

A desire for revenge of the Alamo built as Americans reacted—Mexicans became the archetypal hostile brethren. Border disputes were many. James K. Polk's election as president in November 1844 was interpreted as a mandate from the people for the annexation of Texas, since Polk had come out strongly in favor of it. On March 1, 1845, Congress jointly resolved to admit Texas into the Union, and the Mexican government promptly broke off diplomatic relations. The Mexican-American War of 1846–48 settled certain political issues but slurred feelings about Mexicans persisted (and do even to the present day).

Crockett was first fictionalized into superhero status by Boston literary hacks who produced the *Crockett Almanacs* (1835–56). They concocted tall tales wherein he single-handedly saved the earth by moving the sun from its axis. He also cured his pet bear's stomach disorder by killing and boiling an Indian for proper dietary results.[6]

Sam Colt invented the revolving cylinder gun the year Crockett died. By the 1950s, firearm advertising, fictional accounts by easterners, and radio and Hollywood Westerns gave the American public and the rest of the world the popular misconception that guns were more prevalent on the frontier than they truly were. For instance, in Massachusetts Bay Colony in 1640, it was illegal to shoot a gun for any unnecessary occasion, excepting at a Native American or at any game, excepting a wolf.[7] During the Revolutionary War, most citizens in the colonies did not own guns and most of the guns that were owned by Americans were acutely antiquated. Guns were manufactured in Europe at that time, but not in the United States. Gun ownership was exceptionally rare in the seventeenth, eighteenth, and even early nineteenth centuries. Guns became a common commodity much later, during the period of American industrialization in the mid-nineteenth century and, contrary to legend, gun owners were concentrated mostly in the urban areas and not the western frontier.

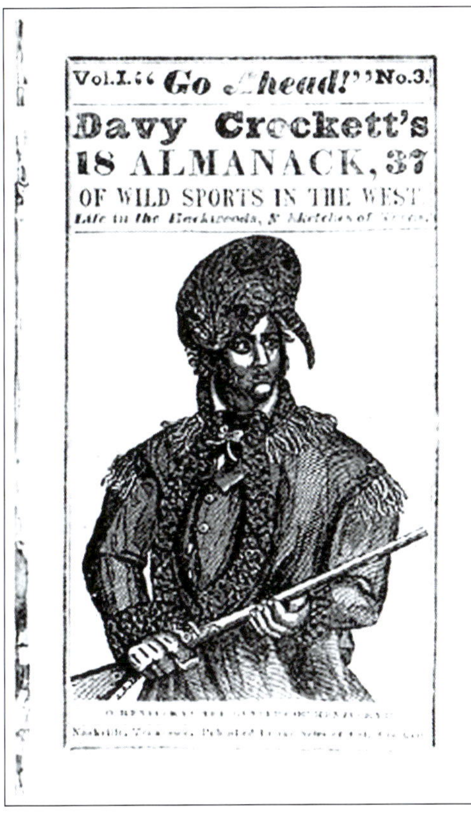

Davy Crockett's Almanack of Wild Sports in the West, book cover, vol. 1, no. 3, 1837

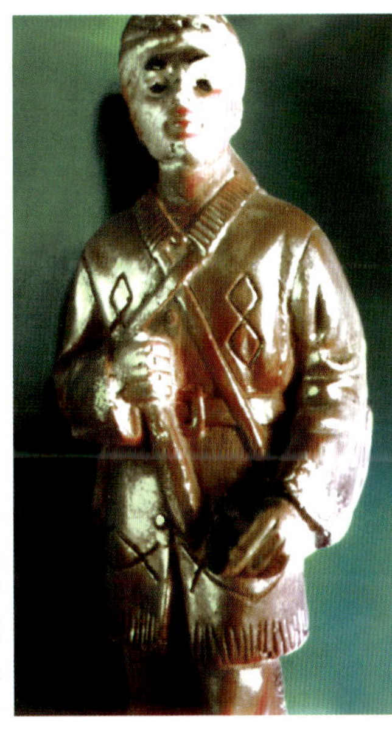

Davy Crockett twelve-inch carnival chalk prize, "Davy Crockett" written on the base

HOLLOWEEN BOY

Halloween is certainly the most ancient of holidays, although corporations have attempted to turn it into a candy-and-costume capitalist blitz and moralists have attempted to take away "Mischief Night." But All Hallow's Eve icons—the mask, costume, and jack-o'-lantern—are still in use. The mask gave its wearer protection against the dead who were returning to Earth on October 31—the day that the ancients considered the last day of summer. This was the day when the sun moved into its least powerful phase and when hostile spirits were most likely to return. A costume increased the wearer's protection. To prevent natural catastrophes from occurring, masks were often worn on other days, as well as in ceremonies. Masks and costumes are archetypal symbols for power, protecting its empowered wearer.

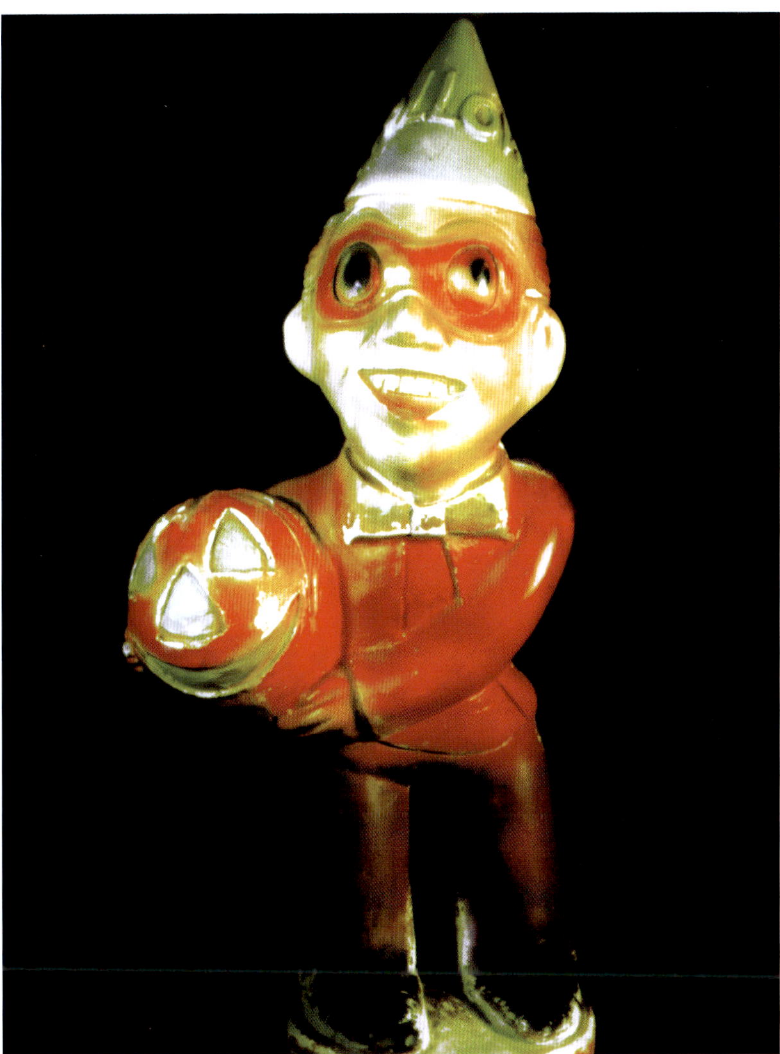

Holloween (spelled with an "o") Boy sixteen-inch carnival chalk prize, wearing a mitre cap that does not suggest he's a dunce, for in ancient times it would have offered him increased ritualistic power against unknown night spirits. He is a valuable carnival chalk prize sought by collectors of Halloween memorabilia.

Many variants of All Hallow's Eve still exist. In Mexico, sweets, flowers, and music are used to invite good spirits of departed family members, particularly children, back to Earth, not to haunt but for a visitation and remembrance, as in the modernized Day of the Dead ceremony on November 2.

The ancients considered light a protection against hostile power at night. Torches and bonfires were lit on October 31 to flood the tops of hills with protective light against the Lord of the Dead. A candle was placed inside a large carved-out turnip or potato (now pumpkins are used—a lot easier to carve). This predecessor to the jack-o'-lantern was an ignus fatuus, something that was used to mislead or delude the evil spirits and keep them from seeing the living. A similar illusion was created by a myriad of white seashells being placed on and around the early graves of African Americans buried on the coastal regions of the South. The shells were placed there by relatives so that the flying spirit of the dead could not see his or her grave—preventing that spirit from returning— thus assisting the departed one on its journey.

When Christianity pushed aside earlier religious beliefs (demeaning them as pagan), the ancients' Lord of the Dead was replaced by the Christian devil and the witch. The witch was an easy slur for Christianity to use against the ancients' nonconventional person. Most witches were women (the word "witch" is not far from the word "bitch"). By the time of the various Inquisitions, any person who was thought to have sold their soul to the devil was then ill considered, therefore a witch, therefore destroyed.

All Hallow's Eve became Halloween and the ancients' evil spirits of the night became witches, goblins (grotesque elfin creatures), and ghosts. It was thought that witches left their beds and flew up chimneys and off through the night sky on a broomstick. A broom is an archetypal symbol for a woman keeping house. Witches were always attended by evil black cats—still considered a sign of bad luck.

Most Halloween customs were brought to America by Irish immigrants. One of their myths explained the history of the jack-o'-lantern. It tells of "Stingy Jack," who invited the devil to pay for his barroom drink. The devil had to change into a sixpence in order to do this, but instead of paying for the drink, Stingy Jack placed the sixpence beside a silver cross, which prevented the devil from changing back. Stingy Jack made a deal with the devil before letting him free. For one year, the devil could not harm Stingy Jack. Next Hallow-een, the devil met Stingy Jack again. Jack made another deal with the devil, again to be left alone. Ah, but Stingy Jack died within the year, and since he had sinned through trickery and drinking, was turned back from Heaven and went to the gates of Hell. Here the devil refused to let him in—because the devil had promised not to claim Stingy Jack's soul. Jack didn't want to leave—it was dark and he couldn't find his way. The devil tossed Jack a glowing coal, which Jack put inside a turnip. Ever since, Stingy Jack roams the Earth with his jack-o-lantern looking for a place to rest. (Stingy Jack is probably a distant cousin to spring-heeled Jack on page 93.)

Forked branches of witch hazel are used for dowsing (still slurred as "water witching"). It was thought that witches made a tingling oil from witch hazel and other herbs, which rubbed on their skin made flying easier. Playing on the idea of witch hazel oil aiding witches in flying was the basis for a witch hazel oil ad from 1909. The ad demonstrates how deeply Halloween witch flight was ingrained into the public's mindset and also the savvy of a corporate medicine seller using an airplane to advertise their product (the Wright brothers first flight was six years ear-lier). The little boy is holding an apple (reminiscent of Eve and a devil). Hold-ing the witch hazel oil sign is a figure dressed in red with a pointed cap—does it represent a devil? The figure is barely visible on this postcard ad.

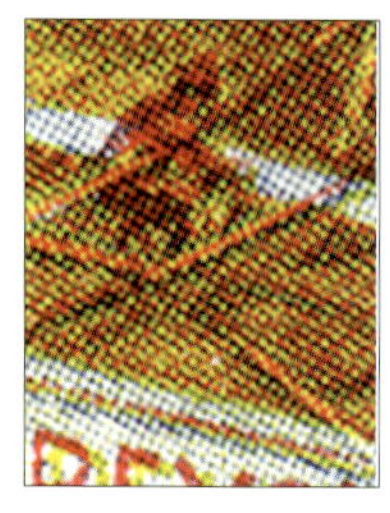

Detail of postcard ad

Flying has always had magical properties attached to it—any object in the air is an archetype for earthly escape and airborne freedom. Birds have been associated with the soul's flight; owls in particular—as birds of the night—are thought to be harbingers of death; they transport the soul away.

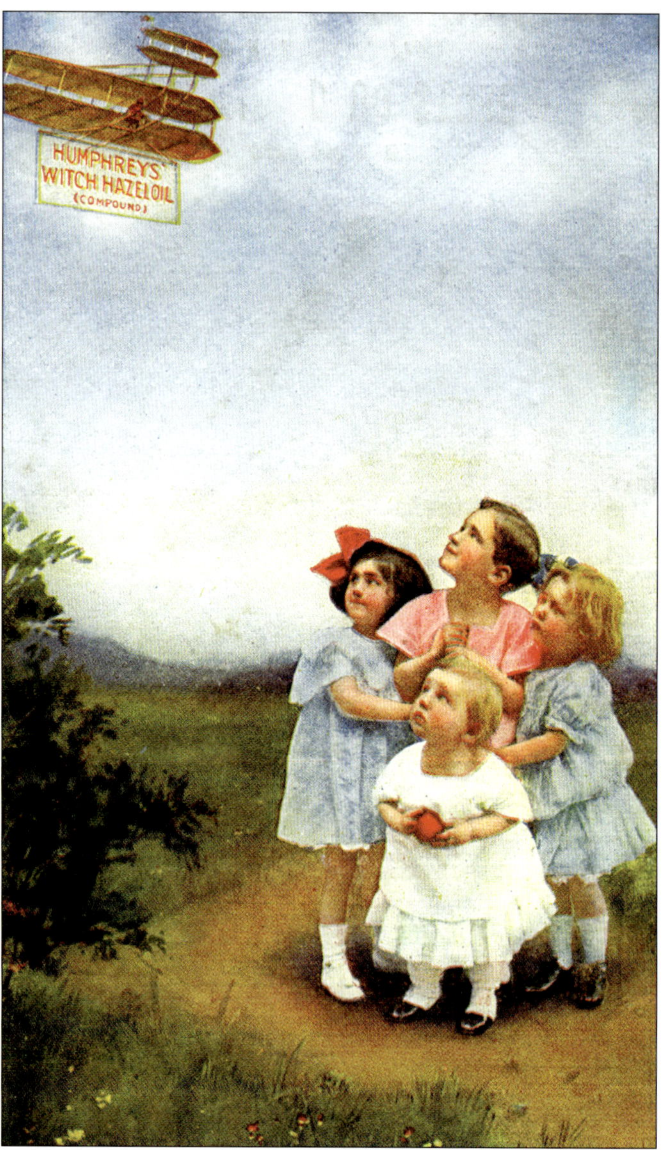

Humphrey's Witch Hazel Oil, postcard ad, 1909

Clown

There's nothing funny about a clown in the moonlight.
— Lon Chaney

Everyone is familiar with the distinctive makeup, costume, and buffoonery of a clown. The clown is meant to entertain by use of graphic absurdity and hearty, foolish physicality.

Clowns in ancient Greece wore padded costumes and had shaved heads (for anyone with a bald head, this archetypal symbol explains why you might feel your baldness creates unwarranted humor—I have one). Clowns in ancient Rome wore patchwork clothes, later evolving into the diamond-shaped harlequin look, similar to the joker on playing cards.

Clowns have always made their audience laugh by playing the fool. The court jester has a slightly different role—less likened to clown routines and more specialized: how to make the king, queen, and court laugh. Usually a court jester had a risky job, particularly if the kingdom was about to collapse, likened to a precarious house of cards.

Traveling English clowns of the seventeenth century invented the stereotypical clown costume, still in vogue today: oversize shoes, waistcoat with giant ruff around the neck, and clownish hat. During that era, whiteface makeup was introduced by Pierrot, a French clown with a bald head and flour-whitened face. Dressing in clown garb and with a painted clown face, the clown had an empowered but disguised personality meant as funny or sad. But no longer. The media has changed all that. Political satirists used and abused the clown stereotype for more than a century. They took the foolish part of clowning and turned the clown into a scapegoat for a stinging projected persona aimed at anyone they deemed an empowered fool. Next, Hollywood films made clowns scary, abnormal people alienated from a normal world. (The secretive group known as Shriners attempt to be funny clowns in their miniature parade cars—most children who see Shriner clowns think of them as weirdly funny, but mostly scary because they look abnormal.)

Through this surfeit of strange Hollywood alterations, the clown paradigm increased to include the clown as deadly maniacal. The feared yet admired Joker in the 1940s Batman comics is one example (long before Jack Nicholson got the role). *Batman's* death-defying Joker appropriation was fashioned after the sewed-on permanently diabolic smile worn by Conrad Veidt in *The Man Who Laughs* (1928). The Joker ploy pitted the clown as a humorous psycho-agent against Batman, a dark but constant hero. The clownish part of the Joker's stereotype kept readers thinking that his ways were funny—but he now embodied a gruesome disguise—a burlesque that pointed him toward a macabre death archetype.

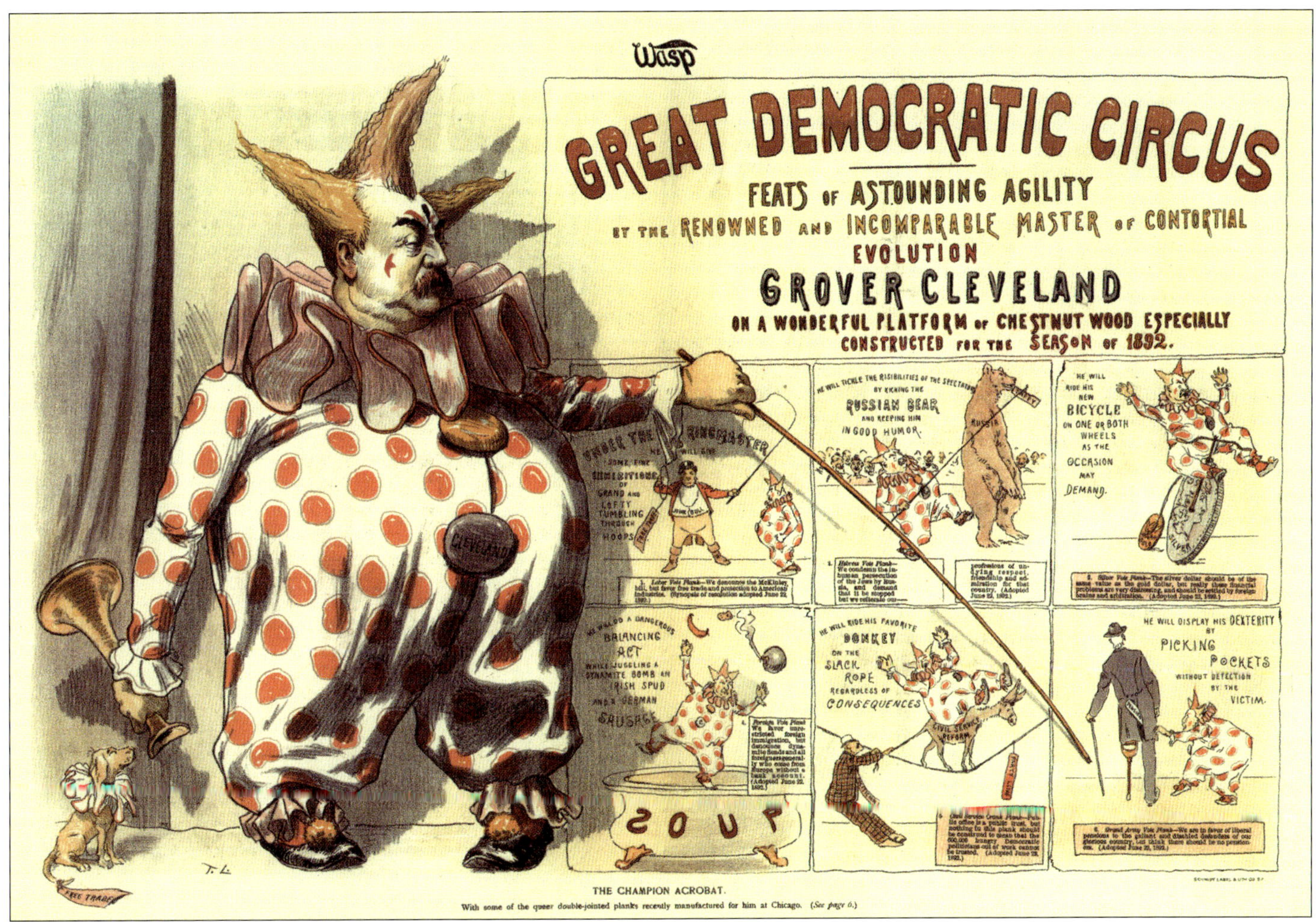

"The Champion Acrobat," cartoon Theodore Langguth, which ridiculed Grover Cleveland in a highly partisan campaign against Benjamin Harrison; published on the *San Francisco Wasp* cover, July 2, 1892. There is an early "Nipper" dog and a horn in the lower left corner; these would later become RCA's logotype.

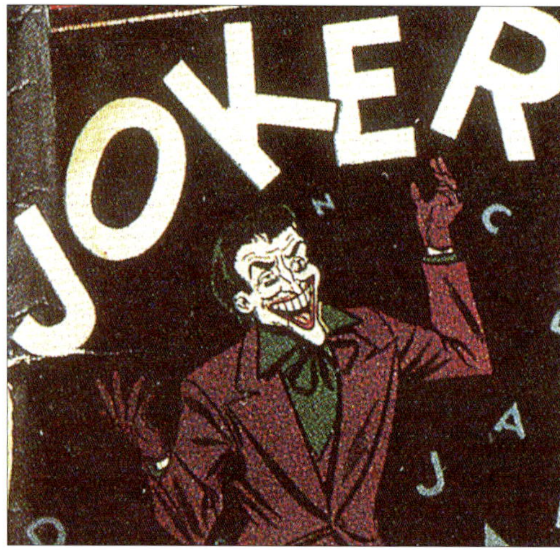
The Joker, *Batman*, cover detail © Detective Comics #114, 1940s

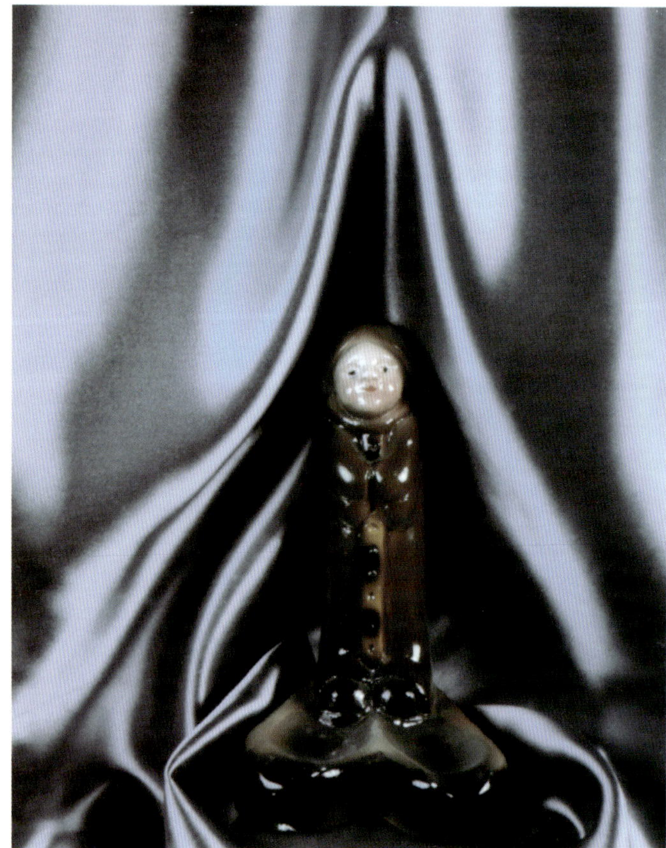
Capuchin monk six-inch carnival chalk prize, painted bright pink as a penis on the reverse

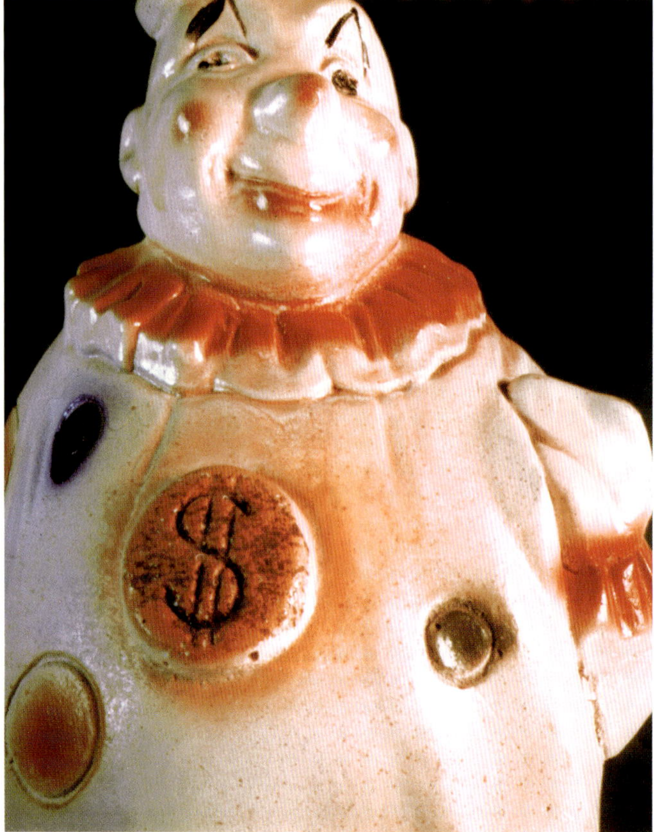
Clown twelve-inch carnival chalk prize

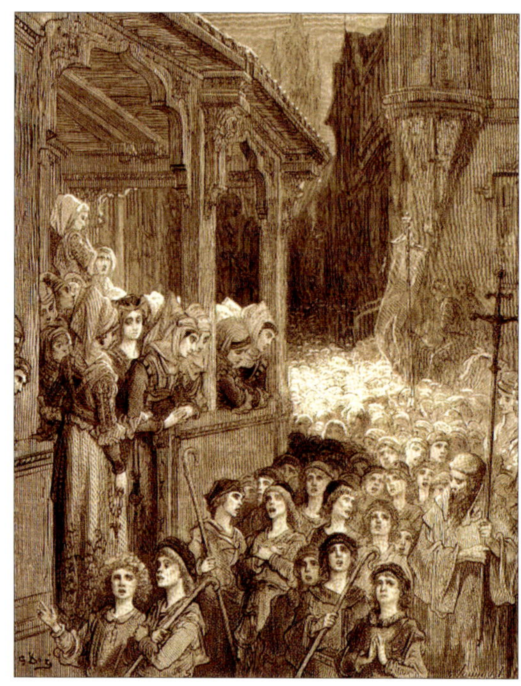
"The Crusade of the Children," *History of the Crusades*,
Joseph-Francois Michuad, Book XII, illustration Gustave Dore

A perfect example of a stereotype which also embodies a burlesque is the Capuchin monk chalk prize. From the front he looks like a monk in brown robes—a simple man of God. When the monk prize is seen from the side or back, he resembles an erect penis. His robes and dogma have supplied him with the ultimate disguise—in them he is expected to represent godliness. Ahem, what's underneath the robe? What's in his mind? If you wear the robes of a monk or priest, your abuse of others might go unchecked. Children are often prey and targeted—for most children accept godliness as a fantasy archetype and feel admiration. The brash monk undermines this godliness. One of the most horriible uses of children propagandized through religious fantasy, and then used as gullible pawns, was the Children's Crusade of 1213. The Crusade consisted of fifty thousand French and German children, most of whom were convinced through the hearing of a revelation that the next summer's drought would dry up the Mediterranean Sea, allowing them to walk to the Holyland unharmed. Heathens would be automatically overcome because God was on the children's side. Almost all of the children died in shipwrecks or were taken into slavery.

CASPER THE FRIENDLY GHOST

(1947-

As a panacea to World War II, Casper the Friendly Ghost proved to children and adults alike that even a ghost could be a cute, smiling, personable, helpful fellow full of goodness. Previously ghosts were generally thought of as scary, but not Casper—when he appeared in 1945, his creators Joe Oriolo and Sy Reit, turned the scary ghost stereotype around.

World War II created a large number of ghosts. After the war the world had to move on, rebuild and find happiness, if that was possible. One unspoken projection lay in Casper, an already dead yet pleasing round white ghost-of-a-fellow (who could not die again), so he could be a humorous risk-taker, as witnessed by the allegorical William Tell apple myth replayed on the 1954 cover of *Casper the Friendly Ghost*, where the archer pig missed the apple and hit Casper (reflecting back to the images on pages 9 and 10). But by 1954, the U.S. had been through yet another war (Korean War 1950-53), making more ghosts while "keeping the world safe for capitalism."[1]

Casper was really a perfect superhero in disguise. He could perform any task that Superman could, and better yet, he couldn't die. Like any ghost he was a spirit of the dead, an archetypal symbol relevant to every culture.

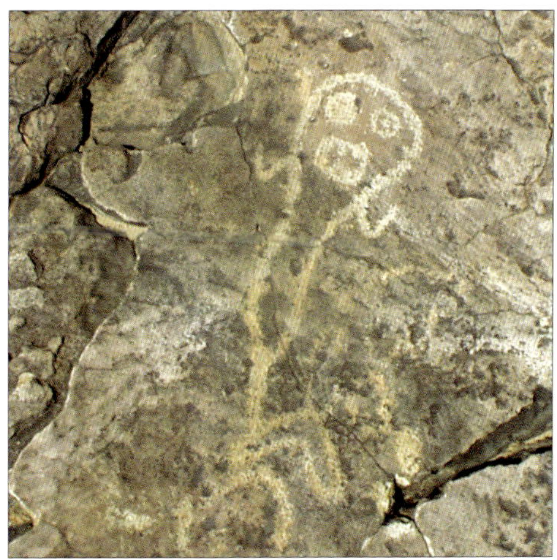

Native American petroglyph, Pony Hills, New Mexico, circa 1000 AD

Each of us has our own personal ghost stories. Mine began when I was a child. At night I had a vivid recurring dream of being a small boy in a tiny boat on a large body of water. Gradually the boat got smaller and I too got smaller, until at the last moment we both would disappear as a mere speck in the water. At the point of disappearance—my imminent death—I would awaken! Later I wondered: was I a ghost of a previous life? Hundreds of times this dream occurred, and every time I was horrified. I could not have invented the story—it was just there and I spoke to no one else about it because it was so scary. After years of pondering what had happened then, I see it as a near-death dream experience. It was clearly archetypal. I was feeling a child's fear of death—I was not a ghost.

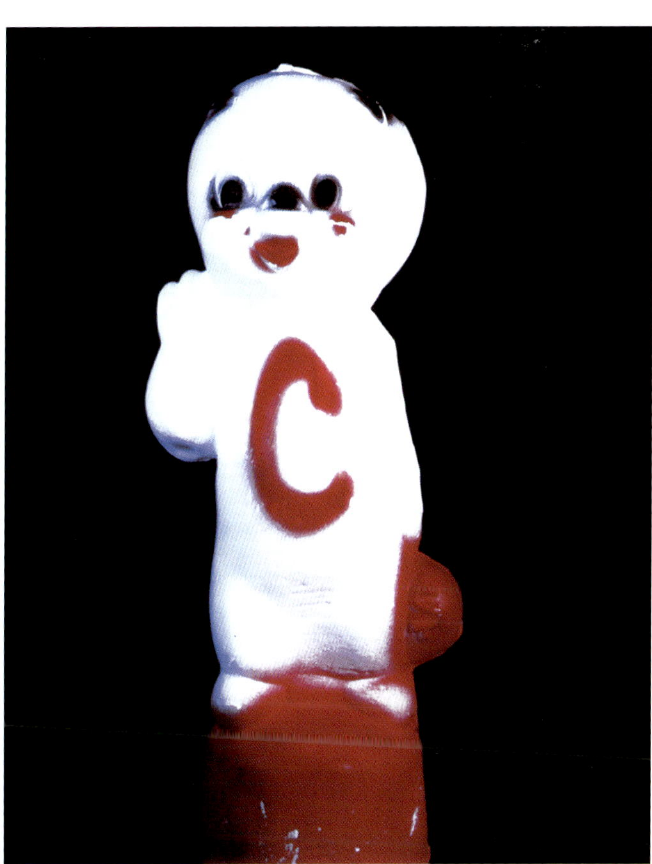

Casper the Friendly Ghost, cover, Joe Oriolo, Sy Reit © Family Comics and Paramount Pictures, vol. 1, no. 25, 1954

Casper the Friendly Ghost twelve-inch carnival chalk prize.

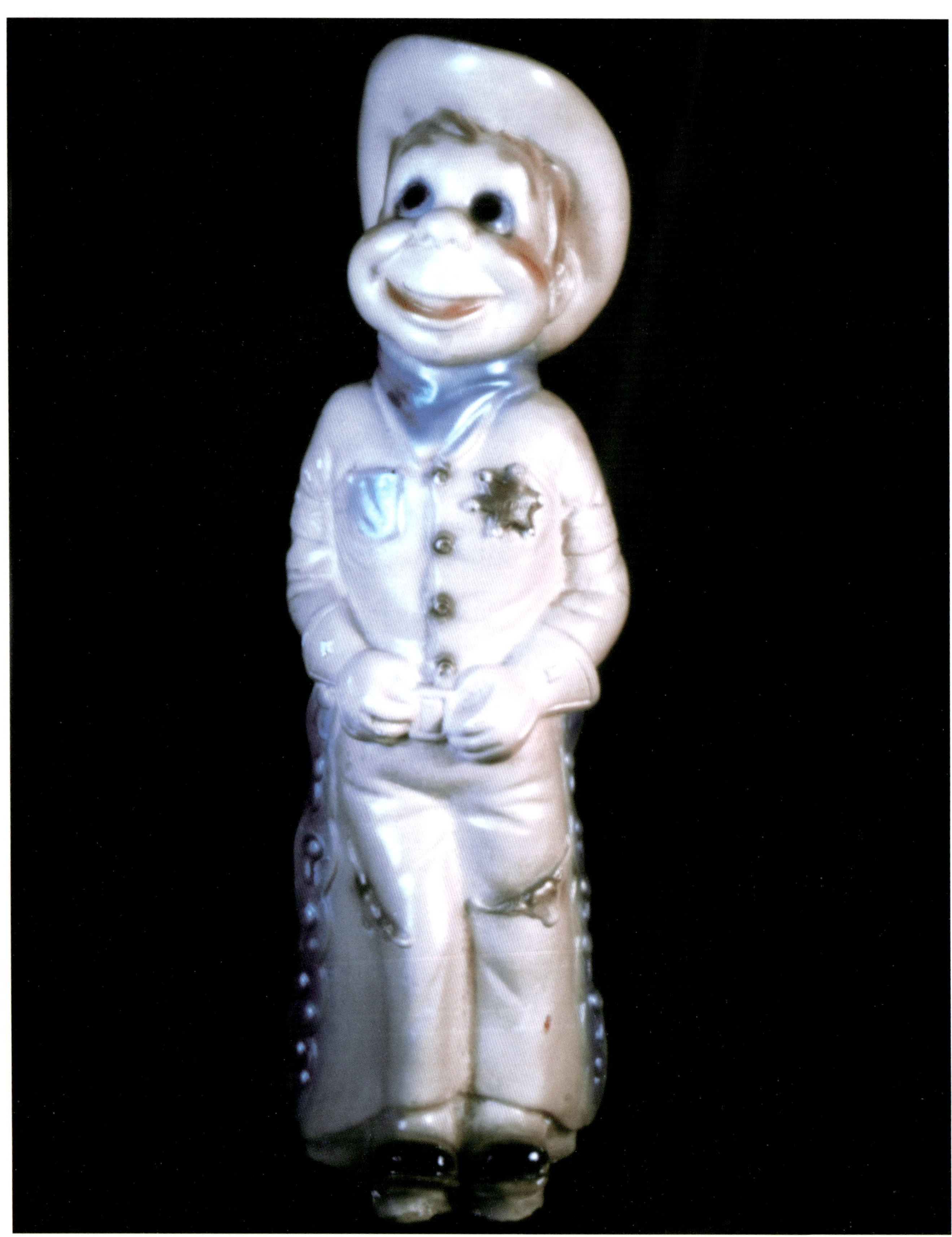

Howdy Doody thirteen-inch carnival chalk prize

Notes

Acknowledgements:

1. Barbara G. Walker, *The Woman's Encyclopedia of Myths and Secrets* (Edison, NJ: Castle Books, 1996).
2. Thomas Morris, *The Carnival Chalk Prize, vol. I and II* (Medford, OR: Prize Publishers, 1985 and 1994).
3. Thomas Morris, *A Price Guide to Chalkware/Plaster Carnival Prizes* (Medford, OR: Prize Publishers, 1995).
4. Althea Aurandt, *Secrets the Church Never Told You* (Silver City, NM: Paracelsus Press, 2000).
5. Norman Schur, *2000 Most Challenging and Obscure Words* (New York: Galahad Books, 1994).
6. Randy Johnson, Johnny Meah, Jim Secreto, and Teddy Verndell, *Freaks, Geeks, and Strange Girls* (San Francisco: Last Gasp Press, 2004).

Introduction:

1. Thomas Jefferson, *Notes on the State of Virginia*, Query XVII "The different religions received into that state?," paragraph 2, 1781-1782, published Feb 27, 1787. This specific quote falls within:
Introduce the bed of Procrustes then, and as there is danger that the large men may beat the small, make us all of a size, by lopping the former and stretching the latter. Difference of opinion is advantageous in religion. The several sects perform the office of a Censor morum over each other. Is uniformity attainable? Millions of innocent men, women, and children, since the introduction of Christianity, have been burnt, tortured, fined, imprisoned; yet we have not advanced one inch towards uniformity. What has been the effect of coercion? To make one half the world fools, and the other half hypocrites. To support roguery and error all over the earth. Let us reflect that it is inhabited by a thousand millions of people. That these profess probably a thousand different systems of religion. That ours is but one of that thousand. That if there be but one right, and ours that one, we should wish to see the 999 wandering sects gathered into the fold of truth. But against such a majority we cannot effect this by force. Reason and persuasion are the only practicable instruments.
2. Franklin Steiner, *Religious Beliefs of Our Presidents* (Girard, KS: Haldeman-Julius Publications, 1936).
3. Apparently Jane McManus Storm Cazneau, a staff writer for O'Sullivan, wrote the words "manifest destiny."
4. Sally Roesch Wagner, *Rapid City Journal*, August 10, 1991: 2.
5. Letter dated November 13, 1861, to Salmon P. Chase, U.S. Treasury Department records.
6. William Scott Green, "Otherness Within: Towards a Theory in Difference in Rabbinic Judaism," in Jacob Neusner and Ernest S. Frerichs, eds., *To See Ourselves as Others See Us* (Chico, CA: Scholars Press, 1985), 46–69.
7. Elaine Pagels, *The Origin of Satan* (New York: Random House, 1995), xix.
8. Carl G. Jung, *Man and His Symbols* (New York: Doubleday, 1983), 67–68.
9. W. Terrence Gordon, *Marshall McLuhan: Escape into Understanding, a Biography* (New York: Basic Books, 1997), 257.
10. Ibid., 315.
11. Ibid., 220, 406. National Archives of Canada, Allen Maruyama, "Conversation with Marshall McLuhan."
12. Attributed to Malcolm X, source unknown.
13. Lary May, *The Big Tomorrow* (Chicago: University of Chicago Press, 2000), 175, from Eric Johnston, *America Unlimited* (Garden City, NJ: Doubleday and Doran and Co., 1944).
14. James W. Loewen, *Lies My Teacher Told Me* (New York: The New Press, 1995), 210.
15. Attributed to Albert Einstein, source unknown.

p. 29 Charlie Chaplin:

1. Kenneth S. Lynn, *Charlie Chaplin and His Times* (New York: Simon & Shuster, 1997), 406.
2. Ibid., 462.
3. Ibid., 539.

p. 33 Buster Brown:

1. Vivian Burnett, *The Romantick Lady* (New York: Charles Scribner's Sons, 1927), 113.
2. New York Herald Company, *Buster Brown in Foreign Lands* (New York: Cupples and Leon Company, 1910).

p. 38 Broncho Billy:

1. Jane and Michael Stern, *Way Out West* (New York: Harper Collins, 1993), 5.
2. Joe McKennon, *The Pictorial History of the American Carnival* (Sarasota, FL: Carnival Publishers, 1974), 67.
3. Ibid.

p. 44 Little Black Sambo:

One of the first small children's books in the United States was *Cries of New York*, (New York: Samuel Wood and Sons, 1809), describing the various calls of vendors and city workers. It was two-and-three-quarter-inches by four-and-three-quarter-inches.

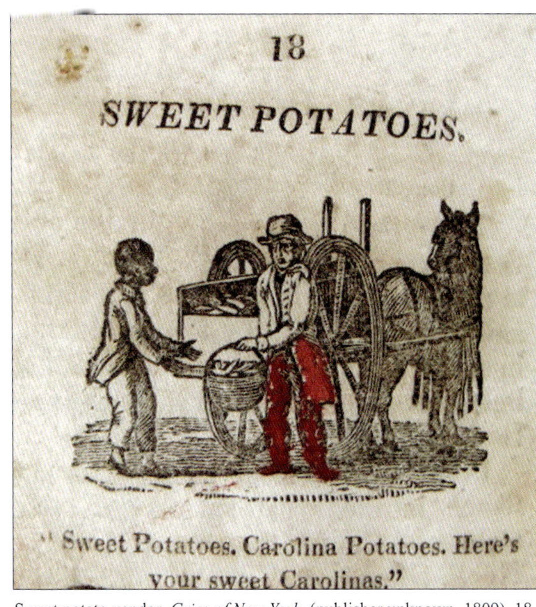

Sweet potato vendor, *Cries of New York*, (publisher unknown, 1809), 18

p. 48 Topsy:

1. Alexis de Tocqueville, *Democracy in America*, translated by George Lawrence (New York: Anchor Books, 1969), 341–342.
2. Leonard Dinnerstein and David M. Reimers, *Ethnic Americans* (New York: Harper and Row, 1988), 4.
3. Sylvaine A Diouf, *Servants of Allah: African Muslims Enslaved in the Americas* (New York: New York University Press, 1998), 145.
4. Ibid., 145–46.
5. Anna Karlina Nichols, communication with the author, January 15, 2005.
6. Harriet Beecher Stowe, *Uncle Tom's Cabin* (New York: New American Library, 1966), 258.

p. 50 Jackie Coogan:

1. Diana Serra Cary, *Hollywood's Children* (Dallas, TX: Southern Methodist University Press, 1997), 59–60.

p. 52 Little Egypt:

1. Joe McKennon, *A Pictorial History of the American Carnival* (Sarasota, FL: Carnival Publications, 1972), 34.
2. James Thornton, copyright 1895, sung by his wife Lizzie Cox who used the stage name Bonnie Thornton. From *Favorite Songs of the Nineties,* Ed. by Robert A. Fremont (New York: Dover Publications Inc., 1973).

p. 57 Cross-dresser:

1. Bourgeois de Paris, *Le Journal d'un Bourgeois de Paris, 1405–99*, edited by A. Tuetey, (Paris. 1881), translated by J. Shirley (Oxford, 1968), p. 263-264 and referenced in Marina Warner, *Joan of Arc*, (New York: Alfred A. Knopf, 1981), 14.
2. Vern L. Bullough and Bonnie Bullough, *Cross Dressing, Sex and Gender* (Philadelphia: University of Pennsylvania Press, 1993), 55–57.
3. Ibid., 167.
4. C. J. Bulliet, *Venus Castina* (New York: Friede Publishers, 1933), 5–6.

5. Ibid., 7.
6. Althea Aurandt, letter to the author, August 3, 2001.
7. Bullough and Bullough, 55–56.
8. Barbara G. Walker, *The Woman's Encyclopedia of Myths and Secrets* (Edison, NJ: Castle Books, 1996), 476–478.
9. Bullough and Bullough, 239.

p. 61 Little Red Riding Hood:
1. Marina Warner, *From the Beast to the Blonde* (New York: Farrar, Straus and Giroux, 1994), 182.
2. Ibid., 182-183.

p. 63 Ku Klux Klan:
1. Philip Dray, *At the Hands of Person's Unknown: The Lynching of Black America* (New York: Random House, 2002).

p. 66 Buddy Lee:
1. Andrew Goliszek, *In the Name Of Science* (New York: St Martin's Press. 2003), 139-141.

p. 67 Sheba:
1. Thomas G. Morris, *The Carnival Chalk Prize I* (Ashland OR: Able Printing, 1985), 19.
2. Althea Aurandt, letter to the author, September 16, 2001.
3. *The Interpreter's Dictionary of the Bible*, supplementary volume (Nashville, TN: Abingdon Press, 1976), 836–38.
4. Althea Aurandt, letter to the author, September 6, 2001.
5. *Harper's Bible Dictionary*, Madeleine S. Miller and J. Lane Miller, editors (New York: Harper & Brothers Publishers, 1958), 630–32.
6. Althea Aurandt, *Secrets Your Church Never Told You* (Silver City, NM: Paracelsus Press, 2002).
7. Althea Aurandt, letter to the author, September 17, 2001.
8. Althea Aurandt, letter to the author, September 9, 2001.

p. 71 Lotus:
1. Helen Zia, *Asian American Dreams* (New York: Farrar, Straus and Giroux, 2000), 23–24.
2. Ibid., 25.
3. Herbert Asbury, *The Barbary Coast* (New York: Garden City Publishing Company, 1933), 177–178.
4. Albert Evans, *A la California: Sketch of Life in the Golden State* (San Francisco: A. L. Bancroft and Company, 1873), from Virtual Museum of the City of San Francisco at sfmuseum.org, unpaginated.
5. Zia, 28.
6. *Life* magazine (August 11, 1941): 65.
7. Zia, 113–114 (compiled by Mary Lee).
8. Thomas Morris, *The Carnival Chalk Prize I* (Medford, OR: Prize Publishers, 1985), 85.

p. 80 Gold Digger:
1. Constance Rosenblum, *Gold Digger* (New York: Henry Holt, 2000), 104.
2. Anita Loos, *A Girl Like I* (New York: Viking Press, 1966), 265.

p. 83 Frenchie:
1. C. J. Bulliet, *Venus Castina* (New York: Covici, Friede, Inc., 1933), 92.

p. 84 Tom Mix:
1. Paul E. Mix, *The Life and Legend of Tom Mix* (Cranbury, NJ: A. S. Barnes and Co. Inc., 1972), 176.

p. 86 Clara Bow:
1. Tom Morris, e-mail to the author, June 8, 2003, as told to him by Dorothy Arthur Walter, who was June Yates Jenkins's niece. When she was growing up, Walter was told the Clara Bow/Frenchie story by Jenkins.

p. 87 Native American:
1. "Columbus's Letter to the Sovereigns on His First Voyage, 15 February–4 March, 1493," in Samuel Eliot Morison, ed., *Journals and Other Documents on the Life and Voyages of Christopher Columbus* (New York: The Heritage Press, 1963), 182.
2. Ibid., 183.

3. Arthur Helps, *The Spanish Conquest in America*, vol. 1 (London: John Lane, 1900), 264–67.
4. David Stannard, *American Holocaust* (New York: Oxford University Press, 1992), 119, 120.
5. Ibid., 121.
6. Ibid., 119.
7. Library of Congress, microfilm reel 34/40, item 305.
8. Library of Congress, microfilm reel 34/41, item 114.
9. Stannard, 126.
10. Ibid., 127.
11. Rebecca Blevins Faery, *Cartographies of Desire* (Norman, OK: University of Oklahoma Press, 1999), 156-220.

p. 100 Miss America:
1. Charles Panati, *Panati's Parade of Fads, Follies, and Manias* (New York: Harper Collins Publishers, 1991), 125.

p. 102 William Jennings Bryan:
1. The lower court was upheld on appeal against every legal attack levied against its rulings and against arguments that the Butler Act was unconstitutional. A technical matter pertaining to the Judge setting the dollar amount of the fine rather than the jury caused the case to be remanded to the lower court.
2. Tom Morris, e-mail to the author, September 21, 2001.
3. Chicago Democratic National Convention, 1896

p. 103 Jesus:
1. *Catholic Encyclopedia*, Doctrinal Explanation, 1, paragraph (e) at newadvent.org.
2. Althea Aurandt, letter to the author, August 5, 2001.
3. John Holland Smith, *The Death of Classical Paganism* (New York: Charles Scribner's and Sons, 1976), 146.
4. Amaury de Riencourt, *Sex and Power in History* (New York: Dell Publishing Co., 1974), 135.
5. Barbara G. Walker, *The Woman's Encyclopedia of Myths and Secrets* (Edison, NJ: Castle Books, 1996), 663.
6. E. O. James, *The Ancient Gods* (New York: G. P. Putnam's Sons, 1960), 250.
7. Walker, 663.
8. Francis Legge, *Forerunners and Rivals of Christianity* (New York: University Books Inc., 1964), Vol. 2, 261.
9. S. Angus, *The Mystery-Religions* (New York: Dover Publications, 1975), 205.
10. C. J. Bulliet, *Venus Castina* (New York: Friede Publishers, 1933), 34.
11. Web Chronology Project, Mediterranean Basin Chronology, The Creed of Nicea at thenagain.info. copyrighted by David W. Koeller, History Department, North Park University.
12. Sir E. A. Wallis Budge, *Egyptian Magic* (New York: Dover Publications, 1971), 116.
13. Mark Tatz and Jody Kent, *Rebirth* (New York: Anchor Press/Doubleday, 1977), 167.
14. Morton Smith, *Jesus the Magician* (San Francisco: Harper & Row, 1978), 25, 120.
15. Walker, 466.
16. Ibid., 466.
17. Ibid., 188.
18. Althea Aurandt, letter to the author, November 5, 2001.

p. 106 Casey Jones:
1. Letter to J. T. Harahan, Offices of the General Superintendent, Illinois Central Railroad, Chicago, May 10, 1900.
2. Lyrics by Robert Hunter, music by Jerry Garcia (Ice Nine Publishing).
3. "The Union Scab" by Joe Hill was first published in *Industrial Worker,* "Little Red Songbook," July 11, 1912.

p. 109 Will Rogers:
1. John Dunning, *On the Air: The Encyclopedia of Old-Time Radio* (New York: Oxford University Press, 1998), 723.

p. 110 Elsie Janis:

1. Diana Serra Cary, *Hollywood's Children* (Dallas, TX: Southern Methodist University Press, 1997), 39-40.
2.William F. Howard, "The Sweetheart of the A. E. F." *New York Archives*, Winter, 2005, 4#3, 4.

p. 113 Virgin Mary:
1. Barbara G. Walker, *The Woman's Encyclopedia of Myths and Secrets* (Edison, NJ: Castle Books, 1996), 603.
2. G. L. Simons, *Sex and Superstition* (New York: Harper and Row, 1973), 103.
3. Amaury de Riencourt, *Sex and Power in History* (New York: Dell, 1974), 258.
4. Ibid., 227.
5. Walker, 609.
6. Geoffrey Ashe, *The Virgin* (London: Routledge & Kegan, 1976), 231.
7. Ibid., 610.
8. Althea Aurandt, e-mail to the author, August 11, 2001.

p. 117 Jean Harlow:
1. David Stenn, *Bombshell: The Life and Death of Jean Harlow* (New York: Doubleday, 1993), 245.
2. Lary May, *The Big Tomorrow* (Chicago: University of Chicago Press, 2000), 217.

p. 119 Mickey Mouse:
1. Marc Eliot, *Walt Disney: Hollywood's Dark Prince* (New York: Birch Lane Press, 1993), 35–36.
2. Charles Solomon, *Enchanted Drawings: The History of Animation* (New York: Wings Books, 1994), 47.
3. Eliot, 27.
4. Ibid., 13–14.
5. See censorship specifics under Betty Boop entry, page 260.

p. 121. Popeye:
1. Bud Sagendorf, *Popeye: The First Fifty Years* (New York: Workman Publishing, 1979), 18.
2. E. C. Segar, "Thimble Theater starring Popeye," Sunday Comics, August 3. 1936.

p. 126 Amos 'n' Andy:
1. Freeman Gosden and Charles Correll, *All About Amos 'n' Andy* (New York: Rand McNally: 1929), 118.
2. Ibid, 51-52.
3. Jon Tuska, *The Films of Mae West* (Secaucus, NJ: The Citadel Press, 1973), 72.
4. Information about Aunt Jemima's history appears on page 17.
5. Jim Lowe, "Tim Moore," August 15, 1951 NAACP Bulletin http://www.geocities.com/~jimlowe/tmoore/tmoordex.html.
6. Octavio Paz, *The Labyrinth of Solitude* (London: Allan Lane/Penguin, 1967), 9.

p. 129 King Kong:
1. Source unknown.

p. 132 Betty Boop:
1. Talkartoon film cartoon "Boop-Oop-A-Doop," 1932.
2. *Life* (July 18, 1938): 50–55.

p. 142 Shirley Temple:
1 Jean-Yves Soucy with Annette, Cécile & Yvonne Dionne, *Family Secrets* (Toronto, Canada: Stoddart Publishing Company, 1996), 104-106.

p. 151 Lana Turner:
1. Lou Valentino, *The Films of Lana Turner* (Secaucus, NJ: The Citadel Press, 1976), 20.

p. 155 Snow White:
1. The first feature-length cartoon was *The Apostle* (1917), a satire on Argentine President Hipolito Irigoyen, by Quirino Cristiani, an Italian living in Argentina. It was seventy minutes long and used 73,000 drawings. No copies exist.

p. 158 Gypsy Rose Lee:
1. H. M. Alexander, *Strip Tease* (New York: Knight Publishers, 1938), 120–123.

p. 160 Mt. Rushmore:
1. James W. Loewen, *Lies My Teacher Told Me* (New York: The New Press, 1995).
2. Douglas L. Wilson, "Thomas Jefferson and the Character Issue," *The Atlantic Monthly* 270, 5 (November 1992): 73.
3. Sylviane A. Diouf, *Servants of Allah, African Muslims Enslaved in the Americas* (New York: New York University Press, 1998), 16.
4. Roy Basler ed., *Collected Works of Abraham Lincoln*, vol. II (New Brunswick, NJ: Rutgers University Press, 1953), 408–409.
5. Thomas G. Dyer, *Theodore Roosevelt and the Idea of Race* (Baton Rouge: Louisiana State University Press, 1980), 78, 86, 159–164.
6. Andrew Goliszek, *In the Name of Science* (New York: St Martin's Press, 2003), 86-87, see Sanger, *The Pivot of Civilization* (NY: Brentano's Press, 1922).

p. 168 Li'l Abner:
1. Elliott Caplin, *Al Capp Remembered* (Bowling Green, OH: Bowling Green State University Popular Press, 1994), 115. To see Capp in action in his right wing attack against John Lennon, see the documentary *Imagine* (1988).
2. Juhn Steinbeck, Introduction to *The World of Li'l Abner*, by Al Capp (New York: Farrar, Straus & Young, 1953) unpaginated.

p. 173 William Powell:
1. Charles Francisco, *Gentleman: The William Powell Story* (New York: St. Martin's Press, 1985), 47–48.

p. 175 Superman:
1. Maria Brenner, "Mr. and Mrs. California," *Vanity Fair* (Dec 1, 2004): 163.
2. Women had their own Superwoman motif in 1900s vaudeville with the muscle-woman trapeze-artist named Charmion.
3. Paul Sassienie, *The Comic Book* (Edison, NJ: Chartwell Books, 1994), 23. (Also in this quote is a possible mistake by Sassienie—most historians say Batman originated in 1939.)

p. 179 Pinocchio:
1. Marc Eliot, *Walt Disney: Hollywood's Dark Prince* (New York: Birch Lane Press, 1993), 116.
2. Ibid., 7. Eliot's information came from John Taylor, *Storming the Magic Kingdom* (New York: Knopf, 1987), 11.
3. Ibid., 152. This complicated story has been the subject of Spanish journalists for fifty years. More on the story can be found in the Eliot book.
4. Ibid., 224.

p. 182 Louis Armstrong:
1. Laurence Bergreen, *Louis Armstrong: An Extravagant Life* (New York: Broadway Books, 1997), 327.
2. Ibid., 382.
3. Louis Armstrong, *Louis Armstrong in His Own Words* (New York: Oxford University Press, 1999), 13–14.
4. Bergreen, 216.

p. 185 Carnival Stripper:
1. John Kenrick e-mail to the author, May 8, 2003.
2. Iceberg Slim, *Pimp* (Los Angeles: Holloway House Publishing Co., 1987), dust jacket.
3. Ibid., 19–20.

p. 189 Little Genevieve:
1.Rose-Marie and Painer Hagen, *What Great Paintings Say* (Kohn: Taschen,

Charmion, circa 1901

2005), 17.

p. 190 Johnny Appleseed:
1. W. D. Haley, "Johnny Appleseed—A Pioneer Hero," *Harper's New Monthly Magazine* XLIII, no. CCLVIII (November 1871): 833–835.

p. 193 The Lone Ranger:
1. Sandy Sturdivant, "Our Favorite Westerns." womenswritersblock.com, unpaginated.
2. "Frequently Asked Questions about The Lone Ranger," geocities.com, unpaginated.

p. 196 Batman:
1. Chip Kidd, *Batman Collected* (Boston: Bulfinch Press, 1996), 21.
2. Paul Sassienie, *The Comic Book* (Edison, NJ: Chartwell Books, 1994), 58.

p. 198 Captain Marvel:
1. Paul Sassienie, *The Comic Book* (Edison, NJ: Chartwell Books, 1994), 59.
p. 200 Confucius:
1. *The American Educator Encyclopedia* (Chicago: The United Educators, Inc., 1942), 912.
2. Ibid.

p. 202 Betty Grable:
1. Robert Heide and John Gilman, *Starstruck: The Wonderful World of Movie Memorabilia* (New York: Doubleday and Company, 1986), 164.
2. Ibid., 166.
3. Ibid., 169.

p. 205 Franklin Delano Roosevelt:
1. Anthony Rhodes, *Propaganda, the Art of Persuasion: World War II* (New York: Chelsea House Publishers, 1976), 148.
2. National Archives, Washington, D.C.

p. 205 Adolf Hitler:
1. Norman H. Baynes, editor, *The Speeches of Adolf Hitler, April 1922–August 1939*, vol. I (London: Oxford University Press, 1942), 19-20
2. Speech in Munich to the "Old Guard."
3. Robert J. Lifton, *The Nazi Doctors : Medical Killing and the Psychology of Genocide* (New York: Basic Books, 1986), 482.
4. Ibid.
5. Susanne K. Langer, *Mind: An Essay on Human Feeling*, vol. III (Baltimore, MD: Johns Hopkins University Press, 1982), 70, 83.
6. Lifton, 431.

p. 210 Benito Mussolini:
1. R. J. B. Bosworth, *Mussolini* (London: Oxford University Press, 2002).

p. 211 Hideki Tojo:
1. First published in 1991 by Sanae Sato in the August and September issues of *Hoseki*; translation by General Hideo Miki and Henry Symington.

p. 213 Winston Churchill:
1. Speech, House of Commons, June 4, 1940.
2. First Speech as Prime Minister, House of Commons, May 13, 1940.

p. 214 Josef Stalin:
1. *J. Stalin, Speeches Delivered at Meetings of Voters of the Stalin Electoral District, Moscow* (Moscow: Foreign Languages Publishing House, 1950), 11–13.

p. 217 U.S. Servicemen and Servicewomen:
1. encyclopedia.thefreedictionary.com
2. National Association of Radiation Survivors, "Summary of Issues," Revised Edition, 2002, Marysville, CA, 4.

p. 223 Skull and Rattlesnake:
1. Barbara G. Walker, *The Woman's Encyclopedia of Myths and Secrets* (Edison, NJ: Castle Books, 1996), 213.

2. Georges Dumézil, *Archaic Roman Religion*, 2 vols. (Chicago: University of Chicago Press, 1970), 566.
3. Frank Kermode, *The Sense of Ending* (London: Oxford University Press, 1966), 27.
4. *Selected Poems of Robert Lowell* (New York: Farrar, Straus and Giroux, 1993).
5. Walker, 290.
6. Ibid.

p. 226 Kilroy was Here:
1. Arthur Helps, *The Spanish Conquest in America*, vol. 1 (London: John Lane, 1900), 264–267.
2. Charles Panati, *Panati's Parade of Fads, Follies, and Manias* (New York: Harper Collins, 1991), 208.

p. 228 George Washington:
1. *The Life of Washington*, Ed. by Marcus Cunliffe (Cambridge: Harvard University Press, 1998), 101.

p. 229 Paul Revere:
1. Jayne E. Triber, *A True Republican: The Life of Paul Revere* (Boston: University Press, 1999), 101.
2. Ibid., 103.
3. Ibid.
4. Ibid., 104.
5. Leonard Dinnerstein and David M. Reimers, *Ethnic Americans* (New York: Harper and Row, 1988), 4, 10.

p. 231 Rita Hayworth:
1. The image painted onto the bomb has been impossible for the author to find. Anyone supplying me with that image will receive a reward!
2. Jonathan M. Weisgall, *Operation: Crossroads: The Atomic Tests at Bikini Atoll* (Annapolis, MD: Naval Institute Press, 1994), 261–262.
3. Lary May, *The Big Tomorrow* (Chicago: Univ. of Chicago Press, 2000), 211.

p. 240 Esther Williams:
1. Esther Williams, *The Million Dollar Mermaid* (New York: Simon & Schuster, 1999), 26.
2. Ibid.,16-17.
3. Anthony Piccolo, "Women of the Deep: A Light History of the Mermaid," in *Sea History* 68 (Winter 1993–94): 45.
4. Ibid., 44.

p. 241 Charlie McCarthy:
1. John Dunning, *On the Air: The Encyclopedia of Old-Time Radio* (New York: Oxford University Press, 1998), 227.
2. Ibid., 229
3. John Tuska, *The Films of Mae West* (Secaucus, NJ: The Citadel Press, 1973), 134.
4. Dunning, 229.

p. 245 Hopalong Cassidy:
1. Clarence Edward Mulford, *Bar-20* (New York: A. L. Burt Company, 1907), 25.
2 .http://www.hopalong.com/creed.htm

p. 247 Annie Oakley:
1. New York Public Library, Ms. leaf recto ("A Death Sonnet for Custer"), 1876, Collection: Walt Whitman Manuscripts, Humanities and Social Sciences Library, Henry W. and Albert A. Berg Collection of English and American Literature.
2. Annie Oakley House, Cambridge, MD, Report by Stephen G. Del Sordo, Senior Associate Heritage Resource Group, report at http://www.dorchesterlibrary.org.
3. Isabelle S. Sayers, *Annie Oakley and Buffalo Bill's Wild West* (New York: Dover Publications Inc., 1981), 23.
4. http://www.stlyrics.com/lyrics/anniegetyourgun/imanindiantoo.htm

p. 250 Lucille Ball:
1. Lucille Ball, *Love Lucy* (New York: G. P. Putnam's Sons, 1996), 18.

2. Ibid., 49.

3. Ibid., 222.

p. 253 Gort:

1. http://www.presidentreagan.info/speeches/sdi.cfm

2. The 1951-1953 atomic bomb tests in the Nevada desert left their mark on an unsuspecting Hollywood. After the 1954 filming of "The Conqueror" starring John Wayne and Susan Hayward, near St. George, Utah, many of the cast and production crew began dying. By 1980, *People* magazine reported in their November 10, 1980 issue (pages 42-47) that 90 out of 220 people connected to the film had died of various cancers, including all the major stars (this statistic did not include the 200 Native Americans who were extras for the filming). Radiation fallout from the bomb tests had created hot spots; the film was apparently made on or near one in the dunes by St. George.

p. 254 Davy Crockett.

1. Marc Eliot, *Walt Disney: Hollywood's Dark Prince* (New York: Birch Lane Press, 1993), 229.

2. David Crockett, *A Narrative of the Life of David Crockett of the State of Tennessee*, Ed. by Paul Andrew Hutton, (Lincoln: The University of Nebraska Press, 1987), 49.

3. Ibid., 125.

4. http://en.wikiquote.org/wiki/Davy_Crockett

5. Ibid.

6. C. R. Wilson and W. Ferris, *Encyclopedia of Southern Culture* (Chapel Hill, NC: University of North Carolina Press, 1989), 683.

7. David Stannard, *American Holocaust* (New York: Oxford University Press, 1992), 241.

p. 261 Casper the Friendly Ghost:

1. John Wood, spoken to the author, describing U.S. wars which were propagandized as against the spread of communism, 1970.

Possibly the Last Carnival Chalk Prizes:

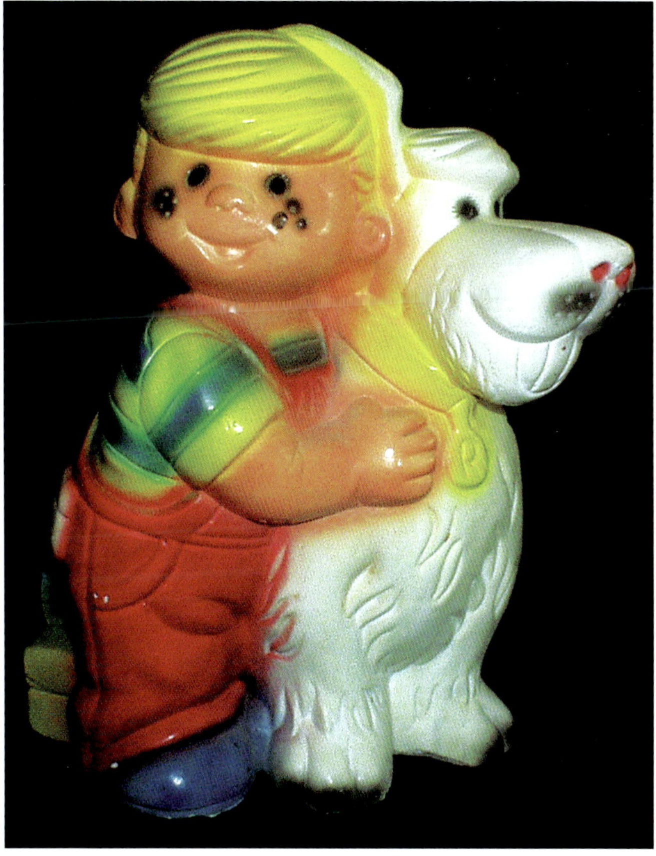

Dennis the Menace nine-and-one-half-inch carnival chalkware bank prize?, 1950s-60s

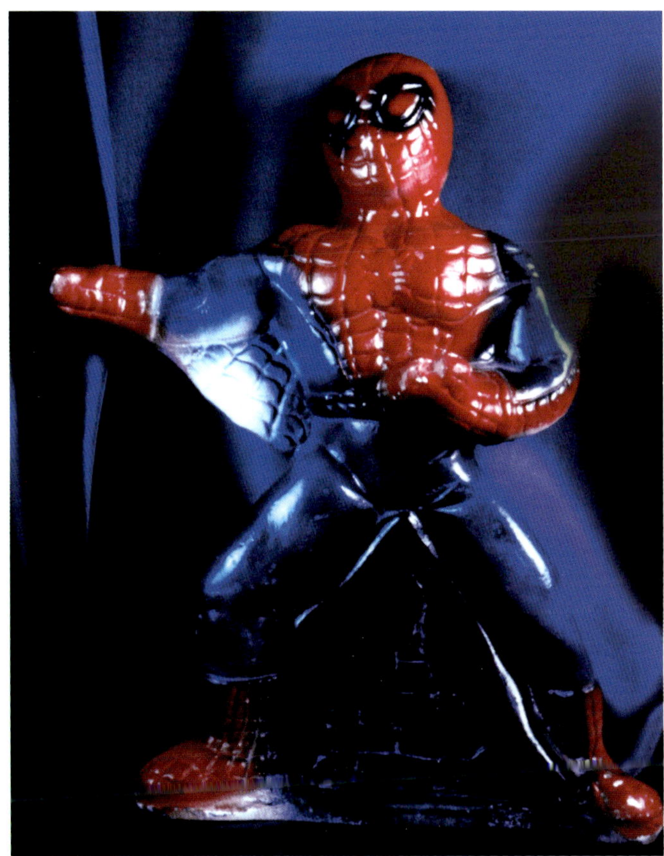

Spiderman twelve-inch carnival chalk prize?, 1960s

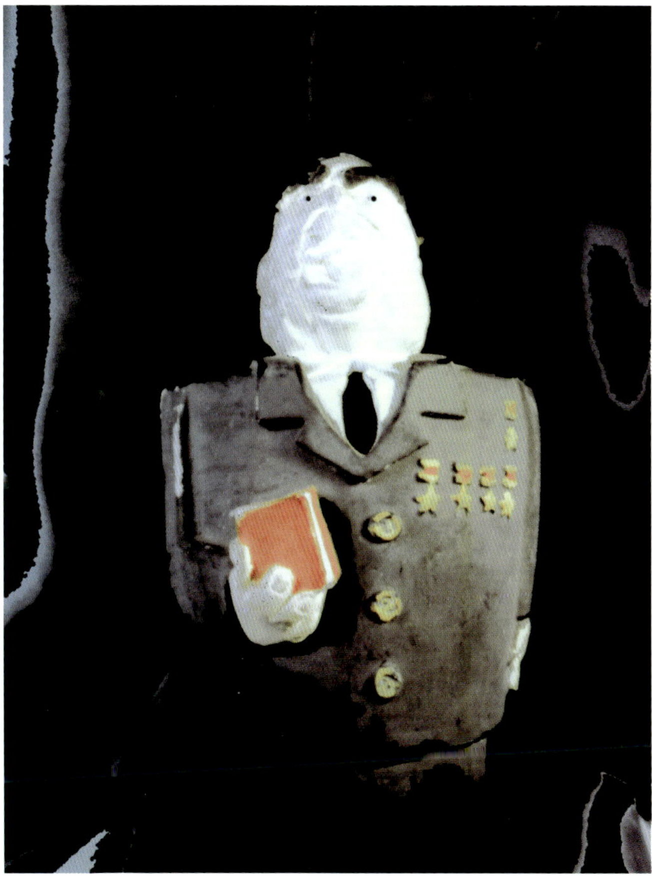

Leonid Breshnev seven-and-one-half-inch carnival chalk bank prize?, coin slot is his tie, 1960s

INDEX

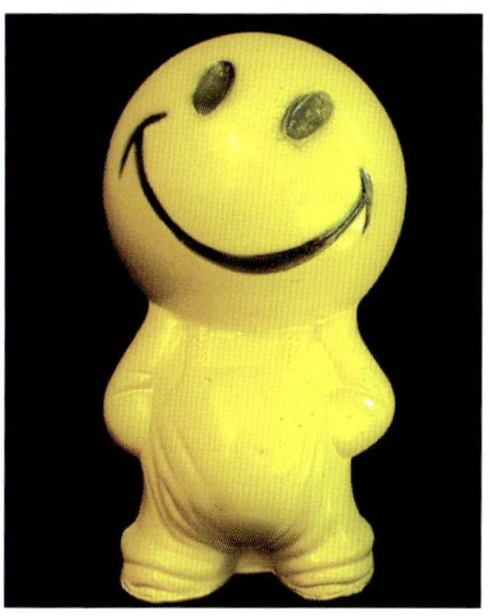

Smiley Face nine-inch carnival chalk bank
prize?, late 1960s. Harvey Ball is credited
with the Smiley Face design for the State
Mutual Life Insurance Company in 1963.
(he was paid $45 for the design). Later the
design was placed into the public domain.
Smiley Face objects became a craze during
the Vietnam War era. By 1971, fifty million
Smiley Face buttons were sold. Is there
someone alive who remembers this bank in
the carnivals?